Tafsīr al-Qurṭubī

Vol. 7

Sūrat al-An'ām – Cattle

& *Sūrat al-A'rāf* – The Ramparts

Tafsīr al-Qurṭubī

The General Judgments of the Qur'ān and Clarification of what it contains of the *Sunnah* and *Āyah*s of Discrimination

Abū 'Abdullāh Muḥammad ibn Aḥmad ibn Abī Bakr ibn Farḥ al-Anṣārī al-Khazrajī al-Andalusī al-Qurṭubī

Vol. 7

Sūrat al-An'ām – Cattle
& *Sūrat al-A'rāf* – The Ramparts

translated by
Aisha Bewley

Diwan Press
Classical and Contemporary Books on Islam and Sufism

Published by: Diwan Press Ltd.
Website: www.diwanpress.com
E-mail: info@diwanpress.com

By: Abu 'Abdullah Muhammad ibn Ahmad al-Qurtubi
Translated by: Aisha Abdarrahman Bewley
Edited by: Abdalhaqq Bewley

A catalogue record of this book is available from the British Library.

ISBN13: 978-1-914397-22-6 (PB)
978-1-914397-23-3 (CB)
978-1-914397-24-0 (ePub Kindle)

Contents

Translator's note	vii
6. Sūrat al-An'ām – Cattle	1
7. Sūrat al-A'rāf – The Ramparts	221
Table of Contents for Āyats	425
Glossary	433

Table of Transliterations

ء	’
ا	a
ب	b
ت	t
ث	th
ج	j
ح	ḥ
خ	kh
د	d
ذ	dh
ر	r
ز	z
س	s
ش	sh
ص	ṣ
ض	ḍ
ط	ṭ
ظ	ẓ
ع	‘
غ	gh
ف	f
ق	q
ك	k
ل	l
م	m
ن	n
ه	h
و	w
ي	y

Long vowel

ا	ā
و	ū
ي	ī
أَوْ	aw
أَيْ	ay

Short vowel

ـَ	a [*fatḥah*]
ـُ	u [*ḍammah*]
ـِ	i [*kasrah*]

Translator’s note

The Arabic for the *āyat*s is from the Algerian State edition of the *riwāyah* of Imam Warsh from the *qirā'ah* of Imam Nāfi‘ of Madina, whose recitation is one of the ten *mutawātir* recitations that are mass-transmitted from the time of the Prophet ﷺ.

There are minor omissions in the text. Some poems have been omitted which the author quotes to illustrate a point of grammatical usage or as an example of orthography or the usage of a word, often a derivative of the root of the word used in the *āyah*, but not the actual word used. Often it is difficult to convey the sense in English. Occasionally the author explores a grammatical matter or a tangential issue, and some of these may have been shortened. English grammatical terms used to translate Arabic grammatical terms do not have exactly the same meaning, sometimes rendering a precise translation of them problematic and often obscure.

The end of a *juz'* may vary by an *āyah* or two in order to preserve relevant passages.

6. Sūrat al-An‘ām – Cattle

According to most people it is a Makkan *sūrah.* Ibn ‘Abbās and Qatādah said that it is all Makkan except for two *āyahs* which were revealed in Madīnah: *āyah* 91, which was revealed about the two Jews, Mālik ibn aṣ-Ṣayf and Ka‘b ibn al-Ashraf, and *āyah* 141, revealed about Thābit ibn Qays al-Anṣārī. Ibn Jurayj says that it was revealed about Mu‘ādh ibn Jabal. Al-Māwardī said that. Ath-Tha‘labī said that *Sūrat al-An‘ām* is Makkan except for six *āyahs* revealed in Madīnah: *āyahs* 91 to the end of 93, and 151 to the end of 153. Ibn ‘Aṭiyyah said that they are *āyahs* of judgment. Ibn al-‘Arabī mentioned that the *āyah* beginning: ‘*Say: "I do not find*"' (6:145) was revealed in Makkah on the Day of ‘Arafah. All of this will be discussed, Allah willing.

In tradition, it states that it was revealed all at once except for six *āyahs* and it was accompanied by seventy thousand angels, twelve thousand appearing with one *āyah* of it, which is: ‘*The keys of the Unseen which no one knows but Him*’ (6:59). They descended with it at night glorifying and praising Allah. The Messenger of Allah ﷺ called for scribes who wrote it down that very night. Abū Ja‘far an-Naḥḥās reported from Muḥammad [ibn Aḥmad] ibn Yaḥyā from Abū Ḥātim Rawḥ ibn al-Faraj, the client of al-Ḥaḍārimah from Abū Bakr Aḥmad ibn Muḥammad al-‘Umarī from Ibn Abī Fudayk from ‘Umar ibn Ṭalḥah ibn ‘Alqamah ibn Waqqāṣ from Abū Sahl Nāfi‘ ibn Mālik from Anas ibn Mālik that the Messenger of Allah ﷺ said, ‘*Sūrat al-An‘ām* descended accompanied by an entourage of angels glorifying Allah, blanketing everything between the East and the West. The earth shook under them,’ and the Messenger of Allah ﷺ then said, ‘Glory be to my Lord, the Immense’ three times.

Abū Muḥammad ad-Dārimī reported in his *Musnad* that ‘Umar ibn al-Khaṭṭāb said, ‘*Al-An‘ām* is a prime example of nobility in the Qur'an.’ Ka‘b said that the opening of *al-An‘ām* is the opening passage of the Torah and its ending is the end of *Hūd.* Wahb ibn Munabbih also said that. Al-Mahdawī mentioned that commentators say that the Torah begins with ‘*Praise belongs to Allah Who created the heavens and the earth…*’ (6:1) and ends with ‘*Praise be to Allah Who has had no son and Who has no partner in His Kingdom…*’ (17:111) to the end of the *āyah.*

Ath-Tha'labī reported from Jābir that the Prophet ﷺ said, 'If someone recites three *āyahs* from the beginning of *Sūrat al-An'ām*, as far as "*and He knows what you earn*" (6:3), Allah will entrust forty thousand angels to him who record for him the like of their worship until the Day of Rising and an angel will descend from the seventh heaven with an iron rod. When *Shayṭān* wants to whisper to that person or inspire anything in his heart, that angel will strike *Shayṭān* a blow so that there will be seventy veils between them. On the Day of Rising, Allah Almighty will say, "Proceed in My shade on a Day during which there is no shade except My shade and eat from the fruits of My garden, drink from the water of Kawthar, and wash in the water of Salsabīl. You are My slave and I am your Lord."' In al-Bukhārī, Ibn 'Abbās said, 'If it you want to know about the ignorance of the Arabs, then recite what is after *āyah* 130 of *al-An'ām*: "*those who kill their children foolishly without knowledge … are lost…*" up to "*…They are not guided.*" (6:140)'

NOTE: Scholars say that this *sūrah* provides the basic premises for arguing against the idolaters and other innovators and those who deny the Resurrection and Gathering. This requires it to have been revealed in one go because it constitutes a single argument, even if that takes different forms. It is that on which the *mutakallimūn* base *uṣūl ad-dīn* because it contains clear *āyahs*, which refute the Qadariyyah, rather than other *sūrahs* which are mentioned. We will deal with that more at length later, Allah willing.

ٱلْحَمْدُ لِلَّهِ ٱلَّذِى خَلَقَ ٱلسَّمَٰوَٰتِ وَٱلْأَرْضَ وَجَعَلَ ٱلظُّلُمَٰتِ وَٱلنُّورَ ثُمَّ ٱلَّذِينَ كَفَرُوا۟
بِرَبِّهِمْ يَعْدِلُونَ ۝١

1 Praise belongs to Allah Who created the heavens and the earth and appointed darkness and light. Then those who disbelieve make others equal to their Lord!

Praise belongs to Allah Who created the heavens and the earth

Allah begins by praising Himself and affirming His Divinity, in that it proclaims that all praise belongs to Him and that He has no partner. If it is said that other *sūrahs* begin in this way and that one makes it unnecessary for there to be others, the response is that each of them has a meaning in its particular context because of being connected to a different kind of benefit that the others do not have. Furthermore, there is a proof in each of them against those who make others equal to their Lord.

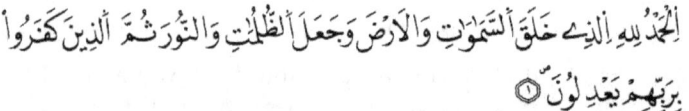

The meaning of 'Praise' was discussed in connection with the *Fātiḥah*. Then the *āyah* speaks about Allah's Power, Knowledge and Will. He says that He is the One who originated, instigated and created. Creation implies invention and it can also imply specification: both meanings are meant here. It indicates the temporality of heaven and earth. He raised the heaven and made it level without the need of any support. He placed in it the sun and moon as signs and adorned it with stars and entrusted it with clouds of varying thickness as indications. He spread out the earth, endowed it with provision and plants and disseminated in it every kind of creature as signs. In it He installed mountains as pegs and valleys as pathways. He made rivers and seas flow in it and made springs gush forth from rocks: all this as indications of His Oneness and the immensity of His Power and that He is Allah, the One, the Conqueror. He made it clear that by virtue of His creating of the heavens and the earth He is the Creator of everything.

Muslim transmitted from Surayj ibn Yūnus and Hārūn ibn 'Abdullāh from Ḥajjāj ibn Muḥammad from Ibn Jurayj from Ismā'īl ibn Umayyah from Ayyūb ibn Khālid from 'Abdullāh ibn Rāfi', the freedman of Umm Salamah, that Abū Hurayrah said, 'The Messenger of Allah ﷺ took my hand and said, "Allah created the earth on Saturday and He created the mountains in it on Sunday, the trees on Monday, disliked things on Tuesday and light on Wednesday. He disseminated creatures in it on Thursday and created Ādam on Friday at the end of creation in the last hour between *'Aṣr* and nightfall."' Scholars say that this *ḥadīth* explains the beginning of this *sūrah*. Al-Bayhaqī said, 'The people with knowledge of *ḥadīth* claim that it is considered to be weak because it contradicts the people of *tafsīr* and histories regarding it.' Some claim that Ismā'īl ibn Umayyah took it from Ibrāhīm ibn Abī Yaḥyā from Ayyūb ibn Khālid. Ibrāhīm is not used as an authority.

Muḥammad ibn Yaḥyā said, 'I asked 'Alī ibn al-Madīnī about the *ḥadīth* from Abū Hurayrah: "Allah created the earth on Saturday." 'Alī said, "This is a Madinan *ḥadīth* which Hishām ibn Yūsuf related from Ibn Jurayj from Ismā'īl ibn Umayyah from Ayyūb ibn Khālid from 'Abū Rāfi', the freedman of Umm Salamah, saying that Abū Hurayrah said, 'The Messenger of Allah ﷺ took my hand.'" 'Alī said, "'Abdullāh ibn Rāfi' took hold of my hand and said to me, 'Abū Hurayrah took hold of my hand and said to me, "Abū al-Qāsim, the Messenger of Allah ﷺ, took my hand and said, 'Allah created the earth on Saturday.'" He mentioned a similar *ḥadīth*. 'Alī ibn al-Madīnī said, 'I can only think that Ismā'īl ibn Umayyah took this from Ibrāhīm ibn Abī Yaḥyā.'"' Al-Bayhaqī said, 'This is corroborated by Mūsā ibn 'Ubaydah az-Zubaydī from Ayyūb ibn Khālid, but Mūsā ibn 'Ubaydah is weak. It is related from Bakr ibn ash-Sharūd from Ibrāhīm ibn Abī Yaḥyā from Ṣafwān ibn Sulaym from Ayyūb ibn Khālid, whose *isnād* is weak. It is reported from Abū Hurayrah that the Prophet ﷺ said, 'There is an hour on Friday in which, if someone asks Allah for anything at that time, He will grant it to him.'

'Abdullāh ibn Salām said, 'Allah began creation and created the earth on Sunday and Monday. He created the heavens on Tuesday and Wednesday and created foods in the earth on Thursday and Friday until the time of *'Aṣr*. Then between *'Aṣr* and sunset He created Ādam.' Al-Bayhaqī transmitted it. This states that Allah began creation on Sunday, not Saturday, and that was reported in *Sūrat al-Baqarah* from Ibn Mas'ūd and other Companions of the Prophet ﷺ. The disagreement about the day has already been adequately discussed.

and appointed darkness and light.

After the creation of essential substances (*jawāhir*), He created incidental attributes (*a'rāḍ*) since the substance (*jawhar*) is necessary and everything that is not independent of temporality is necessarily temporal. In the terminology of the *mutakallimūn*, *jawhar* is something which is not divisible and which can support incidental attributes. This is discussed in *Kitāb al-Asnā*. That which is called *'araḍ* receives its name from the fact that it occurs (*'araḍa*) to the body and the essence and so changes it from one condition to another. The body (*jism*) is the whole. The least of that to which the term 'body' can be applied is to two essences joined together. These are technical terms. Even if these terms do not exist in the original sources, the Book and the *Sunnah* indicate their existence and so there is no reason to deny them. Scholars have used them as technical terms and their discussions are based on them. Some who have specialised in this subject have been killed on account of their use of these terms, as was mentioned in the commentary in *al-Baqarah* (2:170).

Scholars disagree about what 'darkness and light' are intended to mean here. As-Suddī, Qatādah and the bulk of commentators say that what is meant is the darkness of night and light of day. Al-Ḥasan said that they refer to disbelief and belief. Ibn 'Aṭiyyah said, 'This is departing from the apparent meaning.' The expression includes all of this. We find in the Revelation: '*Is someone who was dead and whom We brought to life, supplying him with a light by which to walk among people, the same as someone who is utter darkness?*' (6:122)

The word 'earth' here is generic and its singular form can have the meaning of the plural (lands). The same is true of 'light'. This usage is seen in '*then He brings you out as infants*' (40:67) where the word 'infants' is in the singular. A poet said:

Eat in part of your (pl.) stomach (sing.) and you will be abstinent.

Here the meaning does not allow for a meaning other than 'creation' according to Ibn 'Aṭiyyah. The expression agrees with that and the context gives it that meaning. The plural is used for both the plural and the singular and so the expression is generic and this is clear eloquent Arabic. Allah knows best. It is said that 'darkness' (*ẓulumāt*) is plural and light (*nūr*) singular because light actively strikes things but darkness does not.

Ath-Tha'labī reported that one of the people with expertise in linguistic meanings said that '*ja'ala*' here is redundant. The Arabs sometimes add '*ja'ala*' in statements. [POEM] An-Naḥḥās says that it means 'created' and hence only has one object. The meaning of the verb '*ja'ala*' was fully discussed in *al-Baqarah.*

Then those who disbelieve make others equal to their Lord!

This means: 'Then those who disbelieve make Allah equal to other partners when He alone created these things.' Ibn 'Aṭiyyah said that the use of the conjunction '*then*' indicates the ugliness of what the unbelievers did because it implies: 'His creation of the heavens and the earth is confirmed, His signs are radiant and His blessing in that is clear. Then after all of that, they make others equal to Him!' This is as if you were to say to someone, 'I gave to you and honoured you and was good to you and then you abused me!' If the conjunction had been *wāw*, then the rebuke would not have been as strong as is the case when 'then' is used. Allah knows best.

هُوَ ٱلَّذِى خَلَقَكُم مِّن طِينٍ ثُمَّ قَضَىٰٓ أَجَلًا ۖ وَأَجَلٌ مُّسَمًّى عِندَهُۥ ۖ ثُمَّ أَنتُمْ
تَمْتَرُونَ ۝٢

2 It is He Who created you from clay and then decreed a fixed term, and another fixed term is specified with Him. Yet you still have doubts!

It is He Who created you from clay

Two things are said about its meaning. One of them, which is the best known and most people believe, is that what is being referred to here is Ādam and the creation of his progeny. The branch is ascribed to its root which is why 'you' (*kum*) is in the plural, which is not the normal form of speech, indicating that it refers to Ādam's children. This is the position of al-Ḥasan, Qatādah, Ibn Abī Nājiḥ, as-

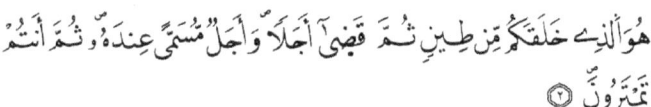

Suddī, aḍ-Ḍaḥḥāk, Ibn Zayd and others. The other thing said is that it is an actual reality. The human being is first formed from clay and then transformed into a human being, which an-Naḥḥās mentioned. As a general rule, when Allah speaks of the creation of the macrocosm, He follows that by speaking of the creation of the microcosm – the human being. He placed in it what he placed in the macrocosm, as we explained in *Sūrat al-Baqarah.* Allah knows best. Praise be to Allah.

Abū Nu'aym related in his book from Murrah from Ibn Mas'ūd that the angel entrusted with the wombs takes the sperm in his hand and then says, 'O Lord, created or not?' If Allah says, 'Created,' He asks, 'O Lord, what is its provision? What is its character? What is its lifespan?' He says, 'Look in the *Umm al-Kitāb*.' The angel looks at the Preserved Tablet and finds in it its provision, character, lifespan and actions. He takes dust from the area where he will be buried and kneads it together with the sperm. That is what the words of the Almighty: '*From it We created you, and to it We will return you.*' (20:55) refer to. He also transmits from Abū Hurayrah that the Messenger of Allah ﷺ said, 'There is no child born but that the dust of his grave is scattered on him.'

On this basis, every human being is created from clay and base fluid, as Allah tells us in *Sūrat al-Mu'minīn*. The *āyah*s and *ḥadīth*s are clearly set out and any uncertainty and contradictions removed, and Allah knows best. As for the reports about the creation of Ādam they were already mentioned in *Sūrat al-Baqarah*. Here we will add some more to that and speak of his description, age and death. Ibn Sa'd mentioned in the *Ṭabaqāt* from Abū Hurayrah that the Messenger of Allah ﷺ said, 'People are the children of Ādam and Ādam was created from earth.' Sa'īd ibn Jubayr said, 'Allah created Ādam from a land called Dajnā'.' Al-Ḥasan said, 'He created his breast from Ḍariyyah.' Al-Jawharī said, 'Ḍariyyah is a settlement of the Banū Kilāb on the road to Basra, closer to Makkah.' Ibn Mas'ūd said, 'Allah sent Iblīs and he took some sweet and salty soil from the crust of the earth and from it Ādam was created. Everyone created from the sweet part goes to the Garden, even if they are the children of an unbeliever, and everyone created from the salty part goes to the Fire, even if they are the children of someone godfearing.' Then Iblīs said: '*Should I prostrate to one You created from clay?*' (17:61) because he brought the clay. Ādam took his name from the fact that he was created from the crust (*adīm*) of the earth.

'Abdullāh ibn Salām said, 'Allah created Ādam towards the end of Friday.' Ibn 'Abbās said, 'When Allah created Ādam, his head touched the sky and when He made him dwell on earth, his height became sixty cubits and his breadth seven cubits. Ubayy ibn Ka'b said, 'Ādam was tall with curly hair like a lofty palm.' Ibn

'Abbās said in a long *ḥadīth*, 'Ādam made forty pilgrimages from India to Makkah walking. When Ādam descended to the earth, his head touched heaven and so he went bald and his children inherited that baldness. The land animals fled from his height and became wild at that time. He did not die until his children and descendants had reached forty thousand in number. He died on top of the mountain to which he had descended. Shīth said to Jibrīl, "Pray over Ādam." Jibrīl said to him, "You go forward and pray over your father. Say thirty *takbīrs* over him: five are for the prayer, and twenty-five are a favour to Ādam."' It is said that he said four *takbīrs* over him. The sons of Shīth put Ādam in a cave and put a guard over him so that none of the sons of Qābīl would approach him. The sons of Shīth used to go there and ask forgiveness for him. Ādam lived for 936 years.

If it is asked whether the *āyah* contains any evidence for saying that substances are all of the same genus, the answer is yes, because, since it is permitted for clay to become a living human being with power and knowledge; it is also possible that it may change to every other state which substances can have, because logic demands the same judgment regarding that, and so it is sound that an inanimate substance can change into a living being based on the proof of this *āyah*.

and then decreed a fixed term, and another fixed term is specified with Him

Aḍ-Ḍaḥḥāk said that the first fixed term is death and the second is the time of the Rising. According to this, it means: 'He determined the time of death and informed you that you will die but did not inform you about the time of the Rising.' Al-Ḥasan, Mujāhid, 'Ikrimah, Khaṣīf and Qatādah said, 'He decreed the term of this world from the time He created you until you die.' '*Another fixed term is specified with Him*' refers to the Next World. It is said that '*decreed*' means firstly, informed us that there will be no Prophet after Muḥammad ﷺ and the second term refers to the Next World. It is said that He informed us firstly about the term of things we know such as the times of the new moons, crops and the like. Then the second fixed term is the time of death as no human being knows when he will die. Ibn 'Abbās and Mujāhid said that the first term is the end of this world and the second is the Next World. It is said that the first is taking the spirits in sleep and the second is taking the spirit in death, as Ibn 'Abbās said.

Yet you still have doubts!

You doubt that He is One God. It is said that '*You still have doubts*' means that you argue as doubters do. 'Doubting' means arguing on the basis of doubt as in the words of Allah: '*What! Do you dispute with him about what he saw?*' (53:12)

وَهُوَ ٱللَّهُ فِى ٱلسَّمَٰوَٰتِ وَفِى ٱلْأَرْضِ يَعْلَمُ سِرَّكُمْ وَجَهْرَكُمْ وَيَعْلَمُ مَا تَكْسِبُونَ ۝ وَمَا تَأْتِيهِم مِّنْ ءَايَةٍ مِّنْ ءَايَٰتِ رَبِّهِمْ إِلَّا كَانُوا۟ عَنْهَا مُعْرِضِينَ ۝ فَقَدْ كَذَّبُوا۟ بِٱلْحَقِّ لَمَّا جَآءَهُمْ فَسَوْفَ يَأْتِيهِمْ أَنۢبَٰٓؤُا۟ مَا كَانُوا۟ بِهِۦ يَسْتَهْزِءُونَ ۝

3-5 He is Allah in the heavens and on the earth. He knows what you keep secret and what you make public and He knows what you earn. Not one of their Lord's Signs comes to them without their turning away from it. They deny the truth each time it comes to them but news of what they were mocking will certainly reach them.

He is Allah in the heavens and on the earth.

The subject of the syntax can be taken in various ways. One is: 'He is Allah, the Esteemed or Worshipped in the heavens and on the earth,' as one says, 'Zayd is the caliph in the east and the west,' in other words rules over them. It is possible that it means: 'He is Allah Who alone has management of the heavens and the earth, and so nothing is concealed from Him.' It is said that it can mean: 'He is Allah in the heavens and He is Allah on the earth.' It is said that the meaning is 'He is Allah Who knows what you conceal and what you make public in the heavens and the earth and so there is no concealing anything from Him.' An-Naḥḥās said: 'This is the best of what is said about it.' Muhammad ibn Jarīr said, 'He is Allah in the heavens and He knows what you keep secret and make public in the earth.' So His knowledge comes first in both cases. The first is sounder and further from doubt. Other things are also said. The rule is to disconnect Him from any kind of movement, movement from one place to another, and occupation of any place.

'*He knows what you earn*' of good and evil. Earning is the action since it brings benefit to or repels harm from oneself, and thus cannot be used of Allah's actions.

Not one of their Lord's Signs comes to them without their turning away from it.

This means such Signs as the splitting of the moon and those like that. '*Min*' here is used for the generic. The second *min* (*min āyāt*) is partitive. '*Turning away from it*' is the predicate of '*kānū*', and turning away implies not seeing the Signs in the creation of the heavens and the earth and what is between them, which are evidence of the oneness of Allah Almighty, and that the signs indicate One who is Timeless, Living and has no need of anything, Who has Power which has no limits, and a Knower from whom nothing is hidden of the miracles which He established for His Prophet ﷺ as proof of his truthfulness in all that he brought.

They deny the truth each time it comes to them but news of what they were mocking will certainly reach them.

'*They*' here are the idolaters of Makkah and '*the truth*' is the Qur'an. It is said that *the truth* means Muḥammad ﷺ. What '*will certainly reach them*' refers to the punishment that will definitely befall them so that the '*news*' will be the punishment. It is said that it refers to the Day of Rising.

أَلَمْ يَرَوْا كَمْ أَهْلَكْنَا مِن قَبْلِهِم مِّن قَرْنٍ مَّكَّنَّٰهُمْ فِي الْأَرْضِ مَا لَمْ نُمَكِّن لَّكُمْ وَأَرْسَلْنَا
السَّمَآءَ عَلَيْهِم مِّدْرَارًا وَجَعَلْنَا الْأَنْهَٰرَ تَجْرِي مِن تَحْتِهِمْ فَأَهْلَكْنَٰهُم بِذُنُوبِهِمْ
وَأَنشَأْنَا مِنۢ بَعْدِهِمْ قَرْنًا ءَاخَرِينَ ﴿٦﴾

6 Have they not seen how many generations We destroyed before them which We had established on the earth far more firmly than We have established you? We sent down heaven upon them in abundant rain and made rivers flow under them. But We destroyed them for their wrong actions and raised up further generations after them.

Have they not seen how many generations We destroyed before them

Grammatically, the question does not refer to what is before it but to what follows it. It means: 'Have they not reflected on the nations whom We destroyed before them because their denial of their Prophets? Have they not recognised that?' *Qarn* is a nation of people. The plural is *qurūn*. A poet says:

When the generation (*qarn*) you are in departs,
and you are left behind in a generation, you are a stranger.

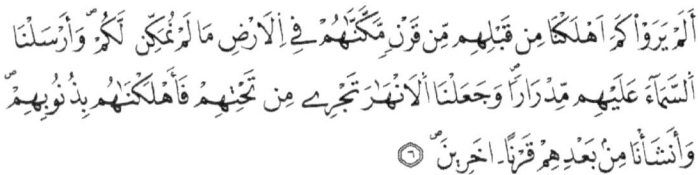

Qarn designates the entire world of its time, taken from *iqtirān* [simultaneous interaction], in other words the contemporary world. The Prophet ﷺ said, 'The best of people is my generation (*qarn*) (meaning the Companions), and then the next generation and then the next one.' This is the soundest of what is said. It is said that it means 'the people of a particular generation,' and there is elision, as in the phrase: '*Ask the town…*' (12:82) The meaning, accordingly, is a period of time. It is said to be sixty, seventy, eighty or a hundred years. Most of the people of *ḥadīth* say that a *qarn* is a hundred years. Their evidence is that the Prophet ﷺ said to 'Abdullāh ibn Busr, 'You will live for a *qarn*,' and he lived to be a hundred. An-Naḥḥās mentioned it. The root of *qarn* is a thing which rises like a horn as animals have horns.

which We had established on the earth far more firmly than We have established you?

Allah moves here from the third person to direct speech. The people of Basra say that in the words '*Have they not seen*,' Allah is talking about them, and the pronoun '*they*' includes Muḥammad ﷺ and his Companions and then them as well. The Arabs say, 'I said of 'Abdullāh, "How noble he is!" and I said of 'Abdullāh, "How noble you are!"' If Allah had continued in the third person, He would have said, '*lam numakkin lahum*'. Also permissible linguistically are: *makkanhu* and *makkan lahu*. So Allah joined both together, 'He gave them what He did not give you of this world.'

We sent down heaven upon them in abundant rain

Here Allah uses heaven to denote rain because rain falls from heaven. A poet said:

When heaven fell on the people's land.

Midrār is an adverbial usage indicating a large amount of something and the nominal form is used for something which produces an abundance. A similar form is *midhkār* which is used for a woman who gives birth to many male children as *mi'nāth* is one who gives birth to daughters. The verb *darra, yadurru* is used of milk when it flows in abundance. '*Midrār*' is in the accusative for the *ḥāl*.

We made rivers flow under them

This was under the trees and their houses as we see in: '*Do not all these rivers flow under me*?' (43:51) It means: 'We gave them ample blessings and they were ungrateful for them.'

But We destroyed them for their wrong actions

Wrong actions are the cause of retribution and removal of blessings.

raised up further generations after them.

'*Raised up*' means 'brought into existence' and so Allah is warning against destruction.

وَلَوْ نَزَّلْنَا عَلَيْكَ كِتَٰبًا فِي قِرْطَاسٍ فَلَمَسُوهُ بِأَيْدِيهِمْ لَقَالَ ٱلَّذِينَ كَفَرُوٓاْ إِنْ
هَٰذَآ إِلَّا سِحْرٌ مُّبِينٌ ٧

7 Even if We were to send down a book to you on parchment pages and they were actually to touch it with their own hands, those who disbelieved would still say, 'This is nothing but downright magic.'

The *āyah* means: 'O Muḥammad, even if We were to do this in front of their very eyes as they demand and solicit and produce written words on parchment...' Ibn 'Abbās said that it means a book suspended between heaven and earth. This makes it clear that there are two aspects to sending down (*tanzīl*). One is the angel actually descending with it and the other is Allah suspending it between heaven and earth. It is said that the use of the words: '*If We were to send down...*' is to stress the length of time of the Book remaining between the heaven and the earth. *Kitāb* (Book) is a verbal noun indicating the fact of it being written and so it is clear that the writing has to be on parchment since it is not logical for writing to be on other than an actual page. The noun '*qirṭās*' means 'page' and is sometimes read as *qurṭās*. The verb *qarṭasa* means to shoot with something so that it hits the target.

'*To touch it with their own hands*' means that even if they had seen that and actually touched it with their own hands as they demanded, and were assiduous about identifying it and turning it over in their own hands so as to remove every doubt and uncertainty about it, they would still be obdurate and continue to disbelieve and say, 'It is obviously magic. He must have put a spell on our eyes.' This *āyah* is a response to their words: '*Unless you bring us down a book to read.*' (17:93) So Allah informs them that He already knows that even if He did send one down, they would still deny it. Al-Kalbī said that it was revealed about an-Naḍr ibn al-Ḥārith, 'Abdullāh ibn Abū Umayyah and Nawfal ibn Khuwaylid who said: '*We will not believe you until you make a spring gush out of the earth for us.*' (17:90)

وَقَالُوا لَوْلَا أُنزِلَ عَلَيْهِ مَلَكٌ وَلَوْ أَنزَلْنَا مَلَكًا لَّقُضِيَ الْأَمْرُ ثُمَّ
لَا يُنظَرُونَ ﴿٨﴾ وَلَوْ جَعَلْنَاهُ مَلَكًا لَّجَعَلْنَاهُ رَجُلًا وَلَلَبَسْنَا عَلَيْهِم
مَّا يَلْبِسُونَ ﴿٩﴾ وَلَقَدِ اسْتُهْزِئَ بِرُسُلٍ مِّن قَبْلِكَ فَحَاقَ بِالَّذِينَ
سَخِرُوا مِنْهُم مَّا كَانُوا بِهِ يَسْتَهْزِئُونَ ﴿١٠﴾

8-10 They say, 'Why has an angel not been sent down to him?' If We were to send down an angel that would be the end of the affair and they would have no reprieve. And if We had made him an angel We would still have made him a man, and further confused for them the very thing they are confused about! Messengers before you were also mocked, but those who jeered were engulfed by what they mocked.

They say, 'Why has an angel not been sent down to him?' If We were to send down an angel, that would be the end of the affair

They also asked for this but Allah responds: '*If We were to send down an angel, that would be the end of the affair.*' Ibn 'Abbās said, "If they were to see the angel in its true form, it would be the death of them since they would not be capable of bearing that sight.' Mujāhid and 'Ikrimah said that it would mean that the Final Hour had arrived. Al-Ḥasan and Qatādah said, 'They would have been destroyed by the punishment of being eradicated because Allah's wont is that if someone demands a sign and it appears to him and he does not believe it, Allah destroys him immediately without any reprieve.'

'*And if We had made him an angel We would still have made him a man*' means that, since they would not be able to see the angel in its true form, the only way they could see one would be by it being given the physicality of a dense body, because every species is at one with its own species and at odds with any other. So if Allah were to make the Messenger to mankind an angel, they would dislike being close to it. If they were close to it, they would be alarmed by its words and fear of it would keep them from speaking to it and from asking it anything and so the benefit would not be universal. If it were to be changed from its angelic form to the like of their form, they would be familiar with it and would then say: 'You are not an angel; you are just a human being. We do not believe in you,' and the same result would ensue. The angels come to Prophets in the form of human beings. They came to Ibrāhīm and Lūṭ in human form. Jibrīl came to the Prophet ﷺ in the form of Diḥyah al-Kalbī. So it means that if an angel had descended, they would have seen it in the form of a man as is the wont with the Prophets. If the angel had descended in its normal form, they would not have seen it. If He made him a man, it would have been more confused for them and they would simply say, 'This is a sorcerer like you.'

Az-Zajjāj said that the meaning of the phrase '*and further confused for them*' means confused their leaders who were confused on account of their own weakness. It used to be said to them, 'Muḥammad is a human being so there is no difference between you and him.' That confused them and caused them to be uncertain. So Allah informed them that if He had sent down an angel in the form of a man, they still would have found a way to be just as confused. *Labs* means mixing. Its root means 'covering with cloth and the like'. '*What they are confused about*' is ascribed to them like earning.

Then Allah consoles the Prophet ﷺ by saying: '*but those who jeered were engulfed by what they mocked*,' meaning that punishment descended on their nations which destroyed them as repayment for their mockery of their Prophets. *Hāqa* (engulfed) means 'to befall'. Allah says: '*Evil plotting envelops (*yaḥīqu*) those who do it.*' (35:43) *Mā* means 'which', and it is also said that it acts like a verbal noun, in other words 'the ultimate consequences of their mocking engulfed them.'

قُلْ سِيرُوا فِي الْأَرْضِ ثُمَّ انظُرُوا كَيْفَ كَانَ عَاقِبَةُ
الْمُكَذِّبِينَ ﴿١١﴾ قُل لِّمَن مَّا فِي السَّمَاوَاتِ وَالْأَرْضِ قُل لِّلَّهِ كَتَبَ عَلَىٰ
نَفْسِهِ الرَّحْمَةَ لَيَجْمَعَنَّكُمْ إِلَىٰ يَوْمِ الْقِيَامَةِ لَا رَيْبَ فِيهِ الَّذِينَ خَسِرُوا
أَنفُسَهُمْ فَهُمْ لَا يُؤْمِنُونَ ﴿١٢﴾

11-12 Say: 'Travel about the earth and see the final fate of the deniers.' Say: 'To whom does everything in the heavens and earth belong?' Say: 'To Allah.' He has made mercy incumbent on Himself. He will gather you to the Day of Rising about which there is no doubt. As for those who have lost their own selves, they do not believe.

Say: 'Travel about the earth

It means: 'O Muḥammad, *say* to the mockers and deniers: "*Travel about the earth* and look and do research and then you will find out about the penalty and painful punishment which befell the unbelievers before you."' This journeying is recommended since it is to reflect on the remains and ruins of the nations who went before. '*The deniers*' are those who deny the truth and its people, not those who deny falsehood.

Say: 'To whom does everything in the heavens and earth belong?'

This is also an argument against them. It means: 'Ask them, Muḥammad, who everything in the heavens and earth belongs to? When they ask, "Who does it belong to?" say "To Allah."' It means: when it is affirmed that everything in the heavens and the earth belongs to Him and that He is the Creator of everything, either by their admission or by establishing the proof against them, then Allah has the power to punish them and to resurrect them after their death. However: '*He has made mercy incumbent on Himself.*' He has promised it as a favour and generosity from Himself. That is why He has given them a reprieve. '*Nafsihi*' (*Himself*) here designates His existence and emphasises His promise and removes any other means than Him. The sense of the words designates kindness on His part to those who turn from Him and then turn back to Him. He tells us that He is merciful to His slaves and will not hasten their punishment and will accept their regret and repentance.

In *Ṣaḥīḥ Muslim* Abū Hurayrah reported that the Messenger of Allah ﷺ said, 'When Allah decreed the existence of creatures, He wrote about Himself in a book which is in His keeping: "My mercy overrides My anger."' This means that when His decree appears and emerges to whomever He wishes, He manifests a book on the Preserved Tablet – or wherever He wishes – and it demands that His promise: 'My mercy overcomes My anger,' is shown to be true, in that it precedes it and is more than it.

He will gather you

The *lām* (*la yajma'anna*) is the *lām* of the oath and the *nūn* at the end is for emphasis. Al-Farrā' and others said that it is possible that the words conclude with the word '*raḥmah*' ('*He has made mercy incumbent on Himself*') and so a new sentence begins. It is for clarification and so the meaning is: 'He will defer and grant a reprieve to all of you.' It is said that the meaning is, 'He will gather you from the grave to the Day which you have denied.' It is said that '*ilā*' means '*fī*', meaning, 'He will gather you on the Day of Rising.' It is said that the phrase '*gather you*' may also be an apodosis for '*mercy*' and so the *lām* here means '*an*' and it signifies: 'Your Lord made it incumbent upon Himself *that* He would gather you.' Many grammarians also say that about 12:35. It is said that it is in the position of the accusative by 'made incumbent' as '*anna*' is in 6:54. That is because '*mercy*' in this instance is explained by az-Zajjāj as meaning reprieve until the Day of Rising.

about which there is no doubt.

'*Rayb*' means doubt.

As for those who have lost their own selves, they do not believe.

Az-Zajjāj said that this is an inceptive and predicate. It is the best that has been said about it. You say, 'The one who honours me will have a *dirham*,' and the *fā'* contains the meaning of the precondition and apodosis. Al-Akhfash said, 'If you wish, "*those*" is in the position of the accusative as an apodosis for the "*kum*" in "*gather you*". It means: "He will gather the idolaters who have lost their own selves."' Al-Mubarrad negates that and says that it is an error because there is no apodosis for the one addressed or the one who addresses. [EXAMP] Al-Qutabī said, 'It is possible that "*those*" is in the genitive as the apodosis of the "*deniers*" who were already mentioned, or a description of them.' It is also said that '*those*' is a single vocative.

وَلَهُۥ مَا سَكَنَ فِي ٱلَّيۡلِ وَٱلنَّهَارِۚ وَهُوَ ٱلسَّمِيعُ ٱلۡعَلِيمُ ﴿١٣﴾ قُلۡ أَغَيۡرَ ٱللَّهِ أَتَّخِذُ
وَلِيّٗا فَاطِرِ ٱلسَّمَٰوَٰتِ وَٱلۡأَرۡضِ وَهُوَ يُطۡعِمُ وَلَا يُطۡعَمُۗ قُلۡ إِنِّيٓ أُمِرۡتُ
أَنۡ أَكُونَ أَوَّلَ مَنۡ أَسۡلَمَۖ وَلَا تَكُونَنَّ مِنَ ٱلۡمُشۡرِكِينَ ﴿١٤﴾ قُلۡ إِنِّيٓ أَخَافُ إِنۡ
عَصَيۡتُ رَبِّي عَذَابَ يَوۡمٍ عَظِيمٖ ﴿١٥﴾ مَّن يُصۡرَفۡ عَنۡهُ يَوۡمَئِذٖ فَقَدۡ
رَحِمَهُۥۚ وَذَٰلِكَ ٱلۡفَوۡزُ ٱلۡمُبِينُ ﴿١٦﴾

13-16 All that inhabits the night and the day belongs to Him. He is the All-Hearing, the All-Knowing. Say: 'Am I to take anyone other than Allah as my protector, the Bringer into Being of the heavens and the earth, He Who feeds and is not fed?' Say: 'I am commanded to be the first of the Muslims,' and, 'Do not be among the idolaters.' Say: 'I fear, were I to disobey my Lord, the punishment of a dreadful Day.' Anyone from whom punishment is averted on that Day has been shown great mercy by Allah. That is the Clear Victory.

All that inhabits the night and the day belongs to Him.

This is further confirmation of the truth of this reality. It is an argument against them. It is said that the *āyah* was revealed because they said, 'We know that it is only need that compels you to do what you do. We will make a collection from our wealth for you so that you will be the wealthiest among us.' Allah said,

'Tell them that everything belongs to Allah and say, "He has the power to enrich me."'

The meaning of *sakana* (inhabit) here is 'to remain and be settled'. What is meant is what is still and what moves. The elision is known. It is said that He singled out mentioning *sākin*, which is stillness, since it is more inclusive than speaking of things that move. It is said that it means: 'what He created' and so it is general to all creatures, moving or still. The night and day flow over them. So what is meant is not stillness as the opposite of movement, but what is meant is creation. This is the best of what is said because it includes all the views. Allah 'hears' their voices and 'knows' their secrets.

Say: 'Am I to take anyone other than Allah as my protector, the Bringer into Being of the heavens and the earth

When they called him to idolworship, the religion of his forefathers, Allah revealed, '*Say*, Muḥammad, "*Am I to take anyone other than Allah as my protector*?",' i.e. a worshipped Lord and Helper other than Allah? '*The Bringer into Being of the heavens and the earth*' is added. If it is in the genitive, it is describing the appellative '*Allah*'. Al-Akhfash says that it can be in the nominative by an implied inchoative. Az-Zajjāj said that it can be in the accusative as praise. Abū 'Alī al-Fārisī said that it can be in the accusative by the action of an elided verb, as if he were saying, 'Am I to abandon the Bringer into being of the heavens and earth?' because the words denote abandoning His protection. That is implied by the strength of the evidence.

He Who feeds and is not fed?

This wording (*yuṭ'imu walā yuṭ'amu*), meaning '*He Who feeds and is not fed*' is how the majority recite, corroborating His words elsewhere: '*I do not require provision from them and I do not require them to nourish Me.*' (51:57) Sa'īd ibn Jubayr, Mujāhid and al-A'mash recite instead '*yuṭ'imu walā yaṭ'amu*', a good reading which would mean that He feeds His slaves and does not require the food which creatures do require. When it is recited with the passive in both cases, it means Allah provides for His slaves and feeds them. The Protector does not feed himself. The second verb is also read '*walā yuṭ'im*' and feeding is singled out to be mentioned rather than other blessings because all mankind is continually in need of it.

Say: 'I am commanded to be the first of the Muslims,

This means the first to submit to the command of Allah. It is also said to mean, 'The first of those who are sincere,' of my people and family, as al-Hasan and others said. '*Do not be among the idolaters*' means: 'It is said to me, "Do not be among the idolaters."'

Say: 'I fear, were I to disobey my Lord, the punishment of a Dreadful Day.'

If I were to worship other than Him, I would have fear of Him punishing me. Fear is anticipation of something disliked. Ibn 'Abbās said that '*I fear*' means 'I know'.

Anyone from whom punishment is averted on that Day has been shown great mercy by Allah.

What is averted is the punishment and the Day is the Day of Rising. Whoever is shown mercy by Allah is successful, saved and shown mercy. The Kufans read '*yuṣraf – is averted*' as 'He averts from him – *yaṣrif 'anhu*' rather than '*yuṣraf*' and that is preferred by Abū Ḥātim and Abū 'Ubayd because of His words: '*Say: 'To whom does everything in the heavens and earth belong?*'' and because He says: 'He has shown him mercy' (*raḥimahu*) and not 'he was shown mercy – *ruḥima*'. The reading of Ubayy is '*yaṣrifhu*'. Sībawayh preferred the reading of the people of Madīnah and Abū 'Amr: *yuṣraf.* The recitation '*yaṣrif*' implies: 'whoever Allah averts the punishment from him.' If one recites '*yuṣraf 'anhu*', it means 'from whom punishment is averted.' '*Clear Victory*' means 'clear salvation.'

وَإِن يَمْسَسْكَ ٱللَّهُ بِضُرٍّ فَلَا كَاشِفَ لَهُۥٓ إِلَّا هُوَ ۖ وَإِن يَمْسَسْكَ بِخَيْرٍ فَهُوَ
عَلَىٰ كُلِّ شَىْءٍ قَدِيرٌ ١٧

17 If Allah touches you with harm, none can remove it but Him. If He touches you with good, He has power over all things.

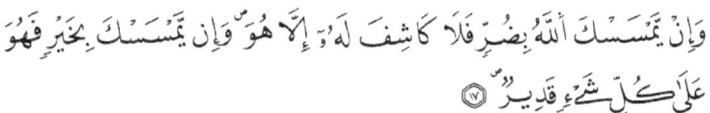

Touching and removing are physical attributes. Here the meaning is metaphorical and a broader understanding is taken. It means: 'If, Muḥammad, the hardship of poverty or illness descends on you, none can remove it and avert it except Him. If He touches you with well-being, ease and blessing, "*He has power over all things*": both benefit and harm.' Ibn 'Abbās said, 'I was riding behind the Messenger of Allah ﷺ and he said to me, "Lad – or my son – shall I teach you some words by which Allah will benefit you?" "Yes indeed," I replied. He said, "Be careful regarding Allah and He will take care of you. Be careful regarding Allah and you will find Him in front of you. Recognise Allah in ease and He will recognise you in hardship. When you ask, ask Allah and when you seek help, seek help from Allah. The pen has dried (after writing) everything that will be. If all creation wanted to harm you in some way which Allah had not decreed for you, they would not be able to do it. Act for Allah with thankfulness and certainty, and know that there is much good in fortitude in the face of what you dislike. Help comes with fortitude and relief with affliction and ease with hardship.' Khaṭīb Abū Bakr ibn Thābit transmitted it in *Kitāb al-Faṣl wa-l-Waṣl.* It is a sound *ḥadīth* and at-Tirmidhī transmitted it. This is a more complete version.

وَهُوَ الْقَاهِرُ فَوْقَ عِبَادِهِۦ وَهُوَ الْحَكِيمُ الْخَبِيرُ ﴿١٨﴾ قُلْ أَيُّ شَيْءٍ
أَكْبَرُ شَهَادَةً قُلِ اللَّهُ شَهِيدٌ بَيْنِي وَبَيْنَكُمْ وَأُوحِيَ إِلَيَّ هَٰذَا الْقُرْءَانُ لِأُنذِرَكُم
بِهِۦ وَمَنْ بَلَغَ أَئِنَّكُمْ لَتَشْهَدُونَ أَنَّ مَعَ اللَّهِ ءَالِهَةً أُخْرَىٰ قُل لَّا أَشْهَدُ قُلْ إِنَّمَا
هُوَ إِلَٰهٌ وَاحِدٌ وَإِنَّنِي بَرِيٓءٌ مِّمَّا تُشْرِكُونَ ﴿١٩﴾

18-19 He is the Absolute Master over His slaves. He is the All-Wise, the All-Aware. Say: 'What thing is greatest as a witness?' Say: 'Allah. He is Witness between me and you. This Qur'an has been revealed to me so that I may warn you by it, and anyone else it reaches. Do you then bear witness that there are other gods together with Allah?' Say: 'I do not bear witness.' Say: 'He is only One God, and I am free of all you associate with Him.'

He is the Absolute Master over His slaves.

The meaning of '*Absolute Master over*' here signifies dominance and overpowering, meaning that they are totally in His power. '*Uqhira*' is used when a man is in a state of subjugation and abasement. A poet said:

Ḥuṣayn hoped that his group would rule,
but in the evening Ḥuṣayn was abased and overcome (*uqhira*).

The meaning of the preposition '*over*' here is the figurative one of having power over them, of their being under His rule. There is no spatial element involved. It is like saying, 'The sultan is over His subjects,' meaning by virtue of position and elevation. The word '*qahr*' has a meaning which is not contained in the word '*qudrah*' (power): it is to prevent someone else from achieving their desire. "*He is the All-Wise*' in His command and '*All-Aware*' of the actions of His slaves, and so the One who has this description cannot have any associate assigned to Him.

Say: 'What thing is greatest as a witness?'

This resulted from the idolaters saying to the Prophet ﷺ, 'Who will bear witness that you are the Messenger of Allah?' and the *āyah* was revealed, as al-Ḥasan and others said. The word '*thing*' here is in place of the Name of Allah. It means that Allah is the greatest Witness, in that He alone has Lordship, and His establishing proofs of His Oneness is the greatest and most authoritative testimony. 'He is Witness between me and you in respect of what I have conveyed to you that I have spoken the truth in what I have said and claimed with regard to being a Messenger.'

This Qur'an has been revealed to me so that I may warn you by it, and anyone else it reaches

This means that 'the Qur'an is a witness to my Prophethood': '*so that I may warn you by it*', people of Makkah, '*and anyone else it reaches*', in other words anyone else whom the Qur'an reaches. The *hā'* of the object is elided (which would be *balaghahu*) because of the length of the words. It is also said that it means: 'whoever has reached puberty'. This indicates that someone who has not reached puberty is not deemed responsible nor made to worship.

We are commanded to transmit the Qur'an and *Sunnah* just as the Prophet ﷺ was commanded to transmit them. Allah says: '*O Messenger, transmit what has been sent down to you from your Lord.*' (5:67) In *Ṣaḥīḥ al-Bukhārī*, 'Abdullāh ibn 'Umar reported that the Prophet ﷺ said, 'Transmit from me, even if it is only an *āyah*, and you may relate from the Children of Israel without harm. Anyone who deliberately tells a lie regarding me will take his seat in the Fire.' It also says in another report: 'Anyone who has an *āyah* of the Book of Allah conveyed to him has had the command of Allah conveyed to him. He takes it or leaves it.' Muqātil said, 'Any of the jinn or men who has the Qur'an reach them has been warned.' Al-Quraẓī said, 'If the Qur'an reaches someone, it is as if he had seen Muhammad ﷺ and listened to him.' Abū Nahīk recited '*Awḥā ilayya hādha-l-Qur'āna* – He revealed to me this Qur'an' which has the same meaning as the normally accepted recitation.

Do you then bear witness that there are other gods together with Allah?

This question is a rebuke. It is recited with the two *hamzahs* (*a'innakum*) on the root. If the second *hamzah* is lightened, you would recite '*ayinnakum*'. Abū 'Amr recited from Nāfi': '*ā'innakum*' which is a known dialect. An *alif* is put between the two *hamzahs* out of the dislike of them being joined. [POEM] If it is recited as '*innakum*' as a statement, it is based on the fact that they really are idolaters. Allah uses the feminine '*ukhrā*' with '*ālihah*' (gods) and not the masculine *ākhar* and al-

Farrā' says that that is because *ālihah* is a plural, and the plural takes a feminine adjective as we see in 7:180 and 20:51. It would be valid to say '*uwal*' and '*ukhar*'. The phrase: '*Say: "I do not bear witness"*' means: 'I do not testify with you,' 'with you' being elided because the words indicate that. It is similar to Allah's words: '*If they testify, do not testify with them.*' (6:150)

ٱلَّذِينَ ءَاتَيْنَٰهُمُ ٱلْكِتَٰبَ يَعْرِفُونَهُۥ كَمَا يَعْرِفُونَ أَبْنَآءَهُمُ ٱلَّذِينَ خَسِرُوٓا۟ أَنفُسَهُمْ فَهُمْ
لَا يُؤْمِنُونَ ٢٠

20 Those We have given the Book recognise it as they recognise their own children. As for those who have lost their own selves, they do not believe.

'*Those We have given the Book*' are the Jews and Christians who recognise the truth, but are stubborn. This was discussed in *Sūrat al-Baqarah* (2:146). The words '*recognise it*' can mean that they recognise the Prophet ﷺ, i.e. 'recognise him', as al-Ḥasan and Qatādah said. That is the position of az-Zajjāj. It is also said that it refers to the Book, i.e. they recognise it and what it indicates of the truth of the mission of the Messenger of Allah ﷺ. The words '*those who have lost their own selves*' are an adjectival usage and can also be an inchoative whose predicate is '*they do not believe.*'

وَمَنْ أَظْلَمُ مِمَّنِ ٱفْتَرَىٰ عَلَى ٱللَّهِ كَذِبًا أَوْ كَذَّبَ بِـَٔايَٰتِهِۦٓ إِنَّهُۥ لَا يُفْلِحُ ٱلظَّٰلِمُونَ ٢١
وَيَوْمَ نَحْشُرُهُمْ جَمِيعًا ثُمَّ نَقُولُ لِلَّذِينَ أَشْرَكُوٓا۟ أَيْنَ شُرَكَآؤُكُمُ ٱلَّذِينَ كُنتُمْ تَزْعُمُونَ ٢٢

21-22 Who could do greater wrong than someone who invents lies against Allah or denies His Signs? The wrongdoers are certainly not successful. On the Day We gather them all together, We will say to those who associated others with Allah, 'Where are the partner-gods, for whom you made such claims?'

'*Who could do greater wrong*' means: no one could do a greater wrong. '*Denies His Signs*' refers to the Qur'an and the miracles of the Prophet ﷺ. '*The wrongdoers are certainly not successful*' means lack of success in this world. Then Allah begins a new sentence with the words: '*On the Day We gather them all together,*' meaning 'Remember the Day We gather them.' So it means: 'they will not be successful in this world nor on the Day We gather them together.' Taking it this way would mean that there is no stop at '*wrongdoers*'. It is said that it is connected by an elided

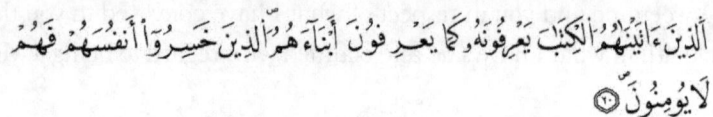

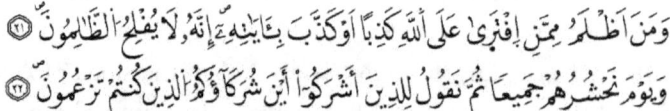

'See', in other words: 'See how they will be punished on the Day We gather them.' '*Where are the partner-gods, for whom you made such claims?*' refers to the fact that they claimed that they would intercede for them with Allah and bring them near to Him. This rebukes them. Ibn 'Abbās said that every time the word *claim* (*za'm*) is used in the Qur'an, it refers to a lie.

ثُمَّ لَمْ تَكُن فِتْنَتُهُمْ إِلَّآ أَن قَالُوا۟ وَٱللَّهِ رَبِّنَا مَا كُنَّا مُشْرِكِينَ ٢٣

23 Then they will have no recourse except to say, 'By Allah, our Lord, we were not idolaters.'

Then they will have no recourse except to say,

Fitnah (*recourse*) in this *āyah* refers to the result of their examination, meaning that their answer, when they are asked this question and see the truth and their claims are negated, is that they will have no option but to say this. They seek to free themselves of *shirk* and be purified of it when they see Allah's pardon and His forgiveness of the believers. Ibn 'Abbās said, 'Allah Almighty will forgive the people of sincerity for their wrong actions and no wrong action will be too great for Him to forgive. When the idolaters see that, they will say, "Our Lord forgives wrong actions but does not forgive *shirk*. So let us say, 'We were people of wrong actions and were not idolaters!'" Allah will reply, "Since you concealed *shirk*, there is a seal on your mouths," and a seal will be placed on their mouths and their hands will speak and their feet testify to what they were doing. Then the idolaters will recognise that not a single thing is concealed from Allah, as evinced by His words: "*On that day those who rejected and disobeyed the Messenger will wish that they were one with the level earth. They will not be able to hide a single circumstance from Allah.*" (4:42)'

Abū Isḥāq az-Zajjāj said that the interpretation of this *āyah* is very subtle. Allah talks about the idolaters and their being tested on account of their *shirk* and then He says that their only recourse, when they see the truth, is to try and free themselves of *shirk*. This is like seeing a man loving something which seduces him and when he falls into destruction, he declares himself innocent of it but is told, 'Your love of it was only to be free of it.' Al-Ḥasan said, 'This is particular to the hypocrites who act then according to their wont in this world.' The meaning of '*fitnatahum*' is the result of their testing i.e. their disbelief. Qatādah said that it means 'their excuse.'

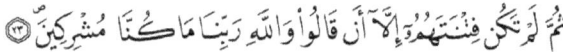

In *Ṣaḥīḥ Muslim*, Abū Hurayrah said, 'Allah will meet the slave and say, "You! Did I not honour you, make you a leader, give you a spouse, subject horses and camels to you and raise you to leadership and rule?" He will say, "Yes, Lord." He will say, "Did you think that you would meet Me?" He will reply, "No." Allah will say, "I will forget you as you forgot Me." Then He will meet a second person and say something similar to him as He said the first time. Then He will meet a third person and say something similar to him and he will say, "Lord, I believed in You and Your Book and Your Messenger. I prayed, fasted, gave *ṣadaqah* and praised as much as I could." He will say, "Stop this." Then he will be told, "We will produce a witness against you." He will think to himself, "Who will testify against me?" A seal will be placed on his mouth and it will be said to his thighs, flesh and bones, "Speak!" and his thighs, flesh and bones will state what he did. That is his attempt to excuse himself. That is the hypocrite and that is the one with whom Allah is angry.'

انظُرْ كَيْفَ كَذَبُوا عَلَىٰٓ أَنفُسِهِمْ وَضَلَّ عَنْهُم مَّا كَانُوا يَفْتَرُونَ ﴿٢٤﴾

24 See how they lie against themselves and how what they invented has forsaken them!

See how they lie against themselves

'*See*' here means 'reflect on'. The idolaters were lying when they said, 'The worship of idols brings us near in proximity to Allah.' They thought that and what they thought was wrong. They will have no excuse and their lying is not removed from them. The hypocrites are relying on what is false in their excuse and their denial is hypocrisy.

and how what they invented has forsaken them!

See how their forgery has forsaken them; it has disappeared and what they thought about their gods interceding for them has been shown to be false. It is said that it means that what they used to worship other than Allah has abandoned them and not helped them at all, as al-Ḥasan said. It is said that the meaning is that their lies are expunged from their minds due to their astonishment and distraction.

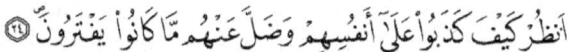

It is said that '*lie*' means 'deny' and the future is here designated by the past tense. It is possible that in the Next World they will deny what they did because it is the place of astonishment, bewilderment and distraction. It is said that it is not permitted for them to lie in the Next World because it is the abode of repayment for what happened in this world – and that is the view of most of the people of discernment – and that this all happens in this world. According to this, the meaning of the words: *'By Allah, our Lord, we were not idolaters'* is 'In our view, we were not idolaters.' The permissibility of denial in the Next World is countered by Allah's words: *'They will not be able to hide a single circumstance from Allah.'* (4:42) There is no contradiction or conflict. No circumstance is hidden from Allah in any place since their tongues, hands and feet will testify to what they did. They will lie against themselves in some places before the limbs testify to what they did, and Allah knows best.

Sa'īd ibn Jubayr said that their words *'By Allah, our Lord, We were not idolaters'* imply that they make excuses and swear oaths.' Ibn Abī Nājiḥ and Qatādah said that. It is related that Mujāhid said, 'When they see that all wrong actions are forgiven except for *shirk* and see people coming out of the Fire, they will say, "By Allah, our Lord, We were not idolaters."' It is said that it means: 'We know that the stones do not harm or help.' This, even if it is true and they spoke the truth and did not conceal, means they are still not excused by that. The stubborn one who is an unbeliever is not forgiven.

Then the words *'they will have no recourse'* have five different readings. Ḥamzah and al-Kisā'ī read *yakun* with *fitnatahum* in the accusative as a predicate its governing noun *'except to say'* i.e. 'except their saying'. This is a clear reading. The people of Madīnah and Abū 'Amr read *takun* with *fitnatahum* in the accusative, i.e. 'they have no recourse except to say.' Ubayy and Ibn Mas'ūd read *mā kāna* instead of *takun* with 'recourse *except to say*'. Ibn 'Āmir, 'Āṣim in the transmission of Ḥafṣ, al-A'mash in the transmission of al-Mufaḍḍal, al-Ḥasan, Qatādah and others have *takun* with *fitnatuhum* in the nominative as the noun of '*takun*' whose predicate is *'except to say.'* These are four readings. The fifth is '*yakun*' and *fitnatuhum*. Allah speaks of *fitnah* because it means trials, as in 2:275. '*Wa-llāhi*' is a vocative with the *wāw* of the oath, and *'our Lord'* is an adjective or appositive. If it is accusative, it is based on the vocative and it means 'O our Lord' which is a good reading because it has the meaning of humility and supplication even though there is a difference between an oath and the vocative.

وَمِنْهُم مَّن يَسْتَمِعُ إِلَيْكَ وَجَعَلْنَا عَلَىٰ قُلُوبِهِمْ أَكِنَّةً أَن يَفْقَهُوهُ وَفِىٓ ءَاذَانِهِمْ
وَقْرًا وَإِن يَرَوْا كُلَّ ءَايَةٍ لَّا يُؤْمِنُوا بِهَا حَتَّىٰٓ إِذَا جَآءُوكَ يُجَٰدِلُونَكَ يَقُولُ ٱلَّذِينَ
كَفَرُوٓا إِنْ هَٰذَآ إِلَّآ أَسَٰطِيرُ ٱلْأَوَّلِينَ ﴿٢٥﴾

25 Some of them listen to you but We have placed covers on their hearts, preventing them from understanding it, and heaviness in their ears. Though they see every Sign, they still do not believe, so that when they come to you, disputing with you, those who disbelieve say, 'This is nothing but the myths of previous peoples!'

Some of them listen to you but We have placed covers on their hearts,

'*Them*' here refers to the idolaters, the unbelievers of Makkah [although the verb is singular]. '*We have placed covers on their hearts*' means: 'We did that to them to repay them for their disbelief.' It does not mean that they do not hear or understand but rather that they do not profit from what they hear and are not guided to the truth and so they are in the position of someone who does not hear or understand. '*Akinnah*' are coverings, the singular of which is *kinān*. The verb means to conceal something in its shelter. *Kinānah* is a quiver, and *kannah* is one's father's wife, or a daughter-in-law or sister-in-law because she is in his protection (*kinn*). '*Preventing them from understanding it*' means disliking them to understand it or so that they do not understand it.

and heaviness in their ears.

This is added to the description. The word '*heaviness*' is used for ears when they are deaf and the verb is '*waqarat, tawqaru, waqr*'. The verbal noun can be vowelled (*waqar*) or it can come with a *sukūn* (*waqr*). When Allah puts heaviness in an ear, the verb is *waqara, yaqiru, waqr*. Abū Zayd said that the Arabs use the expression 'a deaf (*mawqūrah*) ear' without naming the cause. Accordingly, it would be *wuqirat*. Ṭalḥah ibn Muṣarrif recited '*wiqran*'. It means that Allah puts into their ears something that stops them from listening to the words. It resembles the heavy load (*wiqr*) of a camel which is the amount it can bear. *Wiqr* is a heavy load. *Muqīr* and *muqirah* are used for a palm tree when it has a lot a fruit. A man is described as '*dhū qirah*' when he is *waqūr*, someone with gravity. One speaks of a man as *waqura* with the nouns *maqar* and *waqār*.

Though they see every Sign, they still do not believe

Allah is speaking about their obstinacy because when they saw the moon split, they said, 'It is magic,' and Allah reported that they rejected the Signs without proof.

so that when they come to you, disputing with you,

They argue saying, 'You eat what you kill but do not eat what Allah has killed.' Ibn 'Abbās reported that. '*Those who disbelieve*' are Quraysh. Ibn 'Abbās said, 'They asked an-Naḍr ibn al-Ḥārith, "What does Muḥammad say?" He replied, "I saw his lips moving and all he was relating were the myths of previous peoples, like what I tell you about past generations."' An-Naḍr told stories and travelled and listened to the tales in the land of the Persians like the stories of Rustam and Isfandyar which he recounted.

The singular of *asāṭīr* (myths) is *asṭār*, like *abyāt* and *abāyīt*, according to az-Zajjāj. Al-Akhfash said that the singular is *usṭūrah* like *uḥdūthah* and *aḥadīth*, and Abū 'Ubaydah said that it is *isṭārah*, and an-Naḥḥās says *usṭūr*, like *uthkūl*. It is said that it is the plural of *asṭār* and *asṭār* is the plural of *saṭr* and *saṭar*, which is a line, like the line of a book. Al-Qushayrī said that the singular is *asṭīr*. It is also said that it is a plural which has no singular like *madhākīr* and *'abādīd*. It is what the early people wrote in books. Al-Jawharī and others said that it is falsehoods and trifles. One of our shaykhs recited to me:

My night is long and my whisperings afflict me,
    bringing trifles and falsehoods.

وَهُمْ يَنْهَوْنَ عَنْهُ وَيَنْـَٔوْنَ عَنْهُ وَإِن يُهْلِكُونَ إِلَّآ أَنفُسَهُمْ وَمَا يَشْعُرُونَ ﴿٢٦﴾

26 They keep others from it and avoid it themselves. They are only destroying themselves but they are not aware of it.

They keep others from it and avoid it themselves.

'*Keep from*' (*nahy*) means restrain and *na'y* is distance. It is general to all the unbelievers, in that they refuse to follow Muḥammad ﷺ and avoid him, as Ibn 'Abbās and al-Ḥasan said. It is said that it is specific to Abū Ṭālib who forbade the unbelievers to harm Muḥammad ﷺ while he was still far from believing in him, as Ibn 'Abbās also said.

It is related by the people of *Sīrah*: 'The Prophet ﷺ went out to the Ka'bah one day and wanted to pray. When he began the prayer, Abū Jahl – may Allah curse him – said, "Who will go to this man and spoil his prayer?" Ibn az-Ziba'rā got up and took an animal's stomach and blood and used it to splash the face of the Prophet ﷺ. The Prophet ﷺ left his prayer and then went to his uncle, Abū Ṭālib, and said, "Uncle, do you see what has been done to me?" Abū Ṭālib asked, "Who did this?" The Prophet ﷺ said, "'Abdullah ibn az-Ziba'rā." Abu Ṭālib rose and put his sword on his shoulder and he walked with him until he reached the people. When they saw Abū Ṭālib advancing, the people began to get up. Abu Ṭālib said, "By Allah, if a man rises, I will take my sword to him!" So they sat still until he was close to them. He asked, "My son, who did this to you?" He replied, "'Abdullāh ibn az-Ziba'rā." Abū Ṭālib took the stomach and blood and splashed their faces, beards and clothes with it and spoke roughly to them. This *āyah* was revealed: "*They keep others from it and avoid it themselves.*" The Prophet ﷺ said, "Uncle, an *āyah* has been revealed about you." He asked. "What is it?" He said, "You prevent Quraysh from injuring me and yet refuse to believe in me." Abū Ṭālib said:

"By Allah, they will not all reach you
    until I sleep buried in the earth.
State your command! You are not at fault.
    Proclaim the good news of that and eyes will delight in you.
You called me and stated that you have good counsel for me.
    You spoke the truth and you were trusted before.
You presented a *dīn*
    which I recognize is one of the best *dīns* of mankind.
If it had not been for blame or fear of abuse,
    you would have found me with sincere certainty of that."

They asked, "Messenger of Allah, will Abū Tālib benefit from his help to you?" He said, "Yes, because of that manacles are removed from him and he is joined to *shayṭāns* and does not enter into the pit of snakes and scorpions. His punishment is two sandals of fire on his feet by which his brain boils in his head. That is the least of the punishments of the Fire."' Allah revealed to His Messenger ﷺ: '*So be steadfast as the Messengers with firm resolve were also steadfast.*' (46:35)

In *Ṣaḥīḥ Muslim* Abū Hurayrah reported that the Prophet ﷺ said to his uncle, 'Say: "There is no god but Allah." I will testify to it for you on the Day of Rising.' He said, 'If it had not been that Quraysh would blame me, saying, "Anxiety (*jazā'*) has moved him to do this," I would have affirmed it to you.' So Allah revealed, '*You will not guide those you love, but Allah guides whomever He wishes.*' (28:56) This is the well-known transmission. Anxiety here means fear. Another variant has the word *kharā'* instead which is weakness. Again in *Ṣaḥīḥ Muslim*, Ibn 'Abbās reported that the Messenger of Allah ﷺ said, 'The one among the people of the Fire with the least punishment will be Abū Ṭālib. He is wearing a pair of sandals of fire which will make his brain boil.'

'Abdullāh ibn az-Ziba'rā became Muslim in the year of the Conquest and was a good Muslim. He apologised to the Messenger of Allah ﷺ who accepted his apology. He was an excellent poet. He eulogised the Messenger of Allah ﷺ and wrote many poems in praise of him to supplant what he had done when he was an unbeliever. An example of that is:

Anxieties and cares denied sleep.
    The first part of the night is dark and disturbed
At the news that has reached me that Aḥmad has blamed me
    in it, and so I spent the night like someone with a fever.
O best of those borne on a fine camel,
    with an easy gait, steady.
I apologise to you for what I did
    when I was wandering in misguidance
In days which bade me to the most erroneous state
    and bade me to be foolish.
I assisted the means to ruin and the business
    of the seducers led me. Their business is unlucky.
Today my heart has believed in the Prophet Muḥammad,
    and this person in error was replaced.
Enmity has passed and its causes ended.
    Ties and understanding have come between us.
So forgive! Ransom is yours as well as for your father.
    Show mercy! You are merciful and show mercy.
You have the mark of a king:
    a blazing light and fragrant seal.
After love, He gave you His proof
    as honour, and the proof of God is immense.
I have testified that your *dīn* is truthful,
    And true, and you are greatly important among His slaves.
Allah bears witness that Aḥmad is chosen,
    Pre-eminent among the righteous, noble.
A leader who is elevated among the sons of Hāshim,
    a branch firm in peaks and roots.

It is said that the meaning of the words '*They keep others from it*' is that those who listen prevent people from hearing the Qur'an and avoid it themselves, as Qatādah said. So the *hā'* of 'it' according to the first two positions refers to the Prophet ﷺ and in the position of Qatādah it refers to the Qur'an. '*They are only destroying themselves,*' meaning they only destroy themselves by persistence in disbelief and they also bear the burdens of those they bar from it. The '*an*' is negative.

وَلَوْ تَرَىٰٓ إِذْ وُقِفُوا۟ عَلَى ٱلنَّارِ فَقَالُوا۟ يَـٰلَيْتَنَا نُرَدُّ وَلَا نُكَذِّبَ بِـَٔايَـٰتِ رَبِّنَا وَنَكُونَ
مِنَ ٱلْمُؤْمِنِينَ ﴿٢٧﴾

27 If only you could see when they are standing before the Fire and saying, 'Oh! If only we could be sent back again, we would not deny the Signs of our Lord and we would be among the believers.'

If only you could see when they are standing before the Fire

This is when they are made to stand at that time. *Idh* is used in the meaning of *idhā* (when), and *idh* can be used in the place of *idhā* and *idhā* can be used in the place of *idh* and what will be as if it has already been, because the report of Allah is true and this is designated by the past tense. '*When they are standing* (*wuqifū* – they are made to stand)' is when they are held back. The verb is *waqafa* when transitive, *waqf*, and *waqafa* with *wuqūf*. Ibn as-Samayqa' recited '*idh waqafū*' from *wuqūf*. '*Before the Fire*' means above it on the *Ṣirāṭ* when it is under them. It is said that '*alā*' here means *bā'* and so they are made to stand near it seeing it.

Aḍ-Ḍaḥḥāk said, 'They are gathered,' to its gates. It is said that they are made to stand on the back of Hellfire while the Fire is under them. We find in a tradition, 'Everyone will be made to stand on the back of Hellfire, as if it was the back of a sheep's tail. Then a caller will call out, "Take your people and leave my people."' It is said that it means to enter it – may Allah give us refuge from it! – and so it would mean 'in the Fire.'

The apodosis of '*If*' is elided so as to be more effective in causing fear. It means: 'If you were to see them in that state, you would see the worst of states or you would have seen a terrible sight or seen an extraordinary matter or the like.'

saying, 'Oh! If only we could be sent back again, we would not deny the Signs of our Lord and we would be among the believers.'

In the reading of the people of Madīnah, al-Kisā'ī, Abū 'Amr and Abū Bakr from 'Āṣim, all the verbs are read with the *ḍammah* at the end. Ibn 'Āmir has the *ḍammah* in *nukadhdhibu* but *fatḥah* in *nakūna*. All of it has the sense of hoping; they hope to be sent back and not deny and to be believers. Sībawayh prefers a stop after '*deny*', so that it is not included in the hope so that the meaning of '*not deny*' means to be firm in not denying, i.e. 'We will not deny, whether we are returned or not.' Sībawayh said, 'It is like the words, "Leave me. I will not revert." It means: 'I will not revert in any case, whether or not you leave me.'

Abū 'Amr deduced that their state of hopefulness [for a different outcome] ends when Allah says: '*Truly they are liars*,' because hopefulness is not considered to be lying. Lying is a false report. The one who says that the words '*Truly they are liars*' is an aspect of their hopefulness says, 'The meaning is that what they are saying is that they were actually lying in this world when they denied the resurrection and denied the Messengers [but really they believed in it].'

Ḥamzah and Ḥafṣ read '*nukadhdhiba*' and '*nakūna*' as the apodosis of wishing because it is not mandatory. They are both part of wishing, with the meaning that they wish to be returned and to abandon lying and to be with the believers. Abū Isḥāq says that the meaning of '*we would not deny*' is 'If we were to be returned, we will not deny.' '*Nukadhdhiba*' and '*nakūna*' have an implied '*an*' as in the apodosis of a question, command, prohibition or request because none of them are mandatory and have not yet occurred. Therefore, there is a *fatḥah* at the end of the verbs as if it was added to the verbal noun of the first. It is as if they were saying, 'Would that we could be sent back [with a noun rather than the verb], not deny and be among the believers!' So it is based on the verbal noun of '*be sent back*' [*lanā radd*] since it would normally be read as '*nuraddu*' [with a *ḍammah*], and so there must be an implied '*an*' by which the accusative is achieved in the two verbs. Ibn 'Āmir recited '*nakūna*' as the apodosis of wishing as when you say, 'Would that you came to us and we honoured you,' meaning 'would that you would come to us and we would honour you.' So the first two verbs are included in the wish. Or it means: 'we would not deny' and the words stop. This is possible.

Ubayy recited '*lā nukhadhdhiba*' with an additional '*abadan*' (ever) '*the Signs of our Lord*.' Ibn Mas'ūd has, '*falā*' with *fā'* and the verb in the accusative. Because of the *fā'* the apodosis is in the accusative as it would by on account of 'and'. Az-Zajjāj said that. Most of the Basrans only permit the apodosis with *fā'*.

بَلْ بَدَا لَهُم مَّا كَانُوا۟ يُخْفُونَ مِن قَبْلُ ۖ وَلَوْ رُدُّوا۟ لَعَادُوا۟ لِمَا نُهُوا۟ عَنْهُ وَإِنَّهُمْ لَكَٰذِبُونَ ﴿٢٨﴾

28 No, it is simply that what they were concealing before has been shown to them; and if they were sent back they would merely return to what they were forbidden to do. Truly they are liars.

No, it is simply that what they were concealing before has been shown to them;

'*Bal*' is turning away from their wishing and claiming faith if they were to be sent back. Scholars disagree about the meaning of the words '*has been shown to them*' and various things are said about specifying what is meant. It is said that what is meant are the hypocrites because the term '*kufr*' includes them, and so the pronoun refers to some of those mentioned. An-Naḥḥās said, 'This is sweet and eloquent language.' It is said that what is meant are the unbelievers and when the Prophet ﷺ warned them, they were afraid and concealed that fear so that the weak among them would not become aware of their fear. This will all be revealed on the Day of Rising. That is why al-Ḥasan said that it means: 'there appears to some of them what they concealed from others.'

It is said that the *shirk* they denied will appear and they will say, 'Allah is our Lord. We were not idolaters,' and Allah will make their limbs speak and they will bear witness to their disbelief. That is when '*what they were concealing before has been shown to them*'. Abū Rawq said that. It is said that the *kufr* they were concealing will appear to them, in the form of their evil actions, as in Allah's words: '*What confronts them will be the evil actions which they earned.*' (39:47) Al-Mubarrad said, 'The repayment of their *kufr* which they concealed will be shown to them.' It is said that the meaning is that what those in error concealed from those who followed them about the Rising and resurrection will appear to them because it is followed by the words: '*They say, "There is nothing but this life and we will not be raised again."*'

'*If they were sent back*' after seeing the punishment – or it is said that it is before actually seeing it – then they would still revert to the *shirk* which they were forbidden, because Allah knows that they will not believe. Iblīs saw the signs of Allah with his own eyes but then was still obdurate. The words '*Truly they are liars*' tell us about them and their state in this world of denial of the Messengers and the Resurrection, as Allah says: '*Your Lord will judge.*' (16:124) speaking about their future state. It is said that it means that they will lie by saying about themselves that they did not deny and were among the believers. Yaḥyā ibn

Waththāb recited '*riddū*'. The root is '*rudidū*' and the *kasrah* of the *dāl* has been moved to the *rā'*.

وَقَالُوٓاْ إِنۡ هِيَ إِلَّا حَيَاتُنَا ٱلدُّنۡيَا وَمَا نَحۡنُ بِمَبۡعُوثِينَ ٢٩

29 They say, 'There is nothing but this life and we will not be raised again.'

The pronoun '*we*' is the subject noun of *mā* and '*raised again*' is its predicate. This is an inceptive reporting about them and what they said in this world. Ibn Zayd said that this is connected to the prior words and is what the people referred to said in this world. It means that they revert to disbelief and are distracted by immediate pleasure. This is what impels the obstinate as exemplified by *shayṭān*. Or it can mean that Allah confuses them after they had gained knowledge. This is common with the intellect.

وَلَوۡ تَرَىٰٓ إِذۡ وُقِفُواْ عَلَىٰ رَبِّهِمۡۚ قَالَ أَلَيۡسَ هَٰذَا بِٱلۡحَقِّۚ قَالُواْ بَلَىٰ وَرَبِّنَاۚ قَالَ
فَذُوقُواْ ٱلۡعَذَابَ بِمَا كُنتُمۡ تَكۡفُرُونَ ٣٠

30 If only you could see when they are standing before their Lord. He will say, 'Is this not the Truth?' They will say, 'Yes indeed, by our Lord!' He will say, 'Then taste the punishment for your disbelief.'

This is when they are made to stand at Allah's command to them, meaning as Allah has commanded them. It is said that the preposition '*'alā*' (lit. 'upon) here means '*'inda*' ('in the presence of') meaning with the angels and for His repayment to them, since no one has any power except Allah. You say, 'I was made to stand before so-and-so,' and the apodosis of *law* '*if only*' is elided because of the awesomeness of the standing. They will be rebuked and will acknowledge the truth. The angels will say to them, 'Is this Resurrection and Punishment not the truth?' They will answer, 'Yes, indeed it is!'

قَدْ خَسِرَ ٱلَّذِينَ كَذَّبُوا۟ بِلِقَآءِ ٱللَّهِ حَتَّىٰٓ إِذَا جَآءَتْهُمُ ٱلسَّاعَةُ بَغْتَةً قَالُوا۟ يَٰحَسْرَتَنَا
عَلَىٰ مَا فَرَّطْنَا فِيهَا وَهُمْ يَحْمِلُونَ أَوْزَارَهُمْ عَلَىٰ ظُهُورِهِمْ ۚ أَلَا سَآءَ مَا يَزِرُونَ ﴿٣١﴾

31 Those who deny the meeting with Allah have lost, so that, when the Hour comes upon them suddenly, they will say, 'Alas for what we neglected there!' They will bear their burdens on their backs. How evil is what they bear!

Those who deny the meeting with Allah have lost,

It is said that this is about those who deny the Resurrection after death and the Repayment they will face. Its proof is the words of the Prophet ﷺ, 'Whoever swears a false oath in order to take some of the property of a Muslim will meet Allah while He is angry with him,' he will meet His repayment of him, because the one with whom Allah is angry will not see Allah as those who affirm the vision of His face do. Al-Qaffāl and others believed that. Al-Qushayrī said, 'This is not the case because it is clearly indicated that the meeting in the place applies to the repayment. Such an additional interpretation is unnecessary. The meeting is taken literally in this *āyah*. The unbelievers deny the Creator and deny the possibility of seeing Him.'

so that, when the Hour comes upon them suddenly,

The Rising is called the Hour because of the speed of the Reckoning which takes place in it. '*Baghtah*' means 'suddenly' from the verb *baghata*, and it is in the accusative as an adverbial *ḥāl* although Sībawayh said that it is a verbal noun used as a *ḥāl* as when you say, 'he killed him *ṣabran*' (confined him until he died). [POEM]

They will say, 'Alas for what we neglected there!'

The use of the vocative particle *yā'* with *ḥasrah* denotes grief. It is not an actual vocative, but simply indicates a lot of regret. It is like saying, 'How astonishing!' or 'How opulent!' They are not actual vocatives, but call attention to the extent of the marvel and opulence referred to. Sībawayh said, 'It is as if He were saying, "O wonder, come! This is the time for you to come." It is like the words, "O our remorse!" meaning "Come, our remorse. It is your time." Similarly, that which it is not sound to have as a vocative is used in this way. This is more intensive than saying, "I marvelled." A poet said:

O wonder! (*yā 'ajaban*) at the loaded saddle!

It is said that it is calling people's attention to the intensity of the grief they will feel, like saying, 'People! take note of the immensity of my grief!' So the vocative refers to other than the one called to, as when you say, 'I should not see you here' and the prohibition on other than the prohibited is actual.'

The words '*for what we neglected there*!' refer to the Last Day and their lack of preparation for it as al-Ḥasan said. The root of *farraṭa* (*neglected*) is to 'go forward', as when one goes ahead to water, as the Prophet ﷺ said, 'I will be the first of you to reach the Basin.' *Al-fāriṭ* is the one who reaches water first. It is used of a child in supplication: 'O Allah, make him a forerunner for his parents!' It can mean: 'powerlessness preceded us.' It can mean 'We made others go first to obedience of Allah and fell behind them.' '*Fīhā*' can mean in this world by not acting for the Last Hour. Aṭ-Ṭabarī said that the *hā'* refers to the transaction. That is that the loss incurred by them through selling their faith for disbelief and the Next World for this world becomes clear to them. They say, 'Alas for what we neglected in it,' in other words in the transaction they made. Allah does not actually mention it because the words indicate it, such loss only occurring in a sales transaction, as evidenced in Allah's words: '*Their trade has brought no profit.*' (2:16) As-Suddī said, 'It means "what we neglected," referring to the actions of the Garden they failed to do.' In a tradition Abū Sa'īd al-Khudrī reported that the Prophet ﷺ said about this *āyah*, 'The people of the Fire will see their places [they would have had] in the Garden and say, "Alas!"'

They will bear their burdens on their backs.

This means their wrong actions. *Awzār* is the plural of *wizr*. It is a metaphor, likening their situation to the one who carries a burden. The verb is *wazara, yaziru*, and *wazira, yawzaru*. The participles are *wāzir* and *mawzūr*. Its root is *wazr*, which is a mountain. An example of its usage is found in the *ḥadīth* about the women who came out to a funeral, 'They returned burdened (*mawzūrāt*), not rewarded.' Abū 'Ubayd said, 'One generally says "*ma'zūrāt*".' This has no sense because it is derived from *wizr*.' Abū 'Ubayd said, 'It is said to a man when he spreads out his garment and puts goods in it, "Carry your burden (*wizr*)."' *Wazīr* (minister) comes from the same root because the *wazīr* bears the burdens of the management of government. The sentence means that their wrong actions will cling to them and they will be burdened by them. Their burden is evil.

وَمَا ٱلْحَيَوٰةُ ٱلدُّنْيَآ إِلَّا لَعِبٌ وَلَهْوٌ وَلَلدَّارُ ٱلْـَٔاخِرَةُ خَيْرٌ لِّلَّذِينَ يَتَّقُونَ أَفَلَا تَعْقِلُونَ ﴿٣٢﴾

32 The life of this world is nothing but a game and a diversion. The abode of the Next World is better for those who are godfearing. So will you not use your intellect?

The life of this world is nothing but a game and a diversion.

That is due to the shortness of its duration as is said:

This world is like the dream of someone asleep.
There is no good in a life that does not abide.
Reflect! If you obtained a pleasure yesterday,
and spent it. Are you anything except a dreamer?

Another said:

Act gently. You are dead.
Exert yourself, human being!
When it passes, it will be as if it were not.
And it is as if it already was what is already the past.

It is said that the meaning is the enjoyment of the life of this world, saying that they imagine that what they enjoyed in this world will not be subject to an ultimate accounting, and so it is like a game and a diversion and nothing more. Sulaymān ibn 'Abdullāh looked in a mirror and said, 'I am the youthful king.' A slave-girl of his said to him:

You would be the best enjoyment if you would only last,
but no human being lasts for ever.
There is no fault at all in anything we see of you;
it's all a person could possibly have; but you will pass away.

It is said that the expression '*game and diversion*' means falsehood and delusion in that Allah says elsewhere: '*The life of this world is nothing by the enjoyment of delusion.*' (3:185) What is intended by the *āyah* is to say that the unbelievers are lying when they said, '*It is only the life of this world.*' (6:29) The meaning of of the noun '*game*' (*la'ib*) is well-known. *Tal'ābah* means a lot of game playing. *Mal'ab* is the place where game playing takes place. The meaning of '*diversion*' (*lahw*) is also well-known: it is everything that distracts you. The verb is *alhā* from *lahw*. It is said that its root meaning is turning from a thing. Al-Mahdawī said that that is unlikely because the word whose root meaning is turning away has a *yā'* rather than a *wāw*.

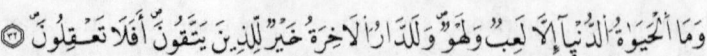

The affairs of the Next World have nothing to do with games and diversion. The reality of a game is that it has no benefit, and diversion is what one diverts oneself with. What is meant for the Next World is outside of them. A man of this world was blamed in the presence of 'Alī ibn Abī Ṭālib and 'Alī said, 'This world is the abode of truthfulness for the one who is true to it, the abode of salvation for the one who understands it, and the abode of stupidity for the one who depends on it.' Maḥmūd al-Warrāq said:

Do not pursue this world and its days
    in a blameworthy way, even if fortune favours you.
Part of the honour of this world and its excellence
    is that you use it in pursuit of the Next World.

Abū 'Umar ibn 'Abd al-Barr related that Abū Sa'īd al-Khudrī reported that the Messenger of Allah ﷺ said, 'This world is cursed and cursed is what is in it, except for the remembrance of Allah Almighty and what leads to it and the teacher and the student who share in the reward. All other people are rabble with no good in them.' At-Tirmidhī reported it from Abū Hurayrah and said it is *ḥasan gharīb*. It is reported that the Prophet ﷺ said, 'Part of the baseness of this world in the sight of Allah is that it is only there that He is disobeyed and that what is with Him is only obtained by leaving it.' At-Tirmidhī reported from Sahl ibn Sa'd that the Messenger of Allah ﷺ said, 'If this world has been worth a gnat's wing in the sight of Allah He would not let an unbeliever have a single drink of water from it.' A poet said:

You hear of days such that, if you have resolve,
    you will be commanding and forbidding in them.
If this world leaves you with your *dīn*,
    anything you miss will not harm you.
This world is not worth a gnat's wing
    nor the weight of a feather of a bird's wing.
This world is not a pleasing reward for a believer
    nor a pleasing reprisal for an unbeliever.

Ibn 'Abbās said, 'This is what the life of the unbeliever is because he spends it in delusion and falsehood. The life of the believer contains righteous actions and so it is not a diversion or a game.'

The abode of the Next World is better for those who are godfearing.

This means the Garden since it will go on forever. It is called *Ākhirah* because it is delayed for us while this world is immediate for us. Ibn 'Āmir reads the word *dār* (abode) with one *lām*: *'wa la-dār'*, which implies: the abode of the final life. The majority read it: *'wa la-d-dār* with the *lām* of the inceptive and *ad-dār* is in the nominative by the inceptive which makes *'Ākhirah'* its adjective. The predicate is '*better for those*'. That is strengthened by the words: '*That is the Next Abode.*' (28:83) and: '*The life of this world is nothing but a game and diversion.*' (29:64) In both cases '*ākhirah*' is an adjective of '*dār*'.

'*Those who are godfearing*' fear *shirk*. The phrase: '*So will you not use your intellect?*' can be read with both *tā'* and *yā'* (will *they* not?) Allah knows best.

قَدْ نَعْلَمُ إِنَّهُۥ لَيَحْزُنُكَ ٱلَّذِى يَقُولُونَ فَإِنَّهُمْ لَا يُكَذِّبُونَكَ وَلَٰكِنَّ ٱلظَّٰلِمِينَ
بِـَٔايَٰتِ ٱللَّهِ يَجْحَدُونَ ﴿٣٣﴾ وَلَقَدْ كُذِّبَتْ رُسُلٌ مِّن قَبْلِكَ فَصَبَرُوا۟ عَلَىٰ مَا
كُذِّبُوا۟ وَأُوذُوا۟ حَتَّىٰٓ أَتَىٰهُمْ نَصْرُنَا وَلَا مُبَدِّلَ لِكَلِمَٰتِ ٱللَّهِ وَلَقَدْ جَآءَكَ
مِن نَّبَإِى۟ ٱلْمُرْسَلِينَ ﴿٣٤﴾

33-34 We know that what they say distresses you. It is not that they are calling you a liar; the wrongdoers are just denying Allah's Signs. Messengers before you were also denied but they were steadfast in the face of the denial and injury they suffered until Our help arrived. There is no changing the Words of Allah. And news of other Messengers has come to you.

We know that what they say distresses you.

'*Inna*' has a *kasrah* because of the addition of the following *lām*. Abū Maysarah said, 'The Messenger of Allah ﷺ passed by Abū Jahl and his people. They said, "Muḥammad! By Allah, we do not say that you are lying. We consider you truthful, but we deny what you have brought." So the *āyah* was revealed: *"It is not that they are calling you a liar; the wrongdoers are just denying Allah's Signs."* Then Allah consoled him by saying: "*Messengers before you were also denied.*"' Ibn 'Abbas said, 'They do not deny you.' It can be recited as '*yukdhibūnaka*' and it is said that that means the same as '*yukadhdhibūnaka*'. Abū 'Ubayd preferred the first reading and it is also the reading of 'Alī. It is related from him that Abū Jahl said to the Prophet ﷺ, 'We do not say you are a liar. We say that what you have brought is a lie.' So this was revealed. An-Naḥḥās said that Abu 'Ubayd is opposed in holding to this opinion, an opposition strengthened by the fact that a man recited to Ibn 'Abbās, '*yukdhibūnaka*' and Ibn 'Abbās said to him, '*yukadhdhibūnaka*' because they called the Prophet ﷺ 'the trustworthy one'. (The meaning of the former is 'they called you a liar' and of the latter 'they denied you'.)

The meaning of '*they deny you*' (*yukadhdhibūnaka*) according to language experts is that they ascribe lying to you and reject what you say. It means: they would not accuse you of telling a lie so as to call you a liar if they were to reflect on what you have brought. It can mean that they do not confirm that you are a liar or, if it is in Form II, that you do not bring a proof or evidence. This is indicated by Allah's words: '*the wrongdoers are just denying Allah's Signs.*' An-Naḥḥās took the position of Abū 'Ubayd regarding this and his justification is because 'Alī related the *ḥadīth* and it is sound that he recited it in Form IV of the verb. Al-Kisā'ī related from the Arabs that you say '*akdhabtu-r-rajul*' when you tell him that he has brought a lie and related it and '*kadhdhabtuhu*' when you tell him that he is a liar. That is also what az-Zajjāj says.

but they were steadfast in the face of the denial and injury they suffered until Our help arrived. There is no changing the Words of Allah.

This means: 'you should be steadfast as they were steadfast.' The words: '*until Our help arrived*' let him know that what he is promised will come to him and the phrase: '*There is no changing the Words of Allah*' makes that help clear, in other words 'Do not doubt what Allah has promised, for no one can annul His judgment or oppose His promise.' This is corroborated by Allah's words elsewhere: '*We will certainly help Our Messengers and those who believe.*' (40:51) and: '*Our Word was given before to Our slaves, the Messengers, that they would certainly be helped. It is Our army which will be victorious.*' (37:171-173) and: '*Allah has written, "I will be victorious, I and My Messengers."*' (58:21)

And news of other Messengers has come to you.

The subject of '*come to you*' is implied. It means: reports concerning the news of other Messengers have come to you.

وَإِن كَانَ كَبُرَ عَلَيْكَ إِعْرَاضُهُمْ فَإِنِ اسْتَطَعْتَ أَن تَبْتَغِيَ نَفَقًا
فِي الْأَرْضِ أَوْ سُلَّمًا فِي السَّمَاءِ فَتَأْتِيَهُم بِآيَةٍ وَلَوْ شَاءَ اللَّهُ لَجَمَعَهُمْ عَلَى
الْهُدَىٰ فَلَا تَكُونَنَّ مِنَ الْجَاهِلِينَ ﴿٣٥﴾

35 If their turning away is hard on you, then go down a tunnel deep into the earth, if you can, or climb up a ladder into heaven, and bring them a Sign. If Allah had wanted to, He would have gathered them all to guidance. So do not be among the ignorant.

Their turning from faith is very difficult for you to bear. The phrase '*go down a tunnel*' (*nafaq*) means seek a means by which you can escape from Him to another place. The word *nāfiqā'* (the hole of the jerboa), which was explained in *Sūrat al-Baqarah* (2:4), comes from the same root. *Munāfiq* (hypocrite) also derives from it. The expression '*a ladder into heaven*' is a metaphor, in that a ladder is also something that is used to go to another place. Qatādah said that it actually means a ladder. Az-Zajjāj said that it is derived from *salāmah* (safety) because it delivers you to another place. The words '*bring them a sign*' are added to it and mean: 'Do it so that they will believe.' The answer is implied since the listener already knows it. Allah commanded His Prophet ﷺ not be deeply sorrowful about them on account of his inability to guide them to belief.

If Allah had wanted to, He would have gathered them all to guidance.

He would have created them believers and sealed them in that state. Allah makes it clear that their disbelief is by the will of Allah, which refutes the Qadariyyah. It is said that it means: 'He would have showed them a sign which have forced them into belief but He wished to reward those of them who believed and acted rightly.'

'

So do not be among the ignorant.

Do not be among those who are sad about them and grieve to the extent that they are moved to deep grief. Do not grieve over their disbelief so as to be close to the state of the ignorant. It is said that although it is addressed to him ﷺ, it is meant for the Community. The hearts of the Muslims were constricted by the disbelief of those people and their harmful behaviour.

إِنَّمَا يَسْتَجِيبُ الَّذِينَ يَسْمَعُونَ ۘ وَالْمَوْتَىٰ يَبْعَثُهُمُ اللَّهُ ثُمَّ إِلَيْهِ يُرْجَعُونَ ﴿٣٦﴾
وَقَالُوا لَوْلَا نُزِّلَ عَلَيْهِ آيَةٌ مِّن رَّبِّهِ ۚ قُلْ إِنَّ اللَّهَ قَادِرٌ عَلَىٰ أَن يُنَزِّلَ
آيَةً وَلَٰكِنَّ أَكْثَرَهُمْ لَا يَعْلَمُونَ ﴿٣٧﴾

36-37 Only those who can hear respond. As for the dead, Allah will raise them up, then to Him they will be returned. They ask, 'Why has no Sign been sent down to him from his Lord?' Say, 'Allah has the power to send down a Sign.' But most of them do not know it.

Only those who can hear respond. As for the dead, Allah will raise them up,

Hearing here means to truly give ear, understand and desire the truth. They are the believers who accept what they hear, benefit by it and act on it. Al-Ḥasan and Mujāhid said that. Then the words end and Allah says: *'Allah will raise them up,'* referring to the unbelievers, as al-Hasan and Mujāhid said. They are like the dead in that they do not accept or listen to evidence. It is said that it means everyone who has died whom Allah will raise up for the Reckoning. According to the first understanding, their raising up is their guidance to faith in Allah and in His Messenger ﷺ. Al-Ḥasan said that it is their being raised up from their *shirk* so that they believe in you, Muḥammad, i.e. when they are dying while still in a state of seeking refuge in this world.

They ask, 'Why has no Sign been sent down to him from his Lord?'

Al-Ḥasan said that *lawlā* (if not) here means *hallā* (why not?) [POEM EXAMP] This is a reference to obduracy on their part after the evidence appeared and the proof of the Qur'an was made manifest when they showed their inability to produce a *sūrah* like it because of the description and knowledge of the Unseen that it contains.

But most of them do not know it.

They do not know that Allah sends down *āyahs* which are beneficial to His slaves. Allah knows that He will bring out from their descendants peoples who will believe and so will not eradicate them. They do not know that Allah has the power to send it down. Az-Zajjāj said, 'They asked him [for a Sign] which would unite them in guidance.'

وَمَا مِن دَآبَّةٍ فِي ٱلْأَرْضِ وَلَا طَٰٓئِرٍ يَطِيرُ بِجَنَاحَيْهِ إِلَّآ أُمَمٌ أَمْثَالُكُم مَّا فَرَّطْنَا فِي ٱلْكِتَٰبِ مِن شَيْءٍ ثُمَّ إِلَىٰ رَبِّهِمْ يُحْشَرُونَ ﴿٣٨﴾

38 There is no creature crawling on the earth or flying creature, flying on its wings, who are not communities just like yourselves – We have not omitted anything from the Book – then they will be gathered to their Lord.

There is no creature crawling on the earth or flying creature, flying on its wings,

The meaning of the word *dābbah* was already discussed in *Sūrat al-Baqarah* (2:164). Its root is from the verb *dabba, yadibbu*. An animal crawls when it moves. '*Flying*' is read *ṭā'irin* in the genitive, conjoined with the previous words. Al-Ḥasan and 'Abdullāh ibn Abī Isḥāq recited *ṭā'irun* in the nominative conjoined with the previous words. The words '*on its wings*' are added for emphasis, and remove any ambiguity, because the Arabs sometimes use the word *ṭayrān* metaphorically for other than birds. Someone might say to a man, 'Fly with wings', meaning that he should go swiftly. Allah mentions '*wings*' to clarify that what He has said actually refers to birds while the word may be metaphorical in respect of other things. It is said that they have 'two wings' for balance so that they do not go to one side rather than the other. We know that birds have wings and yet '*Nothing holds them there (in the air) except Allah.*' (16:79) One wing is *janāḥ* and it is their wings that enable them to fly in the air. The root meaning of *janaḥa* is to incline to one side. and is used of a ship when, beached, it leans on its side and becomes stranded. The word 'bird' is sometimes used of human being in connection with their actions. We find in revelation: '*We have fastened the destiny (*ṭā'ir*) of every man about his neck.*' (17:13)

who are not communities just like yourselves –

They are communities like you in that Allah created and provided for them and is just towards them. Therefore, you must not wrong them and exceed what you are commanded in their respect. The word *dābbah* indicates everything that crawls. Earth rather than heaven is mentioned because it is what they know and see. It is said that they are like us in respect of glorification and guidance. It means: 'There is no animal or bird that does not glorify Allah Almighty.' That clearly indicates His oneness, if the unbelievers were only to reflect. Abū Hurayrah said, 'They are like us in the sense that all of them will be gathered and the hornless will take retaliation from the horned. Then Allah will say to them, "Be dust."' This is preferred by az-Zajjāj. He said, 'Communities like yourselves' in terms of creation, provision, death, resurrection and retaliation, which resembles the first view.

Sufyān ibn 'Uyaynah said, 'There is no category of animal and bird but that its like exists in human beings. Some people attack like lions, some are greedy like pigs, some are rapacious like dogs, and some are vain like peacocks. This is the meaning of resemblance.' Al-Khaṭṭābī preferred this. He said, 'You are dealing with wild animals and beasts of prey, so be careful.' Mujāhid said, 'The species have names by which they are known just as you are known.' Other things, which are not sound, are said about them having the same level of knowledge that we do and that they will be gathered and given bliss in the Garden and recompensed for the pains afflicted on them in this world and that the people of the Garden will be familiar with their forms. The sound view is that '*communities just like yourselves*' means that they are created and directed to their Maker and are in need of Him and provided for by Him just as your provision is up to Allah. What Sufyān said is good. It is like what happens in existence.

We have not omitted anything from the Book

This means from the Preserved Tablet. All the events that will occur are confirmed in it. It is said that it means: in the Qur'an, implying, 'We have not omitted anything of the *dīn* without directing you to it in the Qur'an, either by clear explained guidance or in general terms, which are clarified by the Messenger ﷺ, or by consensus, or analogy, which is based on the text of the Book.' Allah says: '*We have sent down the Book to you making all things clear*' (16:89) and: '*And We have sent down the Reminder to you so that you can make clear to mankind what has been sent down to them*' (16:44) and: '*Whatever the Messenger gives you you should accept and whatever He forbids you you should forgo.*' (59:7) Allah speaks generally in this *āyah* and in the above mentioned *āyah* of *Sūrat an-Naḥl* about what He has not specifically mentioned in a text. So Allah stated that He did not omit anything in the Book: it is mentioned either in detail or in general. He says: '*Today I have perfected your dīn for you.*' (5:3)

then they will be gathered to their Lord.

This will be for repayment, as mentioned in the report from Abū Hurayrah. In *Ṣaḥīḥ Muslim* it is reported that the Messenger of Allah ﷺ said, 'Rights will be given to the people owed them on the Day of Rising until even the hornless sheep takes retaliation from the horned sheep.' This indicates that the animals will be gathered on the Day of Rising. This is the view of Abū Dharr, Abū Hurayrah, al-Ḥasan and others. It is related that Ibn 'Abbās said in one variant, 'The gathering of animals and birds is at their death.' Aḍ-Ḍaḥḥāk said that. The first is sounder based on the literal meaning of *āyah* and the sound report. We read in the Revelation: '*When the wild beasts are all herded together.*' (81:5) Ja'far ibn Barqān related from Yazīd ibn al-Aṣamm that Abū Hurayrah said: 'Allah will gather all creation on the Day of Rising: beasts, animals and birds and everything. Part of the extent of the justice of Allah Almighty on that Day is that He will take from the horned sheep for the hornless one. Then He will say, "Be dust." That is indicated by the words of the Almighty: "*The unbeliever will say, 'Oh, if only I were dust!'*" (78:40)' 'Aṭā' said, 'When they see the sons of Ādam and the anxiety they are in, they will say, "Praise be to Allah Who did not make us like you! We do not desire a Garden or fear a Fire." Allah will say to them, "Be dust." Then the unbeliever will wish that he was dust.'

One group say that the '*gathering*' in the *āyah* refers simply to the unbelievers, and these [words about the animal communities] are parenthetical and the establishment of the evidence [for gathering]. As for the *ḥadīth*, its intention is to demonstrate an aspect of the immensity of the Reckoning, retaliation and concern for it, so that it is understood that it must happen to everyone and that it is unavoidable. They support this by the unsound element added to the *ḥadīth* by some of its transmitters, namely: 'until the hornless sheep takes retaliation from the horned sheep, the stone for what it did to another stone, and the stick for scratching another stick.' Men of knowledge have said, 'It is clear from this that what is meant by it is a useful metaphor bringing about reflection and alarm, because it is not logical that inanimate things should be addressed, rewarded or punished, and no intelligent person believes that they are. It is only imagined by a group of foolish idiots.' Adding, 'Because the pen does not record what they do, it is not possible for them to be punished.'

The sound view is the first one, based on what we mentioned from the *ḥadīth* of Abū Hurayrah. Even if the pen does not record their actions in terms of judgments, they will settle scores between themselves. It is related that Abū Dharr said, 'Two sheep butted one another in the presence of the Prophet ﷺ and he said, "Abū Dharr, do you know why they are butting one another?" I replied, "No." He said, "But Allah knows and will settle it between them."' This is a text. We have offered further explanation about the states of the dead and the Next World in the *Kitāb at-Tadhkirah*. Allah knows best.

وَٱلَّذِينَ كَذَّبُوا۟ بِـَٔايَـٰتِنَا صُمٌّ وَبُكْمٌ فِى ٱلظُّلُمَـٰتِ ۗ مَن يَشَإِ ٱللَّهُ يُضْلِلْهُ وَمَن يَشَأْ يَجْعَلْهُ عَلَىٰ صِرَٰطٍ مُّسْتَقِيمٍ ۝ قُلْ أَرَءَيْتَكُمْ إِنْ أَتَىٰكُمْ عَذَابُ ٱللَّهِ أَوْ أَتَتْكُمُ ٱلسَّاعَةُ أَغَيْرَ ٱللَّهِ تَدْعُونَ إِن كُنتُمْ صَـٰدِقِينَ ۝ بَلْ إِيَّاهُ تَدْعُونَ فَيَكْشِفُ مَا تَدْعُونَ إِلَيْهِ إِن شَآءَ وَتَنسَوْنَ مَا تُشْرِكُونَ ۝

39-41 Those who deny Our Signs are deaf and dumb in utter darkness. Allah misguides whomever He wills, and puts whomever He wills on a straight path. Say: 'What do you think? If Allah's punishment were to come upon you, or the Hour, would you call on other than Allah if you are being truthful?' It is Him you call on and, if He wills, He will deliver you from whatever it was that made you call on Him; and you will forget what you associated with Him.

Those who deny Our Signs are deaf and dumb in utter darkness.

They gain no benefit from their hearing and sight. Every nation of animals and other creatures are guided to their best interests but the unbelievers are not guided. This was discussed in *Sūrat al-Baqarah* (2:18). The '*utter darkness*' referred to is the darkness of disbelief. Abū 'Alī said that the deafness and dumbness referred to may occur in the Next World and it may, therefore, be real and not a metaphor.

Allah misguides whomever He wills, and puts whomever He wills on a straight path.

This indicates that Allah has willed the misguidance of the unbelievers and wanted to carry out His justice on them. He says that He: '…*puts whomever He wills on a straight path*,' in other words on the path of the *dīn* of Islam to fulfil His generosity to him. This invalidates the school of the Qadariyyah. The 'will' refers to those who denied. He will misguide some and will guide some.

Say: 'What do you think? If Allah's punishment were to come upon you or the Hour, would you call on other than Allah if you are being truthful?'

Nāfi' recites this by lightening the two *hamzah*s. Abū 'Ubayd related that the *hamzah* is dropped and replaced by an *alif*. An-Naḥḥās said that those with deep knowledge of Arabic say that this is an error because both the *yā'* and *alif* are silent and two silent letters are not joined together. Makkī said that it is related from Warsh that the *hamzah* is replaced by an *alif* known by the fact that a *maddah* is related from him which can only happen if there is replacement. Replacement is a sub-branch of the roots and the root is to put a *hamzah* between a *hamzah* with a *fatḥah* and an *alif*. It is on that basis that all but Warsh lighten the second. Abū 'Amr, 'Āṣim and Hamzah recite it with both *alifs* and bringing the word on its original base of the *hamzah* because the *hamzah* of the question is added to '*ra'ayta*' and the *hamzah* is part of the root of the verb. The *yā'* is silent because of the connection. 'Īsā ibn 'Umar and al-Kisā'ī recite '*a-raytakum*' with elision of the second *hamzah* which is unlikely in Arabic prose but permitted in poetry.

The position of the Basrans is that '*-kum*' is for the second person and has no position in syntax. That is preferred by az-Zajjāj. The position of al-Kisā'ī, al-Farrā' and others is that '*-kum*' is in the accusative because the seeing (tr. as 'think' here) applies to them. It means: 'Do you see yourselves?' If it is in the second person and added for emphasis, then the '*inna*' is in the accusative as the object of see/think and so '*inna*' is in the position of a second object. The first when the verb *ra'ā* refers to the seeing of the eye when it takes one object. When it means think, it takes two objects.

The words '*or the Hour*' refer to the Hour in which you are resurrected. In the words: '*Would you call on other than Allah if you are being truthful*?' the *āyah* is arguing against the idolaters, who acknowledge that they have a Maker, meaning, 'In times of distress you resort to Allah and you will be returned to Him on the Day of Rising, so why do you insist on *shirk* when you are in a state of ease?' They worshipped idols and then called on Allah to avert punishment from them.

It is Him you call on and, if He wills, He will deliver you; and you will forget what you associated with Him.

'*Bal*' turns away from the first thing mentioned and makes the second necessary. The pronoun '*Him*' is in the accusative through '*call*'. Allah will remove from you the harm which You call on Him to remove if He wishes to remove it. '*You will forget what you associated with Him*' when the punishment arrives. Al-Ḥasan said that it means: 'You turn from it as one who forgets it.' That is due to despair of being helped by it since it contains neither harm nor benefit. Az-Zajjāj said that it is possible that it means 'abandon them'. An-Naḥḥās said that it is like Allah's words: '*We made a contract with Ādam before, but he forgot.*' (20:115)

وَلَقَدْ أَرْسَلْنَآ إِلَىٰٓ أُمَمٍ مِّن قَبْلِكَ فَأَخَذْنَٰهُم بِٱلْبَأْسَآءِ وَٱلضَّرَّآءِ لَعَلَّهُمْ
يَتَضَرَّعُونَ ﴿٤٢﴾

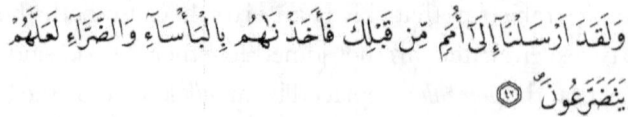

42 We sent Messengers to nations before you, and afflicted those nations with hardship and distress so that hopefully they would humble themselves.

We sent Messengers to nations before you,

The *āyah* is to give solace to the Prophet ﷺ, and there is some elision in it, the literal meaning being 'We sent to the nations before you' with 'Messengers' being implied. It has another elision which the literal text indicates, implying the words 'They denied' before '*We afflicted them*.' This *āyah* is related to the one before it by the connection of one state to another which is close to it. That is because those people followed the course of opposing their Prophet in the way that those before them had also opposed their Prophets. So the affliction that befell them also befell those before them. The meaning of *ba'sā'* (hardship) is affliction in respect of property and *ḍarrā'* (distress) is affliction in respect of the body. Ibn 'Aṭiyyah said, 'On the basis of this *āyah* worshippers have deduced that they should discipline themselves through hardship by lack of property and through distress by imposing hunger and nakedness on themselves.' This is ignorance on the part of the one who does it and who makes this *āyah* a basis for it.

It is in fact a punishment from Allah for whichever of His servants He wishes to afflict it with it. It is not permitted for us to afflict it upon ourselves and burden ourselves in this way based on analogy with this *āyah*. The self is the vehicle by means of which we are enabled to reach the Abode of Honour and be saved from the terrors of the Rising. Allah says: '*O Messengers! Eat of the good things and act rightly*' (23:51) and: '*You who believe! Give away some of the good things you have earned*' (2:267) and: '*You who believe! Eat of the good things We have provided for you.*' (2:172) The command to the believers is to follow the example of the Messengers. The Messenger of Allah ﷺ and his Companions ate good things and and adorned themselves by wearing the best garments. And it was the same with the *Tābi'ūn* after them as we explained in *Sūrat al-Mā'idah* (5:88). Dress will be discussed in *Sūrat al-A'rāf* (7:32).

If it had been as they claim and have deduced, then what is the case with the beneficence of Allah where crops, gardens and all kinds of fruit and plants are concerned, and the domestic animals, which he has allowed us to eat, whose milk we can drink, and whose fur gives us warmth, and other blessings of great benefit? If it had been as they believed about things which bring benefit, then the Messenger of Allah ﷺ and his Companions and the *Tābi'ūn* after them and later scholars would have been more entitled to act in that way. We already discussed in *Sūrat al-Baqarah* (2:283) the excellence of wealth and its benefit and the refutation of those who refuse to amass it, as well as the fact that the Prophet ﷺ forbade continuous fasting out of fear of bodily weakness and that he forbade wasting wealth to deter the ignorant wealthy from doing that.

so that hopefully they would humble themselves.

They will stop doing what they do and show humility. The verb *ḍara'a* is derived from *ḍirā'ah*, which is humbleness and its active participle is *ḍāri'*.

فَلَوْلَآ إِذْ جَآءَهُم بَأْسُنَا تَضَرَّعُواْ وَلَٰكِن قَسَتْ قُلُوبُهُمْ وَزَيَّنَ لَهُمُ
ٱلشَّيْطَٰنُ مَا كَانُواْ يَعْمَلُونَ ﴿٤٣﴾ فَلَمَّا نَسُواْ مَا ذُكِّرُواْ بِهِۦ
فَتَحْنَا عَلَيْهِمْ أَبْوَٰبَ كُلِّ شَيْءٍ حَتَّىٰٓ إِذَا فَرِحُواْ بِمَآ أُوتُوٓاْ أَخَذْنَٰهُم بَغْتَةً
فَإِذَا هُم مُّبْلِسُونَ ﴿٤٤﴾ فَقُطِعَ دَابِرُ ٱلْقَوْمِ ٱلَّذِينَ ظَلَمُواْ وَٱلْحَمْدُ لِلَّهِ رَبِّ
ٱلْعَٰلَمِينَ ﴿٤٥﴾

43-45 If only they had humbled themselves when Our violent force came upon them! However, their hearts were hard and *Shayṭān* made what they were doing seem attractive to them. When they forgot what they had been reminded of, We opened up for them the doors to everything, until, when they were exulting in what they had been given, We suddenly seized them and at once they were in despair. So the last remnant of the people who did wrong was cut off. Praise belongs to Allah, the Lord of all the worlds!

If only they had humbled themselves when Our violent force came upon them! However, their hearts were hard and *Shayṭān* made what they were doing seem attractive to them.

'*Lawlā*' here is for the specification of those mentioned and the verb follows it, and it has the meaning of *hallā* (why do they not?). This is a rebuke for abandoning supplication and tells us that they did not humble themselves when the punishment descended. It is possible that they humbled themselves in the manner of one who is not sincere or only does so when the punishment touches him. Humble entreaty in such cases is of no use. Supplication is commanded in both ease and hardship. Allah says: '*Call on me and I will answer you.*' (40:60) Then He says: '*Those who are too proud to worship Me,*' in other words to call on Me, '*will enter Hell abject,*' (40:60) which is a strong threat. Their hardness of heart refers to their disbelief and insistence on disobedience. We ask Allah for well-being! *Shayṭān* made their error in committing disobedience seem attractive to them and impelled them to it.

When they forgot what they had been reminded of,

If it is asked, 'Why were they blamed for forgetfulness?' the reply is that the verb '*they forgot*' means 'they abandoned what they were reminded of', as Ibn 'Abbās and Ibn Jurayj said and it is also the position of Abū 'Alī. That is because someone who abandons something and turns away from it is in the position of someone who forgets it. There is another view of '*forgot*', which is that they were consciously forgetful and so it is permitted to blame them for it as there is blame for exposing oneself to the wrath and punishment of Allah.

We opened up for them the doors to everything

The noun '*everything*' here means blessings and good things, indicating that Allah gave them a lot of them. With those who know Arabic, it implies: 'We opened up the doors of everything to them which had previously been closed to them.'

until, when they were exulting in what they had been given, We suddenly seized them and at once they were in despair

This means when they were arrogant, insolent and proud and thought that the gifts they had would never end and that they were indicative of Allah's pleasure. '*We suddenly seized them and at once they were in despair*,' meaning 'We attacked and eradicated them.' *Baghtatan* means 'suddenly'. It is seizing something when it is heedless and without any prior indication. When a person is taken when he is heedless, he is seized suddenly. The most damaging matter is one which comes when one is unaware. It is said that the prior reminder which they turned away from was, in effect, a command. Allah knows best. *Baghtatan* (*suddenly*) is a verbal noun used as an adverbial *ḥāl*. It is being led on by Allah in the way He explains in His words: '*I will give them more time. My strategy is sure.*' (7:183). We seek refuge in Allah from His anger and guile!

One of the people of knowledge said, 'May Allah have mercy on someone who reflects on this *āyah*.' Muḥammad ibn an-Naḍr al-Ḥārithī said, 'Allah granted a delay to those people of twenty years.' 'Uqbah ibn 'Āmir related that the Prophet ﷺ said, 'When you see Allah giving people what they desire in spite of their acts of disobedience, that is His leading them on.' Then he recited, '*When they forgot what they had been reminded of...*' Al-Ḥasan said, 'There is no one to whom Allah gives expansion in this world and who does not then fear that he will be deceived by it, but that his actions are deficient and his opinion is of no weight. There is no one from whom Allah withholds and who does not then think that there is good for him in it, but that his actions are deficient and his opinion is of no weight.' In a report it says that Allah Almighty revealed to Mūsā, 'When you see poverty coming towards you, say, "Welcome to the sign of the righteous!" When you see wealth coming towards you, say, "A wrong action whose punishment is hastened."'

The adjective '*mublisūn*' means despairing, disheartened, sorrowful, and having no hope of a good outcome and despairing of being helped because of the enormity of the evil state one is in. Al 'Ajjāj says:

Friend! Do you recognise a mark of the camel droppings?
He said, 'Yes, I recognise them,' and he was without words (*ablasā*).'

It means that he is bewildered at the terror of what he has seen. The name Iblīs is derived from it. The verb *ablasa* is when a man is rendered silent and *miblās* is used of a she-camel when it does not move on account of the intensity its desire for a male camel.

So the last remnant of the people who did wrong was cut off.

Dābir means the last and is used for the last person to arrive. It is used in the *ḥadīth* of 'Abdullāh ibn Mas'ūd: 'There are some people who only come to the prayer at the end of the time (*dabarī*).' It means when all their offspring are cut off and they are wiped out and not a trace of them remains. Quṭrub says that it means that they are eradicated and destroyed. Umayyah ibn Abī-ṣ-Ṣalt said:

They were destroyed by a punishment that took every last one of them (*dābirahum*).
They were not able to avert it and were not helped.

Management (*tadbīr*) comes from the same root because it is making the end of a business firm.

Praise belongs to Allah, the Lord of all the worlds!

Praise be to Allah for destroying them! It is said to be praise for teaching the believers how to praise Him. This *āyah* contains evidence of the obligation to abandon injustice since it ends in eradication and perpetual punishment and the severance of every praiseworthy quality.

قُلْ أَرَءَيْتُمْ إِنْ أَخَذَ ٱللَّهُ سَمْعَكُمْ وَأَبْصَٰرَكُمْ وَخَتَمَ عَلَىٰ قُلُوبِكُم مَّنْ إِلَٰهٌ غَيْرُ ٱللَّهِ
يَأْتِيكُم بِهِ ٱنظُرْ كَيْفَ نُصَرِّفُ ٱلْءَايَٰتِ ثُمَّ هُمْ يَصْدِفُونَ ﴿٤٦﴾ قُلْ أَرَءَيْتَكُمْ إِنْ
أَتَىٰكُمْ عَذَابُ ٱللَّهِ بَغْتَةً أَوْ جَهْرَةً هَلْ يُهْلَكُ إِلَّا ٱلْقَوْمُ ٱلظَّٰلِمُونَ ﴿٤٧﴾

46-47 Say: 'What do you think? If Allah took away your hearing and your sight and sealed up your hearts, what god is there, other than Allah, who could give them back to you?' Look how We vary the Signs, yet still they turn away. Say: 'What do you think? If Allah's punishment were to come upon you suddenly by night or openly by day, would any but the wrongdoing people be destroyed?'

Say: 'What do you think? If Allah took away your hearing and your sight

In other words, obliterated them. The noun '*hearing*' is in the singular because the verbal noun always indicates the plural. The meaning of '*sealed*' was discussed in in *Sūrat al-Baqarah* (2:8). The apodosis of '*in*' (*if*) is elided. It implies, 'Who would bring that back to you?' It is in the accusative because they have the position of a *ḥāl*. It is said that what is meant are the meanings attached to these faculties. Allah will remove the faculties and all the non-essentials and nothing will be left. Allah Almighty says: '*before We obliterate faces*'. (4:47) The *āyah* is an argument against the unbelievers.

what god is there, other than Allah, who could give them back to you?'

'*Man*' (who) is in the nominative by the inceptive and its predicate is '*god*'. The words '*other than Allah*' describe it. Similarly, the phrase '*give them back to you*' is in the nominative as an adjectival clause relating to '*god*'. It is in the form of a question, and the sentence of which it is part is in the position of the two objects of '*think*'.

Say: 'What do you think?

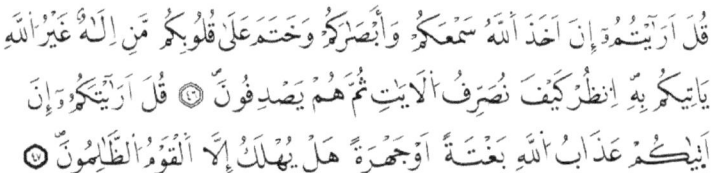

The verb '*ra'ā*' here means 'know', and the singular pronoun in '*bihi*' in the words '*give them back*' is used for the plural and refers to what was mentioned – what is taken. It is said that it refers to the faculty of hearing in particular as in Allah's words: '…*it would be more fitting for them to please Allah and His Messenger*' (9:62). Then sight and hearts are included with it. It is said that it means: 'Who could give any of them back?' referring to each of those things mentioned. It is said that it indicates guidance which the meaning embraces. 'Abd ar-Raḥmān al-A'raj recited '*bihu-n-ẓur*' with a *ḍammah* on the *hā'* based on the root because the root is that there is a *ḍammah* on the *hā'*.

An-Naqqāsh said, 'This *āyah* contains evidence that hearing is better than sight since it is mentioned first here and in other *āyahs*. This was also mentioned at the beginning of *al-Baqarah*.

Look how We vary the Signs, yet still they turn away!

The 'varying' of signs is to bring them in various guises: excusing, warning, encouraging and causing fear, and the like. About the phrase: '*yet still they turn away*!' Ibn 'Abbās, al-Ḥasan, Mujāhid, Qatādah and as-Suddī said that the verb is transitive, and is used for turning away from something. The verb is *ṣadafa*. Someone who turns away is *ṣādif*. *Ṣādafah* is to meet someone after having turned away. Ibn ar-Riqā' said:

When women mention an event, they say the best of it.
They turn away (*ṣuduf*) from every evil which is feared.

Ṣadaf is a camel which splays its front or back foot to the side. It means they turn away from arguments and proofs.

Say: 'What do you think? If Allah's punishment were to come upon you suddenly by night and openly by day

Al-Ḥasan said that '*suddenly*' means at night and '*openly*' is in the day. It is said that it simply means without warning. Al-Kisā'ī said that it means suddenly, as already mentioned.

would any but the wrongdoing people be destroyed?

This is similar to Allah's words: '*Will any be destroyed except for deviant people*?' (46:35) Would any be destroyed except you for your *shirk*? *Ẓulm* here means *shirk* as is made clear in Luqmān's words to his son: '*My son, do not associate anything with Allah. Associating others with Him is a terrible wrong (ẓulm).*' (31:13)

وَمَا نُرْسِلُ الْمُرْسَلِينَ إِلَّا مُبَشِّرِينَ وَمُنذِرِينَ فَمَنْ ءَامَنَ وَأَصْلَحَ فَلَا خَوْفٌ عَلَيْهِمْ
وَلَا هُمْ يَحْزَنُونَ ﴿٤٨﴾

48 We do not send the Messengers except to bring good news and to give warning. As for those who believe and put things right, they will feel no fear and will know no sorrow.

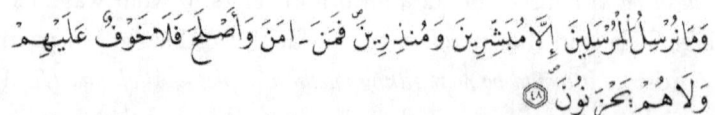

Messengers were sent to encourage and to alarm. Al-Ḥasan said, 'Giving good news of the vastness of provision in this world and reward in the Next World. That is indicated by the words of Allah Almighty: "*If only the people of the cities had believed and been godfearing, We would have opened up to them blessings from heaven and earth.*" (7:96)' The meaning of '*warn*' is to make them fear the punishment of Allah. The meaning is: 'We sent Messengers for this, not for the signs which company them. The signs that they bring are proofs and confirm them.'

وَالَّذِينَ كَذَّبُوا بِآيَاتِنَا يَمَسُّهُمُ الْعَذَابُ بِمَا كَانُوا يَفْسُقُونَ ﴿٤٩﴾

49 The punishment will fall on those who deny Our Signs because they were deviators.

The Signs are the Qur'an and other miracles. It is said that what is meant is denial of Muḥammad ﷺ. They were deviators and disbelieved.

قُل لَّا أَقُولُ لَكُمْ عِندِي خَزَائِنُ اللَّهِ وَلَا أَعْلَمُ الْغَيْبَ وَلَا أَقُولُ
لَكُمْ إِنِّي مَلَكٌ إِنْ أَتَّبِعُ إِلَّا مَا يُوحَىٰ إِلَيَّ قُلْ هَلْ يَسْتَوِي الْأَعْمَىٰ
وَالْبَصِيرُ أَفَلَا تَتَفَكَّرُونَ ﴿٥٠﴾

50 Say: 'I do not say to you that I possess the treasuries of Allah, nor do I know the Unseen, nor do I say to you that I am an angel. I only follow what has been revealed to me.' Say: 'Are the blind the same as those who can see? So will you not reflect?'

Say: 'I do not say to you that I possess the treasuries of Allah,

This is the apodosis of '*Why has no Sign been sent down to him*?' (4:38). The meaning is: 'I do not have access to the treasuries of Allah's Power so as to be able to send down the Sign that you demand. I do not know the Unseen so as to be able to tell you about it.' *Khazānah* (treasury) is a place where treasure is stored. Relating to that is the *ḥadīth*: 'The udders of their livestock store their food for them. Would one of you want to be given his drink and have his store broken open?' The treasuries of Allah are what He has decreed, implying: 'I do not have the power to do what you are asking for.'

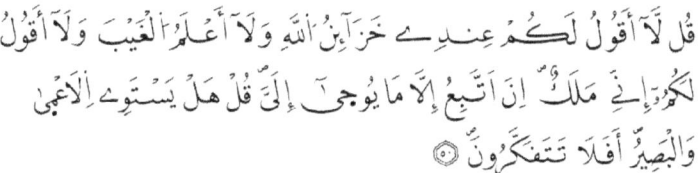

nor do I say to you that I am an angel.

People believed in the superiority of angels. So it means, 'I am not an angel so as to be able to bear witness to the commands of Allah which human beings do not witness.' Those who say that the angels are better than the Prophets use this as evidence. This was discussed in *Sūrat al-Baqarah* (2:32).

I only follow what has been revealed to me.

Its overt meaning is that he ﷺ does not make any command definitive unless there is revelation about it. The sound view is that the Prophets are allowed to make *ijtihād* and analogy based on the text. Analogy is one of the proofs of the *Sharī'ah* and will be discussed in *al-A'rāf* (7:12) as the *ijtihād* of Prophets will be discussed in *Sūrat al-Anbiyā'* (21:89) Allah willing.

Say: 'Are the blind the same as those who can see? So will you not reflect?'

This refers to the unbelievers and believers, as Mujāhid and others said. It is said that it means that they are the knowing and the ignorant. '*So will you not reflect?*' that they are not the same?

وَأَنذِرْ بِهِ ٱلَّذِينَ يَخَافُونَ أَن يُحْشَرُوٓا۟ إِلَىٰ رَبِّهِمْ لَيْسَ لَهُم مِّن دُونِهِۦ وَلِىٌّ
وَلَا شَفِيعٌ لَّعَلَّهُمْ يَتَّقُونَ ﴿٥١﴾

51 Warn by it those who fear they will be gathered to their Lord, having no protector or intercessor apart from Him, so that hopefully they will be godfearing.

Warn by it those who fear they will be gathered to their Lord,

Warn by the Qur'an. Warning is informing and it was talked of in *al-Baqarah* (2:60). It is said that '*by it*' is 'by Him' i.e. by Allah. It is also said that '*it*' is the Last Day. '*Those who fear they will be gathered to their Lord*' will be in fear because the evidence against them will be made manifest then. They fear His punishment and do not vacillate about the Gathering. Here '*fear*' means to anticipate the punishment of the Gathering. It is also said that '*fear*' means 'know' here. If it is a Muslim, he is warned to abandon his acts of disobedience. If it is one of the people of the Book, he is warned to follow the truth. Al-Ḥasan said, 'What is meant here are the believers.' Az-Zajjāj said, 'It refers to everyone who affirms the Resurrection, believer or unbeliever.' It is also said that the *āyah* is about the idolaters who are warned of the Day of Rising. The first is more likely.

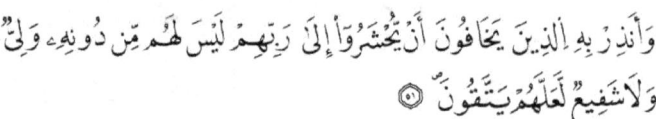

having no protector or intercessor apart from Him,

Apart from Allah. This refutes the Jews and Christians regarding their claim that their 'father' will intercede for them when they say: '*We are the sons of Allah and those He loves.*' (5:18) Although the idolaters wishfully made their idols intercessors with Allah, Allah informs them that there is no intercession for the unbelievers. Those who say that the *āyah* is about the believers say that the Messenger can intercede for them with the permission of Allah and so he is the intercessor who truly has permission. We read in Allah's Book: '*They do not intercede except on behalf of those with whom He is pleased*' (21:28) and '*Intercession with Him will be of no benefit except from someone who has His permission*' (34:23) and '*Who can intercede with Him except by His permission?*' (2:255) '*So that hopefully they will be godfearing*' in the future. That is be firm in their faith.

وَلَا تَطْرُدِ الَّذِينَ يَدْعُونَ رَبَّهُم بِالْغَدَاةِ وَالْعَشِيِّ يُرِيدُونَ وَجْهَهُ ۖ
مَا عَلَيْكَ مِنْ حِسَابِهِم مِّن شَيْءٍ وَمَا مِنْ حِسَابِكَ عَلَيْهِم مِّن شَيْءٍ
فَتَطْرُدَهُمْ فَتَكُونَ مِنَ الظَّالِمِينَ ﴿٥٢﴾

52 Do not chase away those who call on their Lord morning and evening, seeking His Face. Their reckoning is in no way your responsibility and your reckoning is in no way their responsibility. Indeed if you did chase them away, you would be among the wrongdoers.

Do not chase away those who call on their Lord

The idolaters said, 'We do not want to sit with people like that,' meaning Salmān, Ṣuhayb, Bilāl and Khabbāb, 'so chase them away from you.' They asked him to dictate something to that effect for them and the Prophet ﷺ wanted to do that. He called 'Alī to write and the poor stood up and sat at a distance and then Allah revealed the *āyah*. Sa'd indicates this in the sound *ḥadīth*: 'So there occurred to the self of the Messenger of Allah ﷺ what Allah wished to occur,' and it will be mentioned. The Prophet ﷺ inclined towards that out of desire for them to become Muslim and for their people to become Muslim. He thought that his Companions would not be deprived of anything and not be decreased in any way so he inclined towards it. Allah revealed the *āyah* and forbade him to chase them away, not inferring that that had already occurred. Muslim reported that Sa'd ibn Abī Waqqāṣ said, 'There were six of us with the Prophet ﷺ. The idolaters told the

Prophet ﷺ, "Drive them away from you. They should not be impudent towards us." There was myself, Ibn Mas'ūd, a man of Hudhayl, Bilāl and two men I did not name. Whatever Allah wished then occurred to the self of the Prophet ﷺ and then Allah revealed: *"Do not chase away those who call on their Lord morning and evening, seeking His Face."*'"

It is said that what is meant by *'calling'* here is observing the obligatory prayer in a group. Ibn 'Abbās, Mujāhid and al-Ḥasan said that. It is said that it is *dhikr* and recitation of the Qur'an. It is said that it means supplication at the beginning and end of the day so that they began their day with supplication out of desire for success and endd it with supplication seeking forgiveness.

morning and evening, seeking His Face.

This means obeying Him and being sincere in it, sincere in performing their worship and actions for Allah alone, making Him their goal and not aiming for anything else. It is said that their only desire is Allah Who is described by *'Face'* as in the words: *'But the Face of your Lord will remain, Master of Majesty and Generosity'* (55:27) and: *'Those who are steadfast in seeking the Face of their Lord.'* (13:22)

Morning and evening are mentioned because that is when most people are busy. The one who turns to worship at the time of work is more likely to act when he is free of work. After that the Messenger of Allah ﷺ was steadfast with them as Allah had commanded: *'Restrain yourself patiently with those who call on their Lord morning and evening, desiring His face. Do not turn your eyes from them.'* (18:28) It was as if he did not stand unless they did so first. This is clarified by Ibn Mājah in his *Sunan* from what Khabbāb said about this *āyah*. He said, 'Al-Aqra' ibn Ḥābis at-Tamīmī and 'Uyaynah ibn Ḥiṣn al-Farāzī came and found the Prophet ﷺ with Ṣuhayb, Bilāl, 'Ammār and Khabbāb, sitting with some of the poor believers. When they saw them around the Prophet ﷺ, they disdained them. They went up to him and took him aside and said, "We want you to arrange a gathering with us by which the Arabs will acknowledge our excellence. The delegations of the Arabs come to you and we are embarrassed for them to see us in the company of these slaves. We have come to you to ask you to send them away. When we are finished, then sit with them if you wish." He said, "Yes." They said, "Write a document for us to that effect." He called for a paper and summoned 'Alī to write. We were sitting to one side. Then Jibrīl descended and said, *"Do not chase away those who call on their Lord morning and evening, seeking His Face...."*'

Then Allah speaks of al-Aqra' ibn Ḥābis and 'Uyaynah ibn Ḥiṣn saying: *'In this way We try some of them by means of others so that they say, "Are these the people among us to whom Allah has shown His favour?" Does not Allah know best those who are thankful?'* (6:53) Then He says: '*When those who believe in Our Signs come to you, say, "Peace be upon you!" Your Lord has made mercy incumbent on Himself.*' (6:54)

Khabbāb continued, 'We drew near to him until we placed our knees against his. The Messenger of Allah ﷺ used to sit with us. When he wanted to get up, he got up and left us. Then Allah revealed: "*Restrain yourself patiently with those who call on their Lord morning and evening, desiring His face. Do not turn your eyes from them, desiring the attractions of this world.*" (18:28) i.e. do not sit with the nobles, and: "*and do not obey someone whose heart We have made heedless of Our remembrance, and who follows his own whims and desires and whose affair has transgressed all bounds.*" (18:28)' Allah said this in reference to 'Uyaynah and al-Aqra', making an example of these two men and an example of the life of this world. Khabbāb then said, 'We used to sit with the Prophet ﷺ and when the time came for him to get up and leave us, we rose and left him so that he could get up.' It is related from Aḥmad ibn Muḥammad ibn Yaḥyā ibn Sa'īd al-Qaṭṭān from 'Amr ibn Muḥammad al-'Anqazī from Asbāṭ from as-Suddī from Abū Sa'īd al-Azdī, the reciter of Azd, from Abū al-Kanūd from Khabbāb.

It is also transmitted that Sa'd said, 'This *āyah* was revealed about six of us: myself, Ibn Mas'ūd, Ṣuhayb, 'Ammār, al-Miqdād and Bilāl. He said, 'Quraysh said to the Messenger of Allah ﷺ, "We are not happy about being with them, so get rid of them." Whatever Allah wished entered the heart of the Messenger of Allah ﷺ and then Allah revealed: "*Do not chase away those who call on their Lord morning and evening....*"' It is recited as '*bi-l-ghudwati*' as will be mentioned in *al-Kahf*, Allah willing.

Their reckoning is in no way your responsibility and your reckoning is in no way their responsibility.

Their repayment and provision is up to Allah, and your repayment and provision is also up to Allah and no one else. The first '*min*' is partitive and the second is added for emphasis. '*Your reckoning is in no way their responsibility*' means: 'Since that is the case, then turn to them and sit with them and do not drive them away out of concern for the right of someone who does not have their state in the *dīn* and excellence. If you do that, you will be doing wrong and how unlikely that is to happen!' This is clarification of what is correct in order that nothing like that will occur among the people of Islam. It is similar to Allah's words: '*If you associate others with Allah, your actions will come to nothing.*' (39:65) Allah knew very well that he ﷺ would not associate anything with Him nor his actions come to nothing.

Indeed if you did chase them away, you would be among the wrongdoers.

'*You would be among the wrongdoers*' is in the accusative by the *fā'* in the apodosis of the negative. It means: 'Do not drive away those who call on their Lord, making you one of the wrongdoers. Their reckoning is not your responsibility so that you should turn them away.' The root meaning of *ẓulm* is to put a thing in other than its proper place, as was made clear in *Sūrat al-Baqarah* (2:35). The *āyah* and *ḥadīth* constitute a strong prohibition against esteeming anyone on account of their rank and fine clothing and demeaning anyone on account of their obscurity and shabby clothing.

وَكَذَٰلِكَ فَتَنَّا بَعْضَهُم بِبَعْضٍ لِّيَقُولُوٓا۟ أَهَـٰٓؤُلَآءِ مَنَّ ٱللَّهُ عَلَيْهِم
مِّنۢ بَيْنِنَآ ۗ أَلَيْسَ ٱللَّهُ بِأَعْلَمَ بِٱلشَّـٰكِرِينَ ﴿٥٣﴾

53 In this way We try some of them by means of others so that they say, 'Are these the people among us to whom Allah has shown His favour?' Does not Allah know best those who are thankful?

In this way We try some of them by means of others

We tested those before you like that and in the same way We are testing these people. *Fitnah* is testing, i.e. 'We are treating them in as We treat all those who are tested.' '*They say*' refers to the noble and wealthy and' '*these*' are the weak and poor.

to whom Allah has shown His favour?'

An-Naḥḥās said, 'This is problematic because it is asked, "How can their saying this be a trial for them? That is because, if their statement is one of non-acceptance, it is disbelief on their part." There are two responses to this. One is that the meaning is that the wealthy are tested by the poor having the same standing with the Prophet ﷺ as they do, so that they asked that in order to understand, not in order to deny it when they said: "*Are these the people among us to whom Allah has shown His favour*?" The other answer is that when they were tested by this, the end result was that they said this, denying that that could be the case. The situation is similar to that in Allah's words: "*The family of Pharaoh picked him up so that he might be an enemy and a source of grief to them.*" (28:8)'

Does not Allah know best those who are thankful?

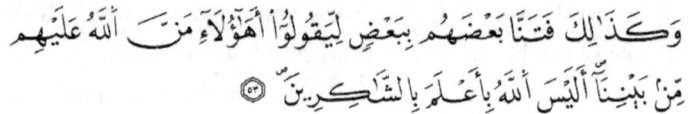

Allah granted them the gift of faith rather than the leaders whom He knew to be unbelievers. So this question is actually confirmation and is the response to their words, *'Are these the people among us to whom Allah has shown His favour?'* It is said that the meaning is: 'Does not Allah know best those who are grateful for being guided to Islam?'

وَإِذَا جَآءَكَ ٱلَّذِينَ يُؤْمِنُونَ بِـَٔايَٰتِنَا فَقُلْ سَلَٰمٌ عَلَيْكُمْ ۖ كَتَبَ رَبُّكُمْ
عَلَىٰ نَفْسِهِ ٱلرَّحْمَةَ ۖ أَنَّهُۥ مَنْ عَمِلَ مِنكُمْ سُوٓءًۢا بِجَهَٰلَةٍ ثُمَّ تَابَ مِنۢ
بَعْدِهِۦ وَأَصْلَحَ فَأَنَّهُۥ غَفُورٌ رَّحِيمٌ ٥٤

54 When those who believe in Our Signs come to you, say, 'Peace be upon you!' Your Lord has made mercy incumbent on Himself. If anyone among you does evil out of ignorance and then afterwards repents and puts things right, He is Ever-Forgiving, Most Merciful.

When those who believe in Our Signs come to you, say, 'Peace be upon you!'

Salām and *salāmah* have the same meaning. The meaning of '*Peace be upon you*!' is: 'May Allah grant you security in your *dīn* and in yourselves.' It was revealed about those whom Allah forbade His Prophet ﷺ to drive away. When he saw them, he was the first to give the greeting. He said, 'Praise be to Allah Who has placed in My community those I am commanded to greet first.' According to this, the *salām* is from the Prophet ﷺ. It is said that it is from Allah and therefore means, 'Convey to them the *salām* from Me.' Both meanings indicate their excellence and position with Allah Almighty.

In *Ṣaḥīḥ Muslim* it is reported from 'Ā'idh ibn 'Amr that Abū Sufyān came to Salmān, Ṣuhayb, Bilāl and a group and they said, 'The swords of Allah have not finished off the enemy of Allah!' Abū Bakr said, 'Do you say this to a shaykh and master of Quraysh?' He went to the Prophet ﷺ and told him. He said, 'O Abū Bakr, perhaps you have made them angry? If you were to make them angry, then you would make your Lord angry.' He went to them and asked, 'Brothers, have I made you angry?' They said, 'No, may Allah forgive you, brother.' This indicates the elevation of their position and the respect in which they are held, as explained in this *āyah*. It is deduced from this that one should respect the righteous and avoid angering or injuring them for that would entail the anger of Allah, in other words the descent of His punishment on those who harm any of His *awliyā'*.

Ibn 'Abbās said, 'This *āyah* was revealed about Abū Bakr, 'Umar, 'Uthmān and 'Alī.' Al-Fuḍayl ibn 'Iyāḍ said, 'A group of Muslims went to the Prophet ﷺ and said, "We have committed wrong actions, so ask forgiveness for us." He turned from them and the *āyah* was revealed.' Anas ibn Mālik related something similar.

Your Lord has made mercy incumbent on Himself.

This means Allah has made it mandatory by His truthful report and true promise. So His servants are addressed since they know that when someone makes something incumbent on himself, it means that he has to do it. It is said that Allah inscribed that on the Preserved Tablet.

If anyone among you does evil out of ignorance He is Ever-Forgiving, Most Merciful.

This means does it accidentally, not deliberately. Mujāhid said, 'He does not know the unlawful from the lawful.' He shows his ignorance by doing what he does. Whoever makes a mistake is ignorant of it. This was discussed in *Sūrat an-Nisā'* (4:17-18). It is said that it is: whoever prefers the close-at-hand to the next World is ignorant.

Ibn 'Āmir and 'Āṣim read '*innahu*' [in 'He is Ever-Forgiving'] as '*annahu*' and '*annahu man 'amila*' and Nāfi' also has '*annahu man 'amila*' while the others have '*innahu*' in both places. If it is '*innahu*', it is a new sentence and it explains the mercy. When '*inna*' is added to sentences, it takes a *kasrah* and what comes after *fā'* is a new sentence and takes a *kasrah*. If it is '*annahu*', it is in the accusative as an appositive for '*mercy*' and so the verb *kataba* acts on it. It is as if Allah were saying, 'Your Lord has made incumbent on Himself that if anyone among you does….'

There are two aspects to the *fatḥah* in '*He is Ever-Forgiving*'. One is that it is nominative by the beginning of the sentence and the predicate is elided. It is as if He were saying, 'to him He is Ever-Forgiving' because what follows the *fā'* is an inchoative, implying 'He has Allah's forgiveness.' The second is that it is implied that the inchoative is '*anna*' and the predicate is what it affects. That implies: 'His business is that he will have Allah's forgiveness.' This is what Sībawayh preferred. He did not permit the first possibility whereas Abū Ḥātim allowed it. It is said that '*kataba*' acts on it, meaning in that case, 'Your Lord has made it incumbent that He is Ever-Forgiving, Most Merciful.' It is related from 'Alī ibn Ṣāliḥ and Ibn Hurmuz that the first *kasrah* is for a new sentence and the *fatḥah* on the second is as an inchoative or the predicate of an inchoative or a regimen. Those, like Nāfi', who have a *fatḥah* on the first, make it an appositive for '*mercy*' and the second is for a new sentence because it is after the *fā'*. It is a clear reading.

وَكَذَٰلِكَ نُفَصِّلُ ٱلْءَايَٰتِ وَلِتَسْتَبِينَ سَبِيلُ ٱلْمُجْرِمِينَ ۝٥٥

55 In that way We make the Signs plain so that you may clearly see the path of the evildoers.

In that way We make the Signs plain

The 'making plain' is the clarification by means of which meanings appear. It implies: 'As We have explained to you Our proofs and argument with the idolaters in this *sūrah*, so We will make plain to you the Signs in respect of everything you need for the *dīn* and in respect of everything that the people of falsehood deny.' Al-Qutaybī said, '*We make the Signs plain*' means 'We will bring them one after another and We will not send them down all joined together.'

so that you may clearly see the path of the evildoers.

The *lām* is connected to the action, but which action? The Kufans say that it is elided, meaning: '*In that way We make the Signs plain* to make them clear to you and so that you may clearly see.' An-Naḥḥās said, 'There is no need for any of this elision. What is implied is: "*In that way We make the Signs plain* and so We have made them plain."' It is said that the inclusion of the *wāw* (and) means 'So that the truth appears and it is clearly seen.' The verb (*yastabīna*) may be read both with *yā'* and *tā'* and *sabīl* may be read both in the accusative and the nominative. If it is read with *tā'*, then it is addressed to the Prophet ﷺ, meaning: 'So that you may see clearly, O Muḥammad, the path of the evildoers.' If it is asked, 'Did the Prophet ﷺ ask for it to be made clear?' the reply according to az-Zajjāj is that when the Prophet ﷺ is addressed, it is actually his whole Community who are intended and so the meaning is: 'so that they may clearly see the path of the evildoers.'

If it is asked why Allah did not mention the path of the believers, there are two replies. One is that it is similar to His words: '*He has made shirts for you to protect you from the heat*' (16:81) and the meaning of 'protect you from the cold' is implied just as here, 'You may clearly see the path of the believers,' is also implied. The second is that the verb *istabāna* can refer to something becoming clear or to someone seeing clearly. When the path of the evildoers is clear, then the path of the believers is clear. The noun *sabīl* (path) can be masculine or feminine. The tribe of Tamīm consider it masculine and the people of the Ḥijāz consider it feminine. We find it in the masculine in 7:146 and in the feminine in 3:99. There it can also be recited as '*tastabīna*' and '*yastabīna*' where the *tā'* is addressed to the Prophet while it is his community who are meant.

قُلْ إِنِّي نُهِيتُ أَنْ أَعْبُدَ الَّذِينَ تَدْعُونَ مِن دُونِ اللَّهِ قُل لَّا أَتَّبِعُ
أَهْوَاءَكُمْ قَدْ ضَلَلْتُ إِذًا وَمَا أَنَا مِنَ الْمُهْتَدِينَ ﴿٥٦﴾

56 Say: 'I am forbidden to worship those you call upon besides Allah.' Say: 'I do not follow your whims and desires. If I did I would go astray and not be among the guided.'

It is said that here '*tad'ūna*' (lit. *call upon*) means 'worship'. It is said: 'You call on them in your important affairs by way of worship,' referring to the idols.

Say: 'I do not follow your whims and desires.

'I do not follow you in worshipping these things and by driving away those you want me to drive away. If I were to follow your whims, then I would go astray and not be on the path of guidance.'

If I did I would go astray and not be among the guided.

The verb '*go astray*' is read as both '*ḍalaltu*' and '*ḍaliltu*'. They are two dialectical usages. Abū 'Amr ibn al-'Alā' said that *ḍaliltu* is the dialect of Tamīm. It is the reading of Yaḥyā ibn Waththāb and Ṭalḥah ibn Muṣarrif. The first is sounder and more eloquent because it is the dialect of the people of the Ḥijāz and the reading of the majority. Al-Jawharī said that *ḍalāl* and *ḍalālah* are the opposite of *rashād* (right guidance). You say, '*ḍalaltu, aḍillu*'. In 34:50 Allah uses that. It is the dialect of Najd, and is eloquent. The people of al-'Āliyah say '*ḍaliltu*'.

قُلْ إِنِّي عَلَىٰ بَيِّنَةٍ مِّن رَّبِّي وَكَذَّبْتُم بِهِ مَا عِندِي مَا تَسْتَعْجِلُونَ بِهِ
إِنِ الْحُكْمُ إِلَّا لِلَّهِ يَقُصُّ الْحَقَّ وَهُوَ خَيْرُ الْفَاصِلِينَ ﴿٥٧﴾

57 Say: 'I stand on a Clear Sign from my Lord and yet you have denied it. I do not have in my possession what you are in such haste to bring about. Jurisdiction over it belongs to Allah alone. He tells the truth and He is the Best of Deciders.'

'*A Clear Sign from my Lord*' means indication, certainty, evidence, and proof, not a whim of any kind. It is a '*Clear Sign*' because it makes the truth clear. The phrase '*Yet you have denied it*', means denied the Clear Sign because the '*it*' here refers to the clarification [provided by the Clear Sign]. It is also said that the pronoun '*it*' is actually 'Him' referring to 'my Lord' because He was mentioned and the meaning is: 'You have denied Him'. It is also said that it is denying the punishment or the Qur'an. Muṣ'ab ibn 'Abdullāh ibn az-Zubayr, an excellent poet, wrote a poem about the meaning of this *āyah* and the one before it:

Shall I sit back after my bones shake
    and death is closer than what is right beside me?
Should I argue with every contrary opponent
    and thus make my *dīn* a target for his *dīn*
So that I leave what I know for the opinion of another?
    Opinion is certainly not like certain knowledge.
What have I to do with argument
    when it is something moving to the right and the left?
The *sunnahs* of support are established for us,
    chanted in every ravine, on every bank.
The Truth is not hidden; it is splendidly radiant
    like the clear radiance of dawn.
For us, the path of Hellfire cannot replace
    the path of Āminah's trustworthy son.
As for what I know, it is enough for me.
    As for what I don't know, just don't ask.

I do not have in my possession what you are in such haste to bring about.

This is the Punishment. Owing to the magnitude of their denial, they asked for it to be hastened out of mockery. This is similar to their words: '*Make the sky, as you claim, fall down on us in lumps*' (17:92) and: '*O Allah! If this is really the Truth from You, rain stones down on us out of heaven.*' (8:32) It is also said to mean, 'I do not have the signs which you ask me for.'

Jurisdiction over it belongs to Allah alone.

There is no judgment except Allah's with respect to delaying or hastening the Punishment. It is said that the judgment which distinguishes between truth and falsehood belongs to Allah alone.

He tells the truth and He is the Best of Deciders.'

He gives the true account. This is used as proof of those who deny the metaphors in the Qur'an. It is the reading of Nāfi', Ibn Kathīr, 'Āṣim, Mujāhid, al-A'raj and Ibn 'Abbās. Ibn 'Abbās said: 'Allah says: "*We tell you the best of stories.*" (12:3).' The rest read *'yaqḍi-l-ḥaqq'* (instead of *yaquṣṣu*), which means 'He decides'. That is the reading of 'Alī, as-Sulamī and Sa'īd ibn al-Musayyab. There is no *yā'* written in the Qur'an [in *yaqḍ*] and one must not stop there. It comes from *qaḍā'*. That is indicated by what follows: *'He is the Best of Deciders.'* A 'decision' (*faṣl*) only takes place after judgment not after giving an account. That is strengthened by the words before it: *'Jurisdiction over it belongs to Allah alone.'* It is also strengthened by the reading of Ibn Mas'ūd, *'yaqḍī'*. He includes the *yā'* at the end of *yaqḍī* which reinforces the meaning. An-Naḥḥās says, 'This is not necessary because the meaning of "judges" is "to come and do" and the meaning is "bring the truth." It can mean "He gives the true judgment."'

Makkī said, 'I prefer the reading with a *ṣād* because Makkah and Madīnah and 'Āṣim agree on that, and because if it had been about judgment, then the *yā'* would have been obliged in it as we find in the reading of Ibn Mas'ūd.' An-Naḥḥās says, 'This is not a conclusive argument because there is often elision in such cases.'

قُل لَّوْ أَنَّ عِندِى مَا تَسْتَعْجِلُونَ بِهِۦ لَقُضِىَ ٱلْأَمْرُ بَيْنِى وَبَيْنَكُمْ
وَٱللَّهُ أَعْلَمُ بِٱلظَّٰلِمِينَ

58 Say: 'If I did have in my possession what you are in such haste to bring about, the affair between me and you would have been decided. Allah has greatest knowledge of the wrongdoers.'

This is again referring to the Punishment: 'I would have brought it down on you to bring the affair to an end.' The verb *istiʻjāl* means to try to hasten something before its time. Allah knows all there is to know about the idolaters and the time of their punishment.

وَعِندَهُۥ مَفَاتِحُ ٱلْغَيْبِ لَا يَعْلَمُهَآ إِلَّا هُوَ وَيَعْلَمُ مَا فِى ٱلْبَرِّ وَٱلْبَحْرِ
وَمَا تَسْقُطُ مِن وَرَقَةٍ إِلَّا يَعْلَمُهَا وَلَا حَبَّةٍ فِى ظُلُمَٰتِ ٱلْأَرْضِ وَلَا رَطْبٍ
وَلَا يَابِسٍ إِلَّا فِى كِتَٰبٍ مُّبِينٍ ٥٩

59 The keys of the Unseen are in His possession. No one knows them but Him. He knows everything in the land and sea. No leaf falls without His knowing it. There is no seed in the darkness of the earth, and nothing moist or dry which is not in a Clear Book.

It is reported that when this *āyah* was revealed, it was accompanied by twelve thousand angels. Al-Bukhārī reported from Ibn 'Umar that the Prophet ﷺ said, 'The keys to the Unseen is one of five things that only Allah knows. No one but Allah knows what the wombs will miscarry except Allah. No one but Allah knows what will happen tomorrow. No one but Allah knows when the rain will fall. No one but Allah knows what land they will die in. And no one but Allah knows when the Hour will come.' In *Muslim*, 'Ā'ishah said, 'Whoever claims that the Messenger of Allah ﷺ reported about what will come in the future has grossly lied against Allah. Allah says: "*Say: 'No one in the heavens and the earth knows the Unseen, except Allah.*'" (27:65)'

Mafātiḥ (keys) is the plural of *miftaḥ*. This is eloquent Arabic. *Miftāḥ* is also used, and the plural of *miftāḥ* is *mafātīḥ*. Ibn as-Samayqa' recited *mafātīḥ*. The word 'key' designates anything that releases something locked, whether physical, like a lock on a house, or intellectual, like research. Ibn Mājah related in his *Sunan* and Abū Ḥātim al-Bustī in his *Ṣaḥīḥ* from Anas ibn Mālik that the Messenger of Allah ﷺ said, 'There are people who are keys to good and locks against evil and there are people who are keys to evil and locks against good. Bliss is for those in whose hands Allah places the keys to good and woe to those in whose hands Allah puts the keys to evil.'

This *āyah* is a metaphor for reaching the unseen worlds as one reaches the visible by having a key to the Unseen. That is why someone said, 'It is taken from the verbal usage. "Open this for me," meaning give it to me or teach me what I need to attain it.' Allah possesses knowledge of the Unseen and the means by which it can be reached are in His hand. None but Him possesses them. If He wishes to acquaint someone with the Unseen, He does so, and if He wishes to veil him, He does so. That is part of what He made occur only to His Messengers as evidenced in His words: '*Allah has not given you access to the Unseen. But Allah chooses those of His Messengers whoever He wills*' (3:179) and He also says: '*He is Knower of the Unseen, and does not divulge His Unseen to anyone – except a Messenger with whom He is well pleased.*' (72:26)

It is also said that what is meant by '*keys*' here are the treasuries of provision, as as-Suddī and al-Ḥasan said. Muqātil and aḍ-Daḥḥāk said that it is a reference to the treasures of the earth. This is a metaphor designating the means by which they are obtained. It is said that part of the meaning of the *ḥadīth* is that Allah knows all lifespans and the time when things will end. It is said: the ends of lives and ends of actions. Other things are said, but the first is preferred, and Allah knows best.

Our scholars say that in more than one *āyah* in His Book Allah ascribes the knowledge of the Unseen to Himself but makes an exception for those of His slaves He chooses. If someone says with conviction, 'There will be a downpour tomorrow,' he is an unbeliever, whether he reports about that on the basis of an indication he claims knowledge of or not. The same holds true for someone who says that he knows what is in the womb: he is an unbeliever. If it is not a definite statement, like saying, 'There is the rising of the star at which Allah usually sends down the rain,' or he says, 'There is usually rain when that happens,' or 'It is the cause of rain according to what Allah has decreed and already knows,' he is not an unbeliever, although it is preferred for him not to say that. That is because it resembles what the people of disbelief say and shows ignorance of the fineness of Allah's wisdom, because He sends it down whenever He wishes, sometimes at the rising of that star and sometimes without it. The Almighty states [in a *ḥadīth qudsī*], 'Some of My slaves believe in Me and disbelieve in the stars, but as for those who say "We had rain by the rising of such-and-such a star," they disbelieve in Me and believe in the stars,' as will be clarified in *Sūrat al-Wāqi'ah*, Allah willing.

Ibn al-'Arabī said, 'The same applies to a doctor when he says, "If there is milk in the right breast it is a boy and if there is milk in the left, it is a girl. Or, if the woman feels the right side heavier, it is a girl." If he claims that this is usually the case but may not necessarily be so, then he is not an unbeliever or impious. If someone claims that he is going to make such and such an amount by predicting the future, he is an unbeliever. If someone claims to know events in the future, whether in general or particular, before they occur, there is no doubt about his disbelief. If he speaks about lunar and solar eclipses, our scholars say that he should be disciplined but not imprisoned. He is not considered an unbeliever because a group say that this is something can be known through reckoning and calculation going by Allah's words: "*And We have decreed set phases for the moon.*" (36:39) As for his being disciplined, it is because he may cause doubt in the common people since they do not know the difference between this and other things and it may confuse their beliefs and they may abandon their certainty in them. They are disciplined to make them conceal such knowledge and not make it public when they know it.'

Also connected to this topic is what is reported in *Ṣaḥīḥ Muslim* from one of the wives of the Prophet ﷺ. The Prophet ﷺ said, 'If anyone goes to a diviner and asks him about something, his prayer will not be accepted for forty days.' An *'arrāf* (diviner) is a diviner or astrologer who claims to know the Unseen. The word comes from *'irāfah* and the one who does it is called an *'arrāf*. He is someone who indicates future matters by means and preliminaries which he claims to know. Some of the people of this craft use sand, divining pebbles, stars and other means for doing that. This craft is called *'iyāfah*. All of that kind of thing is called soothsaying as Qāḍī 'Iyāḍ stated. Soothsaying (*kahānah*) is claiming knowledge of the Unseen.

Qāḍī Ibn 'Abd al-Barr says in *al-Kāfī*: 'Among those earnings which are agreed to be unlawful are usury, the wages of prostitutes, gambling, bribes, taking a wage for wailing and singing, asking money for soothsaying, claiming knowledge of the Unseen and reports from the heavens, and for playing instruments and games and everything earned from falsehood.' Our scholars say, 'Circumstances have changed in our times on account of the advent of astrologers and soothsayers, especially in the cities of Egypt. It is commonplace among our leaders, their followers and commanders to consult astrologers. Indeed, many of those affiliated to *fiqh* and the *dīn* are deluded and go to those soothsayers and prognosticators who glamorise the impossible for them, take money from them and produce mirages and deception in what they say and cause corruption and misguidance in their *dīn*. All of that is a major wrong action since the Prophet ﷺ said, "His prayer is not accepted for forty days." So how is it with someone who uses them and spends on them, relying on what they say?' Muslim reported from 'Ā'ishah, 'Some people asked the Messenger of Allah ﷺ about soothsayers and he said, "They are nothing." They said, "Messenger of Allah, they sometimes speak about things that are true!" The Messenger of Allah ﷺ said, "That single word of truth was snatched by a jinn and put into the ear of his protégé but he mixes a hundred lies with it."' Al-Ḥumaydī said, 'This is the only thing related by Yaḥyā ibn 'Urwah from his father from 'Ā'ishah in the *Ṣaḥīḥ*.

Al-Bukhārī also transmitted from Abū al-Aswad Muḥammad ibn 'Abd ar-Raḥmān from 'Urwah that 'Ā'ishah heard the Messenger of Allah ﷺ say, 'The angels descend in the clouds and mention something that has been decreed in heaven and the *shayṭān*s eavesdrop and hear it and then take it to the soothsayers and they add to it a hundred lies from themselves.' This theme will be further discussed in Sabā', Allah willing.

He knows everything in the land and sea.

They are singled out for mention because they are the largest things in creation in the vicinity of the human being, and mean, 'He knows what dies in the land and sea.' It is said, 'He knows all the plants, seeds and grains in the land of, and all the creatures and provision in the sea.'

No leaf falls without His knowing it.

It is related from Ibn 'Umar that the Prophet ﷺ said, 'There is no crop on the earth nor fruits on the trees nor grain in the darkness of the earth but that written on it is: "In the Name of Allah, the All-Merciful, Most Merciful. Provision for so-and-so." That is in the decisive *āyah* of His Book: "*No leaf falls without His knowing it. There is no seed in the darkness of the earth, and nothing moist or dry which is not in a Clear Book.*"' An-Naqqāsh reported from Ja'far ibn Muḥammad that the falling leaf in this instance is a reference to the miscarriages of children of the sons of Ādam and the seeds are those that do not miscarry. *Moist* here means alive and *dry* means dead. Ibn 'Aṭiyyah said, 'This is a position based on guesswork. It is not soundly transmitted from Ja'far ibn Muḥammad nor must attention be paid to it.'

It is said that the meaning of '*No leaf falls*' is the leaves of the trees, and Allah knows when they will fall, where they will fall and how long they will be in the air. There is no seed but that He knows when it will grow and how much it will grow and who will eat it. '*The darkness of the earth*' means inside it. This is sounder and is in harmony with the *ḥadīth* and the context of the *āyah*. Allah guides to success in guidance. It is also said that '*darkness of the earth*' means the stone which is under the seventh earth. '*Moist or dry*' is in the genitive, added to the expression. Ibn as-Samayqa', al-Ḥasan and others have them in the nominative added to the position of '*leaf*' and the '*min*' is for emphasis. '*In a Clear Book*' means in the Preserved Tablet for the consideration of the angels, not that Allah Himself writes it out of any possibility of forgetfulness. He is far exalted above that. It is said that He writes it while He knows it in order to emphasise the importance of it, meaning, 'Know that this, in respect of which there is neither reward nor punishment, is clearly recorded, so how much more will that be the case with that for which there is reward or punishment?'

وَهُوَ الَّذِي يَتَوَفَّاكُم بِاللَّيْلِ وَيَعْلَمُ مَا جَرَحْتُم بِالنَّهَارِ ثُمَّ يَبْعَثُكُمْ فِيهِ
لِيُقْضَىٰ أَجَلٌ مُّسَمًّى ثُمَّ إِلَيْهِ مَرْجِعُكُمْ ثُمَّ يُنَبِّئُكُم بِمَا كُنتُمْ تَعْمَلُونَ ٦٠

60 It is He Who takes you back to Himself at night, while knowing the things you perpetrate by day, and then wakes you up again, so that a specified term may be fulfilled. Then you will return to Him. Then He will inform you about what you did.

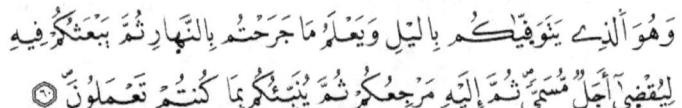

It is He Who takes you back to Himself at night,

He makes you sleep and takes your souls by which you possess discrimination. That is not real death, but it is the divesting the spirits of action by means of sleep similar to the way they are taken in death. 'Taking back' is to take a thing fully. The dead person is taken when the number of the days of his life are completed. In the case of someone who sleeps, it is as if he has exhausted his actions while awake. *Wafā* (fulfilment) is death and the verb is used for receiving payment in full. *Awfā* is to give in full and *istawfā* is to receive in full. A poet has said:

The Banū al-Adram do not count as anyone,
and Quraysh do not include them in their full number (*tawaffā*).

It is said that when the soul leaves the body in sleep, life remains in it. That is why there is movement and breathing. When someone's life ends, his spirit leaves and his life stops and he becomes dead without movement or breath. One of them said, 'The *rūḥ* does not leave him, but consciousness leaves him.' It is said that it is a matter whose reality is only known by Allah. This is the soundest of positions, and Allah knows best.

and then wakes you up again, so that a specified term may be fulfilled.

This is in the daytime. He means wakefulness. The words: '*So that a specified term may be fulfilled*' mean that every human being will have the full term which is set for him. Abū Rajā' and Ṭalḥah ibn Muṣarrif recited '*ajalan*'.

The verb '*jaraḥtum*' (perpetrate) means 'earn', as mentioned in *Sūrat al-Mā'idah* (4:4). There is a reversal of order in the *āyah*. It implies: 'He is the One who takes you back to Himself at night and then wakes you up again and knows what you earn in the day.' He puts the most important part of what occurs in a day first. Ibn Jurayj said that it means to wake you up when you are asleep. The meaning of the *āyah* is that Allah gives the unbelievers a deferment and that is not ignoring their disbelief. It is because He enumerates everything precisely, knows it and establishes it. He will complete their specified term of provision and lifetime and then they will return to Him and He will repay them. This indicates the Gathering and Resurrection because the second formation takes place after the first, just as wakefulness comes after sleep. The One who can do one of them can also do the other.

وَهُوَ ٱلْقَاهِرُ فَوْقَ عِبَادِهِۦ وَيُرْسِلُ عَلَيْكُمْ حَفَظَةً حَتَّىٰٓ إِذَا جَآءَ أَحَدَكُمُ ٱلْمَوْتُ تَوَفَّتْهُ رُسُلُنَا وَهُمْ لَا يُفَرِّطُونَ ﴿٦١﴾ ثُمَّ رُدُّوٓا۟ إِلَى ٱللَّهِ مَوْلَىٰهُمُ ٱلْحَقِّ ۚ أَلَا لَهُ ٱلْحُكْمُ وَهُوَ أَسْرَعُ ٱلْحَٰسِبِينَ ﴿٦٢﴾

61-62 He is the Absolute Master over His slaves. He sends angels to watch over you. Then when death comes to one of you, Our messengers take him, and they do not fail in their task. Then they are returned to Allah, their Master, the Real. Jurisdiction belongs to Him alone and He is the Swiftest of Reckoners.

He is the Absolute Master over His slaves.

The preposition '*over*' here means above in rank and degree, not in place and direction, as was explained at the beginning of the *sūrah.*

He sends angels to watch over you.

Sending is actual and is releasing a thing with any message it bears. The sending of the angels is in order for them to fulfil the task of recording they are charged with. Allah says: '*Standing over you are guardians*' (82:10), meaning the angels who record the actions of people and protect them from disasters. *Ḥafaẓah* is the plural of *ḥāfiẓ*. It is said that there are two angels at night and two in the day. One records good and the other evil. When a man walks, there is one before him and one behind him. When he sits, there is one on his right and the other on his left, as Allah says: '*And the two recording angels are recording, sitting on the right and on the left.*' (50:17) It is also said that every human being has five angels: two at night, two in the day and the fifth which never leaves him, night or day. Allah knows best. 'Umar ibn 'Abd al-'Azīz said:

Some people live in misery with ignorant hearts,
heedless while they are awake.
If they had faithfulness and insight,
they would be cautious of death and fear the guardian angels.
People travel and reside,
so warn the one who resides about what is clear.

Then when death comes to one of you, Our messengers take him, and they do not fail in their task.

Death here means the things that bring it about, as mentioned in *Sūrat al-Baqarah.* (2:133) '*Our messengers take him,*' is in the plural, as in Allah's words:

'*Our Messengers brought them the Clear Signs.*' (5:32) Ḥamzah has '*tawaffāhu*' in the masculine plural. Al-A'mash recited '*yatawaffāhu*' in the masculine but with the additional *yā'*. What is meant are the helpers of the Angel of Death. Ibn 'Abbās and others said that. It is related that they remove the *rūḥ* from the body until, when it is at the point of being taken, the Angel of Death takes it. Al-Kalbī said, 'The Angel of Death takes the *rūḥ* from the body and then hands it over to the angels of mercy if it is a believer or to the angels of punishment if it is an unbeliever.' It is said that with the Angel of Death there are seven of the angels of mercy and seven of the angels of punishment. When he takes a believing soul, he surrenders it to the angels of mercy who give him the good news of the reward and take it to heaven. When he takes the soul of an unbeliever, he gives it to the angels of punishment and they give him the news of the punishment and terrify him. Then they take him to heaven and then deliver him to Sijjīn while the soul of the believer goes to 'Illiyīn.

The 'taking' of the soul is sometimes attributed to the Angel of Death, as in Allah's words: '*Say: "The Angel of Death takes you…"*' (32:11), sometimes to the other angels because they undertake it, as in this *āyah* and elsewhere, and sometimes to Allah Himself, who is the One who truly takes them, as in His words: '*Allah takes back people's selves when their death arrives*' (39:43) and: '*Allah gives you life, then causes you to die*' (45:26) and: '*He Who created death and life.*' (67:2) The angels do everything that they are ordered to do.

The phrase: '*…and they do not fail in their task*', means that they do not neglect or fall short in obeying the command of Allah. The root meaning of the verb '*faraṭa*' is 'to go forward', as already mentioned (6:31), and the meaning of Form II (*farraṭa*) is to fall short. Abū 'Ubaydah said, 'They do not slacken.' 'Amr ibn 'Ubayd reads '*yufriṭūn*' rather than '*yufaṭṭirūn*', indicating that they do not exceed the limit in what they are commanded to do with regard to honouring and abasing.

Then they are returned to Allah, their Master, the Real.

Allah will bring them back to life for the Reckoning. '*Their Master, the Real*' means their Creator, Provider, Resurrector and Master. '*Al-Ḥaqq*' in the genitive is an adjective here to the Name of Allah, according to the reading of most (*their Real Master*). Al-Ḥasan reads '*al-ḥaqqa*' in the accusative implying, 'I mean' or as a verbal noun meaning, 'truly'.

Jurisdiction belongs to Him alone and He is the Swiftest of Reckoners.

Know and say that jurisdiction will be His alone on the Day of Rising, in other words all judgment and decision. '*He is the Swiftest of Reckoners.*' He reckons without any need for thought or consideration.

قُلْ مَن يُنَجِّيكُم مِّن ظُلُمَٰتِ ٱلْبَرِّ وَٱلْبَحْرِ تَدْعُونَهُۥ تَضَرُّعًا وَخُفْيَةً لَّئِنَ اَنجَيْتَنَا
مِنْ هَٰذِهِۦ لَنَكُونَنَّ مِنَ ٱلشَّٰكِرِينَ ﴿٦٣﴾ قُلِ ٱللَّهُ يُنَجِّيكُم مِّنْهَا وَمِن كُلِّ كَرْبٍ ثُمَّ أَنتُمْ
تُشْرِكُونَ ﴿٦٤﴾

63-64 Say: 'Who rescues you from the darkness of the land and sea? You call on Him humbly and secretly: "If you rescue us from this, we will truly be among the thankful."' Say: 'Allah rescues you from it, and from every plight. Then you associate others with Him.'

Say: 'Who rescues you from the darkness of the land and sea?

From its hardships. It is said that a 'dark day' is one of hardship. An-Naḥḥās said that the Arabs say 'a dark day' when it is harsh. When it is worse than that, they say, 'a day of stars' as Sībawayh recited:

If the Banū Asad knew of our affliction
when today is worse than a day of stars.

The word '*darkness*' is in the plural since it means the darkness of land, the darkness of the sea, the darkness of night, and the darkness of clouds, implying, 'When you lose your way and fear destruction, then you are forced to call on Him.' '*If you rescue us from this,*' from these hardships, '*we will truly be among the thankful,*' among the obedient. So Allah is censuring them when they call on Him in times of hardship and then call on others alongside Him when they are in times of ease, made clear by His words: '*Then you associate others with Him.*'

Al-A'mash reads '*khufyah*' (*secretly*) as '*khīfah*', meaning 'in fear'. 'Āṣim reads it as *khifyah* and the rest read *khufyah*, like *ḥubyah* and *ḥibyah*. Al-A'mash's reading is unlikely because humility shows itself but fear does not. The Kufans recite '*la'in anjānā*' and the meaning is expanded with *tā'* (*anjaytanā*) in the reading of the people of Madīnah and Syria.

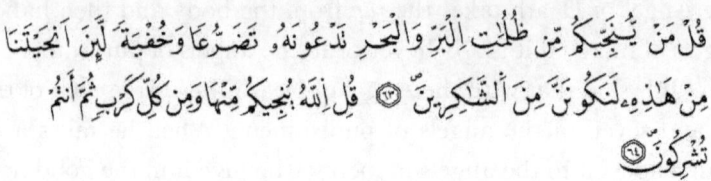

Say: 'Allah rescues you from it, and from every plight. Then you associate others with Him.'

The Kufans read *yunjīkum* in Form II as *yunajjīkum*. The rest have it without the doubled letter. The meaning is the same, like *najā*, *anjā* and *najjā*, although it is said that Form II refers to multiplicity. *Karb* (*plight*) is sorrow that afflicts the soul. A man is called *makrūb* (distressed). 'Antarah said:

A distressed one, I removed distress him
by a decisive thrust when he called for me.

The words: '*Then you associate others with Him*' constitute rebuke and censure, like Allah's words at the beginning of the surah: '*Yet you still have doubts*,' because when the proof is established by their recognition of their Lord, then true sincerity becomes obligatory on them and yet they again assign partners to Him, which is *shirk*, and so they deserve to be rebuked. They were idolaters before being rescued [and revert to idolatry again afterwards].

قُلْ هُوَ ٱلْقَادِرُ عَلَىٰٓ أَن يَبْعَثَ عَلَيْكُمْ عَذَابًا مِّن فَوْقِكُمْ أَوْ مِن تَحْتِ أَرْجُلِكُمْ أَوْ يَلْبِسَكُمْ شِيَعًا وَيُذِيقَ بَعْضَكُم بَأْسَ بَعْضٍ ٱنظُرْ كَيْفَ نُصَرِّفُ ٱلْءَايَٰتِ لَعَلَّهُمْ يَفْقَهُونَ ٦٥

65 Say: 'He possesses the power to send you punishment from above your heads or from beneath your feet, or to confuse you in sects and make you taste one another's violence.' Look how We vary the Signs so that hopefully they will understand.

He has the power to save you from affliction and the power to punish you. The punishment that comes '*from above your heads*' is stoning, flood, the Shout and wind, like that inflicted upon 'Ād, Thamūd, the people of Shu'ayb, the people of Lūṭ and the people of Nūḥ, as Mujāhid, Ibn Jubayr and others said. The one '*from beneath your feet*' is being swallowed up by the earth and quaking, as happened with Qārūn and the people of Madyan. It is said that '*above your heads*' means unjust rulers and '*beneath your feet*' is the lowly and evil slaves, as Ibn 'Abbās and Mujāhid also said.

or to confuse you in sects and make you taste one another's violence

The verb is related from Abū 'Abdullāh al-Madinī as '*yulbisakum*', meaning 'He will envelop you in the punishment and make it cover you.' This is derived from the word *lubs* meaning clothing. The first reading is from the word *labs* meaning confusion. There is some ambiguity but the syntax makes it clear that it means 'He will make the matter confused for you' and one of the two objects is elided as well as the genitive particle. He will make the matter confused for you and also form you into different sects, as Ibn 'Abbās said. It is said that it means: 'He will strengthen your enemies so that they bewilder you. When they bewilder you, you will be confused.'

The noun *shiya'* means 'sects'. It is said: 'He will form you into sects fighting one another.' That is due to their confusion and the disagreement of their rulers brought about by their desire for this world. This will '*make you taste one another's violence*,' through fighting and killing in civil war, as Mujāhid said. The *āyah* is general to the Muslims and unbelievers. It is also said that it is only about the unbelievers. Al-Ḥasan said, 'It is about the people of the prayer.' That is sound; we are witnesses of it. The enemy has confused us in our homes and taken our lives and our property through the civil unrest which has overwhelmed us and made us kill one another and take one another's property. We seek refuge in Allah from sedition, open and hidden.

Al-Ḥasan also interpreted it to refer to what occurred between the Companions. Muslim related from Thawbān that the Messenger of Allah ﷺ said, 'Allah shrank the earth for me and I saw its east and west. My community will rule as far as what was shrunken for me of it. And I was given the two treasures: the red and white (i.e. gold and silver). I asked my Lord not to destroy my Community by a general famine and not to give mastery over them to an enemy from other than themselves, enabling them to take possession of their heartland. My Lord said, "Muḥammad, when I have decided a matter, nothing can stop it happening. I have granted to your community that they will not be destroyed by a general famine and nor will I give mastery over them to an enemy from other than themselves, enabling them to take possession of their heartland – even if they were to gather together from every corner of the earth against them – until they kill one another and imprison one another."'

An-Nasā'ī related from Khabbāb ibn al-Araṭṭ, who had been present at Badr with the Messenger of Allah ﷺ, that he watched the Messenger of Allah ﷺ for the entire night until dawn. When the Messenger of Allah ﷺ said the *salām* for the prayer, Khabbāb came and said, 'Messenger of Allah, may my father and mother be your ransom! You prayed a prayer in the night whose like I have not seen you pray!' The Messenger of Allah ﷺ replied, 'Yes, it is a prayer of desire and fear. In it I asked Allah for three things and He granted me two and denied me one. I asked my Lord not to destroy us in the way that previous nations were destroyed and He granted me that. I asked my Lord not to let our enemy overcome us from other than ourselves, and He granted me that. I asked my Lord not to confuse us into sects but He refused me that.' We have dealt with these reports in the *Kitāb at-Tadhkirah.* Praise belongs to Allah.

It is related that when this *āyah* was revealed, the Prophet ﷺ asked Jibrīl, 'Jibrīl, how will my community endure in that case?' Jibrīl said to him, 'I am a slave like yourself, so call on your Lord and ask Him for your community.' The Messenger of Allah ﷺ rose and performed a full *wuḍū'*, prayed well and then made supplication. Jibrīl descended and said, 'O Muḥammad, Allah Almighty has heard your words and has protected them from two things: punishment from above them and from beneath their feet.' He said, 'Jibrīl, how will my community endure when there are differing sects among them and they taste one another's violence?' Then Jibrīl brought down this ayah: *'Alif Lām Mīm. Do people imagine that they will be left to say, "We believe"?* (29:1-2)'

'Amr ibn Dīnār related that Jābir ibn 'Abdullāh said, 'When the *āyah*: *"He is the Absolute Master over His slaves…"* was revealed, the Messenger of Allah ﷺ said, "I seek refuge with the Face of Allah!" When the words: "*…or confuse you in sects, and make you taste one another's violence,*" was revealed, he said, "These two are easier."'

In the *Sunan* of Ibn Mājah, Ibn 'Umar said, 'The Messenger of Allah ﷺ did not cease to recite these words in the morning and evening: "O Allah, I ask You for well-being in this world and the Next. O Allah, I ask You for pardon and well-being in my *dīn* and this world and my family and property. O Allah, veil my shortcomings and preserve me from my fears! Preserve me from in front of me and behind me, to my right and to my left, and above me. I seek refuge with You from being taken unawares from beneath me."' Wakī' said that it means the earth collapsing.

Look how We vary the Signs so that hopefully they will understand.

See how We make the proofs and evidence clear to them '*so that hopefully they will understand*' the invalidity of any *shirk* and acts of disobedience they continue to hold to.

وَكَذَّبَ بِهِۦ قَوْمُكَ وَهُوَ ٱلْحَقُّ ۚ قُل لَّسْتُ عَلَيْكُم بِوَكِيلٍ ﴿٦٦﴾ لِّكُلِّ نَبَإٍ مُّسْتَقَرٌّ ۚ وَسَوْفَ
تَعْلَمُونَ ﴿٦٧﴾

66-67 Your people deny it and yet it is the Truth. Say: 'I am not here as your guardian. Every communication has its time, and you will certainly come to know.'

Your people deny it and yet it is the Truth.

The pronoun '*it*' refers to the Qur'an. Ibn Abī 'Aqlah recites '*kadhdhabat*' with *tā'* at the end.

Say: 'I am not here as your guardian.

Al-Ḥasan said this means, 'I am not the guardian of your actions in that it is my business to repay you for them. I am a warner and I have conveyed the message.' This is similar to the words: '*I am not set over you as your keeper.*' (11:86) when it is not his business ﷺ to record their actions. Then it is said that this was abrogated by the *Āyah* of the Sword. It is also said that it is not abrogated since it is not within his capacity ﷺ to make them believe.

Every communication has its time.

Every report has a reality, in other words everything has a time when it occurs, not before or later. It is said that it means there is a repayment for every action. Al-Ḥasan said, 'This is a threat from Allah to the unbelievers because they did not affirm the Resurrection.' Az-Zajjāj said, 'It may be a threat about what will happen to them in this world.' As-Suddī said, 'This is a reference to the punishment they were threatened with and it came about on the Day of Badr.' Ath-Tha'labī mentioned that he saw in one of the *tafsīr*s that this *āyah* helps against toothache when it is written on a paper which is then placed on the tooth.

وَإِذَا رَأَيْتَ ٱلَّذِينَ يَخُوضُونَ فِىٓ ءَايَٰتِنَا فَأَعْرِضْ عَنْهُمْ حَتَّىٰ يَخُوضُوا۟
فِى حَدِيثٍ غَيْرِهِۦ ۚ وَإِمَّا يُنسِيَنَّكَ ٱلشَّيْطَٰنُ فَلَا تَقْعُدْ بَعْدَ ٱلذِّكْرَىٰ
مَعَ ٱلْقَوْمِ ٱلظَّٰلِمِينَ ﴿٦٨﴾

68 When you see people engrossed in mockery of Our Signs, turn from them until they start to talk of other things. And if *Shayṭān* should ever cause you to forget, as soon as you remember, do not stay sitting with the wrongdoers.

When you see people engrossed in mockery of Our Signs, turn from them until they start to talk of other things.

The mockery takes the form of denial, rejection and ridicule.

turn from them until they start to talk of other things.

The words '*turn from them*' are addressed solely to the Prophet ﷺ although it is said that the believers are included in it and that is sound. The reason for it was listening to demeaning discussion of the *āyahs* of Allah and that command included them and him. It is said that it means the Prophet ﷺ alone because his standing apart from the idolaters was hard on them. The believers were not like that with them and so he was commanded to separate himself from them by leaving them when they mocked and were engrossed in that activity, in order to discipline them and so that they would leave off this discussion and mockery.

The root meaning of *khawḍ* (*engrossed in*) is to dive into the water, and it is used for the depths of things which are unknown, such as floods, and so an intellectual metaphor is being struck from the sensory meaning. It is said that it is derived from mixing (*khalṭ*). You are mixed with every thing into which you dive as water is mixed with honey. So Allah instructed His Prophet ﷺ by this *āyah* because he used to sit with the idolaters, admonish them and invite them to Islam and then they mocked the Qur'an. So Allah commanded him to turn aside from them in distaste. That indicates that when a man is aware of aversion on the part of another man and he knows that he will not accept something from him, he should turn from him in aversion and not accompany him.

Shibl related from Ibn Abī Najīḥ from Mujāhid about these words, 'They are those who mock the Book of Allah. Allah forbids a person to sit with them unless he forgets. Then when he remembers, he must get up and go.' Warqā' related from Ibn Abī Najīḥ that Mujāhid said, 'They are those who said what was not true about the Qur'an.'

This *āyah* is refutation by the Book of Allah of those who claim that the Imāms who are the authorities and their followers can mingle with the corrupt and assent to their views out of *taqiyyah* (dissimulation). Aṭ-Ṭabarī reported that Muḥammad ibn 'Alī said, 'Do not sit with the people of disputation. They are those who delve into the Signs of Allah.' Ibn al-'Arabī said, 'This is proof that it is not lawful to sit with the people of major wrong action.' Ibn Khuwayzimandād said. 'If someone delves into the Signs of Allah, you should not sit with them and they should be shunned, whether believers or unbelievers.' He said, 'That is why our companions forbade going to the land of the enemy and entering their churches and synagogues and sitting with the unbelievers and people of innovation, and forbade us to love them or listen to their words or debate with them.'

One of the people of innovation said to Abū 'Imran an-Nakha'ī, 'Listen to a word from me.' He turned from him and said, 'Not even half a word.' Something similar is reported from Ayyūb as-Sakhtiyānī. Al-Fuḍayl ibn 'Iyāḍ said, 'Whoever loves one of the people of innovation has his actions cancelled for him and the light of Islam removed from his heart. Whoever has married his daughter to one of the people of innovation has severed her kinship to him. Whoever sits with one of the people of innovation has not been given wisdom. If Allah knows that a man hates the people of innovation, I hope that Allah will forgive him.' Abū 'Abdullāh al-Ḥākim related from 'Ā'ishah that the Messenger of Allah ﷺ said, 'Anyone who esteems one of the people of innovation has helped to destroy Islam.' This invalidates the view of the one who claims that it is permitted to sit with them so long as one protects one's hearing.

And if *Shayṭān* should ever cause you to forget

'*Immā*' is a precondition which usually requires a heavy *nūn*, although it is not absolutely required. [POEM] Ibn 'Abbās and Ibn 'Āmir recited '*yunassiyannaka*' which expresses a great deal. *Nassā* and *ansā* mean the same. A poet said:

Sulaymā said, 'Will you travel today or spend midday?
Laziness has made you forget (*yunassīka*) some of what is needed.

The meaning is: 'If, Muḥammad, *Shayṭān* makes you forget to leave them and you sit with them after the prohibition, "as soon as you remember, do not stay sitting."' The wrongdoers are the idolaters. *Dhikrā* is a noun meaning remembering. It is said that this is addressed to the Prophet ﷺ while what is meant is his community. The people who say that believe that he ﷺ is free of forgetfulness. It is also said that the *āyah* is particular to him and it is conceivable that he might forget. Ibn al-'Arabī said, 'We excuse our companions for what they say because of Allah's words: "*If you associate others with Allah, your actions will come to nothing.*" (39:65) [This is because of the use of the second person singular in both cases.] That is certainly addressed to the Community by way of the Prophet ﷺ since *shirk* is impossible for him. This means they have no excuse for considering forgetfulness conceivable on his part.' The Prophet ﷺ said, 'Ādam forgot and so his descendants forget.' At-Tirmidhī transmitted it and says that it is sound. He said about himself, 'I am a mortal like you. I forget as you forget. When I forget, I am reminded.' It is transmitted in the *Ṣaḥīḥ*. So he ascribed forgetfulness to himself. He ﷺ heard a man reciting and said, 'He reminded me of such-and-such an *āyah* which I forgot.'

After considering forgetfulness conceivable for him, they disagree about whether or not his forgetfulness can be a means of conveying actions and rulings of the *Sharī'ah*. Most scholars and important Imams – among them Qāḍī 'Iyāḍ – believe the first, as it is the apparent meaning of the Qur'an and *ḥadīths*, but the Imams stipulate that Allah Almighty will definitely call his attention to that and not let him remain in it. Then they disagree about when he is alerted, whether it is immediately connected to the event, which is the position of Qāḍī Abū Bakr and most scholars, or whether delay is permitted in that as long as he is still alive and the conveying of the Message continued. That is the position of Abū al-Ma'ālī.

One group of scholars consider forgetfulness inconceivable for him in respect of actions which are transmitted and acts of worship in the *Sharī'ah* as they forbid it by consensus in respect of the words which are conveyed. They make excuses for apparent instances of forgetfulness which are reported. That is the inclination of Abū Isḥāq [al-Isfarāyinī]. The Bāṭiniyyah and a group of the masters of the science of hearts took an aberrant view and said that forgetfulness is not conceivable for him but that he overlooked things deliberately in the form of forgetfulness in order to make a *sunnah*. Many of the meticulous Imāms took this view, among them al-Isfarāyinī, but it is an incorrect approach for it is impossible to join two opposites.

وَمَا عَلَى ٱلَّذِينَ يَتَّقُونَ مِنْ حِسَابِهِم مِّن شَيْءٍ وَلَٰكِن ذِكْرَىٰ
لَعَلَّهُمْ يَتَّقُونَ ۝٦٩

69 Their reckoning is in no way the responsibility of those who are godfearing. But remind them so that hopefully they themselves will be godfearing.

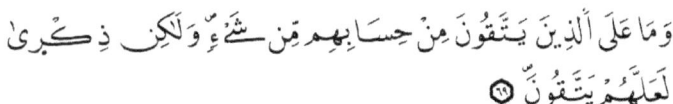

Ibn 'Abbās said, 'When "*Do not sit with the idolaters*," was revealed, by which is meant "turn away from them", the Muslims said, "Then we cannot enter the mosque and do *ṭawāf*," and so the *āyah* was revealed.' '*But remind them*,' in other words if the believers sit with them, they should remind them and '*hopefully they themselves will be godfearing*', show fear of Allah by leaving what they are doing. Then it is said that it is abrogated by Allah's words: '*He has sent down to you in the Book that when you hear Allah's Signs being rejected and mocked at by people, you must not sit with them until they start to talk of other things.*' (4:140) The allowance was before the Conquest, which was a time of *taqiyyah* (dissimulation). By His words: '*He has sent*

down to you in the Book' (4:140), he is indicating His words elsewhere: *'Leave those who take their dīn as a game and diversion.'* (6:79) Al-Qushayrī said, 'The most apparent position is that it is not abrogated. The meaning is: "You are not responsible for any of the reckoning of the idolaters. You must remind them and rebuke them. If they refuse, their reckoning is up to Allah."'

'Dhikrā' is in the accusative based on the verbal noun, and it is also permitted for it to be in the nominative, meaning 'but what they do is a reminder.' Al-Kisā'ī said that it means: 'but this is a reminder.'

وَذَرِ ٱلَّذِينَ ٱتَّخَذُواْ دِينَهُمْ لَعِبًا وَلَهْوًا وَغَرَّتْهُمُ ٱلْحَيَوٰةُ ٱلدُّنْيَا
وَذَكِّرْ بِهِۦٓ أَن تُبْسَلَ نَفْسٌۢ بِمَا كَسَبَتْ لَيْسَ لَهَا مِن دُونِ ٱللَّهِ
وَلِىٌّ وَلَا شَفِيعٌ وَإِن تَعْدِلْ كُلَّ عَدْلٍ لَّا يُؤْخَذْ مِنْهَآ أُوْلَٰٓئِكَ ٱلَّذِينَ
أُبْسِلُواْ بِمَا كَسَبُواْ لَهُمْ شَرَابٌ مِّنْ حَمِيمٍ وَعَذَابٌ أَلِيمٌۢ بِمَا كَانُواْ
يَكْفُرُونَ ﴿٧٠﴾

70 Abandon those who have turned their *dīn* into a game and a diversion and who have been deluded by the life of this world. Remind by it lest a person is delivered up to destruction for what he has earned with no protector or intercessor besides Allah. Were he to offer every kind of compensation, it would not be accepted from him. Such people are delivered up to destruction for what they have earned. They will have scalding water to drink and a painful punishment because they disbelieved.

Abandon those who have turned their *dīn* into a game and a diversion

It means: 'Do not attach your heart to them. They are people of obduracy and you are commanded to admonish them.' Qatādah said, 'This is abrogated.' It is abrogated by the words: *'Kill the idolaters wherever you find them.'* (9:5) The meaning of *'game and diversion'* is mockery of the *dīn* to which you call them. It is said that they mocked the *dīn* which they had and did not act on it. Mockery is not allowed in the *dīn*. It is also said that *'game and diversion'* is falsehood and gaiety. This was already discussed in other places.

The word *'game'* was already used in four places. There is a poem:

When games and diversion come,
  how many places is that mentioned in the Qur'an,

Once in *al-Ḥadīd* (57) and once in *al-Qitāl* (47),
and in two places in *al-An'ām*!

It is said that what is meant by *dīn* here is the *'īd*. Al-Kalbī said that Allah appointed for every people an *'īd* which they esteem and during which they pray to Allah Almighty. Every people made their *dīn* a game and diversion except for the Community of Muḥammad ﷺ. They took it as meaning prayer, *dhikr*, and giving *ṣadaqah*, like *Jumu'ah*, breaking the fast and the Day of Sacrifice.

who have been deluded by the life of this world

It means that they only know the outward aspect of the life of this world.

Remind by it lest a person is delivered up to destruction for what he has earned

In '*Remind by it*' the pronoun '*it*' refers to the Qur'an or the Reckoning. The words '*delivered up to destruction for what he has earned*' mean that he has given himself up as security and will be handed over for destruction, as Mujāhid, Qatādah, al-Ḥasan, 'Ikrimah and as-Suddī said. The verb *absala* means to deliver a person to destruction, a known linguistic usage, and it is also used for offering a person as security. 'Awf ibn al-Aḥwaṣ ibn Ja'far said:

My delivering up my sons (*ibsālī*) for destruction without it being
for a crime we have committed nor for any blood shed.

He offered himself up to a wealthy man of the Banū Qushayr for the two sons of as-Sajafiyyah. They said, 'We are not satisfied with you,' and so he offered his sons as a security, seeking peace. An-Nābighah al-Ja'dī composed:

We are pledged as security to 'Āmir at al-Ufāqah for what happened
to ad-Dardā', and so he was offered for destruction (*ubsilā*).

Ad-Darda' was a squadron of theirs.

Were he to offer every kind of compensation, it would not be accepted from him.

'Adl (compensation) is ransom, as discussed in *Sūrat al-Baqarah* (2:49). *Ḥamīm* is hot water as in Allah's words: '*boiling water (*ḥamīm*) poured over their heads*' (22:19) and: '*They will go back and forth between fire and scalding water* (ḥamīm).' (22:44) This *āyah* was abrogated by the *Āyah* of Fighting. It is also said that it was not abrogated because the words: '*Abandon those who have turned their dīn…*' is a threat, just as: '*Leave them to eat and enjoy themselves,*' (15:3) is also a threat. It means: 'Do not grieve over them. It is your task to convey the Message and remind them they are

offering themselves to destruction.' Whoever delivers himself to destruction has surrendered and been given as a pledge.

It is said that it is basically a prohibition, as one might say, 'This is *basl* for you,' in other words forbidden. So it is as if they were forbidden the Garden and the Garden was forbidden to them. A poet said:

Your granting asylum is forbidden (*basl*) for us
while our neighbour and his wife are lawful for you.

Ibsāl is prohibition.

قُلْ أَنَدْعُواْ مِن دُونِ ٱللَّهِ مَا لَا يَنفَعُنَا وَلَا يَضُرُّنَا وَنُرَدُّ عَلَىٰٓ أَعْقَابِنَا
بَعْدَ إِذْ هَدَىٰنَا ٱللَّهُ كَٱلَّذِى ٱسْتَهْوَتْهُ ٱلشَّيَٰطِينُ فِى ٱلْأَرْضِ حَيْرَانَ لَهُۥٓ
أَصْحَٰبٌ يَدْعُونَهُۥٓ إِلَى ٱلْهُدَى ٱئْتِنَا قُلْ إِنَّ هُدَى ٱللَّهِ هُوَ ٱلْهُدَىٰ
وَأُمِرْنَا لِنُسْلِمَ لِرَبِّ ٱلْعَٰلَمِينَ ﴿٧١﴾ وَأَنْ أَقِيمُواْ ٱلصَّلَوٰةَ وَٱتَّقُوهُ
وَهُوَ ٱلَّذِىٓ إِلَيْهِ تُحْشَرُونَ ﴿٧٢﴾ وَهُوَ ٱلَّذِى خَلَقَ ٱلسَّمَٰوَٰتِ وَٱلْأَرْضَ
بِٱلْحَقِّ وَيَوْمَ يَقُولُ كُن فَيَكُونُ قَوْلُهُ ٱلْحَقُّ وَلَهُ ٱلْمُلْكُ يَوْمَ
يُنفَخُ فِى ٱلصُّورِ عَٰلِمُ ٱلْغَيْبِ وَٱلشَّهَٰدَةِ وَهُوَ ٱلْحَكِيمُ ٱلْخَبِيرُ ﴿٧٣﴾

71-73 Say: 'Are we to call on something besides Allah which can neither help nor harm us, and to turn on our heels after Allah has guided us, like someone the *shayṭāns* have lured away in the earth, leaving him confused and stupefied, despite the fact that he has companions calling him to guidance, saying, "Come with us!"?' Say: 'Allah's guidance, that is true guidance. We are commanded to submit as Muslims to the Lord of all the worlds, and to establish the prayer and have *taqwā* of Him. It is He to Whom you will be gathered.' It is He Who created the heavens and the earth with truth. The day He says 'Be!' it is. His speech is Truth. The Kingdom will be His on the Day the Trumpet is blown, the Knower of the Unseen and the Visible. He is the All-Wise, the All-Aware.

Say: 'Are we to call on something besides Allah which can neither help nor harm us, and to turn on our heels after Allah has guided us,

It does not help us when we call on it or harm us when we do not. This refers to the idols. There is no benefit in our calling upon idols and it brings us no harm when we do not do that. The phrase: '*and to turn on our heels after Allah has guided us*' means to return to misguidance after guidance. The singular of *a'qāb* is *'iqb*. The diminutive is *'uqaybah*. It is said that someone turns on his heels when he turns back. Abū 'Ubaydah said, 'When someone turns from his need without obtaining it, "he turns on his heels."' Al-Mubarrad said that it means to bring evil after good. Its root is *'āqibah* and *'uqbah*, which indicate what necessarily follows something, as in Allah's words: '*The successful outcome* ('āqibah) *is for the godfearing*" (7:128) Also *'uqūbah* is used for punishment because it follows the wrong action and stems from it.

like someone the *shayṭāns* have lured away in the earth,

In '*like someone*' the *kāf* is accusative describing an elided verbal noun. The words '*the shayṭāns have lured away in the earth*' means that they have made him err and made his lower desires attractive to him and called him to them. It is said that the verb *hawā* means to swiftly fall on something. Az-Zajjāj said, 'It comes from the *hawā* (desire) of the self and means that *shayṭān* made his passion seem attractive to him.' Most recite it *istahwat-hu,* meaning 'made him fall', with the feminine singular for a plurality of inanimates whereas Ḥamzah recites it as *istahwāhu* in the masculine plural. Ibn Mas'ūd has '*istahwāhu-sh-shayṭān*' which is also related from al-Ḥasan and is found in the mode (*ḥarf*) of Ubayy.

despite the fact that he has companions calling him to guidance, saying, "Come with us!"?'

The expression '*Come with us*!' means 'Follow us'. The reading of 'Abdullāh also has: 'calling him to guidance clearly (*bayyinan*).' Al-Ḥasan also has '*istahwat-hu-sh-shayāṭūna*'. The word *ḥayrān* means bewildered, someone who is not guided to the proper course in his affair. The verb is *ḥāra*. It is used for water which goes round and round and has no way out. The plural is *ḥūrān*. *Ḥā'ir* is a place in which water collects. A poet says:

She steps on two papyrus plants fed by
    copious water in the long courtyard with water (*ḥā'ir*).

Ibn 'Abbās said, 'It means that someone who worships an idol is like someone whom a ghoul [will-o'-the-wisp] entices and he follows it and morning finds him cast into misguidance and destruction. He is bewildered in that wasteland.'

In a transmission of Abū Ṣāliḥ: 'It was revealed about 'Abd ar-Raḥmān ibn Abī Bakr. He called his father to disbelief while his father and his parents and the Muslims were calling him to Islam and that explains Allah's words: "*despite the fact that he has companions calling him to guidance.*"' Abū 'Umar said, 'His mother was Umm Rūmān bint al-Ḥārith al-Kināniyyah, and he was the full brother of 'Ā'ishah. He was present at the battles of Badr and Uḥud with his people while still an unbeliever. He called on someone to come out and fight him and his father rose to go and fight him. The Messenger of Allah ﷺ said to Abū Bakr, "Let me continue to benefit from you." Then he became a good Muslim and accompanied the Prophet ﷺ in the truce of al-Ḥudaybīyah.' This is what the people of *Sīrah* say. They said that his name was 'Abd al-Ka'bah and the Prophet ﷺ changed it to 'Abd ar-Raḥmān. He was the oldest of Abū Bakr's children. It is said that four generations did not meet the Prophet ﷺ, father and sons, except for Abū Quḥāfah, his son Abū Bakr, his son 'Abd ar-Raḥmān and his son Abū 'Atīq Muḥammad ibn Muḥammad. Allah knows best.

We are commanded to submit as Muslims to the Lord of all the worlds, and to establish the prayer and have taqwā of Him.

We are commanded so that we surrender and establish the prayer because the particles of *iḍāfah* connect them to one another. Al-Farrā' said that the meaning is: 'we are commanded to submit.' Islam is sincerity, and establishing the prayer means to perform it and persevere in it. It can also be added to the meaning: 'Call them to guidance and call them to establish the prayer.'

It is He Who created the heavens and the earth with truth.

He is the one who must be worshipped, not the idols. 'With truth' means by the word of truth, by His command 'Be!'

The day He says 'Be!' it is. His speech is Truth.

This implies 'Remember the day He says, "Be!"' or 'Fear the Day when He says, "Be"' or 'He decrees the Day when He says, "Be!"' It is said that it is joined to 'Him' (meaning fear Him and the Day). Al-Farrā' said that the command '*"Be" it is*' is said to refer to the forms in particular, meaning on the Day when He says to forms, 'Be!' they are. It is said that the meaning is all that He wills of people's death and life. According to these two interpretations the expression: 'His speech is Truth' is a full sentence. It is said that '*qawluhu*' is in the nominative by '*yakūnu*' and it means: 'what He commands is'. '*Truth*' is part of its description and according to this, it ends with '*Truth*'. Ibn 'Āmir recited '*yakūna*' in the subjunctive, and it indicates the speed of Reckoning and the Resurrection. This was already discussed adequately in *al-Baqarah* (2:117).

on the Day the Trumpet is blown

This means the Kingdom will be His on the Day the Trumpet is blown, or He has the Truth on the Day that the Trumpet is blown. It is said that it is an appositive for '*the day He says*'. The Trumpet is a horn of light which will be blown. The first blast is for annihilation and the second for raising. As we will make clear *ṣūr* (*Trumpet*) is not the plural of *ṣūrah* (form), as some claim, meaning that He will blow into the forms of the dead. Muslim related from the *ḥadīth* of 'Abdullāh ibn 'Amr: 'Then the Trumpet will be blown. No one will hear it without inclining his neck towards the sound to listen. The first to hear it will be a man plastering his camels' watering-trough, and he will swoon and everyone will swoon. Then Allah will send – or he said 'Allah will make fall' – rain as if it was dew or a shadow, and through it people's bodies will grow. Then it will be blown a second time and they will be standing, looking round.' That corroborates what is in the Revelation: '*Then it will be blown a second time.*' (39:68) Allah did use the feminine for 'it' here and so it is known that it cannot be the plural of *ṣūrah*.

Nations will be gathered when Isrāfīl blows the Trumpet. Abū al-Haytham said, 'Whoever denies that the *Ṣūr* is a horn is like someone who denies the existence of the Throne, Balance and *Ṣirāṭ* and tries to interpret them esoterically.' Ibn Fāris said that the *Ṣūr* in the *ḥadīth* is like a horn which is blown. *Ṣūr* is the plural of *ṣūrah*. Al-Jawharī said that *ṣūr* is a horn. A poet said:

We gored them in the morning of the two groups
With a severe goring like that done by the two horns (*ṣūrayn*).

Another example of it is: '*On the Day the Trumpet is blown.*' (27:87) Al-Kalbī said, 'I do not know what the *Ṣūr* is.' It is said that it is the plural of *ṣūrah*, like *busrah* and *busr*, meaning that it will be blown into the forms of the dead and souls. Al-Ḥasan recited '*aṣ-ṣuwar*'. *Ṣiwar* is a dialect for this and its singular is *ṣūrah*. *Ṣayrān* is the plural of *ṣiwār*, and *ṣiyār* is one of its dialectical forms. 'Amr ibn 'Ubayd said that 'Iyāḍ recited '*aṣ-ṣuwar*', and this means creation. Allah knows best. Among those who said that what is meant by *ṣūr* in this *āyah* is the plural of *ṣūrah* is Abū 'Ubaydah. Even if this is possible it is refuted by what we have mentioned from the Book and *Sunnah*. The Trumpet is not blown for the Resurrection twice. It is blown once. Isrāfīl blows the Trumpet which is the

Horn and Allah gives life to the forms. In Revelation we find: '*We breathed Our spirit into him.*' (66:12)

the Knower of the Unseen and the Visible.

'*Knower*' is in the nominative as an adjective describing 'who'. It means: He is the One who created the heavens and the earth, the Knower of the Unseen. It can also be in the nominative by an implied inchoative. It is related from some that it is recited '*yanfukhu*' and it is possible that the subject is '*Knower...*' because the blowing is done by the command of Allah and so it is ascribed to Him. '*Knower*' can be in the nominative based on the meaning. [POEM] Al-Ḥasan and al-A'mash recited "*ālim*' in the genitive as an appositive for the *hā'* in '*lahu*'.

وَإِذْ قَالَ إِبْرَٰهِيمُ لِأَبِيهِ ءَازَرَ أَتَتَّخِذُ أَصْنَامًا ءَالِهَةً إِنِّيٓ أَرَىٰكَ
وَقَوْمَكَ فِي ضَلَٰلٍ مُّبِينٍ ﴿٧٤﴾

74 Remember when Ibrāhīm said to his father, Āzar, 'Do you take idols as gods? I see that you and your people are clearly misguided.'

Remember when Ibrāhīm said to his father, Āzar,

Scholars have spoken about this. Abū Bakr Muḥammad al-Juwaynī ash-Shāfi'ī al-Ash'arī said in some points of his *tafsīr*, 'There is no disagreement that the name of the father of Ibrāhīm was Terah yet the Qur'an indicates that his name is Āzar. It is said that *āzar* is censure in their language and so it is as if he were saying to his father, "O one in error, do you take idols as gods?" It is said that Āzar was the name of an idol and it is as if he was saying to his father, "Do you take Āzar as a god and idols as gods?"'

What he claims that there is agreement about is, in fact, not agreed upon. Muḥammad ibn Isḥāq, al-Kalbī and aḍ-Ḍahhāk said, 'Āzar was the father of Ibrāhīm and he is also Terah, like Isrā'īl and Ya'qūb.' I say that these are two distinct names. Muqātil said that Āzar is a title and Terah the name. Ath-Tha'labī related that from Ibn Isḥāq al-Qushayrī. The reverse is also possible. Al-Ḥasan said that his father's name was Āzar. Sulaymān at-Taymī said that it is a term of abuse, and means 'twisted' in their language. Al-Mu'tamir ibn Sulaymān said that his father said, 'I have heard that he was lame.' This is the strongest word which Ibrāhīm directed at his father. Aḍ-Ḍaḥḥāk said, 'The meaning is "senile old man" in Persian.' Al-Farrā' said, 'It is a blameworthy quality in their language.

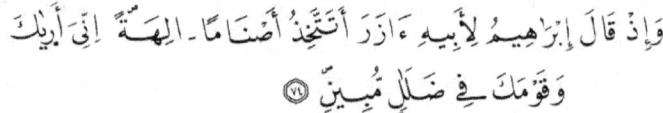

It is as if he were saying, "You who are in error". Or it is as if Allah were saying, "When Ibrāhīm said to his father who was in error."'

Al-Jawharī said, 'It is a foreign name derived from *āzara*, meaning to aid and abet someone. So he is aiding and abetting his people in worshipping idols.' It is also said that it is derived from strength, and *azr* means strength, as Ibn Fāris stated. Mujāhid and Yamān said that it is a name of an idol. According to this interpretation, it is in the accusative, implying, 'Do you take Āzar as a god? Do you take idols?' It is said that there is a change in the normal order and implies: 'Do you take Āzar as idols?' According to this, Āzar is a generic name, and Allah knows best. In *Kitāb al-'Arā'ish*, ath-Tha'labī said, 'The name of Ibrāhīm's father, which was his actual name, was Terah. When he was with Nimrod in charge of the treasures of his gods, he named him Āzar.' Mujāhid said that Āzar was not the name of his father, but the name of an idol. His name was Ibrāhīm ibn Tāriḥ ibn Nākhūr ibn Sārū' ibn Arghū ibn Fāligh ibn 'Ābir ibn Shālikh ibn Arfakhshad ibn Sām ibn Nūḥ.

There are various readings of Āzar. There is A'izrā with two *hamzah*s , the first with a *fatḥah* and the second with a *kasrah*, as is reported from Ibn 'Abbās. He also has A'azrā with two *fatḥah*s on the two *hamzah*s. It is also read in the nominative with *ḍammah* at the end, and that is also related from Ibn 'Abbās. According to the first two readings from him, '*tattakhidu*' (take) is read without a prior *alif.* Al-Mahdawī said, 'A'izrā?' It is said that it is the name of an idol and it is in the accusative as an interrogative, implying, "Do you take Izrā"' It is possible that it is A'izrā as derived from *azr*, meaning back and so it is a direct object. It is also possible that *izr* means *wizr* (heavy load) and the *wāw* is changed into an *alif.*

Al-Qushayrī said, 'The story of Ibrāhīm and his rejection of his father's worship of idols is mentioned as an argument against the idolaters.' The Arabs are the most appropriate people to follow Ibrāhīm as they are his descendants, so it means: 'Remember what Ibrāhīm said' or: '*Remind by it lest a person be delivered up to destruction for what he has earned.*' (6:70) One reading has '*Āzaru*', meaning 'O Āzar' with a singular vocative. That is the reading of Ubayy, Ya'qūb and others. It strengthens the position of those who say that Āzar was the name of Ibrāhīm's father. 'Do you take idols as gods?' is a question conveying disapproval.

وَكَذَٰلِكَ نُرِيٓ إِبْرَٰهِيمَ مَلَكُوتَ ٱلسَّمَٰوَٰتِ وَٱلْأَرْضِ وَلِيَكُونَ مِنَ ٱلْمُوقِنِينَ ۝٧٥

75 Because of that We showed Ibrāhīm the dominions of the heavens and the earth so that he might be one of the people of certainty.

Because of that We showed Ibrāhīm the dominions of the heavens and the earth

Malakūt (*dominions*) is an intensive form of *mulk* (kingdom). The *wāw* is redundant and the *tā'* is for stress in the adjective. Similar forms are: *raghabūt*, *rahabūt* and *jabarūt*. Abū as-Sammāl al-'Adawī recited '*malkūt*', but Sībawayh said that it is not permitted to elide the *fatḥah* because of its lightness. Perhaps it is a dialect. It is said that by it Allah means what is in the heavens of the worship of angels and other wonders and what is in the earth of the disobedience of the sons of Ādam. So it is as if Ibrahim were praying for those he saw disobeying to be destroyed by Allah. So Allah revealed to him, 'Ibrāhīm, refrain from My slaves. Do you not know that one of My Names is aṣ-Ṣabūr?' 'Alī related the same idea from the Prophet ﷺ.

It is said that Allah unveiled the heavens and the earth to him, from the height of the Throne down to the lowest of the earths. It is related by Ibn Jurayj from al-Qāsim that Ibrāhīm an-Nakha'ī said, 'The seven heavens were disclosed to him and he looked up into them as far as the Throne and the earths were disclosed to him and he looked at them until he saw his place in the Garden. That is the meaning of Allah's words: "*We gave him his reward in this world*" (29:37) as as-Suddī said.' Aḍ-Ḍaḥḥāk said, 'He showed him some of the dominions of the heaven as he spoke about the stars and some of the dominions of the earth, the seas, mountains and trees and the like of that which are used as evidence.'

Ibn 'Abbās said something similar to that, saying, 'When he was born, he was put in a burrow and his provision came from the tips of his fingers and he used to lick them. Nimrod had a dream and it was interpreted as meaning that his kingdom would be removed at the hands a child who had been born. So he ordered men to stay away from women. It is said that he commanded every male child to be killed. Āzar was one of those who was close to the King. One day he sent him on an errand and he lay with his wife and she became pregnant with Ibrāhīm. It is said that he lay with her in the temple and she became pregnant and the idols then fell on their faces. He took her to a ravine until she gave birth to Ibrāhīm. He dug a burrow in the earth for Ibrāhīm and placed a stone at its door so that wild animals would not attack him. His mother would go to him and nurse him. She found him sucking his fingers. On one was honey, on another water and on another milk. He grew and at the age of a year he was like a three-year-old. When he left the burrow, people thought that he had been born years before. He asked his mother, 'Who is my Lord?' She said, 'I am.' He asked, 'And who is your Lord?' She answered, 'Your father.' He asked, 'Who is his Lord?' She said, 'Nimrod.' He asked, 'Who is his Lord?' and she slapped him and knew that he was the one at whose hands their kingdom would be destroyed. The story in full is in the Stories of the Prophets by al-Kisā'ī, which is a book which is followed.

Some say that he was born at Harran, but his father moved to Babylon. Most of the early generations among the people of knowledge say that Ibrāhīm was born in the time of Nimrod ibn Kan'ān ibn Sanjārīb ibn Kūsh ibn Sām ibn Nūḥ. This was mentioned in *al-Baqarah* (2:258). There were 1263 years between the Flood and the birth of Ibrāhīm, and that was 3330 years after the creation of Ādam. The words: '*So that he might be one of the people of certainty,*' in other words be one of those whose certainty gives them vision of the unseen dominions of existence.

فَلَمَّا جَنَّ عَلَيْهِ ٱلَّيْلُ رَءَا كَوْكَبًا قَالَ هَٰذَا رَبِّى فَلَمَّآ أَفَلَ قَالَ لَآ أُحِبُّ
ٱلْءَافِلِينَ ﴿٧٦﴾

76 When night covered him he saw a star and said, 'This is my Lord!' Then when it set he said, 'I do not love what sets.'

The words: '*When night covered him,*' mean veiled him with its darkness. The verb (*janna*) gives the nouns *jannah, jinnah, junnah, janīn, mijann* and *jinn*, all with the sense of covering. A poet said:

Were it not for the cover (*janān*) of the night, our gallop
would have reached 'Iyāḍ ibn Nāshib at Dhū ar-Rimth and al-Arṭā.

The *janān* of night is its darkness and covering. *Junūn* is also used for the darkness of night. The verbs *janna* and *ajanna* are used for the night covering someone.

He saw a star.

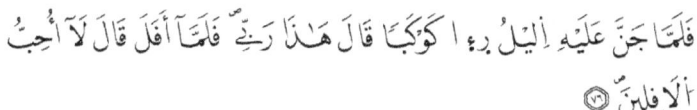

This is different story to that of the dominions being shown to him. It is said that it occurred when the stone at the opening of the burrow split. It is said that it was when his father took him out of the burrow and when the sun was not in the sky. He saw camels, horses and sheep and said, 'They must have a master.' He saw Jupiter or Venus and then the moon and then the sun. This was at the end of the month. Muḥammad ibn Isḥāq said, 'He was fifteen.' It is also said that he was seven years old. It is said that when he argued with Nimrod, he was seventeen.

'This is my Lord!'

There is disagreement about the meaning of this and several things are said. It is said that this was while he was still reflecting and still a child and before the proof was established, and in that state there was neither disbelief nor belief. Those who say this find evidence for it in what is related from 'Alī ibn Abī Ṭalḥah from Ibn 'Abbās, who said about this verse that when Ibrahim said that, he worshipped it until it disappeared and the same happened with the sun and the moon. And when his investigation was complete, he said, '*I am free of what you associate.*' (6:78) There is evidence in the setting because it is the most evident sign of temporality.

Other people say that this cannot be correct. They say, 'It is not conceivable for a Messenger of Allah to be at any time other than someone who affirms Allah's unity and recognises Him and is free of everything worshipped other than Him.' They said, 'How can it be sound for this to be imagined of someone whom Allah has protected and given right-guidance (*rushd*) to before and to whom He showed the extent of His dominions so that he could be one of those with certainty? It is not conceivable for him to be described as lacking in recognition of his Lord. Rather he recognised his Lord at the first glance.'

Az-Zajjāj said, 'I consider this understanding to be an error and a mistake on the part of those who said it. Allah reports Ibrāhīm as saying: "*Keep me and my sons from worshipping idols.*" (14:35) He also says: "*when he came to his Lord with an unblemished heart*" (37:84), meaning that he never associated anyone with Him.' The answer, in my opinion, is that he said, 'This is my Lord' to accord with their view because they were worshipping idols, and the sun and the moon. Something similar to this can be seen in the words of the Almighty: '*Where are My partner gods*?' (16:27) The Almighty has no associate, and so it means: 'Where, according to your position, are My partner gods?'

It is said that when Ibrāhīm emerged from the burrow, he saw the light of the star and he was seeking his Lord and so he thought that it was His light and he said, '*This is my Lord*,' meaning He is showing me His light. '*Then when it set*,' he knew that it was not His Lord. '*Then when he saw the moon come up*' (6:77) and he saw its light, '*He said, "This is my Lord!" Then when it set he said, "If my Lord does not guide me, I will be one of the misguided people."* (6:77)' *Then when he saw the sun come up he said,*

'*This is my Lord!*' (6:78) This is not *shirk*. This is attributing that light to his Lord. When he saw that vanish, his prior knowledge indicated that it did not deserve that appellation and so he negated it in his heart and knew that it was a subject and not a Lord. It is said that '*This is my Lord*' is affirmation of the argument of his people and so he was showing his agreement. When the star set, he affirmed the proof and said, 'That which changes cannot be a true Lord.' They used to esteem the stars and worship them and judge by them.

An-Naḥḥās said, 'One of the best things said about this, which is sound, is reported from Ibn 'Abbās. He said about the words of Allah: "*Light upon light*" (24:35), "That is like the heart of a believer who recognises Allah and is directed to Him by his heart. When he recognises Him, he is increased with light upon light. That was the case with Ibrāhīm. He recognised Allah with his heart and was directed to Him by His proofs. So He knew that he had a Lord and Creator. When Allah made him recognise by himself, his gnosis was increased and he said: "*Do you argue with me about Allah when He has guided me?*" (6:80)' It is said that this is a question and a rebuke to deny their action. In that case it would mean: 'Is this my Lord?' or 'Is the like of this my Lord?' The implied *hamzah* of the question is elided. We find in the Revelation: '*If you die, will they then be immortal?*' (21:34) Al-Hudhalī said:

They calmed me and said, 'Little Khālid, do not fear!'
I said, not recognising the faces, 'Them! Them!'

[ANOTHER POEM]

It is said that it means, 'This is my Lord according to your claim,' as Allah says: '*Where are they, those you claimed to be My partners?*' (28:74). And He says: '*Taste that! You are the mighty one, the noble one!*' (44:49) in yourselves. It is said that it means: 'You say, "This is my Lord."'

فَلَمَّا رَءَا الْقَمَرَ بَازِغًا قَالَ هَٰذَا رَبِّي ۖ فَلَمَّا أَفَلَ قَالَ لَئِن لَّمْ يَهْدِنِي
رَبِّي لَأَكُونَنَّ مِنَ الْقَوْمِ الضَّالِّينَ ﴿٧٧﴾

77 Then when he saw the moon come up he said, 'This is my Lord!' Then when it set he said, 'If my Lord does not guide me, I will be one of the misguided people.'

'*Then when he saw the moon come up*' in other words, rising. The verb *bazagha* is used for the moon when it begins to rise. *Bazgh* means cleaving and so it is as if it splits the darkness by its light. The verb is used for a veterinary surgeon shedding the blood of an animal. The phrase: '*If my Lord does not guide me*' means 'If He does not make me firm in guidance.' He was guided, so this is when he was investigating or asking for more firmness since it is intellectually possible, as Shu'ayb says: '*We could never return to it unless Allah our Lord so willed.*' (7:89) We find in the Revelation: '*Guide us on the Straight Path*' (1:6) which means: 'Make us firm in guidance.'

فَلَمَّا رَءَا ٱلشَّمْسَ بَازِغَةً قَالَ هَٰذَا رَبِّيَ هَٰذَآ أَكْبَرُ فَلَمَّآ أَفَلَتْ قَالَ يَٰقَوْمِ
إِنِّي بَرِيٓءٌ مِّمَّا تُشْرِكُونَ ﴿٧٨﴾

78 Then when he saw the sun come up he said, 'This is my Lord! This is greater!' Then when it set he said, 'My people, I am free of what you associate with Allah!

The accusative is used for the adverbial *ḥāl* because it is connected with seeing with the eye. *Bazagha, yabzughu, buzūgh* is to rise and *afala, ya'filu, ufūl* is to set. In the words: '*Then when it set*': it is said that *shams* (sun) is feminine because of its vastness and immensity. It is like the words describing a man who is *nassābah* (skilful genealogist) and *'allāmah* (great scholar). Ibrahim's words, '*This is my Lord*' mean 'This which is rising is my Lord' as was stated by al-Kisā'ī and al-Akhfash. Others says that he means 'this light'. Abū al-Ḥasan 'Alī ibn Sulaymān says that it means 'this person' as al-A'shā said:

She stood at his grave, weeping for him:
'Who will I have after you, 'Āmir!"
'You have left me in exile in this world.
The one with no helper is abased.'

إِنِّيَ وَجَّهْتُ وَجْهِيَ لِلَّذِي فَطَرَ ٱلسَّمَٰوَٰتِ وَٱلْأَرْضَ حَنِيفًا وَمَآ أَنَا۠ مِنَ
ٱلْمُشْرِكِينَ ﴿٧٩﴾

79 I have turned my face to Him Who brought the heavens and earth into being, a pure natural believer. I am not one of the idolaters.'

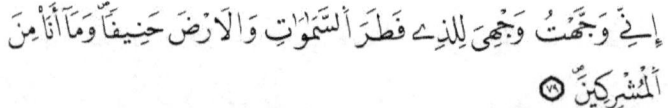

The phrase '*I have turned my face to Him*' means 'I have made Him alone my goal in My worship and *tawḥīd*.' The face is mentioned because it, more than anything else, displays what a man sees in his companion. The noun '*ḥanīf*' (*a pure natural believer*) indicates someone who inclines to the Truth.

I am not one of the idolaters.'

When you stop, you say '*anā*', adding the *alif* to make the vowel clear. It is an eloquent usage. Al-Akhfash said, 'Some Arabs say "*ana*".' Al-Kisā'ī said that some Arabs say '*anah*'. These are three dialectical forms. There are also three dialectical usages in respect of the connection. You can elide the *alif* in interpolation because it is redundant to make the vowel clear in the stop. Some Arabs keep the *alif* in the connection. [POEM] That is the dialect of some of the Banū Qays and Rabī'ah as al-Farrā' said. Some Arabs say in the connection '*ān*'. Al-Kisā'ī related it from some of Quḍā'ah.

وَحَآجَّهُۥ قَوْمُهُۥ ۚ قَالَ أَتُحَٰٓجُّوٓنِّى فِى ٱللَّهِ وَقَدْ هَدَىٰنِ ۚ وَلَآ أَخَافُ مَا
تُشْرِكُونَ بِهِۦٓ إِلَّآ أَن يَشَآءَ رَبِّى شَيْـًٔا ۗ وَسِعَ رَبِّى كُلَّ شَىْءٍ عِلْمًا ۗ أَفَلَا
تَتَذَكَّرُونَ ﴿٨٠﴾

80 His people argued with him. He said, 'Are you arguing with me about Allah when He has guided me? I have no fear of any partner you ascribe to Him unless my Lord should will such a thing to happen. My Lord encompasses all things in His knowledge so will you not pay heed?

His people argued with him.

They argued with him about Allah's unity. Nāfi' reads '*arguing*' with a single *nūn* (*tuḥājjūnī*) in the words: '*Are you arguing with me about Allah*?' whereas the rest have a doubled *nūn* (*tuḥājjūnnī*). Ibn 'Āmir related that, although there is disagreement about the transmission from Hishām. If it has a *shaddah*, then the root is two *nūns*, the first for the sign of the nominative, and the second to separate the verb and the *yā'*. When two *nūns* are together in a verb and that is heavy, then one *nūn* is elided into the other and there is doubling. There must be a *maddah* on the *wāw* so that two silent letters do not meet – the *wāw* and the first doubled letter – and so then the *maddah* becomes the separator between the two silent letters. If someone makes it a single letter, then the second *nūn* is elided for lightening by the joining of two likes [vowelled, and because of the doubling in the verb of the *jīm*] and the first is not elided because it is the marker of the nominative. If it had been elided, then the nominative would resemble the genitive and accusative. It is related from

Abū 'Amr ibn al-'Alā' that this recitation is ungrammatical. Sībawayh allowed it. [OMISSION]

I have no fear of any partner you ascribe to Him

They have no power to help or harm. They used to try to frighten him by the great number of their gods but Allah inspired him and he feared only His harm, which is the meaning of '*unless my Lord should will such a thing to happen*,' in other words: 'if He wishes to afflict me with something hateful for a wrong action which I have done and that is His will.' This is an exception which is independent of the first clause. The *hā'* in '*bihi*' probably refers to Allah, although it can refer to that which is worshipped. '*Unless my Lord should will*' implies that Allah does not wish for me to fear them. The knowledge of Allah encompasses all things.

وَكَيْفَ أَخَافُ مَآ أَشْرَكْتُمْ وَلَا تَخَافُونَ أَنَّكُمْ أَشْرَكْتُم بِٱللَّهِ مَا لَمْ
يُنَزِّلْ بِهِۦ عَلَيْكُمْ سُلْطَٰنًا ۚ فَأَىُّ ٱلْفَرِيقَيْنِ أَحَقُّ بِٱلْأَمْنِ ۖ إِن
كُنتُمْ تَعْلَمُونَ ﴿٨١﴾ ٱلَّذِينَ ءَامَنُوا۟ وَلَمْ يَلْبِسُوٓا۟ إِيمَٰنَهُم بِظُلْمٍ
أُو۟لَٰٓئِكَ لَهُمُ ٱلْأَمْنُ وَهُم مُّهْتَدُونَ ﴿٨٢﴾

81-82 Why should I fear what you have associated with Him when you yourselves apparently have no fear of associating partners with Allah for which He has sent down no authority to you? Which of the two parties is more entitled to feel safe, if you have any knowledge? Those who believe and do not mix up their faith with any wrongdoing, they are the ones who are safe; it is they who are guided.'

Why should I fear what you have associated with Him

The word *kayf* here is a form of denial: Ibrahim denies their attempt to make him fear the idols. They do not fear Allah so why should he fear what is dead when they do not fear Allah Who has power over all things? The noun '*sulṭān*' means authority, as was already mentioned (2:116).

Which of the two parties is more entitled to feel safe,

Which one is more entitled to feel safe from Allah's punishment: the one who affirms His Unity or the idolater? Allah said to judge between them: '*Those who believe and do not mix up their faith with any wrongdoing*', meaning by committing *shirk*.

Abū Bakr aṣ-Ṣiddīq, 'Alī, Salmān and Ḥudhayfah said that. Ibn 'Abbās said that it is said by Ibrāhīm himself, as a scholar might ask himself and answer himself. It is also said that it is part of the words of the people of Ibrāhīm, meaning that they answered with what was a proof against them. Ibn Jurayj said that.

We find in the two *Ṣaḥīḥ* collections that Ibn Mas'ūd reports that this *āyah* was hard on the Companions of the Messenger of Allah ﷺ and they said, 'Which of us does not wrong himself?' The Messenger of Allah ﷺ said, 'It is not as you think. It is as Luqmān said to his son: "*O my son, do not associate anything with Allah. Attributing partners to Him is a terrible wrong.*" (31:13)' '*They who are guided*' means guided in this world.

وَتِلْكَ حُجَّتُنَآ ءَاتَيْنَٰهَآ إِبْرَٰهِيمَ عَلَىٰ قَوْمِهِۦ ۚ نَرْفَعُ دَرَجَٰتٍ مَّن نَّشَآءُ ۗ
إِنَّ رَبَّكَ حَكِيمٌ عَلِيمٌ ﴿٨٣﴾

83 This is the argument We gave to Ibrāhīm against his people. We raise in rank anyone We will. Your Lord is All-Wise, All-Knowing.

This is the argument We gave to Ibrāhīm against his people.

'*This*' refers to all the arguments he used against them and overcame them with. Mujāhid said that it refers to Allah's words: '*those who believe and do not mix up their faith with any wrongdoing.*' It is said that it refers to his argument against them when they said to him, 'Do you not fear that our gods will confuse you because of your abusing them?' and he responded with, 'Do you not fear them since you made small and large equal in worship and esteem and so angered the largest of them causing him to confuse you?'

We raise in rank anyone We will.

This means raise them in knowledge, understanding, imamate and sovereignty. The Kufans read '*darajātin*' with *tanwīn*, which implies an elided 'to' (*ilā*), making it mean, 'We raise *to* ranks.' The people of Makkah and Madīnah and Abū 'Amr read it without *tanwīn*, '*darajāti*' with *iḍāfah* (the ranks of). This reading is strengthened by Allah's words: '*High of rank*' (40:14), showing that the idea of height can be applied to ranks. The two readings are close in meaning because the one whose rank is elevated is elevated, and the one who is elevated has his rank elevated. '*Your Lord is All-Wise*' by placing everything in its proper place.

وَوَهَبْنَا لَهُۥٓ إِسْحَٰقَ وَيَعْقُوبَ كُلًّا هَدَيْنَا وَنُوحًا هَدَيْنَا مِن قَبْلُ وَمِن
ذُرِّيَّتِهِۦ دَاوُۥدَ وَسُلَيْمَٰنَ وَأَيُّوبَ وَيُوسُفَ وَمُوسَىٰ وَهَٰرُونَ
وَكَذَٰلِكَ نَجْزِى ٱلْمُحْسِنِينَ ﴿٨٤﴾ وَزَكَرِيَّا وَيَحْيَىٰ وَعِيسَىٰ وَإِلْيَاسَ كُلٌّ مِّنَ
ٱلصَّٰلِحِينَ ﴿٨٥﴾ وَإِسْمَٰعِيلَ وَٱلْيَسَعَ وَيُونُسَ وَلُوطًا وَكُلًّا فَضَّلْنَا
عَلَى ٱلْعَٰلَمِينَ ﴿٨٦﴾

84-86 We gave him Isḥāq and Ya'qūb, each of whom We guided. And before him We had guided Nūḥ. And among his descendants were Dāwūd and Sulaymān, and Ayyūb, Yūsuf, Mūsā and Hārūn. That is how We recompense the good-doers. And Zakariyyā, Yaḥyā, 'Īsā and Ilyās. All of them were among the righteous. And Ismā'īl, al-Yasa', Yūnus and Lūṭ. All of them We favoured over all beings.

We gave him Isḥāq and Ya'qūb, each of whom We guided.

This was to reward him for arguing in defence of the *dīn* and for expending himself in it and the words '*each of whom We guided*' means that they were both guided. The descendants referred to in the words: '*And among his descendants*' are the descendants of Ibrāhīm. It is also said to mean the descendants of Nūḥ, as al-Farrā' said and as aṭ-Ṭabarī and more than one other commentator said, such as al-Qushayrī, Ibn 'Aṭiyyah and others. The first is the position of az-Zajjāj. His view is countered by the fact that these descendants include Yūnus and Lūṭ, and they were not descendants of Ibrāhīm. Lūṭ was the son of his brother or his sister. Ibn 'Abbās said, 'All those Prophets are described as descendants of Ibrāhīm, even if among them were those who were not connected to him by birth through his mother or father, because Lūṭ was the nephew of Ibrāhīm, and the Arabs consider the paternal uncle to be like a father as Allah reports about the children of Ya'qūb who said: "*We will worship your God and the God of your fathers, Ibrāhīm, Ismā'īl and Isḥāq.*" (2:133) whereas Ismā'īl was the paternal uncle of Ya'qūb.'

'Īsā is considered to be one of the descendants of Ibrāhīm although he was the son of a daughter, and so the children of Fāṭimah are the descendants of the Prophet ﷺ. This is the opinion of those who think that the children of daughters are included in the term 'children'. Abū Ḥanīfah and ash-Shāfi'ī said, 'Whoever establishes a *waqf* for his children and grandchildren includes the children of his sons and the children of his daughters as his lineage. It is the same when he makes a bequest in favour of his near relatives: the children of daughters are included in that.' According to Abū Ḥanīfah, 'near relatives' are everyone with whom marriage is forbidden. In his opinion it does not include the sons of paternal uncles and aunts or maternal uncles and aunts because they are not forbidden. Ash-Shāfi'ī said that near relatives are everyone with whom marriage is forbidden as well as others. For him, it does not stop at the sons of the paternal uncle or anyone else.

Mālik said that the children of daughters are not included in that. The words, 'for my near relatives and descendants' are similar to 'for my children and the children of my children (*walad waladī*).' That includes the children of sons and those who derive from the agnancy (*'aṣabah*) of the father and his loins, but does not include the children of daughters. Something similar to this is reported from ash-Shāfi'ī about *Āl 'Imrān* (3:61). Their argument is found in the words of Allah: '*Allah instructs you regarding your children*' (4:11), and the Muslims did not understand the meaning of the *āyah* to refer to anyone other than the child of the loins and the son's child in particular. The Almighty says: '*To the Messenger and to close relatives*' (8:41), and so the Prophet ﷺ gave to close relatives who included his paternal uncles but not his maternal uncles. It is the same with the children of daughters: they are not ascribed to him paternally by lineage.

Ibn al-Qassār said, 'The argument of those who include daughters among near relatives is backed up by the words of the Prophet ﷺ, "This son of mine is a master." (Referring to al-Ḥasan, the son of his daughter). We do not know of anyone who forbids people to say that the children of daughters are children (*walad*) of their mother's father. The etymology demands that since *walad* (child) is derived from *tawallud* (generation) and they must be those engendered from their mother's father, since that occurs from the father's side as it does from the mother's. The Qur'an indicates that since Allah Almighty says in this *āyah*: "*And among his descendants were Dāwūd and Sulaymān...*" to "*...among the righteous,*" and so 'Īsā is considered one of his descendants when he is the son of a daughter.'

In *Sūrat an-Nisā'* we already discussed those of these names which are not declinable. Dāwūd is not declinable because it is a non-Arabic name as is Ilyās. Everything on the measure *fā'ūl* does not have an *alif-lām* (of the definite article) and is not declinable. Ilyās is not Arabic. Aḍ-Ḍaḥḥāk said that Ilyās was one of the children of Ismā'īl. Al-Qutabī mentioned, 'He was from the tribe of Joshua.' Al-A'raj, al-Ḥasan and Qatādah recited *wa-lyās* with the *alif* joined. The people of Makkah and Madīnah, Abū 'Amr and 'Āṣim recite *wa-l-Yasa'* with a single *lām*. The Kufans, with the exception of 'Āṣim, recite *wa-l-laysa'*. That is how al-Kisā'ī recites it, rejecting the reading of *wa-l-Yasa'*, saying that is because one does not say *al-yaf'al* like *al-yaḥyā*. An-Naḥḥās said, 'This rejection is not necessary. The Arabs say "*al-ya'mal*" and "*al-yaḥmad*". If Yaḥyā is definite, you say, "*al-yaḥyā*".' Abū Ḥātim rejected those who recite '*al-laysa*'' and said that the word *laysa'* does not exist. An-Naḥḥās said, 'This rejection is not necessary. We find such forms in Arabic in the names Ḥaydar and Zaynab. The truth is that it is a non-Arab name. Non-Arab names do not have analogous verbal forms but are taken as heard, although the Arabs alter them a lot and so there is nothing wrong in such a name having more than one form.'

Makkī said, 'If it is read with two *lāms*, then the root of the name is Laysa' and then the *alif-lām* of the definite article is added. If its root had been Yasa', then the *alif-lām* of the definite article would not be added since it is not added to names like Yazīd and Yashkur because they are already definite. If Laysa' is indefinite, then the *alif-lām* of the definite article is added. I prefer the single *lām* because it is more frequent in the recitation.' Al-Mahdawī said, 'If someone recites *al-yasa'* with one *lām*, then the noun is "Yasa'" and the extra definite article is added as it is in "*al-khamsatu 'ashar*" (fifteen).' [POEM] It is added in the imperfect verb. [POEM] Al-Qushayrī said, 'It is read with a double or single *lām*. The meaning is the same. It is the name of a well-known Prophet like Ismā'īl and Ibrāhīm, but it differs from other *lām* names by the inclusion of the *alif-lām*.

Some people imagine that al-Yasa' is the same as Ilyās, but this is not the case because Allah mentioned each of them separately. Wahb said that al-Yasa' was the companion of Ilyās just as Zakariyyā, Yaḥyā and 'Īsā form a group. It is also said that Ilyās is Idrīs, but this is not sound since Idris was the grandfather of Nūḥ and Ilyās was one of his descendants. It is said that Ilyās is al-Khiḍr, and it is said that he is not and that al-Yasa' is al-Khiḍr. Lūṭ is also a non-Arab name, but it is declined because of its simplicity. Its derivation will be mentioned in *al-A'rāf.*

وَمِنْ ءَابَآئِهِمْ وَذُرِّيَّٰتِهِمْ وَإِخْوَٰنِهِمْ ۖ وَٱجْتَبَيْنَٰهُمْ وَهَدَيْنَٰهُمْ إِلَىٰ صِرَٰطٍ
مُّسْتَقِيمٍ ﴿٨٧﴾

87 And some of their forebears, descendants and brothers; We chose them and guided them to a straight path.

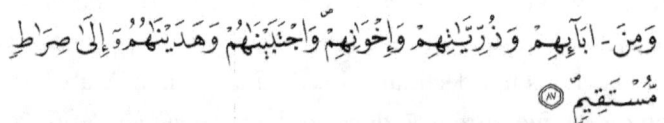

'*Min*' (*some*) is partitive here, meaning 'We guided some of their forbears, descendants and brothers.' The verb '*chose*' here means 'purified' according to Mujāhid. Linguistically it is derived from *jaby* which is used for water collecting in a basin. *Ijtibā'* is making someone you choose one of your close friends. Al-Kisā'ī said, 'I collected (*jabaytu*) water in the basin' with the noun *jabā*. *Al-Jābiyah* is the basin. [POEM] We have already mentioned choosing and guidance.

ذَٰلِكَ هُدَى ٱللَّهِ يَهْدِى بِهِۦ مَن يَشَآءُ مِنْ عِبَادِهِۦ ۚ وَلَوْ أَشْرَكُوا۟ لَحَبِطَ عَنْهُم مَّا كَانُوا۟ يَعْمَلُونَ ﴿٨٨﴾

88 That is Allah's guidance. He guides by it those of His slaves He wills. If they had associated others with Him, nothing they did would have been of any use.

If they had worshipped other than Me, their actions would have come to nothing, but I protected them. *Ḥubūṭ* means invalidation, as was mentioned in *Sūrat al-Baqarah* (2:217).

أُو۟لَٰٓئِكَ ٱلَّذِينَ ءَاتَيْنَٰهُمُ ٱلْكِتَٰبَ وَٱلْحُكْمَ وَٱلنُّبُوَّةَ ۚ فَإِن يَكْفُرْ بِهَا هَٰٓؤُلَآءِ فَقَدْ وَكَّلْنَا بِهَا قَوْمًا لَّيْسُوا۟ بِهَا بِكَٰفِرِينَ ﴿٨٩﴾

89 They are the ones to whom We gave the Book, Judgment and Prophethood. If these people reject it, We have already entrusted it to a people who did not.

'*Judgment*' (*ḥukm*) is knowledge and *fiqh*. '*Reject it*' refers to rejecting Our Signs. '*These people*' are the ones who reject Muhammad ﷺ. '*Entrusted it*' means 'to entrust belief in it,' and '*the people who did not*' reject are the Anṣār among the people of Madīnah and the Muhājirūn among the people of Makkah. Qatādah said that it means the Prophets about whom Allah reports. An-Naḥḥās says that this view is closer to the meaning because Allah says after it: '*They are the ones Allah has guided, so be guided by their guidance.*' Abū Rajā' says that it refers to angels. It is also said that it is general to all who believe, jinn, men or angel. The *bā'* in *bi-kāfirīn* is redundant and for emphasis.

أُوْلَٰٓئِكَ ٱلَّذِينَ هَدَى ٱللَّهُ فَبِهُدَىٰهُمُ ٱقْتَدِهْ قُل لَّآ أَسْـَٔلُكُمْ عَلَيْهِ أَجْرًا إِنْ
هُوَ إِلَّا ذِكْرَىٰ لِلْعَٰلَمِينَ ٩٠

90 They are the ones Allah has guided, so be guided by their guidance. Say, 'I do not ask you for any wage for it. It is simply a reminder to all beings.'

They are the ones Allah has guided, so be guided by their guidance.

Being guided is to seek to be in harmony with the actions of someone else. It is said that it means be steadfast as they were steadfast. It is said that the meaning is *tawḥīd* and different *Sharī'ah*s. Some scholars used this *āyah* as evidence for the obligation to follow the *Sharī'ah*s of the Prophets in matters about which there is no text. That is substantiated by what we find in *Ṣaḥīḥ Muslim* and elsewhere about when the sister of ar-Rubayyi', Umm Ḥārithah, injured someone and they took the case to the Prophet ﷺ. The Prophet ﷺ said, 'Retaliation. Retaliation.' Umm ar-Rubayyi' said, 'Messenger of Allah, is he going to take retaliation from so-and-so? By Allah, he will not take retaliation from her!' The Messenger of Allah ﷺ said. 'Glory be to Allah, Umm ar-Rubayyi', retaliation is the Book of Allah!' She insisted, 'By Allah, he will never take retaliation from her!' She kept on until they accepted the blood money. The Messenger of Allah ﷺ said, 'There are some slaves of Allah Who, if they were to take an oath, Allah would fulfil it.'

The Messenger of Allah ﷺ based his ruling on Allah's words: '*We prescribed in it for them: a life for a life.*' (5:45) There is no text in the Book of Allah about retaliation for a tooth except for this *āyah*. It is speaking about the *Sharī'ah* of the Torah and he ﷺ judged by it and turned to it. This is the position of most of the people of Mālik and ash-Shāfi'ī: that it is obliged to act according to what still exists of it. Ibn Bukayr said, 'That is what the principles of Mālik demand but many of the Mālikīs, Shāfi'īs and Mu'tazilites disagree with that going by Allah's words: "*We have appointed a law and a practice for every one of you.*" (5:48)' This is not evidence because it can refer to limitation, meaning only what is related to you of reports about them which are not in your Book. We find in *Ṣaḥīḥ al-Bukhārī* that al-'Awwām said, 'I asked Mujahid about the prostration in Sura *Ṣād* and he said, "I asked Ibn 'Abbās about the prostration of *Ṣād* and he said, 'Or recite, "*Among his descendants were Dāwūd and Sulaymān...*" to "*...by their guidance.*"'"' Dāwūd was one of those he ﷺ was commanded to follow.'

Ḥamzah and al-Kisā'ī recite '*iqtada'ī*' without the *hā'* in the connection. Ibn 'Āmir recite '*iqtad hiya*' which an-Naḥḥās said is poor grammar because the *hā'* is to clarify the vowel in the stop and does not imply a following *wāw* or *yā'*. Those who avoid poor grammar while following the script recite '*fa-bihudāhumu-qtadih*' and stop without joining because it is poor to join with a *hā'* even if eliding it is contrary to the script. The majority recite it with the *hā'* in the stop with the intention of stopping and the intention of interpolation to follow the writing. Both Ibn 'Ayyāsh and Hishām recite '*iqtadihi*' with a *kasrah* on the *hā'*. That is an error not permitted in Arabic.

Say, 'I do not ask you for any wage for it. It is simply a reminder to all beings.'

This means a wage for the Qur'an so '*it*' here refers to the Qur'an. '*A reminder to all beings*' means that it is admonition for the whole of creation. Guidance is ascribed to them, and '*their guidance*' is since guidance occurs through them. '*Allah has guided*' because He is the Creator of guidance.

وَمَا قَدَرُوا اللَّهَ حَقَّ قَدْرِهِ إِذْ قَالُوا مَا أَنزَلَ اللَّهُ عَلَىٰ بَشَرٍ مِّن شَيْءٍ قُلْ مَنْ
أَنزَلَ الْكِتَابَ الَّذِي جَاءَ بِهِ مُوسَىٰ نُورًا وَهُدًى لِّلنَّاسِ تَجْعَلُونَهُ قَرَاطِيسَ
تُبْدُونَهَا وَتُخْفُونَ كَثِيرًا وَعُلِّمْتُم مَّا لَمْ تَعْلَمُوا أَنتُمْ وَلَا آبَاؤُكُمْ قُلِ اللَّهُ
ثُمَّ ذَرْهُمْ فِي خَوْضِهِمْ يَلْعَبُونَ ﴿٩١﴾

91 They do not measure Allah with His true measure when they say, 'Allah would not send down anything to a mere human being.' Say: 'Who, then, sent down the Book which Mūsā brought as a Light and Guidance for the people?' You put it down on sheets of paper to display it while concealing much. You were taught things you did not know, neither you nor your forefathers. Say: 'Allah!' Then leave them engrossed in playing their games.

They do not measure Allah with His true measure

That is in terms of what is necessarily true for Him, inconceivable for Him, and conceivable for Him. Ibn 'Abbās said, 'They do not believe that He has power over all things.' Al-Ḥasan said, 'They do not esteem Him as they should esteem Him.' 'They do not measure Allah with His true measure (*qadrihi*)' reflects the Arabic expression, 'So-and-so has great value (*qadr*).' The explanation of this is that when they said: '*Allah would not send down anything to a mere human being*,' they were saying that Allah would not establish the proof against His slaves nor command them that in which was their best interests. They did not esteem

Him as He should be esteemed nor recognise Him as He should be recognised. Abū 'Ubaydah said, 'They did not recognise Allah as He should be recognised.' An-Naḥḥās said, 'This is a good meaning because the meaning of "*measure*" is to recognise the true extent of something. That is indicated by His words: "*They say, 'Allah would not send down anything to a mere human being,*'" meaning that they do not recognise Him as He should be recognised since they denied that He would send a Messenger.' The two meanings are close. It is said, 'They did not measure the blessings of Allah as they should be measured. Abū Ḥawyah recited '*qadarihi*' which is a dialectical usage.

They said, 'Allah would not send down anything to a mere human being.'

Ibn 'Abbās and others said that this refers to the idolaters of Quraysh. Al-Ḥasan and Sa'īd ibn Jubayr said, 'It was one of the Jews who said this.' He said. 'Allah has not sent down a Book from heaven.' As-Suddī said, 'His name was Finḥāṣ.' Sa'īd ibn Jubayr said that it was Mālik ibn aṣ-Ṣayf who came to debate with the Prophet ﷺ and the Prophet ﷺ said to him, 'I ask you by the One who sent down the Torah to Mūsā, do you find in the Torah that Allah hates a fat rabbi?' He was fat and he became angry and said, 'By Allah, Allah would not send down anything to a mere mortal.' His companions who were with him said, 'Woe to you! Not even to Mūsā!' He repeated, 'By Allah, Allah would not send down anything to a mere mortal,' and then the *āyah* was revealed.

Allah said to counter their words and reply to them: '*Say: "Who, then, sent down the Book which Mūsā brought as a Light and Guidance for the people?"...*' This was addressed to the Jews when they concealed the description of the Prophet ﷺ and other rulings. Mujāhid said, that the words: '*Say: "Who, then, sent down the Book which Mūsā..."*' are directed at the idolaters, the words '*...put it down on sheets of paper*' are addressed to the Jews and the words: '*You were taught things you did not know*' are addressed to the Muslims. This is sound for the reading with *yā'*: 'they'. It is also read with *tā'* of the second person, and then it is all addressed to the Jews.

The meaning of '*You were taught things you did not know*' is you were taught what neither you nor your fathers knew by way of grace to them through the sending down of the Torah. The Torah was made into pages, and that is why He says: '*...sheets of paper to display it,*' meaning that it was displayed on pages. This is to censure them. That is why scholars dislike writing the Qur'ans in separate *juz'*s. The command: '*Say: "Allah!"*' implies 'Say, O Muḥammad, "Allah is the One who sent down that Book to Mūsā and this Book to me,"' or 'Say: "Allah taught me the

Book.'" The phrase: '*Then leave them engrossed in playing their games.*' is a threat. It is said that it was abrogated by fighting.

It is said that the verb '*put it down*' is like an adjective of '*light and guidance*'. So it is connected although it is possible that it can be a new sentence. It implies: 'They put it on sheets of paper.' The words: '*display it while concealing much*' can also be adjectival describing '*sheets of paper*' because the indefinite can be described by sentences. It is also possible that it is a new sentence as already mentioned.

وَهَٰذَا كِتَٰبٌ أَنزَلْنَٰهُ مُبَارَكٌ مُّصَدِّقُ ٱلَّذِى بَيْنَ يَدَيْهِ وَلِتُنذِرَ أُمَّ ٱلْقُرَىٰ وَمَنْ حَوْلَهَا ۚ وَٱلَّذِينَ يُؤْمِنُونَ بِٱلْءَاخِرَةِ يُؤْمِنُونَ بِهِۦ ۖ وَهُمْ عَلَىٰ صَلَاتِهِمْ يُحَافِظُونَ ﴿٩٢﴾

92 This is a Book We have sent down and blessed, confirming what came before it, so that you can warn the Mother of Cities and the people around it. Those who believe in the Next World believe in it and safeguard their prayer.

The *Book* is the Qur'an and '*blessed*' means that there is blessing in it. The noun *barakah* implies increase and can be used in other than Qur'an as a *ḥāl*. '*What came before it*' are the Books revealed before it which also negate *shirk* and affirm *tawḥīd*. '*The Mother of Cities*' is Makkah and what is meant are its people, and the *muḍāf* is elided, which means: 'We sent it down as both blessing and warning.' The preposition '*around it*' means in all directions. '*Those who believe in it*' are the followers of Muḥammad ﷺ as is shown by Allah's words '...*and safeguard their prayer*'. The belief of those who believe in the Next World but do not believe in the Prophet ﷺ or his Book is not counted.

وَمَنْ أَظْلَمُ مِمَّنِ ٱفْتَرَىٰ عَلَى ٱللَّهِ كَذِبًا أَوْ قَالَ أُوحِىَ إِلَىَّ وَلَمْ يُوحَ إِلَيْهِ شَىْءٌ وَمَن قَالَ سَأُنزِلُ مِثْلَ مَآ أَنزَلَ ٱللَّهُ وَلَوْ تَرَىٰٓ إِذِ ٱلظَّٰلِمُونَ فِى غَمَرَٰتِ ٱلْمَوْتِ وَٱلْمَلَٰٓئِكَةُ بَاسِطُوٓا۟ أَيْدِيهِمْ أَخْرِجُوٓا۟ أَنفُسَكُمُ ٱلْيَوْمَ تُجْزَوْنَ عَذَابَ ٱلْهُونِ بِمَا كُنتُمْ تَقُولُونَ عَلَى ٱللَّهِ غَيْرَ ٱلْحَقِّ وَكُنتُمْ عَنْ ءَايَٰتِهِۦ تَسْتَكْبِرُونَ ۝

93 Who could do greater wrong than someone who invents lies against Allah or who says, 'It has been revealed to me,' when nothing has been revealed to him, or someone who says, 'I will send down the same as Allah has sent down'? If you could only see the wrongdoers in the throes of death when the angels are stretching out their hands, saying, 'Disgorge your own selves! Today you will be repaid with the punishment of humiliation for saying something other than the truth about Allah, and being arrogant about His Signs.'

'*Who could do greater wrong*' means 'No one could do greater wrong.' The person alluded to in the words: '*who says, "It has been revealed to me,"*' is laying claim to Prophethood and the words: '*when nothing has been revealed to him*' are a direct reference to the Raḥmān of Yamāmah (Mūsāylimah), al-Aswad al-'Ansī and Sajjāh, the wife of Mūsāylimah. They all claimed to be Prophets and claimed that Allah had given them revelation. Qatādah said, 'We heard that Allah revealed this about Mūsāylimah.' Ibn 'Abbās said that.

This also addresses those who turn from *fiqh* and the *Sunnah* and the *sunnah*s of the early generations and say, 'Such and such has occurred to me,' or 'My heart tells me.' They judge by what has occurred to their hearts and dominated their thoughts and claim that that is due to their being purified from any impurities and freed from anything other than Allah, and that Divine knowledge and realities have been disclosed to them and so they understand the secrets of universal matters and know the rulings of secondary matters and thus have no need of the universal rulings of the *Sharī'ah*. They say about them, 'These are commonplace legal rulings. They are rulings intended for the stupid and common people. As for the *awliyā'* and people of election, they have no need of such texts.' They say, 'Look to your heart for a *fatwā*, even if the muftis have given you one.' They use al-Khiḍr as evidence for this and say that because of the kind of knowledge Allah had disclosed to him he had no need of Mūsā's understanding of things. This is a statement that amounts to heresy and disbelief. Anyone who makes it should be killed without being asked to repent. There is no need for question or answer. Such a person is calling for the abolition of correct rulings and for the affirmation of Prophethood subsequent to that of our Prophet ﷺ. This will be discussed in *al-Kahf* in greater depth, Allah willing.

Or someone who says, 'I will send down the same as Allah has sent down'

The person meant here is 'Abdullāh ibn Abī Sarḥ who used to write down the Revelation for the Messenger of Allah ﷺ and then apostatised and joined the idolaters. The reason for that is, as the commentators mention, when the *āyah* in al-Mu'minūn: '*We created man from the purest kind of clay*' (23:12) was revealed, the Prophet ﷺ called him and dictated it to him. When he reached: '*Then brought him into being as another creature*' (23:14), 'Abdullāh wondered at the details of the creation of the human being and said, 'Blessed be Allah, the Best of Creators!' The Messenger of Allah ﷺ said, 'That is how it was revealed to me.' 'Abdullāh then doubted and said, 'If Muḥammad is truthful, then I have received revelation as He has. If he is a liar, then I said what he said.' So he left Islam and joined the idolaters. That is his words here. Al-Kalbī related that from Ibn 'Abbās.

Muḥammad ibn Isḥāq mentioned from Sharaḥbīl that it was revealed about 'Abdullāh ibn Sa'd ibn Abi Sarḥ. He apostatised from Islam. When the Messenger of Allah ﷺ entered Makkah, he commanded that he be killed together with 'Abdullāh ibn Khatal and Miqyās ibn Ṣubābah, even if they were found under the curtain of the Ka'bah. 'Abdullāh ibn Abī Sarḥ fled to 'Uthmān, who was his brother by nursing, his mother having also nursed 'Uthmān. 'Uthmān concealed him and then brought him to the Messenger of Allah ﷺ after the people of Makkah were tranquil and asked for security for him. The Messenger of Allah ﷺ was silent for a long time and then he said, 'Yes.' When 'Uthmān left, the Messenger of Allah ﷺ said, 'I was only silent so that one of you would go and strike his neck.' A man of the Anṣār said, 'Why did you not indicate to me, Messenger of Allah?' He answered. 'A Prophet should not be deceitful in that way.'

Abū 'Umar said, "Abdullāh ibn Sa'd ibn Abī Sarḥ became a good Muslim in the days of the Conquest of Makkah and nothing objectionable was seen from him after that. He was one of the noble generous intelligent men of Quraysh and warriors of the Banū 'Āmir. Then 'Umar later appointed him over Egypt in 25 AH. North Africa was conquered in 27 AH at his hands. From there, he attacked the black people in Nubia in 31 AH and concluded a truce with them that remains until today. He attacked the Byzantine navy in 34 AH. When he returned from this expedition, Ibn Abī Ḥudhayfah prevented him from entering

Fusṭāṭ, and he went to 'Asqalān and stayed there until 'Uthmān was murdered. It is said that he stayed in Ramla until he died, fleeing from the civil war, and called on his Lord. "O Allah, make the seal of my actions be the *Ṣubḥ* prayer!" He did *wuḍū'* and then prayed. In the first *rak'ah* he recited the *Fātiḥah* and al-'Ādiyāt, and in the second the *Fātiḥah* and a *sūrah.* Then he said the *salām* to his right and then to his left and Allah took his soul.'

All of that is mentioned by Yazīd ibn Abī Ḥabīb and others. He did not give allegiance to either Mu'āwiyah or 'Alī. He died before the people agreed on Mu'āwiyah. It is also said that he died in North Africa. The sound view is that he died in 'Asqalān in 36 or 37 AH. Ḥafṣ ibn 'Umar transmitted from al-Ḥakam ibn Abān that 'Ikrimah said that the *āyah* was revealed about an-Naḍr ibn al-Ḥārith because he challenged the Qur'an and composed, 'Those grinding wheat, those kneading dough, those making bread, those taking a morsel.'

If you could only see the wrongdoers in the throes of death

Suffering its hardships and agonies. The noun *ghamrah* means hardship. Its root signifies a substance which things are immersed in and covered by and it is used for water flooding. Then it is also used to refer to hardships and hateful things in general. One use of it is the 'adversities (*ghamarāt*) of war'. Al-Jawharī said, '*Ghamrah* means hardship and its plural is *ghumar*, like *nawbah* and *nuwab*.' Al-Qaṭṭāmī said when describing the ship of Nūḥ:

The time was near when those hardships would be removed.

Ghamarāt al-mawt are the difficulties experienced at the time of death.

when the angels are stretching out their hands,

It is said that they are stretching them out to punish them with iron hammers, as al-Ḥasan and aḍ-Ḍaḥḥāk stated. It is said that it is to take their souls. We find in Revelation: '*If only you could see when the angels take back those who disbelieved at their death, beating their faces and their backs.*' (8:51) So this *āyah* combines both possibilities. One says, 'He stretches out his hand to him with what is hateful.'

saying, 'Disgorge your own selves!'

'Save yourselves from the punishment if you can.' It is a rebuke. It is said to mean, 'Bring them out by force!' because the spirit of the believer is eager to leave in order to meet its Lord and the spirit of the unbeliever is dragged out by force. They are told: 'O foul soul! Come out, hating and hated, to the punishment of

Allah and humiliation,' as we find in the *ḥadīth* of Abū Hurayrah and others. We wrote about that in the *Kitāb at-Tadhkirah*. Praise be to Allah. Some have said that it is like the statement of someone who says to the one he is torturing, 'I will make you taste the punishment and disgorge your self!' That is because they do not bring themselves out. The Angel of Death and his helpers bring the soul out. It is also said that these words are said to the unbelievers when they are in the Fire. The answer is elided because of the magnitude of the matter, meaning 'if you could only see the wrongdoers in this state, you would see terrible punishment and humiliation.' The words: '*and being arrogant about His Signs*' mean that they are haughty and too arrogant to accept Allah's signs.

وَلَقَدْ جِئْتُمُونَا فُرَادَىٰ كَمَا خَلَقْنَاكُمْ أَوَّلَ مَرَّةٍ وَتَرَكْتُم مَّا خَوَّلْنَاكُمْ وَرَاءَ
ظُهُورِكُمْ ۖ وَمَا نَرَىٰ مَعَكُمْ شُفَعَاءَكُمُ الَّذِينَ زَعَمْتُمْ أَنَّهُمْ فِيكُمْ شُرَكَاؤُا۟ ۚ
لَقَد تَّقَطَّعَ بَيْنَكُمْ وَضَلَّ عَنكُم مَّا كُنتُمْ تَزْعُمُونَ ﴿٩٤﴾

94 'You have come to Us all alone just as We created you at first, leaving behind you everything We bestowed on you. We do not see your intercessors accompanying you, those you claimed were your partners with Allah. The link between you is cut. Those you made such claims for have forsaken you.'

'You have come to Us all alone just as We created you at first, leaving behind you everything We bestowed on you.

This is an expression which designates the Gathering. The word used for '*alone*' is *furādā*, which is in the accusative for the *ḥāl*, and it is not declined because it is the *alif* of the feminine. Abū Ḥaywah recited it with *tanwīn*, which is the dialect of Tamīm. They say *furādun* in the nominative. Aḥmad ibn Yaḥyā related *furāda* without *tanwīn*, saying that it is like *thulāth* and *rubā'*. *Furādā* is the plural of *fardān*, like *sukārā* is the plural of *sukrān* and *kusālā* is the plural of *kaslān*. It is said that the singular can be *fard* or *fird* or *farīd*. The meaning is: 'You have come to us one by one, each of you alone, without family, wealth, children or helper from among those who followed you in error. What you worshipped other than Allah did not benefit you.' Al-A'raj recited '*fardā*' like *sakrā* and *kaslā*.

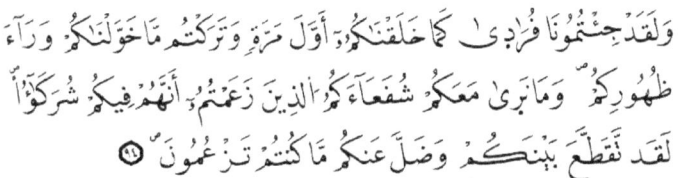

The phrase '*...just as We created you at first,*' implies alone, just as You were created. It is said to mean, 'naked as you emerged from the wombs of your mothers, barefoot, uncircumcised, mute with nothing.' Scholars said, 'A person will be gathered tomorrow and he will have the limbs he was born with. So if someone had a limb severed, it will be restored on the Day of Rising, hence the sense of uncircumcised: what was cut in circumcision will be restored. In the words '... *leaving behind you everything We bestowed on you,' khawl* are the slaves and blessings Allah gives a person and His attributing ownership of them to him.

We do not see your intercessors accompanying you,

'*Your intercessors*' are those you worshipped and made associates of, in other words your idols. The idolaters used to say, 'The idols are the associates of Allah and our intercessors with Him.'

The link between you is cut.

Nāfi', al-Kisā'ī and Ḥafṣ recited it in the accusative as a preposition, meaning, 'The link between you is cut.' The elision of the connective is indicated by Allah's words: '*We do not see your intercessors accompanying you.*' This indicates mutual severance and shunning by them and their partners when they are free of them and are not with them, and their cutting one another off is their abandoning their connection to them. So the elision of the connection after '*cut*' is indicated by the words. The mode of Ibn Mas'ūd indicates the accusative and has '*mā*' (what), meaning 'what is between you'. This is only permitted in the accusative because you mention what is cut off, which is *mā*. So it is as if Allah is saying, 'The connection between you is severed.' It is said that the meaning is that the business between you is cut off. The meaning is similar.

The rest recite it in the nominative (*baynuhum*) as a noun, not an adverb. '*Ja'ala*' strengthens the idea that *bayn* is a noun because the genitive particle is added to it as in 41:5 (*baynika*) and in 18:78 (*baynika*). It is possible that the reading in the accusative is based on the meaning of the reading in the nominative, but it is read as *bayna* because of the frequency of its use in that form even though it is actually in the nominative. That is the position of al-Akhfash. Both readings have the same meaning, so recite whichever you wish.

Those you made such claims for have forsaken you.

The verb '*ḍalla*' (*forsaken*) means 'abandoned'. The '*claims*' are the lies they told in this world. It is related that the *āyah* was revealed about an-Naḍr ibn al-Ḥārith. It is also related that 'Ā'ishah recited this *āyah* and said, 'Messenger of Allah, naked? Men and women will be gathered together looking at one another's private parts?' The Messenger of Allah said ﷺ, 'Every person on that day will have enough to concern them. Men will not look at women nor women at men, being distracted from one another.' It is an established *hadīth* in the *Sahīh*. Muslim transmitted the idea.

إِنَّ ٱللَّهَ فَالِقُ ٱلْحَبِّ وَٱلنَّوَىٰ يُخْرِجُ ٱلْحَىَّ مِنَ ٱلْمَيِّتِ وَمُخْرِجُ ٱلْمَيِّتِ مِنَ ٱلْحَىِّ
ذَٰلِكُمُ ٱللَّهُ فَأَنَّىٰ تُؤْفَكُونَ ﴿٩٥﴾

95 Allah is He Who splits the seed and kernel. He brings forth the living from the dead, and produces the dead out of the living. That is Allah, so how are you perverted?

Allah is He Who splits the seed and kernel.

Allah counts among the smallest wonders of His handicraft something which none of their gods is capable of accomplishing. The word *falq* denotes splitting – the splitting of the dead kernel so that a green shoot emerges from it and the same occurs with grain. This is bringing the living from the dead and the dead from the living, as al-Hasan and Qatādah stated. Ibn 'Abbās and ad-Dahhāk said, 'The meaning of *fāliq* is "creating".' Mujāhid said, 'By splitting what is meant is the splitting of the grain and kernel.' *Nawā* is the plural of *nawāh*. It is used for all fruit that has stones, such as apricots and peaches.

He brings forth the living from the dead,

This refers to His bringing forth the living human being from the dead sperm, and the dead sperm from the living human, as Ibn 'Abbās said. The position of Qatādah and al-Hasan was already mentioned. That was mentioned in *Āl 'Imrān* (3:27). In *Sahīh Muslim*, it is reported that 'Alī said, 'By the One who splits the seed and created the soul, the Unlettered Prophet ﷺ made a contract with me not to love other than a believer nor hate other than a hypocrite.' '*How are you perverted*?' means 'turned from the truth in spite of what you see of the power of Allah.'

فَالِقُ ٱلْإِصْبَاحِ وَجَٰعِلُ ٱلَّيْلِ سَكَنًا وَٱلشَّمْسَ وَٱلْقَمَرَ حُسْبَانًا ذَٰلِكَ تَقْدِيرُ
ٱلْعَزِيزِ ٱلْعَلِيمِ ﴿٩٦﴾

96 It is He Who splits the sky at dawn, and appoints the night as a time of stillness and the sun and moon as a means of reckoning. That is what the Almighty, the All-Knowing has ordained.

It is He Who splits the sky at dawn,

This a description of the Name of Allah – your Lord is the One who makes dawn split. It is said that it means: 'Allah is the One who splits the sky at dawn.' *Ṣubḥ* and *ṣubāḥ* designate the beginning of the day, as does *iṣbāḥ*. Allah makes the sky split with dawn every day. *Isbāh* is a verbal noun, meaning He splits the light from the darkness and removes it.' Aḍ-Ḍaḥḥāk said, 'The one who splits the dawn is the Creator of the day.'

It is definite and *tanwīn* is not permitted according to one of the grammarians. Al-Ḥasan and 'Īsā ibn 'Umar read it as *aṣbāḥ*, the plural of *ṣubḥ*. Al-A'mash related from Ibrāhīm an-Nakha'ī that it is recited as *isbāh*. Al-Ḥasan, 'Īsā, Ḥamzah and al-Kisā'ī read, '*ja'ala*' without *alif* and '*al-layla*' is in the accusative based on the fact that 'Splitter' means 'He splits' in both cases, and the word '*ja'ala*' in the *āyah* can be taken to have the same meaning. It is also followed by verbs in the past tense in 6:97. So the the words at the beginning also apply to the words at the end. That strengthens the consensus that '*sun*' and '*moon*' are in the accusative by an implied verb rather than an active particle. Makkī said that.

An-Naḥḥās said, 'Yazīd ibn Qutayb as-Sakūnī reads "*jā'ili-l-layli sakana wa-sh-shamsi wa-l-qamari*."' Makkī and al-Mahdawī and others meant the consensus on the seven readings, and Allah knows best. Ruways read '*jā'il-l-layla sākinan*' and the people of Madīnah read 'jā'il'l-layla sakinan', meaning 'a place for stillness'.

In the *Muwaṭṭā'*, Yaḥyā ibn Sa'īd reported that the Messenger of Allah ﷺ used to make supplication, saying, 'O Allah, it is You who makes the dawn break and makes the night a time for rest and appoints the sun and moon to reckon by. Relieve me of debt and enrich me from poverty and let my hearing, sight and my strength be devoted to Your way.'

If it is asked, 'How can he say, "let my hearing and my sight be devoted" when in an-Nasā'ī and at-Tirmidhī and other books it says: "Make him my heir?" and that vanishes with the body?' the answer is that there is metaphor in the words. The meaning is: 'O Allah, do not make him cease to exist before me.' It is said that what is meant by hearing and sight here is Abū Bakr and 'Umar since the Prophet ﷺ said, 'They are [my] hearing and sight.' This is an unlikely interpretation. What is meant are the two faculties.

'*Reckoning*' is connected to the best interests of people. Ibn 'Abbās said that it means 'as a means of reckoning'. That is also used in 55:4. Al-Akhfash said that *ḥusbān* is the plural of *ḥisāb* like *shihāb* and *shuhbān*. Ya'qūb said that *ḥusbān* is a verbal noun from *ḥasaba, yaḥsubu* with the nouns *ḥasb, ḥusbān, ḥisāb* and *ḥisbah*. *Ḥisāb* is a noun. Others said that Allah made the courses of the sun and the moon occur by a reckoning in which they do not exceed or fall short of. By that Allah directs people to His power and unity. It is said that '*ḥusbān*' means light. In one dialect *ḥusbān* means fire. Allah Almighty says: '*...and send down on it a fireball* (ḥusbān) *from the sky.*' (18:40). Ibn 'Abbās said 'fire'. *Ḥusbānah* is a small cushion.

وَهُوَ الَّذِي جَعَلَ لَكُمُ النُّجُومَ لِتَهْتَدُوا بِهَا فِي ظُلُمَاتِ الْبَرِّ وَالْبَحْرِ قَدْ
فَصَّلْنَا الْآيَاتِ لِقَوْمٍ يَعْلَمُونَ ﴿٩٧﴾

97 It is He Who has appointed the stars for you so you might be guided by them in the darkness of the land and sea. We have made the Signs clear for people who have knowledge.

Allah has made the perfection of His power very evident. There are many benefits in the stars. He mentions some of their benefits in this *āyah*: things knowledge of which is recommended in the *Sharī'ah*. We find in Revelation: '*Guarded against every defiant shayṭān,*' (37:7) '*We made some of them stones for the shayṭāns.*' (67:5) The verb *ja'ala* (*appointed*) here means 'created'. '*We have made the Signs clear*' – made them clear and distinct so that the lesson gained from them will be greater. The words '*for people who have knowledge*' single them out because they are the people who benefit by them.

وَهُوَ الَّذِي أَنشَأَكُم مِّن نَّفْسٍ وَاحِدَةٍ فَمُسْتَقَرٌّ وَمُسْتَوْدَعٌ قَدْ فَصَّلْنَا
الْآيَاتِ لِقَوْمٍ يَفْقَهُونَ ﴿٩٨﴾

98 It is He Who first produced you from a single self, then from a resting-place and a repository. We have made the Signs clear for people who understand.

It is He Who first produced you from a single self,

This refers to Ādam and was discussed at the beginning of the *sūrah*. Ibn 'Abbās, Sa'īd ibn Jubayr, al-Ḥasan, Abū 'Amr, 'Īsā, al-A'raj, Shaybah and an-Nakha'ī read '*resting-place*' as *mustaqirr* and the rest have *mustaqarr*. It is in the nominative by the inceptive, although if it is read as *mustaqirr*, it implies 'from a resting-place', and if it is read as *mustaqarr*, it implies 'it has a resting-place'. 'Abdullāh ibn Mas'ūd said, 'They have a resting place in the womb and a repository in the earth on which they will die.' This commentary indicates the reading with the *fatḥah* (*mustaqarr*). Al-Ḥasan said, 'Its resting-place is in the grave.' Most commentators say that the resting-place is in the womb and the repository is in the loins. Sa'īd ibn Jubayr reported it from Ibn 'Abbās. An-Nakha'ī said that. Ibn 'Abbās said that the resting place is the earth and the repository is the loins. Sa'īd ibn Jubayr said, 'Ibn 'Abbās asked me, "Are you married?" "No," I replied. He said, "Allah Almighty will bring forth from your back what is lodged in it."' It is also reported from Ibn 'Abbās that the '*resting-place*' is those who have already been created and the '*repository*' are those who are not yet created. Al-Māwardī mentioned it. Ibn 'Abbās also said that the resting-place is with Allah. We find in Revelation: '*You will have residence on the earth and enjoyment for a time.*' (2:36) That indicates their sojourn in the grave until they are raised up for the Reckoning which was discussed in *Sūrat al-Baqarah* (2:5). Qatādah said that '*faṣṣalnā*' means to make clear and confirm. Allah knows best.

وَهُوَ ٱلَّذِىٓ أَنزَلَ مِنَ ٱلسَّمَآءِ مَآءً فَأَخْرَجْنَا بِهِۦ نَبَاتَ كُلِّ شَىْءٍ فَأَخْرَجْنَا مِنْهُ
خَضِرًا نُّخْرِجُ مِنْهُ حَبًّا مُّتَرَاكِبًا وَمِنَ ٱلنَّخْلِ مِن طَلْعِهَا قِنْوَانٌ دَانِيَةٌ
وَجَنَّٰتٍ مِّنْ أَعْنَابٍ وَٱلزَّيْتُونَ وَٱلرُّمَّانَ مُشْتَبِهًا وَغَيْرَ مُتَشَٰبِهٍ
ٱنظُرُوٓا۟ إِلَىٰ ثَمَرِهِۦٓ إِذَآ أَثْمَرَ وَيَنْعِهِۦٓ ۚ إِنَّ فِى ذَٰلِكُمْ لَءَايَٰتٍ لِّقَوْمٍ يُؤْمِنُونَ ٩٩

99 It is He Who sends down water from the sky from which We bring forth growth of every kind, and from that We bring forth the green shoots and from them We bring forth close-packed seeds, and from the spathes of the date palm date clusters hanging down, and gardens of grapes and olives and pomegranates, both similar and dissimilar. Look at their fruits as they bear fruit and ripen. There are Signs in that for people who believe.

It is He Who sends down water from the sky from which We bring forth growth of every kind,

The *water* is rain. The expression '*growth of every kind*' means every type of plant. It is said that it is the provision of every animal. Al-Akhfash said, 'It means green things.' *Khaḍir* are moist vegetables. Ibn 'Abbās said that it means wheat, barley, sult barley, rice and all grains. The expression '*close-packed seeds*' means one on top of another, like are found in an ear of wheat.

and from the spathes of the date palm date clusters hanging down,

Sībawayh said that some Arabs say '*qunwān*' (clusters) rather than '*qinwān*'. Al-Farrā' said that in the Qur'an '*clusters hanging down*" should be added to what is before it. Al-Farrā' said that that is in the dialect of Qays. The people of the Ḥijāz say *qinwān* and Tamīm say *qinyān*. They agree that all of these are plurals of *qinw* or *qanw*. *Ṭal'* (spathe) is the spadix from which a date blossom opens. *Ighrīḍ* also has the same meaning. The spathe is what is seen of the inflorescence of dates. *Qinwān* is plural of *qinw* like *ṣinw* and *ṣinwān*, and the dual is also *qinwān*. The plural is in the dual form. Al-Jawharī and others said that the plural is *ṣinwānu* and the dual is *ṣinwāna*. *Qinw* is the inflorescence and its plural is either *qinwān* or *aqnā'*. Others said that *aqnā'* is the plural of paucity. Al-Mahdawī said that Ibn Hurmuz recited '*qanwān*' and '*qunwān*' is also related from him. If it is read as *qanwān*, it is the noun of an unbroken plural like *rakb*, according to Sībawayh, and *al-bāqir* and *al-jāmil* because the form *fa'lān* is not one of the models of plurals. If it is *qunwān*, it is the plural of *qinw*, which is the spadex. It is a large cluster of dates and *'adhq* is the dates themselves. It is also said that *qinwān* is the pith of the palm.

The adjective *dāniyah* means 'close', so that someone standing or sitting is able to pluck them, as Ibn 'Abbās, al-Barā' ibn 'Āzib and others said. Az-Zajjāj said that some are near and some are far and there is some elision [because it is implied]. Nearness is mentioned because the aim of the *āyah* is to mention power and the granting of blessing, and the enjoyment of a blessing is greater when it is near to hand.

and gardens of grapes

This implies: 'We brought forth gardens.' Muḥammad ibn 'Abd ar-Raḥmān ibn Abī Laylā and al-A'mash recited it as *jannātun* rather than the *jannātin* we find in the reading of 'Āṣim. Abū 'Ubayd and Abū Ḥātim do not acknowledge this reading, and Abū Ḥātim said that it is impossible because '*jannāt*' are not comprised of date palms, while an-Naḥḥās says that the reading is possible, but you cannot understand the *āyah* based on this reading; it is in the nominative by the inceptive whose predicate is elided. It means: 'they will have gardens' as a group of reciters recited '*ḥūrun 'īnun*'. (56:22) That is permitted by Sībawayh, al-Kisā'ī and al-Farrā'. There are many examples of this. It is like '*ḥūran 'īnan*' as Sībawayh related. [POEM] It is said that it implies: 'We produced gardens of grapes'. It is like, 'I honoured 'Abdullāh and his brother' which means that you also honoured his brother. As for 'olives and pomegranates', there is consensus that they can only be in the the accusative case. It is also said that 'gardens' is in the nominative as added to 'spathes', even if they are not the same species.

olives and pomegranates, both similar and dissimilar.

This means similar in terms of leaves, the leaves of the olive resembling those of the pomegranate in the way the leaves are arranged on the branches and the size of the leaves, but they are dissimilar in taste, as Qatādah and others said. Ibn Jurayj said that it means 'similar' in appearance and 'dissimilar' in taste, like two pomegranates that have the same colour but taste different. Olives and pomegranates are singled out because of their familiarity with them. This is like Allah words: '*Have they not looked at the camel – how it was created?*' (88:17) He refers them to camels since they were what they knew best.

Look at their fruits as they bear fruit and ripen.

'*Look*' in this instance means consider, not just look with the eyes without reflecting. *Thamar* is what is harvested from trees. Ḥamzah and al-Kisā'ī read '*thumur*' and the rest '*thamar*' like *baqarah* and *baqar* and *shajarah* and *shajar.* [*Thamar* is the plural of *thamarah.*] Mujāhid said that *thumur* are types of wealth and *thamar* are dates. So, according to Mujāhid, it means: 'Look at the kind of wealth which bears fruit.' *Thumur* is the plural of *thimār*, which is lucrative property. The word is related from al-A'mash as *thumr* where the *ḍammah* is elided for lightness and it can also be the plural of *thamarah. Thumur* can be the plural of a plural.

The verb '*ripen*' is recited by Muḥammad ibn as-Samayqa' as [the active participle,] '*yān'ihi*'. Ibn Muḥayṣin and Ibn Abī Isḥāq recite '*yun'ihi*' [instead of *yan'ihi*]. Al-Farrā' said, 'It is the dialect of the people of Najd. Fruit is said to ripen as *yana'a* and the ripe fruit is *yāni'.*' *Ayna'a* means to become ripe. Al-Ḥajjāj used the verb in his speech which described heads as 'ripe for plucking'. Ibn al-Anbārī said that *yan'* is the plural of *yāni'* which is when fruit reaches the level of complete ripeness. Al-Farrā' said that Form IV is more than ripe. It means red. This meaning is found in the *ḥadīth* about a woman who carried out a *li'ān* divorce in the words: 'If she gives birth to a reddish child like the *yan'ah.*' It is also what a red pearl is called, and said to be agate or a type of it.

The *āyah* indicates that someone who reflects and investigates with his sight and heart will see that things which change necessitate the existence of a Changer, and that is Allah Almighty. Allah says: '*Look at their fruits as they bear fruit and ripen.*' You first look at the spathes, then the opening of the spadix, and the entire process through the whiteness of the inflorescence when the spathe splits, which is also called *ḍaḥk*, then unripe dates (*balaḥ*), then *sayāb*, and then *jadāl* when they are green and round before they are strong. Then they are *busr* when they are large and then *zahw* when they are red. The verb for this is *azhā*. Then they are called *muwakkat* when a spot of ripeness appears. When they begin to be ripe at the stalk, they are called *mudhannabah* or *tadhnūb*. When they are soft, they are *tha'dah*. When half of them are fully ripe, they are *mujazza'ah*. When they are two-thirds ripe, they are *ḥulqānah*. When they are completely ripe, they are *munsabitah*. One refers to ripe dates as '*ruṭab munsabit*'. Then they are dried and become *tamr*. By their transformation from state to state and their existence after they were non-existent Allah calls attention to His oneness and the perfection of His power and to the fact that they have a Maker with Power and Knowledge. It also indicates the expectation of resurrection by the bringing of the plants to life after they were desiccated. Al-Jawharī said that *yana'a* is to become ripe.

Ibn al-'Arabī said that Mālik said, 'Ripening is becoming good without corruption or having to hit them to cause them to ripen.' Mālik said that the people of Basra strike the fruit until it ripens, striking it so that the air enters it quicker which hastens its cropping. That is not the type of ripening referred to in the Qur'an nor that which the Messenger of Allah ﷺ connected to sales; they refer to the ripening which happens naturally without any artificial device. In one of the lands where figs grow, which is cold, they do not ripen until an oiled stick is applied to the bottom of them. When they are good, then they are ripe. That is because it is necessary due to the climate of that land. Were it not for that, they would never become good at the time when fruits are good.

This natural ripeness is the basis on which it is permitted to sell dates and by which they are good for eating and kept free from blight. It happens at the time the Pleaides rise by the *sunnah* of Allah and as ordained by His Wisdom and Power. Al-Mu'allā ibn Asad mentioned from Wuhayb from 'Asl ibn Sufyān from 'Aṭā' from Abū Hurayrah that the Messenger of Allah ﷺ said, 'When the Pleaides rise in the morning, blight is removed from the people of this land.' There is no disagreement that the Pleaides is a constellation of stars which rises on the morning of the 12th of May. We find in al-Bukhārī from Khārijah ibn Zayd ibn Thābit that Zayd ibn Thābit did not sell the fruits of his land until the Pleaides had risen and the yellow colour in the fruits were distinct from the reddish ones. Those who say that blight reduces the amount of harvested fruit use these traditions as evidence. The Prophet ﷺ forbade selling fruits before their ripeness is clear and selling fruits until the blight has passed. 'Uthmān ibn Surāqah said, 'I asked Ibn 'Umar when that was and he said, "After the Pleaides rise."'

Ash-Shāfi'ī said, 'I do not consider that it is proven that Messenger of Allah ﷺ ordered a reduction in price on account of crop damage. Were it in my view confirmed, I would not go against it. The basis on which there is agreement is that if someone buys what it is permitted to buy and takes possession of it, the mishap is his.' He added, 'If I were to allow a reduction on account of crop damage, it would be reduced in both a little and a lot.' That is the view of ath-Thawrī and the Kufans. Mālik and most of the people of Madīnah believe that there is a reduction based on the *ḥadīth* of Jābir that the Messenger of Allah ﷺ ordered a reduction in price on account of crop damage. Muslim transmitted it. That was the ruling given by 'Umar ibn 'Abd al-'Azīz, and it is the position of Aḥmad ibn Ḥanbal and the rest of the People of *Ḥadīth*. The literalists reduce the price on account of it for the seller for both a little and a lot according to the general meaning of the *ḥadīth*, although for Mālik and his people that is only when the crop damage affects a third of the crop or more. They ignore anything less than that and make it a normal consequence since there must be an allowance for a few bad fruits among the good and there will necessarily be a few that are unsound. Aṣbagh and Ashhab did not look at the fruit, but at the price. If the price was a third or more, it was reduced.

According to Ibn al-Qāsim crop damage refers to what cannot be protected against. He also says that theft does not constitute crop damage. That is found in the book of Muḥammad. It also says in the book that it is crop damage. That is related from Ibn al-Qāsim but he is opposed by his fellows and people in general. Muṭarrif and Ibn al-Mājishūn said, 'Fruit that is harmed by rottenness or cold, or lack of water or heat, or breaking of stalks, which has not been done by a human being, is crop damage.' There is disagreement about damage through lack of water. It is transmitted that Ibn al-Qāsim said that it is considered crop damage. What is sound about vegetables is that they suffer crop damage just as fruits do.

If someone sells fruits before they are sound on the basis that the fruits will mature properly, the sale is void and rejected because it is forbidden and because it comes under the heading of of consuming wealth falsely, borne out by the words of the Prophet ﷺ, 'If Allah were to stop the fruits from ripening, how could one of you take his brother's wealth without any right to do so?' This is the view of the majority. Abū Ḥanīfah and his people say that it is sound and make the prohibition one of dislike. The majority believe that it is permitted to sell them before they are ripe with the proviso that they have been already cut down from the tree. Ath-Thawrī and Ibn Abī Laylā forbade it, holding to the prohibition which has come about that. The majority make it specific by clear analogy since it is a known sale which can be validly taken at the time of the contract, and so its sale is valid as is the case with other sales.

وَجَعَلُوا لِلَّهِ شُرَكَاءَ الْجِنَّ وَخَلَقَهُمْ ۖ وَخَرَقُوا لَهُ بَنِينَ وَبَنَاتٍ بِغَيْرِ عِلْمٍ ۚ
سُبْحَانَهُ وَتَعَالَىٰ عَمَّا يَصِفُونَ ١٠٠

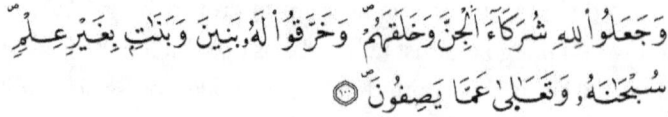

100 Yet they make the jinn co-partners with Allah when He created them! And they attribute sons and daughters to Him without any knowledge. Glory be to Him! He is far above what they describe!

Yet they make the jinn co-partners with Allah when He created them!

This is another aspect of their ignorance, some of them believing that Allah has partners among the jinn. An-Naḥḥās said that '*jinn*' is the first object and '*co-partners*' is a second object. The grammatical structure, which is frequently used in the Qur'an, implies: 'They assigned Allah partners from the jinn.' It is also possible for '*jinn*' to be an appositive of '*partners*'. Al-Kisā'ī permitted '*jinn*' to be in the nominative, meaning 'there are jinn'. Most recite '*when He created them*' as '*khalaqahum*'. It means: 'He created those who then assign Him partners.' It is said that it means: 'He created the partner jinn.' Ibn Mas'ūd adds a '*huwa*' (He) before '*He created*'. Yaḥyā ibn Ya'mar recited '*wa khalqahum*'. He said that it means 'They made what they created co-partners of Allah when they made something and then worshipped it.'

The *āyah* was revealed about the Arab idolaters. The meaning is their attributing partners to Allah from among the jinn. They obey them as Allah should be obeyed. That is related from al-Ḥasan and others. Qatādah and as-Suddī said, 'They are those whom the Arabs called "the daughters of Allah".' Al-Kalbī said, 'It was revealed about the *zindīq*s. They said, "Allah and Iblīs are brothers. (According to them) Allah created people and animals, and Iblīs created the jinn, beasts of prey and scorpions." This is close to the Magian view. The Magians said that the world has two Makers: an eternal God and a temporal devil who sprang from the thought of the eternal God. They claim that the maker of evil is temporal. This is also the view of the Ḥā'iṭiyyah among the Mu'tazilites, who follow Aḥmad ibn Ḥā'iṭ. They claim that the world has two makers: the Eternal God and another temporal one who was first created by Allah after which the management of the world was entrusted to him and who will call creation to account in the Hereafter. '*Allah is high exalted over what the wrongdoers and deniers say*!'

and they attribute

Nāfi' reads this with *tashdīd* (*kharraqū*, Form II intensive) because of their doing it to the highest degree, in that the idolaters claimed that Allah has daughters and they are angels. They called them jinn because they are hidden. The Christians claimed that 'Īsā is the son of Allah and the Jews said that 'Uzayr is the son of

Allah so they are extreme in their unbelief. The verb is in Form II which is in harmony with the meaning, Allah is greatly exalted above what they say! The rest read it is *kharaqū*.

Ḥasan al-Baṣrī was asked about the meaning of '*kharraqū*' and he said that the correct Arabic is actually '*kharaqū*'. When a man lies in an assembly, it is said, 'By the Lord of the Ka'bah, he has made a false attribution (*kharaqa*)!' Linguists say that the meaning of *kharaqū* is 'they disagreed' and *kharraqū* is for doing it to an extreme. Mujāhid, Qatādah, Ibn Zayd and Ibn Jurayj said that *kharaqū* means 'they lied'. It is also said that it means: invented and innovated.

بَدِيعُ ٱلسَّمَٰوَٰتِ وَٱلْأَرْضِ أَنَّىٰ يَكُونُ لَهُۥ وَلَدٌ وَلَمْ تَكُن لَّهُۥ صَٰحِبَةٌ وَخَلَقَ
كُلَّ شَيْءٍ وَهُوَ بِكُلِّ شَيْءٍ عَلِيمٌ ١٠١

101 He is the Originator of the heavens and the earth. How could He have a son when He has no wife? He created all things and He has knowledge of all things.

He is the Originator of the heavens and the earth.

He is the One who first brought them about so how could He have a child? 'Originator' (*badī'*) is in the nominative as the predicate of an implied inceptive. Al-Kasā'ī allows it in the genitive as an attribute of '*Allah*' and also in the accusative, meaning 'Originator of the heavens and the earth.' It is an error according to the Basrans since it refers to something already mentioned.

How could He have a son when He has no wife?

'How could He have a son?' The child of anything resembles it and there is nothing like Him. *Ṣāḥibah* means wife.

He created all things and He has knowledge of all things.

'*He created all things*' is a general statement whose meaning is specific. He created the universe. Neither His words nor any other of His attributes are included in that. It is like His words: '*My mercy extends to all things*' (7:156) but it does not extend to Iblīs nor to someone who dies an unbeliever and like His words: '*destroying everything*' (46:25) when the heavens and earth were not destroyed.

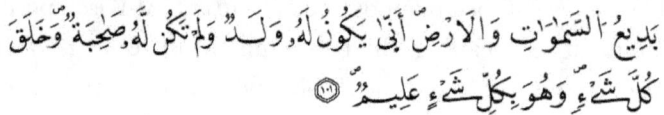

ذَٰلِكُمُ ٱللَّهُ رَبُّكُمْ لَآ إِلَٰهَ إِلَّا هُوَ خَٰلِقُ كُلِّ شَيْءٍ فَٱعْبُدُوهُ وَهُوَ عَلَىٰ
كُلِّ شَيْءٍ وَكِيلٌ ۝١٠٢ لَّا تُدْرِكُهُ ٱلْأَبْصَٰرُ وَهُوَ يُدْرِكُ ٱلْأَبْصَٰرَ وَهُوَ
ٱللَّطِيفُ ٱلْخَبِيرُ ۝١٠٣

102-3 That is Allah, your Lord. There is no god but Him, the Creator of everything. So worship Him. He is responsible for everything. Eyesight cannot perceive Him but He perceives eyesight. He is the All-Gracious, the All-Aware.

That is Allah, your Lord.

'*That*' is in the nominative by the inceptive and the words '*Allah, your Lord*' are an appositive. It is possible for '*your Lord*' to be a predicate and '*Creator*' a second predicate, or it is based on an implied inchoative, in other words 'He is the Creator'. Al-Kisā'ī and al-Farrā' permit it to be in the accusative.

Eyesight cannot perceive Him but He perceives eyesight.

Allah makes it clear that He is free of the qualities of temporality, which include perception with the meaning of encompassment and limitation in the way that other creatures perceive. Seeing is confirmed. Az-Zajjāj said, 'That means it does not reach the core of His reality, as you say, "I perceived such-and-such,' because *ḥadīths* from the Prophet ﷺ confirm the vision on the Day of Rising. Ibn 'Abbās said, '"*Eyesight cannot perceive Him*" in this world but the believers will see him in the Next World since Allah states: *"Faces that Day will be radiant, gazing at their Lord."* (75:22-23)' As-Suddī said, 'That is the best of what is said and is indicated by the Revelation and what traditions have reported about the vision of Allah in the Garden.' It will be dealt with in *Sūrah* Yūnus.

It is said that it means that the sight of the hearts does not perceive Him, i.e. intellects do not perceive Him so as to be able to imagine Him since '*There is nothing like him.*' (42:11) It is said that the meaning is that created eyes cannot perceive Him in this world but that He creates sight and perception by which He can be seen for whomever He wishes to honour, such as Muḥammad ﷺ. His seeing Him in this world is logically possible since, if it had not been possible, the request of Mūsā (to see Him) would then have been impossible and it is not possible for a Prophet to be ignorant of what is conceivable and inconceivable for Allah. So he could only ask for what is possible, not for something impossible.

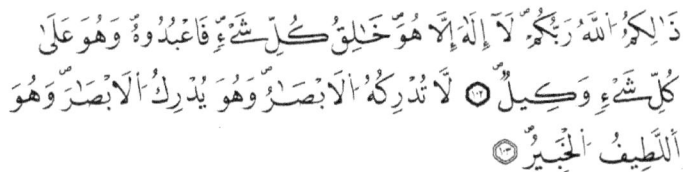

The early generations disagree about the Prophet ﷺ seeing his Lord. In *Ṣaḥīḥ Muslim*, Masrūq said, 'I was reclining in the presence of 'Ā'ishah and she said, "Abū 'Ā'ishah, whoever says one of three things has uttered a terrible lie against Allah." I asked, "What are they?" She answered, "Anyone who claims that Muḥammad saw his Lord has uttered a terrible lie against Allah." I was reclining and sat up and said, "Umm al-Mu'minīn, let me speak and do not rush me. Did not Allah say: '*He saw him on the clear horizon*' (81:23) and: '*He saw him again another time*' (53:13)?" She said, "I was the first of this Community to ask the Messenger of Allah ﷺ about that. He said, 'It was Jibrīl whom I did not see in his form on which he was created except two times. I saw him descending from heaven and the immensity of his form blocked out what was between heaven and earth.'" She said, "Did you not hear Allah say: '*Eyesight cannot perceive Him but He perceives eyesight. He is the All-Penetrating, the All-Aware*'? Did you not hear that Allah says: '*It is not proper for Allah to address any human being except by inspiration, or from behind a veil, or He sends a messenger who then reveals by His permission whatever He wills. He is indeed Most High, All-Wise.*' (42:51)?" She added, "Whoever claims that the Messenger of Allah ﷺ concealed any of the Book of Allah has lied against Allah. Allah says: '*O Messenger! Deliver what has been sent down to you from your Lord. If you do not do it you will not have conveyed His Message.*' (5:67)" She said, "Whoever claims to report about what will happen tomorrow has uttered an immense lie against Allah. Allah says: '*Say: "No one in the heavens and the earth knows the Unseen, except Allah."*' (27:65)"' Ibn Mas'ūd believed what 'Ā'ishah said about his not seeing Allah, and that he saw Jibrīl. The same is reported from Abū Hurayrah about it being Jibrīl, but there is disagreement about it. A group of *ḥadīth* scholars, *fuqahā'* and *mutakallimūn* deny that he ﷺ saw Allah.

Ibn 'Abbās said that he saw Him with his eyes. This is well known from him. His proof is the words of Allah: '*The heart did not lie about what it saw.*' (53:11) 'Abdullāh ibn al-Ḥārith said, 'Ibn 'Abbās and Ubayy ibn Ka'b agree. Ibn 'Abbās said, "We are the Banū Hāshim. We say that Muḥammad saw his Lord twice."' Then Ibn 'Abbās said, 'Are you surprised that Ibrāhīm had friendship, Mūsā speech and that vision was for Muḥammad ﷺ?' He said, 'Ka'b said the *takbīr* until the mountains echoed him. Then he said, "Allah divided His vision and speech between Muḥammad and Mūsā ﷺ. He spoke to Mūsā and Muḥammad ﷺ saw him."'

'Abd ar-Razzāq related that al-Ḥasan used to swear by Allah that Muḥammad ﷺ saw his Lord. Abū 'Umar aṭ-Ṭalamankī reported it from 'Ikrimah and some of the *mutakallimūn* reported it from Ibn Mas'ūd. The first is more famous. Ibn Isḥāq related that Marwān asked Abū Hurayrah, 'Did Muḥammad see his Lord?' He replied, 'Yes.' An-Naqqāsh reported that Aḥmad ibn Ḥanbal said, 'I take the *ḥadīth* of Ibn 'Abbās, "He saw him with his own eyes! He saw him!" which he held to until his death.' Shaykh Abū al-Ḥasan al-Ash'arī and a group of his people held that Muhammad ﷺ saw Allah with his sight and his own eyes. Anas, Ibn 'Abbās, 'Ikrimah, ar-Rabī' and al-Ḥasan said that. Al-Ḥasan used to swear, 'By Allah, there is no god but Him, Muḥammad saw his Lord.'

A group of them, including Abū al-'Āliyah, al-Quraẓī and ar-Rabī' ibn Anas said, 'He saw his Lord with his heart and inner core.' It is also related from Ibn 'Abbās and 'Ikrimah. Abū 'Umar said, 'Aḥmad ibn Ḥanbal said that he ﷺ saw Him with his heart but shrank from the position that He is seen in this world with the eyes.' Mālik ibn Anas said, 'He was not seen in this world because He is eternal and the eternal cannot be seen in anything ephemeral. In the Next World, when they are provided with everlasting sight, then the Everlasting will be seen by the everlasting.' Qāḍī 'Iyāḍ stated, 'These are excellent words.' The words only impute impossibility when there is lack of sufficient capacity. When Allah strengthens whomever He wishes and gives him the power to bear the burden of vision, it is not forbidden for it to take place. Some of this will be mentioned in connection with Mūsā in Surat *al-A'rāf.*

The words: '*But He perceives eyesight*' mean that nothing is hidden from Him. He sees it and knows it. Eyesight is mentioned in a generic way. Az-Zajjāj said, 'These words indicate that creatures cannot perceive sight, in other words they do not recognise the quality of the reality of sight. This applies not only to the eyes, with which a person sees, but to any of his other physical faculties with which he sees.'

He is the All-Gracious, the All-Aware

He is kind to His slaves. *Luṭf* is the action of being kind. *Luṭf* from Allah is giving success and protection. *Luṭf* is a gift and *mulaṭāfah* is mutual kindness, as al-Jawharī and Ibn Fāris said. Abū al-'Āliyah said, 'The meaning of "*al-Laṭīf*" is the One who brings forth things while being aware of their proper place.' Al-Junayd said, '*Al-Laṭīf* is the One who illuminates your heart with guidance. He cares for your body with nourishment and assigns you protection in affliction and guards you when you are enflamed and causes you to enter the Garden of Refuge.' Other things are said whose sense refers to kindness and the like. What scholars say about this will be further discussed in *Sūrat* ash-Shūrā, Allah willing.

قَدْ جَآءَكُم بَصَآئِرُ مِن رَّبِّكُمْ ۖ فَمَنْ أَبْصَرَ فَلِنَفْسِهِۦ ۖ وَمَنْ عَمِىَ فَعَلَيْهَا ۚ وَمَآ أَنَا۠ عَلَيْكُم بِحَفِيظٍ ﴿١٠٤﴾

104 'Clear insights have come to you from your Lord. Whoever sees clearly, does so to his own benefit. Whoever is blind, it is to his own detriment. I am not here as your keeper.'

Clear insights have come to you from your Lord.

The plural of *baṣīrah* is *baṣā'ir* as is shown in the words of the poet:

They came carrying their blood revenge (*baṣā'ir*) on their shoulders,
but my blood revenge (*baṣīrah*) runs with a swift, strong horse.

Here *baṣā'ir* means signs and proofs which are seen and deduced. A 'proof' is described as 'coming' when it is immensely important, since it is like something absent which suddenly occurs to the self, like health comes at the retreat of illness and happiness comes at the retreat of sorrow. The words '*Whoever sees clearly*' refers to direct perception and means those who deduce and recognise benefits themselves. '*Whoever is blind*' and does not deduce, the harm of his blindness is against himself.

I am not here as your keeper.'

I am not commanded to keep you from destroying yourselves. It is also said to mean, 'I cannot protect you from the punishment of Allah.' It is said that *ḥafīẓ* means watcher, i.e. counting your actions. 'I am a Messenger who conveys to you the messages of my Lord. He is the One who preserves you, and none of your actions are hidden from him.' Az-Zajjāj said, 'This was revealed before fighting was made obligatory.' Then he was commanded to stop them worshipping idols by means of the sword.

وَكَذَٰلِكَ نُصَرِّفُ ٱلْءَايَٰتِ وَلِيَقُولُوا۟ دَرَسْتَ وَلِنُبَيِّنَهُۥ لِقَوْمٍ يَعْلَمُونَ ﴿١٠٥﴾

105 That is how We vary the Signs, so that they say, 'You have been studying,' and so We can make it clear to people who know.

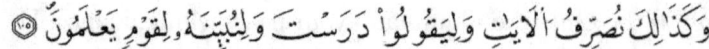

We vary the signs to you in various ways, meaning that We vary them terms of promise, threat, warning and clarification in this *sūrah* and in others. In the phrase '*so that they say, "You have been studying,"*' the conjunction *wa* here implies something being elided, meaning 'We vary the signs to you in order to establish the proof and so that they will say, "You have studied."' Regarding the grammar of '*so that*' (*li*) (which implies a result), az-Zajjāj said, 'This is as you might say, "So-and-so wrote this letter in order to (*li*) encompass his death," i.e. to lead him to that.' So the variety of the *āyahs* leads them to say, 'You studied and learned from Jabr and Yasār,' who were two Christian young men in Makkah. The people of Makkah said, 'He learned from them.' An-Naḥḥās said that there is another idea regarding that, which is that it means: 'We bring them sign after sign, so that they say, "You have studied under us."' They mention the first by the last. (sic.) This is something actual whereas as what Abū Isḥāq said is a metaphor.

There are seven readings of 'You have been studying'. Abū 'Amr and Ibn Kathīr read *dārasta*, which is the reading of 'Alī, Ibn 'Abbās, Sa'īd ibn Jubayr, Mujāhid, 'Ikrimah, and the people of Makkah. Ibn 'Abbas said that the meaning of '*dārasta*' is 'to do it constantly'. Ibn 'Āmir read it as '*darasat*', and it is also the reading of al-Ḥasan. The rest read '*darasta*'. According to the reading *dārasta* it means: 'You study the People of the Book and they study you,' meaning 'you talk to them and they talk to you.' Sa'īd ibn Jubayr said that. This idea is indicated by '*Other people have helped him to do it*' (25:4), implying that the Jews helped the Prophet ﷺ with the Qur'an and discussed it with him. This is all part of the words of the idolaters, like their words: '*They say, "Myths of the earlier peoples which he has had transcribed and which are read out to him in the morning and the evening"*' (25:5) and: '*When they are asked, "What has your Lord sent down?" they say, "Myths and legends of the earlier peoples."*' (16:24) It is also said to have the same meaning as *darasta*. An-Naḥḥās mentioned this and preferred it. Makkī mentioned the former. An-Naḥḥās said that it is metaphorical like:

To death belongs what every mother bears.

If someone reads '*darasat*', the best of what can be said about his reading is that it means: 'So that they do not say that it has ceased and ended and Muḥammad will not bring anything else.' Qatādah recited '*durista*', meaning you were made to recite. Sufyān ibn 'Uyaynah related from 'Amr ibn 'Ubayd that al-Ḥasan recited '*dārasat*' which Abū Ḥātim thought was not permitted because the *āyahs* do not study together. Others say that that reading is permitted, but it does not mean what Abū Ḥātim thought, but means 'your community studies together,' even though they are not mentioned before. That is like 38:32. Al-Akhfash related '*darusat*' which means the same as '*darasat*' although it is more effective. Abū al-'Abbās recited '*wa-l-yaqūlū*' as a command containing a threat, meaning 'They can say whatever they wish. The truth is clear.' We see the same in Allah's words: '*Let them laugh little and weep much.*' (9:82)

All the readings derive from the same thing: making tractable and humble. '*Darasta*' comes from the verb *darasa, yadrusu, dirāsah*, to read out something to someone else. It is said that '*darastahu*' means to master something by frequent reading. Its root is *dars*, threshing grain. The word *diyās* (threshing) is *dirās* in the Syrian dialect. It is said that its root *dars* comes from a garment becoming tattered. This also connects with subduing. It is said that Idrīs got his name from his frequent study of the Book of Allah. The same meaning of study is found in the variants of *darasa: dārasa, tadārasa* and *iddārasa*. The verbal noun for study is *dars* and *dirāsah*. It is also used for a woman menstruating. A woman's vagina is alluded to as 'Abū Adrās, referring to menstruation. *Dars* also means a hidden path. Al-Aṣma'ī related, 'A camel that is not yet subdued (*yudarris*), i.e. ridden.' *Darasa* is also to efface, as when signs of a dwelling have disappeared. Ibn Mas'ūd and his people, Ubayy, Ṭalḥah and al-A'mash recited '*darasa*', meaning 'Muḥammad studied the Signs.' The verb '*make it clear*' may refer to the statement, the variation, or the Qur'an.

اتَّبِعْ مَا أُوحِيَ إِلَيْكَ مِن رَّبِّكَ ۖ لَا إِلَٰهَ إِلَّا هُوَ ۖ وَأَعْرِضْ عَنِ الْمُشْرِكِينَ ١٠٦

106 Follow what has been revealed to you from your Lord – there is no god but Him – and turn away from the idolaters.

What has been revealed is the Qur'an, so the *āyah* implies 'do not occupy your heart and thought with them, rather occupy yourself with worshipping Him.' The phrase '*turn away from the idolaters*' is abrogated (by the command to fight them).

وَلَوْ شَاءَ اللَّهُ مَا أَشْرَكُوا ۗ وَمَا جَعَلْنَاكَ عَلَيْهِمْ حَفِيظًا ۖ وَمَا أَنتَ عَلَيْهِم
بِوَكِيلٍ ١٠٧

107 If Allah had willed, they would not have associated anything with Him. We did not appoint you over them as their keeper and you are not set over them as their guardian.

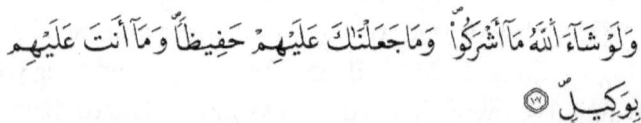

This is a text which demonstrates that *shirk* is willed by Him, which negates the school of the Qadariyyah as already mentioned. The words '*you are not set over them*

as their guardian' mean 'you are not an overseer over their affairs to obtain their best interests for their *dīn* or this world so as to be kind to them by getting them to do what is obligatory for them to do. You are not a guardian or protector in that respect. You are just one who conveys (the Message).' This was before he was commanded to fight.

وَلَا تَسُبُّوا۟ ٱلَّذِينَ يَدْعُونَ مِن دُونِ ٱللَّهِ فَيَسُبُّوا۟ ٱللَّهَ عَدْوًۢا بِغَيْرِ عِلْمٍ
كَذَٰلِكَ زَيَّنَّا لِكُلِّ أُمَّةٍ عَمَلَهُمْ ثُمَّ إِلَىٰ رَبِّهِم مَّرْجِعُهُمْ فَيُنَبِّئُهُم بِمَا كَانُوا۟
يَعْمَلُونَ ﴿١٠٨﴾

108 Do not curse those they call upon besides Allah, in case that makes them curse Allah in animosity, without knowledge. In this way We make the actions of every nation seem attractive to them. Then they will return to their Lord, and He will inform them about what they did.

Do not curse those they call upon besides Allah, in case that makes them curse Allah in animosity, without knowledge.

This is a prohibition. Allah forbids the believers to curse the idolaters' idols because He knows that if they were to curse them, the unbelievers would be antagonistic and their disbelief increased. Ibn 'Abbās said, 'The unbelievers of Quraysh said to Abū Ṭālib, "Either you forbid Muḥammad and his people to curse our gods and disdain them or we will curse his God and satirise Him."' This *āyah* was then revealed.

Scholars say that its ruling continues for this Community in every time and place. If unbelievers are in a protected situation and it is feared that Islam or the Prophet ﷺ or Allah will be abused by them, it is not lawful for a Muslim to abuse their ancestors, *dīn* or churches, nor for them to resort to anything that might lead to that, because it is like an incitement to disobey Allah. The masculine pronoun is used for 'idols', which are not sentient, because of the idolaters' belief about them.

This *āyah* is also a sort of mutual truce, and it also indicates the necessity for the principle of *sadd adh-dharāʾiʿ* (blocking the means) as already mentioned in *al-Baqarah* (2:104). It also is evidence that someone entitled to a right should forgo it if taking it would lead to harm in the *dīn*. This is illustrated by something related from 'Umar ibn al-Khaṭṭāb. He said, 'Do not carry out judgment between relatives when severance [between them] is feared.' Ibn al-'Arabī said, 'If the right is mandatory, then take it in every case. If it is only something acquiesced to, then there is this discussion regarding it.' The word 'animosity' (*'adwan*) here means hostility and aggression.

It is related that the people of Makkah read "*'udduwan*', which is the reading of al-Ḥasan, Abū Rajā', and Qatādah, and it derives from the first reading. Both words mean unjust hostility. The people of Makkah also read "*'aduwan*'. The singular is used for the plural as is the case elsewhere in the Qur'an (26:77), and in 63:4. It is in the accusative as a verbal noun or as a direct object.

In this way We make the actions of every nation seem attractive to them

It means: 'As We make their actions seem attractive to them, so We also made the actions of every other community seem attractive to it.' Ibn 'Abbās said, 'Obedience is made to seem attractive to the people of obedience and disbelief to the people of disbelief. It connects with Allah's words: "*He misguides whomever He wills and guides whomever He wills.*" (74:31)' and it refutes the Qadariyyah.

وَأَقْسَمُوا۟ بِٱللَّهِ جَهْدَ أَيْمَـٰنِهِمْ لَئِن جَآءَتْهُمْ ءَايَةٌ لَّيُؤْمِنُنَّ بِهَا ۚ قُلْ
إِنَّمَا ٱلْـَٔايَـٰتُ عِندَ ٱللَّهِ ۖ وَمَا يُشْعِرُكُمْ أَنَّهَآ إِذَا جَآءَتْ لَا يُؤْمِنُونَ ﴿١٠٩﴾

109 They have sworn by Allah with their most earnest oaths that if a Sign comes to them they will believe in it. Say: 'The Signs are in Allah's control alone.' What will make you realise that even if a Sign did come, they would still not believe?

They have sworn by Allah with their most earnest oaths that if a Sign comes to them they will believe in it.

The strongest oaths are sworn by Allah, and it means the strongest of oaths which they know and which they are capable of swearing. That is because they used to believe that Allah was the greatest God and worshipped these other gods so that they would bring them near to Allah, as He says about them in His words: '*We only worship them so that they may bring us close to Allah.*' (39:3) They used to swear by their fathers, idols and other things and they used also to swear by Allah Almighty and called that their 'most earnest oath' since the oath was by Allah.

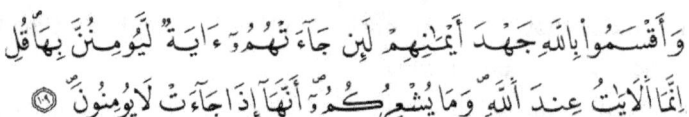

'*Jahd*' is in the accusative for the verbal noun and the regent in it is '*They have sworn*' according to Sībawayh because it has that meaning. The noun '*jahd*' means great effort. You say, 'I did that with great effort (*jahd*).' The noun '*juhd*' means the greatest possible effort, and you say, 'This is as much as I can do (*juhdī*).' Some consider them to mean the same since Allah says: '*Those who can find nothing to give but their own effort* (*juhd*).' (9:79) It is also recited as '*jahd*' by Ibn Qutaybah.

According to commentators, al-Quraẓī, al-Kalbī and others, the reason for the revelation of the *āyah* was that Quraysh said, 'Muḥammad, you tell us that Mūsā struck the stone with his staff and twelve springs burst from it, 'Īsā gave life to the dead, and Thamūd had the She-Camel. So bring us a sign like these so that we can believe in you.' He asked, 'What you do want?' They replied. 'Turn Ṣafā into gold for us. By Allah, if you do that, we will all follow you.' So the Messenger of Allah ﷺ rose to make supplication and Jibrīl came to him and said, 'If you wish, Uḥud will become gold. But if Allah sends a sign and they do not believe when it comes, He will punish them. So leave them until those of them who will repent can repent.' So the Messenger of Allah ﷺ said, 'Rather, let those who will repent do so.' So this *āyah* was revealed. Allah made it clear that He knew before time that such a one would not believe, even if he swore that he would believe.

'*Their most earnest oaths*' are what they consider to be the strongest oaths they can make. There is an extremely important legal question brought up here. It is when a man says that an oath will be binding on him if something specified occurs. Ibn al-'Arabī said, 'This oath was known at the beginning of Islam in other than this form. It was when someone said, "I bind myself with the strongest oath that a person can be bound with." Mālik said, "His wives would be divorced." Then there were a lot of different forms of this until people resorted to a form of which this was the original.' Aṭ-Ṭartūsī said, 'He would be obliged to feed thirty poor people if he broke it because *aymān* is the plural of *yamīn* (oath).' If he said, 'I take an oath,' then one *kaffārah* is obliged for him. If he says, 'I take two oaths,' then there are two *kaffārah*s if he breaks it, and, if he used the plural, then there are three *kaffārah*s.

Aḥmad ibn Muḥammad ibn Mughīth said in his *Wathā'iq*, 'The shaykhs of Qayrawān disagreed about this. Abū Muḥammad ibn Abī Zayd said, "It requires that his wife is triply divorced, that he must walk to Makkah, that he must distribute a third of his property, that he must expiate the oath and that he must free a slave." Ibn Mughīth said, "Ibn Arfa' Ras'ahu and Ibn Badr among the scholars of Toledo, also said that. Shaykh Abū 'Imrān al-Fāsī, Abū al-Ḥasan al-Qābisī, and Abū Bakr ibn 'Abd ar-Raḥmān al-Qarawī said that only one divorce is obliged for him when he does not make a specific intention [about the number of divorces]. Part of their argument regarding that is the transmission of Ibn al-Ḥasan in his *Samā'* from Ibn Wahb: "The maximum amount that anyone can take from another in that instance is the *kaffārah* of an oath."' Ibn Mughīth said, 'Those we named imposed one divorce on someone who says that he "is bound by oaths" because it is not a worse state than someone who says, "The maximum amount that anyone can take from another in that instance is the *kaffārah* of an oath." That is what we say.'

The first cite as evidence the position of Ibn al-Qāsim who spoke about someone who says, 'I swear by the contract of Allah and His strong covenant and guarantee' and the maximum amount that someone can take from someone about not doing something which he then does. He said, 'If he does not mean divorce or emancipation and excepts them from that, then he must do three *kaffārah*s. If he does not have such an intention when he swears, then he must do two *kaffārah*s for his words, "I swear by the contract of Allah and His strong covenant," and must free a slave, divorce his wives, walk to Makkah, and give away a third of his property for his words, "The maximum amount anyone can take from another."'

Ibn al-'Arabī said, 'As for the path of evidence, the definite article in oaths must either be generic or mean previous knowledge. If it is added to denote prior knowledge, then it is made definite by the words, "by Allah". This is what al-Fihrī said. If it is included in generic way, then "divorce" is generic. So it is included in it and no number is detailed. It is sufficient for one meaning to be included in every genus. If all were included in the genus, he would be obliged to give away all his property since giving one's wealth as *ṣadaqah* is a possible oath. Allah knows best.'

Say: 'The Signs are in Allah's control alone.'

This means: 'Say, Muḥammad, "Allah has the power to bring them about, and He will do so if He wishes."'

What will make you realise that even if a Sign did come, they would still not believe?

This means 'What will make you see if that to which you swore to actually does happen?' and the object is elided. Then Allah begins a new sentence with: 'Even if a Sign did come, they would still not believe.' is the reading of Mujāhid, Abū 'Amr and Ibn Kathīr read '*that*' as '*innahā*'. Ibn Mas'ūd attests to this reading where he has '*idhā*' instead [of *innahā*.] Mujāhid and Ibn Zayd said that these words are addressed to the idolaters. Then the words end. Allah has ordained that they will not believe and we know from the following *āyah* that they do not believe. This interpretation resembles those who read the *āyah* with *tā'* as 'you will not believe'. Al-Farrā' and others said that the believers are addressed because the believers said to the Prophet ﷺ, 'O Messenger of Allah, if a sign were to be sent down, perhaps they would believe.' So Allah says, '*What will make you realise?*,' in other words 'what will inform and teach you, O believers?'

The people of Madīnah, al-A'mash and Ḥamzah, however, read it as '*annahā*', meaning: 'Perhaps if it comes, they still will not believe.' Al-Khalīl says that '*annahā*' means 'perhaps', and Sībawayh quoted it. We find in Revelation: '*But how will you know? Perhaps he would be purified.*' (80:3) The Arabs say, 'Go to the market and buy something,' meaning perhaps you will do so. Abū *an-Najm* said:

I told Shaybān, 'Come from meeting him.
  We give a meal to the people from its roast.'

'Adī ibn Zayd said:

O critic! How will you know whether
  My end will be some time today or tomorrow morning?

It means 'perhaps it will be.' [POEM] This usage is used frequently in Arabic: '*ann*' means 'perhaps'. Al-Kisā'ī related that it is like that in the copy of the Qur'an of Ubayy: '*la'allahā*'. Al-Kisā'ī and al-Farrā' said that the '*lā*' is redundant and it means: 'What would make you think that the idolaters would believe when the signs came to them?' So the '*lā*' is redundant as it is in 21:95 where the words: '*There is a ban on any city We have destroyed: they will not return*' mean: 'There is a ban on any destroyed city returning.' This is also the case in 7:12: '*What prevented you from prostrating?*' Az-Zajjāj and an-Naḥḥās and others thought the addition of '*lā*' to be weak and said that it is an error because it is added to what is not ambiguous. It is said that there is some elision in the words and that it means: 'What will make you realise that when the Signs came they would not believe or they would believe?' It is elided because the listener knows it.' An-Naḥḥās and others mentioned it.

وَنُقَلِّبُ أَفْـِٔدَتَهُمْ وَأَبْصَـٰرَهُمْ كَمَا لَمْ يُؤْمِنُوا۟ بِهِۦٓ أَوَّلَ مَرَّةٍ
وَنَذَرُهُمْ فِى طُغْيَـٰنِهِمْ يَعْمَهُونَ ١١٠

110 We will overturn their hearts and sight, just as when they did not believe in it at first, and We will abandon them to wander blindly in their excessive insolence.

This *āyah* is ambiguous (*mushkil*), especially since it says, '*We will abandon them to wander blindly in their excessive insolence.*' It is said that the meaning is: 'We will turn over their hearts and sight on the Day of Rising above the flames of the Fire and the heat of the coals since, in this world, they did not believe.' The words '*We will abandon them*' refer to this world, meaning 'We defer them and do not punish them.' So part of the *āyah* is about the Next World and part is about this world. It is similar to: '*Faces on that Day will downcast.*' (88:2) This is in the Next World and the words: '*labouring, toiling*' apply to this world. It is said that it means, 'We will overturn them in this world,' in other words come between them and belief if that sign comes to them, just as We came between them and belief the first time you called them and showed them miracles. We find in Revelation: '*Know that Allah intervenes between a man and his heart.*' (8:24) The meaning is that they should have believed when the Sign came to them and they saw it with their eyes and recognised it with their hearts. When they did not believe, that was because Allah overturned their hearts and sight.

just as when they did not believe in it at first,

The *kāf* is included to refer to something elided, implying 'They do not believe now just as they did not believe in it at first,' the first time that the Signs came to them which they could not refute, like the Qur'an and other things. It is said that it means: 'We overturn the hearts of those people so that they do not believe in the same way that the unbelievers of previous communities did not believe when they saw the Signs which they had asked for.' It is said that there is a change in the word order and it means: 'When the Signs come, they will not believe as they did not believe the first time and We will overturn their hearts and sight.' The verb '*wander blindly*' means to be confused and was already dealt with in *al-Baqarah* (2:15).

وَلَوْ أَنَّنَا نَزَّلْنَا إِلَيْهِمُ الْمَلَٰٓئِكَةَ وَكَلَّمَهُمُ الْمَوْتَىٰ وَحَشَرْنَا عَلَيْهِمْ كُلَّ
شَيْءٍ قُبُلًا مَّا كَانُوا لِيُؤْمِنُوٓا إِلَّآ أَن يَشَآءَ اللَّهُ وَلَٰكِنَّ أَكْثَرَهُمْ يَجْهَلُونَ ﴿١١١﴾

111 Even if We sent down angels to them, and the dead spoke to them, and We gathered together everything in front of them right before their eyes, they would still not believe unless Allah willed. The truth is that most of them are ignorant.

Even if We sent down angels to them, and the dead spoke to them, and We gathered together everything in front of them

'*Even if We sent down angels to them,*' so that they could see them with their own eyes, '*and the dead spoke to them*' by their being brought to life, '*and We gathered together everything in front of them,'* they would still ask him for signs. '*Qibalan*' means 'directly in front of them' as Ibn 'Abbās, Qatādah and Ibn Zayd said. That is the reading of Nāfi' and Ibn 'Āmir. It is said that it is eye-witnessing. They still would not believe. Muḥammad ibn Yazīd said that it means 'in the direction of' and is an adverb as you say, 'I am due money from (*qibal*) so-and-so.' The rest read it as '*qubulan*' in which case it means 'guarantors,' taking it as the plural of *qabīl*, meaning 'guarantor,' as in Allah's words: '*or bring Allah and the angels here as a guarantee* (*qabīl*)' (17:92), meaning they guarantee that, as al-Farrā' said. Al-Akhfash said that it means 'group by group,' taking *qabīl* to mean 'tribe'. Mujāhid said that. In both cases it is in the accusative as an adverbial *ḥāl*. Muḥammad ibn Yazīd said that it means 'directly in front', as in *Sūrah Yūsuf*, '*If his shirt is torn in front* (*qubul*).' (12:26) Taken from that is the vagina (*qubul*) and anus (*dubur*) of a person. *Qubul* is the site of menstruation. For meeting face-to-face, Abū Zayd used *qubul, muqābalah, qabal* and *qibal*. According to Makkī, the meaning of the two readings is the same. Al-Ḥasan read '*qublan*'. According to the view of al-Farrā', there are words in it which are not spoken, and would make it clear that they would not have grasped the immense sign [if it had occurred]. According to the view of al-Akhfash, it entails combining different categories, which is not well-known. *Ḥashr* is gathering.

They would still not believe unless Allah willed. The truth is that most of them are ignorant.

Only if Allah wills that for them. The exception is for the people of happiness who Allah already knew would believe. This contains solace for the Prophet ﷺ. 'The truth is that most of them are ignorant' meaning they are ignorant of the truth. It is said their ignorance lies in the fact that they do not know that it is not permitted for them to demand more Signs after they have seen one Sign.

وَكَذَٰلِكَ جَعَلْنَا لِكُلِّ نَبِيٍّ عَدُوًّا شَيَٰطِينَ ٱلْإِنسِ وَٱلْجِنِّ يُوحِى بَعْضُهُمْ
إِلَىٰ بَعْضٍ زُخْرُفَ ٱلْقَوْلِ غُرُورًا ۚ وَلَوْ شَآءَ رَبُّكَ مَا فَعَلُوهُ ۖ فَذَرْهُمْ وَمَا
يَفْتَرُونَ ﴿١١٢﴾

112 In this way We have appointed as enemies to every Prophet *shayṭāns* from both mankind and from the jinn, who inspire each other with delusions by means of specious words – if your Lord had willed, they would not have done it, so abandon them and all they fabricate –

In this way We have appointed as enemies to every Prophet

Allah is consoling His Prophet and giving solace to him by saying that as He has tested him by those people, in the same way that He made enemies for every Prophet before him. Then He describes them as being *'shayṭāns from both mankind and from the jinn.'* Sībawayh said *ja'ala* here means 'described'. It is an appositive for *'enemies'*. *'Enemies'* can also be one object and *'shayṭāns'* the second. It is as if Allah were saying, 'He made enemies of *shayṭāns* from both mankind and the jinn.' Al-A'mash recited it with 'jinn' first.

who inspire each other with delusions by means of specious words.

This refers to what the *shayṭāns* of the jinn whisper to human *shayṭāns*. It is called *waḥy* (inspiration) because it is hidden. He called their misrepresentation 'adornments' (*zukhruf*) since they try to make it seem attractive. Part of that usage is calling gold *zukhruf*. Everything which is beautiful and misrepresented is *zukhruf*. A decorator is a *muzakhkharif*. The *zakhārif* of water are the lines which appear on it. The *āyah* means that they inspire one another to that delusion.

Ghurūr (*delusions*) means falsehood. An-Naḥḥās said, 'It is related from Ibn 'Abbās with a weak *isnād* that he said about the words *"inspire each other,"* "There is a *shayṭān* with every jinn and there is a *shayṭān* with every human being. One meets the other and says, 'I misled my person by saying such and such, so mislead your person in the same way.' The other says the same thing. This is their inspiring one another."' 'Ikrimah, aḍ-Ḍaḥḥāk, as-Suddī and al-Kalbī said that. An-Naḥḥās said, 'The first view is indicated by Allah's words: *"The shayṭāns inspire their friends to dispute with you."* (6:121)' This makes the meaning clear.

It is indicated by the sound *ḥadīth* in which the Prophet ﷺ said, 'There is not one of you who does not have a companion of the jinn assigned to him.' It was asked, 'Even you, Messenger of Allah?' He said, 'Even me, except that Allah helped me against him and he surrendered [in Islam] and only commands me to do good' (The reading of the *ḥadīth* can also mean, 'so I was safe from his evil'.) He said, 'None of you,' and did not say, 'nor of the *shayṭāns*' because it is probable that mentioning one of the types includes the other. Allah knows best.

'Awf ibn Mālik related that Abū Dharr reported: 'The Messenger of Allah ﷺ asked me, "Abū Dharr, did you seek refuge with Allah from the evil of the *shayṭāns* of jinn and men?" I asked, "Messenger of Allah, can human beings be *shayṭāns*?" He replied, "Yes, they are worse than the *shayṭāns* of the jinn."' Mālik ibn Dīnār said, 'Human *shayṭāns* are worse for me than the *shayṭāns* of jinn. That is because when I seek refuge with Allah, the *shayṭāns* of the jinn leave me but the human *shayṭāns* come to me to entice me to disobey.' 'Umar ibn al-Khaṭṭāb once heard a woman reciting:

'Women are sweet basil created for you.
All of you desire to smell sweet basil.'

'Umar answered her:

'Women are *shayṭāns* created for us.
We seek refuge with Allah from the evil of *shayṭāns*.'

If your Lord had willed, they would not have done it.

They would not have inspired each other with delusions.

and so abandon them and all they fabricate

'Abandon' is a command implying a threat. Sībawayh said, 'One does not say "*wa dhar*" or "*wada'a*". *Taraka* spares the need for that.' This is only more common. We find in Revelation: *'And abandon (wa dhar) those who'* (6:70): '*leave (wa dhar) them*' (6:91) and: '*has not abandoned (wada'a) you*' (93:4). We find in the *Sunnah*: '...forbid some people from abandoning (*wada'a*) *Jumu'ah*' and: 'when they do acts of disobedience, then leave them.' Az-Zajjāj said, 'The *wāw* (and) is heavy. When it is *taraka*, it has no *wāw* in it and means the same as that with a *wāw*, then that with the *wāw* is left.' This is the meaning of his words and it is his literal expression.

وَلِتَصْغَىٰٓ إِلَيْهِ أَفْـِٔدَةُ ٱلَّذِينَ لَا يُؤْمِنُونَ بِٱلْـَٔاخِرَةِ وَلِيَرْضَوْهُ وَلِيَقْتَرِفُوا۟
مَا هُم مُّقْتَرِفُونَ ﴿١١٣﴾

113 so that the hearts of those who do not believe in the Next World incline towards them and are pleased with them and perpetrate whatever they perpetrate.

so that the hearts of those who do not believe in the Next World incline towards them

Taṣghā means 'to incline', from the verb *ṣaghā, yaṣghū, ṣaghw, ṣughuw*, and *ṣaghā, yaṣghā*. The verb is also read with a *kasrah*: *ṣaghiya, yaṣghā, ṣaghy, ṣughiyy*. *Aṣghā, iṣghā'* both mean the same. A poet said:

You see the ship swerving from all that is firm,
and it is like inclination (*iṣghā'*).

The verb is used to mean 'to tip a vessel on its side to collect what is in it'. Its root is to incline to something because of some desire, and it is also used for the stars when they incline towards setting. We find in Revelation: *'your hearts clearly deviated (ṣaghat).*' (66:4) Abū Zayd said that the verb takes '*ma'a*' (with). The verb is used in a *ḥadīth* for tipping a vessel towards a cat. One also speaks about 'honouring someone in respect of those who incline to him (*ṣāghīyatihi*)', meaning his relatives who incline to him and seek what he has. The verb is used for a camel when it inclines its head towards the saddle, as if it were listening to something when the saddle is tight on it. Dhū ar-Rummah said:

> It inclines close to the ground when the saddle is tight on it
> until its stirrup is level, sitting down.

The *lām* in '*li-tasghā*' is the *lām* of becoming. The regent for this is in the previous *āyah*: the verb '*inspire*', which is also the regent of the verbs '*are pleased with them and perpetrate.*' It is also said that the *lām* is for the imperative, which is an error, because that would require the elision of the *alif.* It is the *lām* of becoming. The same is true in '*are pleased with them and perpetrate*'. Al-Ḥasan, however, recites both with a *sukūn* on the *lām*, making it the *lām* of the command with the meaning of a threat, as you might say, 'Do whatever you like.'

and perpetrate whatever they perpetrate.

The meaning of '*iqtarafa*' (perpetrate) is 'acquire', as Ibn 'Abbās, as-Suddī and Ibn Zayd said. It is used for 'earning' for one's family. *Qārif* is someone who does this. *Qarafa* is also to be suspected of something and it is used for scraping a wound. Its root can mean cutting part of a thing. It is also used for perpetrating a lie. [POEM] The root is to cut something from something else.

أَفَغَيْرَ ٱللَّهِ أَبْتَغِي حَكَمًا وَهُوَ ٱلَّذِيٓ أَنزَلَ إِلَيْكُمُ ٱلْكِتَٰبَ مُفَصَّلًا ۚ
وَٱلَّذِينَ ءَاتَيْنَٰهُمُ ٱلْكِتَٰبَ يَعْلَمُونَ أَنَّهُۥ مُنَزَّلٌ مِّن رَّبِّكَ بِٱلْحَقِّ ۖ
فَلَا تَكُونَنَّ مِنَ ٱلْمُمْتَرِينَ ﴿١١٤﴾

114 'Am I to desire someone other than Allah as a judge when it is He Who has sent down the Book to you clarifying everything?' Those We have given the Book know it has been sent down from your Lord with truth, so on no account be among the doubters.

'Am I to desire someone other than Allah as a judge

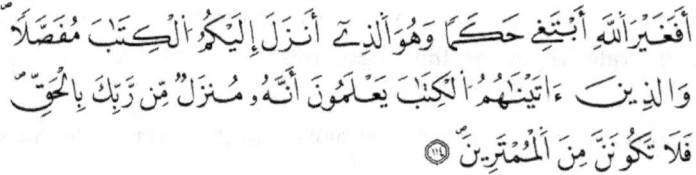

The word '*other*' is in the accusative as the object of the verb '*desire*'. *Ḥakam* (*judge*) is also in the accusative either for determination or as an adverb. The meaning is: 'Do you seek other than Allah as a judge when He will spare you the burden of asking about *āyah*s of the Clarifying Book which are revealed to you?' It is said that the form *ḥakam* is more intensive than *ḥākim* since the name *ḥakam* is only given to someone who judges by the truth because it is an attribute of exaltation in praise. The form *ḥākim* is an adjective which applies to the action, and can be used for someone who judges by other than the truth.

'*Those We have given the Book*' is a reference to the Jews and Christians. It is said that it is only those of them who became Muslim, like Salmān, Ṣuhayb and 'Abdullāh ibn Salām. '*It*' refers to the Qur'an. '*Sent down from your Lord with truth*' means that all it contains of promise and threat is true.

So on no account be among the doubters.

'Do not be one of the doubters when they know that it was revealed from Allah.' 'Aṭā' said, 'Those who were given the Book are the leaders of the Companions of Muḥammad ﷺ: Abū Bakr, 'Umar, 'Uthmān and 'Alī.'

وَتَمَّتْ كَلِمَتُ رَبِّكَ صِدْقًا وَعَدْلًا لَّا مُبَدِّلَ لِكَلِمَٰتِهِۦ وَهُوَ
ٱلسَّمِيعُ ٱلْعَلِيمُ ﴿١١٥﴾

115 The Words of your Lord are perfect in truthfulness and justice. No one can change His Words. He is the All-Hearing, the All-Knowing.

The Words of your Lord are perfect in truthfulness and justice.

The people of Kufa read the plural noun '*Words*' in the singular (*kalimah*) and the rest read it in the plural (*kalimāt*). Ibn 'Abbās said that it refers to the promises of your Lord which are not changed. The '*Words*' here are either verbal expressions or a reference to the promise and threat and other things. Qatādah said that '*Words*' means the Qur'an: there is no changing it and liars cannot add to it or detract from it. The words '*truthfulness and justice*' mean that it contains promises and judgments and that its judgments cannot be refuted nor its promises fail to be kept. Ar-Rummānī reported that Qatādah said, 'There is no changing the judgments in it, even if it were possible to alter the expressions as the people of the Torah and Gospel have changed their book. It is not susceptible to that. The *āyah* indicates the obligation to follow the proofs of the Qur'an because it is true and cannot be changed by anything that might oppose it because it is from a Wise One and none of the details of any affair can be concealed from Him.'

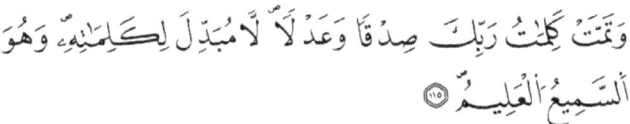

وَإِن تُطِعْ أَكْثَرَ مَن فِي ٱلْأَرْضِ يُضِلُّوكَ عَن سَبِيلِ ٱللَّهِ إِن يَتَّبِعُونَ إِلَّا ٱلظَّنَّ وَإِنْ هُمْ إِلَّا يَخْرُصُونَ ﴿١١٦﴾ إِنَّ رَبَّكَ هُوَ أَعْلَمُ مَن يَضِلُّ عَن سَبِيلِهِۦ وَهُوَ أَعْلَمُ بِٱلْمُهْتَدِينَ ﴿١١٧﴾

116-7 If you obeyed most of those on earth, they would misguide you from Allah's Way. They are only guessing. Your Lord knows best who is misguided from His Way and He knows best those who are guided.

'*Most of those on earth*' are the unbelievers and '*they would misguide you*' from the Path which leads to Allah's reward. The word '*in*' in '*in yattabi'ūna*' means '*ma*' (negation) as does the '*in*' in '*in hum*'. The word *kharaṣ* means guessing and estimating. *Kharṣ* is the noun, and its root is 'to cut' and is used for cutting a branch. A poet said:

You see the fragments of the hard spears thrown at us,
as if they were rods (*khirṣān*) of palm-branches in the hands of the parers.

He means the palm-branches which are cut lengthwise and which are used for counting. It is the plural of *khurṣ*. From that comes the verb *kharaṣa, yakhruṣu kharṣ* which is used when one assesses a tree to take the *kharāj* from it. A *khāriṣ* cuts what is not permitted to cut since he has no certainty. This will be further mentioned in *adh-Dhāriyāt*.

Your Lord knows best

Some people say that '*a'lam*' here simply means 'knows' and quote the words of Ḥātim at-Ta'ī:

Ṭayy' established an alliance with other than us.
Allah knows that we would not disappoint them,

Al-Khansā' said:

The people know that his bowl
Tomorrow will blown by the wind or depart.

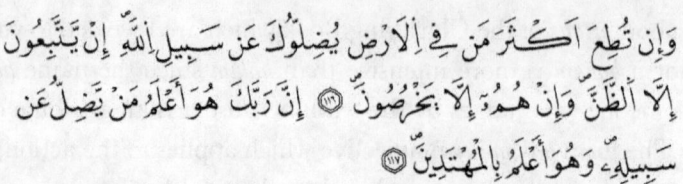

But this is not an argument because it does not tie in with the phrase: '*He knows best those who are guided.*' It is more likely that it has its usual meaning of the comparative or superlative. The preposition '*man*' here means 'which' and so it is the subject of '*are misguided*' and means: 'Your Lord knows best which people are misguided from His Path.' It can also be in the accusative and object of '*knows best*' with removal of the genitive particle meaning: 'who are misguided,' as some Basrans said and it is good because of His words: '*He knows best those who are guided.*' He says in *an-Naḥl*: '*Your Lord knows best who is misguided from His way. And He knows best the guided.*' (16:125). It is also read as '*yuḍillu*' (*who misleads*) with the object elided. The first reading is better because He said, '*He knows best those who are guided.*' If it had been about [their] causing others to be misguided He would have said, 'He knows best the guides.'

فَكُلُوا۟ مِمَّا ذُكِرَ ٱسْمُ ٱللَّهِ عَلَيْهِ إِن كُنتُم بِـَٔايَـٰتِهِۦ مُؤْمِنِينَ ﴿١١٨﴾

118 Eat that over which the name of Allah has been mentioned, if you believe in His Signs.

The *āyah* was revealed because some people came to the Prophet ﷺ and said, 'Messenger of Allah, we eat what we kill, not what Allah kills!' and the *āyah* was revealed: '*Eat that...*' to '*...If you obeyed them you would then be idolaters.*' (6:121) At-Tirmidhī and others transmitted it. 'Aṭā' said, 'This *āyah* is a command to mention the Name of Allah over slaughtering, drinking and all food.' '*If you believe in His Signs*' means to accept His judgments and orders. Faith in them is included and it demands that you both accept them and obey them.

وَمَا لَكُمْ أَلَّا تَأْكُلُوا۟ مِمَّا ذُكِرَ ٱسْمُ ٱللَّهِ عَلَيْهِ وَقَدْ فَصَّلَ لَكُم مَّا حَرَّمَ
عَلَيْكُمْ إِلَّا مَا ٱضْطُرِرْتُمْ إِلَيْهِ ۗ وَإِنَّ كَثِيرًا لَّيُضِلُّونَ بِأَهْوَآئِهِم بِغَيْرِ عِلْمٍ ۗ
إِنَّ رَبَّكَ هُوَ أَعْلَمُ بِٱلْمُعْتَدِينَ ﴿١١٩﴾

119 What is the matter with you that you do not eat that over which the name of Allah has been mentioned, when He has made clear to you what He has made unlawful for you except when you are forced to eat it? Many people lead others astray through their whims and desires without having any knowledge. Your Lord knows best those who overstep the limits.

What is the matter with you that you do not eat that over which the name of Allah has been mentioned,

This means: 'What keeps you from eating that over which the Name of your

Lord has been mentioned, even if you killed it with your own hands?' He has made the *ḥalāl* clear from the *ḥarām* and removed uncertainty and doubt from you. *Mā* is used for a question, but denotes affirmation so the words imply: 'What is it that stops you from eating?' '*An*' is in the genitive implying a genitive particle. It is also sound for it to be in the accusative when a genitive particle is not implied. So the accusative has the meaning of the verb in His words, '*mā lakum*'. It implies: 'What prevents you?' Then there is an exception:

except when you are forced to eat it?

This refers to all that Allah has made *ḥarām*, such as carrion and other things mentioned in *al-Baqarah*. It is a separated exception. Nāfi' and Ya'qūb read '*faṣṣala*' and '*ḥarrama*'. Abū 'Amr, Ibn 'Āmir and Ibn Kathīr read '*fuṣṣila*' and '*ḥurrima*' while the Kufans read '*faṣṣala*' and '*ḥurrima*' and 'Aṭiyyah al-'Awfī reads *faṣala*. The meaning is 'to make clear and manifest'. Abū 'Ubaydah preferred the reading of the People of Madīnah. It is said that it is what is mentioned in *Sūrat al-Mā'idah* (4:3). This is debatable. *Al-An'ām* is Makkan and *al-Mā'idah* is Madinan, so how can it clarify what was not yet revealed unless it means to specify. Allah knows best.

Many people lead others astray through their whims and desires without having any knowledge.

The Kufans read this as *yuḍillūn*, from Form IV and the rest read *yaḍillūn* (Form I). The words: '*through their whims and desires without having any knowledge*' refer to the idolaters when they said, 'What Allah has slaughtered with His knife is better than what you have slaughtered with your knives.' '*Without having any knowledge*' means without any true knowledge of slaughtering since the wisdom in it is to remove the blood that Allah has forbidden which does not happen when an animal has died of suffocation. That is why slaughtering was prescribed in a specific place on the animal so that it becomes the means of removing all the blood in the animal except for what is in its extremities. Allah knows best.

وَذَرُوا۟ ظَـٰهِرَ ٱلْإِثْمِ وَبَاطِنَهُۥٓ ۚ إِنَّ ٱلَّذِينَ يَكْسِبُونَ ٱلْإِثْمَ سَيُجْزَوْنَ بِمَا كَانُوا۟
يَقْتَرِفُونَ ﴿١٢٠﴾

120 Abandon wrong action, outward and inward. Those who commit wrong action will be repaid for what they perpetrated.

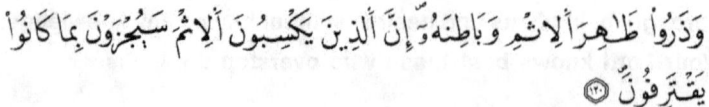

Abandon wrong action, outward and inward.

Scholars say several things about this. In short, the outward referred to applies to physical actions that Allah has forbidden and the inward is the heart's opposition to the commands and prohibitions of Allah. This is a level only reached by those who are godfearing and do good, as evinced by Allah's words: '*...provided they are godfearing and believe and do right actions, and then are godfearing and believe, and then are godfearing and do good.*' (5:93) It is the third rank according to what was already mentioned in the commentary on *al-Mā'idah*. It is said that it refers to what they used to do in the *Jāhiliyyah* by way of outward fornication and taking lovers secretly. We have already discussed all the wrong actions.

وَلَا تَأْكُلُوا۟ مِمَّا لَمْ يُذْكَرِ ٱسْمُ ٱللَّهِ عَلَيْهِ وَإِنَّهُۥ لَفِسْقٌ ۗ وَإِنَّ ٱلشَّيَٰطِينَ
لَيُوحُونَ إِلَىٰٓ أَوْلِيَآئِهِمْ لِيُجَٰدِلُوكُمْ ۖ وَإِنْ أَطَعْتُمُوهُمْ إِنَّكُمْ لَمُشْرِكُونَ ﴿١٢١﴾

121 Do not eat anything over which the name of Allah has not been mentioned. To do so is sheer deviance. The *shayṭāns* inspire their friends to dispute with you. If you obeyed them you would then be idolaters.

Do not eat anything over which the name of Allah has not been mentioned.

Abū Dāwūd said, 'The Jews came to the Prophet ﷺ and said, "We eat from what we kill and not from what Allah kills." Then the Almighty revealed, "*Do not eat anything over which the name of Allah has not been mentioned...*".' An-Nasā'ī related that Ibn 'Abbās said about this, 'The idolaters argued with them and said, "You do not eat what Allah slaughters; you eat what you slaughter." Allah said to them, "Do not eat it. The Name of Allah has not been mentioned over it."'

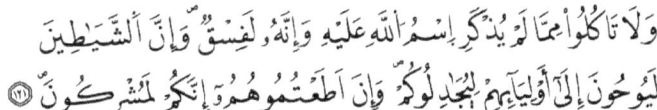

An *uṣūlī* question is derived from this. That is whether the expression which expresses the reason [for the prohibition] is specifically limited or not. Our scholars say that there is no ambiguity regarding the validity of the claim of universality in what the Lawgiver mentions using general non-specific expressions. As for what is mentioned in answer to a question where there is specificity involved, there is elucidation according to what is known about the *uṣūl* of *fiqh* regarding it, unless there is an independent corollary expression used which is connected to the first expression which shows the validity of the intention to make it universal. Allah says: '*Do not eat*' and here that is clearly about the consumption of carrion, and that includes those things over which other than the Name of Allah has been mentioned as part of a general category of things over which the Name of Allah has not been mentioned, so that things over which more than the Name of Allah has been mentioned must be forbidden by the text: '*What has been consecrated to other than Allah.*' (2:173) Does it include that over which a Muslim deliberately fails to mention the Name in slaughter and when releasing hunting animals? Scholars disagree about that, taking five different views on the question.

The first view is that if someone omits it out of forgetfulness, he may eat it all. That is the position of Isḥāq and it is reported from Aḥmad ibn Ḥanbal. If he omits it deliberately, he must not eat it. Mālik and Ibn al-Qāsim said that in the book. It is also the position of Abū Ḥanīfah and his people, as well as ath-Thawrī, al-Ḥasan ibn Ḥayy, 'Īsā and Aṣbagh. Sa'īd ibn Jubayr and 'Aṭā' said that as well. An-Naḥḥās preferred it and said this is better because no one is called *fāsiq* if they forget.

The second view is that if someone omits it either deliberately or due to forgetfulness, he may eat it. That is the view of ash-Shāfi'ī and al-Ḥasan and it is related from Ibn 'Abbās, Abū Hurayrah, 'Aṭā', Sa'īd ibn al-Musayyab, Jābir ibn Zayd, 'Ikrimah, Abū 'Iyāḍ, Abū Rāfi', Ṭāwūs, Ibrāhīm an-Nakha'ī, 'Abd ar-Raḥmān ibn Abī Laylā and Qatādah. Az-Zahrawī reported that Mālik ibn Anas said, 'Slaughtered animals over which the Name has been omitted either deliberately or due to forgetfulness may be eaten. That is also reported from Rabī'ah.' 'Abd al-Wahhāb said, 'Saying the Name is *sunnah*. If the slaughterer omits it forgetfully, the position of Mālik and his people is that the slaughter may be eaten.'

The third view is that if someone omits it deliberately or by overlooking it, it is unlawful to eat it. That is the view of Muḥammad ibn Sīrīn, 'Abdullāh ibn 'Ayyāsh ibn Abī Rabī'ah, 'Abdullāh ibn 'Umar, Nāfi', 'Abdullāh ibn Zayd al-Khatamī, and ash-Sha'bī. Abū Thawr, Dāwūd ibn 'Alī, and Aḥmad in one view also said that.

The fourth view is that if someone omits it deliberately, it is disliked to eat it. Qāḍī Abū al-Ḥasan and Shaykh Abū Bakr among our scholars said that.

The fifth is what Ashhab said: 'An animal slaughtered by someone who omits the Name deliberately may be eaten unless he attaches no importance to it.' Aṭ-Ṭabarī said the same.

[Qāḍī Abū Bakr said, 'It is mandatory to connect these rulings to the Qur'an and *Sunnah* and derive evidence whose basis is the *Sharī'ah*. As for the Qur'an:] the evidence of Allah Almighty is: '*Eat that over which the name of Allah has been mentioned,*' (6:118) and '*Do not eat anything over which the Name of Allah has not been mentioned.*' The two states are therefore clear and the two rulings are clear.'

'Do not eat' is a clear prohibition and it is not permitted to take it as meaning merely dislike since it has some of the requisites of the pure *ḥarām*, and it is not permitted to separate those requisites, in other words, it signifies both prohibition and dislike. This is a fundamental principle. As for the one who forgets, he is not addressed since it is impossible to address him. The precondition is not binding on him.

As for someone who omits the Name deliberately, he must have one of three states. Either he omits it when he makes the animal lie down and says, 'My heart is filled with the Names of Allah and His *tawḥīd*, and so I do not need to mention the Name with my tongue.' His slaughter is allowed because he has remembered Allah. He may say, 'This is not a place for explicit mention since it is not an act of devotion.' His slaughter is also allowed. Or he may say, 'I will not say the Name. What is the point of it?' This is a negligent deviant, and his slaughtered animals may not be eaten. Ibn al-'Arabī said, 'It is extraordinary that the Imām of the Ḥaramayn said, "Mentioning Allah is prescribed in religious acts, and slaughtering is not a religious act." This is contrary to the Book and *Sunnah*. The Prophet ﷺ said in the *Ṣaḥīḥ*, "Eat that which has been bled and had the Name of Allah mentioned over it."'

It may be said that what is meant is mentioning the Name of Allah with the heart because remembrance/mention is the opposite of forgetfulness, and forgetfulness is in the heart, so the place of remembrance is in the heart. It is related from al-Barā' ibn 'Āzib that the Name of Allah is in the heart of every believer, whether or not he says the Name. [That is why the slaughtered animal is permitted when he forgets to say the Name, relying on the Name of Allah being in his heart.] Our response is that the mention should be with both the tongue and the heart. The naming of the idols with the tongue, which was the practice of the Arabs, was abrogated by the Name of Allah being mentioned on the tongue. That is so well-known in the *Sharī'ah* that when Mālik was asked, 'Does one say the Name of Allah when one does *wuḍū'*?' He asked, 'Does he want to slaughter?' As for the *ḥadīth* that is connected to it in the words, 'The Name of Allah is in the heart of every believer,' the *ḥadīth* is weak and no attention is paid to it.

A group of the people of knowledge deduce that saying the Name when slaughtering is not mandatory because of the answer the Prophet ﷺ gave to people who asked him, 'Messenger of Allah, people bring us meat and we do not know whether the Name of Allah has been mentioned over it or not.' The Messenger of Allah ﷺ said, 'Say the Name of Allah over it and eat.' Ad-Dāraquṭnī transmitted it from 'Ā'ishah, and Mālik transmitted it *mursal* from Hishām ibn 'Urwah from his father. There is no disagreement that it is *mursal*. His understanding of the matter is made clear when he says at the end, 'That was at the beginning of Islam,' meaning before Allah's words: '*Do not eat anything over which the Name of Allah has not been mentioned*' were revealed.

Abū 'Umar said, 'This is weak. The contents of the *ḥadīth* itself refutes that. That is because he ﷺ commanded them to say the Name of Allah over the eating. That indicates that the *āyah* about that had already been revealed. One thing that indicates the soundness of what we have said is that this is a Madinan *ḥadīth* and scholars do not disagree that Allah's words: '*Do not eat anything over which the Name of Allah has not been mentioned*' in *Sūrat al-An'ām* were revealed in Makkah.' The meaning of '*sheer deviance*' is disobedience, as Ibn 'Abbās said. *Fisq* is going out (of the *dīn*).

The *shayṭān*s inspire their friends to dispute with you

They whisper and inspire their hearts to argue falsely. Abū Dāwūd related from Ibn 'Abbās about this: 'They say, "You do not eat what Allah has slaughtered; you eat what you slaughter," and then this *āyah* was revealed.' 'Ikrimah said that what is meant by *shayṭān*s in this *āyah* are defiant men among the Magians of Persia. Ibn 'Abbās and 'Abdullāh ibn Kathīr said that the *shayṭān*s are the jinn and the unbelieving jinn who were the friends of Quraysh. It is related that 'Abdullāh ibn az-Zubayr was told, 'Al-Mukhtār says, "I receive revelation."' He said, 'He spoke the truth. *Shayṭān*s reveal to their friends.'

'*To dispute with you*' refers to their words, 'You do not eat what Allah has slaughtered; you eat what you slaughter.' *Mujādalah* is to strongly defend with an argument, derived from *ajdal*, a strong hawk. It is said that it is derived from *jadālah*, which means the ground. It is as if he overcomes someone by the evidence and defeats him, as one is made firm by the ground. It is said that it is derived from *jadl*, which is strong plaiting, and so it is as if each of them twisted the proof of the other until he cut it off, and so it is true in defence of the truth and false in defence of the false.

'*If you obeyed them*' by making carrion lawful, '*you would then be idolaters.*' The *āyah* indicates that anyone who makes lawful what Allah has forbidden becomes an idolater. Allah forbade carrion in a text. If someone accepts it as being lawful from another source, he has committed *shirk*. Ibn al-'Arabī said, 'By obeying an idolater, a believer becomes an idolater if he follows him in respect of belief. If he obeys him in actions and the contract is sound and he remains firm in his *tawḥīd*, he is just a rebel, so understand.' This was already discussed in *al-Mā'idah* (5:81).

أَوَمَن كَانَ مَيْتًا فَأَحْيَيْنَٰهُ وَجَعَلْنَا لَهُۥ نُورًا يَمْشِي بِهِۦ فِي ٱلنَّاسِ
كَمَن مَّثَلُهُۥ فِي ٱلظُّلُمَٰتِ لَيْسَ بِخَارِجٍ مِّنْهَا كَذَٰلِكَ زُيِّنَ
لِلْكَٰفِرِينَ مَا كَانُوا۟ يَعْمَلُونَ ﴿١٢٢﴾

122 Is someone who was dead and whom We brought to life, supplying him with a light by which to walk among people, the same as someone who is in utter darkness, unable to emerge from it? That is how what they were doing is made to seem attractive to the unbelievers.

Is someone who was dead and whom We brought to life,

The majority read '*a wa*' with a *fatḥah* on the *wāw*, adding the interrogative *hamzah* to it. Al-Mūsāyyabī related it from Nāfi' ibn Abī Nu'aym as '*aw*'. An-Naḥḥās said that it can be applied to the meaning, implying: 'Look and reflect. Should I seek other than Allah as a judge?' It is said that it means: 'He was dead when he was a drop and then Allah brought him to life by breathing the *rūḥ* into him.' Ibn Baḥr related it. Ibn 'Abbās said it means: 'Or was an unbeliever and We guided him. It was revealed about Ḥamzah and Abū Jahl.'

Zayd ibn Aslam and as-Suddī said it means: 'We brought 'Umar to life' and '*someone in utter darkness*' is Abū Jahl. The sound view is that it applies generally to every believer and unbeliever. It is said that he was dead through ignorance and Allah brought him to life with knowledge. One of the people of knowledge cited something from one of the poets of Basra that indicates the soundness of this interpretation.

Ignorance before death is death for its people.
    Their bodies are graves before the graves.
One cannot command a corpse to life by knowledge.
    He has no resurrection until the true resurrection.

The '*light*' referred to here is that of guidance and faith. Al-Ḥasan said that it is the Qur'an. It is also said that it is wisdom. It is said that it is the light mentioned in Allah's words: '*...with their light streaming out in front of them and to their right*' (57:12) and '*Wait for us so that we can borrow some of your light.*' (57:13) He walks by the light.

the same as someone who is in utter darkness, unable to emerge from it? That is how what they were doing is made to seem attractive to the unbelievers

The word *mathal* here is redundant. You say, 'I am nobler than one like you,' meaning 'I am nobler than you.' A similar usage is found in Allah's words: '*…the reprisal for it is a livestock animal equivalent (*mithl*) to what he killed*' (5:95) and '*Nothing is like Him.*' (42:11) It is said that it means: 'like one who is in the darkness.' *Mathal* and *mithl* mean the same. *Shayṭān* makes the worship of idols seem attractive and deludes them into thinking that they are better than the Muslims.

وَكَذَٰلِكَ جَعَلْنَا فِي كُلِّ قَرْيَةٍ أَكَٰبِرَ مُجْرِمِيهَا لِيَمْكُرُوا فِيهَا ۖ وَمَا
يَمْكُرُونَ إِلَّا بِأَنفُسِهِمْ وَمَا يَشْعُرُونَ ﴿١٢٣﴾

123 And likewise in every city We set up its greatest wrongdoers to plot in it. They plot against themselves alone, but they are not aware of it.

It means: 'We made what the unbelievers were doing seem attractive to them. That is what We did in every city.' '*Wrongdoers*' is the first object of *ja'ala* and '*greatest*' is the second, and there is a change in word order. *Ja'ala* means to become. *Akābir* is the plural of *akbar.* Mujāhid said that it means the great men. It is said that they are the leaders and great men. They are singled out for mention because they have greater power to corrupt. *Makr* is devising which is the opposite of going straight. Its root means to unravel. Someone who is described as *mākir* veers from what is straight, i.e. turns away from it. Mujāhid said, 'They used to put four men on every pass to warn people against following the Prophet ﷺ, as those of past nations did with their Prophets.' The phrase '*They plot against themselves alone*' means that the evil effects of their plotting will revert to them. It is that Allah will repay the plotters with a painful punishment. '*They are not aware of it*' immediately since they are deeply ignorant of the fact that the evil effects of their plotting will rebound on them.

وَإِذَا جَاءَتْهُمْ آيَةٌ قَالُوا لَن نُّؤْمِنَ حَتَّىٰ نُؤْتَىٰ مِثْلَ مَا أُوتِيَ
رُسُلُ اللَّهِ ۘ اللَّهُ أَعْلَمُ حَيْثُ يَجْعَلُ رِسَالَتَهُ ۗ سَيُصِيبُ الَّذِينَ أَجْرَمُوا
صَغَارٌ عِندَ اللَّهِ وَعَذَابٌ شَدِيدٌ بِمَا كَانُوا يَمْكُرُونَ ﴿١٢٤﴾

124 When a Sign comes to them, they say, 'We will not believe until we have been given the same as the Messengers of Allah were given.' Allah knows best where to place His Message. Debasement in the sight of Allah and a severe punishment will strike those who did wrong for the plots that they concocted.

When a Sign comes to them, they say, 'We will not believe until we have been given the same as the Messengers of Allah were given.'

Allah now explains another aspect of their ignorance, which is that they said, 'We will not believe until we are Prophets and given the same signs as Mūsā and 'Īsā were given.' It is similar to Allah's words: *'In fact each one of them wants to be given an unfurled scroll.'* (74:52) The pronoun *'them'* in *'comes to them'* is an allusion to the great men who were mentioned. Al-Walīd ibn al-Mughīrah said, 'If Prophethood had been true, I would have been more entitled to it than you because I am older and wealthier than you are.' Abū Jahl said, 'By Allah, we are not pleased with him and we will never follow him unless revelation comes to us as it comes to him.' Then the *āyah* was revealed.

It is said that they did not ask for Prophethood but in fact said, 'We will not believe you until Jibrīl and the angels come to us to inform us of your truthfulness.' The first is sounder because the Almighty says: *'Allah knows best where to place His Message'* (6:124), in other words the one who is to be trusted with it. *Ḥaythu* is not an adverb here, but a noun in the accusative as the object to expand it. It means: 'Allah knows best who is worthy of His Message.' The basic sentence would be, 'Allah knows best [the places where to put] His Message,' and then it is elided.

Debasement in the sight of Allah and a severe punishment will strike those who did wrong for the plots that they concocted.

Ṣaghār (debasement) is damage, abasement and humiliation, as is *sughr.* The verbal noun is *ṣaghar.* Its root is 'smallness'. It is as if abasement diminishes a person. It is also said that its root is *ṣaghar* which is meekness. *Ṣāghir* means someone who is meek. Land which is *muṣghirah* has only a few plants which are not tall. Ibn as-Sikkīt said that. *'In the sight of Allah'* i.e. 'Debasement from Allah will smite those who do wrong.' It is said that it means: 'It is confirmed that abasement from Allah will smite those who do wrong.' An-Naḥḥās said that this is the best verdict because the preposition *'inda* is used properly.

فَمَن يُرِدِ ٱللَّهُ أَن يَهْدِيَهُۥ يَشْرَحْ صَدْرَهُۥ لِلْإِسْلَٰمِ ۖ وَمَن يُرِدْ أَن يُضِلَّهُۥ يَجْعَلْ صَدْرَهُۥ ضَيِّقًا حَرَجًا كَأَنَّمَا يَصَّعَّدُ فِى ٱلسَّمَآءِ ۚ كَذَٰلِكَ يَجْعَلُ ٱللَّهُ ٱلرِّجْسَ عَلَى ٱلَّذِينَ لَا يُؤْمِنُونَ ﴿١٢٥﴾

125 When Allah desires to guide someone, He expands his breast to Islam. When He desires to misguide someone, He makes his breast narrow and constricted as if he were climbing up into the sky. That is how Allah defiles those who do not believe.

When Allah desires to guide someone, He expands his breast to Islam.

He makes things more ample for him, gives him success and makes the reward seem attractive to him. It is said that the verb *sharaḥa* means to split, but its root indicates expansion. Allah expands the breast and makes it large enough to accept the evidence of Islam. When a matter is 'expanded', it is made clear and elucidated. Among Quraysh the verb *sharaḥa* was used to describe having intercourse with a woman from the back. *Sharḥ* also means solving, as a riddle is solved. You say, 'I exposed what was hidden.' The verb is also used for cutting meat lengthways in slices. A poet said:

How often I ate liver and stomach
and then stored the sliced (*musharraḥ*) fat tail.

Sharīḥah is a piece of it and is the word used to describe every extended piece of fat meat.

When He desires to misguide someone, He makes his breast narrow and constricted

When Allah desires to make someone err: '*He makes his breast narrow and constricted.*' This refutes the Qadariyyah. Similar to this *āyah* is found in the *Sunnah* in the words of the Prophet ﷺ: 'If He desires good for someone, He gives him understanding of the *dīn*.' It is transmitted in the two *Ṣaḥīḥ* Collections. That only happens by the expansion and illumination of the breast. The *dīn* consists of acts of worship, as Allah says: '*The dīn in the sight of Allah is Islam.*' (3:19). If He does not desire good for a person, He constricts his breast and makes it hard for him to understand so that he does not understand. Allah knows best. It is related that 'Abdullāh ibn Mas'ūd asked, 'Messenger of Allah, does the breast expand?' He answered, 'Yes. Light enters the heart.' He asked, 'Does it have a sign?' The Prophet ﷺ replied, 'Aversion to the abode of delusion, turning to the Abode of Eternity and preparing for death before death comes.'

Ibn Kathīr reads *'narrow'* as *'ḍayqan'* instead of *'ḍayyiqan'*, like *hayn* and *layn*. They are two dialectical forms. Nāfi' and Abū Bakr read *'constricted'* as *'ḥarijan'*, which means narrowness. The meaning is mirrored in the two words in the *āyah*. The rest read it as *ḥaraj*, which is the plural of *harajah*, which is great constriction. A *ḥarajah* is a thicket and its plural can be both *ḥaraj* and *ḥarajāt*. Another expression derived from the verb means 'to constrict oneself to abandon one's passion or acts of disobedience,' as al-Harawī said.

Ibn 'Abbās said, '*Ḥaraj* is an area of dense trees. So it is as if the heart of the unbeliever does not reach wisdom as the shepherd is unable to reach an area densely covered with trees.' It is related that 'Umar ibn al-Khaṭṭāb said this, and Makkī, ath-Tha'labī and others mentioned it. Every narrowness is constriction, *ḥaraj* and *ḥarij*. Al-Jawharī said, 'A place that is *ḥaraj* or *ḥarij* is confined and full of trees so that a shepherd cannot reach it.' *Ḥaraj* and *ḥarij* are like *waḥad* and *waḥid*, *farad* and *farid*, and *danaf* and *danif*. They mean the same and someone else related it from al-Farrā'. The verb is used for the constricting of the breast. *Ḥaraj* means sin, and it is also a thin camel. It is said that it is a tether on the surface of the earth, as Abū Zayd said. So it is a word which has several meanings. *Ḥaraj* also means wood which is tied together as a litter to carry the dead, as al-Asma'ī said. It is what Imru' l-Qays said:

> You will either see me on the saddle of Jābir,
> Or on a bier (*ḥaraj*) like the camel-litter, with the shroud fluttering.

Sometimes it is placed above a woman's bier. In describing a male ostrich, 'Antarah says:

> They follow the crest of his head, as if
> it was a litter (*ḥaraj*) on a bier, tented for them.

Az-Zajjāj said that *ḥaraj* is the most constricted kind of constriction. It is said that someone's bosom is constricted (*ḥaraj*), and it means that there is a constriction in his breast. It is said that *ḥarij* is an active participle. An-Naḥḥās said that *ḥarij* is an active participle and *ḥaraj* is a verbal noun.

as if he were climbing up into the sky.

Ibn Kathīr read it as *'yaṣ'ādu'* (instead of *yaṣṣa''adu*), from the verb meaning to ascend. Allah likens the unbeliever in his aversion to faith and its weight on him to someone on whom is imposed to do something he cannot do, just as he cannot climb up into the sky. Abū Bakr and an-Nahka'ī also read it as *yassā'adu* which also means to impose on someone time after time that which he cannot do. That is heavy for the one who does it. The rest recite it as *yaṣṣa''adu* which means the same: to impose on someone time after time something that he cannot do. This is seen in other verbs like *tajjarra'a* and *taffaraqa*. It is related that 'Abdullāh ibn Mas'ūd recited '*yataṣa''adu*'. An-Naḥḥās said that the meaning is the same as *yaṣṣa''adu* and *yaṣṣā'adu*. It means: the breast of the unbeliever is constricted as if he wanted to climb up into the sky which he is unable to do. It is as if he were being invited to do that. It is also said that the meaning is: his heart almost climbs up into the sky seeking to be far from Islam.

That is how Allah defiles those who do not believe

He does this as well as making their breasts constricted in their bodies. The root of *rijs* is stench. Ibn Zayd said that it is punishment. Ibn 'Abbās said that *rijs* is *shayṭān*, meaning that Allah gives him power over them. Mujāhid said that *rijs* is that which has no good in it. The meaning, and Allah knows best, is that '*those who do not believe*' will be cursed in this world and punished in the Next.

وَهَٰذَا صِرَٰطُ رَبِّكَ مُسْتَقِيمًا ۗ قَدْ فَصَّلْنَا ٱلْـَٔايَٰتِ لِقَوْمٍ يَذَّكَّرُونَ ﴿١٢٦﴾

126 This is the path of your Lord – straight. We have made the Signs clear for people who remember.

The path which you are on, O Muḥammad, and the believers, is the *dīn* of your Lord with no twisting in it. *Faṣṣala* means to make clear.

۞ لَهُمْ دَارُ ٱلسَّلَٰمِ عِندَ رَبِّهِمْ ۖ وَهُوَ وَلِيُّهُم بِمَا كَانُوا۟ يَعْمَلُونَ ﴿١٢٧﴾

127 They will have the Abode of Peace with their Lord. He is their Protector because of what they have done.

'*They*' are those who remember. '*The Abode of Peace*' is the Garden, and the Garden is the Abode of Allah, as the Ka'bah is called the House of Allah. It can mean the Abode of Safety, that in which one is safe from calamities. '*With their Lord*' means what is guaranteed for them with Him is that He will convey them to it. He is their Helper and Aide.

وَيَوْمَ نَحْشُرُهُمْ جَمِيعًا يَٰمَعْشَرَ ٱلْجِنِّ قَدِ ٱسْتَكْثَرْتُم مِّنَ ٱلْإِنسِ وَقَالَ
أَوْلِيَآؤُهُم مِّنَ ٱلْإِنسِ رَبَّنَا ٱسْتَمْتَعَ بَعْضُنَا بِبَعْضٍ وَبَلَغْنَآ أَجَلَنَا ٱلَّذِيٓ
أَجَّلْتَ لَنَا قَالَ ٱلنَّارُ مَثْوَيٰكُمْ خَٰلِدِينَ فِيهَآ إِلَّا مَا شَآءَ ٱللَّهُ إِنَّ رَبَّكَ
حَكِيمٌ عَلِيمٌ ﴿١٢٨﴾

128 On the Day He gathers them all together: 'Company of jinn, you gained many followers among mankind.' And their friends among mankind will say, 'Our Lord, we benefited from one another, and now we have reached the term which You determined for us.' He will say, 'The Fire is your home. You will be in it timelessly, for ever, except as Allah wills. Your Lord is All-Wise, All-Knowing.'

On the Day He gather them all together: 'Company of jinn, you gained many followers among mankind.'

The noun '*Day*' is in the accusative by an implied verb, implying: 'We will say on the Day We gather them.' What is meant is the gathering of all creatures on the Day of Rising. '*Company of jinn*' is a call to them. The phrase '*You gained many followers among mankind*' means they benefited from people. A verbal noun ascribed to the object and genitive particle is elided. It presages Allah's following words: '*Our Lord, we benefited from one another.*'

'Our Lord, we benefited from one another,

This refutes the view of those who say that the jinn are those who listened to mankind, because mankind also listened to them. The sound view is that each of them listened to the other, which is what the Arabic means. The jinn benefit from mankind, since they enjoy the fact that humans obey them, and mankind benefits by being influenced by the jinn so that they fornicate and drink wine at their instigation. It is said that when a man on a journey passes by a valley and fears for himself, he should say, 'I seek refuge with the Lord of this valley from all that I am wary of.' We read in Revelation: '*Certain men of mankind used to seek refuge with certain men of the jinn but they increased them in wickedness.*' (72:6) This is how humans benefit from the jinn. As for how the jinn benefit from letting humans hear them, it is by means of the false tales they give them as well as by inspiring soothsayers and magicians. It is also said that the jinn benefit by people alleging that the jinn are able to defend them from what they fear. The meaning of the *āyah* is to rebuke both those who misguide and those who are misguided and to censure them in the Next World before the eyes of all the worlds.

and now we have reached the term which You determined for us.'

That is death and the grave where they fully acknowledge the regret they feel.

He will say, 'The Fire is your home. You will be in it timelessly, for ever, except as Allah wills.

'*Your home*' is your place of residence. *Mathwā* is where one remains. '*Except as Allah wills*' is an exception to the first sentence. Az-Zajjāj said, 'It refers to the Day of Rising, indicating that they will be in the Fire forever except for the length of time Allah wishes it to take to gather them from their graves and the time of the period of their reckoning.' So the exception is separate. It is said that the exception refers to the Fire, implying except for the punishment Allah wills for them at times without the Fire. Ibn 'Abbās said that the exception is for the people of oaths. He also said that this *āyah* stipulates that all unbelievers will be made to stand. It is said that '*except as Allah wills*' is about them remaining without punishment in this world. The meaning of this will be discussed in *Hūd* (11:106). '*Your Lord is All-Wise*' in punishing them and in all His actions, '*All-Knowing*' of the amount of punishment they will receive.

وَكَذَٰلِكَ نُوَلِّي بَعْضَ الظَّالِمِينَ بَعْضًا بِمَا كَانُوا يَكْسِبُونَ ﴿١٢٩﴾

129 In that way We make the wrongdoers friends of one another because of what they have done.

The meaning is: 'In the same way as I dealt with those I described to you who benefited one another, I also make some wrongdoers friends of one another and then they will declare they have nothing to do with one another.' The meaning of '*nuwallī*' is 'We join in friendship.' Ibn Zayd says that it means: 'We give the wrongdoing jinn power over wrongdoing humans.' So Allah gives some of the wrongdoers power over others so that they destroy and humiliate them. This is a threat to the wrongdoer that if he does not stop his wrongdoing, Allah will give someone else power over him. The *āyah* includes all of those who wrong themselves or wrong those under them or merchants who wrong people in their trade or thieves and others.

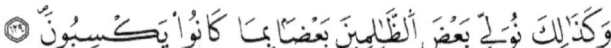

Fuḍayl ibn 'Iyāḍ said, 'When you see a wrongdoer taking revenge on a wrongdoer, stop and look at him in wonder.' Ibn 'Abbās said, 'When Allah is pleased with people, He gives power to the best of them. When Allah is angry with a people, He gives power to the worst of them.' We find in a report from the Prophet ﷺ, 'If someone abets a wrongdoer, Allah will give him power over him.' It is said that it means 'We will entrust them to one another in respect of the unbelief they have chosen, as tomorrow we will consign them to their leaders who will not be able to save them from the punishment. In the same way We do that to them in the Next World, so also We will do it to them in this world.'

It is said that Allah's words: '*We will hand him over to whatever he has turned to*' (4:115) mean 'We will entrust him to what he entrusted himself to.' Ibn 'Abbās said, 'Its explanation is that when Allah desires evil for a people, he gives power to the worst of them.' This is indicated by the words of Allah: '*Any disaster that strikes you is through what your own hands have earned.*' (42:30)

يَٰمَعْشَرَ ٱلْجِنِّ وَٱلْإِنسِ أَلَمْ يَأْتِكُمْ رُسُلٌ مِّنكُمْ يَقُصُّونَ عَلَيْكُمْ ءَايَٰتِى
وَيُنذِرُونَكُمْ لِقَآءَ يَوْمِكُمْ هَٰذَا ۚ قَالُوا۟ شَهِدْنَا عَلَىٰٓ أَنفُسِنَا ۖ وَغَرَّتْهُمُ
ٱلْحَيَوٰةُ ٱلدُّنْيَا وَشَهِدُوا۟ عَلَىٰٓ أَنفُسِهِمْ أَنَّهُمْ كَانُوا۟ كَٰفِرِينَ ﴿١٣٠﴾

130 Company of jinn and men! did not Messengers come to you from among yourselves relating My Signs to you and warning you of the encounter of this Day of yours? They will say, 'We testify against ourselves.' The life of this world deluded them and they will testify against themselves that they were unbelievers.

Company of jinn and men! did not Messengers come to you from among yourselves

On the Day We gather them, We will say to them, '*Did not Messengers come to you?*' They will admit that they did which will disgrace them. The phrase '*from among yourselves*' means in terms of creation, obligation and being addressed with responsibility. Since the jinn are among those who are addressed and responsible, Allah says, 'from among you,' even if the Messengers are from mankind. Mankind dominates in the address in this case as is the case with the masculine in reference to a group of men and women.

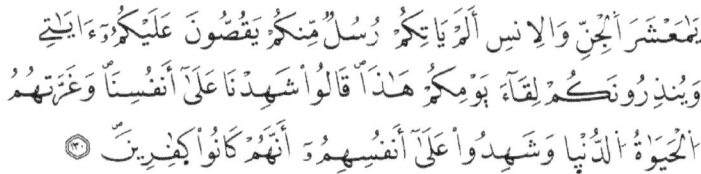

Ibn 'Abbās said that the Messengers of the jinn are those who conveyed to their people any of the Revelation they heard as in His words: '*They went back to their people, warning them.*' (46:29). Muqātil and aḍ-Ḍaḥḥāk said, 'Allah sent Messengers from the jinn in the same way that He sent from them from mankind.' Mujāhid said, 'Messengers from mankind and Warners from the jinn.' Then he recited: '*They went back to their people, warning them.*' (46:29) It is the sense of what Ibn 'Abbās said, and will be dealt with in *al-Aḥqāf.* Al-Kalbī said, 'The Messengers before Muḥammad ﷺ were sent to both men and jinn.' This is not sound. In *Ṣaḥīḥ Muslim* there is the *ḥadīth* of Jābir ibn 'Abdullāh al-Anṣārī in which the Messenger of Allah ﷺ said, 'I was given five things which no Prophet before me was given. Every Prophet was sent only to his people but I was sent to everyone, of all races.' This will be dealt with in *al-Aḥqāf* (46). Ibn 'Abbās said, 'The previous Messengers were sent to mankind alone but Muḥammad ﷺ was sent to both mankind and jinn.' Abū al-Layth as-Samarqandī mentioned it.

It is said, 'Some of the jinn listened to the Prophets and then returned to their people and informed them, as happened with our Prophet ﷺ. They are called Messengers of Allah, even if there is no text about that being the case. We find in Revelation: '*From out of them come glistening pearls and coral*' (55:22), when it actually means from only one of them. They come from the salt water, not the fresh water. That also applies to the Messengers who come from mankind, not the jinn. So the meaning of '*from among yourselves*' is actually 'from one of them.' This is permitted, as we already mentioned.

It is said that the Messengers are included in the expression 'from among you' because both mankind and jinn are included in the presentation at the Rising and the Reckoning, not other creatures. Since in that presentation they will be reckoned together in terms of reward and punishment, so they are addressed in the same way here, as if they were one group because they were both created to worship, and reward and punishment are for worship. Although the source of the jinn is smokeless fire and our source is earth, our creation being different from their creation, some of them are believers and some unbelievers. Our enemy Iblīs is also their enemy, hostile to those of them who believe and a friend to those who reject. They also have Shī'ah, Qadariyyah and Murji'ite sects following our Book. Allah describes them in *Sūrat al-Jinn*: '*Some of us are Muslims and some are degenerates*' (72:14) and: '*Among us there are some who are righteous and some who are other than that. We follow many different paths*' (72:11) as will be explained there. 'They will say, "*We testify against ourselves,*" meaning they testify that the Message was conveyed to them.

The life of this world deluded them.

It is said that this is addressed by Allah to the unbelievers, meaning that they were deluded by the life of this world, being under the delusion of thinking that it would last and fearing that they would lose it if they believed. The words: '*They will testify against themselves,*' mean they will acknowledge their disbelief. Muqātil said that this happens when their limbs testify to their *shirk* and to what they were doing.

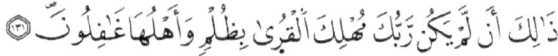

ذَٰلِكَ أَن لَّمْ يَكُن رَّبُّكَ مُهْلِكَ ٱلْقُرَىٰ بِظُلْمٍ وَأَهْلُهَا غَٰفِلُونَ ﴿١٣١﴾

131 That was because their Lord would never have destroyed the cities unjustly while their people were unaware.

Allah would not destroy cities for their injustice, for their idolatry, before Messengers were sent to them, so that they would not be able to say that no herald or warner had come to them. It is said that it means 'I do not destroy the cities on account of the *shirk* of those of them who associate.' So it is like the words: '*No bearer of any burden can bear that of any other.*' (6:154) If Allah does destroy them before sending the Messengers, He is able to do whatever He wishes. 'Īsā said, '*If you punish them, they are Your slaves.*' (5:118). Al-Farrā' said that the initial '*That*' can be in the accusative and means: 'He did that to them because He would not destroy the cities unjustly.'

وَلِكُلٍّ دَرَجَٰتٌ مِّمَّا عَمِلُوا۟ ۚ وَمَا رَبُّكَ بِغَٰفِلٍ عَمَّا يَعْمَلُونَ ﴿١٣٢﴾

132 All have ranks according to what they did. Your Lord is not unaware of what they do.

The words '*All have ranks according to what they did,*' refer to jinn and men, as evidenced by another *āyah*: '*Those are people of whom the statement about the nations, both of jinn and men, who passed away before them, has also proved true. Truly they were the lost.*' (46:18) Allah then says: '*Everyone will be ranked according to what they did. We will pay them in full for their actions and they will not be wronged.*' (46:19) This contains a clear indication that obedient jinn will be in the Garden and those who are disobedient will be in the Fire, the same as mankind. It is the soundest of what is said about the matter. The meaning is that all have ranks in reward according to the extent of their obedience, and ranks in punishment in the Fire according to the extent of their disobedience. '*Your Lord is not unaware,*' means He does not overlook or forget. *Ghaflah* happens when you abandon something because of your being busy with something else. '*They do*' is the reading of all but Ibn 'Āmir, who reads '*ta'malūn*' (you do.)

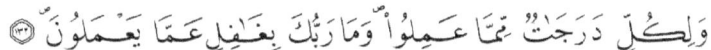

وَرَبُّكَ ٱلْغَنِىُّ ذُو ٱلرَّحْمَةِ إِن يَشَأْ يُذْهِبْكُمْ
وَيَسْتَخْلِفْ مِنۢ بَعْدِكُم مَّا يَشَآءُ كَمَآ أَنشَأَكُم مِّن ذُرِّيَّةِ
قَوْمٍ ءَاخَرِينَ ﴿١٣٣﴾

133 Your Lord is the Rich Beyond Need, the Possessor of Mercy. If He wanted, He could remove you and replace you with anything else He wanted to, just as He produced you from the descendants of another people.

'*Your Lord is the Rich Beyond Need*': He has no need of His creation or their actions. He is '*the Possessor of Mercy*' to His friends and those who obey Him. '*If He wanted, He could remove you*' by making you die and eradicating you by means of His punishment, '*and replace you with anything else He wanted to,*' with another generation better and more obedient than you. The *kāf* in the sentence is in the accusative, meaning: He would appoint after you whatever He wished just as He produced you in the first place. This is similar to His words: '*If you turn away, He will replace you with a people other than yourselves.*' (47:38) The meaning is to put others in your place.

إِنَّ مَا تُوعَدُونَ لَءَاتٍ وَمَآ أَنتُم بِمُعْجِزِينَ ﴿١٣٤﴾

134 What you are promised will come about and you can do nothing to prevent it.

'*What you are promised*' may be something bad, and what is meant here is the punishment of the Next World. It can also refer to the arrival of the Last Day. It can also mean simply what you are promised and the time at which it will arrive, be it good or evil, but it usually refers to good. The same idea is related from al-Ḥasan. You cannot evade it. The verb '*prevent*' here means to be unable to escape.

قُلْ يَٰقَوْمِ ٱعْمَلُوا۟ عَلَىٰ مَكَانَتِكُمْ إِنِّى عَامِلٌ فَسَوْفَ تَعْلَمُونَ
مَن تَكُونُ لَهُۥ عَٰقِبَةُ ٱلدَّارِ إِنَّهُۥ لَا يُفْلِحُ ٱلظَّٰلِمُونَ ﴿١٣٥﴾

135 Say: 'My people, do as you are doing, just as I am doing. You will certainly come to know who will have the best home in the end. The wrongdoers will certainly not be successful.'

Abū Bakr reads *makānātikum,* the plural of *makānatikum. Makānah,* position, is way. It means: 'Be firm on what you have and I will be firm on what I have.' If it is asked, 'How can it be conceivable that they are commanded to be firm on what they have when they are unbelievers?' the answer is that this is a threat similar to Allah's words: '*Let them laugh little and weep much.*' (9:82) This is indicated by what follows: '*You will certainly come to know who will have the best home in the end.*' This means that the end which is praised belongs to the person who is praised, in other words the one who has success in the Abode of Islam and inherits the earth will have the best in the Next World, meaning the Garden.

Az-Zajjāj says that it means your position in this world. Ibn 'Abbās, al-Ḥasan and an-Nakha'ī say that it is your standpoint. Al-Qutabī says 'in your place'. 'Just as I am doing' omits '*'alā makānitī*' since it is implied. The preposition '*man*' in '*who will have*' is in the accusative meaning 'the one who' since that is known. It can also be in the position of object because a question is not affected by what is before it and the verb is connected, and so it means: 'you will know which of us will have the best home in the end.' Something similar is seen in 18:12. '*Who will have*' is read as *takūnu* by most, while Ḥamzah and al-Kisā'ī read *yakūnu.*

وَجَعَلُوا۟ لِلَّهِ مِمَّا ذَرَأَ مِنَ ٱلْحَرْثِ وَٱلْأَنْعَٰمِ نَصِيبًا فَقَالُوا۟
هَٰذَا لِلَّهِ بِزَعْمِهِمْ وَهَٰذَا لِشُرَكَآئِنَا ۖ فَمَا كَانَ
لِشُرَكَآئِهِمْ فَلَا يَصِلُ إِلَى ٱللَّهِ ۖ وَمَا كَانَ لِلَّهِ فَهُوَ
يَصِلُ إِلَىٰ شُرَكَآئِهِمْ ۗ سَآءَ مَا يَحْكُمُونَ ﴿١٣٦﴾

136 They assign to Allah a share of the crops and livestock He has created, saying, 'This is for Allah,' – as they allege – 'and this is for our idols.' Their idols' share does not reach Allah whereas Allah's share reaches their idols! What an evil judgment they make!

Dhara'a, yadhra'u, dhar' means 'to create.' There is some elision and concision in the words, implying 'They assign a share to their idols.' This is indicated by what comes after it. It is one of the things *shayṭān* made seem attractive to them and enticed them to do, so that they claimed to give some of their property to Allah and some to their idols. Ibn 'Abbās, al-Ḥasan, Mujāhid and Qatādah said that. The meanings are similar. They assign Allah a share and their partners a share. Then what they spent on behalf of their idols and their priests was replaced from what was designated for Allah. What was designated for Allah was spent on guests and the poor and not replaced at all. They said, 'Allah has no need of it and our partners are poor.' This is an aspect of their ignorance and their false claim; the claim they made is a lie. Qāḍī Shurayḥ said, 'Everything can be alluded to, and the allusion to a lie is to say, "as they allege."' They used to lie about these things because the *Sharī'ah* had not revealed that.

Sa'īd ibn Jubayr related that Ibn 'Abbās said, 'Whoever wants to learn about the ignorance of the Arabs should recited from *āyah* 130 of *Sūrat al-An'ām* to Allah's words: "*Those who kill their children foolishly without any knowledge have lost.*" (6:140)' Ibn al-'Arabī said, 'These are sound words. They directed their incapable minds to the revision of the *ḥalāl* and the *ḥarām* out of foolishness without any knowledge or right judgment. The one who acts out of ignorance by adopting gods is subject to the worst kind of ignorance and commits the greatest of crimes. Aggression against Allah Almighty is worse than aggression against creatures. The evidence that Allah is One in His Essence, One in His Attributes and One in His creation is clearer and more evident than the evidence that such and such a thing is *ḥalāl* and such and such a thing *ḥarām*.'

It is related that a man said to 'Amr ibn al-'Āṣ, 'In spite of the perfection of your intelligence and your ample discernment, you worship a Stone!' 'Amr said, 'Those are minds outwitted by their Creator.' This is what Allah reports about the Arabs and their ignorance, which was removed by Islam and which Allah nullified by sending the Messenger ﷺ. So it is clear to us that we should put an end to it so that it does not show its face and forget it so that it is not remembered unless our Lord mentions it in a text and explains it as He mentions the disbelief of the unbelievers. The wisdom in doing that, and Allah knows best, is that He already decided that disbelief and confusion will continue until the Day of Rising.

Yaḥyā ibn Waththāb, as-Sulamī, al-A'mash and al-Kisā'ī have '*zu'mihim*' and the rest '*za'mihim*'. They are two dialects. '*Their idols' share does not reach Allah,*' means it does not reach the poor. '*What an evil judgment they make!*' means that their ruling is evil. Ibn Zayd said, 'When they sacrificed what was intended for Allah, they mentioned the name of their idols over it, and when they sacrificed what was for their idols, they did not mention the name of Allah. It was blameworthy for them to omit the mention of Allah, and it is included under not eating that over which the Name of Allah has not been mentioned.'

وَكَذَٰلِكَ زَيَّنَ لِكَثِيرٍ مِّنَ ٱلْمُشْرِكِينَ قَتْلَ
أَوْلَٰدِهِمْ شُرَكَآؤُهُمْ لِيُرْدُوهُمْ وَلِيَلْبِسُوا۟ عَلَيْهِمْ
دِينَهُمْ ۖ وَلَوْ شَآءَ ٱللَّهُ مَا فَعَلُوهُ ۖ فَذَرْهُمْ وَمَا
يَفْتَرُونَ ﴿١٣٧﴾

137 In the same way their associates have made killing their children appear good to many of the idolaters, in order to destroy them and confuse them in their *dīn*. If Allah had willed, they would not have done it; so abandon them and what they fabricate.

In the same way their associates have made killing their children appear good to many of the idolaters

It means: 'As it was made attractive for them to assign a share to Allah and to their idols, so it was made to seem attractive to many idolaters by their associates to kill their children.' Mujāhid and others said, 'Killing daughters was made to seem attractive to them out of fear of poverty.' Al-Farrā' and az-Zajjāj said, 'Their associates here are those who served the idols.' It is said that it is other people who entice them to error. And it is said that it refers to the *shayṭāns*. This is a reference to the secret burying of girls alive out of fear of their being captured, fear of poverty, and fear of having to support them. The *shayṭāns* are called associates because they obeyed them in disobeying Allah and they put them on a par with Allah in making obedience to them obligatory. It is said that a man in the *Jāhiliyyah* would swear by Allah that if he had a certain number of sons born to him, he would sacrifice one of them, as 'Abd al-Muṭṭalib did when he vowed to sacrifice his son 'Abdullāh.

Then it is said that there are four readings of the *āyah*. The majority reading is '*zayyana – qatla – shurakā'uhum*'. This is the reading of the people of Makkah and Madīnah, the people of Kufa and the people of Basra. The noun '*idols*' is in the nominative by being the subject of '*made seem attractive*' because they made that seem attractive, but did not do the killing and so '*qatl*' (*killing*) is in the accusative as the object of '*made seem attractive*' and '*their children*' is a *muḍāf* of the object. The root in the verbal noun is ascribed to the subject because they originated that action and have no need of it and it needs an object, so here it is a *muḍāf* of the subject while in meaning it is actually a *muḍāf* of the object since it implies: 'their idols made it seem attractive to many of the idolaters to kill their children.' Then the *muḍāf* is elided. Makkī said that this recitation is the chosen one because of the soundness of the syntax and because it is the reading of the majority.

The second reading has '*zuyyina – qatlu awlādihim – shurakā'uhum*' which is the reading of al-Ḥasan. Ibn 'Āmir and the people of Syria have *zuyyina – qatlu awlādahim – shurakā'ihum*' as is related by Abū 'Ubayd. Others related that the people of Syria recited *zuyyina – qatlu awlādihim – shurakā'ihum*'. The second reading is good and permitted, and *qatl* is a noun whose subject is not named and '*idols*' is in the nominative by an implied verb indicated by '*made to seem attractive*,' implying their idols made it seem attractive to them. This structure is permissible as in '*ḍuriba Zaydun 'Amrun*,' which means that 'Amr hit him. [POEM]

Ibn 'Āmir and 'Āṣim from the transmission of Abū Bakr recited '*yusabbaḥū lahu*' (24:36-37) which implies 'men who glorify Him'. Ibrāhīm ibn Abī 'Ablah recited '*qutila aṣḥābu-l-ukhdūdi an-nāru dhātu-l-wuqūd*' (85:4-5) meaning 'the fire killed them.'

An-Naḥḥās said, 'As for what Abū 'Ubayd related from Ibn 'Āmir and the people of Syria, it is not permitted in language or in poetry. Grammarians allow a separation between the *muḍāf* and the *muḍāf ilayhi* by an adverb because it does not cut off. That is not the case with nouns that are not adverbs: it is bad grammar. Makkī said, 'This reading contains some weakness because of the separation between the *muḍāf* and the *muḍāf ilayhi* because such separation is possible in poetry with adverbs.' Al-Mahdawī said that this reading has a separation between the *muḍāf* and the *muḍāf ilayhi* [POEMS] Abū Ghānim Aḥmad ibn Ḥamdān the grammarian said that the reading of Ibn 'Āmir is permitted in Arabic. This is a scholar's error, and when a scholar errs, it is not permitted to follow him and one leaves his view for the consensus. As it is obliged to return from an error or oversight on their part to the consensus, so it is even more proper if he insists on other than what is correct. They only permit the separation of the *muḍāf* from the *muḍāf ilayhi* by an adverb due to the exigencies of poetry. [POETIC EXAMPLES]

Al-Qushayrī said, 'People have said that this is ugly, but that is impossible because when a reading is established by multiple transmissions from the Prophet ﷺ, it is eloquent and not ugly. It is found in the words of the Arabs and the copy of 'Uthmān's Qur'an where "*idols*" has a *yā'*. This indicates the reading of Ibn 'Āmir.' In this reading, '*killing*' is connected to the idols because the idols have made that seem attractive to them and called them to do it. So the action is attributed to the doer as obliged in the root, but there is a separation between the *muḍāf* and the *muḍāf ilayhi*. It implies: their idols' killing of their children was made seem attractive to many of the idolaters.

An-Naḥḥās said, 'As for what is related by other than Abū 'Ubayd, which is the fourth reading, it is permitted to make 'associates' (partners, *shurakā'uhum*) an appositive for 'children' because their children share in lineage and inheritance. The verb *irdā'* means 'destroy' and the *lām* is the *lām* of becoming. The phrase 'confuse them in their *dīn*' means in respect of that which was pleasing to them, i.e. they command them to falsehood and make them doubt their *dīn*. They were following the *dīn* of Ismā'īl, and there was no killing of children in it, and so the truth was covered up. This is why they became confused.

If Allah had willed, they would not have done it.

Allah makes it clear that their disbelief was willed by Allah, which refutes the Qadariyyah. 'What they fabricate' is what they say about Allah having partners.

وَقَالُوا هَٰذِهِۦٓ أَنْعَٰمٌ وَحَرْثٌ حِجْرٌ لَّا يَطْعَمُهَآ إِلَّا مَن نَّشَآءُ
بِزَعْمِهِمْ وَأَنْعَٰمٌ حُرِّمَتْ ظُهُورُهَا وَأَنْعَٰمٌ لَّا يَذْكُرُونَ
ٱسْمَ ٱللَّهِ عَلَيْهَا ٱفْتِرَآءً عَلَيْهِ سَيَجْزِيهِم بِمَا كَانُوا يَفْتَرُونَ ﴿١٣٨﴾

138 They say, 'These animals and crops are sacrosanct. No one may eat them except those we wish', – as they allege – and animals on whose backs it is forbidden to ride, and animals over which they do not mention Allah's name, inventing falsehood against Him. He will repay them for the things they have invented.

Then Allah mentions another form of their ignorance. The word '*ḥijr*' is read as *ḥujur* by Abān ibn 'Uthmān and *hajr* by al-Ḥasan and Qatādah. Al-Ḥasan also says *ḥujr*. Abū 'Ubayd said that Hārūn said that al-Ḥasan has a *ḍammah* on *ḥujr* throughout the Qur'an except in 25:53 where he has it with a *kasrah*. It is related from Ibn 'Abbās and az-Zubayr as '*ḥirj*' as it is in the copy of the Qur'an of Ubayy. '*Ḥirj*' is a dialectical form of *ḥaraj*. It designates constriction and sin, and so it means forbidden. *Taḥarraja* as a verb is when someone makes himself refrain from becoming involved in anything that resembles the unlawful. So *ḥijr* is a word with various meanings. Here it means what is forbidden, and so its root is prohibition. The intellect is called *hijr* since it refuses ugly things. A *qāḍī* has *ḥijr*, meaning interdicts. It is used for limitation of legal competence. *Ḥijr* is used for the intellect in Allah's words: '*Is there not in that an oath for the intelligent* (*dhī ḥijr*)?' (89:5) *Ḥijr* is also a mare and kinship. A poet said:

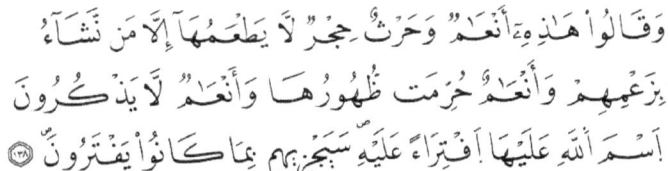

They want to put him far from me.
He has close lineage to me and kinship (*ḥijr*).

A person's bosom or care is both *ḥijr* or *ḥajr*, but *ḥajr* is more common. It means that they made some livestock and crops forbidden and assigned them to their idols.

No one may eat them except those we wish

They are the servants of the idols. Then Allah makes it clear that this judgment was not brought by any *Sharīʿah* and says '*as they allege.*'

and animals on whose backs it is forbidden to ride

This means that they are let loose for their gods as is the case with their share. Mujāhid said that what is meant are the *baḥīrah, waṣīlah* and *ḥām*. The '*animals over which they do not mention Allah's name*' are what they sacrifice to their idols. Abū Wā'il said that they do not perform *ḥajj* on them. They lie about Allah because they said that He is the one who commanded them to so this. So it is in the accusative as the direct object. It is said that they forge lies, and it is in the accusative since it is a verbal noun.

وَقَالُوا۟ مَا فِى بُطُونِ هَٰذِهِ ٱلْأَنْعَٰمِ خَالِصَةٌ لِّذُكُورِنَا وَمُحَرَّمٌ عَلَىٰٓ أَزْوَٰجِنَا ۖ وَإِن يَكُن مَّيْتَةً فَهُمْ فِيهِ شُرَكَآءُ ۚ سَيَجْزِيهِمْ وَصْفَهُمْ ۚ إِنَّهُۥ حَكِيمٌ عَلِيمٌ ﴿١٣٩﴾

139 They say, 'What is in the wombs of these animals is exclusively for our men and unlawful for our wives. But if it is stillborn, they can share in it.' He will repay them for their false depiction. He is All-Wise, All-Knowing.

They say, 'What is in the wombs of these animals is exclusively for our men and unlawful for our wives.

This is yet another type of their ignorance. Ibn 'Abbās said, 'It is about milk which they made lawful for men and unlawful for women.' It is said that it is the foetuses. They said, 'They are for the males. But if any of them are stillborn, men and women may eat it.'

The *tā' marbūṭah* on *khāliṣah* is for emphasis, as a scholar is *'allāmah*, as al-Kisā'ī and al-Akhfash said. *Khāliṣah* is in the nominative as a predicate of the inchoative which is '*mā*'. Al-Farrā' said that it is feminine because it refers to cattle. This is considered an error by some because what is in their wombs is not part of them, and so it is not similar to the words: '*some travellers may discover him*' (12:10) because 'some' travellers are travellers. Al-Farrā', however, says that what is in their wombs are animals like them and so it is feminine for that reason. It is said that it is a plural for what is in the wombs. It is said that '*mā*' may refer to milk or foetuses and that is why it is in the feminine in meaning and masculine in expression which is why the adjective '*unlawful*' is in the masculine rather than the feminine. This is also supported by the reading of al-A'mash who has '*khāliṣ*'.

Al-Kisā'ī said that *khāliṣ* and *khāliṣah* mean the same although the letter *hā'* can be added for emphasis. Qatādah has *khāliṣah* in the accusative as an adverbial *ḥāl* which is connected to *mā*. The predicate of the inchoative is elided as when you say, 'The one who is standing in the house is Zayd.' This is the position of the Basrans. Al-Farrā' says that it is in the accusative on account of the break in the sentence. That is similar to the reading of Sa'īd ibn Jubayr as '*khāliṣan*'. Ibn 'Abbās read '*khāliṣatu*' with *iḍāfah* and so it is a second inceptive whose predicate is '*for our men*'. The sentence is a predicate of *mā* and so it is possible that '*khāliṣ*' is an appositive for *mā*. So there are five readings.

'*Our wives*' means 'our daughters' according to Ibn Zayd and others say that it is 'our women'. '*But if it is stillborn*' (*yakun mayta*) is read as both *yakun* and *takun*. '*They share*' refers to the men and women. *Fīhi* means the stillborn because it is an animal, which strengthened by the reading with *yā'*, and one does not say *fīhā*. '*Maytah*' (*stillborn*) is in the nominative, meaning 'if a stillborn happens or occurs'. If it is in the accusative, it means 'if the child is dead.'

He will repay them for their false depiction.

This is their lies and fabrication, meaning that Allah will punish them for that. '*Waṣfahum*' is in the accusative by the removal of the genitive, which would be '*bi-waṣfihim*'. The *āyah* is evidence for the necessity of scholars learning what their opponents say even though they do not accept it, so that they know its invalidity and how to refute it. This is because Allah informed His Prophet ﷺ and the Companions of the opposition of those who opposed them among the people of their time, so that they would recognise the corruption of what they said.

قَدْ خَسِرَ ٱلَّذِينَ قَتَلُوٓا۟ أَوْلَٰدَهُمْ سَفَهًۢا بِغَيْرِ عِلْمٍ وَحَرَّمُوا۟ مَا رَزَقَهُمُ
ٱللَّهُ ٱفْتِرَآءً عَلَى ٱللَّهِ ۚ قَدْ ضَلُّوا۟ وَمَا كَانُوا۟ مُهْتَدِينَ ﴿١٤٠﴾

140 Those who kill their children foolishly without any knowledge and make what Allah has provided for them unlawful, inventing lies against Allah, such people are lost. They are misguided. They are not guided.

Allah talks of their being lost when they buried their daughters alive and made the *baḥīrah* and other things unlawful on their basis of their own intellection. So they killed their children foolishly out of fear of poverty and forbade themselves their property without fearing consequential poverty, and so Allah explained to them the contradictions inherent in their thinking. Some of the Arabs used to kill their children out of fear of poverty as Allah mentions in other places as well. Some of them killed them foolishly without any rationale for their killing, like the tribes of Rabī'ah and Muḍar. They killed their daughters out of sheer fanaticism. Some said, 'The angels are the daughters of Allah, so join daughters to daughters.'

It is related that one of the Companions of the Messenger of Allah ﷺ was sorrowful in the presence of the Messenger of Allah ﷺ and the Messenger of Allah ﷺ asked him, 'Why are you sad?' He replied, 'Messenger of Allah, I committed a wrong action in the *Jāhiliyyah* and I fear that Allah will not forgive me, even though I have become Muslim!' He told him, 'Tell me about your wrong action.' He said, 'Messenger of Allah, I was among those who used to kill their daughters. A daughter was born to me and my wife asked me to leave her and so I did so until she was grown up and of age. She was one of the most beautiful of women and people asked me for her hand in marriage. Fury entered me and my heart could not bear to give her in marriage and I left her at home without a husband. I told my wife, "I want to go to such-and-such a tribe to visit my relatives. Send her with me." So she was happy to do that and dressed her up in clothes and jewellery and made me promise not to betray her. I took her to the top of a well and I looked into the well and the girl realised that I wanted to throw her down the well. She clung to me and began to weep, saying, "My father, what do you want to do to me!" I felt mercy. Then I looked at the well and fury entered me and she clung to me, saying, "Father, do not break your promise to my mother!" I began to look at the well and then look at her and showed mercy until *Shayṭān* overpowered me and I took her and threw her into the well upside down, while she was crying out, "My father! You have killed me!" I remained there until her voice stopped and went back.' The Messenger of Allah ﷺ and the Companions wept. He said, 'If I had been commanded to punish anyone for what he did in the *Jāhiliyyah*, I would have punished you.'

وَهُوَ ٱلَّذِىٓ أَنشَأَ جَنَّٰتٍ مَّعْرُوشَٰتٍ وَغَيْرَ مَعْرُوشَٰتٍ وَٱلنَّخْلَ وَٱلزَّرْعَ
مُخْتَلِفًا أُكُلُهُۥ وَٱلزَّيْتُونَ وَٱلرُّمَّانَ مُتَشَٰبِهًا وَغَيْرَ مُتَشَٰبِهٍ
كُلُوا۟ مِن ثَمَرِهِۦٓ إِذَآ أَثْمَرَ وَءَاتُوا۟ حَقَّهُۥ يَوْمَ حَصَادِهِۦ وَلَا
تُسْرِفُوٓا۟ إِنَّهُۥ لَا يُحِبُّ ٱلْمُسْرِفِينَ ١٤١

141 It is He Who produces gardens, both cultivated and wild, and palm-trees and crops of diverse kinds, and olives and pomegranates, both similar and dissimilar. Eat of their fruits when they bear fruit and pay their due on the day of their harvest, and do not be profligate. He does not love the profligate.

It is He Who produces gardens, both cultivated and wild,

'*Produces*' here means 'creates'. '*Ma'rūshāt*' are gardens which are held up by trellises and elevated. Ibn 'Abbās said they are what spreads out on the ground like vines, crops and melons. '*Wild*' (*ghayra ma'rūshāt*) means what stands on a trunk such as palms and other trees. It is also said that '*ma'rūshāt*' are those whose trees are tall and that the root of *ta'rīsh* means to elevate. Ibn 'Abbās said that '*ma'rūshāt*' are those gardens which are firm and which people elevate on trellises, and those which are not refers to the fruits produced in the wilderness and mountains. This is indicated by the reading of 'Alī which is '*maghrūsāt*'.

and palm-trees and crops of diverse kinds

The masculine singular noun is used for both (*nakhl, zar'*) and they are part of the gardens because of their excellence as mentioned in *al-Baqarah* (2:98). The term '*diverse kinds*' means the taste of some is excellent and of others not so good. They are called '*food*' (*ukl*) because they are eaten. The noun '*ukluhu*' is in the nominative by the inceptive, and '*diverse*' is its adjective, but since it precedes it and is ruled by the accusative, it is in the accusative, as when you say, 'I have a baker, a slave.' [ANOTHER POEM] It is said that '*diverse*' is in the accusative for the *ḥāl*.

Abū Isḥāq az-Zajjāj said, 'This is a problematic question in grammar because one says, "He raised them and its produce (*ukl*) (meaning its fruit) was not diverse." The response to this is that Allah Almighty raised them since He says: "*Allah is the Creator of everything.*" (39:62) So He informs us that He raised them with their diverse types of food. Another response is that He made them grow, determining diversity in them. Sībawayh made this clear when he said, "I passed by a man with a hawk with which he will hunt tomorrow" which is based on the *ḥāl*. It is as you say, "You will enter the house eating and drinking," meaning that they are determined for that.' A third response is that when He made them grow, their tastes were diverse, meaning that if it has fruits, their taste varies. He did not say '*ukluhā*' because it is sufficient to repeat the masculine for one of them as we see in 62:11. This was already mentioned.

and olives and pomegranates, both similar and dissimilar.

'*Olives and pomegranates*' are added to them and '*similar and dissimilar*' is in the accusative for the *ḥāl*. There are three points in connection with this. One is that the evidence is established by the fact that different things require an agent to make them different.

The second is about Allah's favour. If He had wished, He could have not created nourishment for us, nor nourishment of good appearance and delicious tastes. He also could have made it not easy to harvest. Nothing is obliged for Him.

The third is that it indicates power, in that water, which naturally sinks, rises by the power of Allah the One, Knower of the Unseen worlds, from the bottom of the tree to the top until it reaches its branches and appears in the leaves which grow and in the amply sized, radiantly coloured, delicious tasting fruit it produces and its annually renewed crop. What have scientific categories to do with this? What part in this do philosophers and their followers play? Is it in the power of nature to produce this perfection or is this not an extraordinary order! Intellectually, that is only perfectly achieved by One who possesses knowledge, power and will. Glory be to the One who has a sign and end in everything!

The way this is connected to what is before it is that when the unbelievers lied about Allah and associated others with Him and made things lawful and unlawful, they were indicating His Oneness since He is their Creator and gave them this provision.

Eat of their fruits when they bear fruit and pay their due on the day of their harvest,

Although these are two verbs which come in the imperative tense, the first indicates permissibility, as in Allah's words: '*…spread through the earth*' (62:10) and only the second is mandatory. It is not forbidden in the *Sharī'ah* to join together the permissible and the mandatory. Allah begins with the blessing of eating before giving His command to pay what is due, which indicates that beginning with the blessing is part of His favour before imposition of responsibility.

pay their due on the day of their harvest,

People disagree about what is meant by '*due*' here. Anas ibn Mālik, Ibn 'Abbās, Ṭāwūs, al-Ḥasan, Ibn Zayd, Ibn al-Ḥanafiyyah, aḍ-Ḍaḥḥāk and Sa'īd ibn al-Musayyab said that it refers to obligatory *zakāt*: the tenth and the twentieth. Ibn Wahb and Ibn al-Qāsim related that from Mālik in connection with the explanation of this *āyah* and some of the companions of ash-Shāfi'ī said that.

Az-Zajjāj related that it was said that this *āyah* was revealed in Madīnah. 'Alī ibn al-Ḥusayn, 'Aṭā', al-Ḥakam, Ḥammād, Sa'īd ibn Jubayr and Mujāhid said that it is a due on property for which Allah recommended other than *zakāt*. This is related from Ibn 'Umar and Muḥammad ibn al-Ḥanafiyyah, and Abū Sa'īd al-Khudrī related it from the Prophet ﷺ. Mujāhid said, 'When it is harvested and there are poor people present, give some of the ears to them. If they are cut, then throw them some clusters. When it is threshed and winnowed, then give them some of it. When you know its measure, then take the *zakāt* from it.'

A third verdict is that it was abrogated by *zakāt* because this *sūrah* is Makkan and the *āyah* of *zakāt* was only revealed in Madīnah: '*Take ṣadaqah from their wealth*,' (9:103) and '*Establish the prayer and pay the zakāt*.' (2:43) That is related from Ibn 'Abbās, Ibn al-Ḥanafiyyah, al-Ḥasan, 'Aṭiyyah al-'Awfī, an-Nakha'ī and Sa'īd ibn al-Jubayr. Sufyān said, 'I asked as-Suddī about this *āyah* and he said, "It was abrogated by the tenth and twentieth." I said, "From whom [is this]?" He answered, "From the scholars."'

Abū Ḥanīfah commented on this *āyah* and the general statement in the words of the Prophet ﷺ, 'There is a tenth due on what the sky irrigates, and a twentieth on what is irrigated by watering and buckets,' that it refers to the obligation of *zakāt* on all food or other things that the earth produces. Abū Yusuf said, 'Except for firewood, grass, herbs, figs, palm leaves, rushes, and sugar cane.' The general position is that there is no *zakāt* on such things, relying on the fact that the aim of the *ḥadīth* is to clarify that from which a tenth is taken and that from which a twentieth is taken. Abū 'Umar said, 'There is no disagreement between scholars that *zakāt* is mandatory on wheat, barley, dates and raisins.' One group said, 'There is no *zakāt* due on other than them.' That is related from al-Ḥasan, Ibn Sīrīn and ash-Sha'bī, and among the Kufans, Ibn Abī Laylā, ath-Thawrī, al-Ḥasan ibn Ṣāliḥ, Ibn al-Mubārak, and Yaḥyā ibn Ādam took that position. It is also the position of Abū 'Ubayd. It is related from Abū Mūsā from the Prophet ﷺ

and it is the position of Abū Mūsā. He only took *zakāt* from wheat, barley, dates and raisins. Wakī' mentioned it from Ṭalḥah ibn Yaḥyā from Abū Burdah from his father.

Mālik and his people said, '*Zakāt* is mandatory on every food which is stored.' Ash-Shāfi'ī said that. Ash-Shāfi'ī said, '*Zakāt* is mandatory on what is dried and stored and is a staple foodstuff. There is nothing on olives because they are a condiment.' Abū Thawr said the like of that. Aḥmad has various views, the most evident of which is that *zakāt* is obliged on all that Abū Ḥanīfah said when it is measured in *wasq*s and he also obliges it on almonds, because they are measured, but not on walnuts, which are counted. His evidence is found in the words of the Prophet ﷺ, 'There is no *zakāt* on less than five *wasq*s of dates or grain.' He said, 'The Prophet ﷺ made it clear that the place of the obligation is the *wasq* and he clarified the amount on which the right is taken.'

An-Nakha'ī believed that *zakāt* is taken on everything that the earth produces, even a tenth on bundles of greens. People disagree about that. It is the view of 'Umar ibn 'Abd al-'Azīz. He wrote that a tenth should be collected on that which the earth produces, whether little or a lot. 'Abd ar-Razzāq mentioned it from Ma'mar from Simāk ibn al-Faḍl, who said, "Umar wrote...' It is the position of Ḥammād ibn Abī Sulaymān and his student Abū Ḥanīfah. This is what Ibn al-'Arabī inclined to in his *Aḥkām*: 'Abū Ḥanīfah took the *āyah* as his source and discerned the truth. He used it to support and strengthen the Ḥanafī school.' He said in *Kitāb al-Qabas bimā 'alayhi-l-imām Mālik ibn Anas*: 'Allah says: "*...olives and pomegranates, both similar and dissimilar.*" (6:99) People disagree about all or part of what is included. We explained the core of that in *al-Aḥkām*. *Zakāt* is connected to staple foods rather than vegetables as was made clear. Ṭā'if had pomegranates, peaches and citron and neither the Messenger of Allah ﷺ nor any of his Caliphs went against that or mentioned it.' Even if this is not mentioned in the *Aḥkām*, it is the sound view regarding this question. There is nothing due on green vegetables.

As for the *āyah*, there is disagreement about it. Is it an *āyah* of judgment, abrogated or taken as recommended? There is no definitive evidence for which ruling to accept. What is absolutely sound is what Ibn Bukayr mentioned in his *Aḥkām*: 'Kufa was conquered after the death of the Prophet ﷺ and after the establishment of the rulings in Madīnah. Is it possible that anyone with the least insight could imagine that a ruling of the *Sharī'ah* like this would be invalidated and not acted on in the Abode of the Hijrah and home of Revelation, even in the caliphate of Abū Bakr, until the Kufans acted by it? There is a misfortune for anyone who thinks that!'

Part of the revelation which conveys this meaning is Allah's words: '*O Messenger! deliver what has been sent down to you from your Lord. If you do not do it you will not have conveyed His Message.*' (5:68) Do you think that he ﷺ concealed anything which he was commanded to convey or clarify? Far be it from that! Allah says: '*Today I have perfected your dīn for you and completed My blessing upon you.*' (5:3). Part of the perfection of the *dīn* is that he ﷺ did not collect any *zakāt* on vegetables. Jābir ibn 'Abdullāh is reported as saying in ad-Dāraquṭnī, 'The cucumber vines we have which produce tens of thousands of fruits have no *zakāt* taken on them.' Az-Zuhrī and al-Ḥasan said, '*Zakāt* is taken on the price of vegetables when they are ripe and the price reaches 200 *dirhams*.' Al-Awzā'ī said that about the price of fruits. There is no evidence for their ruling as we mentioned.

At-Tirmidhī related from Mu'ādh that he wrote to the Prophet ﷺ to ask him about vegetables, and he said, 'There is nothing due on them' This is also related from Jābir, Anas, 'Alī, Muḥammad ibn 'Abdullāh ibn Jaḥsh, Abū Mūsā and 'Ā'ishah. Ad-Dāraquṭnī mentioned their *ḥadīth*s. At-Tirmidhī said, 'Nothing attributed to the Prophet ﷺ about this is sound.' Some Ḥanafīs find evidence in the *ḥadīth* of Ṣāliḥ ibn Mūsā from Manṣūr from Ibrāhīm from al-Aswad from 'Ā'ishah who said that the Messenger of Allah ﷺ said, '*Zakāt* is due on the vegetables which the earth produces.' Abū 'Umar said that this *ḥadīth* is not related by any of the reliable companions of Manṣūr. It is part of what Ibrāhīm said.' When deduction based on the *Sunnah* is dropped because of the weakness of the *isnād*s, there only remains what we mentioned about making the generality of the *āyah* specific, and the generality in the words: 'A tenth on what the sky waters' is made specific.

Abū Yūsuf and Muḥammad said, 'There is no *zakāt* owed on vegetables except on that which has fruits which last, except for saffron and the like which is measured. There is *zakāt* due on them.' Muḥammad considered safflower and linen to be seeds. When the seeds of safflower and linen reach five *wasq*s, then the safflower and linen follow the seeds and a tenth or a twentieth is taken from them. As for cotton, there is nothing on it for less than five loads, a load being 300 Iraqi *mann*s. There is nothing on the herb '*wars*' or saffron less than five loads. When one of them reaches five *mann*s, then there is *zakāt* on it, a tenth or a twentieth. Abū Yūsuf said, 'That is also the case with sugar cane which contains sugar and is located in land on which the tenth is due and not *kharāj* land: the same is due on it as is due on saffron.'

'Abd al-Malik ibn al-Mājishūn obliged *zakāt* on the plants from which the fruits come rather than the fruits themselves. This differs from the position of Mālik and his people. They believe that there no *zakāt* on almonds, walnuts, hazelnuts and the like, even though they can be stored. Similarly they believe that there is no *zakāt* on plums, apples or pears, nor on similar fruits which are not dried or stored. There is disagreement about figs. According to the people of the *Maghrib* who follow the school of Mālik, there is no *zakāt* due on figs. An exception to this is 'Abd al-Malik ibn Ḥabīb who thinks that there is *zakāt* on them according to the school of Mālik, making them analogous to dates and raisins. This is also the position of a group of the Baghdadi Mālikī scholars: Ismā'īl ibn Isḥāq and those who follow him.

Mālik said in the *Muwaṭṭā'*: 'The *sunnah* that is undisputed among us and which I have heard from the people of knowledge, is that there is no *zakāt* on any kind of fresh (soft) fruit, whether it be pomegranates, peaches, figs, or anything that is like them or not like them as long as it is fruit.' Abū 'Umar observed, 'Figs are included in this and I think (and Allah knows best) that he did not know that they can be dried, stored and used as a staple. If he had known that, he would not have included them in this context because they are more like dates and raisins than pomegranates.' I heard that al-Abharī and a group of his people used to give a *fatwā* that there is *zakāt* due on them, and they thought that it is the position of the school of Mālik according to his fundamental principles which they know. Figs are measured and one considers five *wasq*s and similar measures in them. They apply to figs the same ruling they think applies to dates and raisins.

Ash-Shāfi'ī said, 'There is no *zakāt* on any fruits other than dates and raisins because the Messenger of Allah ﷺ took *zakāt* on both of them and they were a staple that was stored in the Ḥijāz.' He said, 'Walnuts and almonds are stored, but there is no *zakāt* due on them because, as far I know, they were not a staple in the Ḥijāz. They were fruits. There is no *zakāt* on olives either because Allah says: "*olives and pomegranates*" (6:141) He put them together with pomegranates on which there is no *zakāt*.' Furthermore, figs are more beneficial than them as a staple, but there is no *zakāt* on them. Ash-Shāfi'ī has a position about *zakāt* on olives which he stated in Iraq. The first position was what he stated in Egypt.

So ash-Shāfi'ī's position about olives is confused and Mālik's position about them does not differ. That is proof that they consider the *āyah* to be one of judgment which is not abrogated. They both agree that there is no *zakāt* owed on pomegranates and they would have had to oblige *zakāt* on them. Abū 'Umar said, 'There is agreement that pomegranates are excluded and by that it is clear that it means that the *āyah* is not undefined about them and the pronoun refers to some of the things that were mentioned rather than others. Allah knows best. This is used as evidence by those who oblige the tenth on vegetables. Allah says: '...*pay their due on the day of their harvest'* and olives and pomegranates were mentioned before. There is no dispute that the pronoun normally refers to what was mentioned before. Aṭ-Ṭabarī said that.

It is related that Ibn 'Abbās said, 'No pomegranate is fecundated but that it contains a drop from the Garden.' It is related that 'Alī said, 'When you eat a pomegranate, eat it with its pulp. It treats the intestines.' Ibn 'Asākir related in the *History of Damascus* that Ibn 'Abbās said, 'Do not split open a pomegranate from the top. It contains a worm which causes leprosy.' The benefits of olive oil will be mentioned in *Sūrat al-Mu'minīn*, Allah willing. Those who said that *zakāt* on olives is mandatory were: az-Zuhrī, al-Awzā'ī, al-Layth, ath-Thawrī, Abū Ḥanīfah and his people, and Abū Thawr. Az-Zuhrī, al-Awzā'ī, and al-Layth said that the olives are estimated and pure oil is made from them. Mālik said that they are not estimated, but the tenth is taken after they have been pressed as long as its quantity reaches five *wasqs*. Abū Ḥanīfah and ath-Thawrī said, '*Zakāt* is taken from the olives.'

on the day of their harvest

Abū 'Amr, Ibn 'Āmir and 'Āṣim read *ḥaṣādihi* while the rest read '*ḥiṣādihi*'. Both dialects are well-known, like *ṣarām* and *ṣirām*, *jadād* and *jidād*, and *qaṭāf* and *qiṭāf*.

Scholars have three different verdicts about the time of the obligation. The first view is that it is the time when they are cut, as Muḥammad ibn Maslamah said, based on this *āyah*. The second is that it is on the day they are seen to be ripe because before they are ripe they are not food or nourishment. When they are ripe and ready to eat, then the due which Allah commanded is owed on them, just as gratitude is due when the blessing is complete. The third is that it is after full assessment of its value has taken place because then the obligation has *zakāt* attached to it and that is a precondition for its obligation. Its basis is that the assessor comes to the sheep, and that is what al-Mughīrah says. The first is the sound view because it is what is revealed in the text, while the second is well-known in the Madhhab and ash-Shāfi'ī also said that.

The point of the dispute is that if someone dies after the crop is good, *zakāt* is paid on what he owns, but, if that happens before its value is estimated, then the responsibility falls on the heirs. Muḥammad ibn Maslamah said, 'When the assessment comes, there is allowance for the owners of the fruit. If someone pays the *zakāt* before its value is assessed and before cutting, it is invalid because he paid it before it was due.'

Scholars disagree about the position that the time it is due is when its value is assessed. Ath-Thawrī disliked it and did not allow assessment at all. He said that it is not done but the owner of the garden gives a tenth to the poor when what he gets reaches five *wasqs*. Ash-Shaybānī related that ash-Sha'bī said, 'Assessment today is an innovation.' Most have a different position, but with differing opinions about the crops on which it is permitted. The majority permit it for palm-trees and grape-vines based on the *ḥadīth* of 'Attāb ibn Asīd who said that the Prophet ﷺ sent him with orders to assess the grape-vines as he did palm-trees and take their *zakāt* in raisins as he took the *zakāt* of palm-trees in dates. Abū Dāwūd related it. Dāwūd ibn 'Alī said, 'It is permitted to use assessment for *zakāt* on palm-trees, but not permitted for grape-vines. He ignored the *ḥadīth* of 'Attāb ibn Asīd because it is broken and its *isnād* not connected by a sound path. Abū Muḥammad 'Abd al-Ḥaqq said that.

Assessment is carried out by estimating the dates on the tree and what may be deficient at the time of fruiting, and then there is another assessment of what remains after the amount of loss is clear, and the amounts are added together. The same is done with grape-vines on every trellis. It is alright for the assessment to be carried out by a single person. If the crop produces more than the assessment, the owner is not obliged to pay more because, according to 'Abd al-Wahhāb, the judgment has already been made. The same is true if there is a shortfall: *zakāt* is not reduced. Al-Ḥasan said, 'The Muslims used to have assessment carried out on them and then *zakāt* was taken from them according to that assessment.'

If the owner of the orchard thinks that the assessment is too great, then the assessor gives him a choice about taking what has been assessed against him and accepting it. 'Abd ar-Razzāq mentioned it from Ibn Jurayj from Abū az-Zubayr who heard Jābir ibn 'Abdullāh say, 'Ibn Rawāḥah made an assessment of 40,000 *wasqs* [at Khaybar] and he gave them a choice, and they took the dates and gave him 20,000 *wasqs*.' Ibn Jurayj said, 'I said to 'Aṭā', "When the owner of the property thinks that the estimate is too large, then is the assessor obliged to give him a choice as Ibn Rawāḥah gave the Jews a choice?" He answered, "Yes, by Allah! What *sunnah* is better than the *sunnah* of the Messenger of Allah ﷺ!"'

Assessment is only made after the crop is good based on the *ḥadīth* of 'Ā'ishah: 'The Messenger of Allah ﷺ used to send Ibn Rawāḥah to the Jews to assess the palm-trees when the first of the dates were ripe before any of them were eaten. Then he gave the Jews a choice between taking it by that assessment or giving it to him.' The Messenger of Allah ﷺ commanded assessment so that any *zakāt* due would be collected before the fruits were eaten and divided. Ad-Dāraquṭnī transmitted it from Ibn Jurayj from az-Zuhrī from 'Urwah from 'Ā'ishah. Ṣāliḥ ibn Abī al-Aḥmar related it from az-Zuhrī from Ibn al-Musayyab from Abū Hurayrah. Mālik, Ma'mar and 'Aqīl have it *mursal* from Sa'īd from the Prophet ﷺ.

When the assessor makes his assessment, its ruling is that he should deduct a certain amount from his estimation based on what Abū Dāwūd, at-Tirmidhī and al-Bustī in his *Ṣaḥīḥ* related from Sahl ibn Abī Ḥathmah that the Prophet ﷺ used to say, 'When you assess, take it and deduct a third. If you do not deduct a third, then deduct a quarter.' Abū Dāwūd said, 'The assessor deducts a third for picked ones (*khurqah*).' That is what Yaḥyā ibn al-Qaṭṭān said.

Abū Ḥātim al-Bustī said, 'There are two qualities mentioned in this report. One is that he deducts a third or a quarter of the tenth. The second is that he deducts that from the dates themselves before a tenth is taken if it is a large garden that will support it.' The word *khurqah* refers to dates which are picked when they are ripe. It is said that dates referred to here are those that are picked by someone fasting [to break their fast]. Al-Jawharī and al-Harawī said that. What is well-known in the school of Mālik is that the assessor does not leave out any dates or grapes in his assessment. Some of the Madinans related that he should go easy on the assessment and deduct some of *'arīyah* loans, gifts to kin and the like. If the fruits are hit by blight after assessment and before cutting, the *zakāt* is dropped from them by the consensus of scholars unless there are five *wasq*s or more in what remains.

There is no *zakāt* on less than five *wasq*s. That was clearly stated by the Prophet ﷺ and it is referred to in a general way in the Book when Allah says: '*You who believe! Give away some of the good things you have earned and some of what the earth produces for you*' (2:267) and '*pay their due*'. Then clarification was made about the tenth and the twentieth. That is the amount and when it is reached, the right is taken from it as explained by the Prophet ﷺ: 'There is no *zakāt* on less than five *wasq*s of dates or grain.' He negated *zakāt* on vegetables since they are not measured by *wasq*s, and there is *zakāt* on dates or grain when the amount of them reaches five *wasq*s and the same applies to raisins. This is called the *niṣāb*. A *wasq* is sixty *ṣā'*s, and a *ṣā'* is four *mudd*s. A *mudd* is 1 $^1/_3$ Baghdadi *raṭl*s. In *mudd*s, a *wasq* is 1200 which measures 1600 *raṭl*s.

Someone who has both dates and raisins which, when combined, reach five *wasq*s, is not obliged to pay *zakāt* by consensus because they are two different categories. They also agree that dates are not added to wheat nor wheat to raisins nor camels to cattle nor cattle to sheep. Goats and sheep are put together by consensus. There is disagreement about adding wheat to barley and sult-barley with the following positions: Mālik allowed it only in the case of these three grains because they are like a single category owing to their similarity in use, growth and harvesting. The difference in name does not oblige a difference in ruling, as is also the case with cattle and water buffalo and sheep and goats. Ash-Shāfiʿī and others said that they may not be combined because they are different categories with different qualities, different names and different tastes. That obliges that they should considered separately. Allah knows best.

Mālik said, 'All pulses are one category and are added together.' Ash-Shāfiʿī said, 'Grains known by a separate name are not added to each other if they are clearly different in character and taste. Members of one category are added to one another, the poor quality to good quality, such as dates and their varieties, raisins and their black and red varieties, and wheat and all its varieties.' That is the position of ath-Thawrī, Abū Ḥanīfah and his followers, Abū Yūsuf and Muḥammad, and Abū Thawr. Al-Layth said that all grains should be added together: pulses and others are added together in *zakāt*. Aḥmad ibn Ḥanbal shrank from adding gold to silver and adding grains to one another. Then, at the end of his life, he took the same position as ash-Shāfiʿī.

Mālik said that any part of a crop the owner destroys after it is sound or has been husked is reckoned against him, and any amount the owner gives away of what he has harvested or cut or olives that he has picked, is noted and reckoned against him [as far as *zakāt* is concerned]. Most *fuqahā'* differ from him regarding that and only oblige *zakāt* on what remains after threshing. Al-Layth said regarding the *zakāt* on grains: 'One reckons the whole harvest without taking account of maintenance [of family], so that any of the ground grain that his family eats is not reckoned against him: it is in the same position as fresh dates which are left for the people of the orchard to eat. They are not estimated against them.' Ash-Shāfiʿī said, 'The assessor allow the owner of the orchard any fresh dates that he and his family eat. That is not estimated against them. Any fresh dates someone eats are not counted against him.' Abū ʿUmar said, 'Ash-Shāfiʿī and those who agree with him argue by Allah's words: "*Eat of their fruits when they bear fruit and pay their due on the day of their harvest.*"' On the basis of this *āyah*, they deduce that one does not count what is eaten before the harvest. They also cite the words of the Prophet ﷺ, 'When you assess, deduct a third. If you do not deduct a third, then deduct a quarter." And according to Mālik and others, nothing eaten by camels and cattle at the threshing is counted against the owner.

Sales of broad beans, chickpeas and green vetch are calculated according to the amount of them there would be when dried and then *zakāt* on them is paid in kind. Likewise sales of green fruit are considered and assessed according to their amount when dried and then *zakāt* on them is paid in raisins and dates on the basis of that assessment. It is said that it is paid from the price received for them. As for the fruit of palm-trees not turned into dried dates or grapes from vines, such as the grapes and unripe dates of Egypt and their unpressed olives, Mālik says that their *zakāt* should be paid from their sale price. Nothing more is obliged for the owner. There is no consideration of whether the price reaches twenty *mithqāl*s or 200 *dirham*s or not. One simply looks to see whether they will amount to five *wasq*s or more. Ash-Shāfi'ī said, 'He pays its tenth or twentieth from the median quality of dates when his family eat or give it as food in the form of fresh dates.'

Abū Dāwūd related from Ibn 'Umar that the Messenger of Allah ﷺ said, 'On land watered by rain, rivers, and springs, or in which no artificial irrigation is required, there is a tenth due. On that which is irrigated by water camels or [other forms of] irrigation, there is a twentieth. The same is true of land watered by flowing water (*sayḥ*). There is a tenth owed on it.' Ibn as-Sikkīt said that this refers to water flowing on the surface of the earth. This term is mentioned in *ḥadīth* and an-Nasā'ī transmitted it. If it is watered by flowing water, but the owner of the land does not own the water and it is rented to him, it is like rain according to the well-known position of the School. Abū al-Ḥasan al-Lakhmī thought that it is like irrigation. If it is sometimes watered by rain and sometimes artificially, Mālik said that one observes that by which the crop is achieved and kept alive, and the kind of irrigation more frequently resorted to, and the ruling is connected to that. This is what Ibn al-Qāsim transmitted from him. Ibn Wahb related from him that, when they are watered for half the year by rain and then that stops and the rest of the year they are watered by irrigation, then half of the *zakāt* is a tenth and half is a twentieth.' Once he said that the *zakāt* is only based on what is fully grown.

Ash-Shāfi'ī said that *zakāt* is paid according to the amount of each method used. For instance, if someone waters for two months by irrigation and relies for four on rain, then in such a case two-thirds of the tenth is paid on the basis of rain and a sixth of the tenth on the basis of irrigation. Thus it increases and decreases according to the method used. This was the *fatwā* of Bakkār ibn Qutaybah. Abū Ḥanīfah, and Abū Yūsuf said, 'One looks at the dominant method and *zakāt* is paid accordingly. No attention is paid to other than that.' That is also related from ash-Shāfi'ī. Aṭ-Ṭaḥāwī said, 'All agree that if someone irrigates by rain water for one or two days, no consideration is given to that and it does not play any part. It indicates that what is considered predominant is counted. Allah knows best.

This is a summary of the rulings of this *āyah*. Someone else may bring more according to what Allah opens for him. Some of the ideas of this *āyah* were already mentioned in connection with *al-Baqarah*. Praise be to Allah.

As for the words of the Prophet ﷺ, 'There is no *zakāt* due on grains or dates [on less than...],' transmitted by an-Nasā'ī, Ḥamzah al-Kinānī said, 'Only Ismā'īl ibn Umayyah mentioned "grains" in this *ḥadīth*. He is a trustworthy Qurashī from the descendants of Sa'īd ibn al-'Āṣ.' He said, "None of his Companions related this *sunnah* from the Prophet ﷺ except Abū Sa'īd al-Khudrī."' Abū 'Umar said, 'It is as Ḥamzah said. This is a majestic *sunnah* that all are taught to accept but only Abū Sa'īd related it from the Prophet ﷺ by a firm preserved path. Jābir related something similar to that from the Prophet ﷺ but it is *gharīb*. We found it from the *ḥadīth* of Abū Hurayrah with a good *isnād*.'

do not be profligate.

Linguistically *isrāf* means error. When a Bedouin is looking for some people and says, 'I looked for you and I erred (*sariftu*) about your location,' it means that he was mistaken about their location. A poet said:

Someone said while the horses were trampling on them,
'You are acting with profligacy (*asraftum*).' We answered,
"We are profligate (*saraf*)."

Isrāf with respect to spending is squandering. '*Musrif*' is the nickname given to Muslim ibn 'Uqbah al-Murrī, the leader in the Battle of al-Ḥarrah because he was excessive and unjust in it. 'Alī ibn 'Abdullāh ibn al-'Abbās said:

They refused that which I would protect on the day
The squadrons of Musrif came, as well as the Ka'bah.

The *āyah* means: 'Do not take a thing without any right to it and then place it in another place than where it is right to do so.' Aṣbagh ibn al-Faraj said, 'The like of that was said by Iyās ibn Mu'āwiyah when he said, "I did not exceed what Allah commanded," and it is *saraf* and *isrāf*.' Ibn Zayd said, 'It is addressed to the governors: "Do not take more than your right or what it is not mandatory for people to give."' Both meanings are supported by the statement of the Prophet ﷺ: 'The one who oversteps in [taking] *zakāt* is like the one who refuses to pay it.'

Mujāhid said, 'If Abū Qubays had been gold and belonged to a man and he spent it in obedience to Allah, he would not be profligate. If he spends a *dirham* or *mudd* in disobedience of Allah, then he is profligate.' Thus it was said to Ḥātim, 'There is no good in profligacy.' He replied, 'There is no profligacy in good.' This is weak and is refuted by what Ibn 'Abbās related when he reported that Thābit ibn Qays ibn Shammās went to five hundred palm trees, cut the dates and then divided them out on a single day, leaving nothing for his family. Then '*do not be profligate*' was revealed, meaning: 'Do not give away all of it.' 'Abd ar-Razzaq related that Ibn Jurayj said, 'Mu'ādh ibn Jabal cut some dates and continued to give them as *ṣadaqah* until he had nothing left and "*do not be profligate*" was revealed.' As-Suddī said, 'It means: "do not give away all your property so that you become poor."' It is related that Mu'āwiyah was asked about this and said, 'Profligacy is what falls short of the right of Allah Almighty.'

According to this, giving away all one's property as *ṣadaqah* or denying the right of the poor are included within the ruling of profligacy. Justice is the opposite of this. People should give *ṣadaqah* and leave themselves with something. The Prophet ﷺ said, 'The best *ṣadaqah* is that which comes from wealth.' When someone is strong in himself, rich by Allah, relying on Him, and has no dependants, then such a person may give away all his property. Similarly one must pay the obligatory right of *zakāt* on it and any other of the specific rights on property that may arise at certain times.

'Abd ar-Raḥmān ibn Zayd ibn Aslam said, 'Profligacy (*isrāf*) is that which cannot be restored to rightness. Intemperance (*saraf*) is that which can be restored to rightness.' An-Naḍr ibn Shumayl said, 'Profligacy is squandering and excess. Unmindful immoderation is heedlessness and ignorance.' Jarīr said:

They gave a hundred camels, driven by eight people.
Their gift did not entail an obligating favour or intemperance (*saraf*).

He either means intemperance or error. A man whose heart is '*sarif*' is one who is mistaken in his heart and heedless. Ṭarafah said:

When a person has an intemperate (*sarifa*) heart, he sees
honey in the water of the cloud as my abuse.

وَمِنَ ٱلْأَنْعَٰمِ حَمُولَةً وَفَرْشًا كُلُوا۟ مِمَّا رَزَقَكُمُ ٱللَّهُ وَلَا تَتَّبِعُوا۟
خُطُوَٰتِ ٱلشَّيْطَٰنِ إِنَّهُۥ لَكُمْ عَدُوٌّ مُّبِينٌ ١٤٢

142 And also animals for riding and for haulage and animals for slaughtering and for wool. Eat what Allah has provided for you and do not follow in the footsteps of *Shayṭān*. He is an outright enemy to you.

And also animals for riding and for haulage

This is added to the previous *āyah*. It means: 'He gave us animals for riding and haulage.' Scholars say three things about *an'ām*. One is that it refers to camels in particular, and this will be discussed in *an-Naḥl*. The second is that it refers to camels alone, but if there are cattle and sheep with them, they are also called *an'ām*. The third, which is the soundest, is stated by Aḥmad ibn Yaḥyā: 'It is all the animals which Allah has made lawful.' The soundness of this is indicated by the words of Allah Almighty: *'All livestock animals are lawful for you, except those that are recited to you now.'* (5:1)

Animals '*for riding and for haulage*' are those animals used for carrying and work, as Ibn Mas'ūd and others said. It is also said that the expression is specific to camels, and it is also said that it refers to all animals which can carry, be they donkeys, mules or asses, as Ibn Zayd said, whether or not they are actually used for that. 'Antarah said:

We were only surprised by the haulage (*ḥamūlah*) animals of the people
in the middle of the houses, eating black seeds.

The verbal form *fa'ūlah* (*ḥamūlah*) can be the active participle and is applied to both male or female. It is as a man or woman can be described as '*farūqah*,' which is someone who is a coward or fearful, and a man or woman can be described as '*ṣarūrah*', that is someone who has not performed *ḥajj*. It has no plural. If it indicates the passive participle, there is a difference between masculine and feminine by the *hā'* (*tā' marbūṭah*), like *ḥalūbah* and *rakūbah*. The word *ḥumūlah* means loads and *ḥumūl* are camels with howdahs on them whether there are women in them or not. Abū Zayd said that.

Regarding the term '*for slaughtering and for wool*' (*farsh*): aḍ-Ḍaḥḥāk said that *ḥamūlah* refers to camels and cattle and *farsh* to sheep. An-Naḥḥās said that there is support for this view in the words '*...eight pairs*' in the following *āyah*. He said that '*eight*' is an appositive for '*animals for riding and for haulage and for slaughtering and for wool*'. Al-Hasan said that *ḥamūlah* are camels and *farsh* are sheep. Ibn 'Abbas said that *ḥamūlah* refers to all animals which carry burdens: camels, cattle, horses, mules and donkeys, and *farsh* is sheep. Ibn Zayd that the *ḥamūlah* is what is ridden and *farsh* is what is eaten and milked, like sheep, young camels and calves. They are called *farsh* because their bodies are small and close to the *farsh*, which is the level ground on which people walk. A poet said:

He left me camels for riding and earth (*farsh*)
on which I walk every day.

Another said:

We got the *farsh* from your livestock,
as well as the *ḥamūlāt* and mothers of calves.

Al-Aṣma'ī said, 'I did not hear of it having a plural.' He said, 'It is possible that it is a verbal noun used as a name.' People say, '*farashā-llāhu farshan*,' i.e. 'Allah spread out the young camels.' *Farsh* are household goods that are spread out. *Farsh* are crops when they are spread out. *Farsh* is a wide expanse of land, and it is used for the foot of a camel when it is a little wide, which is praised. The verb *iftarsha* means to expand. It is a word with many meanings. An-Naḥḥās said that one of the best things that is said about these two words is that the *ḥamūlah* is tamed and submissive and accepts carrying, and the *farsh* is what Allah created for skin and wool which are sat on and laid on. The rest of the *āyah* has already been discussed.

ثَمَٰنِيَةَ أَزْوَٰجٍ مِّنَ ٱلضَّأْنِ ٱثْنَيْنِ وَمِنَ ٱلْمَعْزِ ٱثْنَيْنِ
قُلْ ءَآلذَّكَرَيْنِ حَرَّمَ أَمِ ٱلْأُنثَيَيْنِ أَمَّا ٱشْتَمَلَتْ عَلَيْهِ أَرْحَامُ
ٱلْأُنثَيَيْنِ نَبِّـُٔونِى بِعِلْمٍ إِن كُنتُمْ صَٰدِقِينَ ﴿١٤٣﴾ وَمِنَ ٱلْإِبِلِ ٱثْنَيْنِ
وَمِنَ ٱلْبَقَرِ ٱثْنَيْنِ قُلْ ءَآلذَّكَرَيْنِ حَرَّمَ أَمِ ٱلْأُنثَيَيْنِ أَمَّا ٱشْتَمَلَتْ
عَلَيْهِ أَرْحَامُ ٱلْأُنثَيَيْنِ أَمْ كُنتُمْ شُهَدَآءَ إِذْ وَصَّىٰكُمُ ٱللَّهُ بِهَٰذَا
فَمَنْ أَظْلَمُ مِمَّنِ ٱفْتَرَىٰ عَلَى ٱللَّهِ كَذِبًا لِّيُضِلَّ ٱلنَّاسَ بِغَيْرِ عِلْمٍ
إِنَّ ٱللَّهَ لَا يَهْدِى ٱلْقَوْمَ ٱلظَّٰلِمِينَ ﴿١٤٤﴾

143-4 There are eight in pairs: a pair of sheep and a pair of goats – Say: 'Is it the two males He has made unlawful, or the two females, or what the wombs of the two females contain? Tell me with knowledge if you are being truthful.' And a pair of camels and a pair of cattle – Say: 'Is it the two males He has made unlawful, or the two females, or what the wombs of the two females contain? Were you then witnesses when Allah gave you this instruction?' Who could do greater wrong than someone who invents lies against Allah thus leading people astray without any knowledge? Allah does not guide the people of the wrongdoers.

There are eight in pairs:

'*Eight*' is in the accusative by the action of an implied verb, implying, 'He produced eight in pairs,' as al-Kisā'ī said. Al-Akhfash said that it is in the accusative as an appositive for '*animals for riding and for haulage and for slaughtering and for wool*'. 'Alī ibn Sulaymān al-Akhfash said that it is accusative by the implied verb 'eat', meaning 'Eat the flesh of eight pairs.' It can also be in the accusative as an appositive for '*mā*' and it can be in the accusative on the basis of meaning: 'Eat what is permitted: eight in pairs: a pair of sheep…'

The *āyah* was revealed about Mālik ibn 'Awf and his people when they said, '*What is in the wombs of these animals is only for our men, and forbidden to our wives.*' (6:139) Allah informed His Prophet ﷺ and the believers in this *āyah* about what is lawful to them so that they are not in the position of those who make unlawful what Allah has made lawful.

Zawj is the opposite of 'one alone (*fard*)' as is said, odd or even (*khasan aw zakan*), even or odd (*shaf aw witr*). '*Eight in pairs*' means eight individuals. With the Arabs, each single one needs a mate, and so *zawj* is used for either one of a couple and it is used for one or two as well. They are the same. You say, 'I bought a pair (*zawjā*) of doves,' when you mean a male and female.

a pair of sheep and a pair of goats –

This means a male and female of each. *Ḍa'n* are sheep with wool. It is the plural of *ḍā'in*. The feminine is *ḍā'inah* and the plural is *ḍawā'in*. It is also said that it is a plural that has no singular. It is also said that the plural is *ḍa'īn* like *'abd* and *'abīd*. It is called *ḍi'īn* and *sha'īr* is called *shi'īr* with a *kasrah* on the *ḍād*. Ṭalḥah ibn Muṣarrif recited '*ḍa'an*' with a *fatḥah* on the *ḥamzah*. It is a dialectical usage heard among the Basrans while the Kufans recite it in the case of everything that has a pharyngeal as the second letter. That is also the case with the *fatḥah* and *sukūn* in *ma'z*. Abān ibn 'Uthmān recited '*athnān*' as does Ubayy. '*Goats*' is read *ma'z* by most, but Ibn 'Āmir and Abū 'Amr read it *ma'az*. An-Naḥḥās said that in Arabic it is more common with *sukūn*. This is indicated by their statement that the plural of *ma'z* is *ma'īz*, like *'abd* and *'abīd*. [POEM]

Ma'z are different to *ḍa'n*. They have hair and short tails. It is a generic noun. That is the case with *ma'az, ma'īz, am'ūz*, and *mi'zā*, the singular of *ma'z* being *mā'iz*, like *ṣāḥib* and *ṣahb*, and *tājir* and *tajr*. The feminine form is *mā'izah*. They are goats. The plural is *mawā'iz*. Someone who is *am'az* has many goats. *Ma''āz* is someone with goats. Abū Muḥammad al-Faq'isī said when he described camels with abundant milk and how they are superior to sheep during hard times:

They eat a measure that is not wiped out
    when a goat-herd is content with mere lickings.

Ma'az is hard ground and *am'az* is a hard location with numerous pebbles. *Ma'zā'* is the same. The verb *istim'aza* is to be hard in a matter.

Say: 'Is it the two males He has made unlawful, or the two females, or what the wombs of the two females contain? Tell me with knowledge if you are being truthful.'

'*Say: "Is it the two males*"' is in the accusative by '*made unlawful*' and '*or the two females*' is added to it. The same is true of '*what they contain*'. They are added together with the *alif* of the connection with a *maddah* to distinguish between the question and the report. It is also permitted to elide the *hamzah* because '*am*' indicates the question. [POEM]

Scholars say that the *āyah* is an argument against the idolaters about the *baḥīrah* and what was said about it. That is their words in the earlier *āyah*: '*What is in the wombs of these animals is for our men and is unlawful for our wives.*' That indicates the need to establish discussions about knowledge because Allah commanded His Prophet ﷺ to debate with them and make it clear to them that their view was unsound; and it also confirms taking a view based on evidence and analogy. It is also evidence that when a clear text exists, then analogy about any matter is invalid. It is said it is when it is contradicted, because Allah commanded sound analogy and commanded them to discard their efficient cause (*'illah*). So it means: 'Say to them, "If the male is unlawful, is every male unlawful, or if the female is unlawful, is every female unlawful? If what is in the wombs of the females is unlawful, referring to sheep and goats, is every offspring, male or female, unlawful? Are all that are born unlawful because the existence of the efficient cause makes it unlawful?"' So he makes it clear that their efficient cause is null and void and their verdict unsound, and so Allah knows that what they did in that is a forgery against Him.

'*Tell me with knowledge*' means with the knowledge you have. What is the source of this prohibition which you observe? They had no knowledge because they did not read the Scriptures.

And a pair of camels and a pair of cattle...

The words in '*and a pair of camels*' and what follows are the same as the previous *āyah*. The question '*Were you then witnesses?*' means 'Did you witness Allah forbidding this?' Then you must provide evidence for your concocted words when you said, 'This is what Allah commanded.' Allah responds with His words: '*Who could do greater wrong than someone who invents lies against Allah thus leading people astray without any knowledge?*' He clearly states that they are lying since they stated something without providing any evidence for it.

قُل لَّآ أَجِدُ فِى مَآ أُوحِىَ إِلَىَّ مُحَرَّمًا عَلَىٰ طَاعِمٍ يَطْعَمُهُۥٓ إِلَّآ أَن يَكُونَ مَيْتَةً
أَوْ دَمًا مَّسْفُوحًا أَوْ لَحْمَ خِنزِيرٍ فَإِنَّهُۥ رِجْسٌ أَوْ فِسْقًا أُهِلَّ لِغَيْرِ ٱللَّهِ
بِهِۦ فَمَنِ ٱضْطُرَّ غَيْرَ بَاغٍ وَلَا عَادٍ فَإِنَّ رَبَّكَ غَفُورٌ رَّحِيمٌ ﴿١٤٥﴾

145 Say: 'I do not find, in what has been revealed to me, any food it is unlawful to eat except for carrion, flowing blood, and pork – for that is unclean – or some deviance consecrated to other than Allah. But if anyone is forced to eat it, without desiring to or going to excess in it, your Lord is Ever-Forgiving, Most Merciful.'

Say: 'I do not find, in what has been revealed to me, any food it is unlawful to eat

Allah informs us in this *āyah* what is unlawful. The meaning is: 'Say, Muḥammad, "I do not find, in what has been revealed to me anything which is unlawful except for these things, not what you have made unlawful by your whims."' The *āyah* is Makkan, and at that time there was nothing unlawful in the *Sharī'ah* other than these things. Then *Sūrat al-Mā'idah* was revealed in Madīnah, and it added strangled animals, animals killed by a blow, animals fallen to their death, animals which have been gored, wine and other things. In Madīnah the Messenger of Allah ﷺ also forbade every beast of prey with fangs and every bird with talons.

Scholars disagree about the ruling and interpretation of this *āyah* and have various views. The first is what we have indicated about the *āyah* being Makkan. All that the Messenger of Allah ﷺ made unlawful, or what comes in the Book in addition to this is an additional judgment from Allah on the tongue of His Prophet ﷺ, according to most of the people of knowledge and among the people of investigation, *fiqh* and traditions. The same is true of marrying a woman while married to her aunt when He says: '*Lawful to you is what is beyond that*' (4:24) and the ruling of the oath with the witness when He says: '*If there are not two men, then one man and two women.*' (2:282)

It is said that it is abrogated by the words of the Prophet ﷺ, 'Eating every beast of prey with fangs is unlawful' which Mālik transmitted, and it is a sound *ḥadīth*. It is said that the *āyah* is *muḥkam* and only what is in it is forbidden. That is a verdict related from Ibn 'Abbās, Ibn 'Umar and 'Ā'ishah, and the opposite of it is also related from them. Mālik said, 'There is nothing clearly unlawful except what is mentioned in this *āyah*.' Ibn Khuwayzimandād said, 'This *āyah* contains the making lawful of every animal and other things except the carrion, spilled blood and pig meat that are excepted in this *āyah*. This is why we said that the flesh of animals of prey and of all other animals except for human flesh and pigs is lawful.' Aṭ-Ṭabarī said, 'That is ash-Shāfi'ī's basis for all that one is silent about, as derived from this *āyah*, except what other evidence indicates.'

It is said that the *āyah* is a response to someone who asked about something in particular and it is a specific response.' This is the position of ash-Shāfi'ī. Ash-Shāfi'ī related from Sa'īd ibn Jubayr that this *āyah* contains things which the Messenger of Allah ﷺ was asked about and answered regarding which of those things are unlawful. It is said that it means, 'I do not find in what is revealed to me,' meaning in this moment of revelation and the moment of its descent. That does not preclude the arrival of revelation after that forbidding other things. Ibn al-'Arabī claimed that this *āyah* is Madinan, but according to most it is Makkan. It was revealed to the Prophet ﷺ on the day on which: *'Today I have perfected your dīn for you'* (5:3) was revealed and no abrogation was revealed after it and so it is an *āyah* of judgment, and there is nothing forbidden except what is in it. I incline to this.

I saw that others stated this. Abū 'Umar ibn 'Abd al-Barr mentioned the consensus that *Sūrat al-An'ām* was Makkan except for the words: *'Say: "Come and I will recite to you what your Lord has made unlawful for you…"'* (6:151-153): A lot of Qur'an and many *sunnahs* were revealed after it. The prohibition of wine was revealed in Madīnah. Ismā'īl ibn Isḥāq said, 'All of this indicates that it was in Madīnah after the revelation of "*Say: 'I do not find, in what has been revealed to me…*'"' because that is Makkan. This provokes disagreement between scholars. One group turned from the sound *ḥadīths* reporting the prohibition against eating any beast of prey with fangs because the *ḥadīths* were later than the *āyah*. It is more fitting to confine oneself to the apparent and adopt it because this either abrogates what was before it or is preferred to those *ḥadīths*. Others say that beasts of prey are forbidden, and they maintain that *Sūrat al-An'ām* is Makkan and was revealed before the Hjrah. This *āyah* is meant to refute the *Jāhiliyyah* prohibition of the *baḥīrah*, *sā'ibah*, *waṣīlah* and *ḥām*. After that he ﷺ forbade many things, like domestic donkeys, the flesh of mules and other things, and every beast of prey with fangs and every bird with talons.

Abū 'Umar said, 'It is necessary according to those who say, "Only what is in it is unlawful," that what does not have the Name of Allah mentioned over it deliberately is not unlawful. Forbidden wine is allowed by a group of Muslims while the consensus of the Muslims is that prohibition of grape wine is clear evidence that the Messenger of Allah ﷺ prohibited more than what was in *Sūrat al-An'ām* based on what afterwards was revealed to him of the Qur'an.'

There are various transmissions from Mālik about the flesh of beasts of prey, donkeys and mules. Sometimes he says it is forbidden because of its reported prohibition by the Prophet ﷺ. This is sound as reported from him in the *Muwaṭṭā'*. At other times he said that it is disliked and that is the position of the *Mudawwanah*, based on the apparent meaning of the *āyah* and what was related from Ibn 'Abbās, Ibn 'Umar, 'Umar and 'Ā'ishah that it is permissible to eat it. That is the position of al-Awzā'ī. Al-Bukhārī related from the transmission of 'Amr ibn Dīnār, 'I said to Jābir ibn Zayd that they claimed that the Messenger of Allah ﷺ had forbidden the flesh of domestic animals. He said, "Al-Ḥakam ibn 'Amr al-Ghifārī stated that in our presence in Basra, but Ibn 'Abbās rejected it and recited: '*Say: "I do not find, in what has been revealed to me, any food it is unlawful to eat....*"""

It is related that Ibn 'Umar was asked about the flesh of beasts of prey and he said that there was nothing wrong with it. Someone said to him, '[What about] the *ḥadīth* of Abū Tha'labah al-Khushanī?' He said, 'We do not leave the Book of Allah, our Lord, for the *ḥadīth* of a Bedouin who urinates standing.' Ash-Sha'bī was asked about the flesh of elephants and lions and he recited this verse. Al-Qāsim said that when 'Ā'ishah heard people say that every beast of prey with fangs is unlawful, she said that they were lawful and she recited this *āyah*. Then she observed, 'Even when the water of the cooking pot was yellow from blood, when the Messenger of Allah ﷺ saw it, he did not forbid it.' The correct view about this matter is what we first mentioned. What is related of forbidden things after this *āyah* should be added to it.

Qāḍī Abū Bakr ibn al-'Arabī indicated this in his *Qabs* while deriving something different in his *Aḥkām*. He said that it is reported from Ibn 'Abbas that this *āyah* was one of the last to be revealed. The Baghdādīs among our companions say, 'All that is other than it is lawful, even though it is disliked to eat beasts of prey.' According to the *fuqahā'* of the cities, including Mālik, ash-Shāfi'ī, Abū Ḥanīfah and 'Abd al-Malik, it is unlawful to eat beasts of prey with fangs. That does not prevent there being something added after this *āyah* when there is evidence for it, as the Prophet ﷺ said, 'The blood of a Muslim man is only lawful on account of three,' and he mentioned disbelief, fornication and murder.

Our scholars then say that there are ten reasons for execution, based on evidential reports since the Prophet ﷺ relayed knowledge which reached him from the Creator Who rescinds whatever He wishes, confirms and abrogates and determines. It is confirmed that the Prophet ﷺ said, 'Every best of prey with fangs is unlawful.' It is related that he forbade eating every beast of prey with fangs and every bird with talons. Muslim related from Ma'n from Mālik, 'It is forbidden to eat birds with talons.' The first opinion is sounder, and the prohibition of every beast of prey with fangs is the explicit position. Mālik makes that clear in the *Muwaṭṭā'* when he gives the section title, 'The prohibition of every beast of prey with fangs,' and then mentioned the *ḥadīth* and followed that with, 'It is the way with us.' So he reported that the practice is in harmony with the tradition.

Al-Qushayrī said that the statement of Mālik, 'This *āyah* was one of the last to be revealed' does not keep us from saying that the prohibition of certain things was established after this *āyah*. Allah allowed wholesome things and forbade foul things. The Messenger of Allah ﷺ forbade every beast of prey with fangs and every bird with talons and the flesh of domestic donkeys in the year of Khaybar. The soundness of this interpretation is indicated by the consensus of the prohibition of faeces, urine, dirty insects and donkeys which are not mentioned in this *āyah*.

Ibn 'Aṭiyyah said that when the expression of making something *ḥarām* (*taḥrīm*) comes on the tongue of the Messenger of Allah ﷺ, it is valid that the thing forbidden be an absolute prohibition or that it is a linguistic usage which stops short of the definitive and implies dislike and the like. Whatever is connected to the consent of the Companions who can interpret and on whose opinion all agree, when there is no confusion regarding the words of the *ḥadīth*s, is obliged in the *Sharī'ah* to be a prohibition which reaches actual prohibition. That is connected to pigs, carrion and blood. This is also the rank of the prohibition of wine.

That which is accompanied by confusion regarding the words of the *ḥadīth*s and about which the Imams differ, although they act by the *ḥadīth*s, is like his words ﷺ, 'Every beast of prey with fangs is unlawful.' It is reported that the Messenger of Allah ﷺ forbade eating every animal of prey with fangs and then the Companions and those after them disagreed about whether that is prohibited. This is why it is permitted for those who investigate to apply the expression of 'making unlawful' to a prohibition which has the status of dislike and the like.

As for that which is connected to interpretation, like the prohibition by the Prophet ﷺ of the meat of domestic donkeys, some of the Companions present interpreted that as being because of impurity, others that it was to avert the loss of people's transport, and still others interpreted it as pure prohibition. The disagreement of the community about the prohibition of their meat is confirmed. It is permitted for those scholars who apply the term 'making *ḥarām*' to it being disliked and so on according to the *ijtihād* and analogy applied. This is a good point on the subject of reasons for disagreement. It is said that donkeys are not eaten because of their essential impurity since they are prone to mounting males and committing sodomy. So they are called an 'impurity'. Muḥammad ibn Sīrīn said, 'There are no animals that commit sodomy other than pigs and donkeys.' At-Tirmidhī mentioned it in *Nawādir al-Uṣūl.*

'Amr ibn Dīnār related from Abu-sh-Sha'thā' that Ibn 'Abbās said, 'The people of the time of the *Jāhiliyyah* used to eat certain things and leave other things. Then Allah sent His Prophet ﷺ and revealed His Book and made some things lawful and others unlawful. What He made lawful is lawful and what He made unlawful is unlawful and there is allowance for what He is silent about.' He recited this *āyah*, '*Say: "I do not find...*"' It means that when something's prohibition is not clear, its consumption is permitted by the literal meaning of the *āyah.*

Az-Zuhrī related that 'Ubaydullāh, the son of Ibn 'Abbās, recited, '*Say: "I do not find in what has been revealed to me...*"' and said, 'It is forbidden to eat carrion and that refers to its meat. As for its skin, bones, wool and hair, they are lawful.' Abū Dāwūd related from Milqām ibn Talibb that his father said, 'I accompanied the Prophet ﷺ and I did not hear that there was any prohibition of the vermin of the earth.' *Ḥasharah* refers to small vermin like jerboas, lizards, hedgehogs and the like. A poet said:

> We ate mice, Umm 'Amr,
> and we do not consider it strange to eat vermin.

Al-Khaṭṭābī says that this is not evidence that it is permissible, since it is possible that someone else heard that. People disagree about jerboas, hyraxes, and similar vermin. There is an allowance for eating jerboas according to 'Urwah, 'Aṭā', ash-Shāfi'ī, and Abū Thawr. Ash-Shāfi'ī says that there is nothing wrong with hyraxes. Ibn Sīrīn, al-Ḥakam, Ḥammād and the People of Opinion disliked that.

The People of Opinion disliked eating hedgehogs. Mālik ibn Anas was asked about it and answered, 'I do not know.' Abū 'Amr related that Mālik said that there is nothing wrong in eating hedgehogs. Abū Thawr did not see any anything wrong in it and related that from ash-Shāfi'ī. Ibn 'Umar was asked about it and recited: '*Say: "I do not find, in what has been revealed to me, any food it is unlawful to eat.*"' A shaykh said, 'I heard Abū Hurayrah say, "This was mentioned in the presence of the Prophet ﷺ and he said, 'A foul thing among foul things.'" Ibn 'Umar said, "If the Messenger of Allah ﷺ said that, it is as he said."' Abū Dāwūd mentioned that.

Mālik said that there is no harm in eating lizards, jerboas and large lizards. He considered that it is permitted to eat snakes when they are slaughtered. That is the verdict of Ibn Abī Laylā and al-Awzā'ī. The same applies to adders, scorpions, mice, hedgehogs and frogs. Ibn al-Qāsim said, 'There is nothing wrong in eating vermin, scorpions and worms in the opinion of Mālik because he said, "Its death in water does not pollute it (the water)."' Mālik said, 'There is no harm in eating the eggs of bees and worms in cheese and dates and the like.' The evidence for that is the *ḥadīth* reported by Milqām ibn Talibb and the statement of Ibn 'Abbās and Abū ad-Dardā': what Allah has made lawful is lawful and what He has made unlawful is unlawful, and what He is silent about is allowed. 'Ā'ishah said that mice are not unlawful, and she recited this *āyah*. A group of the scholars of the people of Madīnah do not permit eating any vermin and creatures such as snakes, lizards, mice and the like. These people consider that anything that it is not permitted to kill may not be eaten either, nor may it be slaughtered in their view. That is the verdict of Ibn Shihāb, 'Urwah, ash-Shāfi'ī, Abū Ḥanīfah and his people and others.

According to Mālik and his people, no beast of prey may be eaten nor may domestic or wild cats because they are predators. Nor may hyenas or foxes be eaten. There is nothing wrong in eating birds of prey: vultures, eagles, and others, whether they eat carrion or not. Al-Awzā'ī said that all birds are lawful although they dislike eating vultures. The evidence of Mālik is that none of the people of knowledge disliked eating birds of prey and he does not accept the *ḥadīth* from the Prophet ﷺ that he forbade every bird with talons. It is related that Ashhab said, 'There is nothing wrong in eating elephants if they are slaughtered.' That is the verdict of ash-Sha'bī while ash-Shāfi'ī forbade it.

An-Nu'mān and his people disliked eating hyenas and foxes while ash-Shāfi'ī allowed that. It is related that Sa'd ibn Abī Waqqāṣ used to eat hyenas. The evidence of Mālik is a general prohibition of eating any beast of prey with fangs and no beasts are specified. The *ḥadīth* about the hyena, allowing its consumption, which an-Nasā'ī transmitted is not one by which the *ḥadīth* of prohibition can be validly countered because it is a *ḥadīth* with only one transmitter, 'Abd ar-Raḥmān ibn Abī 'Ammār, who is not known for transmitting knowledge. It is not used as evidence when there is a different *ḥadīth* which is firmer than it. Abū 'Umar said that the prohibition of eating beasts of prey with fangs is transmitted by multiple lines of transmission, and a group of trustworthy *imāms* related that. It is impossible for that to be contradicted by the *ḥadīth* of 'Abd ar-Raḥmān ibn Abī 'Ammār.

Abū 'Umar said that there is a consensus among the Muslims that it is not permitted to eat monkeys because the Messenger of Allah ﷺ forbade eating them. It is not permitted to sell them [as meat] because there is no benefit in it. He said, 'I do not know of anyone who allows them to be eaten except what 'Abd ar-Razzāq mentioned from Ma'mar from Ayyūb. Mujāhid was asked about eating monkeys and said, 'They are not part of livestock.' Ibn al-Mundhir mentioned that it was related to them that 'Aṭā' was asked about monkeys killed in the Ḥaram and said, 'Two men of integrity should arbitrate it.' He said, 'According to the school of 'Aṭā', it is permitted to eat them because reparation is not obliged for someone who kills an animal which is not game.' In *Baḥr al-Madhhab* by ar-Rūyānī on the school of ash-Shāfi'ī, he stated that as-Shāfi'ī said that it is permitted to sell monkeys because they can be trained and used to guard goods. Al-Kashfulī related from Abū Shurayḥ that it is permitted to sell them because they have a use. He was asked what their use was and he replied that they were used to amuse children. Abū 'Umar said that dogs, elephants and animals with fangs are all in the same category as monkeys. The proof is in the words of the Messenger of Allah ﷺ and not the words of anyone else. People claim that none of the Arabs ate dogs except for some people from [the tribe of] Faq'as.

Abū Dāwūd reported that Ibn 'Umar said, 'The Messenger of Allah ﷺ forbade eating a *jalālah* animal and its milk. One version has, '...riding camels which are *jalālah* or drinking their milk.' Abū 'Abdullāh al-Ḥalīmī said, 'A *jalālah* is an animal or free range chicken which eats excrement. The Prophet ﷺ forbade their meat.' Scholars say that if the meat or food of any animal smells like excrement, it is unlawful. If that is not apparent, then it is lawful. Al-Khaṭṭābī said that this prohibition is one of cleanliness and fastidiousness. That is because when an animal eats excrement, its flesh has a foul smell. This is when most of its diet consists of that. When it eats fodder and grain and also consumes some excrement, then it is not *jalālah*. It is like free range chickens and other animals which might eat some of it while most of their food and fodder is other than that. Then it is not disliked to eat them. The People of Opinion, ash-Shāfi'ī and Aḥmad said that such an animal should not be eaten until it has been kept for some days and fed with something else. When its flesh is good, then it can be eaten. A *ḥadīth* is related: 'A cow is fed for forty days and then its meat can be eaten.' Ibn 'Umar said that a chicken should be kept for three days and then slaughtered. Isḥāq said that there is nothing wrong in eating it after the meat has been thoroughly washed. Al-Ḥasan did not see anything wrong in eating the meat of a *jalālah* animal, and Mālik ibn Anas said the same. Another aspect of this subject is forbidding excrement to be thrown on the ground. It is related that one of them said, 'We used to rent land from the Messenger of Allah ﷺ and he stipulated that the one who rented it should not throw dung on it.' Ibn 'Umar reported that he rented out his land and stipulated that it should not be fertilised with excrement. It is related that a man used to cultivate his land with excrement and 'Umar told him, 'You are feeding people what issues from them!'

There is disagreement about eating horses. Ash-Shāfi'ī allowed it, and that is sound, and Mālik disliked it. As for mules, which are the issue of a donkey and a horse, eating one of them is allowed or disliked, which is the horses, and the other is forbidden, which is the donkey. The ruling of prohibition is weightier because when there is both lawfulness and prohibition in the same thing, then the ruling of prohibition takes precedence. This will be discussed in full in *Sūrat an-Naḥl*, Allah willing. Locusts will be discussed in *Sūrat al-A'rāf.*

The majority of the early generations and later ones permit eating rabbits, although there is a report from 'Abdullāh ibn 'Amr ibn al-'Āṣ that it is unlawful and from Ibn Abī Laylā that it is disliked. 'Abdullāh ibn 'Amr said, 'A rabbit was brought to the Messenger of Allah ﷺ while I was sitting with him and he did not eat it or forbid eating it. He stated that it was menstruating.' Abū Dāwūd mentioned it. An-Nasā'ī related *mursal* that Mūsā ibn Ṭalḥah said, 'The Prophet ﷺ was brought a rabbit that a man had roasted. He said, "Messenger of Allah, I saw some blood in it." So the Messenger of Allah ﷺ left it without eating it. He said to those with him, "Eat it. Had I wanted it, I would have eaten it."' None of the reports about it indicates that it was forbidden. It is like the words of the Prophet ﷺ, 'It is not found in the land of my people and I do not find that I like it.' Muslim related in his *Ṣaḥīḥ* that Anas ibn Mālik said, 'We passed by Marr aẓ-Ẓahrān and we startled a rabbit and the people ran after it until it was exhausted. I ran and caught it. I took it to Abū Ṭalḥah who slaughtered it. He sent its hip and thigh to the Messenger of Allah ﷺ and I brought it to the Messenger of Allah ﷺ who accepted it.'

In '*any food … to eat*', it refers to an eater eating. It is related that Ibn 'Āmir recited '*awḥā*' and 'Alī ibn Abī Ṭālib recited '*yaṭṭa'imuhu*'. 'Ā'ishah and Muḥammad ibn al-Ḥanafiyyah recited the verb in the past tense.

except for carrion

It is recited as *yakūna* and *takūna*. If it is *takūna*, it means 'except for a dead corpse,' and with *yakūna*, it means what happens to be dead.

flowing blood

'*Masfūḥ*' mean 'flowing, spilled out', and such blood is forbidden, but other blood is overlooked. Al-Māwardī related that if the blood is not flowing, as when it is in the veins and becomes solid like liver and spleen, then it is lawful since the

Prophet ﷺ said, 'Two dead things and two bloods are lawful for us.' As for blood in the veins with the meat, there are two rulings about it. One is that it is unlawful because it is part of what is spilled, and the liver and spleen are an exception, and the second is that it is lawful because what is specified is that which is spilled.

The latter is correct. 'Imrān ibn Ḥuḍayr said, 'I asked Abū Mijlaz about meat mixed with blood and about a pot which becomes red from the blood. He said, "There is no harm in it. Allah forbade flowing blood."' 'Ā'ishah and others said something similar to that. 'Ikrimah said, 'If it were not for this *āyah*, the Muslims would seek out the veins as the Jews do.' Ibrāhīm an-Nakha'ī said, 'There is nothing wrong with blood which remains in veins or the brain.' This ruling and that of someone forced to eat was already discussed in *al-Baqarah* (2:183). Allah knows best.

وَعَلَى ٱلَّذِينَ هَادُوا۟ حَرَّمْنَا كُلَّ ذِى ظُفُرٍ وَمِنَ ٱلْبَقَرِ وَٱلْغَنَمِ
حَرَّمْنَا عَلَيْهِمْ شُحُومَهُمَآ إِلَّا مَا حَمَلَتْ ظُهُورُهُمَآ أَوِ ٱلْحَوَايَآ
أَوْ مَا ٱخْتَلَطَ بِعَظْمٍ ذَٰلِكَ جَزَيْنَٰهُم بِبَغْيِهِمْ وَإِنَّا لَصَٰدِقُونَ ﴿١٤٦﴾

146 We made unlawful for the Jews every animal with an undivided hoof and, in respect of cattle and sheep, We made their fat unlawful for them, except what is attached to their backs or guts or mixed up with bone. That is how We repaid them for their insolence. And We certainly speak the truth.

We made unlawful for the Jews every animal with an undivided hoof,

When Allah mentioned what has been made unlawful for the community of Muḥammad ﷺ, He followed that by mentioning what was forbidden for the Jews since there was denial in their words, 'Allah has not forbidden us anything. We made things unlawful for ourselves as Israel made things unlawful for himself.' The meaning of '*hādū*' was discussed in *Sūrat al-Baqarah* (2:62). This prohibition for the Jews is an imposition, affliction and penalty.

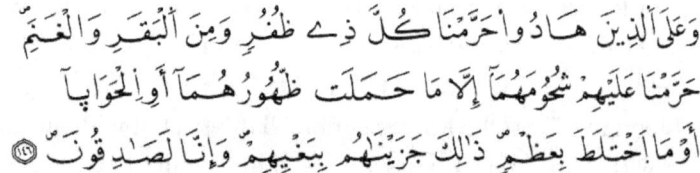

The first prohibition was about hooves (*ẓufur*). Al-Ḥasan recited '*ẓufr*' and Abū as-Simāl recited '*ẓifr*'. Abū Ḥātim did not acknowledge that recitation and did not mention it. It is a dialect. The plurals are *aẓfār, uẓfūr* and *aẓāfīr*. Al-Jawharī said that. An-Naḥḥās added from al-Farrā' *aẓāfīr* and *aẓāfīrah*. Ibn as-Sikkīt said that a man is called *aẓfar* who has long nails as *ash'ar* is used for a man with long hair. Mujāhid and Qatādah said that it refers to animals and birds that do not have divided hooves, like camels, ostriches, geese and ducks. Ibn Zayd said that it only refers to camels. Ibn 'Abbās said that it is camels and ostriches because the ostriches have feet like camels. It is said that it is every bird with talons and animals with hooves. *Ḥāfir* is called *ẓufur* as a metaphor.

At-Tirmidhī al-Ḥakīm said that *ḥāfir* means nails as well as talons. This is based on an assumption and there is no metaphor here. Do you not see that both of them are clipped and shortened and so they form the same category: a soft flexible bone which grows and is clipped like human nails? It is called a 'hoof' (*ḥāfir*) because it digs (*ḥafara*) into the earth. Talons (*mikhlab*) get their name because they are used to seize (*khalaba*) birds with their pointed ends. Nails (*ẓufr*) get their name because things are seized with nails, in other words it takes (*ẓafara*) things with its nails, whether it is a human being or bird doing it.

and in respect of cattle and sheep, We made their fat unlawful for them

Qatādah said that it means the fat of the intestines and the fat of the kidneys, as as-Suddī said. Ibn Jurayj said that every kind of fat is forbidden except for that mixed with a bone or on a bone. They were allowed the fat on the side and rump because it is on the coccyx.

except what is attached to their backs or guts or mixed up with bone

Mā is in the accusative for the exception. The noun '*backs*' is in the nominative by the verb '*attached*' and '*guts*' is also in the nominative added to '*backs*', meaning 'or what is on their guts.' The definite article is an appositive for the *iḍāfah*. According to this, the guts are part of what is lawful. In the phrase '*mixed up with bone*' *mā* is in the accusative through being added to '*attached*'. This is the soundest of what is said about it. It is the position of al-Kisā'ī, al-Farrā' and Aḥmad ibn Yaḥyā. Investigation obliges that a thing is added to what follows it unless the meaning is not sound or there is evidence which indicates something else. It is also said that the exception in the making lawful is what is attached to the backs in particular and that the phrase '*or guts or mixed up with bone*' is added to what is unlawful. In which case it means: forbidden to them is their fat or guts or what is mixed with bone, except any fat attached to backs which is not unlawful. Ash-Shāfi'ī used this *āyah* as evidence that someone who swears not to eat fat breaks his oath when he eats the fat from the back.

The word '*guts*' (*ḥawāyā*) means the intestines (*mabā'ir*) as Ibn 'Abbās and others said. *Mabā'ir* is the plural of *mab'ar* which takes its name from the concentration of dung (*ba'r*) within them. The singular of '*ḥawāyā*' is *ḥawiyā*'. It is also said that the singular is *ḥawiyyah*. Abū 'Ubaydah said that it is the coiled and circular part of the intestines. It is said that the guts are where the milk collects and are connected to the intestines, and they are where the milk settles. It is also said that it is just the intestines which contain fat. In other usages *ḥawāyā* means a garment that is wound around the hump of a camel. Imru al-Qays said:

> They put the garments [on the hump] and put on the garlands
> and encircled them with adorned weaving.

Allah tells us that He prescribed the prohibition of this in the Torah to refute their lie. He says, 'Forbidden to you are carrion, blood, the flesh of pigs, and every animal which does not have a cloven hoof and every fish without scales.' Then Allah abrogated all of that by the *Sharī'ah* of Muḥammad ﷺ and allowed some animals which had been prohibited and removed constriction by Muḥammad ﷺ and imposed the *dīn* of Islam on creation with its lawful and unlawful, commands and prohibitions.

When they slaughter their animals and eat what Allah made lawful for them in the Torah and leave what is unlawful for them, is that which they leave lawful for us? Mālik said in the book of Muḥammad that it is forbidden. He said in *al-Mabsūṭ* that it is lawful and Ibn Nāfi' stated that. Ibn al-Qāsim said that it is disliked. The reason for the first ruling is that its prohibition is part of their *dīn* and so they did not intend it when they slaughtered, and so it is forbidden to us just as blood is forbidden. The reason for the second ruling [making it lawful], which is the sound one, is that Allah Almighty removed the prohibition by Islam, and their belief about it has no effect because it is a false belief, and Ibn al-'Arabī stated that.

I say that its soundness is indicated by what the two *Ṣaḥīḥ* Collections relate from 'Abdullāh ibn Mughaffal. He said, 'While we were laying siege to the fortress of Khaybar, someone threw down a leather bag containing fat and I rushed to get it. I turned and there was the Prophet ﷺ and I was embarrassed before him.' This is found in al-Bukhārī. In Muslim we find: "Abdullāh ibn Mughaffal said, "I got a bag of fat on the Day of Khaybar. I kept it and I said, 'Today I will not give anyone any of this.' I turned and there was the Messenger of Allah smiling."' Our scholars say that he smiled when he saw the intensity of the eagerness of Ibn Mughaffal to take the bag and its contents. He did not command him to cast it away or forbid him.

The position of the schools of Abū Ḥanīfah, ash-Shāfi'ī and most scholars is that it is permitted to eat it, although it is reported from Mālik that it is disliked because of the disagreement concerning it. Ibn al-Mundhir related from Mālik that it is forbidden, and that was the view of some of the great companions of Mālik as we said. The *ḥadīth* is evidence against them. If, for instance, they were to slaughter an animal with claws, Aṣbagh states, 'Animals they have slaughtered which are mentioned in the Book of Allah as being forbidden to them cannot lawfully be eaten because they are forbidden in their *dīn*.' Ashhab and Ibn al-Qāsim said that. Ibn Wahb allowed it. Ibn Ḥabīb said, 'As for what they slaughter which is forbidden for them and we know that from our Book, it is not lawful to us either. Slaughtered animals which are not unlawful except by their words and discretion are not forbidden to us.'

That is how We repaid them

The word '*That*' refers to the prohibition, meaning the command of prohibition. The phrase '*how We repaid them*' means it was a punishment for their wrongdoing in their killing the Prophets, barring people from the Way of Allah, taking usury and making other people's property lawful by false means. This contains evidence that the prohibition is because of wrong action since it is constriction. There is no turning from expansiveness except in punishments. '*And We certainly speak the truth*' in what We say about those Jews regarding the meat and fat forbidden to them.

فَإِن كَذَّبُوكَ فَقُل رَّبُّكُمْ ذُو رَحْمَةٍ وَاسِعَةٍ وَلَا يُرَدُّ بَأْسُهُۥ عَنِ الْقَوْمِ
الْمُجْرِمِينَ ﴿١٤٧﴾

147 If they call you a liar, say: 'Your Lord possesses boundless mercy, but His violent force cannot be averted from the people of the evildoers.'

One aspect of Allah's immense mercy is that He is forbearing to you and did not punish you in this world. Then He reports about the punishment that He has prepared for them in the Next World when He says: '*but His violent force cannot be averted from the people of the evildoers*.' It is said that it means: 'The wrongdoers cannot ward off His force when He desires it to occur in this world.'

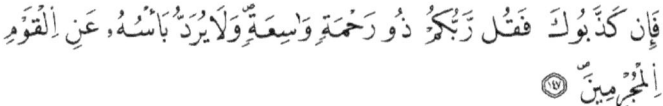

سَيَقُولُ ٱلَّذِينَ أَشْرَكُواْ لَوْ شَآءَ ٱللَّهُ مَآ أَشْرَكْنَا وَلَآ ءَابَآؤُنَا
وَلَا حَرَّمْنَا مِن شَيْءٍ كَذَٰلِكَ كَذَّبَ ٱلَّذِينَ مِن قَبْلِهِمْ حَتَّىٰ
ذَاقُواْ بَأْسَنَا قُلْ هَلْ عِندَكُم مِّنْ عِلْمٍ فَتُخْرِجُوهُ لَنَآ إِن تَتَّبِعُونَ
إِلَّا ٱلظَّنَّ وَإِنْ أَنتُمْ إِلَّا تَخْرُصُونَ ﴿١٤٨﴾

148 Those who associate others with Allah will say, 'If Allah had willed we would not have associated anything with Him, nor would our fathers; nor would we have made anything unlawful.' In the same way the people before them also lied until they felt Our violent force. Say: 'Do you have some knowledge you can produce for us? You are following nothing but conjecture. You are only guessing.'

Those who associate others with Allah will say, 'If Allah had willed we would not have associated anything with Him, nor would our fathers; nor would we have made anything unlawful.'

Mujāhid said that this refers to the idolaters of Quraysh. The phrase '*nor would we have made anything unlawful*' refers to the animals made *baḥīrah*, *sā'ibah* and *waṣīlah*. Allah Almighty is aware in the Unseen about what they will say. They think that this will hold for them when the proof against them is at hand and they know for certain that what they held to was false. The meaning is: 'If Allah had so willed, He could have sent a Messenger to our fathers and forbidden them *shirk* and making unlawful what is lawful for them, and so they would have stopped. So we merely followed them in that.' Allah refutes them and says: '*Do you have some knowledge you can produce for us?*' in other words do you have any evidence for all of this?

You are following nothing but conjecture. You are only guessing.'

Saying this is based on mere conjecture. '*You are only guessing*' since you imagine that you have the proof. '*Our fathers*' is joined to the *nūn* of '*We would not have associated.*' Allah does not say 'Neither we nor our fathers ' because '*wa-lā*' takes the position of emphasising what is implied.

قُلْ فَلِلَّهِ ٱلْحُجَّةُ ٱلْبَٰلِغَةُ فَلَوْ شَآءَ لَهَدَىٰكُمْ أَجْمَعِينَ ﴿١٤٩﴾

149 Say: 'Allah's is the conclusive argument. If He had willed He could have guided every one of you.'

Say: 'Allah's is the conclusive argument.

It cuts off the excuses of the one whose argument is defeated and removes doubt from the one who examines it. So His eloquent evidence for this is a clarification that He is One and that He sent the Messengers and Prophets, and *tawḥīd* is made clear by reflecting on creation. He supported His Messengers by miracles and made His command obligatory for every responsible person. As for His Knowledge, Will and Speech, it is unseen and human beings are not aware of it – except for a Messenger with whom He is pleased. It is enough in respect of responsibility that if human beings truly want to do what Allah has commanded them to do, He will give them the power to do so.

The Mu'tazilites were confused by Allah's words: '*If Allah had so willed, we would not have associated.*' They said that this is Allah's censure of those who claimed that their *shirk* was by His will. Their conclusion regarding that is false because Allah Almighty is criticising them for not striving to seek the truth. They were saying that by way of mockery and jest. If they had said it with veneration and respect and recognition, He would not have criticised them since He says: '*If Allah had willed, they would not have associated anything with Him*' (6:107) and: '*...they still would not believe unless Allah willed*' (6:111) and: '*If He had wished, He could have guided every one of you.*' (16:9) There are many examples of that. The believers say that because of their knowledge of Allah.

قُلْ هَلُمَّ شُهَدَآءَكُمُ ٱلَّذِينَ يَشْهَدُونَ أَنَّ ٱللَّهَ حَرَّمَ هَٰذَا فَإِن شَهِدُوا۟
فَلَا تَشْهَدْ مَعَهُمْ وَلَا تَتَّبِعْ أَهْوَآءَ ٱلَّذِينَ كَذَّبُوا۟ بِـَٔايَٰتِنَا وَٱلَّذِينَ
لَا يُؤْمِنُونَ بِٱلْـَٔاخِرَةِ وَهُم بِرَبِّهِمْ يَعْدِلُونَ ﴿١٥٠﴾

150 Say: 'Produce your witnesses to testify that Allah made this unlawful.' If they do testify, do not testify with them and do not follow the whims and desires of people who deny Our Signs, and who do not believe in the Next World and make others equal to their Lord.

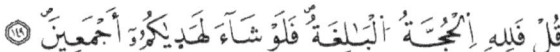

Say: 'Produce your witnesses

Say to those idolaters, 'Bring your witnesses to the fact that Allah forbade what you have made forbidden.' '*Halumma*' is a word which indicates an address to something and the people of the Ḥijāz use the same form for the singular and plural and for male and female. In the Najdī dialect different forms for each are used. It is the language of Ḥijāz which is used in the Qur'an. '*Halumma*' is also used in 33:18. It means: attend, come near, bring the food. Here it means, 'Bring your witnesses.' The *mīm* has a *fatḥah* because of two silent letters meeting. It is not permitted for it to have a *ḍammah* or a *kasrah*. Al-Khalīl says that the root is '*hā*' to which '*lumma*' is added and then the *alif* is elided because the term is so frequently used. Another said that '*hā*' is extra. We also find in *Kitāb al-'Ayn* by al-Khalīl that the root is: '*hal a'ummu*', meaning 'Shall I direct you?' Then it also is changed because of frequency of use. '*If they do testify*' to one another, do not affirm their testimony unless it is from a Divine Book or the words of a Prophet. They have nothing like that.

قُلْ تَعَالَوْا أَتْلُ مَا حَرَّمَ رَبُّكُمْ عَلَيْكُمْ ۖ أَلَّا تُشْرِكُوا بِهِ شَيْئًا ۖ
وَبِالْوَالِدَيْنِ إِحْسَانًا ۖ وَلَا تَقْتُلُوا أَوْلَادَكُم مِّنْ إِمْلَاقٍ ۖ نَّحْنُ نَرْزُقُكُمْ
وَإِيَّاهُمْ ۖ وَلَا تَقْرَبُوا الْفَوَاحِشَ مَا ظَهَرَ مِنْهَا وَمَا بَطَنَ ۖ وَلَا تَقْتُلُوا
النَّفْسَ الَّتِي حَرَّمَ اللَّهُ إِلَّا بِالْحَقِّ ۚ ذَٰلِكُمْ وَصَّاكُم بِهِ لَعَلَّكُمْ
تَعْقِلُونَ ﴿١٥١﴾ وَلَا تَقْرَبُوا مَالَ الْيَتِيمِ إِلَّا بِالَّتِي هِيَ أَحْسَنُ حَتَّىٰ
يَبْلُغَ أَشُدَّهُ ۖ وَأَوْفُوا الْكَيْلَ وَالْمِيزَانَ بِالْقِسْطِ ۖ لَا نُكَلِّفُ نَفْسًا
إِلَّا وُسْعَهَا ۖ وَإِذَا قُلْتُمْ فَاعْدِلُوا وَلَوْ كَانَ ذَا قُرْبَىٰ ۖ وَبِعَهْدِ اللَّهِ أَوْفُوا ۚ ذَٰلِكُمْ
وَصَّاكُم بِهِ لَعَلَّكُمْ تَذَكَّرُونَ ﴿١٥٢﴾ وَأَنَّ هَٰذَا صِرَاطِي مُسْتَقِيمًا
فَاتَّبِعُوهُ ۖ وَلَا تَتَّبِعُوا السُّبُلَ فَتَفَرَّقَ بِكُمْ عَن سَبِيلِهِ ۚ ذَٰلِكُمْ
وَصَّاكُم بِهِ لَعَلَّكُمْ تَتَّقُونَ ﴿١٥٣﴾

151-3 Say: 'Come and I will recite to you what your Lord has made unlawful for you': that you do not associate anything with Him; that you be good to your parents; that you may not kill your children because of poverty – We will provide for you and them; that you may not approach indecency – outward or inward; that you may not kill any person Allah has made inviolate – except

with the right to do so. That is what He instructs you to do so that hopefully you will use your intellects. And that you do not go near the property of orphans before they reach maturity – except in a good way; that you give full measure and full weight with justice – We impose on no self any more than it can bear; that you be equitable when you speak – even if a near relative is concerned; and that you fulfil Allah's contract. That is what He instructs you to do, so that hopefully you may pay heed. This is My Path and it is straight, so follow it. Do not follow other ways or you will become cut off from His Way. That is what He instructs you to do, so that hopefully you will be godfearing.

Say: 'Come and I will recite to you

'Come forward and I will recite with truth and certainty as my Lord has revealed to me, not with falsehood or conjecture as you claim.' Then Allah makes that clear and says: '*that you do not associate anything with Him.*' Grammatically this is in the accusative case by an understood implied verb in the first part of the expression, namely: 'I will recite to you not to associate,' meaning of the prohibition of associating others with Allah. Coming forward is made into a sort of elevation and rising, because someone who is commanded to come forward is undertaking this action. As when someone seated is told, 'Come,' it means 'Elevate yourself by rising and coming forward.' They have extended its usage to include some standing or walking. Ibn ash-Shajarī said that.

what your Lord has made unlawful for you

Mā has the nature of a predicate made accusative by the verb '*recite*'. This means: 'Come and I will recite to you what your Lord has made unlawful to you.' If you connect '*for you*' to '*made unlawful*', that is correct because it is what is closest. That is what the Basrans prefer. But if you connect it to '*recite*' that is also good because it comes first. That is what the Kufans prefer. What is then implied is: 'I recite to you what your Lord has made unlawful to you.' The phrase '*not associate anything*' is made accusative by an implied verb from the first expression and means: 'I recite to you that you should not associate others with Him,' in other words: 'I recite to you the prohibition of *shirk*.' It is also possible that it can be in the accusative based on the instigation in '*alaykum* which is then severed from what is before it, implying: 'You must abandon associating others, and you must also be good to your parents, not kill your children and not approach indecency.' This is like the usage in 5:105. Ibn ash-Shajarī said all of that. An-Naḥḥās said that '*an* (that)' can be in the accusative as an appositive for '*mā*' and it means: 'I recite to you the prohibition of associating others.' Al-Farrā' said that '*lā*' can be a prohibition because Allah says after it: '*you may not kill*'.

This *āyah* is a command from Allah Almighty to His Prophet ﷺ to summon everyone to listen to the recitation of things that Allah has forbidden. Thus it is mandatory for scholars after him to convey that to people and differentiate for them what Allah has forbidden them from what He has made lawful. Allah Almighty says: '*You must make it clear to people and not conceal it.*' (3:187)

Ibn al-Mubārak mentioned that Rabī' ibn Khaytham said to someone sitting with him, 'Would you be happy to be given a page from the Prophet ﷺ whose seal has not been broken?' 'Yes,' he replied. He said, 'Then recite: "*Come and I will recite to you what your Lord has made unlawful for you…*" to the end of the three *āyahs*.'

Ka'b al-Aḥbar said, 'This *āyah* is the beginning of the Torah.' Ibn 'Abbās said, 'These are *āyahs* of judgment which Allah also mentioned in *Sūrat Āl 'Imrān* and which contain the normative laws of creation which have not been abrogated in any religion.' It is said that they are the Ten Commandments revealed to Mūsā.

that you be good to your parents;

This is by being dutiful to them, taking care of them, attending to them, obeying them, emancipating them from slavery and not domineering over them.

that you may not kill your children because of poverty –

Imlāq is poverty, and so it means 'do not bury your daughters alive out of fear of poverty. I will provide for you and them.' Some of them used to do that to boys and girls out of fear of poverty and it is the evident meaning of the *āyah*. *Amlaqa* is to become poor and to make someone poor. An-Naqqāsh related from Mu'arrij that *imlāq* means hunger in the dialect of Lakhm. Mundhir ibn Sa'īd said that *imlāq* means spending. It is mentioned that 'Alī said to his wife, 'Spend (*amliqī*) whatever you wish of your property.' A man who is *maliq* is a flatterer who says on his tongue what is not in his heart. So it is a word with various meanings.

This is used as evidence for those who forbid coitus interruptus because burying alive eradicates progeny and coitus interruptus prevents progeny and so there is a resemblance between the two, although the murder of a soul is the greater sin and the more horrific action. That is why scholars have said that what is understood from the words of the Prophet ﷺ about coitus interruptus: 'That is hidden burying alive,' that it is a matter of dislike and not prohibition. A group of Companions and others said that. A group of scholars among the Companions, *Tābi'ūn* and *fuqahā'* allow coitus interruptus because the Prophet ﷺ said, 'You do not have to not do it. It comes from the decree,' implying that there is nothing wrong in doing it. Al-Ḥasan and Muḥammad ibn al-Muthannā, however, understood that this forbids coitus interruptus, but the first interpretation is more fitting since the Prophet ﷺ said, 'When Allah desires to create something, nothing can prevent it.'

Mālik and ash-Shāfi'ī said that it is not permitted to practise coitus interruptus with a free woman without her permission. It seems that they thought that ejaculation is part of her full pleasure and part of her right to a child. They did not think that that applied to a slave since she did not have the same right.

that you may not approach indecency – outward or inward

This is like *'Abandon wrong action, outward and inward.'* (6:120) The word *'outward'* forbids all sorts of indecency, which are acts of disobedience. The word *'inward'* refers to opposition on which the heart resolves. Outward and inward are two states, each of which contains various things. *'Outward'* is accusative as an appositive for *'indecency'* and *'inward'* is added to it.

that you may not kill any person Allah has made inviolate except with the right to do so.

The noun *'person'* is definite because it is defines the genus as when you say, 'Love of the *dirham* and *dīnār* has destroyed people.' It is the same as: *'Man was created headstrong.'* (70:19) which is followed by: *'except for those who do the prayer'* (70:21); and His words: *'By the afternoon. Truly man is in loss'* (103:1-2) after which He says: *'except for those who believe.'* (103:3)

This *āyah* forbids taking life, which is sacred, whether that of a believer or of someone with an alliance, except when there is a legal right demanding his death. The Messenger of Allah ﷺ said, 'I was commanded to fight people until they say, "There is no god but Allah," If anyone says "There is no god but Allah", his property and life are safe except when there is a legal right to them, and his reckoning is up to Allah.' This legal right exists in several cases. One is refusing to pay *zakāt* and another abandonment of the prayer. Abū Bakr aṣ-Ṣiddīq fought those who refused to pay *zakāt*. We find in Revelation: *'If they turn in repentance and establish the prayer and pay zakāt, let them go on their way.'* (9:5) This is clear. The Prophet ﷺ said, 'The blood of a Muslim is only lawful in one of three cases: a fornicator who has been previously married, a life for a life, and one who abandons his *dīn* and leaves the Community.' The Messenger of Allah ﷺ also said, 'When allegiance is given to two caliphs, kill the second of them.' Muslim transmitted it. Abū Dāwūd related from Ibn 'Abbās that the Prophet ﷺ said, 'If you find someone doing the action of the people of Lūṭ, kill both the active and passive partner in it.' This will be explained in *Sūrat al-A'rāf.*

We find in Revelation: '*The reprisal against those who wage war on Allah and His Messenger, and go about the earth corrupting it, is that they should be killed…*' (5:33) and '*If two parties of the believers fight…*' (49:9). The same applies to those who break their solidarity with the Muslims and oppose the ruler of the Community and split their unity and strive for corruption in that land by looting family and property and attacking the ruler and denying his authority: they are killed. This is the meaning of Allah's words: '*except with the right*'. The Prophet ﷺ said, 'The blood of the believers is the same, and the least of them may give protection. A Muslim is not killed for an unbeliever or one with a treaty when under treaty, and the people of two different religions do not inherit from one another.'

Abū Dāwūd and an-Nasā'ī related from Abū Bakrah that the Messenger of Allah ﷺ said, 'If someone kills someone with a treaty for other than protection of life, Allah will forbid the Garden to him.' In another transmission of Abū Dāwūd, 'Whoever kills a man of the *dhimmah* will not experience the scent of the Garden, and its scent can be perceived at a distance of seventy years.' Al-Bukhārī says in this *ḥadīth*: 'its scent can be perceived at a distance of forty years.' He transmitted it from 'Abdullāh ibn 'Amr ibn al-'Āṣ.

That is what He instructs you to do

The word '*That*' indicates prohibitions. The '*kum*' is for direct address and not declined. In the phrase '*He instructs you to do*' *waṣiyah* is the stressed command. The pronoun refers to Allah.

Maṭar al-Warrāq related from Nāfi' from Ibn 'Umar that 'Uthmān ibn 'Affān looked down at his companions and said, 'What is your reason for killing me? I heard the Messenger of Allah ﷺ say, "The blood of a Muslim man is not lawful except in three cases: a man who commits fornication after he has been married who is stoned; someone who kills intentionally and there is retaliation taken on him; or he apostasies after Islam and he is killed. By Allah, I have not committed fornication either in the *Jāhiliyyah* or Islam. I have not killed anyone so that retaliation should be taken from me, and I have not apostasised after I became Muslim. I testify that there is no god but Allah and that Muḥammad is His slave and Messenger. That is what I remind you and counsel you – perhaps you will understand!"'

And that you may not go near the property of orphans except in a good way

This means in a way that is good for them and brings them benefit. That is by maintaining their capital and making it profitable. This is the best position on this because it is general. Mujāhid says that it means that '*in a good way*' is through trade, not by lending it.

before they reach maturity

This means reaching full strength. That may be physically or mentally. Both aspects must be attained. The maturity referred to here is general. The state of the orphan is clarified in *Sūrat an-Nisā'* and specifically when Allah says: '*Keep a close check on orphans until they reach a marriageable age.*' (4:6) He combined physical strength, which is marriageable age, and mental capacity, which is awareness of good sense. If he were to give the orphan authority over his property before mental awareness but after physical strength, he would waste it through his appetites and end up penniless.

Orphans are specifically mentioned because people tend to neglect them. Fathers assess their children, and children without fathers must be assessed as well. Reaching maturity might allow them access to their property in other than '*a good way*' because respect for adults is a generally accepted thing. Orphans are mentioned because guardians will be answerable to Allah. It means: 'Only ever go near the property of an orphan in a good way until he becomes an adult. When he is an adult and shows good sense, then give him his property.'

Scholars disagree about exactly when an orphan reaches maturity. Ibn Zayd said that it is the time of puberty. The people of Madīnah say that it is both puberty and good sense. Abū Ḥanīfah says that it is at the age of twenty-five. Ibn al-'Arabī says, 'It is extraordinary that Abū Ḥanīfah thinks that age is not settled by analogy or investigation, but by transmission. He confirms that on the basis of weak *ḥadīth*s but he resided in the abode of the mint from which much counterfeit currency emerged. If he had resided in the birthplace of the *dīn*, as Allah granted to Mālik, then only the pure gold of the *dīn* would issue from it.' It is said that maturity is achieved by full strength as was stated by Suḥaym ibn Wathīl:

I am fifty years old, possessing my full power (*ashuddī*).
The trickery of events has made me reach it.

Ashudd is a singular noun which has no plural like *ānuk*, which means lead. It is also said that the singular is *shadd*, like *falas* and *aflus*. Its root is *shadd an-nahār*, the time when the sun is high. It is when the day is well advanced. Muḥammad ibn aḍ-Ḍabbī quoted a verse of 'Antarah:

My arrangement with you is when the day is advanced (*shadd an-nahār*),
as if his chest and head were dyed with indigo.

Another said:

The woman in the sedan went around him when it was well (*shadda*)
into the day, tall, with pure hands.

Sībawayh said that the singular is *shiddah.* Al-Jawharī said that that is good because one says, 'The boy reached full strength (*shiddatahu*)' although the form *fi'lah* does not have the plural form *af'ul*. There are those who say, based on analogy, that it is the plural of *shadd.* Abū Zayd said that *shuddā* (hardship) is *shiddah.* The verb *ashadda* is used of a man who has a strong riding camel with him.

that you give full measure and full weight with justice –

This means being fair in giving and taking when buying and selling. *Qisṭ* means justice.

We impose on no self any more than it can bear,

It means: 'We only impose on it what is within its capacity to fulfil in measure and weighing.' This demands that these matters are within the capacity of man to maintain and observe. So that any disparity between the two measures it is not possible to avoid and is beyond human capacity to achieve is overlooked. It is said that *kayl* means *mikyāl.*

One of the scholars said, 'Since Allah knew that many of His slaves feel constricted about being generous to someone else when they do not have to be, He commanded the giver to give the one with a right his full right and he is not obliged to give more since giving more than that would be constricting himself. He commanded the one with a right to take his right and he is not obliged to be content with less than it since that would be a diminishment which would grieve him.'

In the *Muwaṭṭā'* of Mālik it is related that Yaḥyā ibn Sa'īd heard 'Abdullāh ibn 'Abbās say, 'Stealing from the spoils does not appear in a people without terror being cast into their hearts. Fornication does not spread in a people without there being much death among them. A people do not lessen the measure and weight without provision being cut off from them. A people do not judge unjustly without blood spreading among them. A people do not betray their pledge without Allah giving their enemies power over them.' Ibn 'Abbās also said, 'You company of non-Arabs are involved with two [grave] matters on account of which those before you were destroyed: the measure and the weight.'

that you be equitable when you speak

This includes judgments and testimony. '*Even if a near relative is concerned*', in other words even if the right is owed by one of your relatives as we read in *Sūrat an-Nisā'* (4:134).

and that you fulfil Allah's contract.

This is general to everything that Allah has made a covenant with His slaves about. It can also refer to contracts between two people. The contract is ascribed to Allah since He commanded that it be preserved and one be faithful to it. Perhaps you may be admonished.

This is My Path and it is straight, so follow it.

This immense *āyah* is connected to what is before it. When Allah forbids a matter and cautions here against following other than His Path, He commands people to follow His Path according to what has been made clear by sound *ḥadīths* and the statements of the early generations. '*Anna*' can be in the accusative, implying 'Recite: "*This is My Path*",' according to al-Farrā' and al-Kisā'ī. Al-Farrā' said that it is genitive, implying 'He orders you to it and this is My Path.' According to al-Khalīl and Sibawayh, it can imply, 'Because this is My Path.' Al-A'mash, Hamzah and al-Kisā'ī read it as '*inna hādhā*,' as a new sentence, implying 'What I mention in the *āyahs* is My Path, straight.' Ibn Abī Isḥāq and Ya'qūb recite '*an hādhā*', which is like the doubled form (*anna*), unless it contains the pronoun of what is mentioned in it, i.e. '*annahā hādhā*'. This is in the nominative although it can be considered to be in the accusative. The an can also be added for stress as we see in 12:96.

Ṣirāṭ is the Path which is the *dīn* of Islam. The adjective '*straight*' is in the accusative for the *ḥāl* and means straight, level and even without any crookedness. Allah commands people to follow His Path which He set out and legislated on the tongue of His Prophet Muḥammad ﷺ, and its end is the Garden. There are minor roads which branch off from it. Whoever follows the main path is saved and if someone goes off on those branches, they will take him to the Fire.

Do not follow other ways or you will become cut off from His Way.

This means to incline to them. Abū Muḥammad ad-Dārimī mentioned in his *Musnad* from 'Affān from Ḥammād ibn Zayd from 'Āṣim ibn Bahdalah from Abū Wā'il that 'Abdullāh ibn Mas'ūd said, 'One day the Messenger of Allah ﷺ drew a line for us and then said, "This is the Path of Allah." Then he drew lines to the right of it and lines to the left of it and said, "These are other paths. Every path has a *shayṭān* who calls to it." Then he ﷺ recited this *āyah*.' Ibn Mājah transmits it in the *Sunan* from Jābir ibn 'Abdullāh. He said, 'While we were with the Prophet ﷺ, he drew a line and then two lines to right of it and two lines to the left of it. Then put his hand on the middle line and said, "This is the Path of Allah."' Then he recited this *āyah*: '*This is My Path and it is straight, so follow it. Do not follow other ways or you will become cut off from His Way.*' These '*ways*' include Judaism, Christianity, Magianism, and the people of other religions, innovations and misguidance, the people of sects and deviance as well as other people who engage themselves in argumentation and delving into *kalām*. All of this leads to error and doubt in their belief, as Ibn 'Aṭiyyah said.

This is sound. Aṭ-Ṭabarī mentioned in the *Book of the Adab of Selves* that a man asked Ibn Mas'ūd, 'What is the Straight Path?' He replied, 'Muḥammad ﷺ left us near the beginning of it and it ends up in the Garden, and to its right are paths and to its left are paths. There are men calling out to whoever passes by them. Anyone who goes down those paths will end up in the Fire.' 'Abdullāh ibn Mas'ūd said, 'Learn knowledge before it is taken away. It will be taken away by the removal of its people. Beware of extravagance, delving too deeply and innovations. You should follow the old ways.' Ad-Dārimī transmitted it. Mujāhid said that the words 'Do not follow other ways' refer to innovations.

Ibn Shihāb said, 'This is like Allah's words: "*As for those who divide up their* dīn *and form into sects*" (6:159). Flight is flight and salvation is salvation! [It is] holding to the Straight Path and upright *sunnah*s which the righteous *Salaf* followed, and it contains the true profit.' The *imāms* related from Abū Hurayrah that the Messenger of Allah ﷺ said, 'Take what I command you and leave what I forbid you.' Ibn Mājah and others related from al-'Irbāḍ ibn Sāriyah: 'The Messenger of Allah ﷺ admonished us with an admonition which made eyes weep and hearts tremble. We said, "Messenger of Allah, this admonition is a farewell. So what do you enjoin on us?" He answered, "I have left you that which is clear and whose night is like its day. After me no one will swerve from it but that he will be destroyed. Any among you who live long will see much disagreement, so you must hold to my *Sunnah* and the *Sunnah* of the rightly-guided and guiding caliphs. Hold onto it with your teeth. Beware of new matters. Every innovation is misguidance. You must obey even if it is an Abyssinian slave. The believer is like the haughty camel. When it is bound, it follows.' At-Tirmidhī related something along those lines and said it was sound.

Abū Dāwūd related from Ibn Kathīr that Sufyān said, 'A man wrote to 'Umar ibn 'Abd al-'Azīz to ask him about *qadar* (free will). He wrote back to him, "I advise you to have *taqwā* of Allah, to be moderate in respect of His commands, to follow the *Sunnah* of the Messenger of Allah ﷺ and to abandon any new things which have been originated after what his *Sunnah* brought and spare yourselves trouble. You must hold fast to the Community. It is a protection for you by Allah's permission. Then know that people do not innovate an innovation without what gave rise to it occurring before it. The *Sunnah* was set down by one who, unlike you, was not known to have any error or mistake or stupidity or prolixity. Content yourself with what the early community were themselves content with. They had knowledge and refrained [from certain matters] with piercing insight. They were stronger in discovering matters and were more entitled to excellence. If guidance were what you have, then you would have preceded them in it. If you said that it occurred after them, it was only originated by those who followed other than their path and desired other than what they desired. They are the Forerunners. What they said about it was enough and what they described is adequate. Those below them fall short and those above them are impudent. People fell short compared to them and were coarse, and desired other than what they had and were excessive. In spite of that, they are on a straight path.' And he mentioned the *ḥadīth*.

Sahl ibn 'Abdullāh at-Tustarī said, 'You must follow the tradition and the *Sunnah*. I fear that there will soon come a time when a man mentions the Prophet ﷺ and following him in all his states and they will criticise him and be averse to him and free themselves of him, and humiliate and abuse him.' Sahl also said, 'Innovation appeared at the hands of the people of the *Sunnah* because they expounded and spoke to one another and so their positions became public and spread among the common people. Then the one who had not heard it heard it. If they had left it and not spoken to them, each of them would have died on what is in his breast and not shown any of it and taken it with him to his grave.' Sahl said, 'None of you originates an innovation but that Iblīs makes him innovate a new form of worship and then he worships by it and then makes that into an innovation. When he then talks about that innovation and calls people to it, he wrests that [from *Shayṭān*) to himself.' Sahl said, 'I do not know of any *ḥadīth* which has come about innovation stronger than this *ḥadīth*: "Allah has veiled the Garden from a person with innovation."' He added, 'The Jew and the Christian have more hope than them.' Sahl said, 'Whoever wants to honour his *dīn* should not go to the ruler nor mix with women nor argue with the people of sects.' He also said, 'Follow and do not innovate. You will have enough.'

In the *Musnad* of ad-Dārimī, it states that Abū Mūsā al-Ash'arī went to 'Abdullāh ibn Mas'ūd and said, 'Abū 'Abd ar-Raḥmān, yesterday I saw something in the mosque which I did not recognise, but, praise be to Allah, I only saw good.' He asked, 'What is it?' He replied, 'In the evening you will see it.' He said, 'In the mosque I saw people sitting in circles waiting for the prayer. There was a man in each circle and they had pebbles in their hands. He would say to them, "Do a hundred *takbīrs*," and they did a hundred *takbīrs*. "Do a hundred '*lā ilāha illa-llāh*'," and they did a hundred. "Do a hundred '*subḥānallāh*', and they did a hundred.' He asked, 'What did you say to them?' He answered, 'I did not say anything to them, waiting for your opinion and your command.' He said, 'Did you not command them to count their evil deeds and guarantee for them that their good deeds would not be lost?' Then he went and we went with him to one of the circles and he stood over them and said, 'What is this which I see you doing?' They answered, 'Abū 'Abd ar-Raḥmān, we use the pebbles to count *takbīr, lā ilāha illa-llāh* and *tasbīḥ*.' He said, 'Count your evil deeds and I guarantee that you will not lose any of your good deeds. Judge, community of Muḥammad! How swift is your destruction! (Or opening a door of misguidance)!' They said, 'By Allah, Abū 'Abd ar-Raḥmān, we only desire good.' He said, 'How many a one who desires good will not get it!'

It is reported that 'Umar ibn 'Abd al-'Azīz was asked by a man about the people of sects and innovations. He said, 'Your *dīn* should be that of the of the Bedouin and boys in the schools (*kuttāb*). Turn from what is other than that.' Al-Awzā'ī said, 'Iblīs asked his friends, "How do you come at the sons of Ādam?" They replied, "From all directions." He asked, "Have you come to them from the aspect of asking forgiveness?" He answered, "Unlikely! That is something which is connected to *tawḥīd*!" He said, "I will spread among them something for which they will not ask for Allah's forgiveness."' He said, 'He spread sects among them.' Mujāhid said, 'I do not know which of the two blessings I have is greater: that Allah guided me to Islam or saved me from these sects.' Ash-Sha'bī said, 'They are called the people of sects (*ahwā'*) because they fall into the Fire.' All of that is in ad-Dārimī.

Sahl ibn 'Abdullāh was asked about praying behind the Mu'tazilites and marrying them, and he said, 'No, and it is no honour! They are unbelievers! How can someone believe who says that the Qur'an is created and that neither the Garden nor the Fire are created, and that Allah has no *Ṣirāṭ* nor intercession, and that none of the believers of the Community of Muḥammad ﷺ who commit wrong actions will enter the Fire or leave the Fire, and that there is no punishment in the Grave, and no Munkar nor Nakīr, and that our Lord will not be seen in the Next World, and that faith is not subject to increase and that the knowledge of Allah is created? They do not believe in the ruler nor *Jumu'ah*, and they declare that those who believe are unbelievers.'

Al-Fuḍayl ibn 'Iyāḍ said, 'If someone loves a person with an innovation, Allah makes his actions come to nothing and removes the light of Islam from his heart.' This has already been discussed. Sufyān ath-Thawrī said, 'Innovation is dearer to Iblīs than disobedience. One repents from disobedience but does not repent from innovation.' Ibn 'Abbās said, 'Just looking at a man of the people of the *Sunnah* who calls to the *Sunnah* and forbids innovation is worship.' Abū al-'Āliyah said, 'You must have the original practice they followed before they split up.' 'Āṣim al-Aḥwal said, 'Al-Ḥasan reported it and he said, "By Allah, he advised you well and spoke the truth to you."' The words of the Prophet ﷺ about the division of the tribe of Israel into seventy-two sects was discussed in *Sūrat Āl 'Imrān* (3:103) and that the division of this community will be into seventy-three. One of the gnostic scholars said, 'This additional sect in the Community of Muḥammad ﷺ consists of a people who oppose scholars and hate the *fuqahā'*. That did not exist in the previous communities.'

Rāfi' ibn Khadīj related, 'I heard the Messenger of Allah ﷺ say, "There will be in my Community people who reject Allah and reject the Qur'an without being aware of doing so, just as the Jews and Christians rejected." I said, "May I be your ransom, Messenger of Allah! How is that?" He answered, "They will confirm some of it and deny some." I asked, "May I be your ransom, Messenger of Allah! What will they say?" He said, "They will make Iblīs an equal to Allah in His creation and His strength and provision. They will say that good is from Allah and evil is from Iblīs." He said, "They will reject Allah, but in spite of that, will recite the Book of Allah. They will reject the Qur'an after faith and recognition." He added, "How much enmity, hated and argumentation will be cast into My Community originating with them! Those are the *zindīq*s of this Community."'

We already mentioned the prohibition against sitting with the people of innovation and sects here and in *Sūrat an-Nisā'* and that whoever sits with such people will be judged to be the same as them. Allah says: '*When you see people engrossed in mockery of Our Signs…*' (6:68) Then in *Sūrat an-Nisā'*, which is Madinan, He elucidates the punishment for doing that and opposing what Allah has commanded in His words: '*It has been sent down to you in the Book…*' (4:140) He connected them to those who sit with them.

This was the ruling made by a number of the imams of this Community, among whom were Aḥmad ibn Ḥanbal, al-Awzā'ī, and Ibn al-Mubārak, and it is a ruling obliged by these *āyah*s about those who associate and mix with the people of innovations. They said that if a man is known to sit with the people of innovations, he is forbidden from doing so. If he does not stop, then he is ruled to be the same as them. 'Umar ibn 'Abd al-'Azīz also used the same principle regarding those who sit in a gathering where people are drinking – they receive the same penalty as they do. He was told that that someone may sit with them to tell them they are wrong. He said that he is forbidden to sit with them, and if he does not stop, he is ruled to be one them.

ثُمَّ ءَاتَيْنَا مُوسَى ٱلْكِتَٰبَ تَمَامًا عَلَى ٱلَّذِىٓ أَحْسَنَ وَتَفْصِيلًا
لِّكُلِّ شَىْءٍ وَهُدًى وَرَحْمَةً لَّعَلَّهُم بِلِقَآءِ رَبِّهِمْ يُؤْمِنُونَ ﴿١٥٤﴾ وَهَٰذَا كِتَٰبٌ
أَنزَلْنَٰهُ مُبَارَكٌ فَٱتَّبِعُوهُ وَٱتَّقُوا۟ لَعَلَّكُمْ تُرْحَمُونَ ﴿١٥٥﴾

154-5 Then We gave Mūsā the Book, complete and perfect for him who does good, elucidating everything, and a guidance and a mercy, so that hopefully they will believe in their encounter with their Lord. And this is a Book We have sent down and blessed, so follow it and be godfearing so that hopefully you will gain mercy.

'*We gave Mūsā the Book*' is two objects and '*complete*' is either an object or a verbal noun. The phrase '*for him who does good*' can be recited in both the accusative and nominative. If it is recited in the nominative, which is the reading of Yaḥyā ibn Ya'mar and Ibn Abī Isḥāq, it implies: 'complete for the one who does good'. Al-Mahdawī says that it is unlikely because of the elision of the inchoative that refers to 'which'. Sībawayh related that he heard from al-Khalīl: '*mā anā bi-lladhī qā'ilun laka shay'an.*' If it is in the accusative, it is on the basis that it is a verb in the past tense. This is the view of the Basrans. Al-Kisā'ī and al-Farrā' allow it to be a noun describing 'which'. They permit '*marartu billadhī akhīk*', with both describing 'which' in the definite and what is close to it. An-Naḥḥās says that this is impossible in the view of the Basrans because it is an adjective of the noun before it is complete. They believe that the meaning is: 'for the one who does good'.

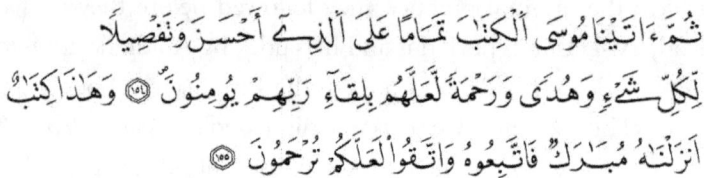

Mujāhid said that '*complete and perfect*' is a description of a believer who does good. Al-Ḥasan said about the meaning of '*complete and perfect for him who does good*': 'Among them were those who did good and those who did not do good, so Allah sent down the Book complete and perfect for those who do good.' The evidence for the soundness of this view is that Ibn Mas'ūd recited, '*Tamāman 'alā-llādhīna aḥsanu*'. It is said that the meaning is: 'We gave Mūsā the Torah in addition to the good-doing which Mūsā used to do which Allah had taught him before the Torah was sent down on him.' Muḥammad ibn Yazīd said, 'The meaning is: perfect according to that which Allah made good to Mūsā in the Message and other things.' 'Abdullāh ibn Zayd said, 'It means Allah's goodness to His Prophets by giving them the Message and other things.' Ar-Rabī' ibn Anas said, 'Complete and perfect for the good-doing of Mūsā in his obeying Him.' Al-Farrā' said that.

'*Thumma*' (then) usually indicates that the second thing follows the first. The story of Mūsā and his being given the Book is before this, and so here '*thumma*' means '*and*', i.e. '*We gave Mūsā the Book*' because they are both conjunctive particles. It is said that words imply: 'We gave Mūsā the Book before We sent down the Qur'an on Muḥammad ﷺ.' It is said that it means: 'Come. I will recite to you how your Lord has forgiven you, and then I will recite what We gave Mūsā in terms of perfection.' '*Elucidating everything*' is added to it, as is '*a guidance and a mercy*'. '*Blessed*' is an adjective and means that it contains much good. Outside of the Qur'an it is permitted to have the accusative as '*mubārakan*' for the *ḥāl*. '*So follow it*' means 'learn what is in it.' '*Be godfearing*' means fear altering it. '*Hopefully you will gain mercy*' so that you will hope for mercy and not be punished.

أَن تَقُولُوٓا إِنَّمَآ أُنزِلَ ٱلْكِتَٰبُ عَلَىٰ طَآئِفَتَيْنِ مِن قَبْلِنَا وَإِن كُنَّا عَن
دِرَاسَتِهِمْ لَغَٰفِلِينَ ﴿١٥٦﴾ أَوْ تَقُولُوا لَوْ أَنَّآ أُنزِلَ عَلَيْنَا ٱلْكِتَٰبُ لَكُنَّآ
أَهْدَىٰ مِنْهُمْ فَقَدْ جَآءَكُم بَيِّنَةٌ مِّن رَّبِّكُمْ وَهُدًى وَرَحْمَةٌ فَمَنْ
أَظْلَمُ مِمَّن كَذَّبَ بِـَٔايَٰتِ ٱللَّهِ وَصَدَفَ عَنْهَا سَنَجْزِى ٱلَّذِينَ
يَصْدِفُونَ عَنْ ءَايَٰتِنَا سُوٓءَ ٱلْعَذَابِ بِمَا كَانُوا يَصْدِفُونَ ﴿١٥٧﴾

156-7 So you cannot say: 'The Book was only sent down to the two groups before us and we were ignorant of their studies.' Nor can you say: 'If the Book had been sent down to us, We would have been better guided than they were.' For a Clear Sign has come to you from your Lord, and guidance and mercy. Who could do greater wrong than someone who denies Allah's Signs and turns away from them? We will repay those who turn away from Our Signs with the worst kind of punishment because they turned away.

'*So you cannot say*': the Kufans say that means: 'So that you will not say,' and the Basrans say, 'We sent it down out of dislike of your saying.' Al-Farrā' and al-Kisā'ī say, 'Fear lest you say, "O people of Makkah!"' '*The Book*' here means the Torah and Gospel. '*The two groups before us*' are the Jews and Christians. This is so that they do not say, 'No Book was sent down on us.' The phrase '*And we were ignorant of their studies*,' refers to reading their books and knowing their languages. Allah did not say 'the studies of both of them' because each group had their own community.

For a Clear Sign has come to you from your Lord, and guidance and mercy.

The excuse was removed when Muḥammad ﷺ came. *Bayyinah* and *bayān* mean the same. What is meant is Muḥammad ﷺ whom Allah here calls a *Clear Sign*. The '*guidance and mercy*' is for the one who follows him. '*Who could do greater wrong*,' means that if you lie, then no one could do more wrong than you. The verb *ṣadafa* means to turn away.

هَلْ يَنظُرُونَ إِلَّآ أَن تَأْتِيَهُمُ ٱلْمَلَٰٓئِكَةُ أَوْ يَأْتِىَ رَبُّكَ أَوْ يَأْتِىَ بَعْضُ ءَايَٰتِ رَبِّكَ
يَوْمَ يَأْتِى بَعْضُ ءَايَٰتِ رَبِّكَ لَا يَنفَعُ نَفْسًا إِيمَٰنُهَا لَمْ تَكُنْ ءَامَنَتْ مِن قَبْلُ أَوْ كَسَبَتْ
فِىٓ إِيمَٰنِهَا خَيْرًا قُلِ ٱنتَظِرُوٓا۟ إِنَّا مُنتَظِرُونَ ١٥٨

158 What are they waiting for but for the angels to come to them or for your Lord Himself to come, or for one of your Lord's Signs to come? On the day that one of your Lord's Signs does come, no belief which a self professes will be of any use to it if it did not believe before and earn good in its belief. Say: 'Wait, then; We too are waiting.'

What are they waiting for but for the angels to come to them

This means that the proof has been established against them and the Book has been revealed to them and yet they still do not believe. What are they waiting for? Ibn 'Abbās and aḍ-Ḍaḥḥāk said that this question is asked at the moment of death when their souls are taken.

or for your Lord Himself to come,

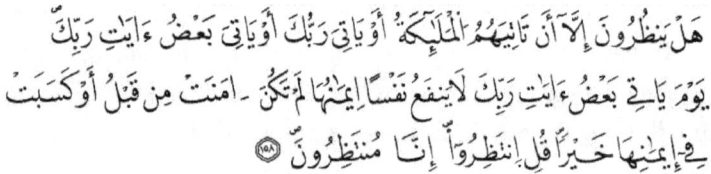

Ibn 'Abbās and aḍ-Ḍaḥḥāk said, 'Your Lord's command regarding them is that they should be killed or something else. It is ascribed to Him in a relative way, like "*Ask the town*" (12:82), meaning "the people of the town" or "*They were made to drink*

the Calf into their hearts" (2:930 which means "love of the Calf". Here it means, "the command of your Lord to come", meaning the punishment of your Lord and the penalty of your Lord.' It is said that this is one of the ambiguous (*mutashabih*) verses whose interpretation is only known by Allah, and this topic was already discussed in *Sūrat al-Baqarah* (2:196).

or for one of your Lord's Signs to come?

This refers to the rising of the sun from the west. By this Allah makes it clear that their punishment is deferred in this world, but then when the Final Hour comes, there will be no deferral. It is said that it refers to when Allah comes to judge finally between His creatures in the Standing on the Day of Rising, as in His words: '*Your Lord arrives with the angels rank upon rank.*' (89:22) His coming does not involve movement, transference or departure because that would make the Comer a body or substance. The majority of the Imāms of the people of the *Sunnah* believe that 'He comes and descends,' but they do not say 'how' because, '*There is nothing like Him, and He is the All-Hearing, All-Seeing.*' (42:11)

We find in *Ṣaḥīḥ Muslim* that Abū Hurayrah reported that Messenger of Allah ﷺ said, 'When three appear, then belief will not help any self which has not believed before nor will its belief then be of any good to it: when the sun rises from the west, the Dajjāl, and the beast of the earth.' Safwān ibn 'Assāl al-Murādī said that he heard the Messenger of Allah ﷺ say, 'In the west there is a door which is open for repentance and its width is a distance of seventy years. It will not be shut until the sun rises from the same place (the west).' Ad-Dāraquṭnī, ad-Dārimī and at-Tirmidhī transmitted it. He said that it is a *ṣaḥīḥ ḥasan ḥadīth*. Sufyān said, 'In the direction of Syria. Allah created it on the day He created the heavens and the earth. The door is open for repentance and will not be closed until the sun rises from it.' He said that it is a *ṣaḥīḥ ḥasan ḥadīth*. The Mu'tazilites and Kharijites deny all of this, as was already mentioned.

Ibn 'Abbās related, 'I heard 'Umar ibn al-Khaṭṭāb say, "O people, stoning is a duty, so do not be deceived about it. The evidence for that is that the Messenger of Allah ﷺ stoned and Abū Bakr stoned. We stoned after them. There will be some people of this Community who deny stoning and deny the Dajjāl. They will deny that the sun will rise from the west. They will deny the punishment of the grave. They will deny the intercession and deny that some people will emerge from the Fire after they have been burned by the Fire."' Abū 'Umar related it.

Ath-Tha'labī mentioned a long *ḥadīth* from Abū Hurayrah from the Prophet ﷺ which states that the sun will be held back from the people when there is a lot of disobedience in the earth and the right disappears so that no one commands it and the wrong spreads and is not forbidden. It will be held back for the length of a night under the Throne. When it prostrates and asks permission from its Lord about where it should rise, it will not receive an answer until the moon comes and prostrates with it and asks permission about where to rise. They will receive no answer until the sun has been held back for three nights and the moon for two. The length of that night will only be known by those who perform night prayers in the earth. On that day they will only be a small group in every Muslim land. When three 'nights' are over, Allah will send Jibrīl to them and he will say, 'The Lord – glory be to Him and may He be exalted – commands you to return to your west and rise from it. There will be no light or illumination for you from us.' They will rise dark from the west with no illumination for the sun or light for the moon, like they are when they are eclipsed. That is the meaning of the words of Allah: '*The sun and moon are fused together*' (75:9) and '*When the sun is compacted in blackness.*' (81:1) They will rise like that as two joined camels. When the sun and moon reach the middle of the sky, Jibrīl will come to them and take their horns and return them to the west and so they will not set from their west but will set from the Door of Repentance and then the doors will be closed and joined together and so it will be as if they had never been open. When the Door of Repentance is closed, then after that no repentance will be accepted from a person and no good action he does after that will help him unless he was a good-doer before it, and he will continue as he was before that day. That is referred to in the words of Allah Almighty: '*On the day that one of your Lord's Signs does come, no belief which a self professes will be of any use to it if it did not believe before and earn good in its belief.*' Then after that the sun and moon will be clothed in light and illumination and they will rise and set for people as they did before.

Scholars say, 'Faith will not help a soul after the sun rises from the west because it will lead to such anxiety in the hearts that every appetite of the self will be deadened and all physical strength removed and all people will be certain that the Rising is very near, just as one who is on the point of death is certain that things that lead to different types of disobedience have also been cut off. If someone repents in such a state, his repentance will not be accepted from him, just as repentance is not accepted when someone is on the point of death. The Prophet ﷺ said, "Allah accepts the repentance of the slave as long as he is not gurgling," in other words his spirit has not reached the top of his throat. That is the time of direct vision in which a person will see his seat in the Garden or the Fire. It is the same with someone who witnesses the sun rising from the west.'

According to this, the repentance of anyone who sees that, or is like someone who sees it, is disregarded as long as he lives, because his knowledge of Allah, His Prophet ﷺ and His promise has become involuntary. If the days of this world continue until people forget this immense matter and only few discuss it, to the point that the report about this matter becomes an individual matter and multiple transmission about it has ceased, then if someone becomes Muslim at that time or repents, his repentance may be accepted. Allah knows best.

In *Ṣaḥīḥ Muslim*, 'Abdullāh said, 'I memorised a *ḥadīth* from the Messenger of Allah ﷺ which I have never forgotten. I heard the Messenger of Allah ﷺ say, "The first of the Signs will be the rising of the sun from the west and the emergence of the Beast to the people in the mid-morning. Whichever of them comes first, the next will soon follow it."'

Ḥudhayfah reported, 'The Messenger of Allah ﷺ was in a room and we were below him. He came out to us and asked, "What are you discussing?" "The Last Hour," we replied. He said, "The Last Hour will not come until ten signs have come about: a collapse of the earth in the east, a collapse of the earth in the west, and a collapse of the earth in the Arabian peninsula, the Smoke, the Dajjāl, the Beast of the earth, Ya'jūj and Ma'jūj, the rising of the sun from the west, and a fire which will emerge from the depths of Aden which will travel with the people."' Shu'bah said that 'Abd al-'Azīz ibn Rufay' related something similar from Abū aṭ-Ṭufayl from Abū Sarīḥah but he did not mention the Prophet ﷺ. One of them said that the tenth is the descent of 'Īsā, the son of Maryam. Another said that it is a wind that will blow people into the sea.

This *ḥadīth* agrees about the order of the signs. Some have already occurred, which are the collapses, as Abū al-Faraj al-Jawzī mentioned, which occurred in Iraq and in the west, and many people were killed because of them. It is mentioned in *Kitāb Fuhūm al-Athār* and elsewhere. The Beast will be discussed in *an-Naml* and Ya'jūj and Ma'jūj in *al-Kahf.* It is said that the signs will follow one another like pearls on a thread year by year.

It is said that the ruling about the rising of the sun from the west is indicated in what Ibrāhīm said to Nimrod: '"*Allah makes the sun come from the East. Make it come from the West." And the one who rejected was dumbfounded.*' (2:258). The atheists and astrologers to a man deny it and say that it will not happen. Therefore, one day Allah Almighty will make the sun rise from the west to demonstrate His power to the deniers, since the sun is under His dominion. If He wishes, it rises from the east, and if He wishes, it will rise from the west. According to this, it is possible that repentance and faith will be repudiated from those who deny this and reject the report of the Prophet ﷺ that it would rise, and then repent and believe. As for those who affirmed that, their repentance is accepted and their belief benefited them before that.

It is related from 'Abdullāh ibn 'Abbās that no action or repentance will be accepted from an unbeliever if he becomes Muslim on seeing it, unless he is a child. If a child becomes Muslim after that, that will be accepted. If someone is a believer and wrongdoer and then repents of sin, that will be accepted from him. It is related that 'Imrān ibn Ḥusayn said, 'His repentance will not be accepted at the time the sun rises [from the west], when the Shout occurs, and then many people will be destroyed. If someone becomes Muslim or repents at that moment and then is destroyed, his repentance will not be accepted. If someone repents after that, his repentance will be accepted.' Abū al-Layth as-Samarqandī mentioned this in his *tafsīr*. 'Abdullāh ibn 'Umar said, 'People will remain after the rising of the sun from the west for another hundred and twenty years, to the point that they start planting date palms.' Allah has the best knowledge of His Unseen.

Ibn 'Umar and Ibn az-Zubayr recite '*yawm ya'tī*' (instead of '*yawm ta'tī*). Al-Mubarrad says that feminine form is because of the proximity of the feminine, not because of the basic form. Ibn Sīrīn recited: '*lā tanfa'u*'. Abū Ḥātim said that they say that this is an error on the part of Ibn Sīrīn. An-Naḥḥās said, 'There is a fine point of grammar here which was remarked on by Sībawayh. That is that *īmān* (faith) and *nafs* (self) each contain the other and so *īmān* can be feminine because it comes from *nafs*.' Sībawayh quoted:

They went as the spears, and their tops
were in motion from the passage (f) of the winds.

Al-Mahdawī said, 'They often make the verb of the masculine *muḍāf* feminine since it is attributed to something feminine. The *muḍāf* is part of the *muḍāf ilayhi* or from it or by it. That is the case in the above verse by Dhū ar-Rummah. 'Passage' (*marr*) is feminine by its relation in *iḍāfah* to 'winds' which is feminine since the 'passage' stems from 'the winds'. An-Naḥḥās said that there is another view, which is that '*īmān*' (faith) is feminine because it is a verbal noun, just as a feminine verbal noun can be masculine, as in the case of *maw'iẓah* in 2:275. [POEM]

Say: 'Wait, then; We too are waiting.'

This refers to waiting for the punishment.

إِنَّ ٱلَّذِينَ فَرَّقُوا۟ دِينَهُمْ وَكَانُوا۟ شِيَعًا لَّسْتَ مِنْهُمْ فِى شَىْءٍ ۚ إِنَّمَآ أَمْرُهُمْ إِلَى ٱللَّهِ
ثُمَّ يُنَبِّئُهُم بِمَا كَانُوا۟ يَفْعَلُونَ ﴿١٥٩﴾

159 As for those who divide up their *dīn* and form into sects, you have nothing whatsoever to do with them. Their affair will go back to Allah and then He will inform them about what they did.

As for those who divide up their *dīn* and form into sects,

Ḥamzah and al-Kisā'ī recited it as *fāraqū* which is the reading of 'Alī ibn Abī Ṭālib, derived from *mufāriqah* and *firāq*. It means that they left their *dīn* and came out of it. 'Alī used to say, 'By Allah, they did not divide (*farraqū*) it, but they split (*fāraqū*) from it.' The rest read it as *farraqū* except for an-Nakha'ī who read it *faraqū*, i.e. believe in some and reject some. According to Mujāhid, Qatādah, as-Suddī and aḍ-Ḍaḥḥāk, what is meant are the Jews and the Christians. They are described as breaking up into sects. Allah Almighty says elsewhere: '*Those who were given the Book did not divide into sects until after the Clear Sign came to them*' (98:4) and: '*They desire to make division between Allah and His Messengers.*' (4:150) It is also said that it is about the idolaters. Some of them worshipped idols and others worshipped angels. And it is said that the *āyah* is general to all unbelievers. Whoever innovates and brings something that Allah did not command has divided up his *dīn*. Abū Hurayrah related from the Prophet ﷺ about this *āyah*: '*As for those who divide up their dīn...*' that it is about the people of innovations and doubt and the people of misguidance in this community.

Baqiyyah ibn al-Walīd related from Shu'bah ibn al-Ḥajjāj from Mujālid from ash-Sha'bī from Shurayḥ from 'Umar ibn al-Khaṭṭāb that the Messenger of Allah ﷺ said to 'Ā'ishah, 'Those who divide up their *dīn* and form into sects are the people of innovations, the people of sects, and the people of misguidance in this community. There is repentance, 'Ā'ishah, for everyone with a wrong action except for the people of innovations and the people of sects. There is no repentance for them and I am quit of them, and they are quit of us.' Layth ibn Abī Sulaym related from Ṭāwūs from Abū Hurayrah that the Prophet ﷺ recited this *āyah* and that the *shiya'* referred to are sects and parties. Every group of people of a single mind who follow one another are a sect.

you have nothing whatsoever to do with them.

This means that one is obliged to be free of them. That is like the words of the Prophet ﷺ, 'Whoever cheats us is not one of us,' meaning we are free of him. It is like the poem:

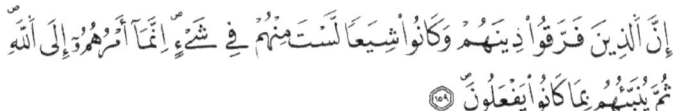

If you try to corrupt Asad, I am not part of you nor you of me.

It means, 'I am free of you.' *'Nothing whatsoever'* is in the accusative for the *ḥāl* based on what is implied in the report as Abū 'Alī said. Al-Farrā' said that it is based on the elision of a *muḍāf.* It means: 'You have nothing to do with their punishment. All you have to do is to warn.' The words: '*Their affair will go back to Allah*' are to console the Prophet ﷺ.

مَن جَآءَ بِٱلْحَسَنَةِ فَلَهُۥ عَشْرُ أَمْثَالِهَا ۖ وَمَن جَآءَ بِٱلسَّيِّئَةِ فَلَا يُجْزَىٰٓ إِلَّا مِثْلَهَا وَهُمْ
لَا يُظْلَمُونَ ﴿١٦٠﴾

160 Those who produce a good action will receive ten like it. But those who produce a bad action will only be repaid with its equivalent and they will not be wronged.

Those who produce a good action will receive ten like it.

This means ten good deeds like it. 'Good deeds' is elided and '*amthāl*' (*like*) is put in its place. It is the plural of *mithl.* Al-Ḥasan, Sa'īd ibn Jubayr and al-A'mash read: '*'ashirun amthāluhā*' (the others have *'ashru amthālihā*). It implies: he has ten good actions like them, in other words the reward for them is ten times more than what he is due. Here the good deed is faith. So anyone who testifies that there is no god but Allah has ten times the reward for every action he does in this world.

But those who produce a bad action will only be repaid with its equivalent

The bad action is *shirk* and '*its equivalent*' is to be forever in the Fire because *shirk* is the worst of wrong actions and the Fire is the worst punishment. That is what is indicated by the words of the Almighty: *'An adequate repayment*' (79:26), in other words an action appropriate to it.

As for the good action, it is different from that because of the text of Allah about that. We find in tradition: 'A good deed is worth ten like it and I give more, and an evil deed is one and I forgive. Woe to the one whose ones are greater than his tens.' Al-A'mash related that Abū Ṣāliḥ said, 'The good action is "*lā ilāha illa-llāh*" and the evil action is *shirk*.'

and they will not be wronged.

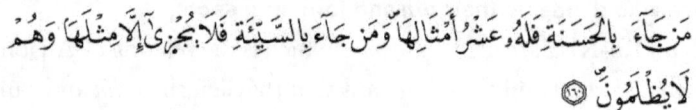

The reward for their actions will not be lessened. This was already discussed in *Sūrat al-Baqarah* (2:261). This is different from spending in the Way of Allah. That is why one of the scholars said, 'Ten are for other good actions and seven hundred is for spending in the Way of Allah, and private and public are the same where that is concerned.' Another of them said that the common man has ten and the elite have seven hundred and more, without limit. A reliable source for such a statement is needed. The first position, however, is sounder because of the *ḥadīth* of Khuraym ibn Fātiḥ from the Prophet ﷺ which says: 'As for the good action multiplied by ten, whoever has does a good action has ten like it. As for the good action multiplied by seven hundred, it is spending in the Way of Allah.'

قُلْ إِنَّنِي هَدَىٰنِي رَبِّيٓ إِلَىٰ صِرَٰطٍ مُّسْتَقِيمٍ دِينًا قِيَمًا مِّلَّةَ إِبْرَٰهِيمَ حَنِيفًا وَمَا كَانَ
مِنَ ٱلْمُشْرِكِينَ ١٦١ قُلْ إِنَّ صَلَاتِي وَنُسُكِي وَمَحْيَايَ وَمَمَاتِي لِلَّهِ رَبِّ ٱلْعَٰلَمِينَ ١٦٢
لَا شَرِيكَ لَهُۥ وَبِذَٰلِكَ أُمِرْتُ وَأَنَا۠ أَوَّلُ ٱلْمُسْلِمِينَ ١٦٣

161-3 Say: 'My Lord has guided me to a straight path, a well-founded *dīn*, the religion of Ibrāhīm, a man of pure natural belief. He was not one of the idolaters.' Say: 'My prayer and my rites, my living and my dying, are for Allah alone, the Lord of all the worlds, Who has no partner. I am commanded to be like that and I am the first of the Muslims.'

Say: 'My Lord has guided me to a straight path, a well-founded *dīn*, the religion of Ibrāhīm, a man of pure natural belief.

When Allah explained that the unbelievers split up, He makes it clear that He has guided him ﷺ to the straight *dīn*, which is the *dīn* of Ibrāhīm. '*Dīn*' is in the accusative for the adverbial *ḥāl* according to Quṭrub. Al-Akhfash said that it because of the verb '*guided*'. Others said that it is in the accusative because that is what is implied by the meaning: 'He acquainted me about a *dīn*.' It can also be an appositive for '*path*', meaning, 'He guided me to straight path, a *dīn*.' It is said that it is in the accusative by an implied verb such as: 'follow a *dīn*' or 'recognise a *dīn*.' The word '*qiyam*' (*straight*) is the reading of the Kufans and Ibn 'Amr, being a verbal noun. The rest read it as '*qayyim*'. They are two dialectical forms. The root of the *yā'* is a *wāw*: *qayūm* and the *wāw* is assimilated into the *yā'* (*qayyim*). It means: a straight *dīn* with no crookedness in it.

'*The religion of Ibrāhīm*' is an appositive. Az-Zajjāj said that '*ḥanīf*' is a *ḥāl* describing Ibrāhīm. 'Alī ibn Sulaymān said that it is in the accusative by something implied.

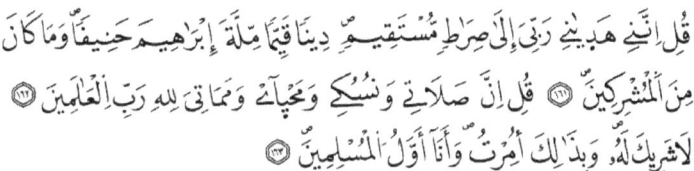

Say: 'My prayer and my rites, my living and my dying, are for Allah alone, the Lord of all the worlds,

The derivation of *ṣalāt* has already been discussed (2:3). It is said that what is meant here is the night prayer and it is also said that it means the *'Īd* prayer. The noun *nusuk* (*rites*) is the plural of *nasīkah,* which means a sacrifice. That is what Mujāhid, aḍ-Ḍaḥḥāk, Sa'īd ibn Jubayr and others said. It means, 'My sacrifices in *ḥajj* and *'umrah*.' Al-Ḥasan said, '"*My rites*" means "my *dīn*."' Az-Zajjāj said that it means 'my worship.' From that comes the person who is *nāsik*, who is someone who draws near to Allah through worship. Some people say that *nusuk* in this *āyah* means all actions of good and obedience as the verb *nasaka* means 'to worship'.

'*My living*' means 'what I do in my life' and '*my dying*' is what I leave after my death. Allah's words '...*are for Allah alone, the Lord of all the worlds*' make it specific to being a means of drawing near to Allah. It is said that '*my living and my dying*' means 'my living and dying are for Him'. Al-Hasan recited, '*nuskī*' (rather than *nusukī*) and the people of Madīnah recite *maḥyāy* with a *sukūn* while the others recite *maḥyāya*. An-Naḥḥās said, 'Only Yūnus among grammarians permits it. He allows it because there is an *alif* before it and the *alif* with a *maddah* takes the place of a vowel.' If someone follows the recitation of the people of Madīnah and wants to be safe from non-grammatical Arabic, he should stop at '*maḥyay*' and then he will be correct in all grammatical positions. Ibn Abī Isḥāq, 'Īsā ibn 'Umar and 'Āṣim al-Jaḥḍarī recite '*maḥyayya*' with the second *yā'* doubled and no *alif*. It is the dialect of 'Ulyā Muḍar.

Aṭ-Ṭabarī states that ash-Shāfi'ī uses this *āyah* as evidence for it being the *iftitāḥ* (opening formula) of the prayer. Allah commanded His Prophet ﷺ and revealed it to Him in His Book. Then he mentioned the *ḥadīth* of 'Alī: 'When the Prophet ﷺ began the prayer he said, "I have turned my face to the One who originated the heavens and the earth, a *ḥanīf*, and I am not one of the idolaters. My prayer and my rites, my living and my dying are for Allah alone the Lord of all the worlds... to ... I am the first of the Muslims."' Muslim related in the *Ṣaḥīḥ* from 'Alī ibn Abī Ṭālib that when the Messenger of Allah ﷺ rose to pray, he said, 'I have turned my face to the One who originated the heavens and the earth, a *ḥanīf*, and I am not one of the idolaters. My prayer and my rites, my living and my dying are for Allah alone the Lord of all the worlds Who has no partner. I am commanded to be like that and I am the first of the Muslims. O Allah, You are the King. There is no god but You. You are My Lord and I am Your slave. I have wronged myself and admitted my wrong action, so forgive me all my wrong actions. None forgives wrong actions but You. Guide me to the best character and only You guide to the best of it. Avert evil from me, and none averts evil but You. At Your service! All good in Your hand and evil does not approach You. You are blessed and exalted. I ask Your forgiveness and turn in repentance to You.' Ad-Dāraquṭnī transmitted it as well. He said at the end of it, 'It reached us from an-Naḍr ibn Shumayl, one of the scholars of language, and others, that the meaning of the words of the Messenger of Allah ﷺ, "evil does not approach you," mean "evil is not something that brings one near to You."'

Mālik said, 'The *tawjīh* in the prayer is not obligatory for people. What is mandatory is the *takbīr*, and then the recitation.' Ibn al-Qāsim said, 'Mālik did not think that one should say this before recitation: "Glory be to You, O Allah, and by Your praise."' We find in the *Summary of what is not in the Summary*: 'Mālik used to say it when he was on his own based on the soundness of the *ḥadīth* regarding it, but he did not think that people should do it, fearing that they would believe that it was mandatory.' Abū al-Faraj al-Jawzī said, 'In my youth I used to pray behind our Shaykh Abū Bakr ad-Dīnawarī, the *faqīh*. Once he saw me doing this and he said, "My son, the *fuqahā'* disagree about the obligation of reciting the *Fātiḥah* behind the *imām* but they do not disagree that the *iftitāḥ* is only *sunnah*. Therefore occupy yourself with the mandatory and leave the *sunnahs*."' Evidence supporting Mālik is found in the words of the Prophet ﷺ to the Bedouin to whom he taught the prayer: 'When you rise for the prayer, say the *takbīr* and then recite.' He did not say to him, 'Say "*Subḥānallāh*"' as Abū Ḥanīfah says, and he did not mention *tawjīh* or *tasbīḥ*, as ash-Shāfi'ī says. He said to Ubayy, 'How do you recite when you begin the prayer?' He answered, 'I say, "*Allāhu akbar*. Praise be to Allah, the Lord of the worlds."' He did not mention *tawjīh* or glorification.

If it is said that 'Alī reported that the Prophet ﷺ used to say it, our reply is that it is possible that he said it before the *takbīr* and then said the *takbīr*, and we consider that to be good. If it is said that an-Nasā'ī and ad-Dāraquṭnī related that when the Prophet ﷺ began the prayer, he said the *takbīr* and then said, '*My prayer and my rites…*', we reply that that may apply to *nāfilah* prayers in night prayers, as it is reported in the book of an-Nasā'ī that Abū Sa'īd said, 'When the Prophet ﷺ began the prayer at night, he said, "Glory be to You, O Allah, and by Your praise. Blessed is Your Name and Exalted are You and there is no God but You,"' or it could be in *nāfilah* prayers in general. The *nāfilah* is lighter than the *farḍ* because one can pray it standing, sitting and riding, toward the *qiblah* or elsewhere in a journey. Therefore it is easier.

An-Nasā'ī related from Muḥammad ibn Maslamah that when the Messenger of Allah ﷺ used to pray a voluntary prayer, he said, '*Allāhu akbar*. I have turned my face to the One who originated the heavens and the earth, a *ḥanīf*, and I am not one of the idolaters. My prayer and my rites, my living and my dying are for Allah alone, the Lord of all the worlds Who has no partner. I am commanded to be like that and I am the first of the Muslims. O Allah, You are the King. There is no god but You. Glory be to You and by Your praise,' and then he would recite. This text is about the voluntary prayers, not the mandatory prayers. If it were about the *farḍ* prayer after the *takbīr*, then it could apply to permission and recommendation. The *sunnah* is recitation [of the fatiḥa] after the *takbīr* and Allah has the best knowledge of the truth of matters. If he says that, he does not say, 'I am the first of the Muslims.'

and I am the first of the Muslims.

Since only Muḥammad ﷺ is the first of them, if someone points out that Ibrāhīm and the Prophets were before him, there are three answers to this. The first is that he was the first of creation in meaning, as in the *ḥadīth* of Abū Hurayrah where the Prophet ﷺ said, 'We are the first and the last on the Day of Rising, and we will be the first to enter the Garden.' We find in the *ḥadīth* of Ḥudhayfah, 'We are the last of the people of this world and the first on the Day of Rising to be judged before other creatures.' The second is that he is the first of them since he came before them in creation. The Almighty says: '*When We made a covenant with all the Prophets: with you and with Nūḥ...*' (33:7) Qatādah said that the Prophet ﷺ said, 'I was the first of the Prophets in creation and the last of them to be sent.' For that reason he is mentioned here before Nūḥ and others. The third is that he is the first of the Muslims among the people of his religion. Ibn al-'Arabī said that. It is the view of Qatādah and others.

Transmissions vary about 'first'. Some confirm it and some do not. 'Imrān ibn Ḥusayn related that the Messenger of Allah ﷺ said, 'Fāṭimah, rise and witness your sacrifices. You will be forgiven every wrong action you have done at the first drop of its blood. Then say, "My prayer and my rites, my living and my dying are for Allah alone the Lord of all the worlds Who has no partner. I am commanded to be like that and I am the first of the Muslims."' 'Imrān said, 'Messenger of Allah, is this for you and the people of your house in particular or for the Muslims in general?' He replied, 'For the Muslims in general.'

قُلْ أَغَيْرَ اللَّهِ أَبْغِي رَبًّا وَهُوَ رَبُّ كُلِّ شَيْءٍ وَلَا تَكْسِبُ كُلُّ نَفْسٍ إِلَّا عَلَيْهَا
وَلَا تَزِرُ وَازِرَةٌ وِزْرَ أُخْرَىٰ ثُمَّ إِلَىٰ رَبِّكُم مَّرْجِعُكُمْ فَيُنَبِّئُكُم بِمَا كُنتُمْ فِيهِ
تَخْتَلِفُونَ ١٦٤

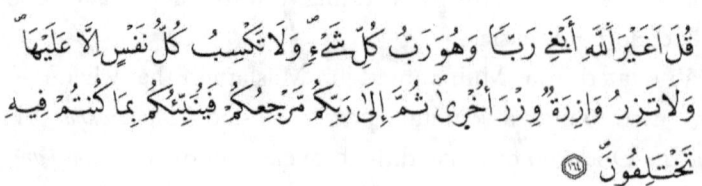

164 Say: 'Am I to desire other than Allah as Lord when He is the Lord of all things?' What each self earns is for itself alone. No burden-bearer can bear another's burden. Then you will return to your Lord, and He will inform you regarding the things about which you differed.

Say: 'Am I to desire other than Allah as Lord when He is the Lord of all things?'

He is their Master. It is related that the unbelievers said to the Prophet ﷺ, 'Revert to our *dīn*, Muḥammad, and worship our gods and leave what you hold and we will take on ourselves all that consequences that befall you in this world and the Next,' and this *āyah* was revealed. It is a question which demands rebuke.

What each self earns is for itself alone.

This means, 'Seeking a Lord other than Allah will not help me in that respect.' That is because what a soul earns is for itself alone since only it is punished for its own disobedience and errors. Some later scholars use this *āyah* as evidence that the sale of an uncommissioned agent is not valid. That is the view of ash-Shāfi'ī. Our scholars say that what is meant by the Allah's words: '*No burden-bearer can bear another's burden*' is the reward and punishment [of the Next World] rather than rulings which pertain to this world. We believe that the sale of an uncommissioned agent is dependent on the granting of permission by the owner. If he allows it, it is allowed. 'Urwah al-Bāriqī bought and sold for the Prophet ﷺ and made a transaction without his command, and the Messenger of Allah ﷺ allowed the transaction. Abū Ḥanīfah said that.

Al-Bukhārī and ad-Dāraquṭnī related that 'Urwah ibn Abī al-Ja'd said, 'Some flocks arrived where the Prophet ﷺ was and he gave me a *dīnār* and said, "'Urwah, go to the flocks which have come and buy us a sheep with this *dīnār*." I went to the flocks and bargained and bought two sheep for a *dīnār* and I drove (or led) them. A man met me on the way and bargained with me and I sold him one of the sheep for a *dīnār*. I brought the other sheep and the *dīnār* and said, "Messenger of Allah, here is the sheep and here is your *dīnār*." He asked, "How did you do it?" And I told him. He said, "O Allah, bless him in the transaction of his right hand!"' 'Urwah said, 'I used to stand in the Kunāsah of Kufa and make a profit of forty thousand before returning to my people.' Abū 'Umar said, 'It is an excellent *ḥadīth* which contains the soundness of the Prophet's affirmation of the two sheep. If it had not been for that, he would not have taken the *dīnār* nor allowed the sale.'

It is evidence for the permissibility of agency (*wakālah*). There is no disagreement about it among scholars. If the one who commissions tells his agent, 'Buy this,' and then the agent buys more than what he was entrusted to do, is that business binding or not? It is like one man saying to another, 'Buy a *riṭl* of meat with this *dirham*,' which he describes, and then the man purchases four *riṭls* of that type of meat with that *dirham*. What Mālik and his people believe is that every such transaction is binding provided that it has the same description and is of the same type, because he acted well. That is the view of Abū Yūsuf and Muḥammad ibn al-Ḥasan. Abū Ḥanīfah said that the buyer has the extra and used this *ḥadīth* as evidence.

No burden-bearer can bear another's burden.

It cannot bear the burden of another, meaning that a soul will not punished for another person's wrong action. Rather each soul is punished for its own crimes and sins. The root of *wizr* means burden, as in Allah's words: '*We removed your burden from you*' (94:2). Here, however, it means wrong action, as in Allah's words: '*They bear their burdens on their backs*' (6:31), as was discussed earlier. Al-Akhfash said that the verb is *wazira, yawzaru, wazara, yaziru*, and *wazura, yawzaru* with the verbal noun *wazar* or *izr*. The *āyah* was revealed about al-Walīd ibn al-Mughīrah. He used to say, 'Follow my way and I will bear your burdens.' Ibn 'Abbās mentioned it. It is said that this *āyah* was revealed to refute the Arabs in the *Jāhiliyyah* for punishing a man because of his father, his son, or for a crime committed by his ally.

It is possible that that this *āyah* refers to the Next World. The same applies to what is before it. As for this world, some people are punished for the crimes of others, especially when those who obey Allah do not stop those who disobey Him, as stated in the *ḥadīth* of Abū Bakr about the words of Allah: '*You are only responsible for yourselves*' (5:105), '*Be fearful of trials which will not afflict only those among you who do wrong*' (8:25) and '*Allah never changes a people's state until they change what is in themselves.*' (13:11) Zaynab bint Jaḥsh said, 'Messenger of Allah, will we be destroyed when there are righteous people among us?' He replied, 'Yes, when there is a lot of depravity.' Our scholars said that 'depravity' means bastards as *khabath* (depravity) means fornication.

On the tongue of His Messenger ﷺ, Allah obliged the *'āqilah* (paternal kin) to pay blood money for an accidental killing so that the blood of the free Muslim is not shed, out of respect for life. The people of knowledge agree on that without any disagreement between them regarding it. So it indicates what we said. It is possible that this phrase is meant to refer to this world in that Zayd is not punished for 'Amr's action and that everyone who commits a crime is responsible for its consequences. Abū Dāwūd related that Abū Rimthah said, 'I went with my father to the Prophet ﷺ and the Prophet ﷺ asked my father, "Is this your son?" He said, "Yes, by the Lord of the Ka'bah." He said, "Truly?" He said, "I testify to it." The Messenger of Allah ﷺ smiled, laughing at the confirmation of my suspicion about my father and that my father swore an oath about me. Then he said, "He should not wrong you nor you wrong him." The Messenger of Allah ﷺ then recited, "*No burden-bearer can bear another's burden.*"' This is not incompatible with Allah's words: '*They will bear their own burdens and other burdens together with their own.*' (29:13) This is explained by another *āyah*: '*So on the Day of Rising they will carry the full weight of their own burdens and some of the burdens of those they misguided without knowledge.*' (16:25) So whoever is a leader in misguidance and calls to it and is followed will bear the burden of those he misguided without that decreasing the burden of the misguided at all as will be clarified, Allah willing.

وَهُوَ ٱلَّذِى جَعَلَكُمْ خَلَٰٓئِفَ ٱلْأَرْضِ وَرَفَعَ بَعْضَكُمْ فَوْقَ بَعْضٍ
دَرَجَٰتٍ لِّيَبْلُوَكُمْ فِى مَآ ءَاتَىٰكُمْ ۗ إِنَّ رَبَّكَ سَرِيعُ ٱلْعِقَابِ وَإِنَّهُۥ لَغَفُورٌ
رَّحِيمٌۢ ١٦٥

165 It is He Who appointed you caliphs on the earth and raised some of you above others in rank so He could test you regarding what He has given you. Your Lord is Swift in Retribution; and He is Ever-Forgiving, Most Merciful.

It is He Who appointed you caliphs on the earth

Khalā'if (caliphs) is the plural of *khalīfah*. Anyone who comes after someone who has passed before is a *khalīfah*, and so it means: 'He made you follow the past communities and previous generations.' Ash-Shammakh said:

Death smites them and steps over me
 and I go after them (*akhluf*) from one campsite to another.

and raised some of you above others in rank so He could test you regarding what He has given you.

Rank here refers to physique, provision, strength, expansion, favour and knowledge. The verb *ibtilā'* means putting to the test, so that things resulting in either reward or punishment emerge from you while He continues to be Rich [and not in need of this information] because of His [prior] knowledge of you. So the wealthy are tested in their wealth and asked to be thankful, and the poor are tested in their poverty and asked to be steadfast. It is said that the testing is by one another, as in Allah's words: *'But We have made some of you a trial for others'* (25:20), as will be clarified.

Your Lord is Swift in Retribution; and He is Ever-Forgiving, Most Merciful.

Then He alarms them by saying: *'Your Lord is Swift in Retribution'* against those who disobey Him but: *'He is Ever-Forgiving, Most Merciful'* towards those who obey Him. He says: *'Swift in retribution'* while He is also described as deferring. Although the punishment of the Fire is in the Next World, everything which is 'coming' is near-at-hand and so in this sense He is swift. As He says: *'The matter of the Hour is only the blink of an eye away, or even nearer'* (16:77) and also: *'They see it as something distant. But We see it as very close.'* (70:6-7) He is also swift in punishing those who deserve it in this world and so it cautions the one who falls into error in this way, and Allah knows best.

7. Sūrat al-A'rāf – The Ramparts

It is Makkan except for the eight *āyahs* from 163 to 171. An-Nasā'ī related from 'Ā'ishah that the Messenger of Allah ﷺ recited *Sūrat al-A'rāf* in the *Maghrib* prayer and divided it between two *rak'ahs*. Abū Muḥammad 'Abd al-Ḥaqq said that it is sound.

الٓمٓصٓ ﴿١﴾ كِتَٰبٌ أُنزِلَ إِلَيْكَ فَلَا يَكُن فِي صَدْرِكَ حَرَجٌ مِّنْهُ لِتُنذِرَ بِهِۦ وَذِكْرَىٰ
لِلْمُؤْمِنِينَ ﴿٢﴾

1-2 Alif Lām Mīm Ṣād. It is a Book sent down to you – so let there be no constriction in your breast because of it – so that you can give warning by it and as a reminder to the believers.

'Alif Lām Mīm Ṣād' was already discussed in *Sūrat al-Baqarah.* (2:1) *'A Book sent down'* means 'this Book' as al-Kisā'ī said.

so let there be no constriction in your breast because of it –

'No constriction' means: 'your breast should not be constricted about conveying it' because it is related that the Prophet ﷺ said, 'I fear that they will pound my head and leave it like broken dough.' Muslim transmitted it. Aṭ-Ṭabarī said that its literal meaning is a prohibition, while the meaning is to negate constriction, i.e. 'Do not be grieved if they do not believe it. You must convey, and you only have to warn by it and have nothing to do with their belief or disbelief.' It is similar to Allah's words: *'Perhaps you may destroy yourself with grief...'* (18:6) and: *'Perhaps you will destroy yourself with grief because they will not become believers.'* (26:3)

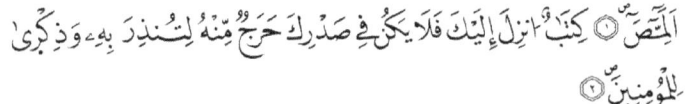

The position of Mujāhid and Qatādah is that *ḥaraj* here means doubt. This is not the doubt of disbelief, but the doubt of constriction, as He says: *'We know that your breast is constricted by what they say.'* (15:97) It is said that it is addressed to the Prophet ﷺ, but it is his Community which is meant. This is somewhat unlikely. The *hā'* in 'of it' refers to the Qur'an, and it is also said that it refers to *'warning'*, meaning 'He sent it down to you to warn by it so let there be no constriction in your breast because of it,' and the normal linguistic order is altered. It is said that it is denial, meaning 'you should feel no constriction at the denial of those who deny you.'

and as a reminder to the believers.

'*Dhikrā*' can be in the nominative, accusative or genitive. There are two reasons for the nominative: it can be in the nominative because of an implied inchoative or, as al-Kisā'ī said, as added to '*Book*'. It can be in the accusative as a verbal noun, as the Basrans said, or added to the '*hā*' in 'sent it down' as al-Kisā'ī said. The genitive is based on the place of '*so that you can give warning* by *it*'. The warning is for the unbelievers and the reminder for the believers because they will benefit from it.

اتَّبِعُوا مَا أُنزِلَ إِلَيْكُم مِّن رَّبِّكُمْ وَلَا تَتَّبِعُوا مِن دُونِهِ أَوْلِيَاءَ قَلِيلًا مَّا
تَذَكَّرُونَ ۝٣

3 Follow what has been sent down to you from your Lord and do not follow any protectors apart from Him. How little you remember!

Follow what has been sent down to you from your Lord

This means the Book and the *Sunnah*. Allah Almighty says: '*Take what the Messenger gives you and leave what He forbids you.*' (59:7). A group said that this command is general to the Prophet ﷺ and his community. The literal meaning is that it is a command to all people except him, telling them to follow the religion of Islam and the Qur'an, make lawful what is lawful in it and make unlawful what is unlawful in it, and obey Allah's commands and avoid what He has forbidden. The *āyah* indicates that one should not follow opinion when a text exists.

and do not follow any protectors apart from Him.

'*Him*' here refers to the Lord. It means: 'Do not worship any other with Him and do not take as protectors those who turn away from the *dīn* of Allah.' When someone is pleased with a position, the people of that school are his protectors. It is related that Mālik ibn Dīnār recited this as meaning 'Do not seek.' *Mā* is redundant. It is said that it acts as a verbal noun with a verb.

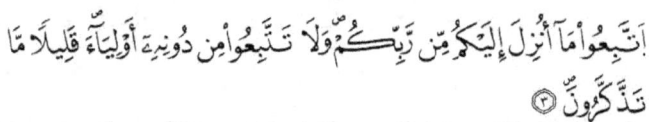

وَكَم مِّن قَرْيَةٍ أَهْلَكْنَـٰهَا فَجَآءَهَا بَأْسُنَا بَيَـٰتًا أَوْ هُمْ قَآئِلُونَ ۞ فَمَا كَانَ دَعْوَىٰهُمْ إِذْ جَآءَهُم بَأْسُنَآ إِلَّآ أَن قَالُوٓا۟ إِنَّا كُنَّا ظَـٰلِمِينَ ۞

4-5 How many cities We have destroyed! Our violent force came down on them during the night, or while they were asleep during the day. And their only utterance, when Our violent force came down upon them, was the cry: 'Truly we have been wrongdoers!'

How many cities We have destroyed!

Kam means 'many' as *rubbah* means 'few'. This means: 'We have destroyed many towns,' which are places where people gather. It is also possible that '*kam*' is in the accusative by a following implied verb, not one before it, because a question does not act on what comes before. The first view is strengthened by the *āyah*: '*How many generations We destroyed after Nūḥ!*' (17:17) '*We have destroyed*' can also be an adjective of '*cities*' and '*kam*' means the cities. So it is as if you were describing '*kam*'. Something similar is seen in 53:26. So the pronoun refers to '*kam*' in the meaning since the angels did it in the meaning. Therefore it is not sound to imply that '*kam*' is in the accusative by a following implied verb.

Our violent force came down on them during the night,

There is some ambiguity about the use of the *fā'* in '*Our violent force came down (fa jā'a) on them*'. Al-Farrā' says that it means 'and' and that no order is obliged. It is said that it means, 'How many cities We desired to destroy and so Our force came upon them.' It is said that destruction occurred to some people and so it implies: 'How many cities We have partially destroyed and then Our violent force came down on it, and so We destroyed all of it.' It is said that it means: 'How many cities We destroyed by Our judgment and so Our violent force came down on them.' It is said, 'We destroyed them by sending the angels of punishment to them and so Our violent force came,' and it implies eradication.

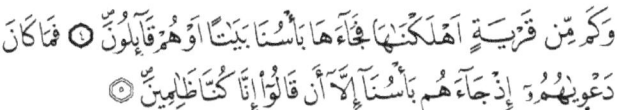

The noun *ba's* (*violent force*) means the coming punishment. It is said that it means, 'Our destruction of them at a certain time,' and so '*force*' here means destruction. It is also said that *ba's* does not mean destruction as we mentioned. Al-Farrā' also related that since the meaning of the two verbs is the same: 'I will send whichever of them I wish. Our force has come to many cities and We destroyed them.' It is like saying, 'He drew near and was near' or 'He was near and drew near,' or 'he insulted me and acted badly,' or 'he acted badly and insulted me' because insulting and acting badly are the same. The same is true of His words: '*The Hour*

has drawn near and the moon has split' (54:1) which equally means that 'the moon has split and the Hour has drawn near.' Allah knows best. The adverb *bayāt* means 'at night'. *Bayt* (house) is derived from it, because one spends the night in it. The verb is *bāta, yabītu, bayt, bayāt*. The phrase '*or while they were asleep during the day*' has a *wāw* elided as it would normally be (*aw wa hum*) because that is heavy, according to al-Farrā'. Az-Zajjāj says that this is an error. When something is mentioned again, then there is no need for the *wāw*. Al-Mahdawī says that one does not use the extra *wāw* in the sentence because the sentence contains a pronoun that refers to the first, and so there is no need for the *wāw*. Az-Zajjāj says something similar. The noun *qā'ilūn* comes from *qā'ilah*, which is the sleep at midday. It is said that it is resting at midday when it is very hot, even if one does not sleep. The meaning is: 'Our punishment comes to them while they are heedless, either at night or in the day.' *Da'wā* means supplication as is seen in Allah's words: '*The end of their call is…*' (10:10) Grammarians say: 'O Allah, we share in the righteous call of those who call on You!' It can mean 'pretense'. It means: they were not delivered up to destruction for other than admitting that they were wrongdoers. It is in the accusative as the predicate of *kāna* and its noun is '*their only utterance*'. It is like 27:56. It can also be in the nominative and '*their only utterance*' is in the accusative as is seen in 2:177 and 30:10.

فَلَنَسْـَٔلَنَّ ٱلَّذِينَ أُرْسِلَ إِلَيْهِمْ وَلَنَسْـَٔلَنَّ ٱلْمُرْسَلِينَ ۝٦ فَلَنَقُصَّنَّ عَلَيْهِم بِعِلْمٍ ۖ وَمَا كُنَّا غَآئِبِينَ ۝٧

6-7 We will question those to whom the Messengers were sent, and We will question the Messengers. We will tell them about it with knowledge. We are never absent.

We will question those to whom the Messengers were sent,

This is evidence that unbelievers will be called to account. We read in the Revelation: '*Then their Reckoning is Our concern*' (88:26) and in *Sūrat al-Qaṣaṣ*: '*The evildoers will not be questioned about their sins*' (28:78), when they are firmly entrenched in the punishment. There are different places in the Next World. There is a place where people are questioned at the Reckoning and there is a place where they are not questioned. Their questioning consists of admission, rebuke and disgrace. The questioning of the Messengers is one of giving testimony and declaration about the response their people gave them. We find that in Allah's words: '*…so that He would be able to question the truly sincere about their sincerity.*' (33:8) It is said that '*those*' here are the Prophets, and the '*Messengers*' are the angels who were sent to them. The *lām* in '*We will question*' is the *lām* of the oath which here is used for emphasis as in 'We will tell'. '*We are never absent*' means 'We witnessed their actions'. The *āyah* proves that Allah is All-Knowing in His knowledge.

وَالْوَزْنُ يَوْمَئِذٍ الْحَقُّ فَمَن ثَقُلَتْ مَوَازِينُهُ فَأُولَٰئِكَ هُمُ الْمُفْلِحُونَ ۝٨ وَمَنْ
خَفَّتْ مَوَازِينُهُ فَأُولَٰئِكَ الَّذِينَ خَسِرُوا أَنفُسَهُم بِمَا كَانُوا بِآيَاتِنَا يَظْلِمُونَ ۝٩

8-9 The weighing that Day will be the truth. As for those whose scales are heavy, they are the successful. As for those whose scales are light, they are the ones who have lost their own selves because they wrongfully rejected Our Signs.

The weighing that Day will be the truth.

The sentence is an inceptive and predicate, and it is also possible that '*truth*' is its adjective and '*that Day*' is the predicate. '*Truth*' can be in the accusative as a verbal noun.

The word '*weighing*' refers to the weighing of actions of people in the Scales. Ibn 'Umar said, 'The pages containing people's actions will be weighed.' This is sound. It is what is related in tradition as will be mentioned. It is said that '*the scales*' refers to the book containing people's actions. Mujāhid said that the actual good actions and bad actions are what is in the Scales. Aḍ-Ḍaḥḥāk and al-A'mash said that the weighing and scales designate justice and decision and that scales is used as a metaphor. It is as you describe words as having a certain 'weight' when they actually have no physical weight. Az-Zajjāj said that this is allowable linguistically. What is appropriate is to follow what has come in sound *isnāds* which talk of the scales.

Al-Qushayrī said that this is the best of what is said since if the scales had been used in this metaphorical way, then the *Ṣirāṭ* would mean the True *Dīn*, the Garden and the Fire for what comes to the spirits rather than bodies, and the *shayṭāns* and jinn for blameworthy character and the angels for praiseworthy faculties. The community agreed to accept these things with their regular meaning without interpretation. When they agree that interpretation is forbidden, then it is mandatory to take the regular meaning, and these apparent statements become texts.

Ibn Fūrak said, 'The Mu'tazilites denied the Scales on the basis that it is impossible to weigh non-essentials since they themselves cannot be estimated.'

Some *mutakallimūn* say that Allah Almighty will transform the non-essentials into physical bodies so that they will be weighed on the Day of Rising. We do not consider this to be sound. The sound view is that the scales will be heavy or light with the books which contain the recorded deeds. There are traditions that verify that. It is related that 'the scale with good actions of some of the sons of Ādam will be light and so there will be placed in it a paper on which will be written "There is no god but Allah," and it will become heavy.' It is known that that refers to the weight of that on which the actions are written, not the actual actions. Allah makes the scale light when He wills and heavy when He wills, by what is placed in it of the pages which contain the actions.

In *Ṣaḥīḥ Muslim*, Ṣafwān ibn Muḥriz mentioned that a man asked Ibn 'Umar, 'What did you hear from the Messenger of Allah ﷺ in private conversation?' He replied, 'I heard him say, "On the Day of Rising, the believer will come near to his Lord until He places His veil over him and he will be made to acknowledge his sins. He will say, 'Do you confess?' He will reply, 'Lord, I confess.' He will say, 'I concealed them for you in the world and I will forgive you for them today.' He will be given the page containing his good actions. As for the unbelievers and hypocrites, there will be a proclamation about them before people, 'These are those who denied Allah.'"' His words, 'given the page containing his good actions' is evidence that actions are written on pages and then weighed.

Ibn Mājah related from the *ḥadīth* of 'Abdullāh ibn 'Umar that the Messenger of Allah ﷺ said, 'There will be loud call for a man of my community in front of people on the Day of Rising and ninety-nine scrolls will be unrolled, and each scroll will extend as far as the eye can see. Then Allah Almighty will demand, "Do you deny any of this?" He will answer, "No, Lord." He will ask, "Have the recording scribes wronged you?" "No," he will reply. Then He will ask, "Do you have an excuse? Do you have any good actions?" The man will be in awe and say, "No." He will say, "Yes, you do. You have good actions with Me. No injustice will be done to you today." A card will be produced for him on which will be, "I testify that there is no god but Allah and that Muhammad is His slave and Messenger." He will say, "Lord, what is this card in comparison to these scrolls?" He will say, "You will not be wronged." So the scrolls will be place in one pan and the card in the other pan and the scrolls will vanish and the card be heavy."' At-Tirmidhī added, 'Nothing is heavy in comparison to the Name of Allah.' He said that the *ḥadīth* is *ḥasan gharīb*. More will be said in *al-Kahf* and *al-Anbiyā'*.

As for those whose scales are heavy, they are the successful. As for those whose scales are light, they are the ones who have lost their own selves

The noun *mawāzīn* (scales) is the plural of *mīzān*. Its root is *miwzān* and the *wāw* has been changed into a *yā'* because of the *kasrah* before it. It is said that it is permitted for there to be scales for each person in which each scale weighs one category of his actions. It is possible that that is just one set of scales since the plural is used. It is said that *mawāzīn* is the plural of *mawzūn*, not *mīzān*, by which the weighed actions are meant [rather than the scales themselves], and '*as for those whose scales are light*' means the same.

Ibn 'Abbās said that good and bad actions are weighed in a set of scales which has a tongue and two pans. The believer will be given his actions in the best possible form and they will placed in the pan of the scales and his good deeds will be heavier than his bad deeds. That is why Allah says: '*As for those whose scales are heavy, they are the successful.*' The actions of the unbelievers will be brought in the worst possible form and placed in the pan of the scales and they will be light so that he falls into the Fire. As for what Ibn 'Abbās indicated, it is close to what has been said about this, namely that Allah will create every category of the actions of people into a gem and the weighing will be done with those gems. Ibn Fūrak and others reject that.

We read in a report: 'If the good deeds of a believer are light, the Messenger of Allah ﷺ will produce a card like a finger and put it into the right hand pan, in which his good deeds are placed, and the good deeds will be heavier. That believer will say to the Prophet ﷺ, "By my father and mother! How beautiful your face is! How excellent your physique? Who are you?" He will answer, "I am Muḥammad, your Prophet, and these are the prayers which you prayed on me. You are more in need of them."' Al-Qushayrī related this in his *tafsīr*. He mentioned that the word for card (*biṭānah*) is a word in the Egyptian dialect meaning a piece of paper on which the number of goods in a transaction is written. Ibn Mājah said that Muḥammad ibn Yaḥyā said that '*biṭānah*' is the word the people of Egypt use for a piece of paper.

Ḥudhayfah said that the one holding the scales on the Day of Rising will be Jibrīl. The Almighty will say, 'Jibrīl, weigh them and return some to others.' He said, 'There will be neither gold nor silver. If the wrongdoer has good deeds, some of his good deeds will be taken and given to the one he wronged. If he has no good deeds, some of the bad actions of the one he wronged will be taken and be given to the wrongdoer who will bear their weight. A man will return bearing the weight of mountains.'

It is related that the Prophet ﷺ said, 'Allah Almighty will say on the Day of Rising, "Ādam, come forward beside the Throne at the Scales and see the actions of your children which will be presented to you. Anyone who has a grain's weight of more good than evil will be in the Garden. Anyone who has a grain's weight of more evil than good will be in the Fire. This is so that you know that I only punish wrongdoers."'

وَلَقَدْ مَكَّنَّٰكُمْ فِي ٱلْأَرْضِ وَجَعَلْنَا لَكُمْ فِيهَا مَعَٰيِشَ قَلِيلًا
مَّا تَشْكُرُونَ ١٠

10 We have established you firmly on the earth and granted you your livelihood in it. What little thanks you show!

We have made it stable for you, and a bed, and We have prepared for you the means of livelihood. *Ma'āyish* is the plural of *ma'īshah*, meaning the food and drink that is sought as sustenance (*ta'ayyasha*) and those things through which life subsists. The verb is *'āsha, ya'īshu* and the verbal nouns are *'aysh, ma'āsh, ma'īsh, ma'īshah* and *'īshah*. Az-Zajjāj said, 'Livelihood (*ma'īshah*) is that which is connected to life (*'aysh*).' According to al-Akhfash and many grammarians the form of *ma'īshah* is *maf'īlah*. Al-A'raj recited *'ma'ā'ish'* with *hamzah*. That is how Khārijah ibn Muṣ'ab related it from Nāfi'. An-Naḥḥās said that the *hamzah* is poor grammatically and not permitted because the singular is *ma'īshah*. Its root is *ma'yīshah* and the connective *alif* is added in the plural, and it and the *yā'* are silent. There must be vowelling since there is no way to elide. The *alif* is not vowelled and so the *yā'* is vowelled with what is necessary for it in the singular. The same is true of *wāw*: *manārah* and *manāwir*, and *maqām* and *maqāwim*. [POEM] And the same is true of *muṣībah* and *maṣāwib*. This is excellent, and a rare dialectical form of *maṣā'ib*. Al-Akhfash said that *maṣā'ib* is permitted because the singular is defective. Az-Zajjāj said, 'This is an error. It must be said *maqā'im*, but the position is that it is like *wisādah* and *isādah*.' It is said that the *hamzah* is not permitted in *ma'āyish* because the form of *ma'īshah* is *maf'īlah*. So the *yā'* is part of the root. There is a *hamzah* when the *yā'* is extra as in *madīnah* and *madā'in*, *ṣaḥīfah* and *ṣaḥā'if*, *karīmah* and *karā'im*, *waṣīfah* and *waṣā'if* and the like.

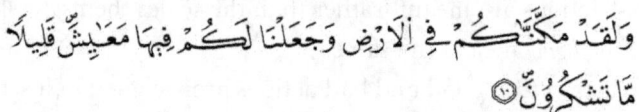

وَلَقَدْ خَلَقْنَٰكُمْ ثُمَّ صَوَّرْنَٰكُمْ ثُمَّ قُلْنَا لِلْمَلَٰٓئِكَةِ ٱسْجُدُوا۟ لِءَادَمَ
فَسَجَدُوٓا۟ إِلَّآ إِبْلِيسَ لَمْ يَكُن مِّنَ ٱلسَّٰجِدِينَ ﴿١١﴾

11 We created you and then formed you and then We said to the angels, 'Prostrate before Ādam,' and they prostrated – except for Iblīs. He was not among those who prostrated.

We created you and then formed you

When Allah mentions His blessings, He then mentions the beginning of His creation. The meaning of *khalq* was discussed elsewhere (2:21,29). '*Formed you*' means 'He created you as a drop and then formed you. Then We inform you that We said to the angels, "Prostrate to Ādam."' Ibn 'Abbās, aḍ-Ḍaḥḥāk and others said that it means, 'We created Ādam, and then formed you in his back.' Al-Akhfash said that *thumma* means 'and' here. It is said that it means; 'We created you, Ādam, and then told the angels to prostrate to Ādam, and then We formed you,' and there is a change in the order. It is said that '*We created you*' refers to the creation of Ādam and the plural is used because he was the father of mankind, and '*then formed you*' also refers to him. Ibn 'Abbās said that there is no change in the order of the words. It is said that it means, 'We created you (Ādam and Ḥawwā') and Ādam was created from earth and Ḥawwā' from one of his ribs.' Formation then occurred after that, and it means: 'We created your parents and then formed them.' Al-Ḥasan said that. It is said that it means: 'We created you in the back of Ādam and then formed you when We took the covenant from you.' This is the view of Mujāhid. Ibn Jurayj and Ibn Abī Najīḥ related it from him. An-Naḥḥās said that it is the best of the views. Mujāhid believed that Allah created them in the back of Ādam, then formed them when He took the covenant from them, and then the prostration occurred. This view is supported by Allah's words: '*When your Lord took out all their descendants from the loins of the children of Ādam*' (7:172) and the *ḥadīth*: 'He produced them like atoms and took the covenant from them.' It is said that the word '*then*' is a report, implying, 'We created you (in the back of Ādam), and then formed you in the wombs.' An-Naḥḥās said that it is sound from Ibn 'Abbās.

All these views are possible. The sound view is that which is supported by Revelation. The Almighty says: '*He created man from the purest kind of clay*' (23:13), meaning Ādam, and '*and created its mate from it*' (4:1). Then He says: '*We made him*', his offspring, '*a drop in a secure receptacle.*' (23:13) Ādam was created from clay and then formed, and was honoured by prostration. His offspring were formed in the wombs of their mothers after they were created in them and in the loins of their fathers. It was already mentioned in *Sūrat al-An'ām* (6:2) that every human being was created from sperm and earth, so reflect on it there. Here Allah says: '*We created you and then formed you*' and He says at the end of *al-Hashr*: '*He is Allah, the Creator, the Maker, the Giver of Form.*' (59:24) He mentioned formation after creation. That will be explained there. It is also said that the meaning of '*We created you*' is 'We created the souls first and then formed the bodies afterwards.'

except for Iblīs. He was not among those who prostrated.

This is an exception from other than the genus or from the genus. Scholars disagree about whether he was one of the angels or not. This was discussed in *al-Baqarah* (2:34).

قَالَ مَا مَنَعَكَ أَلَّا تَسْجُدَ إِذْ أَمَرْتُكَ قَالَ أَنَا خَيْرٌ مِّنْهُ خَلَقْتَنِي مِن نَّارٍ وَخَلَقْتَهُ مِن طِينٍ ﴿١٢﴾

12 He said, 'What prevented you from prostrating when I commanded you to?' He replied, 'I am better than him. You created me from fire and You created him from clay.'

'What prevented you from prostrating

In '*What prevented you*', the pronoun *mā* is nominative for the inceptive, implying 'what thing prevented you?' This question is a rebuke. '*From prostrating*' is in the accusative, i.e. 'from being one who prostrates,' and the *lā* is redundant. This is also seen in 38:75. [POEM] It is also said that the *lā* is not redundant, and preventing contains some words and calling. It is as if Allah were saying, 'Who told you not to prostrate?' or 'Who called on you not to prostrate?' It is as you say, 'I told you not to do it.' It is said that there is something elided which implies: 'What prevented you from obeying and made you want not to prostrate?'

Scholars say that that which made him want not to prostrate was his pride and envy. He concealed that inside himself when he was commanded to do that. The command to do it was made before Ādam as created. Allah Almighty says: '*I am going to create a human being out of clay. When I have formed him and breathed My Rūḥ into him, fall down in prostration to him!*' (38:71-72) It is as if a great matter was contained in His words: '...*fall down in prostration to him.*' Falling down entails humility on the part of one who falls down and honour for the one before whom he falls down. He concealed in himself that he would not prostrate when he was commanded to do that. When the *rūḥ* was breathed into Ādam and the angels fell down in prostration, Iblīs remained among them standing, his standing and lack of prostration displaying what he had inside himself. So Allah asked, '*What prevented you from prostrating?*' meaning, 'What kept you from obeying My command?' Then he disclosed the secret hidden inside him and said, '*I am better than him.*'

when I commanded you to?'

This indicates what scholars have said about a command stipulating obligation in general no matter what the context because censure is connected to abandoning the general command in Allah's words to the angels: '*Prostrate to Ādam.*' This is clear.

He replied, 'I am better than him.

Iblīs says, 'What prevented me from prostrating to him is the fact that I am better than him.' This is an answer from Iblīs based on the words: '*You created me from fire and You created him from clay.*' He thought that fire was nobler than clay since it is high, rises and is light and because it is a luminous substance. Ibn 'Abbās, al-Ḥasan and Ibn Sīrīn said, 'Iblīs was the first to employ analogy and his analogy was erroneous. Anyone who makes an analogy about matters of the *dīn* based on his personal opinion is joined to Iblīs.' Ibn Sīrīn said, 'The sun and moon are only worshipped by analogy.' The wise say that the enemy of Allah erred since he considered fire better than clay while they are in fact the same, both being inanimate creation.

Clay, in fact, is better than fire in four ways: Firstly, the essence of clay contains gravity, stillness, sedateness, deliberation, forbearance, modesty and forbearance. That is what led Ādam to repentance, humility and humble entreaty to Allah after losing the happiness which he previously had. So it brought him forgiveness, election and guidance. Part of the essence of fire is lightness, fickleness, sharpness, elevation and confusion. After the happiness which he had had, that led Iblīs to pride and obstinacy, and so it brought him destruction, punishment, the curse and wretchedness. Al-Qaffāl said that. Secondly, the report says that the earth of the Garden is fragrant musk, and the report does not say that there is fire in the Garden or that there is earth in the Fire. The third way is that fire is a means of punishment, and it is Allah's punishment of His enemies. Earth is not a means of punishment. The fourth point is that earth has no need of fire while fire needs a place, which is the earth. A possible fifth point is that the earth is a mosque and purifying, as is stated in the sound *ḥadīth*. Fire causes fear and punishment as the Almighty says: *'By that Allah strikes fear into His slaves.'* (39:16) Ibn 'Abbās said, 'It would have been more appropriate for Iblīs to obey than to use analogy and disobey his Lord. He was the first to use analogy based on his personal opinion. When analogy opposes the text, it is rejected.'

People disagree about analogy: there are those who espouse it and those who reject it. Those who espouse it are the Companions, the *Tābi'ūn* and the majority after them, and they say that worship by it is permitted logically and occurs legally. That is sound. Al-Qaffāl among the Shāfi'īs and al-Ḥasan al-Basrī believe that it is logically obligatory to worship by means of the use of analogy. An-Naẓẓām believes that it is possible to worship by it both logically and legally. Some of the people who rely on the literal text reject it. The first view is sound. Al-Bukhārī says in 'The Book of Holding to the Book and *Sunnah*' that which means that people should not hold to anything except the Book of Allah, the *Sunnah* of His Prophet or the consensus of scholars if a ruling exists about a matter. If there is no ruling, then analogy may be resorted to. He refers to this in the 'Chapter on rulings which are known by proofs and the meaning of evidence and its explanation'.

Aṭ-Ṭabarī said that *ijtihād* and deduction from the Book of Allah, the *Sunnah* of His Prophet ﷺ and the consensus of the Community is an obligatory duty and binding obligation for the people of knowledge. There are reports confirming that from the Prophet ﷺ and the group of the Companions and *Tābi'ūn*. Abū Tammām al-Maliki said, 'The community agree about consensus. An aspect of that is that they agree that gold and silver are analogous in *zakāt*. Abū Bakr said, "Release me from the allegiance you gave to me." 'Ali said, "By Allah, we will not take back our allegiance nor ask you to give it back. The Messenger of Allah ﷺ was pleased with you for our *dīn*, so should we not be pleased with you for our worldly portion?" He made imamate (leadership) analogous to the prayer. Abū Bakr made *zakāt* analogous to the prayer and said, "By Allah, I will not separate what Allah has joined together." 'Alī clearly articulated an analogy in the presence of the Companions in the case of someone who drank wine. He said, "If he is drunk, he prattles. If he prattles, he lies. So his *ḥadd* punishment is the *ḥadd* of the slanderer." 'Umar wrote a letter to Abū Mūsā al-Ash'arī which said, "Understanding: understanding is what moves in your breast about something not conveyed to you in the Book and the *Sunnah*. Recognise similarities and likenesses, and then use analogy in matters on that basis. Rely on that which is most beloved to Allah and more like the truth in what you see." Ad-Dāraquṭnī mentioned the account in full.' Abū 'Ubaydah said to 'Umar in the *ḥadīth* about the plague when 'Umar returned from Sargh, 'Are we fleeing from Allah's decree?' 'Umar replied,

'Yes, we are fleeing from Allah's decree to Allah's decree.' Then 'Umar asked him, 'Do you think…' and so he used analogy and discussed it with him using something that resembled the matter in the presence of the Muhājirūn and Anṣār. That is enough for you.

There are also numerous reports and *āyah*s of Qur'an about this. It indicates that analogy is one of the fundamentals of the *dīn* and one of the protections of the Muslims to which the *mujtahid*s refer and scholars of action devote themselves, and so rulings are deduced by using it. This is the view of the Community who are the proof and there is no need to pay attention to the aberrant. As for blameworthy opinions and forbidden artificial analogy, they are something that is not based on these principles which have been mentioned and are mere opinion and an impulse from *shayṭān*. Allah Almighty says: '*Do not pursue what you have no knowledge of.*' (17:36) All the weak *ḥadīth*s and weak reports that an opponent may bring in censure of analogy are considered to be part this sort of blameworthy analogy which has no known basis in the *Sharī'ah*.

قَالَ فَاهْبِطْ مِنْهَا فَمَا يَكُونُ لَكَ أَن تَتَكَبَّرَ فِيهَا فَاخْرُجْ إِنَّكَ مِنَ الصَّاغِرِينَ ﴿١٣﴾

13 He said, 'Descend from Heaven. It is not for you to be arrogant in it. So get out! You are one of the abased.'

'*It is not for you to be arrogant in it*' because its inhabitants are humble angels. '*So get out! You are one of the abased.*' indicates that someone who disobeys his master is abased. Abū Rawḥ and al-Bajalī said that it means 'Descend from the form you have been given,' because he boasted that he was made from fire; so his form became mixed with darkness and his radiance was removed. It is said that it means to move from the earth to islands in the sea. He then only enters the land like a thief until he leaves it. The first view is more evident. It was already mentioned in *al-Baqarah* (2:38).

قَالَ أَنظِرْنِي إِلَىٰ يَوْمِ يُبْعَثُونَ ﴿١٤﴾ قَالَ إِنَّكَ مِنَ الْمُنظَرِينَ ﴿١٥﴾

14-15 He said, 'Grant me a reprieve until the day they are raised up.' He said, 'You are one of the reprieved.'

He asked for deferral and delay until the Day of Resurrection and Reckoning. He asked not to die because there will be no death after the Day of Resurrection.

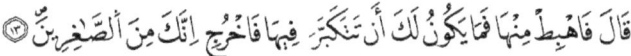

Allah said, '*You are one of the reprieved.*' Ibn 'Abbās, as-Suddī and others said, 'He granted him reprieve until the first blast because then all creation will die. He sought a reprieve until the second blast when people stand for the Lord of the worlds and Allah refused him that.' The words '*they are raised up*' refer to Ādam and his descendants even though those who were going to be raised up were not mentioned before, because the story is about Ādam and his descendants. It indicates that they will be resurrected.

قَالَ فَبِمَآ أَغْوَيْتَنِى لَأَقْعُدَنَّ لَهُمْ صِرَٰطَكَ ٱلْمُسْتَقِيمَ ﴿١٦﴾ ثُمَّ لَءَاتِيَنَّهُم مِّنۢ بَيْنِ أَيْدِيهِمْ وَمِنْ خَلْفِهِمْ وَعَنْ أَيْمَٰنِهِمْ وَعَن شَمَآئِلِهِمْ ۖ وَلَا تَجِدُ أَكْثَرَهُمْ شَٰكِرِينَ ﴿١٧﴾

16-17 He said, 'By Your misguidance of me, I will lie in ambush for them on Your straight path. Then I will come at them, from in front of them and behind them, from their right and from their left. You will not find most of them thankful.'

He said, 'By Your misguidance of me,

Misguiding (*ighwā'*) happens by error being put into the heart, so what is meant is 'by the error, obstinacy and pride You made occur in my heart.' This is because the disbelief of Iblīs was not disbelief based on ignorance, but disbelief resulting from obstinacy and pride, as was mentioned in *al-Baqarah*. It is said that the meaning of the words is an oath, implying, 'Because of Your misguiding of me, I will lie in wait for them on Your Path, or in Your path.' There is elision and there is evidence for this view in Allah's words in *Sūrah Ṣād*: '*By Your might, I will mislead all of them.*' (38:82) It was as if Iblīs exalted Allah's misguidance of him because of the subjugation of Allah's slaves it entailed. His swearing by it is his exaltation of Allah's power.

It is said that the *bā'* here signifies the *lām* of the oath, as if he were saying, 'By Your misguidance of me.' It is said that it means 'with' and means 'with Your misguiding me'. It is said that it is a question, as if he were asking, 'For what reason did You misguide me?' It is said that it means, 'Because You have destroyed me by Your cursing me.' Misguidance is destruction. Allah says: '*They will plunge into the Valley of Evil* (*ghayy*).' (19:59) It is said that misguidance is putting someone far away. Ibn 'Abbās said that. It is said that it means 'disappointed me of Your mercy.' A poet said:

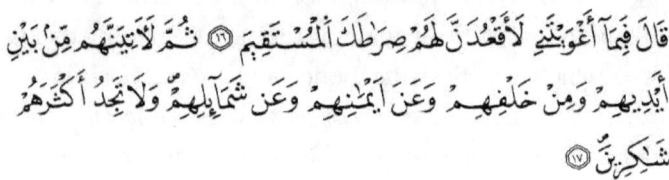

If someone errs, there are no lack of critics of error.

Ibn al-A'rabī said, 'The verb *ghawā, yaghwī* is used for someone whose business is unsound or who is unsound in himself.' It is one of the meaning of the words of Allah when He says: '*Ādam disobeyed his Lord and erred*' (20:121), meaning that his life in the Garden was ruined. The verb is also used for a weaned young camel when its mother's milk does not flow. The position of the people of the *Sunnah* is that Allah Almighty misguided him and created unbelief in him. That is why he here ascribes his misguidance to Allah. It is the reality. There is nothing in existence but that it was created by Him and issues from His will.

The Imāmiyyah Shī'ah, the Qadariyyah and others have differed about this. Their Shaykh is Iblīs, whom they obey in all that he makes seem attractive to them, although they do not obey him in this matter and say that 'Iblīs erred. They say, 'He is in error when he ascribes his misguidance to his Lord. Allah is exalted above that.' The answer given to them is that even though Iblīs was in error, what do you say about the noble protected Prophet Nūḥ when he told his people: '*My counsel will not benefit you, for all my desire to counsel you, if Allah desires to lead you into error. He is your Lord and you will return to Him.*' (11:34) It is related that a man, who was suspected of espousing the Qadariyyah position, and was one of the great *fuqahā'*, approached Ṭāwūs in the Masjid al-Ḥarām. He sat beside him and Ṭāwūs said, 'Do you get up or are you made to get up?' Ṭāwūs was asked, 'Do you say this to a man who is *faqīh*?' He retorted, 'Iblīs has more *fiqh* than he does! Iblīs said, "*My Lord, by Your misguidance of me,*" while this one says, "I misguide myself."'

I will lie in ambush for them on Your straight path

He will block it and make falsehood seem attractive so that they will be destroyed as he was destroyed, misguided as he was misguided, or disappointed as he was disappointed, according to the prior three meanings of the words '*misguided me*'. The Straight Path is the path which leads to the Garden. '*Your straight path*' is in the accusative based on an elided 'on' or 'in' as Sībawayh related. [POEM]

Then I will come at them, from in front of them and behind them, from their right and from their left.

There is an excellent interpretation of this, namely that it means: 'I will bar them from the Truth and make them desire this world and doubt the Next World.' This is the furthest extent of misguidance, as he says, '*I will misguide them.*' (4:119) Sufyān related from Manṣūr that al-Ḥakam ibn 'Uyaynah said that '*in front*' means prevent them from benefitting in this world, '*behind them*' means prevent them from profiting in the Next World,' '*from their right*' means corrupting their good actions and '*from their left*' means encouraging their evil deeds. An-Naḥḥās said, 'This is a good view. Its explanation is that the meaning is: "*I will come at them from in front of them*" in this world until they deny the signs and reports of earlier nations it contains, "*and behind them*" regarding their Next World so that they deny it, "*from their right*" discouraging their good actions and matters of the *dīn*, and "*from their left*," encouraging them in their evil deeds, so that they will follow their lower appetites because they are made to seem attractive to them.' '*You will not find most of them thankful*,' by declaring Allah's unity, obeying Him and showing gratitude to Him.

قَالَ ٱخْرُجْ مِنْهَا مَذْءُومًا مَّدْحُورًا لَّمَن تَبِعَكَ مِنْهُمْ لَأَمْلَأَنَّ جَهَنَّمَ مِنكُمْ أَجْمَعِينَ ﴿١٨﴾

18 He said, 'Get out of it, reviled and driven out. As for those of them who follow you, I will fill up Hell with every one of you.'

'*Get out of it* (the Garden).' *Madh'ūm* means *madhmūm. Dha'm* means 'a vice'. Ibn Zayd said that *madh'ūm* and *madhmūm* mean the same. The verbs *dha'ama*, *dhamma* and *dhāma* mean the same. Al-A'mash recited '*madhūman*' and it means the same although it is lightened of the *hamzah*. Mujāhid said that *madh'ūm* means exiled. *Madḥūr* means 'cast away and put far away', as Mujāhid and others said. Its root means 'to push back'.

As for those of them who follow you, I will fill up Hell with every one of you.'

The *lām* used here is for the oath and its apodosis is '*I will fill*.' It is said that the first *lām* is for stress and the one connected to '*I will fill*' is for the oath. The evidence for this is that it is permitted to elide the first *lām* in other than the first reading but not in the second. The words contain the meaning of the precondition and requital, meaning: 'I will punish whoever follows you.' 'Āṣim recited from the transmission of Abū Bakr ibn 'Ayyāsh: '*liman tabi'aka*' with a *kasrah* on the *lām*. Some grammarians object to this. An-Naḥḥās said: 'It implies, and Allah knows best, "for those who follow you" in the same way that you say, "I honoured so-and-so because of you (*laka*)." The meaning can be "being driven out is for those who follow you."' The meaning of '*every one of you*' is you and the children of Ādam, and the masculine plural is used when addressing the children of Ādam.

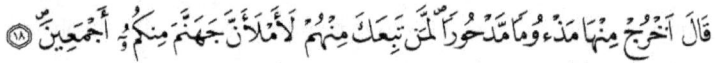

وَيَـٰٓـَٔادَمُ ٱسْكُنْ أَنتَ وَزَوْجُكَ ٱلْجَنَّةَ فَكُلَا مِنْ حَيْثُ شِئْتُمَا وَلَا تَقْرَبَا هَـٰذِهِ
ٱلشَّجَرَةَ فَتَكُونَا مِنَ ٱلظَّـٰلِمِينَ ١٩

19 'Ādam, live in the Garden, you and your wife, and eat of it wherever you like. But do not go near this tree lest you become wrongdoers.'

After Iblīs was expelled from his place in heaven, Allah said to Ādam, 'You and Hawwā' live in the Garden.' This was already discussed in *al-Baqarah* (2:35). '*Do not go near this tree*' was already mentioned (2:35).

فَوَسْوَسَ لَهُمَا ٱلشَّيْطَـٰنُ لِيُبْدِيَ لَهُمَا مَا وُۥرِيَ عَنْهُمَا مِن سَوْءَٰتِهِمَا وَقَالَ مَا
نَهَىٰكُمَا رَبُّكُمَا عَنْ هَـٰذِهِ ٱلشَّجَرَةِ إِلَّآ أَن تَكُونَا مَلَكَيْنِ أَوْ تَكُونَا مِنَ ٱلْخَـٰلِدِينَ ٢٠

20 Then *Shayṭān* whispered to them, disclosing to them their private parts that had been concealed from them. He said, 'Your Lord has only forbidden you this tree lest you become angels or among those who live for ever.'

Then *Shayṭān* whispered to them,

He is said to have got inside the Garden by means of sending the serpent into it. It is said that it was from outside by the power which he was given. This was discussed in *al-Baqarah* (2:36). 'Whispering' (*waswasah*) is a light sound and it is also the self talking internally. One says, '*waswasat ilayhi nafsuhu waswasatan* or *wiswās*' (his self whispered to him). *Waswās* is a proper noun like *zilzāl* and *zalzāl* (earthquake), and it is used for the faint sound made by a hunter and his dogs and the tinkle of jewellery. Al-A'shā said:

You hear twinkling (*waswās*) of jewellery when she goes,
as the senna plant is helped by the wind.

It is a name of *shayṭān*. Allah says, '*From the evil of the slinking whisperer.*' (114:4)

disclosing to them their private parts that had been concealed from them.

'*Disclosing*' means 'showing them'. The *lām* is the *lām* of indicating the end or it means 'in order to'. '*Wuriya*' is concealed and covered. Outside of the Qur'an '*ūriya*' is permitted. '*Private parts*' are called '*awrah* because disclosing them is bad for the person. This indicates that it is ugly to disclose them. It is said that he showed their evil to them, not to others. There was light covering them so that their private parts were not seen and then the light was removed. It is said that it was a garment, and it fell to pieces. Allah knows best.

lest you become angels or among those who live for ever.'

In '*lest you become angels*' *an* is accusative, meaning '*lest*' as the Basrans say. It is 'disliking that...' The Kufans said that it means: 'so that you do not.' It is said that it means: 'Lest you become angels who know good and evil.' It is said that Ādam desired immortality because he knew that the angels would not die until the Day of Rising. An-Naḥḥās said, 'Allah clarified the excellence of the angels over all creation elsewhere in the Qur'an. Indicating that is: "*lest you become angels*" as is: "*I do not say that I am an angel*" (11:31) and: "*nor would the angels who are close to Him.*" (4:172)' Al-Ḥasan said, 'Allah favoured the angels with forms, wings and honour.' Someone else said, 'He favoured them with obedience and lack of disobedience. This is why they are preferred in everything.' Ibn Fūrak said that there is no proof in this *āyah* because it can mean simply that angels do not have desire for food.

Ibn 'Abbās, az-Zajjāj and many scholars preferred to say that believers are better than angels. That was discussed in *al-Baqarah.* (2:33) Al-Kalbī said, 'They are better than all creatures except for a small group of angels: Jibrīl, Mikā'īl, Isrāfīl and the Angel of Death, because they are part of the group of the Messengers of Allah.' Each group holds to the outward texts of the *Sharī'ah*, and excellence is in the hand of Allah.

Ibn 'Abbās recited *malikayn* (two sovereigns), which is the reading of Yaḥyā ibn Abī Kathīr and aḍ-Ḍaḥḥāk. Abū 'Amr ibn al-'Alā' objected to the *kasrah* on the *lām*, saying that there were no sovereigns before Ādam, so how they could they want to become sovereigns? An-Naḥḥās said, 'According to this reading, it is permitted to have a *sukūn* on the *lām* (*malkayn*), but not permitted in the first reading because of the lightness of the *fatḥah*.' Ibn 'Abbās said, 'The cursed one came to him by way of the kingdom (*mulk*). This is why he said: "*Shall I show you the way to the Tree of Everlasting Life and to a kingdom (mulk) which will never fade away?*" (20:120)' Abū 'Ubaydah claimed that Yaḥyā ibn Abī Kathīr used Allah's words: '*...to a kingdom which will never fade away*,' as clear evidence for this reading, but people leave it and this is why we left it. An-Naḥḥās said that it is rare reading, but Abū 'Ubayd objected to these words and said that it is a huge error. Is it conceivable to imagine that Ādam could reach further than the kingdom of the Garden which is the goal of seekers? Rather what the words '*a kingdom which* *will never fade away*' mean is residing in the kingdom of the Garden and being immortal in it.

وَقَاسَمَهُمَآ إِنِّي لَكُمَا لَمِنَ ٱلنَّٰصِحِينَ ٢١

21 He swore to them, 'I am one of those who give you good advice.'

He swore to them. The verb *aqsama* (*iqsām*) means to swear. A poet said:

He swore to them strongly by Allah:
'You are more delicious than quail when they spread.'

Form III (*fāʿala*) can be used for one person. This refutes those who say that the form is only used of two people. This was already mentioned in *al-Māʾidah* (5:89). The pronoun '*lakumā*' is not included in the connective. It implies, 'I give good advice to you from among those who give good advice.' Hishām an-Naḥawī said that and something similar was mentioned in *al-Baqarah* (2:130). The meaning of the words is, 'Follow me, and I will guide you.' Qatādah mentioned it.

فَدَلَّىٰهُمَا بِغُرُورٖۚ فَلَمَّا ذَاقَا ٱلشَّجَرَةَ بَدَتۡ لَهُمَا سَوۡءَٰتُهُمَا وَطَفِقَا يَخۡصِفَانِ
عَلَيۡهِمَا مِن وَرَقِ ٱلۡجَنَّةِۖ وَنَادَىٰهُمَا رَبُّهُمَآ أَلَمۡ أَنۡهَكُمَا عَن تِلۡكُمَا ٱلشَّجَرَةِ وَأَقُل
لَّكُمَآ إِنَّ ٱلشَّيۡطَٰنَ لَكُمَا عَدُوّٞ مُّبِينٞ ٢٢ قَالَا رَبَّنَا ظَلَمۡنَآ أَنفُسَنَا وَإِن لَّمۡ
تَغۡفِرۡ لَنَا وَتَرۡحَمۡنَا لَنَكُونَنَّ مِنَ ٱلۡخَٰسِرِينَ ٢٣ قَالَ ٱهۡبِطُواْ بَعۡضُكُمۡ لِبَعۡضٍ
عَدُوّٞۖ وَلَكُمۡ فِي ٱلۡأَرۡضِ مُسۡتَقَرّٞ وَمَتَٰعٌ إِلَىٰ حِينٖ ٢٤

22-24 So he enticed them to do it by means of trickery. Then when they tasted the tree, their private parts were disclosed to them and they started stitching together the leaves of the Garden in order to cover themselves. Their Lord called out to them, 'Did I not forbid you this tree and say to you, "*Shayṭān* is an outright enemy to you"?' They said, 'Our Lord, we have wronged ourselves. If you do not forgive us and have mercy on us, we will be among the lost.' He said, 'Go down from here as enemies to each other! You will have residence on the earth and enjoyment for a time.'

So he enticed them to do it by means of trickery.

He made them fall into destruction. Ibn 'Abbās said that he tricked them by using the oath. Ādam thought that no one would lie when he swore by Allah and so he tricked them by his whispering and swearing to them. Qatādah said that he swore to them by Allah and so deceived them by doing that. It is possible for those who believe in Allah to be deceived. One of the scholars said, 'Whoever deceives us by Allah deceives us.' It says in a *ḥadīth*: 'A believer is noble and gullible and an unbeliever is blameworthy and cunning.' Niftawah said:

You can trick the noble whenever you wish to do so,
but you see that the blameworthy are experienced and not gulled.

The verb in '*he enticed them*' is *adlā*, which means 'to release', and *dallā* means 'to bring out'. It is also said that it is derived from *dālla*, which is boldness, implying that he enticed them to disobey and thus removed them from the Garden.

Then when they tasted the tree, their private parts were disclosed to them

This was when they ate from it, and the disagreement about what this tree was and how Ādam ate from it was mentioned in *al-Baqarah* (2:35). Ḥawwā' ate first and experienced nothing. When Ādam ate, the punishment occurred because the prohibition was addressed to both of them. Ibn 'Abbās said that the light which clothed them contracted and became confined to the fingernails and toenails.

'*Stitching*': (*yakhṣifāna*) is recited by al-Ḥasan as '*yakhiṣṣifāna*'. The root is '*yakhtaṣifāna*' and there has been elision. Ibn Buraydah and Ya'qūb recite it with a *fatḥah* on the *khā'* because of the vowel on the *tā'*. It is also permitted to have '*yukhaṣṣifāna*' from Form II. Az-Zuhrī recited '*yukhṣifāna*' from Form IV. Both are transmitted with the *hamzah* or doubling. It means they cut up leaves and stuck them on to use them to cover themselves. From it comes *khasf* (sandal) and a *khaṣṣāf* is the cobbler who cuts them out. *Mikhṣaf* means 'awl'. Ibn 'Abbās said that they were fig leaves. It is related that when his private parts were disclosed to him, Ādam went around the trees of the Garden trying to pull off leaves with which to cover his private parts but the trees of the garden all rebuked him until the fig tree had mercy on him and gave him a leaf. This action was done by Ādam and Hawwā'. Allah repaid the fig by making its inside and outside the same in sweetness and use and gave it two crops in the same year.

The *āyah* contains evidence of the great immodesty entailed in disclosing the private parts and the fact that Allah made it obligatory for them to be covered. That is why they set out to conceal them. That does not preclude them being commanded to do that in the Garden as they had been told: '*Do not go near this tree.*'

The author of *al-Bayān* related from ash-Shāfi'ī that the one who does not find anything to cover his private parts with, except for the leaves of trees, is obliged to do that, because it is a clear kind of covering which one is able to achieve as Ādam did in the Garden. Allah knows best.

They said, 'Our Lord, we have wronged ourselves.

Allah said to them, '*Did I not forbid you*?' and they said, '*Our Lord*!' The *yā* ['O!'] before '*rabb*' is elided which is a mark of esteem. They admitted their error and repented, may Allah bless both of them. The rest was already mentioned.

قَالَ فِيهَا تَحْيَوْنَ وَفِيهَا تَمُوتُونَ وَمِنْهَا تُخْرَجُونَ ﴿٢٥﴾

25 He said, 'On it you will live and on it die and from it you will be brought forth.'

All the pronouns '*it*' refer to the earth.

يَٰبَنِيٓ ءَادَمَ قَدْ أَنزَلْنَا عَلَيْكُمْ لِبَاسًا يُوَٰرِي سَوْءَٰتِكُمْ وَرِيشًا وَلِبَاسُ
ٱلتَّقْوَىٰ ذَٰلِكَ خَيْرٌ ذَٰلِكَ مِنْ ءَايَٰتِ ٱللَّهِ لَعَلَّهُمْ يَذَّكَّرُونَ ﴿٢٦﴾

26 Children of Ādam! We have sent down clothing to you to conceal your private parts, and fine apparel, but the garment of *taqwā* – that is best! That is one of Allah's Signs, so that hopefully you will pay heed.

Children of Ādam! We have sent down clothing to you to conceal your private parts,

Many scholars said that this *āyah* is evidence for the obligation to cover the private parts because Allah says: '*to conceal your private parts.*' Some people, however, said that it does not constitute evidence for that but is simply evidence of blessing. The first view is sounder. One aspect of blessing is concealing the private parts. It is clear that Allah Almighty gave Ādam's descendants what they could cover their private parts with and commanded them to cover them. There is no disagreement among scholars that it is obligatory to conceal your private parts from the eyes of other people. They disagree about exactly what the private parts are. Ibn Abī Dhi'b said that for a man it is the private parts themselves: front and back, and nothing else. That is the view of Dāwūd and the literalists, Ibn Abi 'Ablah and aṭ-Ṭabarī by His words: '*...clothing to conceal your private parts,*' '*...disclosing to them their* *private parts*' (7:22), and '...*disclosing to them their private parts*' (7:27). It is reported in al-Bukhārī that Anas said, 'The Messenger of Allah ﷺ rode quickly through the lanes of Khaybar...' He says in it, 'He had removed the wrapper from his thigh so that I could see the whiteness of the thigh of the Prophet of Allah ﷺ.'

Mālik said, 'The navel is not one of the private parts.' But he disliked a man uncovering his thigh in the presence of his wife. Abū Ḥanīfah said that the knee is a private part. That is the view of 'Aṭā'. Ash-Shāfi'ī said, 'Neither the navel nor the knees are private parts in the sound view.' Abū Ḥāmid at-Tirmidhī related that ash-Shāfi'ī had two views about the navel. Mālik's evidence is the words of the Prophet ﷺ to Jarhad, 'Cover your thigh. The thigh is one of the private parts.' Al-Bukhārī transmitted it in his commentary and said: 'The *ḥadīth* of Anas is stronger but the *ḥadīth* of Jarhad is more complete in respect of resolving the disagreement of the scholars.' The *ḥadīth* of Jarhad indicates a disagreement with what Abū Hanīfah said. It is related that Abū Hurayrah kissed the navel of al-Ḥasan ibn 'Alī and said, 'I kiss that part of you which the Messenger of Allah ﷺ used to kiss.' If the navel had been a private part, Abū Hurayrah would not have kissed it and al-Ḥasan would not have allowed it.

In the case of free women, it is everything except for the face and palms, according to most of the people of knowledge. The Prophet ﷺ said, 'Whoever wants to marry a woman should look at her face and hands.' And it is mandatory that they be uncovered in *iḥrām*. Abū Bakr ibn 'Abd ar-Raḥmān ibn al-Ḥārith ibn Hishām said, 'The whole of a woman is a private part, even her nails,' and the same is related from Aḥmad ibn Ḥanbal. As for an *umm walad*, al-Athram said, 'I heard him (Aḥmad ibn Ḥanbal) reply when he was asked about how an *umm walad* should pray: "She should cover her head and her feet, because she cannot be sold, and she prays as a free woman prays." In the case of a slave-girl, her private parts are what is below her breasts, and she can show her head and wrists. It is said that her ruling is the same as that of a man. It is also said that it is disliked for a slave-girl to uncover her head and chest, but 'Umar used to hit slave-girls for covering their heads saying, 'Do not look like free women!' Aṣbagh said, 'If a slave-girl uncovers her thigh, she should repeat the prayer as long as it still in its time.'

Abū Bakr ibn 'Abd ar-Raḥmān ibn al-Ḥārith ibn Hishām said, 'All of a slave-girl is a private part, even her nails.' This is outside the views of the *fuqahā'* since they have a consensus that a free woman should pray the obligatory prayer with her hands and face uncovered so that she touches the ground with them. So that applies even more to a slave-girl. An *umm walad* has a more honoured status than a slave-girl. The private parts of small children have no particular sanctity but when a girl reaches the point where she catches the eye and is desirable, then she covers her private parts. The evidence of Abū Bakr ibn 'Abd ar-Raḥmān is the words of the Almighty: '*O Prophet! Tell your wives and daughters and the women of the believers to draw their outer garments closely round themselves*' (33:59) and the *ḥadīth* of Umm Salamah when she was asked what clothes a woman may pray in. She said, 'She should pray in a shift and ample veil which covers the tops of her feet.' It was related *marfū'*. Those who make it stop at Umm Salamah are more numerous and have a better memory. They include Mālik, Ibn Isḥāq and others. Abū Dāwūd said, "Abd ar-Raḥmān ibn 'Abdullāh ibn Dīnār has it *marfū'* from Muḥammad ibn Zayd from his mother that Umm Salamah asked the Messenger of Allah ﷺ ...' Abū 'Umar said, 'They consider this 'Abd ar-Raḥmān to be weak although al-Bukhārī has some of his *ḥadīth*s. The consensus about this is stronger than the report.

In the words '*We have sent down clothing to you*' the 'sending down' refers to the rain which makes cotton and linen grow and supports the animals from which there is wool, hair and fur. It is a metaphorical usage we also find in the words: '*He sent down livestock to you – eight kinds in pairs*' (39:6). It is said that this 'sending down' is some sort of clothing that was given to Ādam and Hawwā' so that it would be example for others. Sa'īd ibn Jubayr said that it means, 'We created for you.' It is said that it means: 'We inspired you how to make clothing.'

and fine apparel

'*Rīsh*' (*fine apparel*) is recited by Abū 'Abd ar-Raḥmān, al-Ḥasan and 'Āṣim in the reading of al-Mufaḍḍal aḍ-Ḍabbī, while Abū 'Amr in the reading of al-Ḥasan ibn 'Alī al-Ju'fī recited *riyāsh*, the plural of *rīsh*. He only has it from al-Ḥasan. It refers to property and clothing. Al-Farrā' said that *rīsh* and *riyāsh* are both used, and the feathers (*rīsh*) of a bird are what Allah uses to cover it. It is said that it refers to abundance and furnishings. Most linguists say that it is clothing that provides covering or comfort. Sibawayh composed:

My apparel (*rīsh*) is from you and my desire is with you
even if your visit is only rare.

Abū Ḥātim related from Abū 'Ubayd: 'I gave him a camel with its *rīsh*,' meaning with the cloths that are on it.

but the garment of *taqwā* – that is best!

Allah makes it clear that *taqwā* is the best garment as in the poem:

If a person does not wear the garment of *taqwā*
he becomes naked, even if he is dressed.
The best garment of a person is his obedience of his Lord.
There is no good in someone who disobeys Allah.

Qāsim ibn Mālik related that 'Awf said that Ma'bad al-Juhanī said that the garment of *taqwā* is modesty. Ibn 'Abbās said that it is righteous actions. He also said that it is a good demeanour. It is said that it is that by which Allah teaches and guides. It is said that it is wearing wool and rough garments which is an aspect of humility before Allah, and that worshipping Him is better than anything else. Zayd ibn 'Alī said that it is armour, a helmet, and the two arm and leg coverings by which one is protected in war. 'Urwah ibn az-Zubayr said that it is fear of Allah. It is said that it is an awareness of *tawqā* of Allah in what He commands and forbids. This is sound, and the view of Ibn 'Abbās and 'Urwah refers to it. The view of Zayd ibn 'Alī is good, and it is encouraging *jihād*. Ibn Zayd said that it is covering the private parts. This involves repetition since that was mentioned before. As for the one who says that it is wearing coarse clothing, that is closer to humility and seriousness. Excellent scholars, however, wear fine clothes while also having *taqwā* as will be made clear.

The people of Madīnah and al-Kisā'ī recited *libās* in the accusative, added to the first *libās*. It is said that it is in the accusative by an implied verb, namely 'We sent down the garment of *taqwā*.' The rest have it in the nominative for the inceptive. The word '*that*' is its adjective and '*best*' is the predicate of the inceptive. The meaning is: '*the garment of taqwā*, which is indicated, is better for you than wearing clothes which conceal your private parts and than the fine apparel which has been sent down on you, so wear it.' It is said that it is nominative as the pronoun 'it' is implied, i.e. 'It is the garment of *taqwā*' meaning the concealing of the private parts, which is the basis of the view of Ibn Zayd. It is said that the meaning is 'The garment of *taqwā* is better' and so '*that*' means 'it'. The first syntax is the best of what is said about it. Al-A'mash recited, '*libāsu-t-taqwā khayrun*' without '*dhālika*', which differs from the text of the Qur'an. '*That is one of Allah's Signs*' indicates that He is its Creator. '*That*' is in the nominative as an adjective, an appositive, or the addition of clarification.

يَٰبَنِيٓ ءَادَمَ لَا يَفۡتِنَنَّكُمُ ٱلشَّيۡطَٰنُ كَمَآ أَخۡرَجَ أَبَوَيۡكُم مِّنَ ٱلۡجَنَّةِ يَنزِعُ عَنۡهُمَا
لِبَاسَهُمَا لِيُرِيَهُمَا سَوۡءَٰتِهِمَآۚ إِنَّهُۥ يَرَىٰكُمۡ هُوَ وَقَبِيلُهُۥ مِنۡ حَيۡثُ لَا تَرَوۡنَهُمۡۗ
إِنَّا جَعَلۡنَا ٱلشَّيَٰطِينَ أَوۡلِيَآءَ لِلَّذِينَ لَا يُؤۡمِنُونَ ٢٧

27 Children of Ādam! do not let *Shayṭān* tempt you into trouble as He expelled your parents from the Garden, stripping them of their covering and disclosing to them their private parts. He and his tribe see you from where you do not see them. We have made the *shayṭāns* friends of those who do not believe.

Children of Ādam! do not let *Shayṭān* tempt you into trouble

His words, '*do not let Shayṭān tempt you*' mean: 'Do not let *Shayṭān* divert you from the *dīn* as he tempted your ancestors causing their expulsion from the Garden.' *Ab* is masculine and *abah* is for the feminine. According to this, it is said *abawayn*.

stripping them of their covering and disclosing to them their private parts.

'*Stripping them of their covering*' is in the accusative for the adverbial *ḥāl*. It is a new sentence and so one stops at '*Garden*.' '*Disclosing to them*' is also in the accusative by the *lām*. The word '*tribe*' is added for stress. Something in which the pronoun is concealed is the same as that in which it is openly expressed. This also indicates the obligation of covering the private parts since Allah says: '*disclosing to them their private parts*'. Others said that it is a warning about blessing being removed as it was removed from Ādam. This would be the case if it were confirmed that the *dīn* of Ādam is binding on us, but that is not the case.

He and his tribe see you from where you do not see them.

'*His tribe*' is his army. Mujāhid said that it means the jinn and *shayṭāns*. Ibn Zayd said that it means his generation. Regarding the phrase '*from where you do not see them*,' some scholars have said that this indicates that the jinn are invisible. Others have said that they can be seen because, when Allah Almighty wants them to be seen, He reveals their bodies so that they become visible. An-Naḥḥās said that it indicates that the jinn can only be seen in the time of a Prophet in order that that should be evidence of his Prophethood, because Allah Almighty created them in a form that makes them invisible. They become visible when they are changed from their original form and that is one of the miracles which only occur in the time of the Prophets ﷺ. Al-Qushayrī said, 'Allah made it the norm that the children of Ādam do not see the *shayṭāns* today.

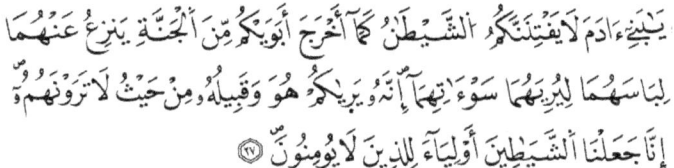

We read in a report, '*Shayṭān* flows through the son of Ādam like his blood flows,' and the Almighty says: '...*who whispers in the breasts of people.*' (114:5) The Prophet ﷺ said, 'An angel has a touch and *shayṭān* has a touch, felt by the heart. As for the touch of the angel, it promises good and affirms the truth. As for the touch of *Shayṭān*, it promises evil and denies the truth.' This was already mentioned in *al-Baqarah* (2:268). There are sound reports about seeing them. Al-Bukhārī transmitted that Abū Hurayrah said, 'The Messenger of Allah ﷺ put me in charge of guarding the *zakāt* of Ramaḍān,' and he mentioned a long story in which he seized a jinn who was taking some dates. The Prophet ﷺ asked him, 'What did you do with your captive last night?' The story was mentioned in *al-Baqarah* (2:24). It states in *Ṣaḥīḥ Muslim* that the Prophet ﷺ said, 'By Allah, were it not for the supplication of my brother Sulaymān, he would have been chained up so that the children of the people of Madīnah could play with him.' This was about the *'ifrīt* who rushed at him, which will be mentioned in *Ṣād* (38:35)

'*We have made the shayṭāns friends of those who do not believe*' refers to increasing their punishment and making them the same in their abandonment of the truth.

وَإِذَا فَعَلُوا۟ فَٰحِشَةً قَالُوا۟ وَجَدْنَا عَلَيْهَآ ءَابَآءَنَا وَٱللَّهُ أَمَرَنَا بِهَا ۗ قُلْ إِنَّ
ٱللَّهَ لَا يَأْمُرُ بِٱلْفَحْشَآءِ ۖ أَتَقُولُونَ عَلَى ٱللَّهِ مَا لَا تَعْلَمُونَ ﴿٢٨﴾

28 Whenever they commit an indecent act, they say, 'We found our fathers doing it and Allah commanded us to do it too.' Say: 'Allah does not command indecency. Do you say things about Allah you do not know?'

The '*indecent act*' referred to here, in the view of most commentators, is performing *ṭawāf* of the House while naked. Al-Ḥasan said that it is *shirk* and disbelief. The idolaters used their imitation of their ancestors as evidence for that and said that Allah had commanded them to do it. Al-Ḥasan said that they said, 'Allah commanded us to do it,' and they said, 'If Allah had disliked what we are doing, we would have ceased doing it.' The words: '*Say: "Allah does not command indecency"*' make it clear that they are making an arbitrary decision and have no evidence that Allah commanded them to do what they claim. The censure of their imitation and their great ignorance was already mentioned (2:170). This is part of it.

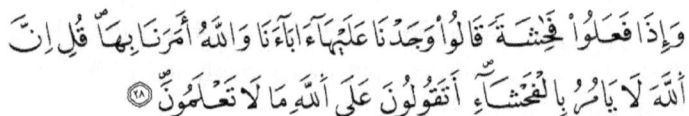

قُلْ أَمَرَ رَبِّي بِالْقِسْطِ ۖ وَأَقِيمُوا وُجُوهَكُمْ عِندَ كُلِّ مَسْجِدٍ وَادْعُوهُ
مُخْلِصِينَ لَهُ الدِّينَ ۚ كَمَا بَدَأَكُمْ تَعُودُونَ ﴿٢٩﴾ فَرِيقًا هَدَىٰ وَفَرِيقًا حَقَّ
عَلَيْهِمُ الضَّلَالَةُ ۗ إِنَّهُمُ اتَّخَذُوا الشَّيَاطِينَ أَوْلِيَاءَ مِن دُونِ اللَّهِ
وَيَحْسَبُونَ أَنَّهُم مُّهْتَدُونَ ﴿٣٠﴾

29-30 Say: 'My Lord has commanded justice. Stand and face Him in every mosque and call on Him, making your *dīn* sincerely His. As He originated you, so you will return.' One group He guided; but another group got the misguidance they deserved. They took the *shayṭāns* as friends instead of Allah and thought that they were guided.

Say: 'My Lord has commanded justice.

Ibn 'Abbās said, '[Justice is contained in] "No god except Allah."' It is also said that it means fairness, i.e. He commanded justice, so obey Him. There is something elided in it.

Stand and face Him in every mosque and call on Him, making your *dīn* sincerely His.

'*Stand and face Him*' means to face Him in every prayer by facing the *qiblah*. '*In every mosque*' means in any mosque where you are. '*And call on Him, making your dīn sincerely His*' means 'Proclaiming His unity and not associating others with Him.'

As He originated you, so you will return.'

This is like Allah's words: '*You have come to Us all alone just as We created you at first.*' (6:94). The *kāf* is in the position of the accusative and means that you will return as He began you. 'As He created you the first time, so He will restore you.' Az-Zajjāj said that it is connected to what was before it, implying, 'From it you will emerge as you began, and so you will also return.'

One group He guided; but another group got the misguidance they deserved.

In the words '*One group He guided*' the word *farīq* (*group*) is in the accusative for the adverbial *ḥāl* or the pronoun in '*you will return*,' meaning they will return as two groups: one happy and one wretched. This is strengthened by the reading of Ubayy, '*farīqayn*', as al-Kisa'ī said. Muḥammad ibn Ka'b al-Quraẓī said, 'Whoever Allah initially created for misguidance will be moved to misguidance, even if he performs the actions of guidance. Whoever Allah initially created for guidance will be moved to guidance, even if he performs the actions of misguidance. Allah initially created Iblīs for misguidance and he performed actions with the angels that would lead to happiness. Then Allah returned him to what He initially created him for, saying: *'He was one of the unbelievers.'* (2:34) This is a clear refutation of the Qadariyyah and those who follow them. It is said that *'group'* is in the accusative by the verb *'He guided'* and the second *'group'* is in the accusative by an implied verb, 'He misguided a group.' [POEM] Al-Farrā' said that it is also permitted it for it to be in the nominative. In the phrase *'they took the shayṭāns,'* 'Īsā ibn 'Umar recited *'annahum,'* meaning 'since they took'.

يَٰبَنِيٓ ءَادَمَ خُذُواْ زِينَتَكُمۡ عِندَ كُلِّ مَسۡجِدٖ وَكُلُواْ وَٱشۡرَبُواْ وَلَا تُسۡرِفُوٓاْۚ
إِنَّهُۥ لَا يُحِبُّ ٱلۡمُسۡرِفِينَ ٣١

31 Children of Ādam! wear fine clothing in every mosque and eat and drink but do not be profligate. He does not love the profligate.

Children of Ādam! wear fine clothing in every mosque

'Children of Adam' is addressed to the entire world, even if what is meant by it are those Arabs who went around the House naked. It is general and applies to every mosque because the expression is general and not related to a specific cause. Some scholars deny that what is meant is *ṭawāf* because *ṭawāf* is only performed in one mosque, and that which is general to every mosque is the prayer. This is a view of someone for whom the aims of the *Sharī'ah* are concealed. In *Ṣaḥīḥ Muslim* it is reported that Ibn 'Abbās said, 'A woman used to perform *ṭawāf* of the House naked, saying, "Who will blame me for doing *ṭawāf*?" She covered her genitals, saying:

"Today some or all of it shows
I do not make lawful what appears of it."'

Then *'wear fine clothing in every mosque'* was revealed. This woman was Ḍubā'ah bint 'Āmir ibn Qurṭ. Qāḍī 'Iyāḍ said that.

We also find in *Ṣaḥīḥ Muslim* from Hishām ibn 'Urwah that his father said, 'All the Arabs, except for Ḥums, used to perform *ṭawāf* of the House naked. Ḥums consisted of Quraysh and their descendants. People used to perform *ṭawāf* of the House naked unless the Ḥums gave them clothing. The men would give to the men and the women to the women. The Ḥums did not leave Muzdalifah. All the people used to stand at 'Arafat.'

Elsewhere in other than *Ṣaḥīḥ Muslim* it says: 'We are the people of the Ḥaram. None of the Arabs should perform *ṭawāf* except in our clothes and they should only eat from our food when they enter our land.' Any of the Arabs who did not have friends in Makkah to lend them a garment, nor wealth with which to rent it, would do one of two things: they would perform *ṭawāf* of the House naked or perform *ṭawāf* in their clothes and when they finished their *ṭawāf*, they would throw their clothes away and no one would touch them. Such a garment was called a cast-off. One of the Arabs said:

It is enough sorrow that he is seen
like a forbidden cast-off among those who do *ṭawāf.*

They were subject to this ignorance, innovation and misguidance until Allah sent Muḥammad ﷺ and then Allah revealed: '*Children of Ādam! wear fine clothing in every mosque.*' The herald of the Messenger of Allah ﷺ announced, '*Ṭawāf* of the House should be not be performed naked.'

If someone says that what is meant is the prayer, his '*fine clothing*' is his sandals since Kurz ibn Wabrah related from 'Aṭā' from Abū Hurayrah that the Prophet ﷺ said one day, 'Take the '*fine clothing*' of the prayer.' He was asked, 'What is the '*fine clothing*' of the prayer?' He said, 'Wear your sandals, and pray in them.'

The *āyah* indicates the obligation to cover the private parts. The majority of the people of knowledge believe that doing that is one of the obligatory elements of the prayer. Al-Abharī said that it is a general obligation. A human being must conceal them from the eyes of people in the prayer and other situations. That is sound according to the words of the Prophet ﷺ to al-Miswar ibn Makhramah: 'Put your garment over your thigh and do not walk naked.' Muslim transmitted it. Qāḍī Ismā'īl, however, believed that covering the private parts is one of the *sunnahs* of the prayer, and he argues that if it had been obligatory, a naked person would not be obliged to pray because all the obligations of the prayer must be met when one is able to do them, or substituted when lacking, or else the entire prayer would be cancelled, and that is not the case.

Ibn al-'Arabī said, 'If we said that covering the private parts is an obligation in the prayer, and then the garment of the imam slips down and his bottom shows while he is bowing and then he comes up and covers it, the prayer is still valid.' Ibn al-Qāsim said that. Saḥnūn said, 'Any of the followers who look at it should repeat the prayer.' It is also related from him that both the *imām* and the followers must repeat the prayer because covering the private parts is one of the preconditions of the prayer. When the private parts show, then the prayer is invalid. Its root is purity. Qāḍī Ibn al-'Arabī said, 'Those who say that the prayer is not invalid do not consider that a precondition has been missed. As for someone who says that if someone else takes over the prayer where he is, then his prayer is valid and the prayer of those who look at him is invalid, that is a page which should be erased and it is not permitted to concern oneself with it.'

It is reported by al-Bukhārī and an-Nasa'ī that 'Amr ibn Salamah said, 'When my people returned from the Prophet ﷺ they said, "The one who leads you in the prayer should be the one with the most recitation of the Qur'an."' He added, 'They summoned me and taught me to bow and prostrate, and I used to lead them in the prayer wearing an open robe. They said to my father, "Will you not cover your son's buttocks for us?"' This is the version of an-Nasā'ī. It is confirmed that Sahl ibn Sa'd said, 'The men tied their waist-wrappers to their necks due to shortage of cloth, like children, while praying behind the Messenger of Allah ﷺ. Someone said, "Company of women! do not lift your heads until the men have risen."' Al-Bukhārī, an-Nasa'ī and Abū Dāwūd transmitted it.

They disagreed about someone seeing his own private parts. Ash-Shāfi'ī said, 'If the garment is tight and buttoned or has some sort of a gap so that the shirt opens and one's nakedness can be seen through it, and a person does nothing about it and sees his own nakedness, he should repeat the prayer.' That is also the view of Aḥmad. Mālik allowed the prayer in a shirt with open buttons for someone who is not wearing trousers. That is the view of Abū Ḥanīfah and Abū Thawr. Sālim used to pray in an unbuttoned waist-wrapper. Dāwūd at-Ta'ī said, 'When someone has a large beard, there is nothing wrong with it.' Al-Athram related that idea from Aḥmad.

If he is an *imām*, he should pray in his cloak because it is part of '*fine clothing*'. It is said that an aspect of '*fine clothing*' is praying in sandals. Anas related that from the Prophet ﷺ, but it is not sound. It is said that the adornment of the prayer is raising the hands in *rukū'* and in coming up from it. Ibn 'Umar said, 'Everything has an adornment, and the adornment of the prayer is the *takbīr* and raising the hands.' 'Umar said, 'When Allah enriches you, then spend more (on clothing). A man should combine garments and pray in a waist-wrapper and cloak (*ridā'*), in a wrapper and a shirt, in a wrapper and *qabā'* (outer garment with long sleeves), in trousers and a cloak, in trousers and a shirt, in trousers and a *qabā'*, in long shorts and a *qabā'*, and in long shorts and a shirt (I think he also said 'in long shorts and a cloak.').' Al-Bukhārī and ad-Dāraquṭnī related it.

eat and drink but do not be profligate.

Ibn 'Abbās said, 'In this *āyah* Allah made it lawful to eat and drink as long it is not out of extravagance or arrogance.' As for that for which there is need, which is what will prevent hunger and quell thirst, that is recommended logically and legally since it entails preservation of the self and guarding the senses. That is why the *Sharī'ah* prohibits continuous fasting because it weakens the body, debilitates the self and makes it too weak to worship. That is forbidden by the *Sharī'ah* and rejected logically. Anyone who denies themselves what they need has no portion of piety nor of asceticism because prevents them from doing voluntary worship due to incapacity and weakness, which would have had a great reward and wage.

There is disagreement about taking more than what one needs and there are two views: unlawful or disliked. Ibn al-'Arabī said that this is sound. The amount required for satisfaction varies in different lands, times, ages, and foods. Then it is said that there are many benefits in a small amount of food. One of them is that the man has a healthier body, more ample memory, purer understanding, less sleep and a lighter self. A lot of food makes the intestines heavy, causes indigestion, and produces various illnesses. So someone who has that needs medical treatment more than someone who only eats little.

Some sages have said that the greatest medicine is limiting the amount of food. The Prophet ﷺ adequately expressed this idea without needing the words of doctors. He said, 'The son of Ādam did not fill a worse vessel than the belly. Enough for the son of Ādam are a few morsels to keep his back upright. If it is necessary, then a third is for food, a third for drink and a third for breath.' At-Tirmidhī transmitted it from the *ḥadīth* of al-Miqdām ibn Ma'dīkarib. Our scholars said, 'If Socrates had heard this division, he would be amazed at its wisdom.'

It was mentioned that ar-Rashīd had a clever Christian doctor who said to 'Alī ibn al-Ḥusayn, 'There is nothing of the science of medicine in your Book. There are two types of knowledge: knowledge of the *dīn* and knowledge of physical bodies.' 'Alī said to him, 'Allah has collected all medicine in half an *āyah* of the Book.' The doctor asked him, 'What is it?' He answered, 'The words of Allah: "*eat and drink but do not be profligate.*"' The Christian then said, 'There is nothing about medicine related from your Messenger.' 'Ali said, 'The Messenger of Allah ﷺ has compiled medicine in a few words.' 'What are they?' he asked. He replied, 'The intestines are the home of ailments. Fever is the head of every illness. Give the body what will restore it.' The Christian said, 'Neither your Book nor your Messenger have left any medicine to Galen.'

It is said that the treatment of sick people has two parts: half is the remedy and half is fever. When they are united, it is as if the ill person was healed and sound.

But if not, fever is more appropriate to it since the remedy will not help when fever is omitted. Fever may benefit with lack of medicine. The Messenger of Allah ﷺ said, 'The root of every remedy is fever.' He meant by it, and Allah knows best, is that it spares the use of every remedy. That is why it is said, 'Most of the medical treatment of India relies on fever which prevents the sick person from eating, drinking or speaking for a number of days so that he recovers.'

Muslim related that Ibn 'Umar said, 'I heard the Messenger of Allah ﷺ say, "An unbeliever eats in seven intestines and the believer eats in one."' This is encouragement from him ﷺ to make do with a little of this world, be ascetic in and content with basic subsistence. The Arabs used to praise a little food and censure consuming a lot of it. One of them said:

A piece of grilled liver is enough for him if he gets it
and his thirst is quenched by a drink of water.

Umm Zar' said about Abū Zar': 'a shoulder of lamb is enough for him.' Hātim aṭ-Ṭā'ī said when criticising eating too much:

If you give your stomach what it asks for
and your private parts also: they will both bring you blame.

Al-Khaṭṭābī said that the meaning of his words ﷺ, 'The believer eats from one intestine' is that he takes less than what will fill him and prefers others to himself and leaves some of his provision for others and so he is content with what he eats.' The first interpretation is more likely, and Allah knows best. It is said that his words ﷺ, 'the unbeliever eats in seven intestines' is not general because experience refutes that. There may be an unbeliever who eats less than a believer and when the unbeliever becomes Muslim, his eating does not increase or decrease. It is also said that it indicates a particular person. The Prophet ﷺ gave hospitality to an unbeliever who was said to be al-Jahjāh al-Ghifārī, Thumāmah ibn Athāl, Naḍlah ibn 'Amr al-Ghifārī or Basrah ibn Abī Basrah al-Ghifāri. He drank the milk of seven sheep and then in the morning became Muslim and drank the milk of one sheep and did not finish it. Then the Prophet ﷺ said that. It is said as if he said, 'This unbeliever…' and Allah knows best.

It is said that when the heart is illuminated with the light of *tawḥīd*, it looks at food with the eye of *taqwā* to eat what is sufficient for obedience and so takes only what it needs. When it is dark with unbelief, the person concerned eats like an animal that grazes and eats until it has diarrhoea. There is disagreement about whether these seven intestines are actual intestines or not. It is said that they are real and they have known names among the people with knowledge of medicine and anatomy. It is said that they are allusions to the seven means by which the glutton eats. He eats for need, experience, smell, look, touch, taste and simply to take it. It is said that he eats as someone with seven intestines eats. Because the believer eats lightly, he eats like one with only one intestine, and so he shares with a portion of what the unbeliever eats, but the unbeliever has seven more like it.

When this is confirmed, know that it is recommended for people to wash their hands both before and after eating since the Prophet ﷺ said, 'Washing (*wuḍū'*) before and after food is a blessing.' The same is said in the Torah. Zādhān related it from Salmān. Mālik used to dislike washing clean hands, but it is more fitting to follow the *ḥadīth*. You should not eat food until you know whether it is cold or hot. If it is hot, you may be harmed by it. It is related that the Messenger of Allah ﷺ said. 'Cool food. The hot does not have blessing.' It is a *Ṣaḥīḥ ḥadīth* and was already mentioned in *al-Baqarah* (2:124). Do not sniff at it. That is something that animals do. If you want it, eat it. If you dislike it, leave it. Make the morsels small and chew it a lot so that you are not considered greedy. Say the Name of Allah Almighty at the beginning and praise Him at the end. You should not raise your voice with praise unless your companions are finished eating because raising your voice might prevent them from eating more. There are many behaviours related to eating and these are some of them. Some of them will be mentioned in *Sūrat Hūd*, Allah willing. There are also behaviours connected to drinking which have not been mentioned because they are well-known. In *Ṣaḥīḥ Muslim* Ibn 'Umar related that the Messenger of Allah ﷺ said, 'When one of you eats, he should eat with his right hand. When he drinks, he should drink with his right hand. *Shayṭān* eats with his left hand and drinks with his left hand.'

'*Do not be profligate*' by eating a lot and connected with that is drinking a lot. That is heavy on the intestines and a man will be too ponderous to obey his Lord and engage in voluntary acts of good. If that leads to consuming so much that it will prevent someone from fulfilling the obligations which are mandatory for him, then it is unlawful for him and he is considered prodigal in the matter of his food and drink. Asad ibn Mūsā related from the *ḥadīth* of 'Awn ibn Abī Juḥayfah that his father said, 'I ate broth with fat meat and the Prophet ﷺ came while I was belching. He said, "Refrain from your belching, Abū Juḥayfah. Many people who are full in this world have the greatest hunger on the Day of Rising."' After that Abū Juhayfah did not eat his fill until he died. When he ate in the day, he did not eat at night, and when he ate at night he did eat during the day. This is the meaning of the words of the Prophet ﷺ, 'The believer eats in one intestine,' in other words with full faith because someone who has good Islam and full faith like Abū Juḥayfah reflects on death and what comes after it. Then fear and apprehension of those terrors will keep him from fulfilling his appetites. Allah knows best.

Ibn Zayd said that the command '*do not be profligate*' means do not eat what is unlawful. It is said, 'Part of profligacy is to eat everything you want to.' Anas ibn Mālik related it from the Prophet ﷺ. Ibn Mājah transmitted it in the *Sunan*. It is said that part of profligacy is eating after you have satisfied your hunger. All of that is forbidden. Luqmān told his son, 'My son, do not eat until you are full beyond being full. It is better for you to toss it to the dog than to eat it.' Samurah ibn Jundub asked what his son was doing. They replied, 'He suffered from indigestion yesterday.' 'Indigestion?' he said. 'Yes,' they answered. He exclaimed, 'If he were to die, I would not pray over him!'

It is said that in the time of the *Jāhiliyyah* the Arabs did not eat fat during the days of Hajj and were content with a small amount of food and performed *ṭawāf* naked. So they were told: '*Wear fine clothing in every mosque and eat and drink but do not be profligate.*' It means: 'Do not be profligate in making forbidden that which was not made unlawful for you.'

قُلْ مَنْ حَرَّمَ زِينَةَ ٱللَّهِ ٱلَّتِىٓ أَخْرَجَ لِعِبَادِهِۦ وَٱلطَّيِّبَـٰتِ مِنَ ٱلرِّزْقِ ۚ قُلْ هِىَ لِلَّذِينَ ءَامَنُوا۟ فِى ٱلْحَيَوٰةِ ٱلدُّنْيَا خَالِصَةً يَوْمَ ٱلْقِيَـٰمَةِ ۗ كَذَٰلِكَ نُفَصِّلُ ٱلْـَٔايَـٰتِ لِقَوْمٍ يَعْلَمُونَ ﴿٣٢﴾

32 Say: 'Who has forbidden the fine clothing Allah has produced for His slaves and the good kinds of provision? 'Say: 'On the Day of Rising such things will be exclusively for those who believed during their life in this world.' In this way We make the Signs clear for people who know.

Say: 'Who has forbidden the fine clothing

This makes it clear that on their own initiative they made unlawful things that Allah has not made unlawful. *Zīnah* here refers to good clothing when someone is able to wear it. It is also said that it is all clothing, as is related from 'Umar: 'When Allah expands things for you, then expand' as was already mentioned. It is related that 'Alī ibn al-Husayn ibn 'Alī ibn Abī Ṭālib, the shaykh of Mālik, used to wear a robe woven of wool and silk (*khazz*) worth fifty *dīnār*s which he wore in the winter.

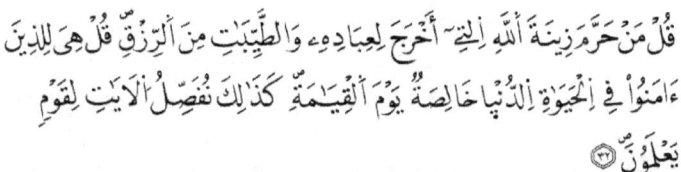

In the summer, he would give it as *ṣadaqah* or sell it and give its price as *ṣadaqah*. In the summer, he used to wear two woven Egyptian garments. He quoted this *āyah*.

If this is the case, the *āyah* indicates wearing fine clothes and adorning oneself with them in gatherings, *'īd*s and when meeting people and visiting brothers. Abū al-'Āliyah said, 'When Muslims visit one another, they adorn themselves.' We find in *Ṣaḥīḥ Muslim* from 'Umar ibn al-Khattab that he saw some silk robes being sold at the door of the mosque. He said, 'Messenger of Allah, you should buy them to wear on Fridays and when delegations come to you.' The Messenger of Allah ﷺ said, 'Such clothing is worn by someone who has no portion in the Next World.' He was not objecting to the mention of adornment but he disliked the fact that they were silk robes.

Tamīm ad-Dārī bought a robe for a thousand *dirhams* in which he used to pray. Mālik ibn Dīnār used to wear good 'Adanī garments. The garment of Ahmad ibn Ḥanbal cost about a *dīnār*. Where is this in respect of those who do not like such clothes and prefer to wear rough linen and wool and say, '*The garment of tawqā – that is better*' (7:26)? How unlikely! Do you think that those we mentioned abandoned the garment of *taqwā*? No, by Allah! Rather they are the people of *taqwā* and people of knowledge and intelligence and the others are the people of claims whose hearts are empty of *taqwā*. Khālid ibn Shawdhab said, 'I saw al-Hasan when Farqad came to him. Al-Hasan took hold of his robe, extended it to him, and said, "Little Farqad, son of the mother of little Farqad. Piety does not lie in the robe. Piety is what is heavy in the breast and confirmed by action."' Abū Muḥammad ibn Abī Mar'ūf al-Kharkhī related from Abū al-Ḥasan ibn Yasār who was wearing a woollen robe. Abū al-Ḥasan said to him, 'Abū Muhammad, has your heart or body become Sufi? Make your heart Sufi and then wear white Qūhī garments on top of Qūḥī garments.' A man said to ash-Shibli, 'A group of your companions came while they were in the mosque.' He went and saw patched garments and rags on them. He said:

> The tents are our tents
>   but I see that the women of the quarter are not its women.

Abū al-Faraj ibn al-Jawzī said, 'I dislike wearing rags and patches for four reasons. One is that it is not what the early generations wore. They only wore rags out of necessity. The second is that it entails a claim of poverty and the human being is commanded to show the effects of the blessing of Allah on himself. The third is making a show of asceticism, and we are commanded to conceal it. The fourth is that such people resemble those who are outside of the *Sharī'ah* and whoever resembles a people is one of them.' Aṭ-Ṭabarī said, 'Anyone who prefers wearing hair and wool to wearing cotton and linen when it is possible to wear them errs as does anyone who eats vegetables and lentils rather than eating wheat bread and anyone who stops eating meat out of fear of being exposed to lust for women.' Bishr ibn al-Ḥārith was asked about wearing wool and that was offensive to him and dislike was clear in his face. Then he said, 'I prefer wearing a fabric woven of wool and silk (*khazz*) and what is dyed with saffron to wearing wool in the cities.'

Abū al-Faraj said, 'The early generations used to wear clothes of medium quality, not patches or inferior clothing, and they preferred the best for *Jumu'ah*, *'Īd*s and meeting their brothers. They did not consider it a bad thing to prefer the best. As for clothing that demeans the wearer, it gives rise to making a display of asceticism and poverty. It is almost like making a complaint about Allah Almighty and brings about the debasing of the wearer. All of that is disliked and forbidden.'

It has been said, however, that wearing excellent clothing is an appetite of the lower self and we are commanded to strive against that. In adorning ourselves, it must be that our actions are for Allah not for other people. The response to that is that not all that the lower self desires is blameworthy and not all that one adorns oneself with is disliked. It may be forbidden when the *Sharī'ah* forbids it for being showing off in respect of the *dīn*. A person should be seen with a beautiful appearance. That is a portion of the self that is not blameworthy. This is why you comb your hair and look in the mirror and straighten your turban and wear simple clothing inside and fine clothing on the outside. There is nothing in any of that which is disliked or blameworthy.

Makḥūl related that 'Ā'ishah said, 'A group of the Companions of the Messenger of Allah ﷺ were waiting for him at the door. He was going to come out to them and in the house was a vessel containing some water. He began to look in the water and smooth his beard and hair. I asked, "Messenger of Allah, so you do this?" "Yes," he answered, "When a man goes out to his brothers, he should prepare himself. Allah is beautiful and loves beauty."'

We find in *Ṣaḥīḥ Muslim* that Ibn Mas'ūd reported that the Prophet ﷺ said, 'Anyone with an atom's worth of pride in his heart will not enter the Garden.' A man said, 'A man might like his garment to be good and his sandals to be good.' He replied, 'Allah is beautiful and loves beauty. Pride is to disregard the truth and to despise people.' There are many *ḥadīth*s along these lines which all indicate the need for cleanliness and good appearance. Muḥammad ibn Sa'd related that the Messenger of Allah ﷺ travelled with a comb, mirror, oil, *siwāk* and kohl. Ibn

Jurayḥ related, '…an ivory comb which he used.' Ibn Sa'd reported from Anas ibn Mālik that the Messenger of Allah ﷺ used often to oil his hair and comb his beard with water. Ibn 'Abbās said, 'The Messenger of Allah ﷺ had a kohl stick which he used three times in each eye before going to sleep.'

and the good kinds of provision?

The word *ṭayyibāt* is a general noun for what is good and wholesome. Ibn 'Abbās and Qatādah said that it means the good provision represented by *baḥīrah*, *sā'ibah*, *wāṣīlah* and *ḥām*, which the people of the *Jāhiliyyah* made forbidden. It is also said that it is all tasty food. There is disagreement about leaving good things and turning away from things that give pleasure. Some people say that doing that is not an act of devotion and that doing it or not doing it is the same in the case of permitted things. Others say that it is not an act of devotion in itself but that it can be the means to asceticism in this world, restricting aspiration for it and not burdening oneself for its sake. It is recommended and what is recommended is an act of devotion. Others have said that it is transmitted that 'Umar ibn al-Khaṭṭāb said, 'If we wish, we could have roast meat, loaves and mustard sauce, but I have heard Allah Almighty censure people in His words: "*You dissipated the good things you had in your worldly life.*" (46:20)' *Ṣalā'iq* is related as *ṣarā'iq* which are large loaves and *ṣalā'iq* is roasted (*yuṣlaqu*) meat and vegetables. *Ṣilā'* is roasting. *Ṣināb* is mustard mixed with vinegar.

Others differentiated between whether that is had by effort or without effort. Abū al-Ḥasan 'Alī ibn al-Mufaḍḍal al-Muqaddasī, the shaykh of our shaykhs, said that it is sound (to make that distinction), Allah willing. It is not transmitted that the Prophet ﷺ forbade any food on account of its goodness. He used to eat sweets, honey, melon and fresh dates. He disliked people burdening themselves since that is a sign of preoccupation with the appetites of this world, which distract people from the concerns of the Next World. Allah knows best.

Some Sufis dislike eating good things. They use as evidence the words of 'Umar, 'Beware of meat. It is addictive in the way that wine is addictive.' The answer is that this statement by 'Umar was directed at someone he feared would prefer the luxury of this world, devote himself to his lower appetites, indulge himself with pleasure, forget the Next World and turn to this world. This is why 'Umar wrote to his governors: 'Beware of luxury and wearing the clothing of foreigners. Live simply.' He did not mean to prohibit anything which Allah has made lawful nor to make unlawful what Allah has permitted. The words of Allah are the most fitting to be obeyed and to rely on. He says: '*Say: "Who has forbidden the fine clothing*

Allah has produced for His slaves and the good kinds of provision?"' The Prophet ﷺ said, 'The master of the condiments of this world and the Next is meat.' 'Urwah related that 'Ā'ishah reported that the Prophet ﷺ used to eat watermelon with fresh dates and said, 'The heat of this one breaks the cold of that one and the cold of that one breaks the heat of this one.' The refutation of someone who prefers coarse food is found in *al-Mā'idah*. (5:82) This *āyah* and others refute him. Praise be to Allah.

Say: 'On the Day of Rising such things will be exclusively for those who believed during their life in this world.'

This was by the right of their belief in the *tawḥīd* of Allah Almighty and their affirmation of it. Allah gives blessing and provision. If someone declares the Blesser to be One and affirms Him, he has undertaken what is duly owed for blessings received. If he does not do that, he has given *Shayṭān* power over himself. We find in a sound *ḥadīth*, 'There is no one who is more patient than Allah in the face of maltreatment. He gives people health and provides for them when they claim that He has a wife and child.'

The words end with '*the life of this world*.' Then He says '*exclusively*' which is in the nominative in the reading of Ibn 'Abbās and Nāfi'. It means that in the Next World Allah will single out good things for those who believe. The idolaters will have none of them in the way they have share of them in this world. The implication of the *āyah* is: 'Say: "The believers share them with others in this world but they are exclusively for the believers on the Day of Rising."' '*Exclusively*' is part of a new sentence as the predicate of an implied inceptive. This is the view of Ibn 'Abbās, aḍ-Ḍaḥḥāk, al-Ḥasan, Qatādah, as-Suddī, Ibn Jurayḥ and Ibn Zayd.

It is said that the meaning is that the good things which exist in this world will, on the Day of Rising, be exclusively for those who believed while they were in this world, and the 'exclusivity' refers to the fact that they are not punished or penalised for [their enjoyment of them in this world.] So Allah's words: '*in the life of this world*' are connected to '*believe*'. This is indicated by the *tafsīr* of Sa'īd ibn Jubayr.

The rest read it in the accusative for the adverbial *ḥāl* and then stop because the words end at it. According to this reading, it is not permitted to stop at '*this world*' because what is after it is connected to Allah's words: '*to those who believe*' as an adverb of it implying, 'Say: "It is confirmed for those who believe during their lives in this world that it will be exclusively for them on the Day of Rising."' Abū 'Alī said that. The phrase '*in this way We make the Signs clear*' means making clear the lawful and unlawful, meaning, 'I will explain to you what you need to know.'

قُلْ إِنَّمَا حَرَّمَ رَبِّيَ ٱلْفَوَٰحِشَ مَا ظَهَرَ مِنْهَا وَمَا بَطَنَ وَٱلْإِثْمَ وَٱلْبَغْيَ بِغَيْرِ ٱلْحَقِّ
وَأَن تُشْرِكُوا۟ بِٱللَّهِ مَا لَمْ يُنَزِّلْ بِهِۦ سُلْطَٰنًا وَأَن تَقُولُوا۟ عَلَى ٱللَّهِ مَا لَا تَعْلَمُونَ ٣٣

33 Say: 'My Lord has forbidden indecency, both open and hidden, and wrong action, and tyranny, and associating anything with Allah for which He has sent down no authority, and saying things about Allah you do not know.'

Al-Kalbī said, 'When the Muslims wore clothes and did *ṭawāf* of the House, the idolaters thought that they had changed things and this *āyah* was revealed.' *Fawāḥish* are actions which are excessively ugly, both what is open and what is hidden. Rawḥ ibn 'Ubādah related from Zakariyyā ibn Isḥāq from Ibn Abī Najīḥ that Mujāhid said, 'What was '*open*' was men marrying their mothers in the *Jāhiliyyah* and what was '*hidden*' was fornication.' Qatādah said that it is the secret and public facets of indecency. This is debatable. It mentions wrong action and tyranny, and this indicates that what is meant by indecency is part of that. If that is the case, then fornication is part of indecency, and Allah knows best. Al-Ḥasan said that '*wrong action*' is wine. A poet said:

I drank wrong action until my senses were lost.
That is how wrong action takes away the minds.

Another said:

I drank wrong action openly with the goblet
and you see that among us 'musk' is metaphorical.

'*Baghy*' is injustice and exceeding the limits, as was already mentioned (2:173). Tha'lab said that *baghy* is for a man to attack another man, talk about him and attack him without justification, unless he is seeking help in getting something he is owed by him. Wrong action and tyranny are made separate from indecency, although they are part of it, because of the enormity of the indecency in them. They are specifically mentioned to stress them and to forbid them.

The verbs in '*associating anything with Allah*' and '*saying things about Allah*' are nominative as added to what is before them. One group said that '*wrong action*' does not mean wine here. Al-Farrā' said, '"*Wrong action*" is something less than the *ḥadd* and is arrogance towards people.' An-Naḥḥās said, 'As for "*wrong action*" meaning wine, it is not known. The reality of '*wrong action*' is all acts of disobedience as the poet said:

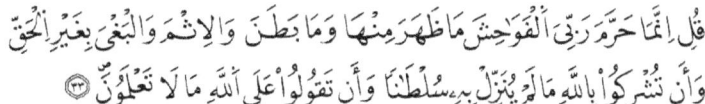

I find the matter which entails the greatest guidance is *taqwā* of Allah
and the worst of matters to be wrong action.'

Ibn 'Arabī also denied it being wine. He said, 'There is no evidence in the verse because if the poet had said, "I drank a sin or burden," that would have been the case. His words do not make wrong action necessarily to mean wine here. Saying this indicates ignorance of the language and of the method of attributing meaning.' This was mentioned from al-Ḥasan. In *aṣ-Ṣiḥāḥ*, al-Jawharī said, 'Wine is called a wrong action,' and he cited a verse proving it from al-Harawī in which he called wine 'wrong action'. It is not unlikely that '*wrong action*' can be applied to all acts of disobedience and to wine as well linguistically and there is no inherent contradiction. *Baghy* is transgression in wrongdoing. It is also said that it is corruption.

وَلِكُلِّ أُمَّةٍ أَجَلٌ فَإِذَا جَآءَ أَجَلُهُمْ لَا يَسْتَـْٔخِرُونَ سَاعَةً وَلَا يَسْتَقْدِمُونَ ﴿٣٤﴾

34 Every nation has an appointed time. When their time comes, they cannot delay it a single hour or bring it forward.

This is the time known by Allah. Ibn Sīrīn recited '*time*' in the plural (*ājāl* instead of *ajal*). '*They cannot delay it*' an hour or less than an hour. '*Hour*' is mentioned because it is the name for the least of the units of time and it is an adverb of time. This indicates that a person who is killed is killed according to his allotted term, and the term of his death is the time of his death, as the term of the debt is the time when it is due. Everything which has a time is something which has a term. The term of a man is the time at which Allah knows that he must die. He is not permitted to die later than it inasmuch as it is not decreed that it be delayed. Many of the Mu'tazilites, except for the odd one, say that a person who is killed dies at other than the term set for him and, if he had not been killed, he would have lived. This is a mistake because the victim did not die at the term at which another killed him. The time he was struck was the term which Allah set for his soul to be removed.

If the question is asked, 'Why then, if he died at his term, do they kill the one who struck the blow in retribution?' the answer is, 'He is killed for his transgression and doing what he should not do, not for the death and removal of the soul. That was not part of his action. If people were left to transgress without retaliation, that would have led to corruption and people's destruction.' This is clear.

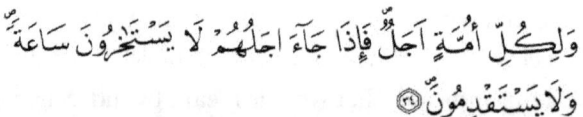

يَٰبَنِيٓ ءَادَمَ إِمَّا يَأْتِيَنَّكُمْ رُسُلٌ مِّنكُمْ يَقُصُّونَ عَلَيْكُمْ ءَايَٰتِي فَمَنِ اِتَّقَىٰ وَأَصْلَحَ
فَلَا خَوْفٌ عَلَيْهِمْ وَلَا هُمْ يَحْزَنُونَ ۝٣٥ وَالَّذِينَ كَذَّبُواْ بِـَٔايَٰتِنَا وَاسْتَكْبَرُواْ
عَنْهَآ أُوْلَٰٓئِكَ أَصْحَٰبُ النَّارِ هُمْ فِيهَا خَٰلِدُونَ ۝٣٦

35-36 Children of Ādam! if Messengers come to you from among yourselves, recounting My Signs to you, those who are godfearing and put things right will feel no fear and will know no sorrow. But as for those who reject Our Signs and are arrogant regarding them, they are the Companions of the Fire, remaining in it timelessly, for ever.

Children of Ādam! if Messengers come to you from among yourselves,

This is a precondition. The *nūn* is included for stress by the inclusion of *mā*. It is said that the *mā* is connective, meaning 'if they come to you'. Allah is telling them that He sends to them Messengers from among themselves so that it is more likely that they will respond. The verb 'recounting' means to speak to one another. 'My Signs' means 'My obligations and judgments'.

those who are godfearing and put things right,

This is a precondition, and what is after is the apodosis, which is the apodosis of the first, implying 'put right what is between you and him'. The phrase '*will feel no fear and will know no sorrow*' indicates that on the Day of Rising the believers will not fear or sorrow, nor will they be touched by terror and anxiety. It is said that they will be affected by the terrors of the Day of Rising but hope for security. It is said that the apodosis of 'come to you' is indicated by the words in the *āyah*, meaning 'you should obey them,' instructing 'whoever is godfearing and puts things right'. The first view is that of az-Zajjāj.

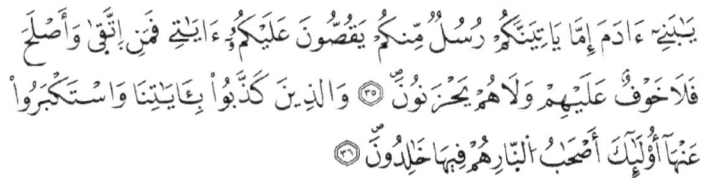

فَمَنْ أَظْلَمُ مِمَّنِ ٱفْتَرَىٰ عَلَى ٱللَّهِ كَذِبًا أَوْ كَذَّبَ بِـَٔايَـٰتِهِۦٓ ۚ أُو۟لَـٰٓئِكَ يَنَالُهُمْ
نَصِيبُهُم مِّنَ ٱلْكِتَـٰبِ ۖ حَتَّىٰٓ إِذَا جَآءَتْهُمْ رُسُلُنَا يَتَوَفَّوْنَهُمْ قَالُوٓا۟ أَيْنَ مَا كُنتُمْ
تَدْعُونَ مِن دُونِ ٱللَّهِ ۖ قَالُوا۟ ضَلُّوا۟ عَنَّا وَشَهِدُوا۟ عَلَىٰٓ أَنفُسِهِمْ أَنَّهُمْ
كَانُوا۟ كَـٰفِرِينَ ﴿٣٧﴾

37 Who could do greater wrong than someone who invents lies against Allah or denies His Signs? Such people's portion of the Book will catch up with them so that when Our messengers come to them to take them in death, saying, 'Where are those you called upon besides Allah?' they will say, 'They have forsaken us' testifying against themselves that they were unbelievers.

Who could do greater wrong than someone who invents lies against Allah or denies His Signs?

The meaning is: 'What wrongdoing could be worse than lying against Allah and denying His Signs?' Then He says:

Such people's portion of the Book will catch up with them so that when Our messengers come to them to take them in death,

According to Ibn Zayd the *Book* referred to is the provision, lifespan and actions that are written for them. Ibn Jubayr said that it is about their misery or happiness [in the Next World]. Ibn 'Abbās said that it is about evil and good. Al-Ḥasan and Abū Ṣāliḥ said that it is their portion of the punishment according to their unbelief. Aṭ-Ṭabarī preferred that the meaning be that it is the portion that is written for them, namely what is decreed for them of good and evil, provision, actions and term of life, including all that was already said by Ibn Zayd, Ibn 'Abbās and Ibn Jubayr. He said, 'Do you not see that Allah follows that with His words: "*so that when Our messengers come to them to take them in death*," meaning the messengers of the Angel of Death.'

It is said that the Book here is the Qur'an because the punishment of the unbelievers is mentioned in it. It is also said that the Book is the Preserved Tablet. Al-Ḥasan ibn 'Alī al-Ḥulwānī related, "Alī ibn al-Madīnī dictated to me and said, "I asked 'Abd ar-Raḥmān ibn Mahdī about the Decree and he said to me, 'Everything is by the Decree. Both obedience and disobedience are by the Decree.'" It is a terrible thing to say that acts of disobedience are not by a Decree.' 'Alī said, "Abd ar-Raḥmān ibn Mahdī said to me, "Knowledge, the Decree and the Book are the same." Then I presented the words of 'Abd ar-Raḥmān ibn Mahdī to Yaḥyā ibn Sa'īd and he said, "After this, nothing remains, neither a little nor a lot."'

Yaḥyā ibn Ma'īn related from Marwān al-Fazārī from Ismā'īl ibn Sumay' from Bukayr aṭ-Ṭawīl from Ibn 'Abbās that this refers to people who do actions which they could not avoid doing. '*Ḥattā*' (*so that*) is not the end of a statement. It is the beginning of a new statement about them. '*Where are those you called upon besides Allah*?' is both a question and a rebuke. The meaning of '*call upon*' is 'worship'. '*They will say, "They have forsaken us*,"' means that they have been of no use and vanished away. It is said that this is in the Next world. '*Testifying against themselves that they were unbelievers*' means that they confessed to their own unbelief.

قَالَ ٱدْخُلُوا۟ فِىٓ أُمَمٍ قَدْ خَلَتْ مِن قَبْلِكُم مِّنَ ٱلْجِنِّ وَٱلْإِنسِ فِى ٱلنَّارِ كُلَّمَا
دَخَلَتْ أُمَّةٌ لَّعَنَتْ أُخْتَهَا حَتَّىٰٓ إِذَا ٱدَّارَكُوا۟ فِيهَا جَمِيعًا قَالَتْ أُخْرَىٰهُمْ لِأُولَىٰهُمْ
رَبَّنَا هَٰٓؤُلَآءِ أَضَلُّونَا فَـَٔاتِهِمْ عَذَابًا ضِعْفًا مِّنَ ٱلنَّارِ قَالَ لِكُلٍّ ضِعْفٌ
وَلَٰكِن لَّا تَعْلَمُونَ ﴿٣٨﴾ وَقَالَتْ أُولَىٰهُمْ لِأُخْرَىٰهُمْ فَمَا كَانَ لَكُمْ عَلَيْنَا مِن فَضْلٍ
فَذُوقُوا۟ ٱلْعَذَابَ بِمَا كُنتُمْ تَكْسِبُونَ ﴿٣٩﴾

38-39 He will say, 'Enter the Fire together with the nations of jinn and men who have passed away before you.' Each time a nation enters, it will curse its sister nation, until, when they are all gathered together in it, the last of them will say of the first, 'Our Lord, those are the ones who misguided us, so give them a double punishment in the Fire.' He will say, 'Each will receive double. But you do not know it.' The first of them will say to the last, 'You are in no way superior to us so taste the punishment for what you earned.'

He will say, 'Enter the Fire together with the nations of jinn and men

This means '*with the nations*' as *fī* here means 'with'. It is also said that it has its normal significance and means 'enter with all of them'. The Speaker here is Allah Almighty in other words Allah will say, '*Enter*.' It is also said that it is Mālik, the Keeper of the Fire.

Each time a nation enters, it will curse its sister nation, until, when they are all gathered together in it,

Its sister nation is the one that preceded it into the Fire. It is its sister in *dīn* and religion. '*Gathered together*' here means 'collected'. Al-A'mash recited '*tadārakū*,' which is the root. Then there is assimilation and it needs the connective *alif.* Al-Mahdī related that from Ibn Mas'ūd. An-Naḥḥās said that Ibn Mas'ūd recited '*iddarakū*,' which would mean 'reach one another'. 'Iṣmah reported '*iddārakū*' from Abū 'Amr, keeping the *alif* in spite of two silent letters being joined. Abū 'Amr also related '*iddarakū*' with the connective *alif* separate so that it is as if there were a silent letter on '*idhā*'. When there is a long silence, the connective *alif* is separate just as is the case when it is in the beginning. This is also found in poetry. [POEM] Mujāhid and Ḥumayd ibn Qays related '*ḥattā idha-ddarakū*' with the *alif* at the end of '*idhā*' elided because of two silent letters meeting, and the *alif* after the *dāl* is elided. 'All' is in the accusative for the adverbial *ḥāl.*

the last of them will say of the first, 'Our Lord, those are the ones who misguided us, so give them a double punishment in the Fire.'

This is the last of them to enter, who are the followers of the first of them, who are the leaders. The *lām* in '*of the first of them*' is the *lām* of attribution, because they did not address the first of them, but said in respect of the first of them, 'Our Lord, they misguided us.' The doubling refers to something added which is the same as it or more. Ibn Mas'ūd related that doubling here relates to vipers and snakes. We find the same usage in the *āyah*: '*Our Lord, give them double the punishment and curse them many times over*!' (33:68) We will later speak of a doubling which entails worse than this and the consequent rulings based on it, Allah willing.

He will say, 'Each will receive double. But you do not know it.'

Each means both the follower and the followed. This becomes 'But they do not know it' when read with a *yā'* and means that each group does not know what will happen to the other group since, if those who are in the Fire knew that the punishment of one is worse than his own punishment, that would have been a sort of solace for him. It is said that the meaning of '*But you do not know*' with *tā'* means: but you do not know the punishment those addressed will experience. It is also possible that the meaning is: 'But you, people of this world, do not know the extent of the punishment they will have there.' '*The first of them will say to the last, "You are in no way superior to us*,"' means, 'You disbelieved and did what we did, so you do not deserve to have the punishment lightened, so taste the punishment for what you earned.'

إِنَّ ٱلَّذِينَ كَذَّبُوا۟ بِـَٔايَـٰتِنَا وَٱسْتَكْبَرُوا۟ عَنْهَا لَا تُفَتَّحُ لَهُمْ أَبْوَٰبُ ٱلسَّمَآءِ
وَلَا يَدْخُلُونَ ٱلْجَنَّةَ حَتَّىٰ يَلِجَ ٱلْجَمَلُ فِى سَمِّ ٱلْخِيَاطِ ۚ وَكَذَٰلِكَ نَجْزِى
ٱلْمُجْرِمِينَ ﴿٤٠﴾ لَهُم مِّن جَهَنَّمَ مِهَادٌ وَمِن فَوْقِهِمْ غَوَاشٍ ۚ وَكَذَٰلِكَ نَجْزِى
ٱلظَّـٰلِمِينَ ﴿٤١﴾

40-41 As for those who deny Our Signs and are arrogant regarding them, the Gates of Heaven will not be opened for them, and they will not enter the Garden until a camel goes through a needle's eye. That is how We repay the evildoers. They will have Hell as a resting-place and covering layers on top of them. That is how We repay wrongdoers.

As for those who deny Our Signs and are arrogant regarding them, the Gates of Heaven will not be opened for them,

This means for their souls. There are sound reports about that which we spoke about in *Kitāb at-Tadhkirah*. One of them is the *ḥadīth* of al-Barā' ibn 'Āzib which mentions the taking of the soul of an unbeliever. It says: 'A smell will come from it like the stench of a corpse found on the surface of the earth. They will take it up and will not pass by any group of angels who will not ask, "Who is this foul soul?" They will answer, "So-and-so the son of so-and-so," using the ugliest of the names by which he was called in this world. When they bring it to the lowest heaven, they will ask for it to be opened and it will not be opened for them.' Then the Messenger of Allah ﷺ recited, '*The Gates of Heaven will not be opened for them.*' It is said that the gates of heaven will not be opened for them when they call. Mujāhid and an-Nakha'ī said that.

It is said that it means the gates of the Garden will not be opened for them because the Garden is in heaven. This is indicated by His words: '*...and they will not enter the Garden until a camel goes through a needle's eye.*' The camel will not be able to do that and so they will never enter it. This is a definite proof that it is not possible for them to be pardoned. There is a consensus of the Muslims about this, with which one is not permitted to disagree, that Allah Almighty will not forgive any of them at all.

Qāḍī Abū Bakr ibn aṭ-Ṭayyib said, 'If someone asks, "How can this be said to be a consensus of the community when some *mutakallimūn* claim that people who emulate the Jews and Christians and other people of unbelief are not in the Fire? They are told, "Those are people who deny that such emulators are unbelievers because of their uncertainty about them [and whether that constitutes unbelief]. They did not state that emulators are unbelievers and, in addition to that, say they are not in the Fire." The means to knowing whether an emulator is an unbeliever or not is to examine him continually or base his unbelief on an actual text.'

Hamzah and al-Kisā'ī recited *yufattaḥū* as a masculine plural. The rest recited it with a *tā'* for the feminine plural as Allah says: '*...whose gates will be open to them...*' (38:50) which is feminine. The feminine gender of the plural '*doors*' is not a real feminine and it is permitted for it to be considered masculine plural. It is the reading of Ibn 'Abbās who has it with the *yā'*. Abū 'Amr, Hamzah and al-Kisā'ī made it an undoubled verb it since that is used for a little and a lot and the double form is for a lot and repetition time after time. The double form here is more fitting because it indicates a lot.

Jamal are camels. Al-Farrā' said, '*Jamal* is the mate of the she-camel.' That is what 'Abdullāh ibn Mas'ūd said when he was asked about *jamal*. He said, 'It is the mate of the she-camel,' as he thought the person ignorant when he asked about what all people know. The plural is *jimāl, ajmāl, jamālāt* and *jamā'il*. The reading of 'Abdullāh has 'the yellow camel'. Abū Bakr al-Anbārī mentioned it from his father from Naṣr ibn Dāwūd from Abū 'Ubayd from Ḥajjāj from Ibn Jurayj from Ibn Kathīr from Mujāhid from 'Abdullāh. Ibn 'Abbās recited it as '*jummal*' which is the rope of the ship called a hawser. It is a composite rope. Aḥmad ibn Yaḥyā Tha'lab stated that. It is said that it is a thick rope made from cane. It is said that it is the rope used to climb a palm tree. It is also related from him and Sa'īd ibn Jubayr as '*juml*' which is a cable and rope as we already mentioned. It is also related from him as '*jumul*', the plural of *jamal*, like *asad* and *usad*, and '*juml*' is like *asad* and *usd*. Abū as-Sammāl has '*jaml*' which is a lightened form of *jamal*.

The eye of a needle is the opening in it, as Ibn 'Abbās and others said. Every fine opening in the body is called *samm* and *summ*, the plural being *sumūm*. The plural of *summ* meaning poison is *simām*. Ibn Sīrīn recited '*summ*'. *Khayāṭ* is the needle, the implement used for sewing. Both *khiyāṭ* and *mikhyaṭ* are said, like *izār* and *mi'zar*, and *qinā'* and *miqna'*. *Mahād* is a bed. *Ghawāsh* is the plural of *ghāshiyah*, meaning that fires cover them. '*That is how We repay the wrongdoers*' means the unbelievers, and Allah knows best.

وَالَّذِينَ ءَامَنُوا وَعَمِلُوا الصَّٰلِحَٰتِ لَا نُكَلِّفُ نَفْسًا إِلَّا وُسْعَهَا أُولَٰٓئِكَ
أَصْحَٰبُ الْجَنَّةِ هُمْ فِيهَا خَٰلِدُونَ ﴿٤٢﴾

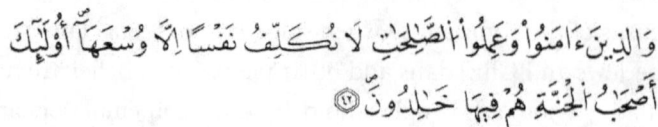

42 As for those who believe and do right actions – We impose on no self any more than it can bear – they are the Companions of the Garden, remaining in it timelessly, for ever.

'*We impose on no self any more than it can bear*' are interposed words, the basic sentence being that those who believe and do right actions are the Companions of the Garden who will be in it forever. It means: 'Allah does not impose on anyone the maintenance of wives unless he has the means and is able to do it and does not ask him for what he does not have and cannot obtain. The ability to pay is only established at the actual time of payment.' Aṭ-Ṭayyib said that it is like: '*Allah does not demand from any self more than He has given it.*' (65:7)

وَنَزَعْنَا مَا فِي صُدُورِهِم مِّنْ غِلٍّ تَجْرِي مِن تَحْتِهِمُ الْأَنْهَارُ وَقَالُوا الْحَمْدُ لِلَّهِ
الَّذِي هَدَانَا لِهَٰذَا وَمَا كُنَّا لِنَهْتَدِيَ لَوْلَا أَنْ هَدَانَا اللَّهُ لَقَدْ جَاءَتْ
رُسُلُ رَبِّنَا بِالْحَقِّ وَنُودُوا أَن تِلْكُمُ الْجَنَّةُ أُورِثْتُمُوهَا بِمَا كُنتُمْ
تَعْمَلُونَ ﴿٤٣﴾

43 We will strip away any rancour in their hearts. Rivers will flow under them and they will say, 'Praise be to Allah Who has guided us to this! We would not have been guided, had Allah not guided us. The Messengers of our Lord came with the Truth.' It will be proclaimed to them: 'This is your Garden which you have inherited for what you did.'

Allah tells us that one of the blessings given to the people of the Garden is the removal of rancour from their hearts. *Naz'* is extraction and *ghill* is the envy hidden in the heart. The plural is *ghilāl*. It means: 'In the Garden We will remove the rancour which troubles their hearts in this world.' The Prophet ﷺ said, 'Rancour will be like a kneeling camel at the door of the Garden. Allah will remove it from the hearts of the believers.' It is related that 'Alī said, 'I hope that I, 'Uthmān, Talḥah and az-Zubayr will be among those about whom Allah says, "*We will strip away any rancour in their hearts.*"' It is said that the removal of rancour will occur in the Garden preventing them from having any envy of one another for the disparity of their degrees there. It is said that that is a quality of the drink of the Garden, being the reason why Allah says: '*And their Lord will give them a pure draught to drink*' (76:21) one that will purify their hearts of all uncleanness, as will be made clear in *Sūrat al-Insān* and *az-Zumur*, Allah willing.

they will say, 'Praise be to Allah Who has guided us to this! We would not have been guided, had Allah not guided us.

He has brought us to this reward by guiding us and creating guidance for us. This refutes the Qadariyyah. '*Mā kunnā*' is the reading of Ibn 'Āmir without the *wāw* while the rest have a *wāw* ('*Wa mā kunnā*'). '*Guided*' has the *lām* of 'in order to'. 'Had Allah not guided us' is in the nominative.

It will be proclaimed to them: 'This is your Garden which you have inherited for what you did.'

The root of *nūdū* (proclaimed) is *nūdiwa*. *An* is accusative and is lightened from the heavy form (*anna*). It explains that to which they were called because the call is a word and it has no place, in other words they will have the Garden because they were promised it in this world. They will be told: 'This is that Garden which you were promised.' Or it will be said to them before they enter it when they see it from afar. It is said that '*that*' means 'this'.

The meaning of the words: '*which you have inherited for what you did*' is that they will inherit their ranks by their actions and enter into them by the mercy of Allah and His favour,' as Allah says elsewhere: '*That is favour from Allah*' (4:70) and: '*He will admit them into mercy and favour from Him*.' (4:175) We read in *Ṣaḥīḥ Muslim*: 'None of you will enter the Garden by his actions.' They asked, 'Not even you, Messenger of Allah?' He answered ﷺ, 'No, not even me unless Allah covers me with His mercy and favour.' We read in other than the *Ṣaḥīḥ*: 'There is no unbeliever or believer who does not have a place both in the Garden and the Fire. When the people of the Garden enter the Garden and the people of the Fire enter the Fire, the Garden will be elevated above the people of the Fire and they will see their places in it. They will be told, "These would have been your places if you had obeyed Allah." Then it will be said, "People of the Garden, inherit them for what you did." So their places will be divided between the people of the Garden.'

We read in *Ṣaḥīḥ Muslim*, 'No Muslim man dies without Allah putting a Jew or Christian in his place in the Fire.' This is also inheritance. By His favour Allah grants the Garden to whomever He wishes and by His justice He punishes whomever He wishes. In general, the Garden and its degrees are only obtained by His mercy. People entering it by their actions are in fact inheriting it by His mercy since their actions are a mercy from Him to them and by His favour to them. '*Ūrithtumūhā*' is recited both with and without *idghām*.

وَنَادَىٰٓ أَصۡحَٰبُ ٱلۡجَنَّةِ أَصۡحَٰبَ ٱلنَّارِ أَن قَدۡ وَجَدۡنَا مَا وَعَدَنَا رَبُّنَا حَقّٗا فَهَلۡ
وَجَدتُّم مَّا وَعَدَ رَبُّكُمۡ حَقّٗاۖ قَالُواْ نَعَمۡۚ فَأَذَّنَ مُؤَذِّنُۢ بَيۡنَهُمۡ أَن لَّعۡنَةُ ٱللَّهِ
عَلَى ٱلظَّٰلِمِينَ ٤٤

44 The Companions of the Garden will call out to the Companions of the Fire, 'We have found that what our Lord promised us to be true. Have you found what your Lord promised you to be true?' They will say, 'Yes, we have!' Between them a herald will proclaim: 'May the curse of Allah be on the wrongdoers

This is a question entailing rebuke and censure. '*We have found*' is like '*that Garden*,' in other words 'We did find it.' It is said that it is the same call. The herald will call out with a voice which comes from among the angels. '*Between them*' is adverbial as you say, 'announce in their midst.' Al-Aʿmash and al-Kisāʾī recited '*naʿam*' (Yes) and it is permitted in this dialect to have a *sukūn* on the '*ayn* (*naʿm*). Makkī said that if someone uses *naʿima*, he wants to distinguish between the *naʿam* which is the answer 'Yes' and the *niʿim* which is a name for camel, cattle and sheep. It is related that 'Umar did not recognise *naʿam* as the answer. He said, 'Say, "*naʿima*".' *Naʿam* and *naʿim* are two dialectical forms meaning promise and affirmation. When someone asks about the negative, then the answer is *balā*. So '*naʿm*' is the answer to a question which is affirmative, as in this *āyah*, and *balā* is the answer to a negative question, as when the Almighty says: '"*Am I not your Lord?" They said, "Balā."*' (7:172) meaning, 'Yes, You are.'

Al-Bazzī, Ibn 'Āmir, Ḥamzah and al-Kisāʾī recited '*anna laʿnata*' (May the curse…). The rest recite '*an laʿnatu*' for the inceptive, so *an* is accusative in both readings with the omission of the genitive. It is permitted to be lightened as *an*. It is related that al-Aʿmash recited *inna* and there is something implied.

It is related that Ṭāwūs visited Hishām ibn 'Abd al-Malik and said to him, 'Fear Allah and beware of the day of Proclamation.' He asked, 'What is the Day of Proclamation?' and he answered, 'The words of Allah: "*Between them a herald will proclaim: 'May the curse of Allah be on the wrongdoers*,"' and Hisham fainted. Ṭāwūs said, 'This is the abasement that comes from the description, so how will be the abasement of seeing it with one's own eyes?'

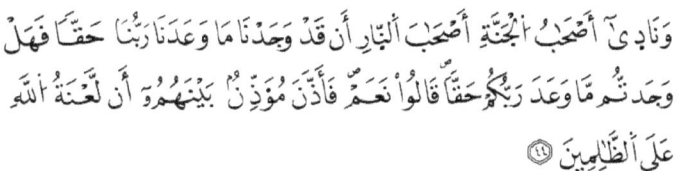

ٱلَّذِينَ يَصُدُّونَ عَن سَبِيلِ ٱللَّهِ وَيَبۡغُونَهَا عِوَجٗا وَهُم بِٱلۡأٓخِرَةِ كَٰفِرُونَ ٤٥

45 those who bar access to the Way of Allah, desiring to make it crooked, and reject the Next World.'

This is in the position of the genitive because of describing what is in the previous *āyah*. It can also be nominative or accusative by an implied 'They are,' those who bar people from the Way of Islam in this world. It is the aspect of barring which entails preventing others from reaching something. Or it may be that they bar themselves from the Way of Allah, in other words turn away from it. This is from *ṣudūd*.

desiring to make it crooked, and disbelieve in the Next World.'

This is seeking to twist it. They criticise it and so do not believe in it. This meaning was already mentioned (3:98). '*Disbelieve in the Next World*' means that they reject it, and such elision is frequent in language.

وَبَيۡنَهُمَا حِجَابٞۚ وَعَلَى ٱلۡأَعۡرَافِ رِجَالٞ يَعۡرِفُونَ كُلَّۢا بِسِيمَىٰهُمۡۚ وَنَادَوۡاْ
أَصۡحَٰبَ ٱلۡجَنَّةِ أَن سَلَٰمٌ عَلَيۡكُمۡۚ لَمۡ يَدۡخُلُوهَا وَهُمۡ يَطۡمَعُونَ ٤٦

46 There will be a dividing wall between them and on the ramparts there will be men who recognise everyone by their mark. They will call out to the people of the Garden: 'Peace be upon you!' They have not entered it for all their ardent desire to do so.

There will be a dividing wall between them and on the ramparts there will be men who recognise everyone by their mark.

The dividing wall is between the Garden and the Fire because they were already mentioned. A wall is a barrier and it is the wall which Allah mentions in His words: '*And a wall will be erected between them*' (57:13). The phrase '*and on the ramparts there will be men*' means on the ramparts of the walls, which are its high points. The word is derived from the mane (*'urf*) of a horse and the crest (*'urf*) of a cock. 'Abdullāh ibn Abī Yazīd related that Ibn 'Abbās said, '*A'rāf* is something elevated.' Mujāhid related that Ibn 'Abbās said, '*A'rāf* are walls which have an elevated part like the crest of the cock.' Linguistically *a'rāf* means an elevated place, being the plural of *'urf*. Yaḥyā ibn Ādam said, 'I asked al-Kisā'ī about the singular of *a'rāf* and he was silent, so I said that Isrā'īl had related to me from Mujāhid from Ibn 'Abbās that *a'rāf* are walls with an elevation (*'urf*) like the crest of a cock. He said,

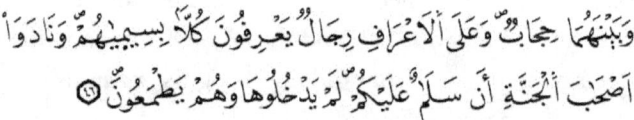

"Yes, by Allah, that is its singular, and the plural is *a'rāf.* Lad! Bring paper!" and he wrote it down.' These words convey praise in the same way as do the words in the phrase: '*...men not distracted by trade or commerce from the remembrance of Allah.*' (24:37)

Scholars have spoken about the people of the Ramparts and they say ten things. 'Abdullāh ibn Mas'ūd, Ḥudhayfah ibn al-Yamān, Ibn 'Abbās, ash-Sha'bī, aḍ-Ḍaḥḥāk and Ibn Jubayr said that they are the people whose good actions and bad actions are equal. Ibn 'Aṭiyyah said 'We read in the *Musnad* of Khaythamah ibn Sulaymān at the end of part 15 the *ḥadīth* of Jābir ibn 'Abdullāh in which the Messenger of Allah ﷺ said, "The scales will be set up on the Day of Rising and good and bad actions will be weighed. Whoever has his good actions outweigh his bad actions by the weight of a flea will enter the Garden. Whoever has his bad actions outweigh his good actions by the weight of a flea will enter the Fire." It was asked, "Messenger of Allah, what about the one whose bad actions and evil actions are equal?" He answered, "Those are the people of the Ramparts. They will not enter it despite their desire to do so."'

Mujāhid said, 'They are righteous people, *fuqahā'* scholars.' It is said that it is the martyrs. Al-Mahdawī mentioned that. Al-Qushayrī said that it is said that they are the excellent from among the believers and the martyrs. They have finished their work and look at the state of the people. When they see the people of the Fire, they will seek refuge with Allah from being sent to the Fire. Everything is in the power of Allah and what is known is different from what is decreed. When the people of the Garden see the Garden when they have not yet entered it, they will hope to enter it.

Sharaḥbīl ibn Sa'd said, 'They are those who desired martyrdom in the Way of Allah Who went out in disobedience to their parents.' Aṭ-Ṭabari mentioned a *ḥadīth* about that from the Prophet ﷺ and that their disobedience to their parents and seeking martyrdom are equal. Ath-Tha'labī mentioned with an *isnād* from Ibn 'Abbās that the Ramparts are high places on the Path. On them will be al-'Abbās, Ḥamzah, 'Alī ibn Abi Ṭālib and Ja'far with wings. They will recognise those who love them by the whiteness of their faces and those who hate them by the blackness of their faces.

Az-Zahrāwī related that they are the just people of the Rising who will testify about people's actions. They are found in every community. An-Naḥḥās preferred this view. He said, 'It is the best that is said about it. They are on the walls between the Garden and the Fire.' Az-Zajjāj said, 'They are the people of certain Prophets.' It is said that they are people who had minor wrong actions not expiated by pains and afflictions in this world. So they are held back from the Garden so that they grieve by that and so it is put opposite their minor wrong actions. Sālim, the freedman of Abū Hudhayfah, wished that he were one of the people of the Ramparts because he believed that they were sinners. It is also said that they are the children of fornication. Al-Qushayrī mentioned that from Ibn 'Abbās.

It is also said that they are angels in charge of these walls who distinguish between the unbelievers and the believers before they enter the Garden and the Fire. Abū Mijlaz mentioned that. It was said to him, 'Angels are not called men.' He retorted, 'They are male and not female and so it is not unlikely for the term "*men*" to be applied to them, as it is applied to the jinn in Allah's words: "*Certain men from among mankind used to seek refuge with certain men from among the jinn.*" (72:6) They are angels who recognise the believers by their signs and the unbelievers by their signs. So they give good news to the believers before they enter the Garden when they have not yet entered it but desire it. When they see the Fire, they pray for safety from the punishment for themselves.' Ibn 'Aṭiyyah said, 'What the *āyah* means is that there are men on the Ramparts from the people of the Garden who are late in entering it, and those men speak about both groups [the People of the Garden and the People of the Fire.]'

The phrase '*who recognise everyone by their mark*' refers to their distinguishing signs, which are the whiteness and beauty of the faces of the People of the Garden and the blackness and ugliness of the People of the Fire and other features which distinguish the one from the other. Allah is not specific about the marks and details. Allah knows the realities of matters.

Then it is also said that *a'rāf* is the plural of *'urf* which is every high elevated place because its appearance is better recognised than that which is low. Ibn 'Abbās said that the Ramparts are the high parts of the Path. It is said that it is the mountain of Uḥud which will be placed there. Ibn 'Aṭiyyah said that az-Zahrāwī mentioned a *ḥadīth* in which the Messenger of Allah ﷺ said: 'Uḥud is a mountain which loves us and we love it, and on the Day of Rising it will take on a form between the Garden and the Fire where some people will be held, each recognised by their mark. They will enter the Garden, Allah willing.' He mentioned another *ḥadīth* from Safwān ibn Sulaym that the Prophet ﷺ said, 'Uḥud is one of the pillars of the Garden.' Abū 'Umar mentioned from Anas ibn Mālik that the Prophet ﷺ said, 'Uḥud is a mountain which loves us and we love it. It will be on one of the canals of the Garden.'

They will call out to the people of the Garden:

The People of the Ramparts will call out to the People of the Garden: '*Peace be upon you*'. It is said that the meaning is 'you are safe from the punishment'.

They will not enter it, for all their ardent desire to do so.

The People of the Ramparts have not entered the Garden, implying that they have not yet entered it '*for all their desire to do so*'. According to this interpretation, they know that they will enter it. It is known in language that 'to desire' (*tami'a*) can mean 'to know'. An-Naḥḥās mentioned it. This is the view of Ibn Mas'ūd, Ibn 'Abbās and others: what is meant are the People of the Ramparts. Abū Miljiz said, 'They are the People of the Garden,' meaning that the People of the Ramparts say to them, '*Peace be upon you*,' to believers who pass them by, being People of the Garden who have not yet entered the Garden and desire to do so. The stop is after '*Peace be upon you*' and at '*have not entered it*'. Then it starts: '*They desire*' with the meaning, 'they desire to enter it.' It is permitted for this to be an adverbial *ḥāl*, and it means, 'The believers who pass by the People of the Ramparts and have not yet entered it desire to enter it while those who have entered it no longer have that desire,' and so there is no stop at '*have not entered it*'.

وَإِذَا صُرِفَتْ أَبْصَٰرُهُمْ تِلْقَآءَ أَصْحَٰبِ ٱلنَّارِ قَالُوا۟ رَبَّنَا لَا تَجْعَلْنَا مَعَ
ٱلْقَوْمِ ٱلظَّٰلِمِينَ ﴿٤٧﴾

47 When they turn their eyes towards the Companions of the Fire, they will say, 'Our Lord, do not place us with the people of the wrongdoers!'

This means turning away from looking directly at the People of Garden. There are only two verbal nouns on the measure *tif'āl*: *tilqā'* and *tibān*. The subject of '*they will say*,' is 'the People of the Ramparts' and their words '*Our Lord, do not place us with the people of the wrongdoers*!' mean they have asked Allah not to put them with them. They know that He will not place them with them. This is by way of humility, as the People of the Garden say: '*Our Lord, perfect our light for us*.' (66:8) They say, '*Praise be to Allah*' by way of thankfulness to Allah and they have pleasure with that.

وَنَادَىٰٓ أَصۡحَٰبُ ٱلۡأَعۡرَافِ رِجَالٗا يَعۡرِفُونَهُم بِسِيمَىٰهُمۡ قَالُواْ مَآ أَغۡنَىٰ عَنكُمۡ
جَمۡعُكُمۡ وَمَا كُنتُمۡ تَسۡتَكۡبِرُونَ ﴿٤٨﴾ أَهَٰٓؤُلَآءِ ٱلَّذِينَ أَقۡسَمۡتُمۡ لَا يَنَالُهُمُ ٱللَّهُ
بِرَحۡمَةٍۚ ٱدۡخُلُواْ ٱلۡجَنَّةَ لَا خَوۡفٌ عَلَيۡكُمۡ وَلَآ أَنتُمۡ تَحۡزَنُونَ ﴿٤٩﴾

48-49 The Companions of the Ramparts will call out to men they recognise by their mark, saying, 'What you amassed was of no use to you, nor was your arrogance. Are these the people you swore that Allah's mercy would never reach?' 'Enter the Garden. You will feel no fear and know no sorrow.'

The Companions of the Ramparts will call out to men they recognise by their mark,

Those they recognise are people in the Fire.

saying, 'What you amassed was of no use to you, nor was your arrogance.

This means 'what you did for the sake of this world and being too arrogant to believe.'

Are these the people you swore that Allah's mercy would never reach?'

This is a reference to people among the poor believers like Bilāl, Salmān, Khabbāb and others. '*You swore*' in this world that it '*would never reach*' them in the Next World. They criticised them in that way. They are given sorrow and regret for what they said to them.

'Enter the Garden. You will feel no fear and know no sorrow.'

'Ikrimah recites this as '*dakhalū*', 'they entered. Ṭalḥah ibn Muṣarrif recited '*idkhilū*' in the past tense. The *āyah* indicates that the Companions of the Ramparts are angels or Prophets. These words are a report from Allah. For those who consider the Companions of the Ramparts to be wrongdoers, their words to the people of the Fire end with '*nor was your arrogance*', and then the words from '*these the people*' to the end of the *āyah* are part of the words of the Almighty to the People of the Fire to rebuke them for what they said in this world. This is related from Ibn 'Abbās. The first was reported from al-Ḥasan. It is said that it is part of the words of the angels entrusted with the People of the Ramparts. The people of the Fire swear that the People of the Ramparts will enter the Fire with them, and so the angels say to the People of the Ramparts: '*Enter the Garden. You will feel no fear and know no sorrow.*'

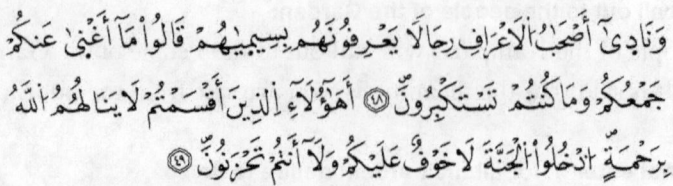

وَنَادَىٰٓ أَصۡحَٰبُ ٱلنَّارِ أَصۡحَٰبَ ٱلۡجَنَّةِ أَنۡ أَفِيضُواْ عَلَيۡنَا مِنَ ٱلۡمَآءِ أَوۡ مِمَّا رَزَقَكُمُ
ٱللَّهُۚ قَالُوٓاْ إِنَّ ٱللَّهَ حَرَّمَهُمَا عَلَى ٱلۡكَٰفِرِينَ ٥٠

50 The Companions of the Fire will call out to the Companions of the Garden, 'Throw down some water to us or some of what Allah has given you as provision.' They will say, 'Allah has forbidden them to the unbelievers:

About the verb '*call out*' it is said that when the People of the Ramparts go to the Garden, the People of the Fire will have their hopes raised and say, 'Our Lord, we have relatives in the Garden. Give us permission to see them and speak to them.' The People of the Garden will not recognise them because of the blackness of their faces. They will say: '*Throw down some water to us or some of what Allah has given you as provision*.' It is clear that the children of Ādam must have food or water, even if they are in the Fire. Those in the Garden will say '*Allah has forbidden them to the unbelievers*' meaning the food and drink of the Garden. The root of '*afīdū* (throw down)' is showing liberality and the verb is used for showering down blessings.

This *āyah* is evidence for the fact that bringing water is one of the best actions you can do. Ibn 'Abbās was asked, 'Which *ṣadaqah* is best?' He said, 'Water. Do you not see when the people of the Fire ask for help from the people of the Garden, they say "*Throw down some water to us or some of what Allah has given you as provision*"?' Abū Dāwūd related that Sa'd went to the Prophet ﷺ and asked, 'Which *ṣadaqah* do you like best?' 'Water,' he answered. In one version, 'He dug a well and said, "This is for Umm Sa'd."' Anas said that Sa'd said, 'Messenger of Allah, Umm Sa'd used to like to give *ṣadaqah*. Will it help her if I give *ṣadaqah* on her behalf?' He said, 'Yes, and you should give water.' In one version the Prophet ﷺ commanded Sa'd ibn 'Ubādah to give water on her behalf. It indicates that giving water is one of the greatest acts of devotion in the sight of Allah Almighty.

One of the *Tābi'ūn* said, 'Whoever has a lot of wrong actions should give water. Allah forgave the wrong actions of the one who gave water to a dog, so how will it be with someone who gives water to a true believer and gives him life?' Al-Bukhārī related from Abū Hurayrah that the Messenger of Allah ﷺ said, 'Once while a man was walking on a path, he became very thirsty and went down to a well and drank from it and then went out and there was a dog eating the earth because it was so thirsty. He said, "This dog must be as thirsty as I was." So he filled his leather sock and held its end and went up and gave the dog water. So Allah thanked him and forgave him.' They asked, 'Messenger of Allah, will we have a reward for (good action towards) animals?' He said, 'There is a reward for everything with a moist liver.' This is the converse of what Muslim related from 'Abdullāh ibn 'Umar, that the Messenger of Allah ﷺ said, 'A woman was punished for a cat which she imprisoned until it died. She entered the Fire on account of it. She did not feed or water it from the time she took it and did not leave it to eat from the vermin of the earth.' We find in the *hadīth* of 'Ā'ishah from the Prophet ﷺ: 'If anyone gives a Muslim a drink of water when there is no water to be found, it is as if he set a human being free. If anyone gives water to a Muslim when there is no water, it is as if he has given him life.' Ibn Mājah transmitted it in the *Sunan*.

This *āyah* is used as evidence by the those who say that the owner of a water basin or waterskin is more entitled to its water and he can deny it to whomever he wishes, because the words of the people of the Garden: *'Allah has forbidden them to the unbelievers'*, mean that they had no right to it. Al-Bukhārī has a chapter on this called, 'Chapter on the one who thought that the owner of a basin or waterskin was more entitled to its water.' In the chapter he included the *ḥadīth* from Abū Hurayrah that the Prophet ﷺ said, 'By the One who has my soul in His hand, I will drive men away from my basin as strange camels are driven away from a basin.' Al-Muhallab said, 'There is no disagreement that the owner of a basin is more entitled to its water based on these words of the Prophet ﷺ.'

ٱلَّذِينَ ٱتَّخَذُواْ دِينَهُمْ لَهْوًا وَلَعِبًا وَغَرَّتْهُمُ ٱلْحَيَوٰةُ ٱلدُّنْيَا فَٱلْيَوْمَ نَنسِيٰهُمْ
كَمَا نَسُواْ لِقَآءَ يَوْمِهِمْ هَٰذَا وَمَا كَانُواْ بِـَٔايَٰتِنَا يَجْحَدُونَ ﴿٥١﴾

51 those who took their *dīn* as a diversion and a game, and were deluded by the life of this world.' Today We will forget them just as they forgot the encounter of this Day and denied Our Signs.

The pronoun '*those*' stems from their adjectival connection with '*unbelievers*'. It can be nominative or accusative by something implied. It is said to be part of the words of the people of the Garden. The phrase '*Today We will forget them*' means, 'We Will leave them in the Fire' and the words '*Just as they forgot the encounter of this Day*' mean 'they did not act for it and they denied it.' *Mā* acts as a verbal noun. Added to it is '*and denied Our Signs*'.

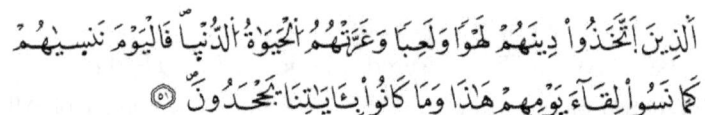

وَلَقَدْ جِئْنَٰهُم بِكِتَٰبٍ فَصَّلْنَٰهُ عَلَىٰ عِلْمٍ هُدًى وَرَحْمَةً لِّقَوْمٍ يُومِنُونَ ﴿٥٢﴾

52 We have brought them a Book elucidating everything with knowledge, as guidance and a mercy for people who believe.

The '*Book*' referred to here is the Qur'an and '*elucidating*,' means making clear, so that someone who reflects on it will recognise it. It is said that '*elucidating*' means 'We sent it in sections.' '*With knowledge*' means 'with Our knowledge of it.' There is no oversight nor error in it. Az-Zajjāj said that the words '...*as guidance and a mercy*' mean 'guiding and having mercy'. He made it an adverbial *ḥāl* of the *hā'* (it) in '*elucidating it*'. Az-Zajjāj said that it is permitted for '*guidance and mercy*' to be nominative. It is said that it is permitted for them to be genitive as appositives for '*Book*'. Al-Kisā'ī and al-Farrā' said that it is permitted for them to be genitive as an adjective of '*Book*'. Al-Farrā' said that it is similar to the words: '*And this is a Book We have sent down and blessed*' (6:155). '*People who believe*' are singled out because they are the ones who benefit from it.

هَلْ يَنظُرُونَ إِلَّا تَاوِيلَهُۥ يَوْمَ يَاتِے تَاوِيلُهُۥ يَقُولُ ٱلَّذِينَ نَسُوهُ مِن قَبْلُ قَدْ
جَآءَتْ رُسُلُ رَبِّنَا بِٱلْحَقِّ فَهَل لَّنَا مِن شُفَعَآءَ فَيَشْفَعُواْ لَنَآ أَوْ نُرَدُّ فَنَعْمَلَ
غَيْرَ ٱلَّذِے كُنَّا نَعْمَلُ قَدْ خَسِرُوٓاْ أَنفُسَهُمْ وَضَلَّ عَنْهُم مَّا كَانُواْ
يَفْتَرُونَ ﴿٥٣﴾

53 What are they waiting for but its fulfilment? The Day its fulfilment occurs, those who forgot it before will say, 'The Messengers of our Lord came with the Truth. Are there any intercessors to intercede for us, or can we be sent back so that we can do something other than what we did?' They have lost their own selves and what they invented has forsaken them.

What are they waiting for but its fulfilment?

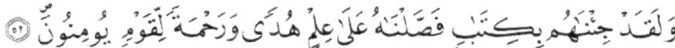

The word for '*fulfilment*' is *ta'wīl* from the verb *āla*. The people of Madīnah remove the *hamzah*. The verb *naẓara* means to wait, in other words, 'Are they waiting for anything except the punishment and reckoning they were promised in the Qur'an?' It is said that *naẓr* is waiting for the Day of Rising. The '*it*' alluded to in '*its fulfilment*' is the Book. The result of the Book is the resurrection and reckoning that Allah has promised. Mujāhid that that it refers to the repayment they will receive for their denial of the Book. Qatādah said that it is its end. The meanings are similar.

The Day its fulfilment occurs, those who forgot it before will say, 'The Messengers of our Lord came with the Truth.

'*The Day its fulfilment occurs*' is when its consequences appear on the Day of Rising. '*Day*' is in the accusative by the verb '*say*', namely that 'those who forgot it before will say on the day that it fulfilment occurs "*The Messengers of our Lord came with the Truth.*"

Are there any intercessors to intercede for us, or can we be sent back so that we can do something other than what we did?'

This is a question which expresses hopefulness. The verb '*to intercede*' is accusative because it is the apodosis of a question. Al-Farrā' said about the words: '*Or can we be sent back*' that their meaning is 'Or will we be sent back?' Az-Zajjāj said that the words: '*so that we can do something other than what we did*' is added to the meaning, implying, 'Will anyone intercede for us or can we return?' Ibn [Abī] Isḥāq recited '*aw nuradda fa-na'mala*' with a *fatḥah* on the end of both verbs which means: 'unless we can be sent back so that we can do.' [POEM] Al-Ḥasan recited: '*aw nuraddu fa-na'malu*' with a *ḍammah* at the end of both.

They have lost their own selves and what they invented has forsaken them.

The phrase '*They have lost their own selves*' means 'They have not helped themselves, and anyone who does not help his self has lost it.' It is said that they have lost blessings and their souls' portion of them. The words '*and what they invented has forsaken them*' mean that what they said about there being another god with Allah is shown to be false.

إِنَّ رَبَّكُمُ ٱللَّهُ ٱلَّذِى خَلَقَ ٱلسَّمَٰوَٰتِ وَٱلْأَرْضَ فِى سِتَّةِ أَيَّامٍ ثُمَّ ٱسْتَوَىٰ
عَلَى ٱلْعَرْشِ يُغْشِى ٱلَّيْلَ ٱلنَّهَارَ يَطْلُبُهُۥ حَثِيثًا وَٱلشَّمْسَ وَٱلْقَمَرَ وَٱلنُّجُومَ
مُسَخَّرَٰتٍۭ بِأَمْرِهِۦٓ ۗ أَلَا لَهُ ٱلْخَلْقُ وَٱلْأَمْرُ ۗ تَبَارَكَ ٱللَّهُ رَبُّ ٱلْعَٰلَمِينَ ﴿٥٤﴾

54 Your Lord is Allah, Who created the heavens and the earth in six days and then settled Himself firmly on the Throne. He covers the day with the night, each pursuing the other urgently; and the sun and moon and stars are subservient to His command.

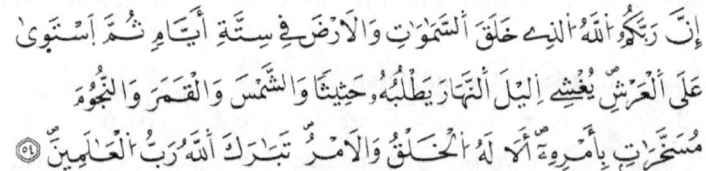

Both creation and command belong to Him. Blessed be Allah, the Lord of all the worlds.

Your Lord is Allah, Who created the heavens and the earth in six days

This makes it clear that He is the only one who has the power to bring anything into existence. So He is the one who must be worshipped. The root of *sittah* (*six*) is *sidsah* and the *dāl* is assimilated into the *sīn* and they meet where the *tā'* is pronounced and dominates them. If you wish, you could say that one of the *sīn*s is changed into a *tā'*, and is elided in the *dāl* because you say *sudaysah* for the diminutive and the plural is *asdās*. The plural and the diminutive return nouns to their roots. They say (for sixth) *sādisan*, *sādiyan*, and *sāttan*. In *sādiyan*, the *sīn* is changed for a *yā'*.

The noun '*day* (*yawm*)' covers the period from sunrise to sunset. If there were no sun, there would be no '*day*'. Al-Qushayrī said that. He said that the meaning of '*in six days*' here is the days of the Next World. Each day is a thousand years because of the immensity of the creation of the heavens and the earth. It is also said that it is the days of this world. Mujāhid and others said that the first of them was Sunday and the last Friday. Allah mentions this period, but if He had wished to create it in an instant, He could have done that since He has the power to say it to it, 'Be' and it will be. But He wanted to teach His slaves compassion and being firm in matters and to manifest His power to the angels by creating one thing after another. This is according to the view of those who say that He created the angels before He created the heavens and the earth.

Another wisdom in His creating them in six days is because each thing has a fixed term with Him. By this He made it clear that He does not hasten punishment for those who obey Him because everything has a fixed term with Him. This is like His words: '*We created the heavens and the earth, and everything between them, in six days and We were not affected by fatigue. So be patient in the face of what they say*' (50:38-39) and: '*How many generations before them We destroyed who had greater force than them.*' (50:36)

and then settled Himself firmly on the Throne.

The issue here is the meaning of '*settling*' (*istiwā'*). The scholars have spoken about it at length. We clarified the views of scholars about it in *Kitāb al-Asnā fī sharḥ asmā' Allāh al-ḥusnā wa ṣifātihi-l-'ulā*. In it we mentioned fourteen views. Most of the early and later people say that it is obliged to free the Creator – glory be to Him – from any notion of spatial direction and encompassment and from the necessity of that and the necessary consequences of that. So, according to most early scholars and the leaders among later scholars, it is necessary to free Him from any notion of directionality. In their view, 'above' is not a direction, because they say that if a single direction were singled out, that would necessitate it being in a place or contained, and place and encompassment demand movement and stillness from that which is encompassed, as well as change and temporality. This is the view of the *mutakallimūn*.

The first generations, may Allah be pleased with them, did not speak about negation of direction nor did they articulate that. Rather they said that it is enough to affirm for Allah Almighty what His Book has stated and Messengers reported. None of the righteous *Salaf* denied that He truly settled on His Throne. The Throne is singled out for that because it is the greatest of His creations. How the settling occurs is not known and its reality is not known. Mālik said, '"Settling" is known (meaning linguistically), but the how of it is unknown, and asking about it is innovation.' That is what Umm Salamah said. This is enough. Whoever wants more should look for it in its place in the books of the scholars.

'*Istiwā*'' in Arabic means exaltedness and stability. Al-Jawharī said, 'It is being straightened after being crooked, and being upright on the back on an animal,' in other words sitting up straight. It also means 'to aim upwards for something' and it can mean 'to overcome and conquer'. A poet said:

Bishr took control (*istawā*) of Iraq
without sword or bloodshed.

It is used for reaching the end of youth and being balanced. Abū 'Umar ibn 'Abd al-Barr related that Abū 'Ubaydah said that '*the All-Merciful, established firmly upon the Throne*' (20:5) means 'to be high'. A poet said:

I got water for them in a flat desert.
The Yemeni star circled and was high (*istawā*).

It designates the exaltedness of Allah's glory, attributes and domain. It means that there is none above Him in any conception of majesty nor any with Him who would share in His exaltedness. He is the Absolutely High.

'Arsh (*throne*) is a word which has several possible meanings. Al-Jawharī and others said that it is the seat of a King. It says in revelation: '*Disguise her throne*' (27:41) and: '*He raised his parents up onto the throne.*' (12:100) The noun *'arsh* is used for the roof of a house and the instep of the foot. *'Arsh as-Simāk* (the Throne of Simāk) are four small stars lower than *al-'Awwā'* which is called *'Ajuz al-Asad*. The word *'arsh* is also used for the wood encasing the upper part of a well after its bottom has

been encircled with stones. That wood is called *'arsh* and the plural is *'urūsh. 'Arsh* is a name of Makkah and *'arsh* is the kingdom and the Sultan. One says, '*Thulla 'arshu fulān*", 'the kingdom of so-and-so departed.' Zuhayr said:

> You brought peace between 'Abs when its power (*'arshuhā*) had departed
> and Dhubyān when sandals humbled their feet.

In this *āyah*, the word '*throne*' can be interpreted as meaning 'kingdom', namely the kingdom rightly belongs to Him alone. That is the view of al-Ḥasan, but it is debatable. We have explained the various views in our book, and praise is due to Allah.

He covers the day with the night

He makes it like a covering; He removes the light of the day to complete what is needed to support life in this world by the coming of night. Night is for rest and day is for gaining livelihood. It is also recited as *yughashshī* as in *Sūrah ar-Ra'd*. That is the reading of Abū Bakr from 'Āṣim, Ḥamzah and al-Kisā'ī. The rest have it in the single form (*yughshī*). They are two dialectical usages of forms IV and II. They agree that Form II is correct in 53:54 and Form IV in 36:9. The readings mean the same, while Form IV has a meaning of repetition and frequency. 'Covering' is to clothe something with something else. In this *āyah* Allah does not mention the day entering the night, it being enough to mention one to imply the other. Ḥumayd ibn Qays recited *an-nahāru*, which means that the day covers the night.

each pursuing the other urgently;

They do this constantly without ever flagging. The phrase '*covers the night with the day*' is in the accusative as a *ḥāl*. It implies: 'He settled on the Throne, making the night cover the day,' and so '*pursuing the other urgently*' is an adverbial *ḥāl* of '*night*', meaning that the night covers the day, seeking it. It is possible that it is a new sentence and not a *ḥāl*. The adverb '*urgently*' is an appositive for the seeker, who is implied, or an adjective describing the seeker or a description of an elided verb, i.e. 'seeking it swiftly'. *Ḥaththa* means 'to hasten and rush'.

The sun and moon and stars are subservient to His command.

Al-Akhfash says that this is added to '*heavens*,' namely 'He created the heavens and created the sun.' It is related from 'Abdullāh ibn 'Āmir all in the nominative.

Both creation and command belong to Him.

Allah is truthful in saying this. He owns creation and He has command. He created creatures and commanded them to do what He loves. This command necessarily also entails prohibition. Ibn 'Uyaynah said, 'There is a difference between creation and command. Whoever makes them one thing is an unbeliever. Creation is created and the command is His word 'Be', which is not created: "*His command when He desires something is that He says to it "Be!" and it is.*"' (16:40)

This difference between creation and the command is clear evidence of the incorrectness of anyone who says that the Qur'an is created, since if His words, which are the command, were created, He would be saying here, 'Both creation and creation belong to Him.' That would be a clear error of expression and defective and corrupt. Allah is too exalted to say something that has no benefit in it. This is corroborated by His words: '*Among His Signs is that heaven and earth hold firm by His command*' (30:25) and: '*The sun, moon, and stars are subservient to His command.*' (7:54) So He tells us that creatures stand firm by His command. If the command were created, it would need another command to establish it and that command would need another command ad infinitum. That is impossible. It is confirmed that His command, which are His words, is timeless, pre-eternal and uncreated in order for it to be the case that creatures are sustained by it.

This is also indicated by His words: '*We did not create the heavens and earth and everything between them, except with truth.*' (15:86) He reported that He created them with truth, namely the word which is His command to beings: 'Be'. If the truth were created, it would not be valid for creatures to be created by it because what is created cannot create what is created. This is indicated by Allah's words: '*Our Word was given before to Our slaves, the Messengers*' (37:171): '*Those for whom the Best from Us was pre-ordained, will be far away from it*' (21:101) and: '*But now My Words are shown to be true.*' (31:12). This all indicates that the Word preceded the existence of time, which makes its pre-eternal existence necessary. This is sufficient to refute them.

They have *āyah*s which they use for evidence for their position like His words: '*No fresh reminder comes to them from their Lord*' (21:2), '*Allah's command is a pre-ordained decree*' (33:35), and '*Allah's command is carried out*' (33:37) and the like. Qāḍī Abū Bakr said, 'The meaning of "*no fresh reminder comes to them*" is admonition, promise and threat from the Prophet ﷺ, "*without their listening to it as if it was a game*" because the admonition and cautioning by the Messenger ﷺ is a reminder.' The Almighty says: '*Remind, You are only a reminder.*' (88:21) It is said, 'So-and-so is in a gathering of *dhikr*.' The meaning of '*Allah's command is a pre-ordained decree*' and '*Allah's command is carried out*' is that He willed punishment and revenge for the unbelievers and help for the believers as well as the judgments He made and determined. Another example of that is His words, '*Until our command comes*' (11:40) and '*Pharaoh's command was not rightly guided*' (11:97), meaning his business, actions, and methods. A poet said:

She has charge (*amr*) until when she masters
the pasture with her hooves, she has a place to sleep.

When this is confirmed, know that the term '*command*' has no connection to will. The Mu'tazilites say that the command is the same as the will, but this is not correct. Allah commands things He does not desire and prevents things He does desire from occurring. Do you not see that he commanded Ibrāhīm to sacrifice his son but did not desire him to do it, and that He commanded His Prophet ﷺ to pray fifty prayers with his community but only desired five prayers from him? He desired the martyrdom of Hamzah as is shown by His words: '*and can gather martyrs from among you*' (3:140). He forbade the unbelievers to kill him but nevertheless commanded them to do it. This is a correct and valuable understanding of this subject, so reflect on it.

Blessed be Allah, the Lord of all the worlds.

The verb '*Blessed*' is Form VII from blessing, which is abundance and expansion. Ibn 'Arafah said that. Al-Azharī said that 'He is blessed' means 'exalted and high'. It is said that it is by His name which has blessing. This was mentioned in the commentary on *al-Fātiḥah*.

ٱدْعُوا۟ رَبَّكُمْ تَضَرُّعًا وَخُفْيَةً ۚ إِنَّهُۥ لَا يُحِبُّ ٱلْمُعْتَدِينَ ﴿٥٥﴾

55 Call on your Lord humbly and secretly. He does not love those who overstep the limits.

'*Call on your Lord*' is a command to call on Him and worship Him. Then He combines the command with attributes which it is good to accompany it with: humility, humbleness and entreaty. *Khufyah* means '*secretly*', internally, so that the person is far away from showing off. Allah praised His Prophet Zakariyyā for that when He says about him: '*When he called on his Lord secretly.*' (19:3) Similar to that are the words of the Prophet ﷺ, 'The best *dhikr* is that which is hidden, and the best provision is that which is adequate.' The *Sharī'ah* affirms that secretly in that context means that there are some actions which have a greater reward when done secretly than when done openly. This was already mentioned in *al-Baqarah*

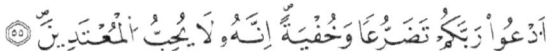

(2:271). Al-Ḥasan ibn Abī al-Hasan said, 'We met some people who could not do any action secretly but always acted openly. The Muslims strove in supplication and not a sound was heard from them except a whispering between them and their Lord. That is because Allah Almighty says: "*Call on your Lord humbly and secretly.*" He mentions a righteous slave and says: "*When he called on his Lord secretly.*" (19:3)' The people of Abū Ḥanīfah use this as evidence that it is more appropriate to say '*Āmīn*' silently than to say it aloud because it is a supplication. This was already discussed in the commentary on *al-Fātiḥah*. Muslim related that Abū Mūsā said, 'We were with the Prophet ﷺ on a journey – 'an expedition' in one variant – and people began to say the *takbīr* aloud – one variant has, 'whenever they went up a hill, a man would say, "There is no god but Allah" – the Messenger of Allah ﷺ said, "People! Be kind to yourselves. You are not calling on One Who is deaf nor absent. You are calling One Who is with you, near and hearing."'

Scholars disagree about raising the hands when making supplication. One group disliked it – including Jubayr ibn Muṭ'im, Sa'īd ibn al-Musayyab and Sa'īd ibn Jubayr. Shurayḥ saw a man with his hands raised and said, 'Who will take them? You are motherless!' Masrūq said to people who raised their hands, 'May Allah cut them off!' When someone calls on Allah in need they preferred him to indicate with his index finger. They said, 'That is sincerity.' Qatādah used to indicate with his index finger and not raise his hands. Raising the hands was disliked by 'Aṭā', Ṭāwūs, Mujāhid and others. Raising the hands was permitted by a group of Companions and *Tābi'ūn*. It was related from the Prophet ﷺ and al-Bukhārī mentioned it. Abū Mūsa al-Ash'arī said, 'The Prophet ﷺ made supplication and raised his hands. I saw the whiteness of his armpits.' Something similar is related from Anas. Ibn 'Umar said, 'The Prophet ﷺ raised his hands and said, "O Allah, I am free of what Khālid did."'

In *Ṣaḥīḥ Muslim* it is reported that 'Umar ibn al-Khaṭṭāb said, 'On the day of Badr, the Messenger of Allah ﷺ looked at the idolaters who were a thousand while his Companions only numbered three hundred and seventeen. The Prophet of Allah ﷺ faced the *qiblah*, stretching out his hands, and began to speak to his Lord.' He mentioned the *ḥadīth*. At-Tirmidhī related that he said, 'When the Messenger of Allah ﷺ raised his hands, he did not lower them until he had wiped his face with them.' He said that this is a *gharīb* sound *ḥadīth*. Ibn Mājah related from Salmān that the Prophet ﷺ said, 'Your Lord is alive, noble, and is ashamed that His slave who lifts his hands to Him should return them with them empty or disappointed.'

The first people use as evidence what Muslim related from 'Umārah ibn Rubaybah and the opinion of Bishr ibn Marwān who raised his hands on the *minbar* and said, 'May Allah make these two hands ugly! I saw that the Messenger of Allah ﷺ did not do more with his hands when he spoke than this,' and he pointed with his glorifying finger. They also used what Sa'īd ibn Abī 'Arūbah related from Qatādah that Anas ibn Mālik related to him that the Prophet ﷺ did not raise his hands in any supplication except for the Rain Prayer. Then he would raise them so far that the whites of his armpits could be seen. The first has sounder paths of transmission and is firmer than the *ḥadīth* of Sa'īd ibn Abī 'Arūbah. Sa'īd's mind became unsettled towards the end of his life. Shu'bah differed from him in his transmission from Qatādah from Anas ibn Mālik. He said, 'The Messenger of Allah ﷺ used to raise his hands so that the white of his armpits could be seen.' It is said that when some disaster befalls the Muslims, raising the hands in that way is excellent and beautiful, as the Prophet ﷺ did that in the Rain Prayer and at the Battle of Badr.

Supplication is good in whatever way it is done. What is desired of a person is to show his poverty and need of Allah Almighty, humility before Him and humbleness. If he wishes, he can face the *qiblah* and raise his hands, and that is good. If he wishes, he need not. According to what has come in *ḥadīth*s, the Prophet ﷺ did that. The Almighty says: '*Call on your Lord humbly and secretly*' and did not speak of raising the hands or anything else. He also says: '*those who remember Allah, standing, sitting...*' (3:191) and He praised them and did not stipulate other than what He mentions. The Prophet ﷺ made supplication in his Friday *khuṭbah* while facing *qiblah*.

He does not love those who overstep the limits.

Allah means in supplication here, even if the expression is general. The person who oversteps the limits is the one who goes beyond the bounds and does something unlawful. Such people vary according to how they transgress. It is related that the Prophet ﷺ said, 'There will be people who overstep the limits in supplication.' Ibn Mājah transmitted from Abū Bakr ibn Abī Shaybah from 'Affān from Ḥammād ibn Salamah from Sa'īd al-Jurayrī from Abū Na'āmah that 'Abdullāh ibn Mughaffal heard his son say, 'O Allah, I ask you for a white castle on the right hand side of the Garden when I enter it.' He said, 'My son, ask Allah for the Garden and seek refuge with Him from the Fire. I heard the Messenger of Allah ﷺ say, "There will be people who overstep the limits in supplication."'

There are various ways of overstepping the limits in supplication. One of them is doing much of it aloud and shouting, as already stated. Another is for someone to ask to have the station of a Prophet or ask for something else impossible and other things like that. Another is to ask for wrong actions and other such things. Another is making supplication with something that is not in the Book or *Sunnah* and by doing so choosing bad expressions and rhyming words found in small books that have no basis and are not reliable, making them his refrain and leaving that which Allah's Messenger ﷺ used in supplication. All of this prevents the supplication being answered, as explained in *al-Baqarah* (2:186).

وَلَا تُفْسِدُوا فِي الْأَرْضِ بَعْدَ إِصْلَاحِهَا وَادْعُوهُ خَوْفًا وَطَمَعًا إِنَّ رَحْمَتَ اللَّهِ قَرِيبٌ مِنَ الْمُحْسِنِينَ ﴿٥٦﴾

56 Do not corrupt the earth after it has been put right. Call on Him fearfully and eagerly. Allah's mercy is close to the good-doers.

Do not corrupt the earth after it has been put right.

The Almighty here forbids every type of corruption, great or small, after the earth has been put right in any way, great or small. So it is taken generally according to the sound view. Aḍ-Ḍaḥḥāk said that it means: 'Do not let the water of a well drain away or cut down fruit trees to cause harm.' It is related that clipping *dīnār*s is an aspect of corruption of the earth. It is said that the bribery of judges is part of corruption of the earth. Al-Qushayri said, 'What is meant is: "Do not associate others with Allah." So it is a prohibition of *shirk*, of spilling blood and bloodshed in the earth and a command to abide by the law after it has been put right by Allah by sending His Messenger, affirming the *Sharī'ah*, and making clear the religion of Muḥammad ﷺ.' Ibn 'Aṭiyyah said, 'Someone who does such things aims for the greatest corruption after the greatest putting right and so he is singled out.' What aḍ-Ḍaḥḥāk mentioned is not part of its general meaning. It only applies when it entails harm for believers. As for that which causes harm to the idolaters, in that case it is permitted. The Prophet ﷺ stopped up the water at Badr and cut down trees belonging to unbelievers. Clipping *dīnār*s will be discussed in Hūd, Allah willing.

Call on Him fearfully and eagerly.

This is a command telling human beings to be in a state of watchfulness, fear and hope in Allah Almighty, so that hope and fear are like the wings of a bird carrying them on the path of rectitude. If someone has only one wing, he will inevitably come to grief. Allah says: '*Tell My slaves that I am the Ever-Forgiving, the*

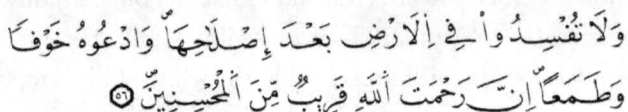

Most Merciful, but also that My punishment is the Painful Punishment' (15:49-50), and He encourages hope and fear. Man makes supplication in fear of His punishment and hoping for His reward. Allah Almighty says: '*...calling out to Us in yearning and in awe*' (21:90). This will be discussed in its place. Fear is anxiety about harm from which one is not safe and hope is expectation of what is desired. Al-Qushayrī said that. Some of the people of knowledge said, 'Fear should dominate hope throughout one's life but when death is near, then hope should dominate. The Prophet ﷺ said, "One should only die with a good opinion of Allah." It is sound and transmitted by Muslim.'

Allah's mercy is close to the good-doers.

Allah does not use the feminine adjective (*qarībah*) for '*close*' [even though the word for '*mercy*' is feminine]. There are seven reasons for that. The first is that *raḥmah* and *ruḥum* are the same and mean pardon and forgiveness. Az-Zajjāj said that and an-Naḥḥās preferred it. An-Naḍr ibn Shumayl said that *raḥmah* is a verbal noun, and the verbal noun should be masculine, just as *maw'iẓah* (admonition) takes a masculine verb in 2:275. This is close to the view of az-Zajjāj because admonition means warning. It is said that '*mercy*' means 'doing good', and because it is not a real feminine, it becomes masculine. Al-Jawharī mentioned that. It is said that what is meant by '*mercy*' here is rain. Al-Akhfash said that. It is permitted to be masculine as some feminine nouns are masculine. [POEM] Abū 'Ubaydah said that it is masculine because 'place' (*makān*) is masculine, i.e. 'a close place'. 'Alī ibn Sulaymān said that this is an error. If that had been the case, 'place' would be in the accusative in the Qur'an as you say, 'Zayd is close to you.' It is said that it is masculine for relationship reasons as is said, 'The mercy of Allah has nearness'. Al-Farrā' said that when 'near' refers to spatial distance, it can be masculine or feminine. If it has the meaning of family relationship, it is feminine without any disagreement. Al-Jawharī mentioned it. Those other than al-Farrā' say that it is masculine. One says about lineage (*nasab*) '*qarībah*' while it is permitted to be masculine or feminine in other than *nasab*. One says, 'Your house is close [fem.] to us' and 'So-and-so [f.] is near [m.] to us.' Allah says: '*What will make you understand? It may be that the Last Hour is very near* [m.] (33:63) Those who use that as an argument say that the words of the Arabs are like that. [POEM] Az-Zajjāj said that this is an error because masculine and feminine act according to their verbs.

وَهُوَ ٱلَّذِى يُرْسِلُ ٱلرِّيَٰحَ نُشُرًۢا بَيْنَ يَدَىْ رَحْمَتِهِۦ ۖ حَتَّىٰٓ إِذَآ أَقَلَّتْ سَحَابًا ثِقَالًا سُقْنَٰهُ لِبَلَدٍ مَّيِّتٍ فَأَنزَلْنَا بِهِ ٱلْمَآءَ فَأَخْرَجْنَا بِهِۦ مِن كُلِّ ٱلثَّمَرَٰتِ ۚ كَذَٰلِكَ نُخْرِجُ ٱلْمَوْتَىٰ لَعَلَّكُمْ تَذَكَّرُونَ ﴿٥٧﴾

57 It He is who sends out the winds, bringing advance news of His mercy, so that when they have lifted up the heavy clouds, We dispatch them to a dead land and send down water to it, by means of which We bring forth all kinds of fruit. In the same way We will bring forth the dead, so that hopefully you will pay heed.

It He is who sends out the winds, bringing advance news of His mercy,

This is added to His words: '*He covers the night with the day*' (13:3). He mentions other blessings He gives and indicates His oneness and affirms His divinity. The word '*wind*' (*rīḥ*) was already discussed in *al-Baqarah* (2:104). *Riyāḥ* (*winds*) is the plural, indicating a lot of winds, and *arwāḥ* the plural, indicating a few. The root of *rīḥ* is *rawḥ*. Those who say that the plural of few is *aryāḥ* are mistaken. There are seven readings of '*bringing advance news*'. The people of Makkah and Madīnah and Abū 'Amr read *nushuran*, the plural of *nāshir* with the relative meaning, i.e. 'with *nashr*'. It is like *shāhid* and *shuhud*. It is permitted for it to be the plural of *nashūr* like *rasūl* and *rusul*. It is said that wind is called *nushūr* when it veers in different directions. *Nashūr* means 'spread', like *rakūb* means ridden (*markūb*). This means He is the One who sends the winds which spread. Al-Ḥasan and Qatādah recited *nushran* as a lightened form of *nushur*, as is done with *kutb* and *rusl*. Al-A'mash and Ḥamzah recited *nashran* as the verbal noun, and it is as if Allah were saying, 'He is the One who sends the winds spreading.' It is as if something were rolled up and then spread out by the winds. It is permitted for it to be a verbal noun in the position of an adverbial *ḥāl* describing winds, and then it is as if He were saying, 'He sends the winds spreading,' meaning reviving. When Allah resurrects (*anshara*) someone dead, he gets up. It is said that *nashran* is from *nashr* which is the opposite of rolling up as we mentioned. So it is as if the wind, when it is still, is wrapped up and then released from its coil and becomes as if it has been opened up. Abū 'Ubaydah explained it with the meaning of separated in all directions according to the meaning of 'spreading them here and there'.

'Āṣim recited *bushran*, the plural of *bashīr*, implying that the winds bring good news of rain. There is evidence for that in Allah's words: '*Among His signs is that He sends the winds bringing good news.*' (30:46) The root has a *ḍammah* on the *shīn*, but it has been elided and lightened, like *rusl*. It is related as *basharan*. An-Naḥḥās said that it is recited *bushuran* and *bashr*, the verbal noun of *bashara*, meaning 'to give good news'. These are five readings. Muḥammad al-Yamānī recited *bushrā* and the seventh reading is *bushurā*.

so that when they have lifted up the heavy clouds,

The noun '*clouds*' can be masculine or feminine. That is the case with several plurals which have a final *hā'* in the singular. You can use both masculine and feminine adjectives for it. The meaning is: 'The wind bears the clouds which are laden with water,' i.e. which are heavy. '*We dispatch them*,' meaning the clouds, '*to a dead land*', one without plants. *Saqā* and *saqā ilā* are used for watering land. It is also said that it is 'for the sake of a dead land' and the *lām* is the *lām* of purpose. The noun *balad* is every place on the earth, occupied or not occupied, empty or inhabited. *Balad* and *baldah* are the singulars of *buldān* and *bilād*. *Balad* is also a trace and its plural is *ablād*. A poet said:

After decay encompassed their traces (*ablād*).

Balad also means the place where an ostrich lays an egg. One says that someone is more humble than 'the egg of the *balad*' and it is the egg which an ostrich lays and then abandons. *Baldah* means land. One says, 'This is our land (*baldah*).' *Baldah* is one of the Mansions of the Moon, which is six stars in Sagittarius which the sun enters on the shortest day of the year. *Baldah* is also used for the breast, and a person is described as having a wide breast (*wāsi' aṣ-ṣadr*). A poet said:

The [camel] was made to lie down
 and put her breast (*baldah*) on the ground (*baldah*),
Making little noise except grumbling.

Buldah of *baldah* is the space between the eyebrows. So it is a word with many meanings.

send down water to it,

The pronoun '*it*' here refers to the land. It is said, 'We send down water by the clouds because the clouds are the tool of sending down water.' It is also possible that the meaning is: 'We sent down water from them,' like Allah's words: '…*a spring from which Allah's slaves will drink*" (76:6), i.e. from it.

by means of which We bring forth all kinds of fruit. In the same way We will bring forth the dead, so that hopefully you will pay heed.

The *kāf* here is in the position of the accusative, implying: 'the like of this bringing forth is the same way We bring the dead to life'. Al-Bayhaqī and others transmitted that Abū Razīn al-'Uqayli said, 'I asked, "Messenger of Allah, how will Allah bring back creation, and what is the instrument of doing that in His creation?" He answered, "Have you not passed by the valleys of your people in a drought and then passed by it when it quivers with water?" "Yes," I answered, He said, "That is the Sign of Allah in His creation."' It is said that the aspect of the resemblance is that Allah will bring them to life from their graves by means of a rain which He sends down on their them and the graves will split open from them, and their spirits will return to them.

In *Ṣaḥīḥ Muslim,* we read in a *ḥadīth* that 'Abdullāh ibn 'Amr reported from the Prophet ﷺ: 'Then Allah will release – or send down – a rain like dew and the bodies of people will grow from it. Then it will be said, "People, hasten to your Lord!" and they will be made to stand and they will be questioned.' He mentioned the *ḥadīth.* We mentioned it in full in *Kitāb at-Tadhkirah*, praise be Allah. It indicates the Resurrection, and that all affairs return to Allah.

وَالْبَلَدُ الطَّيِّبُ يَخْرُجُ نَبَاتُهُۥ بِإِذْنِ رَبِّهِۦ وَالَّذِى خَبُثَ لَا يَخْرُجُ إِلَّا نَكِدًا
كَذَٰلِكَ نُصَرِّفُ الْآيَٰتِ لِقَوْمٍ يَشْكُرُونَ ﴿٥٨﴾

58 Good land yields up its plants by its Lord's permission, but that which is bad only yields up scantily. In this way We vary the Signs for people who are thankful.

Good land yields up its plants by its Lord's permission, but that which is bad only yields up scantily.

There is good earth, and the bad is that in which there are stones or thorns, as al-Ḥasan said. It is said that it is a metaphor. The Almighty likened a person with quick understanding to good earth and a stupid person to the bad, as an-Naḥḥās said. It is said that this is a metaphor for the hearts. One heart accepts admonition and the reminder, while another heart is deviant and far from that. Al-Ḥasan also said that. Qatādah said, 'It is a metaphor for the believer who acts voluntarily in expectation of a reward and the hypocrite who does not expect a reckoning.' The Messenger of Allah ﷺ said, 'By Him in whose hand my soul is, if any of them had known they would find a meaty bone or two good hooves there, they would have attended *'Ishā'*.'

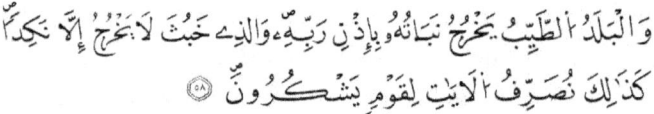

Nakid is in the accusative as an adverbial *ḥāl*. It is a difficulty which prevents giving good. This is a likeness. Mujāhid said, 'It means that there are both good and bad among the children of Ādam.' Ṭalḥah recited, '*illā nakdan*', eliding the *kasrah* since it is heavy. Ibn al-Qa'qā' recited *nakadan* which is a verbal noun. It means 'with scantiness', [POEM NOT ABOUT MEANING] It is said that *nakid* and *nakad* mean the same, like *danif* and *danaf*. They are two dialects.

'*In this way We vary the Signs*' means 'as We made the signs different', and they are evidence and proofs of the invalidity of *shirk*. That is how We vary the signs in all that people need. '*For people who are thankful*': the thankful are singled out because they benefit from it.

لَقَدْ أَرْسَلْنَا نُوحًا إِلَىٰ قَوْمِهِ فَقَالَ يَٰقَوْمِ ٱعْبُدُوا۟ ٱللَّهَ مَا لَكُم مِّنْ إِلَٰهٍ غَيْرُهُۥٓ إِنِّىٓ أَخَافُ عَلَيْكُمْ عَذَابَ يَوْمٍ عَظِيمٍ ۝

59 We sent Nūḥ to his people and he said, 'My people, worship Allah! You have no other god than Him. I fear for you the punishment of a dreadful Day.'

'*Worship Allah*' since it is clear that He is the Creator Who has total power. He mentions the stories of past nations and the warning they contain for the unbelievers. The *lām* in *laqad* is to stress what is reported about in the oath. The *fā'* indicates that the second action is after the first. '*O My people!*' This is the vocative with the *yā'* elided. It is permitted to have *qawmī* which is the root. Nūḥ was the first Messenger to the earth after Ādam and came to forbid marriage with daughters, sisters, and aunts. An-Naḥḥās said, 'Nūḥ is declined because it has three letters. It is permitted to derive it from *nāḥa, yanūḥu*, and the meaning was mentioned in *Āl 'Imrān* (3:33).'

Ibn al-'Arabī said that any historian who says that Idrīs came before Nūḥ is weak. The evidence for the weakness of that view is the sound *ḥadīth* about the Night Journey when the Prophet ﷺ met Ādam and Idrīs, and Ādam said to him, 'Welcome to a righteous Prophet and a righteous son' while Idrīs said to him, 'Welcome to a righteous Prophet and a righteous brother.' If Idrīs had been earlier than Nūḥ, he would also have said, 'Welcome to a righteous Prophet and a righteous son.' The fact that he said 'righteous brother' indicates that they share in Nūḥ as a father, peace be upon all of them. In fairness there is no discussion after that.

Qāḍī 'Iyāḍ said that the forefathers here are Nūḥ, Ibrāhīm, and Ādam who responded, 'Welcome to a righteous son,' whereas Idrīs said, 'a righteous brother,' as did Mūsā, ʻIsā, Yūsuf, Hārūn and Yaḥyā who were not, by agreement, forefathers of the Prophet ﷺ. Al-Māzirī said that some historians have said that Idrīs was the grandfather of Nūh. If the evidence for this is based on Idrīs being sent, then the words of the genealogists are not true when they say that he was before Nūh, since the Prophet ﷺ stated that Ādam said that Nūḥ was the first Messenger to be sent. If there is no evidence of this then it is permissible for them to say that it is possible that Idrīs was a Prophet who was not sent.

Qāḍī ʻIyāḍ said that this is added to what is said about Allah singling out the sending of Nūḥ to the people of the earth as the *ḥadīth* makes clear that he was sent to the whole of mankind like our Prophet ﷺ. Idrīs was only sent to his people as was also the case with Mūsa, Hūd, Ṣāliḥ, Lūt and others. Some of them use as evidence Allah's words: '*Ilyās was one of the Messengers. When he said to his people, "Will you not be godfearing?"*' (37:123-124). It is said that Ilyās was Idrīs. It is recited '*Idrāsīn*'. Qāḍī ʻIyāḍ said, 'I saw al-Ḥasan ibn Baṭṭāl state that Ādam was not a Messenger, so as to avoid this controversy.' The *ḥadīth* of Abū Dharr aṭ-Ṭawīl indicates that Ādam and Idrīs were both Messengers. Ibn ʻAṭiyyah said, 'Both views can be combined inasmuch as the sending of Nūḥ was known to be for the purpose of putting people right and to impose on them punishment and destruction on the basis of belief or lack of it. What is meant is that he was the first Prophet sent for this purpose, and Allah knows best.'

It is related from Ibn ʻAbbās that Nūḥ became a Messenger at the age of forty. Al-Kalbī said that that was 800 years after Ādam. Ibn ʻAbbās said that he remained among his people calling them to belief for 950 years, as Revelation reports, and then lived for a further sixty years after the Flood until there were many people and they had spread. Wahb said, 'Nūh was sent when he was fifty.' ʻAwn ibn Shaddād said, 'Nūh became a Messenger when he was 350 years old.' It states in many books of *ḥadīth*, at-Tirmidhī and others, that all human beings now are descendants of Nūḥ.

An-Naqqāsh mentioned from Sulaymān ibn Arqam from az-Zuhrī that the Arabs, Persians, Greeks, Syrians and people of Yemen are descended from Sām ibn Nūḥ; Indians (Hind and Sind), the blacks, Abyssinians, Zuṭṭ, Nubians and all those with dark skin are descended from Ḥām ibn Nūḥ; the Turks, Berbers, Transoxianans, Yājūj and Mājūj, and the Slavs are descended from Yāfith ibn Nūḥ. All of them are descendants of Nūḥ.

You have no other god than Him.

The word '*other*' is in the nominative in the reading of Nāfiʻ, Abū ʻAmr, ʻĀṣim and Ḥamzah, meaning 'You have no god but Him,' and describes the subject. It is said that it means '*illā*', in other words 'You have no God except Him.' Abū 'Amr said, 'I do not know of anyone reading it in the genitive or accusative.' Al-Kisā'ī recited it in the genitive based on its position in the sentence. It is permitted to be in the accusative for the exception, but it is not used often that way, although al-Kisā'ī and al-Farrā' allowed '*other*' to be accusative in every place that *illā* (except) can be used whether or not the words end there, so a sentence can end with '*ghayraka*'. Al-Farrā' said that that is the dialect of the Banū Asad and Quḍā'ah. [POEM] Al-Kisā'ī said that it is not permitted to end with '*ghayraka*' if it is in the positive although that is not the case here. An-Naḥḥās said that the Basrans permit '*ghayr*' to be in the accusative when it is not at the end of a sentence. They consider that to be the most ugly form of ungrammatical speech.

قَالَ ٱلْمَلَأُ مِن قَوْمِهِۦٓ إِنَّا لَنَرَىٰكَ فِى ضَلَٰلٍ مُّبِينٍ ﴿٦٠﴾ قَالَ يَٰقَوْمِ لَيْسَ بِى ضَلَٰلَةٌ
وَلَٰكِنِّى رَسُولٌ مِّن رَّبِّ ٱلْعَٰلَمِينَ ﴿٦١﴾ أُبَلِّغُكُمْ رِسَٰلَٰتِ رَبِّى وَأَنصَحُ لَكُمْ
وَأَعْلَمُ مِنَ ٱللَّهِ مَا لَا تَعْلَمُونَ ﴿٦٢﴾

60-62 The ruling circle of his people said, 'We see you in flagrant error.' He said, 'My people, I am not in error at all but rather am a Messenger from the Lord of all the worlds, transmitting my Lord's Message to you and giving you good counsel, and I know from Allah what you do not know.

Malā' are the nobles of a people and their leaders. This was already mentioned in *al-Baqarah* (2:246). *Ḍalāl* and *ḍalālah* refer to turning from the path of the truth and leaving it, so the meaning is: 'In calling us to one god, we see that you are misguided from the Truth.' The verb '*transmitting*' is read in Form II and IV, and it is said that these are two dialectical forms that mean the same. The verb '*giving you good counsel*' – *nuṣḥ* – entails having a sincere intention free of any trace of corrupt behaviour with no element of deceit in it. The verb is *naṣaḥa* which can either take a direct object or one with the preposition *li*. It is more eloquent to have it with *li*. The noun is *naṣīḥah*. The one who gives good counsel is *naṣīḥ* and *nāṣiḥ*, the plural of which is *nuṣaḥā'*. A man whose breast is *nāṣiḥ* has a pure heart. Al-Aṣmā'ī said that *nāṣiḥ* is purified honey, like *nāṣi'*. *Naṣaḥa* is used for everything that is purified. Form VIII is used for accepting good advice. *Nāṣiḥ* is a tailor and *niṣāḥ* is thread and *niṣāḥāt* is also used to mean 'skins'. Al-A'shā said:

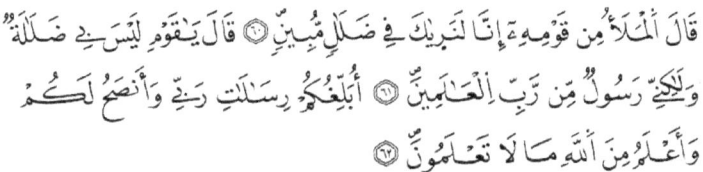

You see the drink we share between all of them,
like what is stretched of the skins (*niṣāḥāt*) of camel foals.

أَوَعَجِبْتُمْ أَن جَاءَكُمْ ذِكْرٌ مِّن رَّبِّكُمْ عَلَىٰ رَجُلٍ مِّنكُمْ لِيُنذِرَكُمْ وَلِتَتَّقُوا
وَلَعَلَّكُمْ تُرْحَمُونَ ﴿٦٣﴾ فَكَذَّبُوهُ فَأَنجَيْنَاهُ وَالَّذِينَ مَعَهُ فِي الْفُلْكِ
وَأَغْرَقْنَا الَّذِينَ كَذَّبُوا بِآيَاتِنَا إِنَّهُمْ كَانُوا قَوْمًا عَمِينَ ﴿٦٤﴾

63-64 Or are you astonished that a reminder should come to you from your Lord by way of a man among you, to warn you and make you godfearing so that hopefully you will gain mercy? But they denied him so We rescued him and those with him in the Ark. And We drowned the people who denied Our Signs. They were a blind people.

In the expression '*or are you astonished*', the *wāw* of *aw* has a *fatḥah* because it is a conjunction. The interrogative *alif* is added to it for confirmation. '*A reminder should come to you*' means an admonition from your Lord. '*By way of a man among you*' is on the tongue of a man. It is said that *'alā* means 'with', meaning 'with a man'. It is said that the meaning is, 'If a reminder comes to you from your Lord, revealed to a man among you, one whose lineage you know, in other words to a human being like yourselves. Implying that if he had been an angel, there may have been natural aversion on your part owing to the difference between the species.' The word '*fulk*' (*Ark*) is both singular and plural, and it was discussed in *al-Baqarah* (2:104). The adjective '*blind*' here means blind to the truth. Qatādah said that. It is also said that it means 'blind to acknowledgment of Allah Almighty and His power'. Someone ignorant is often called blind.

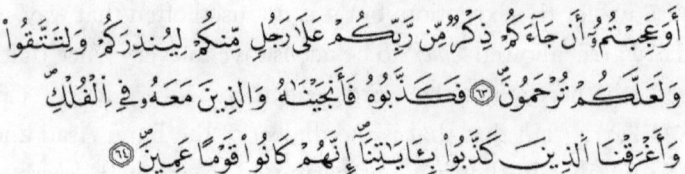

وَإِلَىٰ عَادٍ أَخَاهُمْ هُودًا قَالَ يَٰقَوْمِ ٱعْبُدُوا۟ ٱللَّهَ مَا لَكُم مِّنْ إِلَٰهٍ غَيْرُهُۥٓ أَفَلَا
تَتَّقُونَ ﴿٦٥﴾ قَالَ ٱلْمَلَأُ ٱلَّذِينَ كَفَرُوا۟ مِن قَوْمِهِۦٓ إِنَّا لَنَرَىٰكَ فِى
سَفَاهَةٍ وَإِنَّا لَنَظُنُّكَ مِنَ ٱلْكَٰذِبِينَ ﴿٦٦﴾ قَالَ يَٰقَوْمِ لَيْسَ بِى
سَفَاهَةٌ وَلَٰكِنِّى رَسُولٌ مِّن رَّبِّ ٱلْعَٰلَمِينَ ﴿٦٧﴾ أُبَلِّغُكُمْ رِسَٰلَٰتِ رَبِّى
وَأَنَا۠ لَكُمْ نَاصِحٌ أَمِينٌ ﴿٦٨﴾ أَوَعَجِبْتُمْ أَن جَآءَكُمْ ذِكْرٌ مِّن رَّبِّكُمْ عَلَىٰ
رَجُلٍ مِّنكُمْ لِيُنذِرَكُمْ وَٱذْكُرُوٓا۟ إِذْ جَعَلَكُمْ خُلَفَآءَ مِنۢ بَعْدِ
قَوْمِ نُوحٍ وَزَادَكُمْ فِى ٱلْخَلْقِ بَصْۜطَةً فَٱذْكُرُوٓا۟ ءَالَآءَ ٱللَّهِ
لَعَلَّكُمْ تُفْلِحُونَ ﴿٦٩﴾

65-69 And to ʿĀd We sent their brother Hūd, who said, 'My people, worship Allah! You have no other god than Him. So will you not be godfearing?' The ruling circle of those of his people who disbelieved said, 'We see you as a fool and think you are a liar.' He said, 'My people, I am by no means a fool, but rather am a Messenger from the Lord of all the worlds, and I am a faithful counsellor to you. Or are you astonished that a reminder should come to you from your Lord by way of a man among you in order to warn you? Remember when He appointed you successors to the people of Nūh, and increased you greatly in stature. Remember Allah's blessings, so that hopefully you will be successful.'

And to ʿĀd We sent their brother Hūd, who said, 'My people, worship Allah!

It means: 'We sent to ʿĀd their brother Hūd.' Ibn ʿAbbās said that '*brother*' means the descendant of their ancestor. It is said that he was their brother in tribal terms. It is also said that it means any human being descended from their ancestor Ādam. In the *Muṣannaf* of Abū Dāwūd it says that their brother Hūd was their companion. ʿĀd was a descendant of Sām ibn Nūḥ. Ibn Isḥāq said that ʿĀd was the son of ʿAwṣ ibn Iram ibn Sālikh ibn Arfakhshand ibn Sām ibn Nūḥ. Hūd was Hūd son of ʿAbdullāh ibn Rabāḥ ibn al-Jalūd ibn ʿAwṣ ibn Iram ibn Sālikh ibn Arfakhshand ibn Sām ibn Nūḥ whom Allah sent as a Prophet to ʿĀd. He was from their middle class in respect of lineage and the best of them in personal nobility. ʿĀd is not declined as it is the name of a tribe. Anyone who declines it makes it the name of a quarter. Abū Ḥātim said, 'In the mode (*ḥarf*) of Ubayy and Ibn Masʿūd it is, "*'Ād al-ūlā*" (50:13) without the *alif*.' Hūd is a non-Arabic name. It is declined since it is light because it has three letters. It is possible that it has an Arabic origin derived from *hāda, yahūdu*. The accusative is for the appositive.

Commentators say that there were seven generations between Hūd and Nūḥ. It is related that 'Ād was made up of thirteen tribes who were settled in the hills of Arabia. They had gardens, crops and civilisation. Their land was very fertile. Allah became angry with them and turned their land into a desert. It is related that they lived in the region extending from Hadramawt to Yemen. They worshipped idols. When his people were destroyed, Hūd took those who believed to Makkah and they remained there until they died. '*We consider you a fool*' means someone possessing foolishness and lacking in intelligence. A poet said:

> They walked like shaking spears whose tops
> bend (*tasaffahat*) when the wind passes over them.

This was already dealt with in *al-Baqarah* (2:13). The verb '*see*' here and in the account of Nūḥ may mean the seeing of the eye and may mean thinking something which is probably the case case.

Remember when He appointed you successors to the people of Nūḥ and increased you greatly in stature.

Khulafā' is the masculine plural of *khalīfah* and the meaning is *khalā'if*. Allah was gracious to them by making them inhabitants of the earth after the people of Nūh. In '*and increased you greatly in stature*', the word *baṣṭah* is written with a *ṣād* rather than a *sīn* because it is followed by *ṭā'* and it means that they were tall in stature and large in body. Ibn 'Abbās said, 'The tallest of them was a hundred cubits in height, and the shortest sixty cubits.' This increase is over and above the stature of their ancestors. It is said that it is over and above the stature of the people of Nūḥ. Wahb said, 'The head of one of them was like an immense dome. Wild beasts could hatch in a man's eye-socket. The same was true of their nostrils.' Shakhr ibn Ḥawshab related that Abū Hurayrah said, 'A man of the people of 'Ād could pick up two stone lintels. If five hundred men of this community were to get together to move it, they would not be able to do so. If one of them were to press hard on the earth with his foot, it would sink into it.'

In '*remember Allah's blessings*,' the singular can be *ilā*, *ily*, *ilw* and *alā*, like *ānā'* whose singular can be *innā*, *iniyy*, *inuw* and *anā*.

قَالُوٓاْ أَجِئۡتَنَا لِنَعۡبُدَ ٱللَّهَ وَحۡدَهُۥ وَنَذَرَ مَا كَانَ يَعۡبُدُ ءَابَآؤُنَا
فَأۡتِنَا بِمَا تَعِدُنَآ إِن كُنتَ مِنَ ٱلصَّٰدِقِينَ ﴿٧٠﴾ قَالَ قَدۡ وَقَعَ عَلَيۡكُم
مِّن رَّبِّكُمۡ رِجۡسٞ وَغَضَبٌۚ أَتُجَٰدِلُونَنِي فِيٓ أَسۡمَآءٖ سَمَّيۡتُمُوهَآ أَنتُمۡ
وَءَابَآؤُكُم مَّا نَزَّلَ ٱللَّهُ بِهَا مِن سُلۡطَٰنٖۚ فَٱنتَظِرُوٓاْ إِنِّي مَعَكُم
مِّنَ ٱلۡمُنتَظِرِينَ ﴿٧١﴾ فَأَنجَيۡنَٰهُ وَٱلَّذِينَ مَعَهُۥ بِرَحۡمَةٖ مِّنَّا وَقَطَعۡنَا دَابِرَ
ٱلَّذِينَ كَذَّبُواْ بِـَٔايَٰتِنَاۖ وَمَا كَانُواْ مُؤۡمِنِينَ ﴿٧٢﴾

70-72 They said, 'Have you come to us to make us worship Allah alone and abandon what our fathers used to worship? Then bring us what you have promised us if you are telling the truth.' He said, 'Punishment and anger have come down on you from your Lord. Do you argue with me regarding names which you and your forefathers invented and for which Allah has sent down no authority? Wait, then; I am waiting with you.' So We rescued him and those with him by mercy from Us, and We cut off the last remnant of those who denied Our Signs and were not believers.

They asked for the punishment, which He threatened them with and cautioned them about, and so he said to them, '*It has come down on you*,' meaning that it is bound to come. One says, 'The word and judgment have occurred,' in other words they are inevitable. It is similar to the words: '*Whenever the plague came down on them*' (7:134), meaning befell them, and: '*When the Word is justly carried out against them, We will produce a Beast from the earth may Allah bless him and grant him peace.*' (27:82) The word *rijs* means punishment. It is said that it refers to the rust on the heart which results from an increase in unbelief.

Do you argue with me regarding names which you and your forefathers invented and for which Allah has sent down no authority?

This means the idols which they worshipped which had different names. The phrase '*for which Allah has sent down no authority*' means you have no evidence to justify your worship of them. The name here means the named. It is similar to Allah's words: '*What you serve apart from Him are only names which you and your forefathers have made up.*' (27:23) These are names like al-'Uzzā from al-'Izz and al-A'azz, and al-Lāt which have neither might nor divinity. *Dābir* (last remnant) is the end of them. There is nothing left of them at all.

وَإِلَىٰ ثَمُودَ أَخَاهُمْ صَٰلِحًا قَالَ يَٰقَوْمِ ٱعْبُدُوا۟ ٱللَّهَ مَا لَكُم مِّنْ إِلَٰهٍ غَيْرُهُۥ قَدْ جَآءَتْكُم بَيِّنَةٌ مِّن رَّبِّكُمْ هَٰذِهِۦ نَاقَةُ ٱللَّهِ لَكُمْ ءَايَةً فَذَرُوهَا تَأْكُلْ فِىٓ أَرْضِ ٱللَّهِ وَلَا تَمَسُّوهَا بِسُوٓءٍ فَيَأْخُذَكُمْ عَذَابٌ أَلِيمٌ ﴿٧٣﴾

73 And to Thamūd We sent their brother Ṣāliḥ, who said, 'My people, worship Allah! You have no other god than Him. A Clear Sign has come to you from your Lord. This is the She-Camel of Allah as a Sign for you. Leave her alone to eat on Allah's earth and do not harm her in any way or a painful punishment will afflict you.

And to Thamūd We sent their brother Ṣāliḥ, who said,

The tribe of Thamūd descended from Thamūd ibn 'Ād ibn Iram ibn Sām ibn Nūh. He was one of the tribe of Jadīs. They had ample livelihood and then opposed Allah's command, worshipped other than Him, and corrupted the earth. So Allah sent them the Prophet Ṣāliḥ. He was Ṣāliḥ ibn 'Ubayd ibn Āsaf ibn Kāshih ibn 'Ubayd ibn Ḥādhir ibn Thamūd. They were an Arab people. Ṣaliḥ was from their middle class in lineage and the best of them in personal nobility. He called them to Allah Almighty until he was old and only a few persecuted people among them followed him.

Thamūd is not declined because it is the name of a tribe. Abū Ḥātim said that it is not declined because it is a foreign noun. An-Naḥḥās said, 'This is an error because it is derived from the noun *thamd*, which is a small amount of water.' Reciters recited: '*Inna Thamūdan*' (11:68) as the name of a water. The dwellings of Thamūd were located at al-Hijr between the Ḥijāz and Syria towards Wadī al-Qurā. They were descended from Sām ibn Nūḥ. It was called Thamūd due to lack of water, and this will be discussed in al-Hijr.

This is the She-Camel of Allah as a Sign for you.

A she-camel came out to them from hard rock when they asked him for a sign. It had one day when it drank all the water in the *wadī* and it gave them the like of it in milk and no milk was more pleasant and sweeter. It was according to their need because of the great number of them. Allah Almighty says: '*She has a time for drinking and you have a time for drinking – on specified days.*' (26:155) The she-camel is ascribed to Allah as creation is ascribed to the Creator. That implies honouring and specification.

Leave her alone to eat on Allah's earth

You do not have to provision or feed her.

وَاذْكُرُوٓاْ إِذْ جَعَلَكُمْ خُلَفَآءَ مِنۢ بَعْدِ عَادٍ وَبَوَّأَكُمْ فِى ٱلْأَرْضِ
تَتَّخِذُونَ مِن سُهُولِهَا قُصُورًا وَتَنْحِتُونَ ٱلْجِبَالَ بُيُوتًا
فَاذْكُرُوٓاْ ءَالَآءَ ٱللَّهِ وَلَا تَعْثَوْاْ فِى ٱلْأَرْضِ مُفْسِدِينَ ﴿٧٤﴾

74 Remember when He appointed you successors to 'Ād and settled you in the land. You built palaces on its plains and carved out houses from the mountains. Remember Allah's blessings and do not go about the earth, corrupting it.'

Remember when He appointed you successors to 'Ād and settled you in the land.

The phrase '*Settled you in the land*' contains some elision, implying, 'We settled you in dwellings in the earth.'

You built palaces on its plains and carved out houses from the mountains.

You built castles everywhere. The expression '*carved out houses from the mountains*' means 'made houses in the mountains' on account of the great height of their dwellings. Their roofs and foundations were in ruin before their dwellings vanished. Al-Ḥasan recited it with *fatḥah* on *ḥā'*, which is a dialect. This *āyah* is used as evidence by those who permit tall buildings such as castles and the like, which are also permitted by Allah's words: '*Say: "Who has forbidden the fine clothing Allah has produced for His slaves and the good kinds of provision?"*' (7:32) It was mentioned that a son of Muḥammad ibn Sīrīn built a house and spent a lot of money on it. That was mentioned to Muḥammad ibn Sīrīn who said, 'I do not see any harm in a man building something on which he spends. It is related that the Prophet ﷺ said, "When Allah gives blessing to a slave He likes the effect of His blessing to be seen on him." One of the signs of blessing is fine buildings and good clothing. Do you not see that it is permitted for someone to buy a beautiful slave-girl for a great price, when less than that would be enough for him? The same is true of buildings.'

Others disliked that, including al-Ḥasan al-Baṣrī and others. They used as evidence the words of the Prophet ﷺ, 'When Allah desires evil for a slave, he destroys his wealth in brick and clay.' In another report the Prophet ﷺ said, 'Whoever builds beyond what is enough for him will come bearing it on his neck on the Day of Rising.' This is what I say because of the words of the Prophet ﷺ, 'It is up to Allah Almighty to replace whatever a believer spends on maintenance except for what is spent on buildings or disobedience.' Jābir ibn 'Abdullāh related it and ad-Dāraquṭnī transmitted it. The Prophet ﷺ said, 'The son of Ādam has no right to other than these things: a house to live in, a garment with which to cover his nakedness, and hard bread and water.' At-Tirmidhī transmitted it.

Remember Allah's blessings

This indicates that unbelievers receive blessings. It was already mentioned in *Āl 'Imrān* (3:196-197). Corruption in the earth was mentioned in *al-Baqarah* (2:61). *'Ithy* and *'uthuw* are two dialectical forms.

قَالَ ٱلۡمَلَأُ ٱلَّذِينَ ٱسۡتَكۡبَرُواْ مِن قَوۡمِهِۦ لِلَّذِينَ ٱسۡتُضۡعِفُواْ لِمَنۡ ءَامَنَ
مِنۡهُمۡ أَتَعۡلَمُونَ أَنَّ صَٰلِحٗا مُّرۡسَلٞ مِّن رَّبِّهِۦۚ قَالُوٓاْ إِنَّا بِمَآ أُرۡسِلَ بِهِۦ
مُؤۡمِنُونَ ٧٥ قَالَ ٱلَّذِينَ ٱسۡتَكۡبَرُوٓاْ إِنَّا بِٱلَّذِيٓ ءَامَنتُم بِهِۦ كَٰفِرُونَ ٧٦

75-76 The ruling circle of those of his people who were arrogant said to those who were oppressed – those among them who believed – 'Do you know that Ṣāliḥ has been sent from his Lord?' They said, 'We believe in what he has been sent with.' Those who were arrogant said, 'We reject Him in whom you believe.'

The oppressed people were believers.

فَعَقَرُواْ ٱلنَّاقَةَ وَعَتَوۡاْ عَنۡ أَمۡرِ رَبِّهِمۡ وَقَالُواْ يَٰصَٰلِحُ ٱئۡتِنَا بِمَا
تَعِدُنَآ إِن كُنتَ مِنَ ٱلۡمُرۡسَلِينَ ٧٧ فَأَخَذَتۡهُمُ ٱلرَّجۡفَةُ فَأَصۡبَحُواْ فِي
دَارِهِمۡ جَٰثِمِينَ ٧٨ فَتَوَلَّىٰ عَنۡهُمۡ وَقَالَ يَٰقَوۡمِ لَقَدۡ أَبۡلَغۡتُكُمۡ
رِسَالَةَ رَبِّي وَنَصَحۡتُ لَكُمۡ وَلَٰكِن لَّا تُحِبُّونَ ٱلنَّٰصِحِينَ ٧٩

77-79 And they hamstrung the She-Camel, spurning their Lord's command, and said, 'Ṣāliḥ, bring us what you have promised us if you are one of the Messengers.' So the earthquake seized them and morning found them lying flattened in their homes. He turned away from them and said, 'My people, I transmitted my

Lord's message to you and gave you good counsel. However, you do not like good counsellors!'

And they hamstrung the She-Camel, spurning their Lord's command,

To hamstring (*'aqr*) is to inflict a type of injury. It is said that it is cutting a limb which can prove fatal. It is used for a horse when its legs are hit with a sword. Hamstrung horses are "*aqrā*'. The verb is also used for camels with a galled backs. Imru' al-Qays said:

You say, when we have been long in the saddle,
'You galled the back of my camel, Imru' al-Qays, so dismount.'

Al-Qushayri said that *'aqr* is exposing the hock of the camel. Then it is used for slaughtering because hamstringing is usually a reason for slaughtering.

There are different views about who did the hamstringing. The soundest of them in *Ṣaḥīḥ Muslim* is found in the *ḥadīth* of 'Abdullāh ibn Zam'ah: 'The Messenger of Allah ﷺ gave a speech and mentioned the person who hamstrung her. He said "'*When the worst of them rushed ahead*' (91:12) refers to a strong violent man, unassailable in his clan like Abū Zam'ah, who rushed ahead."' It is said that his name was Quddār ibn Sālif. It is said that their kingdom was ruled by a woman called Malkā who envied Ṣāliḥ when people started to incline towards him. She said to two women who had lovers who desired them, 'Do not give in to them. Ask them to slaughter the she-camel.' They did that. The two men went out and the she-camel took refuge in a narrow place and one of them shot it with an arrow and they killed it. Its foal went up to the rock from which it had emerged and grumbled three times. The rock opened and it entered it. It is also said that it is the Beast which will emerge at the end of time to people as will be made clear in *an-Naml*. Ibn Isḥāq said that the foal was followed by four people from those who hamstrung the camel: Miṣda' and his brother Dhu'awb. Miṣda' shot an arrow and it pierced its heart. Then he dragged it by the leg and put it with its mother and they ate them both together. The first account is sounder.

Ṣāliḥ told them, 'You have three days of your life left.' This is why it grunted three times. It is said that the man who hamstrung it had eight other men with him and they are those about whom Allah says: '*There were a group of nine men in the city*' (27:48), as will be explained in *an-Naml*. This is why Allah says: '*They called on their companion and he set to it and hamstrung her.*' (54:29) They used to drink and ran out of the water with which they used to mix their drink. It was the day of the milk of the she-camel. One of them went and waited for the people and said, 'I will spare people from it,' and he hamstrung it.

spurning their Lord's command

This means they were arrogant. The verb *'aṭā* means 'to be arrogant' and such a person is not prone to obedience. A night which is *'āṭī* is one which is very dark, as al-Khalīl states.

They said: 'Ṣāliḥ! Bring us what you have promised us'

This is a reference to the promised punishment. So the earthquake seized them, a very strong earthquake. It is said that it was a loud shout which seized their hearts, as in the story of Thamūd in *Sūrat Hūd* where it says that the Great Blast (*rajfah*) seized hold of them. The root of the verb *rajafa, yarjufu, rajf, rajafān* is movement with a sound. *Arjafa* is used for the wind causing a tree to rustle. We see this in Allah's words: '*On the Day the first Blast (rajfah) shudders (tarjufu).*' (79:6) A poet said:

When I saw that the time of the *ḥajj* had come,
the mounts of the people resounded (*tarjufu*) with them.

and morning found them lying flattened in their homes.

Dār (homes) means in their land. It is said that it is singular by way of being generic and means 'houses'. In another place we find '*diyār*' (11:68), meaning houses. The adjective '*flattened*' means on the ground on their knees and faces, as a bird perches (*jathama*). They became still due to the intensity of the punishment. The root *jathūm* refers to a hare and its like. *Majtham* is a bird's resting-place. Zuhayr said:

The wild cows and white deer are there, walking one behind the other,
while their young are rising from every resting-place (*majtham*).

It is said that they were burned by lightning and were dead in the morning except for one man who was in the Ḥaram of Allah. When he left the Ḥaram, what had struck his people also struck him.

He turned away from them and said, 'My people, I transmitted my Lord's message to you and gave you good counsel.'

'*He turned away from them*' means 'he despaired of them'. It could be that he said these words to them before they died, and it is also possible that he said it after they were dead, like the words of the Prophet ﷺ to the people of Badr, 'Have you found what your Lord promised you to be true?' He was asked, 'Do you speak to those corpses?' He replied, 'You do not hear better than they do, but they cannot answer.' The first is more evident as indicated by the words: '*However, you do not like good counsellors!*', implying that they did not accept his counsel.

وَلُوطًا إِذْ قَالَ لِقَوْمِهِۦٓ أَتَأْتُونَ ٱلْفَٰحِشَةَ مَا سَبَقَكُم بِهَا
مِنْ أَحَدٍ مِّنَ ٱلْعَٰلَمِينَ ﴿٨٠﴾

80 And Lūṭ, when he said to his people, 'Do you commit an obscenity not perpetrated before you by anyone in all the worlds?

And Lūṭ, when he said to his people,

Al-Farrā' said, 'Lūṭ is derived from the words, "This is glued (*alyaṭ*) to my heart," meaning it clings to it.' An-Naḥḥās said, 'Az-Zajjāj said, "Some grammarians (meaning al-Farra') claimed that Lūṭ can be derived from *lāṭa*, meaning 'smoothed with clay'."' He said that this is an error because foreign nouns, like Isḥāq, are not derived. It is not said that Isḥāq is derived from *suḥq* which means distance. Lūṭ is declined because it is light since it is composed of three letters and it is silent in the middle. An-Naqqāsh said that Lūt is a foreign word, not Arabic. As for using *lāṭa* for applying clay to a basin and other usages, they are sound, but Lūṭ is a foreign name like Ibrāhīm and Isḥāq. Sībawayh said that Nūh and Lūṭ are foreign words, but they are declined because they are light. Allah sent him to a nation called Sodom. He was the nephew of Ibrāhīm. 'Lūṭ' is in the accusative as the object of '*We sent*' as was previously mentioned, or it can be accusative by an implied 'Remember...'

'Do you commit an obscenity not perpetrated before you by anyone in all the worlds?

This means having sex with men. Allah mentioned it as '*an obscenity*' to clarify that it is fornication, as the Almighty says: '*Do not go near fornication. It is an indecent act.*' (17:32) Scholars disagree about what is obliged in terms of punishment for anyone who does that although there is a consensus that it is forbidden. Mālik said that he should be stoned, whether *muḥṣan* or not. The one to whom it is done is stoned if he has reached puberty. It is also related from him that he should be stoned if he is *muḥṣan*, and imprisoned and disciplined if he is not a *muḥṣan*. That is the position of 'Aṭā', an-Nakhā'ī, Ibn al-Musayyab and others. Abū Ḥanīfah said that both the *muḥṣan* and others should be disciplined. That is also related from Mālik. Ash-Shāfi'ī said that he receives the *ḥadd* punishment for fornication by analogy with it.

Mālik used as evidence Allah's words: '*We rained down on them stones of hard-baked clay.*' (15:74) That was a punishment for them and repayment for their action. If it is said that for two reasons there is no evidence in that: firstly the people of Lūṭ were punished for unbelief and denial like other nations and secondly both their young and old were involved in it which indicates that it is outside of the area of the *ḥudūd*, the response is that the first objection is an error. Allah Almighty reports that they were committing acts of disobedience and that He seized them on account of those actions, and this was part of that. As for the second objection, some of them did it and some were pleased with it, and so all were punished because of the silence of the majority about it. That is the wisdom of Allah and His *sunnah* with His slaves. There remains the question of the punishment for those who did it continuously, and Allah knows best.

Abū Dāwūd, Ibn Mājah, at-Tirmidhī, an-Nasā'ī and ad-Dāraquṭnī related that the Messenger of Allah ﷺ said, 'If you find someone doing the action of the people of Lūt, kill the doer and the one to whom it is done.' This is the wording of Abū Dāwūd and Ibn Mājah. At-Tirmidhī said, 'whether *muḥṣan* or not.' Abū Dāwūd and ad-Dāraquṭnī related something from Ibn 'Abbās about a virgin who was found engaged in sodomy. He said, 'He should be stoned.' It is related that Abū Bakr as-Ṣiddīq burned a man called al-Fujā'ah when he performed the deeds of the people of Lūt. That was also the opinion of 'Alī ibn Abī Ṭālib. When Khālid ibn al-Walīd wrote to Abū Bakr about that, Abū Bakr and the Companions of the Prophet ﷺ met and he consulted them about it. 'Alī said, 'This wrong action was not committed any of the nations except for one and Allah did what you know to them. I think that he should be burned with fire.' The Companions of the Messenger of Allah ﷺ agreed that he should be burned with fire. Abū Bakr wrote to Khālid ibn al-Walīd that he should be burned, and so he burned him. Then Ibn az-Zubayr burned them in his time. Hishām ibn al-Walīd burned them. Then Khālid al-Qasrī burned them in Iraq.

It is related that seven were arrested for sodomy in the time of Ibn az-Zubayr. He asked about them and found that four were *muḥṣan*, and so he ordered that they should be taken out of the Ḥaram and stoned to death. He applied the *ḥadd* punishment to the other three. Ibn 'Abbās and Ibn 'Umar were with him and did not object to that. It is what ash-Shāfi'ī believed. Ibn al-'Arabī said, 'What Mālik believed is more correct. It is the sounder transmission and has stronger support.' The Ḥanafīs further add: 'The punishment for fornication is known. When this disobedience is other than it, it is obliged that they do not share with it in its *ḥadd* punishment.' They recount a *ḥadīth* about this: 'Whoever applies the *ḥadd* punishment to other than the *ḥadd* has transgressed and done wrong.' It is also a form of sexual intercourse which is not connected to making re-marriage lawful or rendering someone *muḥṣan*, and does not oblige a dower or the establishment of a lineage, and so the *ḥadd* punishment is not connected to it.

If someone goes to an animal for sex, it is said that neither he nor the animal is killed and it is also said that they are both killed. Ibn al-Mundhir related that from Abū Salamah ibn 'Abd ar-Raḥmān. There is a *ḥadīth* on the topic which Abū Dāwūd and ad-Dāraquṭnī related from Ibn 'Abbās in which the Messenger of Allah ﷺ said, 'If someone has sexual intercourse with an animal, kill him and kill the animal with him.' He said, 'We asked Ibn 'Abbās, "What about the animal?" He answered, "I do not think that he said that, unless it is that he disliked for its meat to be eaten when that action had been done with it."' Ibn al-Mundhir said, 'If the *ḥadīth* is firm, then the view must be what it contains. If it is not firm, then the one who does that must ask for Allah's forgiveness greatly. If the judge punishes him, it is good, and Allah knows best.' It is said that the animal should be killed so that it does not produce tainted offspring, and therefore killing is for welfare in this sense as well as what has come of the *Sunnah* about it. Allah knows best. Abū Dāwūd related that Ibn 'Abbas said, 'There is no *ḥadd* punishment for someone who commits bestiality.' Abū Dāwūd said that that is what 'Aṭā' said. Al-Ḥakam said, 'I think that he should be flogged, but it should not reach the level of the *ḥadd*.' Al-Ḥasan said that he is in the position of a fornicator. Az-Zuhrī said that he should be flogged with a hundred lashes whether he is *muḥṣan* or not. Mālik, Ath-Thawrī, Aḥmad and the people of opinion say that he should be disciplined. That is also related from 'Aṭā', an-Nakhaʿī and al-Ḥakam. The transmission from ash-Shāfiʿī varies. This is more likely according to his position about this matter. Jābir ibn Zayd said that the *ḥadd* punishment is carried out on him unless he owns the animal.

not perpetrated before you by anyone in all the worlds

'*Min*' is used here to include all of the genus, meaning that there was no sodomy in a nation before the people of Lūṭ. The atheists claim that that existed before them. The truth is what was related by the Qur'an. An-Naqqāsh related that Iblīs was the basis of their action by calling them to himself – may Allah curse him. They used to marry one another. Al-Ḥasan said, 'They used to do that to strangers and did not do it to one another.' Ibn Mājah related from Jābir ibn 'Abdullah that the Messenger of Allah ﷺ said, 'What I most fear for my community is the action of the people of Lūt.' Muḥammad ibn Sīrīn said, 'There are no animals which perform the action of the people of Lūṭ except for pigs and donkeys.'

إِنَّكُمْ لَتَأْتُونَ ٱلرِّجَالَ شَهْوَةً مِّن دُونِ ٱلنِّسَآءِ بَلْ أَنتُمْ قَوْمٌ مُّسْرِفُونَ ﴿٨١﴾

81 You come with lust to men instead of women. You are indeed a depraved people.'

'You (*innakum*)': Nāfi' recites it with a single *hamzah* with a *kasrah* as explaining the previously mentioned indecency. It is not good to make it interrogative because it separates what is after it from what is before it. The rest recite it with two *hamzah*s as a question which means rebuke ('Do you come?). That is good because what is before it and after it are separate statements. Abū 'Ubayd, al-Kisā'ī and others prefer the first view. They used as corroborating evidence Allah's words in 21:34: '*We did not give any human being before you immortality. And if you die, will they then be immortal*?' where He does not use the interrogative *alif*, and in 3:144: '*If he were to die or be killed, would you turn on your heels*?' where again, He does not use the interrogative *alif.* This is an extremely egregious error because they are comparing two things which are not similar. The precondition and its apodosis are treated as one thing, as are the inceptive and the predicate. It is not permitted for there to be two interrogatives about the same thing and so it is not permitted to have a second interrogative *alif.* In the story of Lūṭ there are these two sentences. You can ask about either of them. This is the view of al-Khalīl and Sībawayh. An-Naḥḥās, Makkī and others chose it.

The noun '*lust*' is in the accusative by the verbal noun, namely 'you desire them with lust.' It is permitted that it be in the place of an adverbial *ḥāl.* The words: '*You are indeed a depraved people*' is like: '*You are a people who have overstepped the limits.*' (26:166) They share in this depravity.

وَمَا كَانَ جَوَابَ قَوْمِهِۦٓ إِلَّآ أَن قَالُوٓاْ أَخْرِجُوهُم مِّن قَرْيَتِكُمْ إِنَّهُمْ أُنَاسٌ يَتَطَهَّرُونَ ﴿٨٢﴾ فَأَنجَيْنَٰهُ وَأَهْلَهُۥٓ إِلَّا ٱمْرَأَتَهُۥ كَانَتْ مِنَ ٱلْغَٰبِرِينَ ﴿٨٣﴾

82-83 The only answer of his people was to say, 'Expel them from your city! They are people who keep themselves pure!' So We rescued him and his family – except for his wife. She was one of those who stayed behind.

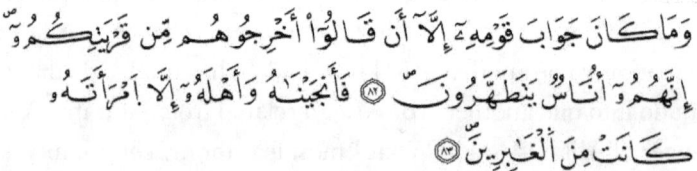

They wanted to expel Lūṭ and his followers. The meaning of '*keep themselves pure*' is that they refrain from doing this action. It is said that a man keeps himself pure in refraining from wrong action. Qatādah said, 'They censured him, by Allah, without there being a fault.' '*Those who stayed behind*' are those who remained to suffer the punishment of Allah. Ibn 'Abbās and Qatādah said that. The verb *ghabara* is used of something when it remains, and goes on. It is one of the words which can have opposite meanings. Some people said that the one who goes on is *'ābir* and the one who remains is *ghābir*. Ibn Fāris related that in *al-Mujmal*. Az-Zajjāj said that it means 'among those without salvation'. It is said that it is because of the great length of their life. An-Naḥḥās said that Abū 'Ubayd believed that the meaning is 'among those who live long,' implying that they were senile. Usually *ghābir* means 'one who remains'. [POEM]

وَأَمْطَرْنَا عَلَيْهِم مَّطَرًا فَانظُرْ كَيْفَ كَانَ عَاقِبَةُ الْمُجْرِمِينَ ﴿٨٤﴾

84 We rained down a rain upon them. See the final fate of the evildoers!

Lūṭ travelled with his people as Allah described, '*in the middle of the night*' (11:81) and then Allah gave the command to Jibrīl and he put his wing under their cities, ripped them up and raised them until the people of heaven could hear the sound of cocks and barking of dogs. Then he turned it upside down and rained down on them stones of baked clay. It is said that the stones also fell on those who were not there with them. The rain also caught the wife of Lūṭ. There was a stone in it that killed her. There were four towns involved. It is said that there were five towns which contained 400,000 people. The full story of Lūṭ will be mentioned in *Sūrat Hūd*, Allah willing.

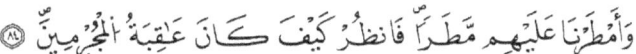

وَإِلَىٰ مَدْيَنَ أَخَاهُمْ شُعَيْبًا قَالَ يَٰقَوْمِ ٱعْبُدُوا۟ ٱللَّهَ مَا لَكُم مِّنْ
إِلَٰهٍ غَيْرُهُۥ قَدْ جَآءَتْكُم بَيِّنَةٌ مِّن رَّبِّكُمْ فَأَوْفُوا۟
ٱلْكَيْلَ وَٱلْمِيزَانَ وَلَا تَبْخَسُوا۟ ٱلنَّاسَ أَشْيَآءَهُمْ وَلَا
تُفْسِدُوا۟ فِى ٱلْأَرْضِ بَعْدَ إِصْلَٰحِهَا ذَٰلِكُمْ خَيْرٌ لَّكُمْ إِن
كُنتُم مُّؤْمِنِينَ ﴿٨٥﴾ وَلَا تَقْعُدُوا۟ بِكُلِّ صِرَٰطٍ تُوعِدُونَ
وَتَصُدُّونَ عَن سَبِيلِ ٱللَّهِ مَنْ ءَامَنَ بِهِۦ وَتَبْغُونَهَا عِوَجًا وَٱذْكُرُوٓا۟
إِذْ كُنتُمْ قَلِيلًا فَكَثَّرَكُمْ وَٱنظُرُوا۟ كَيْفَ كَانَ عَٰقِبَةُ
ٱلْمُفْسِدِينَ ﴿٨٦﴾ وَإِن كَانَ طَآئِفَةٌ مِّنكُمْ ءَامَنُوا۟ بِٱلَّذِىٓ أُرْسِلْتُ
بِهِۦ وَطَآئِفَةٌ لَّمْ يُؤْمِنُوا۟ فَٱصْبِرُوا۟ حَتَّىٰ يَحْكُمَ ٱللَّهُ بَيْنَنَا وَهُوَ
خَيْرُ ٱلْحَٰكِمِينَ ﴿٨٧﴾

85-87 And to Madyan We sent their brother Shu'ayb who said, 'My people, worship Allah! You have no other god than Him. A Clear Sign has come to you from your Lord. Give full measure and full weight. Do not diminish people's goods. Do not cause corruption in the land after it has been put right. That is better for you if you are believers. Do not lie in wait on every pathway, threatening people, barring those who believe from the Way of Allah, desiring to make it crooked. Remember when you were few and He increased your number: see the final fate of the corrupters! There is a group of you who believe in what I have been sent with and a group who do not, so be steadfast until Allah judges between us. He is the best of judges.'

It is said that Madyan is the name of a land and region and it is also said that it is the name of a tribe like Bakr and Tamīm. It is said that they were among the descendants of Madyan, son of Ibrāhīm, the Prophet. Anyone who thinks that Madyan is the name of a man does not decline it because it is a foreign name. If someone thinks that it is the name of a tribe or a land, then it is even more appropriate for it not to be declined. Al-Mahdawī said, 'It is related that he was the son of Lūṭ's daughter. Makkī said, 'He was the husband of the daughter of Lūṭ.'

There is disagreement about the lineage of Shu'ayb. 'Aṭā', Ibn Isḥāq and others said that he was the son of Mīkīl ibn Yashjar ibn Madyan ibn Ibrāhīm. His name in Syriac was Yabrūt and his mother was Mīkā'īl, the daughter of Lūṭ. Ash-Sharqī ibn al-Quṭāmī claimed that Shu'ayb was the son of 'Ayfā' ibn Yawbab ibn Madyan ibn Ibrāhīm. Ibn Sam'ān claimed that Shu'ayb was the son of Jaziyy ibn Yashjar ibn Lāwī ibn Ya'qūb ibn Isḥāq ibn Ibrāhīm. Shu'ayb is the diminutive of Sha'b or Shi'b. Qatādah said that he is Shu'ayb ibn Yawbab. It is said that he was Shu'ayb ibn Ṣafwān ibn 'Ayfā' ibn Thābit ibn Madyan ibn Ibrāhīm. Allah knows best. He was blind. That is why his people said, '*We see you are weak among us.*' (11:91) He was called 'the Orator of the Prophets' because of his excellence in answering his people. His people disbelieved in Allah and skimped in their weight and measure.

A Clear Sign has come to you from your Lord.

This was Shu'ayb bringing the Message. It is not mentioned in the Qur'an that he performed any miracle. It is said that his miracle is what al-Kisā'ī mentioned in the stories of the Prophets.

Do not diminish people's goods.

Bakhs is decrease. In goods it arises through finding fault or carping about them or by cheating about the price. Trickery is in making the measure less and decreasing it. All of that is consuming wealth falsely. That was forbidden in prior communities on the tongues of the Messengers, may Allah bless all of them. Allah is enough for us and the best protector.

Do not cause corruption in the land after it has been put right.

This is added to '*Do not diminish.*' It is an expression which includes all corruption, both small and great. Ibn 'Abbas said, 'Before Allah sent Shu'ayb as a Messenger, acts of disobedience were committed in the land, unlawful things made lawful and blood was spilled in it.' He said, 'That was its corruption. When Allah sent Shu'ayb and he called them to Allah, the land was put right. Every Prophet sent to his people is what puts things right.'

Do not lie in wait on every pathway,

Allah forbade them to sit on the roads and bar people from the path which leads to obedience to Allah. They used to threaten to punish those who believed. Scholars disagree about the meaning of their sitting on the roads, and have three ideas about it. Ibn 'Abbās, Qatādah, Mujāhid and as-Suddī said that they used to sit on the roads which led to Shu'ayb and threaten those who wanted to come there and they would bar the way to them. They would say, 'He is a liar. Do not go to him,' just as Quraysh used to do with the Prophet ﷺ. This is the literal meaning of the *āyah*. Abū Hurayrah said, 'This is a prohibition of sitting on the road and taking spoils. That was part of what they did.' It is related that the Prophet ﷺ said, 'During the Night Journey, I saw a piece of wood on the road which tore every garment which passed it and pierced everything. I asked, "What is this, Jibrīl?" He answered, "This is an example of the people of your community who sit on the road and stop people." Then he recited: "*Do not lie in wait on every pathway, threatening people.*"' Thieves and highwaymen have already been discussed (4:16). Praise belongs to Allah.

As-Suddī also said that they were tax-collectors and bailsmen. Our scholars say that today they are like those tax-collectors who extort financial impositions they are not legally entitled to by force and compulsion. They add what is not permitted to people's basic liability in *zakāt*, inheritance, and various taxes. They are those who are set up on the roads and other places. This is frequently found and is done in all lands. It is one of the greatest, most terrible and worst of wrong actions. It is usurpation, injustice and oppression of people, and spreading wrongdoing, acting on it, remaining on it and affirming it. The worst of it is dealt with by the *Sharī'ah* and the judgments of judges. We belong to Allah and to Him we return. Only the slightest trace of Islam remains and there is nothing of the *dīn* except its name. This view is supported by what was mentioned about weighing and measures and short-changing in respect of property.

barring those who believe from the Way of Allah, desiring to make it crooked.

The pronoun in *bihi* can refer to the Name of Allah and can refer to Shu'ayb in the view of those who say that sitting on the road means to block it and it may refer to the path. In respect of the word '*crooked*', Abū 'Ubaydah and az-Zajjāj said that '*iwaj* is used for ideas and '*awaj* for bodies.

Remember when you were few and He increased your number:

It means: 'when He made your numbers great, or made you great with wealth after poverty, meaning 'you were poor and He made you rich.' '*So be steadfast*' is not a command to remain in disbelief, but is rather a threat. Allah says: '*There is a group of you*' and '*group*' (*ṭā'ifah*) is masculine on account of the meaning. If the word were taken literally, the verb would have been '*kānat*' (feminine).

قَالَ ٱلْمَلَأُ ٱلَّذِينَ ٱسْتَكْبَرُوا۟ مِن قَوْمِهِۦ لَنُخْرِجَنَّكَ يَٰشُعَيْبُ وَٱلَّذِينَ ءَامَنُوا۟ مَعَكَ مِن
قَرْيَتِنَآ أَوْ لَتَعُودُنَّ فِى مِلَّتِنَا قَالَ أَوَلَوْ كُنَّا كَٰرِهِينَ ﴿٨٨﴾ قَدِ ٱفْتَرَيْنَا عَلَى
ٱللَّهِ كَذِبًا إِنْ عُدْنَا فِى مِلَّتِكُم بَعْدَ إِذْ نَجَّىٰنَا ٱللَّهُ مِنْهَا وَمَا يَكُونُ لَنَآ أَن نَّعُودَ
فِيهَآ إِلَّآ أَن يَشَآءَ ٱللَّهُ رَبُّنَا وَسِعَ رَبُّنَا كُلَّ شَىْءٍ عِلْمًا عَلَى ٱللَّهِ تَوَكَّلْنَا رَبَّنَا
ٱفْتَحْ بَيْنَنَا وَبَيْنَ قَوْمِنَا بِٱلْحَقِّ وَأَنتَ خَيْرُ ٱلْفَٰتِحِينَ ﴿٨٩﴾

88-89 The ruling circle of those of his people who were arrogant said, 'We will drive you out of our city, Shu'ayb, you and those who believe along with you, unless you return to our religion.' He said, 'What, even though we detest it? We would be inventing lies against Allah if we returned to your religion after Allah has saved us from it. We could never return to it unless Allah our Lord so willed. Our Lord encompasses everything in His knowledge. We have put our trust in Allah. Our Lord, judge between us and our people with truth. You are the best of judges.'

The ruling circle of those of his people who were arrogant said,

This was already discussed. The meaning of '*unless you return to our religion*' is 'to become part of our religion'. It is said that the followers of Shu'ayb had been unbelievers before. So it means, 'return to us as you were before'. Az-Zajjāj said that '*return*' may mean '*begin*'. One says, 'So-and-so reverted to something disliked,' meaning that he did it even though he had had nothing to do with that disliked thing before that, i.e. 'I found that in him.' Shu'ayb said to them, "'*What, even though we detest it?*,' meaning: 'Will you force us to do it even though we do not want to do it?' i.e. to leave our homeland or to revert to your religion. 'If you do this, then you are doing something terrible.'

We would be inventing lies against Allah if we returned to your religion after Allah has saved us from it.

'*It*' in '*saved from it*' means that there is no prospect of us reverting to your religion. '*We could never return to it unless Allah our Lord so willed.*' Abū Isḥāq az-Zajjāj said, 'This means that it could only happen by the will of Allah Almighty.' He said, 'This is the view of the people of the *Sunnah*, namely: 'We would only revert to unbelief if Allah willed that.' The exception is one denoting separation. It is said that the exception here is by way of submission to Allah Almighty, as in the words:

'My success is only by Allah.' (11:88) The evidence for this is that after it he says: *'Our Lord encompasses everything in His knowledge.'* It is said that it is like someone's words: 'I will not speak to you until the crow becomes white and the camel goes through the eye of a needle.' The crow will never become white and the camel will never go through the eye of a needle.

Our Lord encompasses everything in His knowledge.

This means the knowledge of what was and what will be. The noun *'knowledge'* is in the accusative for the distinction. It is said that the meaning of *'We could never return to it'* means to the town after they hated being there. 'Rather we will leave the town and emigrate elsewhere.' *'Unless Allah our Lord so willed'* that we return to it. That is unlikely because one uses *li* and not *fī* for that meaning.

We have put our trust in Allah.

'We have put our trust in Allah' means 'We have relied on Him.' It has already been discussed (3:122).

Our Lord, judge between us and our people with truth

Qatādah said, 'Allah sent him to two nations, the people of Madyan and the people of Al-Aykah.' Ibn 'Abbās said, 'Shu'ayb prayed a lot. After a long time when his people continued in their unbelief and error, and he despaired of their being put right, he invoked against them, saying: "*Our Lord, judge between us and our people with truth. You are the best of judges.*"' Allah answered his prayer and destroyed them with an earthquake.

وَقَالَ ٱلْمَلَأُ ٱلَّذِينَ كَفَرُوا۟ مِن قَوْمِهِۦ لَئِنِ ٱتَّبَعْتُمْ شُعَيْبًا إِنَّكُمْ إِذًا
لَّخَـٰسِرُونَ ﴿٩٠﴾ فَأَخَذَتْهُمُ ٱلرَّجْفَةُ فَأَصْبَحُوا۟ فِى دَارِهِمْ جَـٰثِمِينَ ﴿٩١﴾ ٱلَّذِينَ كَذَّبُوا۟
شُعَيْبًا كَأَن لَّمْ يَغْنَوْا۟ فِيهَا ٱلَّذِينَ كَذَّبُوا۟ شُعَيْبًا كَانُوا۟ هُمُ ٱلْخَـٰسِرِينَ ﴿٩٢﴾
فَتَوَلَّىٰ عَنْهُمْ وَقَالَ يَـٰقَوْمِ لَقَدْ أَبْلَغْتُكُمْ رِسَـٰلَـٰتِ رَبِّى وَنَصَحْتُ لَكُمْ
فَكَيْفَ ءَاسَىٰ عَلَىٰ قَوْمٍ كَـٰفِرِينَ ﴿٩٣﴾

90-93 The ruling circle of those of his people who disbelieved said, 'If you follow Shu'ayb, you will definitely be lost.' So the earthquake seized them and morning found them lying flattened in their homes. As for those who denied Shu'ayb, it was as if they had never lived there. It was the people who denied Shu'ayb

who were the lost. So he turned away from them and said, 'My people, I transmitted My Lord's message to you and gave you good counsel. Why should I grieve for an unbelieving people?' The ruling circle of those of his people who disbelieved said, 'If you follow Shu'ayb, you will definitely be lost.'

They said this to those under them. '*If you follow Shu'ayb, you will definitely be lost*,' in other words destroyed. '*So the earthquake seized them*': it is said it was an earthquake or the Shout. The People of al-Aykah were destroyed by the Shadow, as will come.

As for those who denied Shu'ayb, it was as if they had never lived there.

Al-Jurjānī said that it is said that this is a new sentence, meaning that those who denied Shu'ayb became as if they were dead. The verb '*yaghnaw*' means 'stayed' in respect of a place. The people remained in their houses, i.e. continued to be there for a long time. The noun *maghnā* means a house and its plural is *maghānī*. Labīd said:

'I remained (*ghanītu*) for a time…'

Ḥātim Ṭayy said:

We lived (*ghanīnā*) for a time in poverty and in wealth,
as time has days of hardship and days of ease.
We wore the vicissitudes of time, both gentle and harsh.
Time made us taste each of them.
Our wealth did not make us prouder towards relatives,
and I do not demean my lineage.

It was the people who denied Shu'ayb who were the lost.

This is the beginning of a statement which stresses censure and blame. It is repeated to exalt the matter and stress its great import. When they said, 'Whoever follows Shu'ayb is lost,' Allah said, 'It is the ones who said this who are lost.' His words: '*Why should I grieve for an unbelieving people?*' mean 'feel sorrow concerning them'. The verb is *asiya*, and the person feeling sorrow is '*āsī*'.

وَمَآ أَرۡسَلۡنَا فِي قَرۡيَةٖ مِّن نَّبِيٍّ إِلَّآ أَخَذۡنَآ أَهۡلَهَا بِٱلۡبَأۡسَآءِ وَٱلضَّرَّآءِ لَعَلَّهُمۡ
يَضَّرَّعُونَ ﴿٩٤﴾ ثُمَّ بَدَّلۡنَا مَكَانَ ٱلسَّيِّئَةِ ٱلۡحَسَنَةَ حَتَّىٰ عَفَواْ وَّقَالُواْ قَدۡ
مَسَّ ءَابَآءَنَا ٱلضَّرَّآءُ وَٱلسَّرَّآءُ فَأَخَذۡنَٰهُم بَغۡتَةٗ وَهُمۡ لَا يَشۡعُرُونَ ﴿٩٥﴾

94-95 We have never sent a Prophet to any city without seizing its people with hardship and distress so that hopefully they would be humble. Then We gave them good in exchange for evil until they increased in number and said, 'Our forefathers too underwent both hardship and ease.' Then We seized them suddenly when they were not expecting it.

'We have never sent a Prophet to any city' contains something elided, which is: 'whose people rejected him,' 'without seizing them'. The terms '*hardship and distress*' have already been mentioned (2:177). The words '*Then We gave them good in exchange for evil,*' mean fertility in exchange for drought and '*until they increased in number*' means became great in number, as Ibn 'Abbās said. Ibn Zayd said that their wealth and children became abundant. The verb *'afā* is one of those words which can mean opposites, meaning both to become abundant and to be effaced. Allah informs us that He seized them with hardship and gave them ease, but they did not abandon their behaviour nor were they thankful. They said, '"*Our forefathers too underwent both hardship and ease,*" so we are like them.' '*Then We seized them suddenly*' so that their regret would be overwhelming.

وَلَوۡ أَنَّ أَهۡلَ ٱلۡقُرَىٰٓ ءَامَنُواْ وَٱتَّقَوۡاْ لَفَتَحۡنَا عَلَيۡهِم بَرَكَٰتٖ مِّنَ ٱلسَّمَآءِ وَٱلۡأَرۡضِ
وَلَٰكِن كَذَّبُواْ فَأَخَذۡنَٰهُم بِمَا كَانُواْ يَكۡسِبُونَ ﴿٩٦﴾

96 If only the people of the cities had believed and been godfearing, We would have opened up to them blessings from heaven and earth. But they denied the truth so We seized them for what they earned.

If only the people of the cities had believed and been godfearing,

A city is called *qaryah* since people gather in it. When the verb *qarā* is used in respect of water, it means collect. It was discussed in *al-Baqarah.* (2:58) The verb '*believed*' means 'affirmed the truth' and '*been godfearing*' means 'guarded themselves against *shirk.*'

We would have opened up to them blessings from heaven and earth.

This refers to water and plants and is about the specific people who were already mentioned. The believers are tested by constriction in their livelihood and for them that is expiation for their wrong actions. Do you not see that Allah reported that Nūḥ said to his people: *'Ask forgiveness of your Lord. Truly He is Endlessly Forgiving. He will send heaven down on you in abundant rain'* (81:10-11) and: *'Then repent to Him. He will send heaven down to you in abundant rain.'* (11:52). He promised them rain and fertility in particular. This is indicated His words: *'But they denied the truth so We seized them for what they earned,'* implying that they denied the Messengers while the believers affirmed and did not deny them.

أَفَأَمِنَ أَهْلُ ٱلْقُرَىٰٓ أَن يَأْتِيَهُم بَأْسُنَا بَيَٰتًا وَهُمْ نَآئِمُونَ ﴿٩٧﴾ أَوَأَمِنَ أَهْلُ
ٱلْقُرَىٰٓ أَن يَأْتِيَهُم بَأْسُنَا ضُحًى وَهُمْ يَلْعَبُونَ ﴿٩٨﴾

97-98 Do the people of the cities feel secure against Our violent force coming down on them in the night while they are asleep? Or do the people of the cities feel secure against Our violent force coming down on them in the day while they are playing games?

This is a question which expects a negative response. The *fā'* is a conjunction as we see elsewhere. What is meant by *'cities'* here is Makkah and the surrounding area because they denied Muḥammad ﷺ. It is said that it is general to all cities. The *'violent force'* is Allah's punishment. *Bayāt* means 'at night'. *'Or do'* is recited by the people of Makkah and Madīnah and Ibn 'Āmir as *'aw'* with a *sukūn* on the *wāw* of the conjunction highlighting the possibility of it happening. The meaning is: 'Or did they feel safe from these types of punishments?' implying 'If you feel safe from them, you still are not safe from the punishment of the Next World.' It is permitted that *aw* be for one of the two things. The rest recite it with a *fatḥah* on the *hamzah* after it and make it the *wāw* of the conjunction and add the *alif* of the question to it (*a wa*).

The meaning of the phrase *'in the day while they are playing games'* means that they are involved in something that is of no benefit to them. It is said that each is involved in something that will harm them and their playing will be of no use to them. An-Naḥḥās mentioned it. According to *aṣ-Ṣiḥāḥ*, *la'ib* (*playing*) is well known and *la'b* means the same. The verb is *la'iba* and *tala''aba* is to play time after time. A man who is *til'ābah* plays often. *Tal'ab* is a verbal noun. *La'ūb* is a coquettish girl.

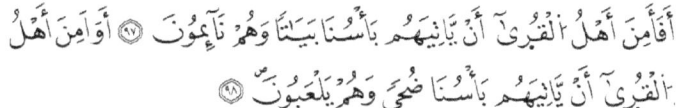

أَفَأَمِنُوا۟ مَكْرَ ٱللَّهِ ۚ فَلَا يَأْمَنُ مَكْرَ ٱللَّهِ إِلَّا ٱلْقَوْمُ ٱلْخَٰسِرُونَ ﴿٩٩﴾

99 Do they feel secure against Allah's devising? No one feels secure against Allah's devising except for those who are lost.

The word '*devising*' means His punishment and repayment for their devising. It is said that His devising is drawing them on by means of blessings and good health.

أَوَلَمْ يَهْدِ لِلَّذِينَ يَرِثُونَ ٱلْأَرْضَ مِنۢ بَعْدِ أَهْلِهَآ أَن لَّوْ نَشَآءُ
أَصَبْنَٰهُم بِذُنُوبِهِمْ ۚ وَنَطْبَعُ عَلَىٰ قُلُوبِهِمْ فَهُمْ لَا يَسْمَعُونَ ﴿١٠٠﴾

100 Is it not clear to those who have inherited the earth after these people that, if We wanted to, We could strike them for their wrong actions, sealing up their hearts so that they cannot hear?

'*Yahdī*' here means 'make clear'. '*Those who have inherited the earth*' is a reference to the unbelievers of Makkah and those around them. '*We could strike them*' means seize them, and '*their wrong actions*' are their unbelief and denial. '*Sealing up*' starts a new sentence, or it may be added to '*strike them*', i.e. strike them and seal them up. The past tense is used here with a future meaning.

تِلْكَ ٱلْقُرَىٰ نَقُصُّ عَلَيْكَ مِنْ أَنۢبَآئِهَا ۚ وَلَقَدْ جَآءَتْهُمْ رُسُلُهُم
بِٱلْبَيِّنَٰتِ فَمَا كَانُوا۟ لِيُؤْمِنُوا۟ بِمَا كَذَّبُوا۟ مِن قَبْلُ ۚ كَذَٰلِكَ
يَطْبَعُ ٱللَّهُ عَلَىٰ قُلُوبِ ٱلْكَٰفِرِينَ ﴿١٠١﴾

101 These cities – We have given you news of them. Their Messengers came to them with Clear Signs, but they were never going to believe in what they had previously rejected. That is how Allah seals up the hearts of the unbelievers.

'*These cities*' are the cities of Nūḥ, 'Ād, Lūṭ, Hūd, and Shu'ayb which were already mentioned. '*Naquṣṣu*' means '*We recite*' and *anbā'* are reports. This is solace for the Prophet ﷺ and the Muslims. The phrase '*but they were never going to believe*' means that those unbelievers would not believe even if Allah revived them after their destruction. Mujāhid said that. It is similar to the words: '*If they were sent back they would merely return to what they were forbidden to do.*' (6:28). Ibn 'Abbās and ar-Rabī' said, 'Allah Almighty knew on the Day He took a covenant with them that they would not believe in the Messengers.'

The words '*...in what they had previously rejected*' is a reference to the Day of the Covenant when Allah brought them out from of Ādam's back and they then believed, willingly or unwillingly. As-Suddī said, 'They believed unwillingly on the day when the covenant was taken from them and so they did not truly believe even then.' It is said that they asked for miracles and when they saw them, they did not believe in what they had denied before seeing them, as in Allah's words: '*just as when they did not believe in it at first.*' (6:110) The sentence: '*That is how Allah seals up the hearts of the unbelievers*' means His sealing the hearts of those who were mentioned. So Allah will seal the hearts of those who reject Muḥammad ﷺ.

وَمَا وَجَدْنَا لِأَكْثَرِهِم مِّنْ عَهْدٍ وَإِن وَجَدْنَآ أَكْثَرَهُمْ لَفَـٰسِقِينَ ۝١٠٢

102 We did not find many of them worthy of their contract.

'*Min*' in '*min 'ahd*' is redundant, and it indicates the genus. If it were not for *min*, it would be permitted to imagine that it was singular in meaning. Ibn 'Abbās said this means the contract which was made with them at the time of when they were merely atoms. If someone breaks a contract it is said, 'He has no contract,' i.e. he does not observe it. Al-Ḥasan said that the contract they had with the Prophets was to worship Allah and not associate anything with Him. It is said that Allah means that unbelievers are in two groups: most of them have neither trustworthiness nor fidelity, while some of them are trustworthy in spite of their unbelief, even if they are few. That is related from Abū 'Ubaydah.

ثُمَّ بَعَثْنَا مِنۢ بَعْدِهِم مُّوسَىٰ بِـَٔايَـٰتِنَآ إِلَىٰ فِرْعَوْنَ وَمَلَإِي۟هِۦ
فَظَلَمُوا۟ بِهَا ۖ فَٱنظُرْ كَيْفَ كَانَ عَـٰقِبَةُ ٱلْمُفْسِدِينَ ۝١٠٣

103 And then, after them, We sent Mūsā with Our Signs to Pharaoh and his ruling circle but they wrongfully rejected them. See the final fate of the corrupters!

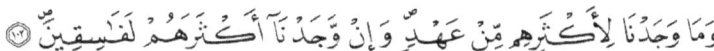

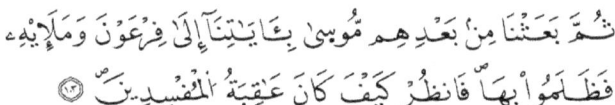

'*And then, after them, We sent,*' in other words after Nūḥ, Hūd, Ṣāliḥ, Lūṭ and Shu'ayb. Mūsā is Mūsā ibn 'Imrān. '*Our Signs*' are miracles. '*They wrongfully rejected*

them,' mean that they rejected and did not affirm the signs. To wrong something is to put it in other than its proper place. 'See the final fate of the corrupters' means see how they end up.

وَقَالَ مُوسَىٰ يَٰفِرْعَوْنُ إِنِّي رَسُولٌ مِّن رَّبِّ الْعَٰلَمِينَ ﴿١٠٤﴾ حَقِيقٌ عَلَىٰٓ أَن
لَّآ أَقُولَ عَلَى اللَّهِ إِلَّا الْحَقَّ قَدْ جِئْتُكُم بِبَيِّنَةٍ مِّن رَّبِّكُمْ فَأَرْسِلْ مَعِيَ بَنِيٓ
إِسْرَٰٓءِيلَ ﴿١٠٥﴾ قَالَ إِن كُنتَ جِئْتَ بِـَٔايَةٍ فَأْتِ بِهَآ إِن كُنتَ مِنَ
الصَّٰدِقِينَ ﴿١٠٦﴾ فَأَلْقَىٰ عَصَاهُ فَإِذَا هِيَ ثُعْبَانٌ مُّبِينٌ ﴿١٠٧﴾ وَنَزَعَ يَدَهُۥ فَإِذَا هِيَ
بَيْضَآءُ لِلنَّٰظِرِينَ ﴿١٠٨﴾ قَالَ الْمَلَأُ مِن قَوْمِ فِرْعَوْنَ إِنَّ هَٰذَا لَسَٰحِرٌ
عَلِيمٌ ﴿١٠٩﴾ يُرِيدُ أَن يُخْرِجَكُم مِّنْ أَرْضِكُمْ فَمَاذَا تَأْمُرُونَ ﴿١١٠﴾
قَالُوٓا۟ أَرْجِهْ وَأَخَاهُ وَأَرْسِلْ فِي الْمَدَآئِنِ حَٰشِرِينَ ﴿١١١﴾ يَأْتُوكَ بِكُلِّ
سَٰحِرٍ عَلِيمٍ ﴿١١٢﴾

104-12 Mūsā said, 'Pharaoh! I am truly a Messenger from the Lord of all the worlds, duty bound to say nothing about Allah except the truth. I have come to you with a Clear Sign from your Lord. So send the tribe of Israel away with me.' He said, 'If you have come with a Clear Sign produce it if you are telling the truth.' So he threw down his staff and there it was, unmistakably a snake. And he drew out his hand and there it was, pure white to those who looked. The ruling circle of Pharaoh's people said, 'This is certainly a skilled magician who desires to expel you from your land, so what do you recommend?' They said, 'Detain him and his brother and send out marshals to the cities, to bring you all the skilled magicians.'

'*Ḥaqīq 'alayya*' means 'it is mandatory for me'. If someone recites '*'alā an lā*', the meaning is: 'I am encouraged to say nothing but…'. In the reading of 'Abdullāh it is '*ḥaqīq allā aqūl*' with the preposition *'alā* omitted. It is also said that the preposition *'alā* here has the meaning of the preposition *bā'*, implying: 'my duty is only to say'. That is how it is in the reading of Ubayy and al-A'mash: '*bi-allā aqūl*', as is said. So according to this, *ḥaqīq* has a passive meaning. The meaning of the phrase '*send the tribe of Israel away with me*' is to let them go free. Pharaoh was employing them in arduous work. The verb in '*so he threw down his staff*' is used of both physical bodies and ideas but was already discussed (3:151). *Thu'bān* is a large male snake. It is the largest of the snakes. The adjective '*mubīn*' means that it was undoubtedly a snake. '*And he drew out his hand*' means that he brought it out and displayed it. It is said that he drew it out of his pocket or from his side, as we find elsewhere in the revelation: '*Put your hand inside your shirt front. It will emerge pure white, yet quite unharmed*' (27:12), meaning not white on account of leprosy. Mūsā was very dark brown and when he put his hand down, it reverted to its original colour. Ibn 'Abbās said that his hand shone with a light that illuminated everything between heaven and earth. It is said that when he brought out his hand it was shining, white as snow and then when he lowered it, it reverted to the colour of the rest of his body.

The meaning of '*skilled*' is specific to magic and '*from your land*' means from 'your kingdom, company of Copts, by virtue of giving the tribe of Israel precedence over you.' '*So what do you recommend*?' is what Pharaoh said, in other words 'What do you instruct me to do?' It is possible that the assembly said that, asking Pharaoh, 'What do you instruct us to do?' as one addresses tyrants and leaders, saying, 'What do you think about this?' It is possible that they said it to him and his companions. *Mā* is nominative since *dhā* means 'which'. It is accusative if *mā* and *dhā* are the same thing. '*They said, "Detain him."*' The people of Madīnah, 'Āṣim, and al-Kisā'ī recited it without *hamzah*, although Warsh and al-Kisā'ī recited it with *ishbā'* of the *kasrah* on the *hā'*. Abū 'Amr recited it with a silent *hamzah* and a *hā'* with *ḍammah*. They are two dialectical forms. It means 'delay'. That is how Ibn Kathīr, Ibn Muḥayṣin and Hishām recited it although they use *ishbā'* on the *ḍammah* of the *hā'*. The rest of the people of Kufa recite *arjih* with *sukūn* on the *ḥā'*. Al-Farrā' said that it is an Arab dialect. They stop at the *hā'*, alluding to it in the connection since what is before it is vowelled as '*Hadhihi Ṭalḥah qad aqbaltu*.' The Basrans do not recognise this.

Qatādah said that it means 'imprison him'. Ibn 'Abbās said it means, 'delay him'. It is said that it is taken from *rajā, yarjū*, implying make him hope and leave him to hope. An-Naḥḥās related it from Muḥammad ibn Yazīd. There is *kasrah* on the *hā'* for following, and it can have a *ḍammah* based on the root. A *sukūn* is incorrect Arabic and only permitted in unusual poems. The words '*and his brother*' are added to the *hā'* and '*bring you all*' is in the accusative on account of the adverbial *ḥāl* and the verb is jussive because it is the answer to the command. That is why the *nūn* is elided from it. The people of Kufa except for 'Āṣim recited *saḥḥār* and the rest recite *sāḥir* for magicians. They are close, although *saḥḥār* is an intensive form.

وَجَآءَ ٱلسَّحَرَةُ فِرْعَوْنَ قَالُوٓا۟ إِنَّ لَنَا لَأَجْرًا إِن كُنَّا نَحْنُ ٱلْغَٰلِبِينَ ﴿١١٣﴾ قَالَ نَعَمْ وَإِنَّكُمْ لَمِنَ ٱلْمُقَرَّبِينَ ﴿١١٤﴾

113-4 The magicians came to Pharaoh and they said, 'We should receive a reward if we are the winners.' He said, 'Yes, and you will be among those brought near.'

The magicians came to Pharaoh

The mention of sending is elided since the listener knows it. Ibn 'Abd al-Ḥakam said, 'There were twelve chiefs. With each chief there were twenty prefects and under each prefect were a thousand magicians.' Their chief was Sham'ūn, according to Muqātil ibn Sulaymān. Ibn Jurayj said that there were nine hundred from al-'Aris, Fayyum and Alexandria divided into three groups. Ibn Isḥāq said that there were fifteen thousand magicians. It is related from Wahb. It is said that they were twelve thousand. Ibn al-Munkadir said that there were eighty thousand. It is said that there were fourteen thousand. It is even said that there were three hundred thousand magicians from the countryside, three hundred thousand from the hills and three hundred thousand from Fayyum and the surrounding area. It is said that they were seventy men and it is said that they were seventy-three. Allah knows best. It is related that they had with them ropes and staves which were carried by three hundred camels. The snake swallowed all of that.

Ibn 'Abbās and as-Suddī said that when it opened its mouth, the size of its jaws was eighty cubits and the bottom its mouth was on the earth and its upper jaw above the walls of the castle. It is said that the size of its mouth was forty cubits. Allah knows best. It went for Pharaoh to swallow him, but he leapt from his throne and fled from it and sought refuge with Mūsā. Mūsā took it and it reverted to a staff. Wahb said that twenty-five thousand people died of fright.

They said, 'We should receive a reward if we are the winners.'

The reward is a prize and wealth. Allah does not use the conjunction *fā'* here because when they came they said this. It is related that, '*We should receive...*' is a statement and that is the reading of Nāfi' and Ibn Kathīr. They were demanding Pharaoh to allot them wealth if they won. So Pharaoh said, '*Yes, and you will be among those brought near,*' meaning highly placed people in our religion, offering them more than what they demanded. It is said that they allotted that for themselves in their judgment if they were successful. This means, 'They said, "We are entitled to a reward if we are victorious."' The rest make it a question (Will we receive...) and have them asking for information. They asked Pharaoh whether he would allot them a reward if they were successful or not. They did not decide that Pharaoh would do it. They asked him whether he would do it. He told them, 'Yes, you will have a reward and nearness to me if you are victorious.'

قَالُوا يَـٰمُوسَىٰٓ إِمَّآ أَن تُلْقِيَ وَإِمَّآ أَن نَّكُونَ نَحْنُ ٱلْمُلْقِينَ ﴿١١٥﴾ قَالَ أَلْقُوا فَلَمَّآ
أَلْقَوْا سَحَرُوٓا أَعْيُنَ ٱلنَّاسِ وَٱسْتَرْهَبُوهُمْ وَجَآءُو بِسِحْرٍ عَظِيمٍ ﴿١١٦﴾
وَأَوْحَيْنَآ إِلَىٰ مُوسَىٰٓ أَنْ أَلْقِ عَصَاكَ فَإِذَا هِيَ تَلَقَّفُ مَا يَأْفِكُونَ ﴿١١٧﴾

115-7 They said, 'Mūsā, will you throw first or shall we be the ones to throw?' He said, 'You throw.' And when they threw, they cast a spell on the people's eyes and caused them to feel great fear of them. They produced an extremely powerful magic. We revealed to Mūsā, 'Throw down your staff.' And it immediately swallowed up what they had forged.

They behaved well towards Mūsā and that was the cause of their becoming believers. *An* is accusative according to al-Kisā'ī and al-Farrā' with the meaning of 'will you throw?' It is like the words of the poet:

They said, 'Riding.' We said, 'That is our custom.'

He said, 'You throw.'

Al-Farrā' said that something is elided in these words. The meaning is: 'Mūsā told them, "You will not defeat your Lord and you will not invalidate His signs."' This is part of the miracle of the Qur'an whose like has not come in the words of people and they are incapable of it. These brief words hold an huge meaning. It is said that it is a threat, implying 'begin by throwing and you will see the disgrace which befalls you' since it is not permitted for Mūsā to command them to do magic. It is said that he commanded them to do that to make their lies and distortion clear. '*And when they threw*' the ropes and staves, '*they cast a spell on the people's eyes*,' in other words created an illusion for them and turned them from true perception to an imaginary one achieved by legerdemain and sleight of hand, as mentioned in *al-Baqarah* (2:102). The meaning of '*aẓīm* (*extremely powerful*) refers to their perception of it because although it seemed great, it was not in reality powerful at all.

Ibn Zayd said, 'The meeting took place in Alexandria and the tail of the serpent reached beyond Buḥayrah.' Others said that it opened its mouth and began to swallow up the ropes and staves they had thrown. It is said that what they threw were ropes of skin which contained quicksilver and so they moved and they said, 'These are snakes.'

And it immediately swallowed up what they had forged.

Ḥafṣ recited *talqafu* and made it the present tense of *laqifa.* The rest recite it in Form II with a *fatḥah* on the *lām*, and they made it the present tense of *talaqqafa* and it is *tatalaqqafa.* One uses '*laqiftu*' and '*talaqqaftu*' for 'I snatched something or swallowed it.' *Talqafu, talqamu* and *talhamu* mean the same. Abū Ḥātim said, 'I heard in one of the readings: "*talaqqama*'. [POEM] It is related: '*talqafu*'. '*What they had forged*' were their deceptions because they brought ropes and put quicksilver in them so that they moved about.

فَوَقَعَ ٱلْحَقُّ وَبَطَلَ مَا كَانُوا۟ يَعْمَلُونَ ﴿١١٨﴾ فَغُلِبُوا۟ هُنَالِكَ
وَٱنقَلَبُوا۟ صَٰغِرِينَ ﴿١١٩﴾ وَأُلْقِىَ ٱلسَّحَرَةُ سَٰجِدِينَ ﴿١٢٠﴾ قَالُوٓا۟ ءَامَنَّا بِرَبِّ
ٱلْعَٰلَمِينَ ﴿١٢١﴾ رَبِّ مُوسَىٰ وَهَٰرُونَ ﴿١٢٢﴾

118-22 So the Truth took place and what they did was shown to be false. They were defeated then and there, transformed into humbled men. The magicians threw themselves down in prostration. They said, 'We believe in the Lord of all the worlds, the Lord of Mūsā and Hārūn.'

Mujāhid says that this means that the Truth was victorious. The people of Pharaoh and Pharaoh with them were abased, defeated and overcome. The magicians believed.

قَالَ فِرْعَوْنُ ءَامَنتُم بِهِۦ قَبْلَ أَنْ ءَاذَنَ لَكُمْ ۖ إِنَّ هَٰذَا لَمَكْرٌ مَّكَرْتُمُوهُ فِى
ٱلْمَدِينَةِ لِتُخْرِجُوا۟ مِنْهَآ أَهْلَهَا ۖ فَسَوْفَ تَعْلَمُونَ ﴿١٢٣﴾ لَأُقَطِّعَنَّ أَيْدِيَكُمْ وَأَرْجُلَكُم مِّنْ
خِلَٰفٍ ثُمَّ لَأُصَلِّبَنَّكُمْ أَجْمَعِينَ ﴿١٢٤﴾ قَالُوٓا۟ إِنَّآ إِلَىٰ رَبِّنَا مُنقَلِبُونَ ﴿١٢٥﴾ وَمَا تَنقِمُ
مِنَّآ إِلَّآ أَنْ ءَامَنَّا بِـَٔايَٰتِ رَبِّنَا لَمَّا جَآءَتْنَا ۚ رَبَّنَآ أَفْرِغْ عَلَيْنَا صَبْرًا وَتَوَفَّنَا
مُسْلِمِينَ ﴿١٢٦﴾

123-6 Pharaoh said, 'Have you believed in him before I authorised you to do so? This is just some plot you have concocted in the

city to drive its people from it. You will soon know. I will cut off your alternate hands and feet and then I will crucify every one of you.' They said, 'We are returning to our Lord. You are only avenging yourself on us because we believed in our Lord's Signs when they came to us. Our Lord, pour down steadfastness upon us and take us back to You as Muslims.'

Pharaoh said, 'Have you believed in him before I authorised you to do so?

This is his objecting to what they did.

This is just some plot you have concocted in the city to drive its people from it. You will soon know.

It means: 'This was pre-planned between you so that you could gain control of Egypt,' and means: 'This was organised by you in the city before you came here.' '*You will soon know*' is a threat against them. Ibn 'Abbās said that Pharaoh was the first to crucify people and cut off their alternate hands and feet, first the right foot and left hand, and then the right hand and left foot. Al-Ḥasan said that.

You are only avenging yourself on us because we believed in our Lord's Signs

The word for revenge is recited with a *fatḥah* on the *qāf* (*tanqamu*). Al-Akhfash said that it is a dialect. It means: 'You only dislike the fact that we have believed in Allah when it is the truth. Allah's Clear Signs have come to us.'

Our Lord, pour down steadfastness upon us and take us back to You as Muslims.'

Ifrāgh is to pour, meaning 'pour it down on us when our limbs are amputated and we are crucified.' '*Take us back to You as Muslims*': it is said that Pharaoh took the magicians and carried out the amputation *on* them on the bank of the river, and that six hundred thousand also believed in Mūsā when the magicians believed.

وَقَالَ ٱلْمَلَأُ مِن قَوْمِ فِرْعَوْنَ أَتَذَرُ مُوسَىٰ وَقَوْمَهُۥ لِيُفْسِدُوا۟ فِى ٱلْأَرْضِ وَيَذَرَكَ وَءَالِهَتَكَ ۚ قَالَ سَنُقَتِّلُ أَبْنَآءَهُمْ وَنَسْتَحْىِۦ نِسَآءَهُمْ وَإِنَّا فَوْقَهُمْ قَٰهِرُونَ ﴿١٢٧﴾ قَالَ مُوسَىٰ لِقَوْمِهِ ٱسْتَعِينُوا۟ بِٱللَّهِ وَٱصْبِرُوٓا۟ ۖ إِنَّ ٱلْأَرْضَ لِلَّهِ يُورِثُهَا مَن يَشَآءُ مِنْ عِبَادِهِۦ ۖ وَٱلْعَٰقِبَةُ لِلْمُتَّقِينَ ﴿١٢٨﴾

127-8 The ruling circle of Pharaoh's people said, 'Are you going to leave Mūsā and his people to cause corruption in the earth and abandon you and your gods?' He said, 'We will kill their sons and let their women live. We have absolute power over them!' Mūsā said to his people, 'Seek help in Allah and be steadfast. The earth belongs to Allah. He bequeathes it to any of His slaves He wills. The successful outcome is for the godfearing.'

The ruling circle of Pharaoh's people said, 'Are you going to leave Mūsā and his people and his people to cause corruption in the earth and abandon you and your gods?'

Causing corruption is effected by causing splits and breaking unity. The verb '*abandon*' has a *fatḥah* on the *rā'* as the answer to the question, and the *wāw* before it takes the place of the *fā'*. About '*your gods*' al-Ḥasan said that Pharaoh worshipped idols and so he both worshipped and was worshipped. Sulaymān at-Taymī said, 'I heard that Pharaoh used to worship cows.' At-Taymī said, 'I asked al-Hasan, "Did Pharaoh worship anything?" He answered, "Yes, he used to worship something which he put around his neck."' It is said that the meaning of '*your gods*' is 'obedience to you', as in Allah's words: '*They have taken their rabbis and monks as lords besides Allah.*' (9:31). They were not objects of worship for them but they obeyed them, so it became a precedent.

Nu'aym ibn Maysarah recited '*yadharuka*' (*leave*) in the nominative, meaning 'he will abandon you'. Al-Ashhab al-'Uqaylī recited '*yadhurka*' in the jussive because of the heavy nature of the *ḍammah*. Anas ibn Mālik recited '*nadharuka*' (we leave) and so they reported about themselves that they would leave his worship if he left Mūsā alive. 'Alī ibn Abī Ṭālib, Ibn 'Abbās and aḍ-Ḍaḥḥāk recited '*ilāhatuka*', meaning 'worship of you'. According to this reading, he was worshipped and did not worship and so it means: 'Abandon your being worshipped.' Abū Bakr al-Anbārī said, 'One reason for the position of the people who espouse this reading is that by saying: "*I am your Lord Most High*" (79:24) and: "*I do not know of any other god for you apart from Me*" (28:38), he was denying that he had a Lord and God so he was told, "We will abandon you and your claim to divinity," meaning "abandon your people's worship of you."'

Most recite '*ālihataka*'. That is based on the fact that Pharaoh claimed lordship outwardly while he knew that he was in reality the subject of the Lord. The proof of this is his words when he was about to die: '*I believe that there is no god but Him in whom the tribe of Israel believe.*' (10:90) This statement was not accepted from him when he came to the door of repentance because he was drowning. Before that he had another god which he worshipped secretly rather than the Lord of the worlds. Al-Ḥasan and others said that. The variant of Ubayy has: 'they have left you (*tarakū*) to be worshipped.'

It is said that the god was a cow which was worshipped. When Pharaoh thought a cow was god, they were commanded to worship it. He said, 'I am your Lord and the lord of this.' This is why Allah says: '*Then he produced a calf for them.*' (20:88) Ibn 'Abbās and as-Suddī mentioned that. Az-Zajjāj said, 'He had small idols which his people worshipped as a means of coming near to him. This is why he said, "*I am your Lord Most High.*"' Ismā'īl ibn Isḥāq said, 'The words of Pharaoh indicate that they worshipped something besides him.' It is said that what is meant by 'your god' in the reading of Ibn 'Abbās is the cow which they worshipped. It is said that the sun was meant by it and that they used to worship that. [POEM]

He said, 'We will kill their sons and let their women live. We have absolute power over them!'

Then he encouraged his people and said, '*We will kill their sons*' in Form I (*sa-naqtulu*) in the reading of Nāfi' and Ibn Kathīr, while the rest recite Form II (*sa-nuqattilu*) which means slaughter. He means, 'You should not fear them. '*We have absolute power over them*' is to gladden them by that information. He did not say, 'We will kill Mūsā' since he knew that he would not be able to do that. Sa'īd ibn Jubayr said, 'Pharaoh was filled with fear of Mūsā. When he saw him, he urinated like a donkey.

Mūsā said to his people, 'Seek help in Allah and be steadfast. The earth belongs to Allah. He bequeaths it to any of His slaves He wills. The successful outcome is for the godfearing.'

When the people of Mūsā heard this about Pharaoh, Mūsā told them, "*Seek help in Allah and be steadfast. The earth belongs to Allah. He bequeaths it to any of His slaves He wills.*"' This was to make them hope that Allah would bequeath the land of Egypt to them. '*He bequeaths it to any of His slaves He wills,*' refers to the Garden, for those who are godfearing. The '*outcome*' of anything is its end, but when it is applied to a person, it is understood to refer to good.

قَالُوٓاْ أُوذِينَا مِن قَبۡلِ أَن تَأۡتِيَنَا وَمِنۢ بَعۡدِ مَا جِئۡتَنَاۚ قَالَ عَسَىٰ
رَبُّكُمۡ أَن يُهۡلِكَ عَدُوَّكُمۡ وَيَسۡتَخۡلِفَكُمۡ فِي ٱلۡأَرۡضِ
فَيَنظُرَ كَيۡفَ تَعۡمَلُونَ ١٢٩

129 They said, 'We suffered harm before you came to us and after you came to us.' He said, 'It may well be that your Lord is going to destroy your enemy and make you the successors in the land so that He can see how you behave.'

They said, 'We suffered harm before you came to us and after you came to us.'

'*Before*' refers to the birth of Mūsā when they suffered harm through the killing of their sons and enslavement of their women, '*and after you came to us*', means that now that was happening to them again, referring to the threat Pharaoh had made. It is said that the first '*harm*' was the forcing of the tribe of Israel to work until the middle of the day and releasing them for the rest of the day to earn for themselves. The second '*harm*' was making them work for the entire day without food or drink. Jubaybir said that. Al-Ḥasan said that the prior and later harm were the same and refers to the taking of the *jizyah*.

He said, 'It may well be that your Lord is going to destroy your enemy

When the verb '*may be*' ('*asā*) is used of Allah, it means that it will definitely happen. He renewed the promise to them and it was realised. They succeeded in Egypt in the time of Dāwūd and Sulaymān and they conquered Jerusalem with Yūsha' ibn Nūn, as already mentioned (2:246). It is related that they said that when Mūsā left with them and Pharaoh pursued them, he was behind them and the sea in front of them. Allah realised this threat by drowning Pharaoh and his people and saving the Israelites.

and make you the successors in the land so that He can see how you behave.'

Something similar was already mentioned, namely Allah will see the actions which bring about reward, because Allah does not reward according to His knowledge of them but requites them for what they do.

وَلَقَدْ أَخَذْنَآ ءَالَ فِرْعَوْنَ بِٱلسِّنِينَ وَنَقْصٍ مِّنَ ٱلثَّمَرَٰتِ لَعَلَّهُمْ
يَذَّكَّرُونَ ﴿١٣٠﴾

130 We seized Pharaoh's people with years of drought and scarcity of fruits so that hopefully they would pay heed.

'*Sinīn*' literally means drought and this is known linguistically. One speaks about being affected by drought (*sanah*). It implies a year's drought. It is used in that way in *ḥadīth*: 'O Allah, impose on them drought (*sinīn*) like that of Yūsuf.' Some Arabs decline the *nūn* in *sinīn*. Al-Farrā' said:

I saw that the passage of years (*sinīn*) took from me
as the last night of the moon takes from the crescent.

An-Naḥḥās said, 'Sībawayh quoted this verse with a *fatḥah* on the *nūn*, but what he quoted in this regard is not permitted by others. It is his words:

I passed the end of forty (*arba'īn*).

Al-Farrā' related that the Banū 'Āmir said, 'I stayed with him for years (*sinīnan*)' and inflected it. He said that the Banū Tamīm do not inflect it and would say *sinīnu* in this sentence. *Sinīn* is the plural of *sanah*. Here *sanah* means drought rather than 'year'. Part of it is the expression, '*asnata al-qawmu*', i.e. they suffered a drought. 'Abdullāh ibn az-Ziba'rī said:

'Amr al-'Ulā [Hāshim] who broke up bread (*hashama*) for *tharīd* for his people
when the men of Makkah were suffering drought (*musnitūn*) and lean.

'*So that hopefully they would pay heed*' means accept the warning and their hearts become soft.

فَإِذَا جَآءَتْهُمُ ٱلْحَسَنَةُ قَالُوا۟ لَنَا هَٰذِهِۦ ۖ وَإِن تُصِبْهُمْ سَيِّئَةٌ يَطَّيَّرُوا۟ بِمُوسَىٰ
وَمَن مَّعَهُۥٓ ۗ أَلَآ إِنَّمَا طَٰٓئِرُهُمْ عِندَ ٱللَّهِ وَلَٰكِنَّ أَكْثَرَهُمْ لَا يَعْلَمُونَ ﴿١٣١﴾

131 Whenever a good thing came to them, they said, 'This is our due.' But if anything bad happened to them, they would blame their ill-fortune on Mūsā and those with him. No indeed! Their ill-fortune will be with Allah. But most of them did not know.

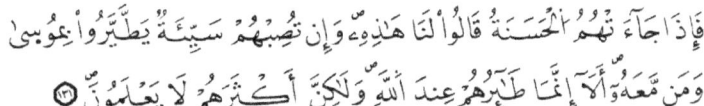

Whenever a good thing came to them, they said, 'This is our due.'

The '*good thing*' is fertility and well-being. They said, 'We have been given it because we deserve it.' 'But if anything bad happened to them' refers to drought and illness.

they would blame their ill-fortune on Mūsā and those with him.

They thought that their bad luck was due to him. It is similar to Allah's words: '*But if a bad thing happens to them, they say, "This has come from you."*' (4:78). The root is '*yataṭayyarū*' which has the *tā'* assimilated into the *ṭā'*. Ṭalḥah recited *taṭayyarū* as the past tense. The root of this is from *ṭayrah* (a slip) and it connects with the prohibition against looking for omens. Then it is used often so that one uses *taṭayyara* for anyone who is seen as a source of bad luck. The Arabs used to see good luck in what comes from the right and bad luck in what comes from the left. They also thought that the sound of a crow was bad luck and interpreted it to mean separation. They used to decide certain matters by how birds answered one another and by their song outside its normal time in the same way. It was the same with a gazelle when it came from the right or the left. They referred to all such things by the word *taṭayyara*. Persians saw bad luck in seeing a child going to his teacher in the morning and good luck in seeing a child returning from his teacher to his house. They saw bad luck in seeing a watercarrier with a waterskin on his back which was very full and good luck in seeing a watercarrier whose waterskin was open. They saw bad luck in a porter burdened with a load and an animal with a heavy load, and good luck in a camel which had set down its load and in an animal whose load had been removed.

Islam came and forbade people to see omens and bad luck in the sound of birdsong, whatever it was and in any case. The Prophet ﷺ said, 'Leave the bird on its nest.' In the *Jāhiliyyah*, it often happened that when people had some need, they would go to a bird in its nest and chase it off. If it went to the right, their need would be settled, and they viewed this as a good omen. If it went to the left, they returned, and they viewed that as a bad omen. The Prophet ﷺ forbade this practice by saying this. He used the word '*makināt*' for nests and some Arabs say '*wukunāt*' as does Imru al-Qays in a verse. *Wuknah* is the name for every bird's nest. A nest is any place where a bird lays its eggs and where they hatch and fledge. It can be a crack in a wall or in a tree. The verb *wakana* is used for a bird brooding on its eggs.

There were also Arabs who did not see any omens in birds and praised those who denied such things. Al-Muraqqish said:

I had my midday meal and I used
 not to have it based on the sparrow-hawk or crow.
The one on the left is the same as the one on the right
 and the one on the right is the same as the one on the left.

'Ikrimah said, 'I was with Ibn 'Abbās when a bird passed by crying out. One of the people said, "Good! Good!" Ibn 'Abbās retorted, "There is neither good nor evil in this."' Our scholars have said, 'As for the sounds of birds, they are not connected to any evidence nor do they have any knowledge of what is now, let alone of what the future holds, so that they could report about it. There is no one who knows the speech of birds except for what Allah Almighty chose for Sulaymān of that. Divination is connected to vain falsehood, and Allah knows best.'

The Prophet ﷺ said, 'Whoever pretends to have had a dream, or consults soothsayers, or returns from his journey because of a bad omen, is not one of us.' Abū Dāwūd related from 'Abdullāh ibn Mas'ūd that the Prophet ﷺ said, 'Seeing omens is *shirk*,' and he repeated it three times, 'That can happen to any of us, but Allah will remove that by our having trust in Him.' 'Abdullāh ibn 'Amr ibn al-'Āṣ related that the Messenger of Allah ﷺ said, 'Whoever consults omens about his need has committed *shirk*.' He was asked, 'What is the expiation for that, Messenger of Allah?' He replied, 'That one of you says, "O Allah, there is no omen except Your omen nor any good except Your good and no god but You," and then attends to his need.' We find in another report, 'When one of you experiences that, he should say, "O Allah, only You can bring good outcomes and only You can remove bad outcomes. There is no strength nor power except by You." Then he should proceed, trusting in Allah. Allah will be enough for him in what he encounters. Allah Almighty will be enough for him in what concerns him.' The difference between a lucky sign and an omen was mentioned in *al-Mā'idah*. (5:2)

Their ill-fortune will be with Allah. But most of them did not know.

Al-Ḥasan recited '*ṭayruhum*', the plural of *ṭā'ir*, meaning what is decreed for and against them. '*But most of them did not know*' that the drought and hardships they suffered came to them from Allah because of their wrong actions, not from Mūsā and his people.

وَقَالُواْ مَهۡمَا تَأۡتِنَا بِهِۦ مِنۡ ءَايَةٖ لِّتَسۡحَرَنَا بِهَا فَمَا نَحۡنُ لَكَ بِمُؤۡمِنِينَ ١٣٢

132 They said, 'No matter what kind of Sign you bring us to bewitch us, we will not believe in you.'

They said, 'No matter what kind of Sign you bring us

The people of Pharaoh said to Mūsā, '*No matter what...*' Al-Khalīl said, 'The root is '*mā mā*'. The first is for the precondition and the second is redundant to stress the repayment as there is an increase in the rest of the letters, for instance either *hathaymā, aynamā* and *kayfuhamā*. They disliked it being two words since it is one expression and so they changed the first *alif* into a *hā'* and said *mahmā*. Al-Kisā'ī said that its root is *mah*, i.e. 'Refrain, whatever sign you bring us.' It is said that it is a single word.

to bewitch us,

It means 'to divert us from our customary practice'. The explanation of this word was already given in *al-Baqarah* (2:102). It is said that after the sorcerers fell down in prostration Mūsā remained among the Copts for twenty years, showing them signs until Allah drowned Pharaoh. This is what they said.

فَأَرۡسَلۡنَا عَلَيۡهِمُ ٱلطُّوفَانَ وَٱلۡجَرَادَ وَٱلۡقُمَّلَ وَٱلضَّفَادِعَ وَٱلدَّمَ ءَايَٰتٖ مُّفَصَّلَٰتٖ فَٱسۡتَكۡبَرُواْ وَكَانُواْ قَوۡمٗا مُّجۡرِمِينَ ١٣٣

133 So We sent down on them floods, locusts, lice, frogs and blood, Signs, clear and distinct, but they proved arrogant and were an evildoing people.

Isrā'īl related from Simāk that Nawf ash-Shāmī said, 'Mūsā remained among the people of Pharaoh for forty years after he defeated the magicians.' Muḥammad ibn 'Uthmān ibn Abī Shaybah related from Munjāb that he spent twenty years showing them the signs: floods, locusts, lice, frogs and blood. '*Floods*' means such an immense amount of water that they had to swim in it. Mujāhid and 'Aṭā' said, 'The "*flood*" is death.' Al-Akhfash said that its singular is *ṭūfānah*. It is said that it is a verbal noun like *rujḥān* and *nuqsān*, and has no singular. An-Naḥḥās said that *ṭūfān* linguistically is a destructive power, death or flood, which comes and annihilates people. As-Suddī said, 'Not a single drop of water fell on the tribe of Israel. It entered the houses of the Copts until they were in water up to their collar-bones, and it remained for seven days or forty days. They said, "*Pray to your Lord to remove it from us and we will believe in you.*" He prayed to his Lord to remove it and the flood was removed from them but they still did not believe. Then Allah made fodder and crops grow for them in that year such as had not grown before that and they said, "That water was a blessing." So Allah sent locusts down upon them which ate their crops and fruits and then ate their roofs and doors to the point that they destroyed the houses yet none of that happened to the houses of the tribe of Israel.'

Scholars disagree about killing locusts if they alight in a land and spoil it. It is said that they should not be killed but all the people of *fiqh* say that they should be killed. The first group use as evidence that locusts are a mighty creation of Allah which consumes the provision of Allah which has not been ordained for us, and it is also related, 'Do not kill locusts. They are the immense army of Allah.' The majority use as evidence the fact that leaving them amounts to corruption of wealth. The Prophet ﷺ permitted fighting a Muslim when he wants to take someone's property. The locusts want to destroy property and so it is more fitting to permit killing them. Do you not see that there is consensus about it being permitted to kill snakes and scorpions because they harm people? That is also the case with locusts. Ibn Mājah related from Jābir and Anas ibn Mālik that the Prophet ﷺ used to pray against locusts. He said, 'O Allah, destroy their adults and kill their young. Corrupt their eggs and eradicate them. Take their mouths from our livelihood and provision. You hear the supplication.' A man said, 'Messenger of Allah, how can you pray for one of the armies of Allah to be eradicated?' He answered, 'The locusts come from the sneezes of the fish in the sea.'

It is confirmed in *Ṣaḥīḥ Muslim* from 'Abdullāh ibn Abī Awfā: 'We went on seven expeditions with the Messenger of Allah ﷺ during which we ate locusts with him.' Scholars do not disagree about eating them in general and that when they are taken alive and their heads cut off, they are lawful by agreement. That is how they are slaughtered. They disagree about whether there needs to be a reason for their death and whether or not they are game. Most of them said that there is no need for that and they may be eaten however they die. The ruling on them in their view is the same as the ruling on snakes. Ibn Nāfi' and Muṭarrif believed that. Mālik believed that there must be a reason for their death, such as cutting off their head, foot or wing when that causes them to die, or being hit or thrown into a fire. This is because he considers them to be land animals and so one must take account of how they died. Similarly al-Layth disliked eating dead locusts except for those which are caught alive and then die. Catching them amounts to slaughter. Sa'īd ibn al-Musayyab believed that. Ad-Dāraquṭnī related from Ibn 'Umar that the Messenger of Allah ﷺ said, 'Lawful for us are two dead animals: fish and locusts, and two kinds of blood: the liver and the spleen.' Ibn Mājah said, 'Ahmad ibn Mani' related to us from Sufyān ibn 'Uyaynah that Abū Sa'īd heard Anas ibn Mālik say, "The wives of the Prophet ﷺ used to give one another locusts on plates."' Ibn al-Mundhir mentioned it as well.

Muḥammad ibn al-Munkadir related from Jābir ibn 'Abdullāh that 'Umar ibn al-Khaṭṭāb said, 'I heard the Messenger of Allah ﷺ say, "Allah Almighty created a thousand nations, 600 of which are in the sea and 400 on the land. The first of these nations to be destroyed will be the locusts. When the locusts are destroyed, then the nations will follow one another like the pearls on a thread when it is broken."' At-Tirmidhī al-Hakīm mentioned it in *Nawādir al-Uṣūl.* He said, 'The locusts will be the first of these nations to be destroyed because they were created from the clay which was left over from the clay of Ādam. Those nations will be destroyed by the destruction of human beings because they are subject to human beings.'

We return to the story of the Copts. They made a covenant with Mūsā that they would believe if the locusts were removed from them. He prayed and the locusts were removed, and some of their crops were left. They said, 'What remains is enough for us,' and they did not believe, so Allah sent '*lice* (*qummal*)' down upon them. This designates small locusts (*dabā*). Qatādah said that *dabā* is the locust before it flies, the singular being *dabāh.* Land whose plants have been eaten by them is called *madbiyyah.* Ibn 'Abbās said *qummal* are the worms that are found in wheat. Ibn Zayd said that they are fleas. Al-Ḥasan said that they are small black creatures. Abū 'Ubaydah said they were small ticks. They ate the animals and crops and clung to their skins as if they had a pox on them and prevented them from sleeping and standing still. Ḥabīb ibn Abī Thābit said that *qummal* are black beetles. The people of language consider *qummal* to be a sort of tick. Abū al-Ḥasan al-A'rābī said that *qummal* are small creatures like ticks but smaller than them and the singular is *qumlah.* An-Naḥḥās said, 'This is not contrary to what the people of *tafsīr* have said because it is permissible that all these things were sent against them, and they were all involved in harming them.' Some commentators said that there was a heap of sand at 'Ayn ash-Shams and when Mūsā hit it with his staff it turned into these creatures. The singular of *qaml* is *qamlah.* 'Aṭā' al-Khurāsānī said it. It is *al-qaml* in the reading of al-Ḥasan.

They entreated him but, when that plague was removed from them, they did not believe. So Allah sent the frogs on them. *Ḍafāḍi'* (*frogs*) is the plural of *ḍifḍi'*. It is the well-known creature that lives in water. There is a report that it is prohibited to kill them. Abū Dāwūd and Ibn Mājah related it with a sound *isnād*. Abū Dāwūd related it from Aḥmad ibn Ḥanbal from 'Abd ar-Razzāq and Ibn Mājah from Muḥammad ibn Yaḥyā an-Nīsābūrī adh-Dhuhlī from Abū Hurayrah who said, 'The Messenger of Allah ﷺ forbade killing sparrow-hawks, frogs, ants and hoopoes.' An-Nasā'ī transmitted from 'Abd ar-Raḥmān ibn 'Uthmān that a doctor mentioned frogs as being useful in remedies in the presence of the Prophet ﷺ and he forbade killing them. Abū Muḥammad 'Abd al-Ḥaqq says that that is sound. Abū Hurayrah said, 'The sparrow-hawk was the first bird to fast. When Ibrāhīm left Syria for the Ḥaram to build the House, the *Sakīnah* [cloud] and sparrow-hawk accompanied him. The sparrow-hawk was his guide to the place and the *Sakīnah* was its size. When he went to the place, the *Sakīnah* descended on the site of the House and called out, "Ibrāhīm, build according to the size of my shadow!" So the Prophet ﷺ forbade killing the sparrow-hawk because it was Ibrāhīm's guide to the House and the frogs because they poured water on the fire of Ibrāhīm.'

When the frogs overwhelmed Pharaoh, they came and took over the whole place. They went to the ovens and, in obedience to Allah, jumped into them when the fire was blazing. Allah made their croaking glorification. It is said that it is the creature which glorifies Allah the most. 'Abdullah ibn 'Amr said, 'Do not kill frogs. The croaking which you hear from them is glorification.' It is related that they filled people's beds, vessels, food and drink. A man would sit up to his chin in frogs. When he spoke, the frogs would leap into his mouth. They complained to Mūsā and said, 'We repent.' Allah removed that from them, and they reverted to their unbelief. So Allah sent the blood down upon them, and the Nile flowed with blood. The Israelites would scoop up water from it and the Copts blood. An Israelite would pour water into the mouth of a Copt and it would become blood. A Copt would pour blood into the mouth of a Israelite and it would become pure water.

Signs, clear and distinct

They were obvious and apparent, as Mujāhid said. Az-Zajjāj said that the phrase is in the accusative as an adverbial *ḥāl*. It is related that the time between the Signs was eight days, or forty days, or a month. This is why '*distinct*' (*mufaṣṣilāt*) is used. '*But they proved arrogant*' means too proud to believe in Allah Almighty.

وَلَمَّا وَقَعَ عَلَيْهِمُ الرِّجْزُ قَالُوا يَٰمُوسَى ادْعُ لَنَا رَبَّكَ بِمَا عَهِدَ
عِندَكَ لَئِن كَشَفْتَ عَنَّا الرِّجْزَ لَنُؤْمِنَنَّ لَكَ وَلَنُرْسِلَنَّ
مَعَكَ بَنِي إِسْرَٰٓءِيلَ ﴿١٣٤﴾ فَلَمَّا كَشَفْنَا عَنْهُمُ الرِّجْزَ إِلَىٰٓ أَجَلٍ هُم
بَٰلِغُوهُ إِذَا هُمْ يَنكُثُونَ ﴿١٣٥﴾ فَانتَقَمْنَا مِنْهُمْ فَأَغْرَقْنَٰهُمْ فِي الْيَمِّ
بِأَنَّهُمْ كَذَّبُوا بِـَٔايَٰتِنَا وَكَانُوا عَنْهَا غَٰفِلِينَ ﴿١٣٦﴾

134-6 Whenever the plague came down on them they said, 'Mūsā, pray to your Lord for us by the contract He has with you. If you remove the plague from us, we will definitely believe in you and send the tribe of Israel away with you.' But when We removed the plague from them – for a fixed term which they fulfilled – they broke their word. Then We took revenge on them and drowned them in the sea because they denied Our Signs and paid no attention to them.

Whenever the plague came down on them they said,

Rijz (*plague*) refers to the punishment. It is recited as *rijz* and *rujz* which are two dialectical forms. Ibn Jubayr said, 'It was a plague in which 70,000 Copts died in a single day.' It is said that it means the Signs which were already mentioned. In the words '*by the contract He has with you*', *mā* means 'which', implying by the knowledge with which He entrusted you or which He singled out for you and informed you of. It is said that this is an oath, implying by His contract with you, unless you pray for us, in which case *mā* is a connective. '*If you remove the plague from us*' through your supplication to your God to remove it from us, '*we will definitely believe in you*,' we will believe in what you have brought, '*and send the tribe of Israel away with you*' whom they had made their servants, as already stated.

for a fixed term which they fulfilled – they broke their word.

This was until the time that was set for their drowning. '*They broke their word*,' broke the contract they had made. The noun *yamm* means '*the sea*'. The pronoun in '*to them*' may be 'to it' and refer to the revenge indicated in the words '*We took revenge*' but is usually said to refer to the Signs which they did not consider so that they became as if they were utterly heedless of them.

وَأَوْرَثْنَا الْقَوْمَ الَّذِينَ كَانُوا يُسْتَضْعَفُونَ مَشَارِقَ الْأَرْضِ وَمَغَارِبَهَا
الَّتِي بَارَكْنَا فِيهَا ۖ وَتَمَّتْ كَلِمَتُ رَبِّكَ الْحُسْنَىٰ عَلَىٰ بَنِي إِسْرَائِيلَ بِمَا صَبَرُوا ۖ
وَدَمَّرْنَا مَا كَانَ يَصْنَعُ فِرْعَوْنُ وَقَوْمُهُ وَمَا كَانُوا يَعْرِشُونَ ﴿١٣٧﴾

137 And We bequeathed to the people who had been oppressed the easternmost part of the land We had blessed, and its westernmost part as well. The most excellent Word of your Lord was fulfilled for the tribe of Israel on account of their steadfastness. And We utterly destroyed what Pharaoh and his people made and the buildings they constructed.

And We bequeathed to the people who had been oppressed the easternmost part of the land We had blessed, and its westernmost part as well.

'*The people*' here are the tribe of Israel, '*who had been oppressed*,' by being humbled in serfdom. Al-Kisā'ī and al-Farrā' claimed that the root is '*in the easternmost*' and the preposition '*fī*' has been elided and so it is in the accusative. The apparent meaning is that they inherited the land of the Copts. It is in the accusative as an explicit object. One says, '*warithu-l-māl*' and '*awrathuhu-l-māl*'. When the verb is transitive with the *hamzah*, then the two objects are in the accusative. The land is the land of Syria and Egypt. The easternmost and westernmost are the directions of the east and the west, and the earth is specific, as al-Ḥasan, Qatādah and others said. It is said that it means all of the land because Dāwūd and Sulaymān were part of the tribe of Israel who ruled the earth. In the '*We had blessed*' the blessing was by the production of crops, fruits and rivers.

The most excellent Word of your Lord was fulfilled for the tribe of Israel on account of their steadfastness.

The noun '*Word*' refers to Allah's words: '*We desired to show kindness to those who were oppressed in the land and to make them leaders and make them inheritors.*' (28:5). '*On account of their steadfastness*' refers to the steadfastness they displayed in the face of the injury on them inflicted by Pharaoh and in the command of Allah after that to believe in Mūsā.

And We utterly destroyed what Pharaoh and his people made and the buildings they constructed.

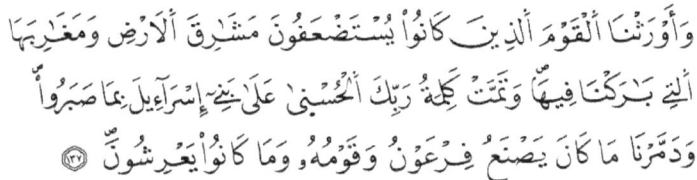

The verb '*arasha*' means 'to build'. Ibn 'Abbās and Mujāhid said that it means the palaces they built and other things. Al-Hasan said that it is setting up of grape vines. Ibn 'Āmir and Abū Bakr recited from 'Āṣim *'ya'rushūna'* (instead of *ya'rishūna*), which al-Kisā'ī said is the dialect of Tamīm. Ibrāhīm ibn Abī 'Ablah recited *yu'arrishūna*.

وَجَٰوَزْنَا بِبَنِيٓ إِسْرَٰٓءِيلَ ٱلْبَحْرَ فَأَتَوْا۟ عَلَىٰ قَوْمٍ يَعْكُفُونَ عَلَىٰٓ أَصْنَامٍ
لَّهُمْ ۚ قَالُوا۟ يَٰمُوسَى ٱجْعَل لَّنَآ إِلَٰهًا كَمَا لَهُمْ ءَالِهَةٌ ۚ قَالَ إِنَّكُمْ قَوْمٌ
تَجْهَلُونَ ﴿١٣٨﴾

138 We conveyed the tribe of Israel across the sea and they came upon some people who were devoting themselves to some idols which they had. They said, 'Mūsā, give us a god just as these people have gods.' He said, 'You are indeed an ignorant people.

Ḥamzah and al-Kisā'ī recite '*devoting*' with a *kasrah* on the *kāf* (*ya'kifūna*) and the rest recite it with a *ḍammah*. The verb is *'akafa, ya'kifu*, which means to rely on something and cling to it. The verbal noun from both of them is based on the form *fu'ūl*. Qatādah said, 'Those people were part of the Lakhm tribe. They used to camp at Raqqa. It was said that their idols were images of cows, and that is why the Sāmirī produced a calf for them.' The words: 'Mūsā, give us a god just as these people have gods' are similar to the words of the ignorant Arabs. They saw a green tree that belonged to the unbelievers called Dhāt Anwāṭ which they revered for a day every year and said, 'Messenger of Allah, appoint Dhāt Anwāṭ for us.' He said, 'Allah is greater. By the One who has my soul in His hand, what you have said is similar to what the people of Mūsā said: "*Give us a god just as these people have gods.*" He said, "*You are indeed an ignorant people.*" You will pursue the traditions of those before you step by step until, if they were to enter a lizard's hole, you would enter it.' This occurred when he was going to Ḥunayn, as will be made clear in *at-Tawbah*, Allah willing.

إِنَّ هَٰٓؤُلَآءِ مُتَبَّرٌ مَّا هُمْ فِيهِ وَبَٰطِلٌ مَّا كَانُوا۟ يَعْمَلُونَ ﴿١٣٩﴾ قَالَ أَغَيْرَ ٱللَّهِ
أَبْغِيكُمْ إِلَٰهًا وَهُوَ فَضَّلَكُمْ عَلَى ٱلْعَٰلَمِينَ ﴿١٤٠﴾

139-40 What these people are doing is destined for destruction. What they are doing is purposeless.' He said, 'Should I seek something other than Allah as a god for you when He has favoured you over all other beings?'

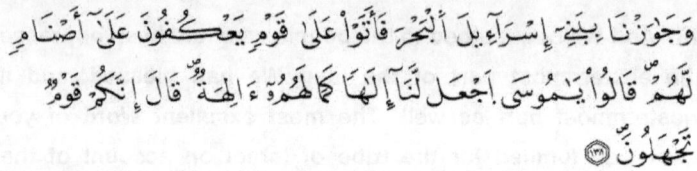

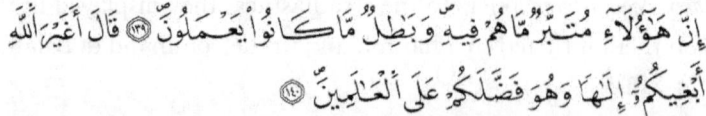

The word *mutabbar* means 'destroyed'. *Tabbār* is destruction. A broken vessel is called *mutabbar* and that also refers to a business, implying that both the worshipper and worshipped are destroyed. The adjective '*bātil*' (*purposeless*) means 'vanishing and disappearing'. In the words '*what they are doing*,' *kānū* is an extra connective. The words '*Should I seek something other than Allah...?*' mean, 'Should I seek a god for you other than Allah Almighty?' And the words '*He has favoured you over all other beings*' mean over all the nations of your time. It is said that He favoured them by destroying their enemy and by the Signs singled out for them.

وَإِذَ اَنجَيْنَٰكُم مِّنَ ـ اٰلِ فِرْعَوْنَ يَسُومُونَكُمْ سُوٓءَ اَلْعَذَابِ يَقْتُلُونَ
أَبْنَآءَكُمْ وَيَسْتَحْيُونَ نِسَآءَكُمْ وَفِے ذَٰلِكُم بَلَآءٌ مِّن
رَّبِّكُمْ عَظِيمٌ ﴿١٤١﴾

141 Remember when We rescued you from Pharaoh's people who were inflicting an evil punishment on you, killing your sons and letting your women live. In that there was a terrible trial from your Lord.

Allah is reminding them of His favour to them. It is said that it is addressed to the Jews at the time of the Prophet ﷺ and implies 'Remember when We saved your ancestors,' as already mentioned in *al-Baqarah*.

وَوَٰعَدْنَا مُوسَىٰ ثَلَٰثِينَ لَيْلَةً وَأَتْمَمْنَٰهَا بِعَشْرٍ فَتَمَّ مِيقَٰتُ
رَبِّهِۦٓ أَرْبَعِينَ لَيْلَةً وَقَالَ مُوسَىٰ لِأَخِيهِ هَٰرُونَ اَخْلُفْنِے فِے قَوْمِے
وَأَصْلِحْ وَلَا تَتَّبِعْ سَبِيلَ اَلْمُفْسِدِينَ ﴿١٤٢﴾

142 We set aside thirty nights for Mūsā and then completed them with ten, so the appointed time of his Lord was forty nights in all. Mūsā said to his brother Hārūn, 'Be my *khalīfah* among my people. Keep order and do not follow the way of the corrupters.'

We set aside thirty nights for Mūsā and then completed them with ten,

Allah is telling us that this was one of the things Allah honoured Mūsā with. His promise to speak with him was to honour him. Ibn 'Abbās, Mujāhid and Masrūq said that the words '*and then completed them with ten*' indicate that the time referred to was Dhū al-Qa'dah and the first ten days of Dhū al-Ḥijjah. He commanded him to fast the month and devote himself completely to worshipping Allah during that period. When he fasted, he disliked the smell of his mouth and so he used a *siwāk*. It was said that it was of carob wood. The angels said, 'We smelt the scent of musk from your mouth and you ruined it with the *siwāk*,' and so ten days of Dhū al-Ḥijjah were added to the period. It is said that when he used the *siwāk* Allah revealed to him: 'Mūsā, I will not speak to you until the smell of your mouth returns to what it was before. Do you not know that I love the smell of the faster more than the scent of musk?' and He commanded him to fast a further ten days. Allah Almighty spoke to Mūsā on the morning of the Day of Sacrifice and it was also [on that day] that Ismā'īl was ransomed from the slaughter and Muḥammad ﷺ completed the *ḥajj*. The *hā'* is elided from *'ashr* (*ten*) because the definite is feminine. The point being made by Allah's words '*so the appointed time of his Lord*' here is that He knew that thirty plus ten is forty, preventing it from being imagined that it means that he completed the thirty days with ten of those days, and so it is clear that the ten were on top of the thirty. If it said that Allah says '*forty*' in *al-Baqarah* (2:51) and '*thirty*' here, so it must form part of the first number, it is said that it is not like that. Allah says: '*We completed them with ten*,' and forty and thirty plus ten are the same with no disagreement. The two views can be separate and combined. He said forty, combining them, and then thirty, meaning a continuous month, plus ten days more, making forty in all.

Our scholars have said that this *āyah* indicates that stipulating a term by a mutual agreement is an old *sunnah*. The meaning of 'old' is that Allah made it a custom in judgments and decreed it for nations. He taught them the lengths of time for actions. The first of them was the term of six days that Allah set in which He created all creatures. He says: '*We created the heavens and the earth, and everything between them, in six days and We were not affected by fatigue*.' (50:38) We explained the meaning of this already in this *sūrah* in 7:54.

Ibn al-'Arabī said, 'When a term is set for some reason, one tries to attain what was stipulated within it. If the term comes to an end and that has not proved feasible, it is increased by insight and excuse. Allah made that clear to Mūsā and He set a term of thirty days for him and then increased it by ten to a full forty. Mūsā's return to his people was delayed by those ten days but they did not know that it was permitted for there to be a delay and so they said, "Mūsā has become lost or he has forgotten," and broke the covenant they had made with him, changing things after him and worshipping a god other than Allah.' Ibn 'Abbas said, 'Mūsā had said to his people, "My Lord has appointed thirty nights for me to receive it, and I put Hārūn in charge of you." When Mūsā reached his Lord, Allah added ten days to that.' Their trial of their worship of the Calf occurred during the ten days that Allah added as will be explained. The increase of the term was determined and the term was determined. An increase can only be added by *ijtihād* on the part of a judge after he has looked at the time, state and action connected to the agreement in question, and it can be a third of the previously agreed period as Allah set for Mūsā. If the judge thinks that there is an agreed basis for the term and the addition is the same period again, that it is permitted, but there must be waiting after it when there is an excuse which happens to people. Ibn al-ʿArabī said that. Al-Bukhārī related from Abū Hurayrah that the Prophet ﷺ said, 'Allah excuses a man whose term is delayed until he reaches the age of sixty.'

This is also a basis of judges allowing an excuse for the person, against whom judgment is made, time after time. This is kindness to creation and so that the right may be justly carried out against them. The greatest granting of excuse to the tribe of Ādam was in Allah sending Messengers to them before assessing the evidence against them. He says: '*We never punish until We have sent a Messenger*' (17:15) and '*And did not the warner come to you?*' (35:37) namely a Messenger.

Ibn 'Abbas said that the time of excusing ends with the coming of white hair, which arrives when the age of maturity is reached and is a sign that someone has left the years of youth behind. He made sixty the end of the time of excuse because sixty is close to the end of people's lives. It is the age of repentance, humility and submission to Allah, and waiting for death and meeting Allah. It entails lack of excuse upon lack of excuse. The first evidence is by the statement of Prophet ﷺ, and the second through whiteness of hair. That is at the end of forty years. Allah Almighty says: '*Then when he achieves his full strength and reaches forty, he says, "My Lord, keep me thankful for the blessing You bestowed on me."*' (46:15) He is telling us that someone who reaches forty has had time to recognise the extent of Allah's blessings to him and his parents and to be thankful for them. Mālik said, 'I met the people of knowledge in our land, and they would seek this world and socialise with people until they reached the age of forty. When they reached that age, they would withdraw from people.'

The *āyah* indicates that Allah's words: '*thirty nights*' indicate that the dates of the days of the month start with the coming of the night rather than the day because that is when the months begin. That is how the Companions used to refer to days [using the term 'nights'] even so far as saying, 'We fasted five with the Messenger of Allah ﷺ.' Non-Arabs differ from that. They count by days because they are based on the sun. Ibn al-ʿArabī said, 'The reckoning by the sun is for worldly benefits and the reckoning of the moon is for religious practices. That is why Allah says: "*We set aside thirty nights for Mūsā*."'

Mūsā said to his brother Hārūn, 'Be my *khalīfah* among my people. Keep order."

When Mūsā wanted to go to talk with Allah and go away to do that, he said to his brother Hārūn, '*Be my representative* (*khalīfah*),' indicating delegation. In *Ṣaḥīḥ Muslim*, Sa'd ibn Abī Waqqāṣ said, 'I heard the Messenger of Allah ﷺ say to 'Alī when he left him in charge when he went on an expedition, "Are you not content to be in relation to me what Hārūn was in relation to Mūsā, although there will no Prophet after me?"'

The Rafiḍites, Imamites and other Shī'ah groups use this as evidence that the Prophet ﷺ appointed 'Alī over the entire Community so that the Imamites – may Allah make them ugly – claim that the Companions became unbelievers because the Imamites consider that the Companions did not act by the text which appointed 'Alī and appointed someone else by their own *ijtihād*. Some of them have gone as far as saying that 'Alī became an unbeliever because he did not demand his right. There is no doubt about the unbelief of such people and those who follow them in what they say. They did not know that this appointment was for a limited period, like guardianship which is cancelled by the retirement or death of the one who instituted it. It does not continue after his death and so undermines the claim that the Imamites and others make. The Prophet ﷺ also put Ibn Umm Maktūm and others in charge of Madīnah. It is agreed that that showed that such an appointment by him was not permanent. Furthermore Hārūn shared with Mūsā in the Message. So they had no evidence in that appointment for the claim they make. Allah is the One who gives success to guidance.

The command in '*Keep order*' is to put things right. Ibn Jurayj said, 'Part of putting things right was to rein in the Sāmirī and change what he was doing.' It is said that it means, 'Be kind to them and put yourself right,' be a reformer. '*Do not follow the way of the corrupters*' means: 'Do not follow the path of disobedience and do not help the wrongdoers.'

وَلَمَّا جَآءَ مُوسَىٰ لِمِيقَٰتِنَا وَكَلَّمَهُۥ رَبُّهُۥ قَالَ رَبِّ أَرِنِىٓ أَنظُرْ إِلَيْكَ ۚ قَالَ
لَن تَرَىٰنِى وَلَٰكِنِ ٱنظُرْ إِلَى ٱلْجَبَلِ فَإِنِ ٱسْتَقَرَّ مَكَانَهُۥ فَسَوْفَ تَرَىٰنِى ۚ
فَلَمَّا تَجَلَّىٰ رَبُّهُۥ لِلْجَبَلِ جَعَلَهُۥ دَكًّا وَخَرَّ مُوسَىٰ صَعِقًا ۚ فَلَمَّآ أَفَاقَ
قَالَ سُبْحَٰنَكَ تُبْتُ إِلَيْكَ وَأَنَا۠ أَوَّلُ ٱلْمُؤْمِنِينَ ﴿١٤٣﴾

143 When Mūsā came to Our appointed time and his Lord spoke to him, he said, 'My Lord, show me Yourself so that I may look at You!' He said, 'You will not see Me, but look at the mountain. If it remains firm in its place, then you will see Me.' But when His Lord manifested Himself to the mountain, He crushed it flat and Mūsā fell unconscious to the ground. When he regained consciousness he said, 'Glory be to You! I repent to You and I am the first of the believers!'

When Mūsā came to Our appointed time and his Lord spoke to him, he said, 'My Lord, show me Yourself so that I may look at You!'

'*Our appointed time*' means within the promised time. '*His Lord spoke to him*,' in other words let Mūsā hear His words without intermediary. '*He said, "My Lord, show me Yourself so that I may look at You!*"' He asked to look at Him and yearned to see Him when he heard His speech.

He said, 'You will not see Me,

Allah means '*You will not see Me* in this world.' It is not permitted to imply that Mūsā meant: 'Show me something tremendous so that I can witness Your power' because he said, '*ilayka*', meaning 'You yourself' and received the reply, '*You will not see Me*.' If Mūsā had asked Allah for a Sign, Allah would have given him what he asked for, in the same way that He had given him all the other Signs. That prevented Mūsā from asking for another Sign and so it is wrong to interpret this in that way.

but look at the mountain. If it remains firm in its place, then you will see Me.'

Allah makes an example for him of something whose structure is stronger and firmer than his, implying, 'If the mountain remains solid and still, then you will see Me. If it does not remain solid, then you will not be able to see Me. If it does not retain its solidity, you would not be able to see me, just as the mountain was not able to see Me.' Qāḍī 'Iyāḍ related from Qāḍī Abū Bakr ibn aṭ-Ṭayyib that it means: 'Mūsā saw Allah and that is why he fell unconscious. The mountain saw its Lord and turned to dust by perceiving that Allah created it.' He derived that from Allah's words: '*but look at the mountain. If it remains firm in its place, then you will see Me.*'

But when His Lord manifested Himself to the mountain, He crushed it flat and Mūsā fell unconscious to the ground.

Tajallā means 'to manifest' as used in 'the bride disclosed herself' when she unveils, and of a sword when it emerges free of dust. *Tajallā* refers to a thing disclosing itself. It is said that Allah's command and power were disclosed. Quṭrub and others said that. The people of Madīnah and Basra read *dakkan*, and the soundness of this reading is indicated in Allah's words: '*the earth is crushed* (*dakkan*)' (89:21) although the noun '*mountain*' is masculine. The people of Kufa recited *dakka'a* implying making it like flat earth, on which no mountain rises, and the masculine is *adakka* and the plural is *dakkawat*. Al-Kisā'ī said that *dakk* in respect of mountains means flat-backed and the singular is *adakk*. Others said that *dakkawat* is the plural of *dakkā'*, which is a low clay hill, and *dakdāk* is similar to that, but is a low sand mound. A she-camel which is *dakkā'* has no hump. It says in commentary that the mountain sank into the earth, and it is still sinking. Ibn 'Abbās said that Allah turned it to dust. 'Aṭiyyah al-'Awfī said it will be like disappearing sand.

'*He fell unconscious*' means that he fainted. That is related from Ibn 'Abbās, al-Ḥasan and Qatādah. It is also said that it means he fell down dead. The verb is used for a man when he is struck down. Qatādah and al-Kalbī said, 'Mūsā fell down on Thursday, the Day of 'Arafah and he was given the Torah on Friday, the Day of Sacrifice.'

When he regained consciousness he said, 'Glory be to You! I repent to You.'

Mujāhid said, 'This repentance was on account of asking to see Allah in this world.' It is said that it was because he asked without asking permission first. That is why he repented. It is said that his repentance to Allah was being humble to Him when the signs appeared. The Community agree that such repentance is normally on account of disobedience and the Prophets are protected from that. According to the people of the *Sunnah* and the Community such vision (of Allah) is permitted. Innovators believe that he asked for the sake of the people in order to make it clear to them that it was not permitted. This does not demand repentance. It is said that it means, 'I have repented to You for killing the Copt.' Al-Qushayrī said that. The explanation of such vision being permitted was already discussed in *al-An'ām*. (6:103)

'Alī ibn Mahdī aṭ-Ṭabarī said, 'If the question of Mūsā had been an impossible demand, his knowledge of Allah would have prevented him from asking it, in the same way that it is not permitted to ask, "O Lord, do you have a spouse and child?"' The position of the Mu'tazilites and refutation of them will be covered in the commentary on *Sūrah al-Qiyāmah* Allah willing.

and I am the first of the believers!'

This is said to mean 'first of my people'. It is also said to mean, 'of the tribe of Israel in this time'. It is said that it means 'You are not seen in this world because of Your prior promise regarding that.' We read in the sound *ḥadīth* related from Abū Hurayrah and others that the Messenger of Allah ﷺ said, 'Do not make rivalry between the Prophets. People will faint on the Day of Rising and I will lift my head and see Mūsā holding on to one of the legs of the Throne. I do not know whether he will be among those who fainted and he regained consciousness before me, or if he was reckoned according to his first fainting,' or he said, 'his first fainting was enough for him.' Abū Bakr ibn Shaybah mentioned that Ka'b said, 'Allah Almighty divided His Words and His Vision between Muḥammad and Mūsā. He spoke to Mūsā twice and Muḥammad ﷺ saw him twice.'

قَالَ يَـٰمُوسَىٰٓ إِنِّيَ ٱصْطَفَيْتُكَ عَلَى ٱلنَّاسِ بِرِسَالَتِي وَبِكَلَـٰمِي فَخُذْ مَآ
ءَاتَيْتُكَ وَكُن مِّنَ ٱلشَّـٰكِرِينَ ۝١٤٤

144 He said, 'Mūsā, I have chosen you over all mankind for My Message and My Word. Take what I have given you and be among the thankful.'

Choosing is preference, so the meaning is 'We have preferred you.' Allah does not say 'over all creation' because this choosing is by His speaking to Him and He also spoke to the angels. He sent him and also sent others. What is meant by '*over all mankind*' is those to whom he was sent. Nāfi' and Ibn Kathīr recited '*bi-risālatī*' (...for My Message) in the singular and the rest recite in the plural. *Risālah* is the verbal noun. It is permitted for it to be the singular. Whoever makes it plural does so on the basis that He sent the Message at different times and in different forms. The verbal noun is the plural because of the different realities, as He says: '*The most hateful of voices is the donkey's bray.*' (31:19) The plural refers to the different categories of voices and different types of sounds. Allah uses the singular here (*My Word*) since He means the whole genus of speech by it. This indicates that his people did not share in speaking nor were they among the seventy, as we explained in *al-Baqarah.* (2:55)

'*Take what I have given you*' indicates contentment, meaning 'Be content with what I have given you.' '*Be among the thankful*' means 'be among those who display My goodness and favour to you.' An animal is described as *shakūr* when it appears to be plump beyond the fodder it is given. The one who is thankful is likely to get more, as in Allah's words: '*If you are grateful, I will certainly give you increase.*' (14:7) It is related that for forty days after Allah spoke to Mūsā, anyone who saw him died because of the intensity of the light of Allah Almighty.

وَكَتَبْنَا لَهُۥ فِى ٱلْأَلْوَاحِ مِن كُلِّ شَىْءٍ مَّوْعِظَةً وَتَفْصِيلًا
لِّكُلِّ شَىْءٍ فَخُذْهَا بِقُوَّةٍ وَأْمُرْ قَوْمَكَ يَأْخُذُوا بِأَحْسَنِهَا سَأُوْرِيكُمْ دَارَ
ٱلْفَـٰسِقِينَ ﴿١٤٥﴾

145 We wrote about everything for him on the Tablets as an admonition and making all things clear. 'Seize hold of it vigorously and command your people to adopt the best in it. I will show you the home of the deviators!'

We wrote about everything for him on the Tablets as an admonition and making all things clear.

'*The Tablets*' means the Torah. It is related in a report that Jibrīl took him in his wings and ascended with him until he brought him so close that he could hear the scratching of the pen when Allah wrote the Tablets for him. At-Tirmidhī al-Hakīm mentioned that. Mujāhid said, 'The Tablets were made of emerald.' Ibn Jubayr said they were made of ruby. Abū al-'Āliyah said that they were made of topaz, and al-Ḥasan said that they were on wood sent down from heaven. It is said that they were made of hard stone which Allah made soft for Mūsa and he cut them with his hand and then split them with his fingers, and the material obeyed him like iron did in the case of Dāwūd. Muqātil said, 'It means, "We wrote for him on the Tablets as stone is engraved."' Rabī' ibn Anas said, 'When the Torah was sent down, it had the weight of the load of seventy oxen. The writing was ascribed to Allah out of honour since they were written at His command. Jibrīl wrote them with the Pen by which the remembrance is written. The ink was taken from the River of Light. It is said that it is writing which Allah manifested and made appear on the Tablets.'

The root of the noun tablet is *lawḥ*. Allah Almighty says: '*It is indeed a Glorious Qur'an preserved on a Tablet.*' (85:21-22) It is as if the *lawḥ* has meanings appear (*talūḥu*) in it. It is related that there were two tablets. The plural is used because two is a plural. It is said that a man 'has immense tablets' when he has large hands and feet.

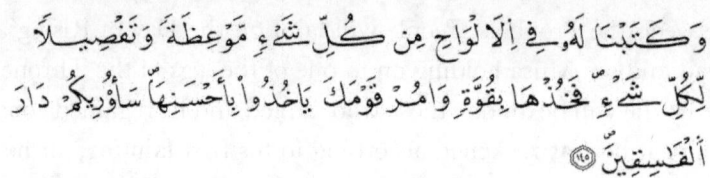

Ibn 'Abbās said, 'The tablets were broken when Mūsā threw them down, and they were taken back except for the sixth.' It is said that a seventh of them remained and six-sevenths were removed. Those that were removed contained the distinction of everything and what remained contained guidance and mercy. Abū Nu'aym related that 'Amr ibn Dīnār said, 'It reached me that Mūsā ibn 'Imrān, the Prophet of Allah, fasted for forty days. When he threw down the Tablets they were broken and he fasted for the same length of time, and then they were returned to him.'

According to ath-Thawrī and others, the meaning of the words '*about everything*' is the rulings needed in Allah's *dīn* and clarification of the lawful and unlawful. It is said that it is an expression which is mentioned for the sake of exaltation and does not imply universality. You say, 'I entered the market and bought everything' and 'So-and-so has everything', and it is seen in Allah's words: '*destroying everything*' (46:25) and: '*I have been given everything*' (27:23) as already mentioned (2:20). '*As an admonition and making all things clear*' means all of the rulings which they were commanded to obey. They did not have *ijtihād*. That was given specifically to the community of Muḥammad ﷺ.

seize hold of it vigorously

In the words '*seize hold of it vigorously*' there is something elided such as 'We said to them…' and it means with seriousness and energy. It is like the words: '*Take hold vigorously of what We have given you.*' (2:63) as was already mentioned there.

command your people to adopt the best in it

This means 'to act by the commands in it and abandon what is forbidden and reflect on its examples and warnings.' It is similar to Allah's words: '*Follow the best that has been sent down to you from your Lord.*" (39:55) and: '*…follow the best of it.*' (39:18) Pardon is better than retaliation, and patience is better than seeking help. It is said that the best of it are its obligations and voluntary actions, and the least of it is what is permissible.

I will show you the home of the deviators.

Al-Kalbī said that this is a reference to the dwellings of 'Ād and Thamūd and the past generations that had been destroyed, which they used to pass by when they travelled. It is said that it refers to Jahannam, as al-Ḥasan and Mujāhid said, implying, 'lest you are mentioned among them and so beware of being from them.' It is said that it means Egypt, implying, 'I will show you the abode of the Copts and the dwellings of Pharaoh which are now empty and abandoned,' as Ibn Jubayr said. Qatādah said that the meaning is 'I will show you the abode of the unbelievers, the tyrants and the Amalekites, where they lived before you, so that you reflect on them, in which case it is about Syria. These two views are indicated by Allah's words: '*We bequeathed to the people…*' (7:137) and '*We desired to show kindness to those who were oppressed in the land*' (28:5), as has already been mentioned. Ibn 'Abbās and Qasāmah ibn Zuhayr recited it in Form II. This is clear.

It is said that *dār* here means destruction and its plural is *adwār*. That is because when Pharaoh and his army drowned, Allah inspired the sea to cast up their bodies on the shore. He said, 'When that happened, the tribe of Israel looked at them and saw the destruction of the deviators.'

سَأَصْرِفُ عَنْ ءَايَٰتِيَ ٱلَّذِينَ يَتَكَبَّرُونَ فِي ٱلْأَرْضِ بِغَيْرِ ٱلْحَقِّ وَإِن
يَرَوْا۟ كُلَّ ءَايَةٍ لَّا يُؤْمِنُوا۟ بِهَا وَإِن يَرَوْا۟ سَبِيلَ ٱلرُّشْدِ لَا يَتَّخِذُوهُ
سَبِيلًا وَإِن يَرَوْا۟ سَبِيلَ ٱلْغَيِّ يَتَّخِذُوهُ سَبِيلًا ذَٰلِكَ بِأَنَّهُمْ كَذَّبُوا۟ بِـَٔايَٰتِنَا
وَكَانُوا۟ عَنْهَا غَٰفِلِينَ ﴿١٤٦﴾ وَٱلَّذِينَ كَذَّبُوا۟ بِـَٔايَٰتِنَا وَلِقَآءِ ٱلْءَاخِرَةِ
حَبِطَتْ أَعْمَٰلُهُمْ هَلْ يُجْزَوْنَ إِلَّا مَا كَانُوا۟ يَعْمَلُونَ ﴿١٤٧﴾

146-7 I will divert from My Signs all those who are arrogant in the earth without any right. If they see every Sign, they will not believe in it. If they see the way of right guidance, they will not take it as a way. But if they see the way of error, they will take that as a way. That is because they denied Our Signs and paid no attention to them. As for those who denied Our Signs and the encounter of the Next World, their actions will come to nothing. Will they be repaid except for what they did?

I will divert from My Signs all those who are arrogant in the earth without any right.

Qatādah said that this means: 'I will prevent them from understanding My Book.' Sufyān ibn 'Uyaynah said that. It is said that it means 'I will divert them from believing in the Signs' or that, 'I will divert them from benefiting from them.' That alludes to their arrogance. It is like Allah's words: '*So when they deviated, Allah made their hearts deviate.*' (61:5) The '*Signs*' according to this, may be miracles or revealed Books. It is said that it is about the creation of the heavens and the earth, meaning 'divert them from seeing them.' The arrogance in '*who are arrogant*' is lies in thinking that they are the best of creation. This is a false view. That is why Allah says: '*without any right*'. They do not follow a Prophet, nor listen to him, because they are arrogant.

If they see the way of right guidance, they will not take it as a way.

'*They*' here are those who are arrogant. Allah tells us that they abandon the path of guidance and follow the path of error and misguidance, in other words they take unbelief as their *dīn*.

That is because they denied Our Signs and paid no attention to them.

They do what they do on account of their denial. The phrase '*paid no attention to them*' refers to their lack of reflection on the truth and so they were like those who are heedless. It is possible that they were heedless of what they were doing.

Mālik ibn Dīnār recited '*in yuraw*' with a *ḍammah* on the *yā'*, meaning 'they were not made to see'. The people of Madīnah and the people Basra recite *rushd* and the people of Kufa, except for 'Āṣim, recite *rashad*. Abū 'Ubayd said that Abū 'Amr made a distinction between *rushd* and *rashad*, and said that *rushd* is putting things right in general and *rashad* is specific to the *dīn*. An-Naḥḥās said that Sībawayh believed that *rushd* and *rashad* are like *sukht* and *sakhat*. That is what al-Kisā'ī said. The sound view from Abū 'Amr and others is what Abū 'Ubayd said. Ismā'īl ibn Isḥāq related from Naṣr ibn 'Alī that he related from his father that Abū 'Amr ibn al-'Alā' said, 'When *rushd* is the middle of an *āyah*, it is read with a *sukūn*. When it is at the beginning of an *āyah*, it is vowelled.' An-Naḥḥās said that the end of an *āyah* is such as we find in 18:10. They are two dialectical forms with the same meaning. One says *rashada, yarshudu*, and *rashuda, yarshudu*. Sībuwayh related *rashida, yarshada*. The reality of *rushd* and *rashad* in language is that a man obtains what he wants. This is the opposite of disappointment.

وَاتَّخَذَ قَوْمُ مُوسَىٰ مِنۢ بَعْدِهِۦ مِنْ حُلِيِّهِمْ عِجْلًا جَسَدًا لَّهُۥ خُوَارٌ ۚ أَلَمْ يَرَوْا
أَنَّهُۥ لَا يُكَلِّمُهُمْ وَلَا يَهْدِيهِمْ سَبِيلًا ۘ ٱتَّخَذُوهُ وَكَانُوا ظَٰلِمِينَ ﴿١٤٨﴾

148 After he left, Mūsā's people adopted a calf made from their ornaments, a form which made a lowing sound. Did they not see that it could not speak to them or guide them to any way? They adopted it and so they were wrongdoers.

After he left, Mūsā's people adopted a calf made from their ornaments

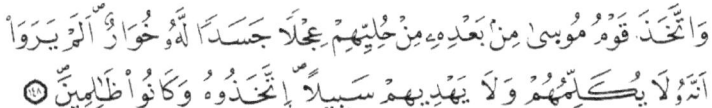

This was after he went to Sinai. The reading '*min ḥulliyyihim*' (from their jewellery) is that of the people of Madīnah and Basra. The people of Kufa recited *ḥillīhim*. Ya'qūb recited *ḥallīhim*. An-Naḥḥās said that it is the plural of *ḥalī*, *ḥullī* and *ḥillī*. The root is *ḥaluwy* and the *wāw* has been elided into the *yā'* and the *lām*

has a *kasrah* because it is close to the *yā'*, and the *ḥā'* has a *kasrah* by the *lām* and a *ḍammah* by the root. The word *'calf'* is the object of the verb.

a form which made a lowing sound.

The noun *'a form'* is an adjective or appositive and the clause *'which made a lowing sound'* is nominative by the inceptive. The verb for the noise a calf makes is *khāra, yakhūru*. In the stories about Calf it is related that the name of the Sāmirī was Mūsā ibn Ja'far, ascribed to a town called Sāmirah. He was born in the year when the sons of the tribe of Israel were killed. His mother hid him in a mountain cave and Jibrīl fed him and he was known for that. When Jibrīl crossed the sea on a mare in heat in front of Pharaoh, the Sāmirī took a handful of the track left by the horse's hooves. That is the meaning of *'I gathered up a handful from the Messenger's footprints.'* (20:96)

Mūsā said he would be away from his people for thirty days and when he was delayed for extra ten, and the thirty had passed, the Sāmirī said to the tribe of Israel, who used to obey him, 'You have jewellery with you from the family of Pharaoh.' They used to have a festival in which they dressed up and borrowed jewellery from the Copts. They had borrowed it for that day and when Allah brought them out of Egypt and drowned the Copts, they still had that jewellery in their possession. The Sāmirī said to them, 'It is unlawful for you. Bring what you have and burn it.' It is said that this jewellery is what the tribe of Israel took from the people of Pharaoh after they drowned. Hārūn told them, 'The jewellery is booty and it is not lawful for you.' So it was collected in a hole which he dug and the Sāmirī took it. It is said that they borrowed the jewellery on the night they wanted to leave Egypt and led the Copts to think that it was for a wedding or gathering.

The Sāmirī heard them say, *'Give us a god just as these people have gods.'* (7:138). Those gods were in the form of cows and so he made the body of a calf for them which was mute, although they heard a lowing from it. It is said that Allah transformed it into flesh and blood. It is said that when he threw that handful of dust into the fire onto the jewellery, it became a calf which lowed, and it lowed once and did not repeat it. Then he told the people, *'This is your god – and Mūsā's god as well, but he forgot.'* (20:88) He said, 'He forgot him here and went to look for him and could not find him. Come and we will worship this calf.' Allah said to Mūsā while he was speaking to him: *'We tried your people after you left and the Sāmirī has misguided them.'* (20:85) Mūsā said, 'Lord, this Sāmirī has produced for them a calf from their jewellery. Who made it into a body? (meaning flesh and blood). Who made it low?' Allah Almighty said, 'I did.' He said, 'By Your might and majesty, it is You alone who have misguided them!' He said, 'You have spoken the truth, wise of the wise.' This is the meaning of Allah's words: '*It was only a trial from You.*' (7:155)

Al-Qaffāl said, 'The Sāmirī made that happen by means of a trick – he hollowed out the calf and made it face the wind, and when the wind blew it made the reported lowing sound, and he made them imagine that it was the calf that was doing that when he threw some of the earth into the body which he took from the earth on the hooves of Jibrīl's horse.' These words have some inconsistency. Al-Qushayrī said that.

Did they not see that it could not speak to them or guide them to any way? They adopted it and so they were wrongdoers.

It was clear that any object worthy of worship must be endowed with speech. '*Or guide them to any way*' means to a path leading to definitive evidence and the words: '*They adopted it*' mean they made it into a god. '*They were wrongdoers*' towards themselves in what they did by adopting it. It is said that they became wrongdoers, in other words idolaters, when they made the Calf a god.

وَلَمَّا سُقِطَ فِىٓ أَيْدِيهِمْ وَرَأَوْا۟ أَنَّهُمْ قَدْ ضَلُّوا۟ قَالُوا۟ لَئِن لَّمْ يَرْحَمْنَا
رَبُّنَا وَيَغْفِرْ لَنَا لَنَكُونَنَّ مِنَ ٱلْخَٰسِرِينَ ﴿١٤٩﴾

149 When they took full stock of what they had done and saw they had been misled, they said, 'If our Lord does not have mercy on us and forgive us, we will certainly be among the lost.'

When they took full stock of what they had done (literally 'fell into their own hands')

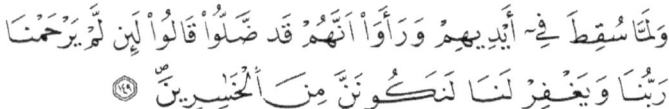

This was after Mūsā returned from the appointment [with His Lord]. This is said of someone who regrets and is confused, literally 'he fell into his own hand'. Al-Akhfash said that Form I and Form IV of the verb are used. He said that it is in the past active tense, and he thinks that the meaning is, 'Regret occurred.' Al-Azharī, an-Naḥḥās and others said that. Regret is located in the heart, but the hand is mentioned because one says about someone who obtains something, 'It fell into his hand like that' because direct contact with things is usually made with the hand. Allah Almighty says: '*That is for what you did* (literally, what your hands advanced).' (22:10) Furthermore, if regret falls into the heart, then its effect appears on the body because the one who is regretful bites his hand and hits one hand against the other. Allah Almighty says: '*He woke up wringing his hands in grief,*

rueing everything that he had spent on it' (18:42), meaning he was regretful. And He says: '*The Day when a wrongdoer will bite his hands*' (25:27), out of regret. The one who regrets puts his chin in his hand.

It is said that the root of 'falling into one's own hand' is when someone is taken as a prisoner. It is said that a man hits another man or floors him, and he throws him with his hands to the earth to capture him or handcuff him. So the one who is thrown down has fallen into the hands of the one who has made him fall.

and saw they had been misled, they said, 'If our Lord does not have mercy on us and forgive us, we will certainly be among the lost.'

Their being misled was by their rebellion against Allah. They began to affirm their slavehood and ask for forgiveness. Ḥamzah and al-Kisā'ī recited it with *tā'* in the second person, 'If You do not have mercy on us and forgive us.' It contains the meaning of asking for help, humble entreaty and a supplication. '*Our Lord*' is in the accusative with the elision of the vocative. It is also more intensive in terms of supplication and humility. Their reading is more in intensive abasement and humility, and so it more appropriate.

وَلَمَّا رَجَعَ مُوسَىٰٓ إِلَىٰ قَوْمِهِۦ غَضْبَٰنَ أَسِفًا قَالَ بِيسَمَا خَلَفْتُمُونِے مِنۢ بَعْدِيٓ
أَعَجِلْتُمْ أَمْرَ رَبِّكُمْ وَأَلْقَى ٱلْأَلْوَاحَ وَأَخَذَ بِرَأْسِ أَخِيهِ يَجُرُّهُۥٓ إِلَيْهِ قَالَ ٱبْنَ أُمَّ
إِنَّ ٱلْقَوْمَ ٱسْتَضْعَفُونِے وَكَادُواْ يَقْتُلُونَنِے فَلَا تُشْمِتْ بِيَ ٱلْأَعْدَآءَ
وَلَا تَجْعَلْنِے مَعَ ٱلْقَوْمِ ٱلظَّٰلِمِينَ ﴿١٥٠﴾ قَالَ رَبِّ ٱغْفِرْ لِے وَلِأَخِے وَأَدْخِلْنَا
فِے رَحْمَتِكَ وَأَنتَ أَرْحَمُ ٱلرَّٰحِمِينَ ﴿١٥١﴾

150-1 When Mūsā returned to his people in anger and great sorrow, he said, 'What an evil thing you did in my absence after I left! Did you want to hasten your Lord's command?' He threw down the Tablets and seized hold of his brother's head, dragging him towards him. Hārūn said, 'Son of my mother, the people oppressed me and almost killed me. Do not give my enemies cause to gloat over me. Do not include me with the wrongdoing people.' He said, 'My Lord, forgive me and my brother and admit us into Your mercy. You are the Most Merciful of the merciful.'

When Mūsā returned to his people in anger and great sorrow,

'*Ghaḍbān*' is not declined because it is the feminine of *ghaḍbā* and because the *alif* and the *nūn* in it have the position of the two *alifs* of the feminine in *ḥamrā'*. It is in the accusative as an adverbial *ḥāl*. The adjective '*asif*' describes intense anger. Abū ad-Dardā' said that it is a state beyond anger which is greater than it. It is *asif, asīf, asfān* and *asūf*. *Asīf* also means 'sad'. Ibn 'Abbās and as-Suddī said, 'He returned full of sorrow about what his people had done.' Aṭ-Ṭabarī said that Allah informed him before he returned that they had been tested by the Calf, and that is why he returned in anger.

Ibn al-'Arabī said that of all people Mūsā was the fiercest in anger but that he was also quick to cool down. Ibn al-Qāsim said, 'I heard Mālik say, "When Mūsā was angry, smoke came out of his cap and the hair of his body lifted up his shirt."' That was because anger is a hot coal kindled in the heart. That is why the Prophet ﷺ commanded someone who was angry to lie down. If his anger did not depart, then he should wash himself. So his lying down is to dampen it down and washing extinguishes it. Being quick to anger was the reason Mūsā slapped the Angel of Death and knocked out his eye. We already mentioned in *al-Mā'idah* (5:11-14) what scholars say about that. At-Tirmidhī al-Hakīm said, 'Mūsā was excused for that because he was the one to whom Allah spoke. It was as if he thought someone was being insolent to him or was stretching out his hand to harm him, and that was terrible in his view. Do you not see that he argued with the angel and said, "How are you going to take my soul? Is it from my mouth when I have spoken with my Lord? Or from my ear when I have heard the words of Allah with it? Or from my hand which has clasped the Tablets or from My foot by which I stood before Him when I spoke to Him at Sinai? Or is it from my eye when my face shone by His light?" So the angel returned, unable to answer, to his Lord.'

In the *Musnad* of Abū Dāwūd, Abū Dharr said, 'The Messenger of Allah ﷺ told us, "When one of you is angry and is standing, he should sit down. If anger does not leave him, he should lie down."' It is also related that Wā'il al-Qāṣṣ said, 'We visited 'Urwah ibn Muḥammad as-Sa'dī, and a man spoke to him and he became angry. He stood up and then came back after having done *wuḍū'*. He said, "My father reported to me from my grandfather, 'Aṭiyyah, who said that the Messenger of Allah ﷺ said, 'Anger is from *shayṭān*. *Shayṭān* was created from fire. Fire is put out by water. When one of you is angry he should do *wuḍū'*.'"'

What an evil thing you did in my absence after I left!

He blamed them, saying 'What an evil action you did while I was away.' The verb *khalafa* is used for what is disliked. It is said that it is also used for good.

Did you want to hasten your Lord's command?

It means: 'Bring it about before its time.' 'Hastening' (*'ajalah*) is to go forward to something before its time and it is blameworthy. Hurrying (*sur'ah*) is to do a thing at the beginning of its time and it is praiseworthy. Ya'qūb said that Form I is used for doing something before something and Form X is used for to attempt to hasten. The meaning of '*Your Lord's command*' is the ordainment of your Lord, meaning He ordained forty days. It is said that you hastened the anger of your Lord. It is said, 'You hastened to worship the Calf before a command came to you from your Lord.'

He threw down the Tablets.

It means that this was something he did out of anger and sorrow when he saw his people devoting themselves to worshipping the Calf and saw his brother ignoring what they were doing. Sa'īd ibn Jubayr said that. This is why it is said that hearing a report is not like seeing something with one's one eyes. One does not pay attention to what is related from Qatādah, if it is sound from him. In other words it is not true that Mūsā threw down the Tablets because he saw that they contained the excellence of the community of Muḥammad ﷺ and that his community would not have that excellence. This is a vile view that should not be ascribed to Mūsā. It was already mentioned that Ibn 'Abbās said that the Tablets broke and that details of discrimination were removed from them and that guidance and mercy remained in them (7:145).

Some ignorant Sufis use this as evidence that it permissible to cast off one's garment when there is intense ecstasy in singing. Then some of them take them off without damaging them and some of them rip them and then throw them away. They say, 'Those are absent from themselves are not blameworthy. When sorrow at his people worship of the Calf overwhelmed Mūsā, he cast down the Tablets and broke them and did not know what he had done.'

Abū al-Faraj al-Jawzī said, 'Where is a sound transmission from Mūsa that he threw them in a manner which broke them? What is said in the Qur'an is: "*He threw them.*" How do we know that they were broken? And even if it is admitted that they were broken, how can we say that he intended to break them? Then if we say that it is true that he did that, we say that he was in a state of self-forgetfulness to such an extent that if he had been in front of a sea of fire, he would have plunged into it. They consider it sound for those people to claim such states of self-forgetfulness, while they still know that the singing is from someone else and they take care to avoid falling into a well if it is there! How can there be an analogy between the states of the Prophets and the state of those fools?' Ibn 'Aqīl was asked about their feigned ecstasy and tearing their garments and said, 'It is an error and unlawful. The Messenger of Allah ﷺ forbade wasting property.' Someone said to him, 'They do not know what they are doing.' He replied, 'If they attend these places while knowing that rapture will overpower them and remove their understanding, they sin by bringing about that tearing and other things which are wrong. The responsibility of the *Sharī'ah* is not cancelled for them because, before attending, they have a responsibility to avoid a place which will lead to that, just as they are forbidden to drink an intoxicant. It is the same with this rapture which the people of *taṣawwuf* call ecstasy if they affirm that it is of an intoxicating nature. If they lie about it, they do wrong while sober, and so there is no safety in either state and it is mandatory to avoid the places of doubt.'

He seized hold of his brother's head, dragging him towards him.

He grabbed him by his beard and chin. Hārūn was three years older than Mūsā and the tribe of Israel loved him more than Mūsā because he was mild-tempered. The schools have four interpretations about his seizing hold of his brother's head. The first is that that was common among them, as the Arabs do when taking hold of the beard of one's brother and friend out of honour and esteem, and that was not intended to humiliate him. The second is that in this intimate conversation he was confiding to him that the Tablets had been sent down to him, but he wanted to conceal what he was saying from the tribe of Israel before [informing them about] the Torah. Hārūn said to him, '*Do not take hold of my beard or head,*' lest the tribe of Israel assumed that what Mūsā was doing was humiliating Hārūn. The third is that he did that to him because it occurred to him that Hārūn had inclined with the tribe of Israel in what they did regarding the Calf. The like of this is not permitted for Prophets. The fourth interpretation is that he brought his brother close to him to learn what he knew and Hārūn disliked that lest the tribe of Israel imagine that he had humiliated him. His brother explained to him that they, the worshippers of the Calf, had victimised him. They almost killed him. When Mūsā heard his excuse, he said, '*Lord, forgive me and my brother,*' in other words, 'forgive my anger because of which I threw the Tablets down and forgive my brother because he thought that he was unable to object to what they were doing, even if he himself did not fall short,' i.e. 'forgive my brother since he did not fall short.'

Al-Ḥasan said, 'All of them worshipped the Calf except for Hārūn since, if there had been a believer other than just himself and Hārūn, Mūsā would not have confined himself to his words: "*Lord, forgive me and my brother,*" and would have prayed for that believer as well.' It is said that he asked forgiveness for himself for what he did to his brother when he was angry with him since it was nothing to do with him, and so he informed him what had happened so that he would return and they could meet them. That is why Allah says: '*What prevented you following me, Hārūn, when you saw that they had gone astray? Did you too, then, disobey my command?*' (20:92) Hārūn explained that he had stopped out of fear that they would kill him. The *āyah* indicates that if someone fears he will be killed on account of changing something wrong, he can remain silent. That was explained in *Āl 'Imrān* (3:21).

Ibn 'Arabī said, 'There is evidence in this *āyah* that anger does not alter rulings as some people claim. Mūsā's anger did not change the ruling of any of his actions. His actions in throwing down the Tablets, rebuking his brother and slapping the angel are treated in the usual way.' Al-Mahdawī said, 'It was because his anger was for Allah Almighty and his silence towards the tribe of Israel out of fear that they would fight one another or divide.'

'Son of my mother, the people oppressed me

He was the son of his mother and father, but these words contain gentleness and kindness. Az-Zajjāj said, 'It is said that Hārūn was the brother of Mūsā by his mother and not his father.' It is recited both with *fatḥah* and *kasrah* on the *mīm*. If someone recites it with a *fatḥah*, he makes 'son of my mother' a single noun like '*khamsata 'ashar*' (fifteen). If someone recites it with a *kasrah*, he annexes it to the pronoun of the speaker and then elides the *yā'* of the annexation because the basis of the vocative includes elision, and so the *kasrah* remains on the *mīm* to indicate the annexation. The reading of Ibn as-Samayqa', '*yā-bna ummī*', indicates this as it keeps the original *yā'*. Al-Kisā'ī and Abū 'Ubayd said, '*yā-bna umma*' which implies: 'son of his mother'. The Basrans say that this statement is an error because the *alif* is light and not elided, but the two nouns are made into a single noun. Al-Akhfash and Abū Ḥātim said, '*yā-bna ummi*'. This is an aberrant dialect and an unlikely reading. This is how it is used when the *iḍāfah* is connected to you. When the *iḍāfah* is connected to something connected to you, then it is proper to say, 'O slave of my slave (*ghulāma ghulāmī*)' and 'O son of my brother (*ibna akhī*)'. They permit '*yā-bna 'amm*' since it is often used in language. Az-Zajjāj and an-Naḥḥās say, 'But it has an excellent, good aspect: making the son with the mother and with the uncle into a single word, as when you say "*yā khamsat 'ashari-qbalū* (O fifteen, advance!)" The *yā'* is elided as in "*yā ghulām*". '*The people oppressed me*' means 'they abased me and threatened me as weak,' and '*almost killed me.*' They came close to doing that. '*Killed me*' has two *nūns* because it is a future verb.

Do not give my enemies cause to gloat over me.

This means: 'Do not make them happy.' *Shamātah* is being happy when hardships in the *dīn* and this world befall your brother, and it is forbidden and prohibited. A *ḥadīth* reported from the Prophet ﷺ says: 'Do not gloat over your brother lest Allah gives him well-being and tests you.' The Messenger of Allah ﷺ used to seek refuge from gloating. He said, 'O Allah, I seek refuge with You from an evil decree, the arrival of wretchedness and the gloating of enemies.' Al-Bukhārī and others transmitted it. A poet said:

When time drags people down,
putting other than us in great distress,
Say to those who gloat over us: 'Wake up!
Those who gloat will encounter what we have encountered.

Mujāhid and Mālik ibn Dīnār recited '*tashmata*' and '*al-a'dā'u*' in the nominative. The meaning is: 'Do not do to me anything that will make my enemies gloat,' meaning that 'that should not be done by them on account of what You do to me.' Mujāhid also said '*tashmat*' with '*al-a'dā'a*' in the accusative. Ibn Jinni said, 'The meaning is, "Do not gloat over me, Lord." This is permitted, as Allah says: "*Allah mocks them*" (2:15) and the like. Then he returns to what is meant and conceals the verb because of which '*enemies*' is in the accusative as if He were saying, "Do not let my enemies gloat over me."' Abū 'Ubayd said that it is related that Humayd said, 'Do not gloat (*tashmit*).' An-Naḥḥās said, 'There is no logic to his recitation because if someone gloats, you must say, "*tashamta*".'

Do not include me with the wrongdoing people

This means among those who worshipped the Calf.

إِنَّ ٱلَّذِينَ ٱتَّخَذُواْ ٱلْعِجْلَ سَيَنَالُهُمْ غَضَبٌ مِّن رَّبِّهِمْ وَذِلَّةٌ فِى ٱلْحَيَوٰةِ
ٱلدُّنْيَا وَكَذَٰلِكَ نَجْزِى ٱلْمُفْتَرِينَ ﴿١٥٢﴾ وَٱلَّذِينَ عَمِلُواْ ٱلسَّيِّـَٔاتِ ثُمَّ تَابُواْ
مِنۢ بَعْدِهَا وَءَامَنُوٓاْ إِنَّ رَبَّكَ مِنۢ بَعْدِهَا لَغَفُورٌ رَّحِيمٌ ﴿١٥٣﴾

152-3 As for those who adopted the Calf, anger from their Lord will overtake them together with abasement in the life of this world. That is how we repay the purveyors of falsehood. But as for those who do evil actions and then subsequently repent and believe, in that case your Lord is Ever-Forgiving, Most Merciful.

As for those who adopted the Calf, anger from their Lord will overtake them together with abasement in the life of this world.

Anger from Allah is punishment. Their '*abasement in the life of this world*' is by their being commanded to kill one another. It is said that the abasement was paying the *jizyah*, but that is unlikely because *jizyah* was not taken from them, but was taken from their descendants. Then it is said that this is the final part of the words spoken by Mūsā, which Allah reports from him, and then the words end.

That is how we repay the purveyors of falsehood.

The statement made by Mūsā was before the people repented by killing themselves. When they repented and Allah pardoned them after extensive killing had taken place, as was already made clear in *al-Baqarah* (2:54), He told them that those of them who had been killed were martyrs and those who remained alive were forgiven. It is said that there was a group of those who drank the Calf into their hearts – meaning love of it – but did not repent, and it is they who are meant by Allah's words: '*those who adopted the Calf.*' It is said that it means those of them who had died before Mūsā returned from the appointment. It is said that it means their children and that it is what happened to the Qurayẓah and an-Nadīr – meaning that it will afflict their descendants. Allah knows best. The words '*That is how we repay the purveyors of falsehood*' mean 'We will do to those who forge lies the like of what We did to these.' Mālik ibn Anas said, 'There is no innovator who will not find himself covered by abasement.' Then he recited: '*As for those who adopted the Calf...*' '*Purveyors of falsehood*' means the innovators.

It is said that Mūsā commanded the Calf to be slaughtered and blood flowed from it. Then it was filed down and thrown with the blood into the sea and he commanded them to drink from that water. If someone who was made to drink had worshipped the Calf, that appeared on the outside of his mouth, and so those who worshipped the Calf were known. This was mentioned elsewhere.

But as for those who do evil actions

This refers to unbelief and acts of disobedience, '*then subsequently repent and believe,*' after they did them, '*in that case your Lord,*' after repentance, '*is Ever-Forgiving, Most Merciful.*'

وَلَمَّا سَكَتَ عَن مُّوسَى ٱلْغَضَبُ أَخَذَ ٱلْأَلْوَاحَ وَفِى نُسْخَتِهَا هُدًى وَرَحْمَةٌ
لِّلَّذِينَ هُمْ لِرَبِّهِمْ يَرْهَبُونَ ﴿١٥٤﴾

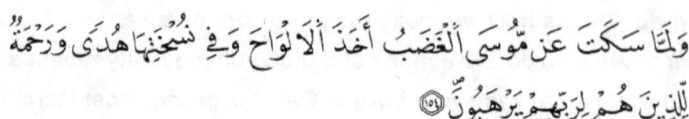

154 When Mūsā's anger abated he picked up the Tablets and in their inscription was guidance and mercy for all of them who feared their Lord.

When Mūsā's anger abated he picked up the Tablets

When he had calmed down. Mu'āwiyah ibn Qurrah recited it as *sakana* instead of *sakata*. The root of *sukūt* is stillness and withholding. One says, 'The river flowed for three days and then was still (*sakana*),' in other words stopped flowing. 'Ikrimah said, 'Mūsā's anger stilled,' and it is reversed, like, 'I put the finger into the ring,' when the ring was put onto the finger, and 'the hat went on my head' when my head went into the cap.

'*He picked up the Tablets*' which he had thrown down, '*and in their inscription was guidance and mercy*,' guidance from misguidance and mercy from punishment. *Naskh* is transmitting what was in the Book to another Book. Both the original from which the copy is made and what is copied is called *nuskhah*. It is said that when the Tablets broke, Mūsā fasted for forty days, and they were returned to him and those Tablets were restored in the form of two tablets. Nothing was missing from them. Ibn 'Abbās mentioned that. Al-Qushayrī said, 'According to this, "*in their inscription*" implies that what was inscribed on the broken tablets and transferred to the new tablets was guidance and mercy. 'Aṭā' said, 'in what remained of them.' That was because only a seventh of them remained and six-sevenths of them were gone. But no limits (*ḥudūd*) or judgments were removed.

It is said that the meaning of '*in their inscription*' is what was copied in them from the Preserved Tablet of guidance. It is said that the meaning is that what Allah wrote for him contained guidance and mercy and it does not need to have a source from which it is copied. This is as it is said, 'Copy (*insakh*) what he told you,' meaning to write it down.

for all of them who feared their Lord.

There are three views about the *lām* (*for*) here. The view of the Kufans is that it is redundant. Al-Kisā'ī said, 'It is related to me that someone heard al-Farazdaq say, "I paid a hundred *dirhams* for it (*lahā*)," meaning "I spent it."' It is said that it is the *lām* of causation, meaning, 'those who fear because of their Lord without showing off or reputation,' as al-Akhfash said. Muḥammad ibn Yazīd said that it is connected to the verbal noun and means: 'those whose fear is of their Lord.' It is said that since the object was first, it is good to include the *lām* as in Allah's words: '*if you are those who can interpret dreams*' (12:43). When the object comes first, the action of the verb is weak and it takes the position of one that is not transitive.

وَاخْتَارَ مُوسَىٰ قَوْمَهُۥ سَبْعِينَ رَجُلًا لِّمِيقَٰتِنَا فَلَمَّآ أَخَذَتْهُمُ الرَّجْفَةُ قَالَ
رَبِّ لَوْ شِئْتَ أَهْلَكْتَهُم مِّن قَبْلُ وَإِيَّٰيَ أَتُهْلِكُنَا بِمَا فَعَلَ
السُّفَهَآءُ مِنَّآ إِنْ هِيَ إِلَّا فِتْنَتُكَ تُضِلُّ بِهَا مَن تَشَآءُ وَتَهْدِي مَن تَشَآءُ
أَنتَ وَلِيُّنَا فَاغْفِرْ لَنَا وَارْحَمْنَا وَأَنتَ خَيْرُ الْغَٰفِرِينَ ﴿١٥٥﴾

155 Mūsā chose seventy men from his people for Our appointed time and when the earthquake seized them he said, 'My Lord, if You had willed, You could have destroyed them previously and me as well. Would you destroy us for what the fools among us did? It was only a trial from You by which You misguided those You willed and guided those You willed. You are our Protector so forgive us and have mercy on us. You are the Best of Forgivers.

Mūsā chose seventy men from his people for Our appointed time and when the earthquake seized them

'*People*' and '*men*' are two objects and the '*min*' is elided before '*people*'. [POEMS] He chose them from the people. The words '*when the earthquake seized them*' means when they died. *Rajfah* is an intense earthquake. It is related that they were shaken until they died.

he said, 'My Lord, if You had willed, You could have destroyed them previously and me as well.

'*Me as well*' means their nation, as the Almighty says: '*if a man dies.*' (4:176). '*Iyyāy*' is conjunctive. The meaning is, 'If You had wished, You could have made us die, in the presence of the tribe of Israel, before we went to keep the appointment so that they would not suspect me.' Abū Bakr ibn Abi Shaybah related from Yaḥyā ibn Sa'īd al-Qaṭṭān from Sufyān from Abū Isḥāq from 'Umārah ibn 'Abd that 'Alī said, 'Mūsā and Hārūn and Shabbar and Shabīr, the sons of Hārūn, went, and they reached a mountain where there was a bed. Hārūn stood on it and his soul was taken. Mūsā returned to his people and they said, "You have killed him. You resented the fact that he was kind to us," or words to that effect. (Sufyān was unsure.) He replied, "How could I kill him when his two sons were with me?" He said, "Choose whomever you wish." They chose ten from each tribe."' He said, 'That is the context of Allah's words: "*Mūsā chose seventy men from his people for Our appointed time*". They went there and asked, "Who killed you, Hārūn?" He replied, "No one killed me; Allah took me." They said, "Mūsā, you were not disobeyed."

So the earthquake seized them and they began to shake right and left, and he said: "*My Lord, if You had willed, You could have destroyed them previously and me as well. Would you destroy us for what the fools among us did?*"' He said, 'He prayed to Allah Who brought them to life and made them all Prophets.'

It is said that the earthquake seized them because of their words: '*Show us Allah openly*' (4:153) and Allah's words: '*And when you said to Mūsā, "Mūsā, we will not believe in you until we see Allah with our own eyes." So the thunder-bolt struck you dead...*' (2:55) as was explained in *al-Baqarah*. Ibn 'Abbās said, 'The earthquake seized them because they did not stop worshipping the Calf and were not content with worshipping Allah.' It is said that those seventy were those who did not say, '*Show us Allah openly*.' Wahb said, 'They did not die, but the earthquake terrified them to the point that their joints almost showed and Mūsā himself feared they would die.' Wahb's statement that they died for a day and a night was already mentioned in *al-Baqarah*. Other than this is said about the reason why they were seized by the earthquake, and Allah knows best the soundness of it. The aim of the question in Allah's words: '*Would You destroy us?*' is denial, meaning You would not do that. That is frequently used in Arabic. When it is negative, it has a positive meaning as in:

> Are you not the best of those who ride mounts,
> and the most generous of the worlds to the tribes?

It is said that the meaning is supplication implying 'Do not destroy us.' He ascribed it to himself when what is meant were the people who died in the earthquake. Al-Mubarrad said that what is meant by the question is to consider something terrible, as if he were saying, 'Do not destroy us.' Mūsā knew that Allah would not destroy anyone for the sin of someone else, but it is like the words of 'Isā, '*If You punish them, they are Your slaves.*' (5:118) It is said that what is meant by the fools are the seventy and so the meaning is, 'Would you destroy us, the tribe of Israel, for what those fools did in saying, "*Show us Allah openly*"?'

It was only a trial from You

This is only Your test and testing. *Fitnah* (*trial*) is here ascribed to Allah, and Mūsā does not ascribe it to himself in the same way that Ibrāhīm said: '*When I am ill, it is He Who heals me*' (26:80), ascribing illness to himself and healing to Allah. Yūsha' said: '*No one made me forget to remember it except Shayṭān.*' (18: 63) Mūsā derived that from the words of Allah to him: '*We tried your people after you left.*' (20:85) When he returned to his people and saw the Calf which lowed set up for worship, he said:

'It was only a trial from You by which You misguided those You willed and guided those You willed.' This refutes the Qadariyyah.

وَاكْتُبْ لَنَا فِي هَٰذِهِ الدُّنْيَا حَسَنَةً وَفِي الْآخِرَةِ إِنَّا هُدْنَا إِلَيْكَ ۚ قَالَ عَذَابِي أُصِيبُ بِهِ مَنْ أَشَاءُ ۖ وَرَحْمَتِي وَسِعَتْ كُلَّ شَيْءٍ ۚ فَسَأَكْتُبُهَا لِلَّذِينَ يَتَّقُونَ وَيُؤْتُونَ الزَّكَاةَ وَالَّذِينَ هُمْ بِآيَاتِنَا يُؤْمِنُونَ ﴿١٥٦﴾

156 Prescribe good for us in this world and the Next World. We have truly turned to You.' He said, 'As for My punishment, I strike with it anyone I will. My mercy extends to all things but I will prescribe it for those who are godfearing and pay *zakāt*, and those who believe in Our Signs:

Prescribe good for us in this world and the Next World. We have truly turned to You.'

This means: 'Give us success in terms of righteous actions through which good actions will be written for us.' And good in '*the Next World*' refers to the repayment for them. '*We have truly turned to You*' means 'we have repented.' Mujāhid, Abū al-'Āliyah and Qatādah said that. *Hawd* is repentance as mentioned in *al-Baqarah*. (2:62)

He said, 'As for My punishment, I strike with it anyone I will.

Allah will strike those who deserve it, meaning 'This earthquake and thunderbolt is a punishment from Me with which I will strike whomever I wish.' It is said that the meaning of '*anyone I will*' means 'whomever I wish to misguide.'

My mercy extends to all things, but I will prescribe it for those who are godfearing and pay *zakāt*,

It is general, meaning that there is no end to it and that whoever enters it will not be deprived of it. It is said, 'It encompasses all of creation. Even the animals show mercy and kindness to their offspring.' Some commentators have said, 'This *āyah* contains hope for everything, even Iblīs. He said, "I am a thing." So Allah Almighty adds: "*but I will prescribe it for the godfearing.*" Then the Jews and the Christians said: "We are godfearing," so Allah Almighty says: "*those who follow the Messenger, the unlettered Prophet*" (7:157) and the *āyah* limits the generality. Praise belongs to Allah.' Ḥammād ibn Salamah related from 'Aṭāh ibn as-Sā'ib from Sa'īd ibn Jubayr that Ibn 'Abbās said, 'Allah prescribed it for this Community.'

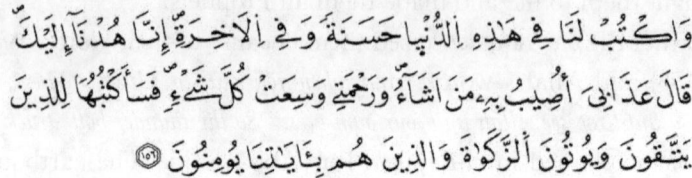

ٱلَّذِينَ يَتَّبِعُونَ ٱلرَّسُولَ ٱلنَّبِيَّ ٱلْأُمِّيَّ ٱلَّذِى يَجِدُونَهُۥ مَكْتُوبًا
عِندَهُمْ فِى ٱلتَّوْرَىٰةِ وَٱلْإِنجِيلِ يَأْمُرُهُم بِٱلْمَعْرُوفِ وَيَنْهَىٰهُمْ عَنِ
ٱلْمُنكَرِ وَيُحِلُّ لَهُمُ ٱلطَّيِّبَٰتِ وَيُحَرِّمُ عَلَيْهِمُ ٱلْخَبَٰٓئِثَ وَيَضَعُ
عَنْهُمْ إِصْرَهُمْ وَٱلْأَغْلَٰلَ ٱلَّتِى كَانَتْ عَلَيْهِمْ ۚ فَٱلَّذِينَ
ءَامَنُوا۟ بِهِۦ وَعَزَّرُوهُ وَنَصَرُوهُ وَٱتَّبَعُوا۟ ٱلنُّورَ ٱلَّذِىٓ أُنزِلَ
مَعَهُۥٓ ۙ أُو۟لَٰٓئِكَ هُمُ ٱلْمُفْلِحُونَ ﴿١٥٧﴾

157 those who follow the Messenger, the Unlettered Prophet, whom they find written down with them in the Torah and the Gospel, commanding them to do right and forbidding them to do wrong, making good things lawful for them and bad things unlawful for them, relieving them of their heavy loads and the chains which were around them. Those who believe in him and honour him and help him, and follow the Light that has been sent down with him, they are the ones who are successful.'

Yaḥyā ibn Abī Kathīr related from Nawf al-Bilākī al-Ḥimyarī that, 'When Mūsā chose seventy men of his people for the appointment with his Lord, Allah Almighty said to Mūsā, "I will make the earth a mosque for you and pure for you to pray wherever the prayer catches you, except in a lavatory, bath-house or grave, and I will place tranquillity (*sakīnah*) in your hearts and I will make you recite the Torah from memory. Men and women, free people and slaves, young and old will recite it." Mūsā told his people that and they said, "We only want to pray in temples and we cannot bear the *Sakīnah* in our hearts, and we want it to remain in the Ark. We cannot recite the Torah by memory and we only want to recite it by seeing it." So Allah Almighty said: "*I will prescribe it for those who are godfearing …to …the ones who are successful.*" He appointed it for this Community. Mūsā said, "Lord, make me their Prophet." He replied, "Their Prophet will be from among them." He said, "Lord, make me one of them." He answered, "You will not meet them." Mūsā said, "Lord, I have brought you a delegation of the tribe of Israel. Give the gift we would normally receive on arrival to someone else." So Allah revealed: "*Among the people of Mūsā there is a group who guide by the truth and act justly in accordance with it.*" (7:159) So Mūsā was satisfied.' Nawf added, 'So praise Allah Who gave you the gift the tribe of Israel would have received on arrival.'

Abū Nu'aym also related this story from the *ḥadīth* of al-Awzā'ī. He related from Yaḥyā ibn Abī as-Saybānī that Nawf al-Bikālī said, when he began an admonition, 'Will you not praise your Lord who made you present after you were absent, took for you your share and gave you the gift that people normally receive on arrival?' That was because Mūsā came to the tribe of Israel and Allah said to them, 'I have made the earth a mosque for you so you could pray on it, and your prayer will be accepted except in three places. If anyone prays in them, his prayer is not accepted: graves, bathhouses and the lavatory.' They said, 'No, only in the temple.' He said, 'So I have made the earth pure for you when you do not find water.' They said, 'No, only water.' He said, 'It has been granted for you that if a man prays alone, his prayer is accepted.' They said, 'No, only in a group.'

those who follow the Messenger, the Unlettered Prophet

These words, as we mentioned, remove the Jews and Christians from sharing in Allah's words: '*I will prescribe it for those who are godfearing*,' and show that this promise is only for the community of Muhammad ﷺ. Ibn 'Abbās, Ibn Jubayr and others said that. '*Follow*' means in respect of his *Sharī'ah*' and *dīn* and what he brought. '*Messenger*' and '*Prophet*' are two nouns indicating two different concepts. '*Messenger*' is more specific than '*Prophet*'. The Messenger is put first out of concern for the meaning of the Message. Otherwise, the meaning of Prophethood precedes it. That is why the Messenger of Allah ﷺ corrected al-Barā' when he said, 'By Your Messenger whom You sent.' He said to him, 'Say, "I have believed in Your Prophet whom You sent."' It is transmitted in the *Ṣaḥīḥ*. Furthermore the words, 'By Your Messenger whom You sent' repeats the Message, which has the same meaning, and so it is like padding which has no use, as opposed to His words, 'Your Prophet whom You sent.' According to this, every Messenger is a Prophet, but not every Prophet is a Messenger, because both Messengers and the Prophets share in the general business, which is Prophethood, but they differ in a specific matter, which is the Message. If you said, 'Muḥammad is a Messenger from Allah,' that contains the fact that he is a Prophet and the Messenger of Allah. That is how it was with other Prophets.

'*Unlettered*' (*ummī*) is ascribed to the unlettered community which is on the root of a newborn, not knowing writing or reading, Ibn 'Azīz said that. Ibn 'Abbās said, 'Your Prophet ﷺ was unlettered, not writing or reading or reckoning. Allah Almighty says: "*You never recited any Book before it nor did you write one down with your right hand.*" (29:48)' It is related in the *Ṣaḥīḥ* from Ibn 'Umar that the Prophet ﷺ said, 'We are an unlettered nation. We do not write or reckon.' It is said that the Prophet ﷺ was ascribed to Makkah, the mother of the cities. An-Naḥḥās mentioned that.

whom they find written down with them in the Torah and the Gospel

Al-Bukhārī related that 'Aṭā' ibn Yasār said, 'I met 'Abdullāh ibn 'Amr ibn al-'Āṣ and he said, "Tell me about the description of the Messenger of Allah ﷺ in the Torah." He replied, "Indeed, by Allah, some of the characteristics by which he is described in the Qur'an can also be found in the Torah: 'O Prophet! We have sent you as a witness, and a bringer of good news and a warner and as a refuge for the unlettered. You are My slave and My Messenger. I have called you the one in whom people put their trust, one who is neither coarse nor vulgar and who neither shouts in the markets, nor repays evil with evil, but rather pardons and forgives.' Allah will not take him back to Himself until the crooked community has been put straight by him and they say, 'There is no god but Allah.' Through him blind eyes, deaf ears and closed hearts will be opened."'

We find in other than al-Bukhārī that 'Aṭā' said, 'Then I met Ka'b and asked him about that description and they did not differ by a single letter, although Ka'b said some of the words in his dialect: "*qulūban ghulūfiyā*" (instead of *ghulfan*), "*ādhānan ṣumūmiyyā*" (instead of *ṣumman*) and "'*ayunan 'umūmiyā*" (instead of '*umyan*).' Ibn 'Aṭiyyah said, 'I think this is weak and non-Arabic.' It is also related that Ka'b said '*ghulūfan*', '*ṣumūmān*' and "*umūmiyān*'. Aṭ-Ṭabarī said that it is the dialect of Ḥimyar.

Ka'b added in the description of the Prophet ﷺ, 'His birthplace will be Makkah, his emigration will be to Ṭābah, his kingdom in Syria, and his community will be praisers. They praise Allah in every state and at every stage. They will perform *wuḍū'* on their limbs and wear their waist-wrappers to the middle of their calves. They will observe the sun, praying the prayer where it catches them, even on top of rubbish heaps. Their rows in battle are like their rows in the prayer.' Then he recited: '*Allah loves those who fight in His Way in ranks like well-built walls.*' (61:4)

commanding them to do right and forbidding them to do wrong,

'Aṭā' said that commanding to do the right is not considering anything to be equal with Allah, possessing noble character and maintaining ties of kinship. '*Forbidding the wrong*' is worshipping idols and cutting off kin.

making good things lawful for them

The position of Mālik is that good things are those which are made lawful. It is as if they are described as good since it is an expression which contains praise and honour. According to this, we say that foul things are forbidden things. That is why Ibn 'Abbās said that bad things are the flesh of pigs, usury and the like. Accordingly, Mālik makes some foul things lawful, like snakes, scorpions, bats and the like. The position of ash-Shāfi'ī is that things are good in respect of taste, although the expression in his view is not an undefined term, because its being undefined in this aspect of food would necessitate making wine and pigs lawful. He thinks that it is specific to that which the *Sharī'ah* made lawful. He thought that '*bad things*' is a general expression for both things forbidden by the *Sharī'ah* and foul things in general, and so he forbids scorpions, bats, geckoes and what is like that. People have these two views which were mentioned in *al-Baqarah* (2:168).

relieving them of their heavy loads

Iṣr is weight. Mujāhid, Qatādah and Ibn Jubayr said that. *Iṣr* is also a contract. Ibn 'Abbās, aḍ-Ḍaḥḥāk and al-Ḥasan said that. This *āyah* includes both meanings. The tribe of Israel had a contract made with them to establish actions that weighed heavily on them, and that contract was removed from them by Muḥammad ﷺ as well as the alleviation of the burden of those actions in the form of things such as the washing off of urine, making booty lawful, and sitting, eating and sleeping with a menstruating woman. When urine got onto one of their garments, the tribe of Israel used to cut it out. When booty was collected, a fire descended from heaven and consumed it. When a woman menstruated, they would not go near her, and there are other things which are confirmed in firm *ḥadīth*s and elsewhere.

and the chains which were around them.

Chains is a metaphorical expression for those burdens. One of the burdens is the prohibition of working on the Sabbath. It is related that on the Sabbath Mūsā saw a man carrying a stalk and struck off his head. This is the view of the majority of commentators. They also had no provision for blood money, but only retaliation. They were commanded to kill themselves as a sign of their repentance. That is likened to chains as a poet said:

It is not like the custom of the house, Umm Mālik,
    but chains encircle the necks.
A young man becomes like a mature man, only speaking fairly,
    and so the critics have a rest.

He likens the limits (*ḥudūd*) of Islam and its prohibitions to its preventing proceeding to forbidden things by having chains around the neck. Part of this idea is what Abū Aḥmad ibn Jaḥsh said to Abū Sufyān:

> Take her away! Take her away!'
> Her collar is the collar of a dove.

It means her shame sticks to her. When someone has a collar, it is as if it sticks.

If it asked how can chains be added to a heavy load when chains is a plural and load is singular, the answer is *iṣr* is a verbal noun which can also be used for the plural. Ibn 'Āmir recited *āṣār* in the plural, like their actions. It is plural because of the different types of sins. The rest have it in the singular because it is a verbal noun which is used for both a little and a lot of the same genus although the word is singular. They agree on the singular in Allah's words: '*Do not make us bear a burden.*' (2:276). It is the same whenever this convention is used to convey the plural.

Those who believe in him and honour him and help him

They respect and help him. Al-Akhfash said, 'Al-Jaḥdarī and 'Īsā recited it in Form I as *'azarūhu*, as is also done in 5:12.' '*The Light*' referred to is the Qur'an and they are '*successful*' in obtaining what is desired as already mentioned.

قُلْ يَٰٓأَيُّهَا ٱلنَّاسُ إِنِّى رَسُولُ ٱللَّهِ إِلَيْكُمْ جَمِيعًا ٱلَّذِى لَهُۥ
مُلْكُ ٱلسَّمَٰوَٰتِ وَٱلْأَرْضِ لَآ إِلَٰهَ إِلَّا هُوَ يُحْىِۦ وَيُمِيتُ فَـَٔامِنُوا۟
بِٱللَّهِ وَرَسُولِهِ ٱلنَّبِىِّ ٱلْأُمِّىِّ ٱلَّذِى يُؤْمِنُ بِٱللَّهِ وَكَلِمَٰتِهِۦ وَٱتَّبِعُوهُ
لَعَلَّكُمْ تَهْتَدُونَ ١٥٨

158 Say: 'Mankind! I am the Messenger of Allah to you all, of Him to whom the kingdom of the heavens and earth belongs. There is no god but Him. He gives life and causes to die. So believe in Allah and His Messenger, the Unlettered Prophet, who believes in Allah and His words, and follow him so that hopefully you will be guided.'

Allah tells us that Mūsā gave the good news of his coming and 'Īsā also gave the good news of his coming. Then He commanded him to say of himself: '*I am the Messenger of Allah to you all.*' '*His words*' are the words of Allah which he transmitted in the Torah, Gospel and Qur'an.

وَمِن قَوْمِ مُوسَىٰٓ أُمَّةٌ يَهْدُونَ بِالْحَقِّ وَبِهِۦ يَعْدِلُونَ ﴿١٥٩﴾

159 Among the people of Mūsa there is a group who guide by the truth and act justly in accordance with it.

They call people to guidance. The meaning of '*act justly*' is in giving judgment. In the *tafsīr*, those were people beyond China, beyond the river of sand, who worshipped Allah with truth and justice. They believed in Muḥammad and abandoned the Sabbath and faced our *qiblah*. None of them reached us and none of us reached them. It is related that when there was disagreement after Mūsā, a nation of them were guided to the truth and were unable to remain in the midst of the tribe of Israel and so Allah brought them out to a part of His earth apart from other people and they had an underground passage through the earth. They walked along it for a year and a half until they emerged beyond China. They are following the truth until today. There is a sea between other people and them because of which they do not reach them.

Jibrīl conveyed the Prophet ﷺ to them during the Night Journey and they believed in him and he taught them some *sūrah*s of the Qur'an and asked them, 'Do you have a measure and a weight?' 'No,' they replied. He asked, 'What is the source of your livelihood?' They answered, 'We go out to the land and cultivate it. When we harvest it, we place what we harvest there, and if one of us needs it, he takes what he needs.' He asked, 'Where are your women?' They answered, 'Apart from us. When one of us needs his wife, he goes to her at the time of need.' He asked, 'Do any of you lie when speaking?' They said, 'If one of us were to do that, a flame would take him. Fire would descend and burn him up.' He asked, 'Why are your houses all the same size?' They answered, 'So that no one is above anyone else.' He asked, 'Why are your graves at your doors?' They said, 'So that we do not forget to remember death.' Then when the Messenger of Allah ﷺ returned to this world on the Night Journey, these words were revealed to him: '*Among those We have created there is a community who guide by the Truth and act justly according to it.*' (7:181) It means the community of Muḥammad ﷺ. Allah told him: 'That which I gave Mūsā for his people I have given you for your community.' It is said that the people referred to are those who believed in our Prophet Muhammad ﷺ among the People of the Book. It is also said that they are a people from the tribe of Israel who hold to the *Sharī'ah* of Mūsā as it was before it was written down and did not alter it nor kill the Prophets.

وَقَطَّعْنَٰهُمُ ٱثْنَتَىْ عَشْرَةَ أَسْبَاطًا أُمَمًا ۚ وَأَوْحَيْنَآ إِلَىٰ مُوسَىٰٓ إِذِ
ٱسْتَسْقَىٰهُ قَوْمُهُۥٓ أَنِ ٱضْرِب بِّعَصَاكَ ٱلْحَجَرَ ۖ فَٱنۢبَجَسَتْ مِنْهُ ٱثْنَتَا
عَشْرَةَ عَيْنًا ۖ قَدْ عَلِمَ كُلُّ أُنَاسٍ مَّشْرَبَهُمْ ۚ وَظَلَّلْنَا عَلَيْهِمُ ٱلْغَمَٰمَ
وَأَنزَلْنَا عَلَيْهِمُ ٱلْمَنَّ وَٱلسَّلْوَىٰ ۖ كُلُوا۟ مِن طَيِّبَٰتِ مَا
رَزَقْنَٰكُمْ ۚ وَمَا ظَلَمُونَا وَلَٰكِن كَانُوٓا۟ أَنفُسَهُمْ يَظْلِمُونَ ﴿١٦٠﴾
وَإِذْ قِيلَ لَهُمُ ٱسْكُنُوا۟ هَٰذِهِ ٱلْقَرْيَةَ وَكُلُوا۟ مِنْهَا حَيْثُ شِئْتُمْ
وَقُولُوا۟ حِطَّةٌ وَٱدْخُلُوا۟ ٱلْبَابَ سُجَّدًا نَّغْفِرْ لَكُمْ
خَطِيٓـَٰٔتِكُمْ ۚ سَنَزِيدُ ٱلْمُحْسِنِينَ ﴿١٦١﴾ فَبَدَّلَ ٱلَّذِينَ ظَلَمُوا۟ مِنْهُمْ
قَوْلًا غَيْرَ ٱلَّذِى قِيلَ لَهُمْ فَأَرْسَلْنَا عَلَيْهِمْ رِجْزًا مِّنَ ٱلسَّمَآءِ
بِمَا كَانُوا۟ يَظْلِمُونَ ﴿١٦٢﴾

160-2 We divided them up into twelve tribes – communities. We revealed to Mūsā, when his people asked him for water: 'Strike the rock with your staff.' Twelve fountains flowed out from it and all the people knew their drinking place. And We shaded them with clouds and sent down manna and quails to them: 'Eat of the good things We have provided you with.' They did not wrong Us; rather it was themselves they wronged. When they were told: 'Live in this town and eat of it wherever you like and say, "Relieve us of our burdens!" and enter the gate prostrating. Your mistakes will be forgiven you. We will grant increase to good-doers.' But those of them who did wrong substituted words other than those they had been given. So We sent a plague on them from heaven for their wrongdoing.

We divided them up into twelve tribes – communities.

Allah enumerated His blessings to the tribe of Israel and made them tribes so that each tribe was known by its leader, making things easy for Mūsā. We read in Revelation: '*We raised up twelve leaders from among them.*' (5:12) That was already discussed. The word '*twelve*' is feminine when the noun '*tribe*' is masculine because it is after '*communities*' and so the feminine is ascribed to them. If it is said it is in the masculine for tribes, that it is permitted according to al-Farrā'. It is said that *asbāṭ* means tribes and parties. That is why the number is feminine. A poet said:

All of Quraysh are ten sub-tribes (*abṭun*),
and you are free of its ten tribes (*qabā'il*).

The noun *batn* is applied to both the tribe and the sub-tribe. That is why it is feminine. *Batn* is masculine and *asbāṭ* is a masculine plural. Az-Zajjāj said that the meaning is 'We divided them into twelve groups.' '*Tribes*' is an appositive for '*twelve*' and '*communities*' is an adjective of tribe. Al-Mufaḍḍal recited 'divided' in Form I from 'Āṣim. *Asbāṭ* is used of the tribes of the descendants of Isḥāq as *qabā'il* is used for the descendants of Ismā'īl. *Asbāṭ* is derived from *sibṭ*, which is a tree which provides fodder for camels and it was fully discussed in *al-Baqarah* (2:136).

Ma'mar related from Hammām ibn Munabbih from Abū Hurayrah from the Prophet ﷺ about Allah's words: '*But those of them who did wrong substituted words other than those they had been given.*' [The words were: '*ḥittatun*' ('*Relieve us of our burdens.*')] They said, '*ḥabbatan fī sha'arah*' ['a grain in a hair'].' They were told: '*enter the gate prostrating*' and they entered creeping forward on their bottoms. '*For their wrongdoing*' is in the indicative mood because it is a future verb although it would normally be in the subjunctive. *Mā* has the meaning of the verbal noun, referring to '*their wrongdoing*'. The ideas and rulings in this *āyah* were already mentioned in *al-Baqarah* (2:58). Praise belongs to Allah.

وَسْـَٔلْهُمْ عَنِ ٱلْقَرْيَةِ ٱلَّتِى كَانَتْ حَاضِرَةَ ٱلْبَحْرِ إِذْ
يَعْدُونَ فِى ٱلسَّبْتِ إِذْ تَأْتِيهِمْ حِيتَانُهُمْ يَوْمَ سَبْتِهِمْ شُرَّعًا
وَيَوْمَ لَا يَسْبِتُونَ لَا تَأْتِيهِمْ كَذَٰلِكَ نَبْلُوهُم بِمَا كَانُوا۟
يَفْسُقُونَ ﴿١٦٣﴾ وَإِذْ قَالَتْ أُمَّةٌ مِّنْهُمْ لِمَ تَعِظُونَ قَوْمًا ٱللَّهُ مُهْلِكُهُمْ أَوْ
مُعَذِّبُهُمْ عَذَابًا شَدِيدًا قَالُوا۟ مَعْذِرَةً إِلَىٰ رَبِّكُمْ وَلَعَلَّهُمْ يَتَّقُونَ ﴿١٦٤﴾

163-4 Ask them about the town which was by the sea when they broke the Sabbath – when their fish came to them near the surface on their Sabbath day but did not come on the days which were not their Sabbath. In this way We put them to the test because they were deviators. When a group of them said, 'Why do you rebuke a people whom Allah is going to destroy or severely punish?' they said, 'So that we have an excuse to present to your Lord, and so that hopefully they will be godfearing.'

Ask them about the town which was by the sea

This means ask about the people of the town. It is used to designate them because they lived there or because of their gathering. It is similar to the words of the Prophet ﷺ, 'The Throne shook at the death of Sa'd ibn Mu'ādh,' meaning the angels, the people of the Throne, at joy and the good news of his arrival. This means: 'Ask the Jews who are your neighbours about the reports of their ancestors and how Allah transformed them into apes and pigs.' This is a question entailing rebuke and confirmation. That is a sign of the truthfulness of the Prophet ﷺ since Allah informed him of these matters without him being taught about them. They used to say, 'We are the sons of Allah and His beloved ones because we are the tribe of His *Khalīl*, Ibrāhīm, and from the tribe of Israel, who are the virgin brides of God, from the tribe of Mūsā, the *Kalīmu-llāh*, and from the tribe of His son 'Uzayr and so we are their children.' Allah said to His Prophet, 'Ask them, Muḥammad, about the town. Did I not punish them for their sins?' That is because they altered one of the rulings of the *Sharī'ah*.

There is disagreement about which town it was. Ibn 'Abbās, 'Ikrimah and as-Suddī said that it was Ayla. Ibn 'Abbās also said that it was Madyan between Ayla and Sinai. Az-Zuhrī said Tiberias. Qatādah and Zayd ibn Aslam said that it was on the coast of Syria between Madyan and 'Aynūn and was called Maqnā. The Jews used to conceal this story since it put them in a shameful light.

The phrase '*which was by the sea*' means close to the sea. One says, 'I was close to the house,' meaning near to it. '*...they broke the Sabbath*' by fishing when they were forbidden to do so. *Sabata* is used for the Sabbath since the Jews abandoned working on it. *Subita* is used to mean 'being lethargic', from which the word *subāt* (lethargy) is derived. *Asbata* means to be still without moving. The word '*Sabbath*' (*sabt*) is derived from rest and cutting off. The plural is *asbut, subūt* and *asbāt.*

It is reported from the Messenger of Allah ﷺ: 'Anyone who is cupped on Saturday and then gets leprosy should only blame himself.' Our scholars say that that is because blood congeals on Saturday. When it is assisted in its emergence, it does not flow properly and that turns into leprosy. Most recite '*ya'dūna*' while Abū Nahīk recited *yu'iddūna.* The first is from [the meaning of] Form VIII and the second from Form IV, implying that they prepared the apparatus with which to catch them. Ibn as-Samayqa' recited '*al-asbāṭ*' in the plural. It is also recited as '*isbātihim*'.

when their fish came to them near the surface on their Sabbath day

'*Shurra'*' means with many clear paths in the water. Al-Layth said that this is when the fish hold their heads high. It is said that it means that the fish of the sea used to come on Saturday in shoals and crowd around Ayla. Allah inspired them to do that since there was no fishing on Saturday because Allah had forbidden the Jews to fish then. It is said that they used to come openly to its gates, like white rams with their heads up high. Some historians related that. So they violated that prohibition and caught them on the Sabbath. Al-Ḥasan said that. It is said that it was Sunday, and that is sounder as will be explained.

on the days which were not their Sabbath

These are the days when they did not observe the Sabbath. One says *sabata, yusbitu* when the Sabbath is esteemed. Al-Ḥasan recited '*yusbitūna*', meaning 'entered the Sabbath'. One says '*ajma'nā*', '*azharnā*' and '*ashharnā*' for 'We entered Friday, we entered *Ẓuhr*, and we entered the month.' The verb '*did not come*' refers to their fish.

In this way We put them to the test because they were deviators.

It means: 'We made worship difficult for them and tested them.' The *kāf* is in the position of the accusative. '*Because they were deviators*' means because of their deviance. Al-Ḥusayn ibn al-Faḍl was asked, 'Do you find in the Book of Allah that the lawful is only what comes to you as nourishing food and the unlawful is what comes to you as excess?' He answered. 'Yes, in the story of Dāwūd and Aylah: "...when their fish came to them near the surface on their Sabbath day but did not come on the days which were not their Sabbath."'

It is related in the stories about this *āyah* that this happened in the time of Dāwūd, and that Iblīs inspired them and said, 'You are only forbidden to take them on Saturday, so make traps.' They used to drive the fish to them on Friday and they would remain in them unable to get out due to lack of water and they would take the fish out on Sunday. Ashhab related that Mālik said, 'Ibn Rūhmān claimed that a man would take a thread and put a loop in it and cast it over the tail of the fish. There was a peg on the end of the thread. He would leave it like that until Sunday. Then the people wanted to employ that stratagem when they saw what this man did and that he was not tried so that he had a lot of fish and took them to the market. The deviants proclaimed that he had fished. A group of the tribe of Israel got up and forbade it and stated the prohibition publicly and then withdrew.'

It is said that those who forbade it said, 'We will not live with you, and they divided the town with a wall. One morning those who forbade it were in their gatherings and none of those who had transgressed came out. They said, 'Something has happened to the people.' They climbed the wall and looked over it and they had become monkeys. They opened the gate and entered and the monkeys recognised their relatives among the people while the people did not recognise their relatives among the monkeys. So the monkeys began to come to their human relatives, and sniff their clothes and weep. The human relative would say, 'Did we not forbid you!' and the monkey would indicate yes with its head. Qatādah said, 'The young men became monkeys and the old men pigs. Those who forbade it were saved and the rest were destroyed.'

According to this view, the tribe of Israel only divided into two groups, and the meaning of that can be seen in Allah's words: '*When a group of them said, "Why do you rebuke a people…*"' namely, 'those who did that said to the warners when they admonished them, "Since you know that Allah will destroy us, why do you admonish us?"' So Allah turned them into monkeys. 'They said, "*So that we have an excuse to present to your Lord, and so that hopefully they will be godfearing.*"' Aṭ-Ṭabarī reports this from Ibn al-Kalbī.

Most commentators say that the tribe of Israel divided into three groups. That is clear from the pronouns in the *āyah.* One group of about seventy thousand disobeyed and fished. One group withdrew and neither forbade nor disobeyed. This group said to those who forbade: '*Why do you forbid a people?*' – meaning forbid their disobedience – '*whom Allah is going to destroy*' or probably punish in the way Allah customarily does to disobedient communities. The group who forbade said, 'Our admonition is our excuse with Allah. Perhaps they will be godfearing.' If they had been two groups, the forbidding group would have said to the disobedient, 'Perhaps you will be godfearing.'

Then after this there is disagreement. One group said that the group which did not forbid and did not disobey were destroyed along with the rebels as a punishment for not forbidding them. Ibn 'Abbās said that. He also said, 'I do not know what was done to them.' That is the literal meaning of the *āyah.* 'Ikrimah said, 'I said to Ibn 'Abbās when he said, "I do not know what was done to them," "Do you not see that they disliked what they did and differed from them and said, '*Why do you admonish a people whom Allah is going to destroy*'?" I continued at him until he admitted that they had been saved and clothed me in this robe.' This is the position of al-Ḥasan. One thing indicating that it was only the transgressing group which was destroyed is that Allah says: '*We seized those who did wrong*' (7:165) and His words: '*You are well aware of those of you who broke the Sabbath.*' (2:65)

'Īsā and Ṭalḥah recited *'excuse'* in the accusative, and al-Kisā'ī says that it is in the accusative for two reasons: one is as a verbal noun and the second is to imply, 'We did that as an excuse.' That is the reading of Ḥafṣ from 'Āṣim, while the rest read it in the nominative, and that is preferred because they did not mean that they wanted to be excused from something new, but they were asked, *'Why did you admonish?'* and they replied, 'Our admonishment of them is our excuse.' If a man were to say to another man, 'My excuse is to Allah and to yourself for such-and-such,' meaning excusing himself, it is in the accusative. This is the view of Sībawayh.

This *āyah* indicates the principle of 'blocking the means' (*sadd adh-dharā'i'*). This was already discussed in *al-Baqarah* (2:65) and there was discussion about whether or not the transmogrified people reproduced. Praise belongs to Allah. Commanding the right and forbidding the wrong were discussed in *Āl 'Imrān* and *al-Mā'idah* (3:21, 5:2). Withdrawing from the people of corruption and avoiding them was discussed in *an-Nisā'*, and that whoever sits with them is like them (4:140). There is no need to repeat it here.

فَلَمَّا نَسُوا۟ مَا ذُكِّرُوا۟ بِهِۦٓ أَنجَيْنَا ٱلَّذِينَ يَنْهَوْنَ عَنِ ٱلسُّوٓءِ وَأَخَذْنَا ٱلَّذِينَ
ظَلَمُوا۟ بِعَذَابٍۭ بَـِٔيسٍۭ بِمَا كَانُوا۟ يَفْسُقُونَ ١٦٥

165 Then when they forgot what they had been reminded of, We rescued those who had forbidden the evil and seized those who did wrong with a harsh punishment because they were deviators.

Forgetting can be both inadvertent and deliberate abandonment of something, as is shown by Allah's words: *'Then when they forgot what they had been reminded of,'* meaning that they intentionally abandoned it. Another example can be seen in His words: *'They have forgotten Allah, so He has forgotten them.'* (9:67) The meaning of *'harsh'* is 'severe'. There are ten readings of the word used for it. The first is the reading of Abū 'Amr, Ḥamzah and al-Kisā'ī: *'ba'īs'* from the form *fa'īl*. The second is the reading of the people of Makkah which is *bi'īs* with same form but with *kasrah* on the *bā'*. The third is the reading of the people of Madīnah as *bīsin*. There are two views about it. Al-Kisā'ī said that the root of it is *biyis* and the two *yā's* meet and one of them has been elided and there is a *kasrah* on the first, like *raghīf* and *shahīd*. It is said that it means *bi's* on the form of *fi'l*, with a *kasrah* on the first and lightened *hamzah* and the *kasrah* elided, as one says *raḥim* and *riḥm*.

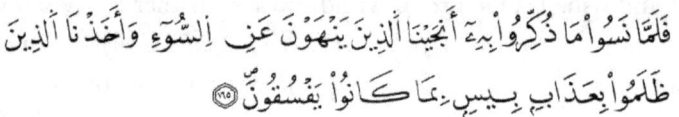

The fourth reading is that of al-Hasan where the *bā'* has a *kasrah*, followed by silent *hamzah*, followed by, a *sīn* with a *fatḥah* (*bi'sa*). The fifth is recited by Abū ʿAbd ar-Raḥmān al-Muqrī as *ba'isin* with a *bā'* with a *fatḥah*, a *hamzah* with a *kasrah* and a *sīn* with a *kasrah* and *tanwīn*. The sixth is that Yaʿqūb al-Qāri' who said that some recited *ba'isa* with a *fatḥah* on the *bā'*, a *kasrah* on the *hamzah* and a *fatḥah* on the *sīn*. The seventh is the reading of al-Aʿmash which is *bay'isin* on the measure of *fay'il*. *Bay'asin* on the measure of *fay'al*, and *ba''isin* with a *fatḥah* on the *yā'*, a double *hamzah* and *sīn* with a *kasrah* and *tanwīn* are also related from him. This is in the reading of al-Aʿmash. The tenth is the reading of Naṣr ibn ʿĀṣim: *bayyisin* with a *fatḥah* on the *bā'* and a doubled *yā'* without a *hamzah*. Yaʿqūb al-Qāri' said that some reciters recite '*bi'yasin*'. These are the eleven readings that an-Naḥḥās mentioned.

ʿAlī ibn Sulaymān said that the Arabs use this word to describe something ruinous. When applied to a punishment, it means a ruinous punishment. As for the reading of al-Ḥasan, Abū Ḥātim claimed that there is no sense to it because one does not say, 'I passed by a *bi'sa* man' so that one can say, '*bi'sa-r-rajul*' or '*bi'sa rajulan*'. An-Naḥḥās said, 'What Abū Ḥātim said is rejected because of what grammarians say.' [BIT MORE]

فَلَمَّا عَتَوْا عَن مَّا نُهُوا عَنْهُ قُلْنَا لَهُمْ كُونُوا قِرَدَةً خَاسِئِينَ ﴿١٦٦﴾

166 When they were insolent about what they had been forbidden to do, We said to them, 'Be apes, despised, cast out!'

When they went beyond the limits in disobeying Allah. The verb *khasa'a* means 'to put far away and drive off' was already mentioned in *al-Baqarah* (2:66). It indicates that acts of disobedience are a reason for vengeful requital. This is unconcealed. It is said that Allah said that to them in words which were heard and so they were like that. It is said that the meaning is: 'We made them into monkeys.'

وَإِذْ تَأَذَّنَ رَبُّكَ لَيَبْعَثَنَّ عَلَيْهِمْ إِلَىٰ يَوْمِ الْقِيَامَةِ مَن يَسُومُهُمْ سُوءَ الْعَذَابِ
إِنَّ رَبَّكَ لَسَرِيعُ الْعِقَابِ وَإِنَّهُ لَغَفُورٌ رَّحِيمٌ ﴿١٦٧﴾

167 Then your Lord announced that He would send against them until the Day of Rising people who would inflict an evil punishment on them. Your Lord is Swift in Retribution. And He is Ever-Forgiving, Most Merciful.

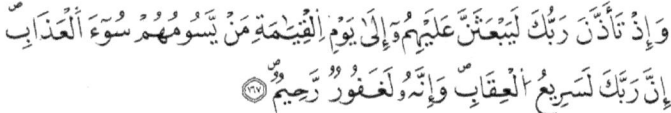

He informed their ancestors that if they altered things and did not believe in the unlettered Prophet, Allah would send against them someone who would punish them. Abū 'Alī said that *ādhana* is to announce and *adhdhana* is to call. Some people say that they both mean announce as is the case with *ayqana* and *tayaqqana* (to be certain). Zuhayr said:

I said, 'You state that game can be surprised.
If you lose it, you can kill it.

Another said:

You state that the worst of people is alive.
He is called Yasār in their motto.

In both cases, the verb means to inform.

The meaning of '*inflict on them*' is to make them experience. It was already mentioned in *al-Baqarah* (2:49). It is said that the one referred to is Nebuchadnezzar. It is said that it means the Arabs. It is said that it is the community of Muḥammad ﷺ which is more likely as they will last until the Day of Rising, and Allah knows best.

Ibn 'Abbās said that the '*evil punishment*' here is paying *jizyah*. If it is said, 'They were transformed, so how could *jizyah* be taken from them?' the answer is that it was taken from their sons and children, who are the most abased of people, the Jews. Sa'īd ibn Jubayr said that it is the *kharāj* and no Prophet at all obliged the *kharāj* before Mūsā who was the first to impose it. He collected it for thirteen years and then stopped; and our Prophet ﷺ [also collected it.]

وَقَطَّعْنَٰهُمْ فِى ٱلْأَرْضِ أُمَمًا مِّنْهُمُ ٱلصَّٰلِحُونَ وَمِنْهُمْ دُونَ ذَٰلِكَ وَبَلَوْنَٰهُم
بِٱلْحَسَنَٰتِ وَٱلسَّيِّـَٔاتِ لَعَلَّهُمْ يَرْجِعُونَ ﴿١٦٨﴾

168 And We divided them into nations in the earth. Some of them are righteous and some are other than that. We tried them with good and evil so that hopefully they would return.

We divided them among the lands. By it He means to unsettle their business and so they are disunited. '*Some of them are righteous*' is nominative for the inceptive. What is meant are those who believed in Muḥammad ﷺ and those among them who did not alter things and then died before the abrogation of the Law of

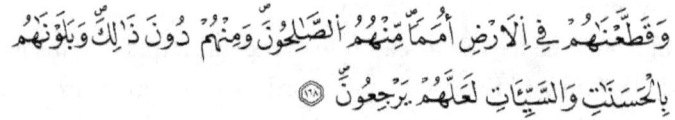

Mūsā, or those who are beyond China, as already stated. The word '*that*' is in the accusative as an adverb. An-Naḥḥās said, 'We do not know of anyone who makes it nominative. What is meant are the unbelievers among them.' '*We tried them*' means, 'put them to the test.' '*Good*' refers to fertility and health, '*evil*' to drought and hardships. The words '*so that hopefully they would return*' mean revert from their unbelief.

فَخَلَفَ مِنۢ بَعْدِهِمْ خَلْفٌ وَرِثُوا۟ ٱلْكِتَـٰبَ يَأْخُذُونَ عَرَضَ هَـٰذَا ٱلْأَدْنَىٰ
وَيَقُولُونَ سَيُغْفَرُ لَنَا وَإِن يَأْتِهِمْ عَرَضٌ مِّثْلُهُۥ يَأْخُذُوهُ ۚ أَلَمْ يُؤْخَذْ
عَلَيْهِم مِّيثَـٰقُ ٱلْكِتَـٰبِ أَن لَّا يَقُولُوا۟ عَلَى ٱللَّهِ إِلَّا ٱلْحَقَّ وَدَرَسُوا۟ مَا فِيهِ ۗ
وَٱلدَّارُ ٱلْـَٔاخِرَةُ خَيْرٌ لِّلَّذِينَ يَتَّقُونَ ۗ أَفَلَا تَعْقِلُونَ ﴿١٦٩﴾

169 An evil generation has succeeded them, inheriting the Book, taking the goods of this lower world, and saying, 'We will be forgiven.' But if similar goods come to them again they still take them. Has not a covenant been made with them in the Book, that they should only say the truth about Allah and have they not studied what is in it? The Final Abode is better for those who are godfearing. Will you not use your intellect?

An evil generation has succeeded them,

These are the children of those whom Allah divided throughout the earth. Abū Ḥātim said that *khalf* means children, and the singular and plural are the same. *Khalaf* is the substitute, a child or stranger. Ibn al-A'rabī said that the word *khalaf* refers to righteous descendants and *khalf* to wicked ones. Labīd said:

'Those who lived in their shelters have departed
and I remain behind (*khalf*) like a skin with scabies.

This is borne out by the use of *khalf* meaning ruinous and by the saying: 'He was silent for a thousand words and then spoke evil (*khalf*).' *Khalf* is used in censure and *khalaf* in praise. This is a well-known usage. The Prophet ﷺ said, 'This knowledge will be borne by the just of every generation (*khalaf*).' The words can also be used as synonyms for one other. Ḥassān ibn Thābit said:

We have taken the first step towards you, and we left (*khalfunā*)
someone to follow the first of us in obeying Allah.

Another said:

> We found successors (*khalaf*) who are the worst successors.
> He closed his door to us and then swore.
> The doorkeeper only admits the one he recognises
> as a slave when he stops groaning under a load.

Khalafa [in the poem] is also related as *khaḍafa* which means to succeed. Censure is meant in the *āyah.*

inheriting the Book,

The commentators said that they are the Jews who inherited the Book of Allah and recited it and taught it and then differed from its rulings and did things that it forbade in spite of their study of it. This is to rebuke them and chide them.

taking the goods of this lower world

Then Allah tells us that they took the goods of this world that were offered to them of out of their extreme avarice and avidity. The words '*and saying, "We will be forgiven,"*' when they do not in fact repent clearly indicate that they do not repent.

But if similar goods come to them again they still take them

'Araḍ are worldly goods, and *'arḍā* is wealth other than *dirham*s and *dīnār*s. This *āyah* designates bribes and corrupt earnings. Then Allah censures them for their delusion of first saying, '*We will be forgiven*' and then, when they are able to do the same again, they do so and yet remain in their delusion of being forgiven while they persist in doing it. They say, '*We will be forgiven* as long as we stop what we were doing and repent.' The behaviour that Allah censures here also exists among us. Abū Muḥammad ad-Dārimī reported from Muḥammad ibn al-Mubārak from Ṣadaqah ibn Khālid from Ibn Jābir from an old man called Ibn 'Amr that Mu'ādh ibn al-Jabal said, 'The Qur'an will decay in the hearts of people as cloth becomes ragged and breaks up. They will recite it and not experience any desire or pleasure. They will wear the clothing of sheep over the hearts of wolves. Their actions are avarice not mixed with fear. If they fall short, they say, "We will get there." If they do evil, they say, "Allah will forgive us. We do not associate anything with Him."' It is said that the pronoun '*them*' refers to the Jews of Madīnah, implying that if similar goods come to the Jews of Yathrib in the time of the Prophet ﷺ they will take them as their ancestors did.

Has not a covenant been made with them in the Book

The *Book* is the Torah. This is emphatic regarding the obligation of speaking the truth in law and when rendering judgment. Judges should not, on account of bribes, show bias in favour of falsehood. That which was obligatory on the Jews, and on whose basis the contract was made with them about speaking the truth, was equally made obligatory for us on the tongue of our Prophet ﷺ and in the Book of Allah as mentioned in *an-Nisā'* (4:154). All *Sharī'ahs* are unanimous about this matter. Praise be to Allah.

and have they not studied what is in it?

This means 'have they not read it?' when they were familiar with the contract. Abū 'Abd ar-Raḥmān recited '*addārasū*' and the *tā'* is assimilated into the *dāl*. Ibn Zayd said, 'Someone who was telling the truth would bring them a bribe and they would produce the Book for him and judge in his favour according to what is in it. When someone who was lying came, they took the bribe and brought out their book which they had written themselves and gave judgment in his favour.' Ibn 'Abbās said, '"*That they should only say the truth about Allah*" rather than the lie they told when they said their sins would be forgiven.' Ibn Zayd said, 'It means in the judgments which they give based on it.'

Some scholars said that the meaning of '*darasū*' means 'erased it' by not acting by it and understanding it. The verb, *darasa*, is used when the wind effaces tracks and *darasa* is when one eradicates and removed traces. This meaning is in agreement with Allah's words: '*A group of those who have been given the Book disdainfully toss the Book of Allah behind their backs?*' (2:101) and '*They threw it behind their backs*' (6:187) as already mentioned in *al-Baqarah* (2:102).

وَالَّذِينَ يُمَسِّكُونَ بِالْكِتَٰبِ وَأَقَامُوا الصَّلَوٰةَ إِنَّا لَا نُضِيعُ أَجْرَ
الْمُصْلِحِينَ ﴿١٧٠﴾

170 As for those who hold fast to the Book and establish the prayer, We will not let the wage of the righteous be wasted.

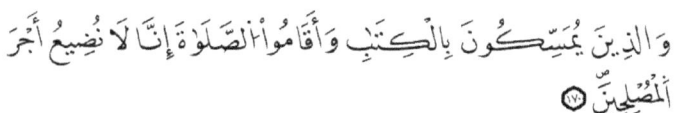

'*Those who hold fast to the Book*' refer to acting according to the Torah. The verb is *massaka*, and *tamassaka* is to seek to hold to something. Abū al-'Āliyah and 'Āṣim, in the transmission of Abū Bakr, recite *yumsikūna* from *amsaka*. The first reading is more appropriate because it contains the meaning of repetition and a lot of holding to the Book of Allah and His *dīn*. They are praised for that. So holding to the Book of Allah and the *dīn* requires cleaving to it and repetition of those actions. Ka‘b ibn Zuhayr said:

> You did not hold to the contract as you claim
> except as water clings to sieves.

It is normal to censure frequent breaking of a contract.

وَإِذْ نَتَقْنَا ٱلْجَبَلَ فَوْقَهُمْ كَأَنَّهُۥ ظُلَّةٌ وَظَنُّوٓا۟ أَنَّهُۥ وَاقِعٌۢ بِهِمْ خُذُوا۟ مَآ
ءَاتَيْنَـٰكُم بِقُوَّةٍ وَٱذْكُرُوا۟ مَا فِيهِ لَعَلَّكُمْ تَتَّقُونَ ﴿١٧١﴾

171 When We uprooted the mountain, lifting it above them like a canopy, and they thought it was about to fall on them: ‘Seize hold vigorously of what We have given you and remember what is in it, so that hopefully you will be godfearing.’

The verb means to ‘raise up’ already mentioned in *al-Baqarah* (2:63). ‘*Like a canopy*’ means as if Allah raised it up to give shade. The meaning of ‘*Seize hold vigorously of what We have given you*’ implies doing it with gravity as was already mentioned (2:63).

وَإِذْ أَخَذَ رَبُّكَ مِنۢ بَنِىٓ ءَادَمَ مِن ظُهُورِهِمْ ذُرِّيَّـٰتِهِمْ وَأَشْهَدَهُمْ عَلَىٰٓ أَنفُسِهِمْ
أَلَسْتُ بِرَبِّكُمْ قَالُوا۟ بَلَىٰ شَهِدْنَآ أَن تَقُولُوا۟ يَوْمَ ٱلْقِيَـٰمَةِ إِنَّا كُنَّا عَنْ هَـٰذَا
غَـٰفِلِينَ ﴿١٧٢﴾ أَوْ تَقُولُوٓا۟ إِنَّمَآ أَشْرَكَ ءَابَآؤُنَا مِن قَبْلُ وَكُنَّا ذُرِّيَّةً مِّنۢ بَعْدِهِمْ
أَفَتُهْلِكُنَا بِمَا فَعَلَ ٱلْمُبْطِلُونَ ﴿١٧٣﴾ وَكَذَٰلِكَ نُفَصِّلُ ٱلْـَٔايَـٰتِ وَلَعَلَّهُمْ يَرْجِعُونَ ﴿١٧٤﴾

172-4 When your Lord took out all their descendants from the loins of the children of Ādam and made them testify against themselves ‘Am I not your Lord?’ they said, ‘We testify that indeed You are!’ Lest you say on the Day of Rising, ‘We knew nothing of this.’ Or lest you say, ‘Our forefathers associated others with Allah before our time, and we are merely descendants coming after them. So are You going to destroy us for what those purveyors of falsehood did?’ That is how We make the Signs clear so that hopefully they will return.

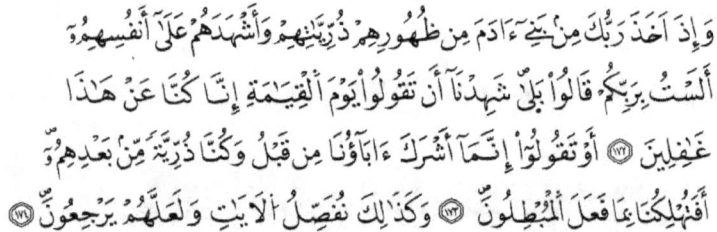

When your Lord took out all their descendants from the loins of the children of Ādam

This means: 'Remind them, in addition to the previous contracts mentioned in their Book, of the contract that I made with people on the Day of Atoms.' This is an ambiguous *āyah.* Scholars have spoken at length about its interpretation and the rulings connected with it. We will mention what they mentioned according to what has reached us.

Some people said, 'The meaning of the *āyah* is that Allah Almighty brought forth one after the other from the loins of the descendants of Ādam.' They said that the meaning of '*made them testify against themselves "Am I not your Lord?"*' is His guiding His creation to knowledge of His Unity, because everyone who is adult knows by necessity that He has one Lord. So He said, '*Am I not your Lord?*' This statement amounts to testimony against them and affirmation on their part, as when the Almighty says about the heavens and the earth that they said, '*We come willingly*' (41:11). Al-Qaffāl believed that. It is said that Allah produced the spirits before the creation of the bodies and that He imbued them with recognition of what was being said to them.

There is a *ḥadīth* from the Prophet ﷺ that expresses other than these two views. It is that Allah produced forms from the back of Ādam which contained souls. Mālik related in his *Muwaṭṭā'* that 'Umar ibn al-Khaṭṭāb was asked about this *āyah* and said, 'I heard the Messenger of Allah ﷺ being asked about it and the Messenger of Allah ﷺ said, "When Allah Almighty created Ādam, He stroked his back with His right hand, and removed progeny from him and said, 'I created these for the Garden and they will act with the behaviour of the people of the Garden.' Then He stroked his back again and brought forth progeny from him and said, 'I created these for the Fire and they will act with the behaviour of the people of the Fire.'" A man asked, "Then of what value are deeds?" The Messenger of Allah ﷺ said, "When Allah creates someone for the Garden, he makes him do the actions of the people of the Garden, so that he dies on one of the actions of the people of the Garden and by it He brings him into the Garden. When He creates someone for the Fire, He makes him do the actions of the people of the Fire, so that he dies on one of the actions of the people of the Fire, and by it, He brings him into the Fire."' Abū 'Umar said, 'This is a *ḥadīth* with a broken *isnād* because Muslim ibn Yasār did not meet 'Umar.' Yaḥyā ibn Ma'īn said that Muslim ibn Yasār is not known. Between him and 'Umar was Nu'aym ibn Rabī'ah whom an-Nasā'ī mentioned, and Nu'aym is not known for having knowledge. Nonetheless the meaning of this *ḥadīth* is sound from the Prophet ﷺ

from many firm paths from the *ḥadīth*s of 'Umar ibn al-Khaṭṭāb, 'Abdullāh ibn Mas'ūd, 'Alī ibn Abī Ṭālib, Abū Hurayrah and others.

At-Tirmidhi related, and said it was sound, that Abū Hurayrah said that the Messenger of Allah ﷺ said, 'When Allah created Ādam, He stroked his back and every soul fell from it which He created from his progeny until the day of Rising and He put between the eyes of every man a nugget of light and then presented them to Ādam who asked, "Lord, who are these?" He answered, "These are your progeny." He saw one man among them and admired a nugget between his eyes and asked, "Lord, who is this?" He answered, "This is a man from one of the last of the nations of your offspring called Dāwūd." He asked, "Lord, how long will he live?" "Sixty years," he was told. He said, "Lord, give him forty years of my life." When Ādam's life ended, the Angel of Death came to him and Ādam said, "Do I not still have forty years of life?" He replied, "Did you not give you them to your descendant Dāwūd?"' He said, 'Ādam denied and his offspring denied. Ādam forgot, so his offspring forgot.' It is found in other than at-Tirmidhī. Then Allah will command the scribes and witnesses. In one variant, he saw among them the weak, the rich, the poor, the abased, the tested and the sound. Ādam asked him, 'Lord, What is this? Have you not made them equal?' He said, 'I wanted to be thanked.'

'Abdullāh ibn 'Amr related that the Prophet ﷺ said, 'They were taken from his back as one uses a comb on the head. Allah gave them intellects like the ant had in the story of Sulaymān and made a contract with them on the basis that He was their Lord and they had no Lord but Him. They affirmed that and made it binding on themselves. He announced that He would send Messengers to them and some of them would testify against others.' Ubayy ibn Ka'b said, 'The seven heavens testified against them, and no one will be born until the Day of Rising without a contract having been made with him.'

There is disagreement about the place where the contract was made when they were brought out, and four things are said. Ibn 'Abbās said that it was on the plain of Na'mān, a valley beside 'Arafah. It is also related from him that it was in Barahbā, a land in India where Ādam descended. Yaḥyā ibn Sallām said that Ibn 'Abbās said about this *āyah*, 'Allah brought Ādam down in India. Then he stroked his back and brought forth from it every soul that He will create until the Day of Rising. Then He said, "*Am I not your Lord?*" They said, "*We testify.*"' Yaḥyā said that al-Ḥasan said, 'Then he put them back in the loins of Ādam.' Al-Kalbī said that it was between Makkah and Ṭā'if. As-Suddi said, 'In the lowest heaven when he descended from the Garden to it. He stroked his back and produced from the right side of his back progeny white like pearls and said to them, "Enter the Garden by My mercy," and He produced from the left side of his back black progeny and said to them, "Enter the Fire, and I do not care."' Ibn Jurayj said, 'Every soul emerged created white for the Garden and black for the Fire.'

Ibn al-'Arabi said, 'If it is asked, "How can it be permitted to punish people when they have not sinned, or punish them for what He Himself willed from them and wrote for them and drove them to?" we say, "On what basis is that forbidden? Is it logically or legally?" If it is said that it is because the merciful and wise among us are not permitted to do that, we answer that it is because above him is a Commander who commands him and One who forbids him. Our Lord is not asked about what He does but they will be asked. It is not permitted to compare creation with the Creator. The actions of Allah's slaves are not comparable to the actions of the Deity. In reality, all actions belong to Allah and creation belongs entirely to Him. He disposes them however He wishes and judges between them as He wills. That which the Ādamic creature feels which gives rise to intrinsic kindness, genetic compassion and love of praise comes about because he anticipates gaining benefit from feeling that. The Creator is free of all that and it is not permitted to consider it.'

There is disagreement about this *āyah* and whether it is specific or general. It is said that the *āyah* is specific because the Almighty says: '*from the loins of the children of Ādam*' and according to this *ḥadīth* the children of Ādam are taken from the loins. The Almighty says: '*Or lest you say, "Our forefathers associated others with Allah before our time,"*' and so it disassociated them from all of those who did not have fathers who were idol-worshippers. It is said that it is particular to those with whom the contract was made on the tongues of the Prophets. It is said that it is general to all mankind because each knows that he was a child and was nourished and nurtured and that He has a Manager and Creator. This is the meaning of '*testify against themselves*'.

The words '*They said, "Indeed"*' mean 'That is mandatory for us.' When creation acknowledged to Allah that He is the Lord and then they forgot it, He reminded them by His Prophets and ended the Reminder with the best of His chosen pure ones so that the proof will be established against them. He says: '*So remind them! You are only a reminder. You are not in control of them.*' (88:21-22) Then he gave him power to control and authority and made his *dīn* firm in the earth. Aṭ-Ṭarṭūshī said, 'This contract is binding on human beings even if they do not remember it in this life, in the same way that, when there is testimony to it, divorce is obliged on someone even when he has forgotten it.'

This *āyah* is used as evidence by those who say that anyone who dies as a child will enter the Garden because of their affirmation in this first contract, but the first contract is not enough for those who reach the age of rationality. This speaker says that the children of the idolaters are in the Garden. That is sound. This is a matter about which traditions differ, but the sound view is what we mentioned, and it will be discussed in *ar-Rūm*, Allah willing. We dealt with it in *Kitāb at-Tadhkirah.*

'*From the loins*' is an inclusive appositive for '*the children of Ādam*'. The words of the *āyah* demand that the contract was with the descendants of Ādam, while Ādam himself is not actually mentioned in the *āyah.* The aspect of the order according to this is: '*when your Lord took all their descendants from the loins of the children of Ādam,*' and he did not mention the loins of Ādam because it is known that they were all his children. They were brought out of his back on the Day of the Contract, and so it is enough to mention '*the children of Ādam*'.

'*Their descendants*': the Kufans and Ibn Kathīr recited it in the plural with a *fatḥah* on the *tā'* (*dhurriyyātihim*) which is used for both one and the plural. He said, '*we are merely descendants coming after them*' and it is plural. The rest recite it in the plural because when the word '*descendants*' is used in the singular, then one uses a word which is not used for one, and so it is single to specify the words of its desired meaning in which nothing else shares, and it is the plural because the backs from which many descendants were produced were many, generation after generation, whose number is only known by Allah, and it is plural because of this.

they said, 'We testify that indeed You are!' Lest you should say

The meaning of the word '*balā*' was already discussed in *al-Baqarah* in 2:81 in full. Reflect on it there. '*Lest you/they should say*' is recited by Abū 'Amr with *yā'* (*an yaqūlū*) in both places referring to the third person repeated before that. The rest recite both with a *tā'* (*you should say*) referring to the second person mentioned in His words, '*Am I not your Lord?*' '*We testify*' can also be part of the words of the angels. When they said, 'Yes,' the angels said, 'We testify that indeed You are, lest you should say.' It is said that the meaning of that is that when they said, 'Yes,' they affirmed His lordship. Allah Almighty said to the angels, 'Testify,' and they said, 'We testify to your affirmation so that you cannot say…' This is the view of Mujāhid, aḍ-Ḍaḥḥāk and as-Suddī.

Ibn 'Abbās and Ubayy ibn Ka'b said that the words, '*We testify*' are the words of the children of Ādam. The meaning is: 'We testify that you are Our Lord and our God.' Ibn 'Abbās said, 'Testify against one another.' The meaning, according to this, is that they said, 'Indeed, some of us testify against others.' If it is the words of the angels, one stops at '*Yes.*' It is not good to stop there if the words are ascribed to the children of Ādam because *an* is connected to what is before '*Yes*' in '*made them testify against themselves,*' *lest they say*… Mujāhid related from Ibn 'Umar that the Prophet ﷺ said, 'Your Lord took from the backs of children of Ādam their descendants as one uses a comb on the head. He said to them, "Am I not your Lord?" They said, "Yes." The angels said, "We testify that you said," i.e. "We testify that you admitted His Lordship so that you do not say …" This indicates the *tā'*.' Makkī said, 'It is chosen because of the soundness of its meaning, and because the group agree on it.'

It is said that words '*We testify*' should be attributed to Allah Almighty and the angels and mean: 'We testified to your admission.' Abū Mālik said that. It is also related also from as-Suddī. The phrase '*We are merely descendants coming after them*' means 'We imitated them' and '*So are You going to destroy us for what those purveyors of falsehood did*?' means 'You would not do that.' There is no excuse for anyone who merely imitates where *tawḥīd* is concerned.

وَٱتۡلُ عَلَيۡهِمۡ نَبَأَ ٱلَّذِيٓ ءَاتَيۡنَٰهُ ءَايَٰتِنَا فَٱنسَلَخَ مِنۡهَا فَأَتۡبَعَهُ ٱلشَّيۡطَٰنُ
فَكَانَ مِنَ ٱلۡغَاوِينَ ١٧٥

175 Recite to them the tale of him to whom We gave Our Signs, but who then cast them to one side and *Shayṭān* caught up with him. He was one of those lured into error.

The People of the Book mentioned a story which they recognised in the Torah and there is disagreement about exactly who the person was to whom the Signs were given. Ibn Mas'ūd and Ibn 'Abbās said that it was Bal'am ibn Bā'ūrā'. It is said it was Nā'im, one of the tribe of Israel in the time of Mūsā. When he looked, he saw the Throne, which is what is meant by the words: '*Recite to them the tale of him to whom We gave Our Signs*' rather than 'Sign'. There were twelve thousand inkwells for the students in his gathering who wrote down what he said. Then he was the first to write a book stating that the world does not have a Maker.

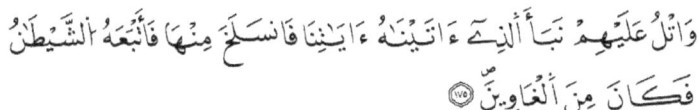

Mālik ibn Dīnār said, 'Bal'am ibn Bā'ūrā' was sent to the King of Madyan to call him to believe and the king was generous to him and paid him close attention and so he followed his religion and left that of Mūsā, and this *āyah* was revealed about him.' Al-Mu'tamir ibn Sulayman related that his father said, 'Bal'am was given prophethood and his prayer was answered. When Mūsā sent the tribe of Israel forward intending to fight the tyrants, the tyrants asked Bal'am ibn Bā'ūrā' to pray against Mūsā. He stood up to pray against him and his tongue was twisted into praying against his companions. He was asked about that and said, "I cannot do more than what you hear." His tongue hung on his chest. He said, 'Now this world and the Next has left me and there only remains trickery, deceit and stratagems. I will tell you what to do. I think that you should send out your young girls to them. Allah hates fornication. If they fall into it, they will be destroyed.' They did that and the tribe of Israel fell into fornication and so Allah sent the plague on them and seventy thousand of them died.' This story is mentioned in full by ath-Tha'labī and others.

It is related that Bal'am ibn Ba'ūra' prayed that Mūsā would not enter the city of the tyrants and it was answered and he remained in the desert. Mūsā said, 'O Lord, for what sin do we remain in the desert?' He answered, 'By the supplication of Bal'am.' He said. 'As You heard his supplication against me, hear my supplication against him.' Mūsā made supplication that Allah would remove the Greatest Name from him. So Allah removed what he had. Abū Ḥāmid said at the end of the book of *Minhāj al-'Ārifīn*, 'I heard one of the gnostics say that one of the Prophets asked Allah Almighty about the business of Bal'am and his expulsion after those signs and miracles. Allah Almighty said, "He did not thank me one day for what I gave him. If he had thanked me for that once, I would not have stripped him of what he had."' 'Ikrimah said, 'Bal'am was a Prophet and was given a Book.' Mujāhid said, 'He was given Prophethood and his people bribed him to be silent and he did that and he left them with what they had.' Al-Māwardī said, 'This is not sound because Allah only selects for His Prophethood those He knows will not abandon obeying Him in favour of disobeying Him.'

'Abdullāh ibn 'Amr ibn al-'Āṣ and Zayd ibn Aslam said, 'It was revealed about Umayyah ibn aṣ-Ṣalt ath-Thaqafī. He used to read books and knew that Allah would send a Messenger at that time and he hoped that he would be that Messenger. When Allah sent Muhammad, ﷺ, he envied him and rejected him. He is the one about whom the Messenger of Allah ﷺ said, "His perception believed while his heart rejected."'

Sa'īd ibn al-Musayyab said, 'It was revealed about Abū 'Āmir ibn Ṣayfī. He used to wear a hair shirt in the *Jāhiliyyah* and he rejected the Prophet ﷺ. That occurred when the Prophet ﷺ entered Madīnah and he asked him, "Muḥammad, what have you brought?" He answered, "I have brought the

Ḥanīfiyyah, the *dīn* of Ibrāhīm." He said, "I am following it." The Prophet ﷺ said, "You are not following it because you have added to it something that is not part of it." Abū 'Āmir said, "May Allah make the one of us who is lying die alone and cast out!" The Prophet ﷺ replied, "Yes, may Allah make the one of us who is lying die like that." This is the one who opposed the Messenger of Allah ﷺ after leaving Madīnah. Abū 'Āmir left for Syria and went to Caesar and wrote to the hypocrites, "Prepare. I will bring you an army from Caesar to expel Muḥammad from Madīnah." He died alone in Syria. About him was revealed: "*and in readiness for those who previously made war on Allah and His Messenger.*" (9:107).' This will be discussed in *at-Tawbah.*

Ibn 'Abbās said in one transmission, 'It was revealed about a man who had three supplications which would be answered. He had a wife called Labsūs and had children by her. She said, "Give me one of the supplications." He said, "You have one. What do you command?" She said, "Pray to Allah to make me the most beautiful woman in the tribe of Israel." When she knew that there was no one like her among them, she was averse to him. So he prayed to Allah to make her a barking dog. So two supplications were used on her. His sons came to him and said, "We cannot endure this. Our mother has become a dog and people blame us for it. Pray to Allah to return her as she was." He prayed and she returned as she was and all the supplications were used on her.' The first view is more famous and most people hold to it.

'Ubādah ibn aṣ-Ṣāmit said, 'It was revealed about Quraysh. Allah brought them His signs which Allah Almighty sent down on Muḥammad ﷺ but they cast them aside and did not accept them.' Ibn 'Abbas said, 'Bal'am was from the city of the tyrants.' It is also said that he was from Yemen.

but who then cast them to one side

This refers to his knowledge of Allah Almighty, meaning that the knowledges he had known were removed from him. We read in a *ḥadīth* from the Prophet ﷺ: 'There are two types of knowledge: knowledge in the heart, which is beneficial knowledge, and knowledge on the tongue, and that is the evidence of Allah Almighty against the son of Ādam.' This is like the knowledge of Bal'am and those like him. We seek refuge with Allah from it. We ask Him for success and dying with realisation. 'Casting aside' is removal, and one uses the verb for a snake sloughing off its skin, i.e. coming out of it. It is said that this is a reversal, implying 'The signs were stripped from him.'

and *Shaytān* caught up with him

He caught him. The verb is used for catching up to the people. It is said that it was revealed about the Jews and the Christians who saw the emergence of Muḥammad ﷺ and then rejected him.

وَلَوْ شِئْنَا لَرَفَعْنَٰهُ بِهَا وَلَٰكِنَّهُۥٓ أَخْلَدَ إِلَى ٱلْأَرْضِ وَٱتَّبَعَ هَوَىٰهُ
فَمَثَلُهُۥ كَمَثَلِ ٱلْكَلْبِ إِن تَحْمِلْ عَلَيْهِ يَلْهَثْ أَوْ تَتْرُكْهُ
يَلْهَث ذَّٰلِكَ مَثَلُ ٱلْقَوْمِ ٱلَّذِينَ كَذَّبُوا۟ بِـَٔايَٰتِنَا فَٱقْصُصِ
ٱلْقَصَصَ لَعَلَّهُمْ يَتَفَكَّرُونَ ﴿١٧٦﴾ سَآءَ مَثَلًا ٱلْقَوْمُ ٱلَّذِينَ كَذَّبُوا۟
بِـَٔايَٰتِنَا وَأَنفُسَهُمْ كَانُوا۟ يَظْلِمُونَ ﴿١٧٧﴾

176-7 If We had wanted to, We would have raised him up by them. But he gravitated towards the earth and pursued his whims and base desires. His metaphor is that of a dog: if you chase it away, it lolls out its tongue and pants, and if you leave it alone, it lolls out its tongue and pants. That is the metaphor of those who deny Our Signs. So tell the story so that hopefully they will reflect. How evil is the metaphor of those who deny Our Signs. It is themselves that they have badly wronged.

If We had wanted to, We would have raised him up by them.

This refers to Bal'am, implying 'If We had wished, We would have made him die before He disobeyed and raised him to the Garden.' *Bihā* is by acting by it.

But he gravitated towards the earth and pursued his whims and base desires.

This means he relied on it as Ibn Jubayr and as-Suddī said. Mujāhid said: 'He relied on it,' meaning relied on its pleasures. The root of *akhlada* means 'to cling'. It is used when someone lives in a place and clings to it. Zuhayr said:

To the one whose houses you visited in the desert
like writing on the stone of a lingering (*mukhlid*) water-course.

The meaning is: 'he clung to the pleasures of the earth' which are implied by '*earth*' because the goods of this world are on the face of the earth. '*His whims and base desires*' were what *shayṭān* made seem attractive to him. It is said that he put his hopes in the unbelievers. It is said that he followed the pleasure of his wife who desired wealth so that she made him pray against Mūsā.

His metaphor is that of a dog: if you chase it away, it lolls out its tongue and pants, and if you leave it alone, it lolls out its tongue and pants.

'*If you chase it away, it lolls out its tongue and pants*' is a precondition and its apodosis. It is in the position of the adverbial *ḥāl*, meaning his metaphor is that of a dog that lolls out its tongue. The meaning is that it is the same thing. He does not refrain from disobedience, like a dog which is like this. The meaning is: it lolls out its tongue in any case, whether you chase it away or not do not chase it away. Ibn Jurayj said the dog has a disconnected intellect, no intelligence. When it is attacked, it lolls out its tongue. If you leave it alone, it lolls out its tongue. That is how it is with the one who abandons guidance: he has no intellect; his intelligence is cut off. Al-Qutabī said, 'Everything which lolls out its tongue does so from fatigue or thirst except for the dog. It lolls out its tongue in a state of tiredness and a state of rest, in a state of illness and a state of health, in a state of satisfied thirst and being thirsty. Allah used it as an example for someone who denies His Signs. He is saying, "If you admonish him, he is misguided. If you leave him, he is misguided. He is like a dog. If you leave it alone, it lolls out its tongue. If you drive it away, it lolls out its tongue," similar to His words: "*If you call them to guidance they will not follow you. It makes no difference if you call them or stay silent.*" (7:193).' Al-Jawharī said the verb *lahatha* is when the tongue comes out of tiredness or thirst. That is how it is with a man when he is tired.

'*If you chase it away, it lolls out its tongue and pants*': because when you attack a dog, it barks, and runs away. If you leave it alone, it attacks you and barks. So it tires itself coming towards you and retreating from you and it experiences thirst in doing that, making its tongue come out. At-Tirmidhi al-Ḥakīm said in *Nawādir al-Uṣūl*, 'Allah likens it to the dog among other animals because the dog has a dead heart. Its lolling its tongue is due to the death of its heart. Other animals are not like that. That is why they do not loll out their tongues. The dog does that because, when Ādam ﷺ descended to earth, the enemy envied him and went to the animals and incited them against Ādam. The dog was the strongest of them in pursuit. Jibrīl brought down the staff that was given to Mūsā at Madyan and made a sign for him to Pharaoh and his Council. He appointed in it immense power. It was taken from the myrtle of the Garden and Allah gave it to Ādam to drive away the animals. It is related that He commanded him to approach a dog and put his hand on its head and because of that it became one of the guardians of his children. When it is taught and learns to hunt, it absorbs the knowledge and accepts training. That is referred to in Allah's words: "*which you have trained as Allah has taught you.*" (5:4)'

As-Suddī said that after that Bal'am used to loll out his tongue as a dog would do. This example is used in the words of many people who know interpretation to be general to all of those who are given the Qur'an but do not act by it. It is said that it is about every hypocrite, but the first view is sounder.

Mujāhid said about these words, that if you attack with the animal you are riding or your foot, it lolls out its tongue, or if you leave it alone, it lolls out its tongue. That is how it is with someone who reads the Book and does not act by what it contains. Someone else said that this is an evil likeness because Allah likens him, in his being overcome by his desires until he does not possess harm or benefit for himself, to a dog which always lolls out its tongue if you attack it or do not attack it. It cannot stop itself from lolling out its tongue. It is said that one of the characteristics of the dog is to attack the one it does not fear will be harsh to it. Then its rage is calmed by any little sop given to it. Allah likens it to someone who accepts a bribe in the *dīn* in that by doing so he casts aside the Signs of his Lord. For someone who reflects on it, the *āyah* indicates that no one should be deluded by his actions or his knowledge since he does not know what his seal will be. It indicates the prohibition of taking a bribe to invalidate a right or change it. It was explained in *al-Mā'idah.* It also indicates the prohibition of imitating a scholar except by a proof he makes clear because Allah Almighty reported that He gave this one His Signs and he cast them aside, so you should fear the like of this in another and only accept from him on the basis of evidence.

How evil is the metaphor of those who deny Our Signs

This is the metaphor of all unbelievers. Allah's words: '*How evil is the metaphor of those*' mean that it is ugly. This is necessary. The verb *sā'a, yasū'u* is transitive, meaning their metaphor is a ugly one. It implies: 'An evil metaphor is that of such people' and the *muḍāf* is elided. '*Metaphor*' is in the accusative for the distinction. Al-Akhfash said, 'The likeness being made of such is a metaphor.' '*People*' is nominative for the inceptive, or for an implied inchoative. The implication is: 'The metaphor made, which is an evil metaphor, is that of these people.' Abū 'Alī took it to mean: 'An evil metaphor is that of these people.' 'Āṣim al-Jaḥdarī and al-A'mash recited, '*sā'a mathalu-l-qawm.*'

مَن يَهْدِ ٱللَّهُ فَهُوَ ٱلْمُهْتَدِى ۖ وَمَن يُضْلِلْ فَأُو۟لَـٰٓئِكَ هُمُ ٱلْخَـٰسِرُونَ ۝١٧٨

178 Whoever Allah guides is truly guided; but those He misguides are the lost.

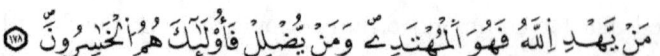

The meaning of this was discussed elsewhere. This *āyah* refutes the Qadariyyah as stated before and it refutes those who say that Allah guided all of those who are responsible and did not permit any of them to be misguided.

وَلَقَدْ ذَرَأْنَا لِجَهَنَّمَ كَثِيرًا مِّنَ الْجِنِّ وَالْإِنسِ لَهُمْ قُلُوبٌ لَّا يَفْقَهُونَ بِهَا وَلَهُمْ أَعْيُنٌ
لَّا يُبْصِرُونَ بِهَا وَلَهُمْ آذَانٌ لَّا يَسْمَعُونَ بِهَا أُولَٰئِكَ كَالْأَنْعَامِ بَلْ هُمْ أَضَلُّ
أُولَٰئِكَ هُمُ الْغَافِلُونَ ١٧٩

179 We created many of the jinn and mankind for Hell. They have hearts they do not understand with. They have eyes they do not see with. They have ears they do not hear with. Such people are like cattle. No, they are even further astray! They are the unaware.

Allah reported that He has created people for the Fire by His justice and then He describes them, saying: '*They have hearts they do not understand with,*' meaning they are in the position of someone who does not understand because they do not benefit from guidance and do not understand the reward nor fear the penalty. '*They have eyes they do not see with*', they do not see guidance, and '*they have ears they do not hear*' the warnings '*with*'. The goal is not to deny the senses having perception at all as we explained in *al-Baqarah* (2:18).

'*Such people are like cattle. No, they are even further astray*' because they are not guided to a reward, making them like cattle in that their only concern is food and drink. They are further astray because cattle are aware of what benefits and harms them and follow their master. They are different to that. 'Aṭā' said. 'Cattle recognise Allah but the unbeliever does not recognise Him.' It is said that cattle obey Allah Almighty but the unbeliever does not obey. '*They are the unaware,*' in that they do not reflect and turn away from the Garden and the Fire.

وَلِلَّهِ الْأَسْمَاءُ الْحُسْنَىٰ فَادْعُوهُ بِهَا وَذَرُوا الَّذِينَ يُلْحِدُونَ فِي أَسْمَائِهِ سَيُجْزَوْنَ
مَا كَانُوا يَعْمَلُونَ ١٨٠

180 To Allah belong the Most Beautiful Names, so call on Him by them and abandon those who desecrate His Names. They will be repaid for what they did.

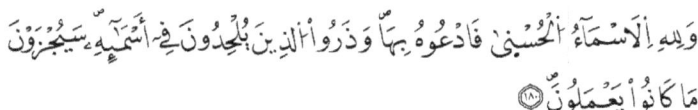

To Allah belong the Most Beautiful Names, so call on Him by them

Allah commands sincere worship of Him and the avoidance of idolaters and heretics. Muqātil and other commentators said, 'The *āyah* was revealed about a Muslim man who used to say in his prayer, "O All-Merciful, Most Merciful." One of the idolaters of Makkah said, "Do not Muḥammad and his companions claim that they worship one god? Why is this one calling on two gods?" So Allah revealed this.'

A *ḥadīth* from Abū Hurayrah is reported in the book of at-Tirmidhī, the *Sunan* of Ibn Mājah and others from the Prophet ﷺ which is a text about Allah having ninety-nine names, each report having something that is not in the others. We explained that in *Kitāb al-Asnā*. Ibn 'Aṭiyyah mentioned the *ḥadīth* of at-Tirmidhī and said that it is not *mutawātir*. Abū 'Īsā said about it, 'This is a *gharīb ḥadīth*. We only know it from the *ḥadīth* of Ṣafwān ibn Ṣāliḥ, who is considered trustworthy by the people of *ḥadīth*.' The *mutawātir ḥadīth* is the words of the Prophet ﷺ: 'Allah has ninety-nine names, one hundred less one. Whoever memorises them will enter the Garden.' The meaning of *aḥṣā* is 'to count and memorise'.

Other things are said which we explained in our book. We mentioned there the verification of the *ḥadīth* of at-Tirmidhī. We also mentioned the names which are agreed upon and those about which there is disagreement, which we found in the books of our imams and which include about two hundred names. Whoever wants them, should go there and to other books written on the subject. Allah is the One who gives success and there is no Lord but Him.

Scholars disagree about the Name and the Named. We mentioned what scholars said about that in our book. Ibn al-Ḥaṣṣār said, 'In this *āyah* the Name is applied to the Named, and it is used for naming.' His words '*To Allah*' are applied to the Named. '*Asmā*'' is the plural of *ism*, which is also used for the named. The soundness of what we said is indicated by His words: '*call on Him by them*.' The *hā'* (*Him*) refers to the Named – Glorious is He – and He is the One who is called upon and the *hā'* (*them*) refers to names, which are the namings by which one calls and nothing else. This is what the Arabic demands. An example of that is the words of the Messenger of Allah ﷺ, 'I have five names. I am Muḥammad and Aḥmad....' Some of this was mentioned in *al-Baqarah* (2:31).

That which the people of the truth believe is that the Name is the Named, or an adjective connected to Him and it is not naming. Ibn al-'Arabī said in his books about this that there are three views concerning it. Some of our scholars have said that that indicates the Name is the named because if it had been other than Him, it would be obliged that the names belong to other than Allah Almighty. The second view is that others said that what is meant by it are the namings because He is one and the names are several. Ibn 'Atiyyah mentioned in his *tafsīr* that the names in the *āyah* means the namings according to the consensus of the interpreters and nothing else is permitted. Qāḍī Abū Bakr said in the *Kitāb at-Tamhīd*, 'The words of the Prophet ﷺ, "Allah has ninety-nine names. Whoever memorises them will enter the Garden" is interpreted as Him having ninety-nine namings without disagreement. These are expressions for the fact of Allah having different attributes. Some of them are only for Himself and some He deserves by an attribute connected to Him. His names which refer to Himself are Him, and what is connected to an attribute of His are names of His. Some of them are attributes of His Essence and some are attributes of actions. This is the interpretation of His words: "*To Allah belong the Most Beautiful Names*," in other words the most beautiful namings. The third view is that Allah has attributes.'

Allah called His Names most beautiful because they are good in renown and hearts. They indicate His Unity, Generosity, Nobility, Mercy and Favour. *Ḥusnā* is a verbal noun which describes them. It is permitted to say that it is the feminine of *aḥsan* in the same way that *kubrā* is the feminine of *akbar*. The plural is *kubar* and *ḥusan*. According to the first view it is singular, as the singular is used for that which is not sentient as we see elsewhere in the Qur'an.

His words, '*so call on Him by them*,' mean 'ask of Him by His Names. So one asks by each Name what is appropriate to it. You say, 'O Merciful, have mercy on Me,' 'O Wise, judge for me,' 'O Provider, provide for Me,' 'O Guide, guide me,' 'O Opener, give me an opening,' 'O Turner, turn to me,' and so on. If you ask by a general name, you say: 'O King, have mercy on me, O Mighty, judge for me, O Kind, provide for Me.' If you call by the Most Universal, Most Majestic Name, you say, 'O Allah,' and it contains every name. You do not say, 'O Provider, guide me' unless you mean, 'O Provider, provide me with good.' Ibn al-'Arabī said, 'That is how you order your supplication if you are among the sincere.' The preconditions of supplication were mentioned in *al-Baqarah* (2:186). Allah knows best.

Qāḍī Abū Bakr ibn al-'Arabi included a number of names in His Names, like 'He whose Light is Perfect, the Best of Heirs, the Best of Plotters, the Fourth of Three, the Sixth of Five, the Good, the Teacher and the like of that.' Ibn al-Ḥaṣṣār said, 'He followed Ibn Barrajān when he mentioned "the Clean" (*an-Naẓīf*) among the names and others which are not reported in the Book or the *Sunnah*.'

As for what he mentioned of names 'which are not reported in the Book or the *Sunnah*,' 'Good (*Ṭayyib*)' has come in *Ṣaḥīḥ Muslim*. At-Tirmidhī transmitted 'the Clean'. It is related from Ibn Abbās that the Prophet ﷺ said in his supplication,

'Lord, assist me and do not assist against me. Help me and do not help against me. Plot for me and do not plot against me.' He said that is a *ḥasan ṣaḥīḥ ḥadīth.* According to this it is permitted to say, 'O Best of plotters, plot for me and do not plot against me.' Allah knows best.

We mentioned the names Good and Clean in our books and elsewhere as part of what has come from the early generations and which is permitted to use to call Him by and pray to Him with, and what it is not permitted to call Him by nor pray to Him with, and what is not permitted to call on Him by nor use to name Him, according to what Shaykh Abū al-Ḥasan al-Ash'arī mentioned. That will be made clear to you, Allah willing.

and abandon those who desecrate His Names. They will be repaid for what they did

The word for '*desecrate*' – *ilḥād* – means to incline to the side and abandon the goal. The verb is used for a man who does this in the *dīn.* There is also the word *laḥd* (niche) in the grave which is called that because it is in a corner. It is also recited *yalḥadūna* (instead of *yulḥidūna*) as a dialect. There are three aspects of *ilḥād.* The first is by changing the names, as was done by the idolaters. That is because they turned them away from what they were and named their idols after them. So they derived *al-Lāt* from Allāh, *al-'Uzzā* from al-'Azīz and *Manāt* from al-Mannān. Ibn 'Abbās and Qatādah said that. The second aspect is by adding to them. The third is by omitting some of them as some of the ignorant people do who originate supplications in which Allah Almighty is named by other than His Names and they mention Him with other than what is mentioned of His actions and other things which are not appropriate.

Ibn al-'Arabī said. 'Beware of them, and no one should make supplication except by what is in the Book of Allah and the five books: al-Bukhārī, Muslim, at-Tirmidhī, Abū Dāwūd and an-Nasā'ī. These are the books around which Islam revolves, and included in them is what is in the *Muwaṭṭā'*, which is the basis of these works, and they should leave other than them. No one should say that he selected such-and-such a supplication. Allah has chosen for him and sent His Messenger to creation with that.'

The meaning of adding to the names is by *tashbīh* and decrease is by divesting Him of these attributes (*ta'ṭīl*). Those who practise *tashbīh* describe Him with what is not conceivable for Him, and the ones who deny strip him of what he is correctly described with. That is why the people of truth say, 'Our *dīn* is a path between the two paths: neither *tashbīh* nor *tanzīh*.' Shaykh Abū al-Hasan al-Bushanjī was asked about *tawḥīd* and said, 'It is affirmation of an essence not likened to other essences and not denied attributes.' It is said that this *āyah* means: 'Abandon them and do not argue with them and do not confront them.' The *āyah*, according to this, was abrogated by fighting. Ibn Zayd said that. It is said that it implies a threat like: '*Leave the person I created on his own to Me alone*' (74:11) and: '*Leave them to eat and enjoy themselves.*' (15:3) It is clear in this *āyah* because He says: '*They will be repaid for what they did.*' Allah knows best.

وَمِمَّنْ خَلَقْنَآ أُمَّةٌ يَهْدُونَ بِالْحَقِّ وَبِهِۦ يَعْدِلُونَ ﴿١٨١﴾

181 Among those We have created there is a community who guide by the Truth and act justly according to it.

The Prophet ﷺ said, 'They are this community.' It is related that he said, 'This is for you, and Allah gave the people of Mūsā the like of it.' He recited this *āyah* and said, 'Among my community are a people who will remain on the truth until 'Īsā ibn Maryam descends.' The *āyah* indicates that Allah will not leave this world at any time without someone who calls to the truth.

وَالَّذِينَ كَذَّبُوا بِـَٔايَٰتِنَا سَنَسْتَدْرِجُهُم مِّنْ حَيْثُ لَا يَعْلَمُونَ ﴿١٨٢﴾

182 But as for those who deny Our Signs, We will lead them, step by step, into destruction from where they do not know.

The Almighty reported that He would lead on those who denied His Signs. Ibn 'Abbās said that this refers to the people of Makkah. 'Leading on' is to seize gradually, stage by stage. *Darj* means to wrap something up, and the verb is used in Form IV and II. It is used for wrapping the dead in their shrouds. It is said that it is from *daraja*, and so meaning to come down step by step to the goal.

Aḍ-Ḍaḥḥāk said it means, 'Whenever they disobey Us anew, they are given a new blessing.' Dhū an-Nūn was asked, 'What is the limit of the way a person can be deceived?' He answered, 'By kindness, and tokens of honour. That is why the Almighty says: "*We will lead them, step by step, into destruction from where they do not know.*" We will pour down blessings on them and make them forget to be grateful for them.' They wrote:

You thought well of days when they were good
 and did not fear any evil which fate may bring.

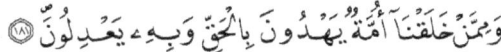

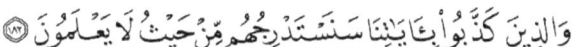

The nights wished you peace and you were beguiled by them.
In nights of pardon, impurities occur.

وَأُمْلِي لَهُمْ إِنَّ كَيْدِي مَتِينٌ ﴿١٨٣﴾

183 I will give them more time. My strategy is sure.

'I will give them longer and defer them and delay their punishment.' '*My strategy*' is My plotting. The adjective '*matīn*' means strong and firm. It comes from *matn*, which is the thick flesh at the side of the spine. It is said that it was revealed about those of Quraysh who mocked. Allah killed them in a single night after He had given them a long delay. It is like Allah's words: '*When they were exulting in what they had been given, We suddenly seized them.*' (6:44)

أَوَلَمْ يَتَفَكَّرُوا مَا بِصَاحِبِهِم مِّن جِنَّةٍ إِنْ هُوَ إِلَّا نَذِيرٌ مُّبِينٌ ﴿١٨٤﴾

184 Have they not reflected? Their companion is not mad. He is only a clear warner.

'*Have they not reflected*?' on what Muḥammad ﷺ has brought them. It is good to stop at '*reflected*'. Then Allah says: '*Their companion is not mad*' to refute their words: '*You, to whom the Reminder has been sent down, are clearly mad.*' (15:6) It is said that it was revealed because the Messenger of Allah ﷺ stood in the night on Ṣafā calling Quraysh tribe by tribe, saying, 'O tribe of so-and-so!' warning them about the force and punishment of Allah. One of them said, 'This companion of yours is mad! He spoke the whole night until morning came.'

أَوَلَمْ يَنظُرُوا فِي مَلَكُوتِ السَّمَاوَاتِ وَالْأَرْضِ وَمَا خَلَقَ اللَّهُ مِن شَيْءٍ وَأَنْ
عَسَىٰ أَن يَكُونَ قَدِ اقْتَرَبَ أَجَلُهُمْ فَبِأَيِّ حَدِيثٍ بَعْدَهُ يُؤْمِنُونَ ﴿١٨٥﴾

185 Have they not looked into the dominions of the heavens and the earth and what Allah has created, and seen that it may well be that their appointed time is near? In what discourse after this will they believe?

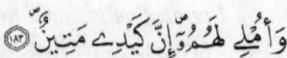

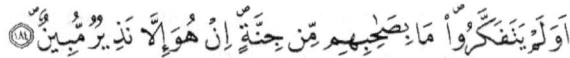

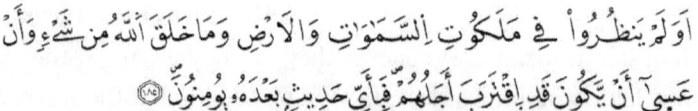

Have they not looked into the dominions of the heavens and the earth

The words '*Have they not looked*' are an expression of amazement at their turning away from looking at Allah's Signs and failing to recognise the perfection of His power as we made clear in *al-Baqarah* (2:15). *Malakūt* (*dominions*) is an intensive form which means 'immense kingdom'. This *āyah* is used as evidence by those who say that it is mandatory to look at Allah's Signs and reflect on His creation, along with other similar *āyahs* such as His words: '*Say: "Look at what there is in the heavens and on the earth"*' (10:101): '*Have they not looked at the sky above them: how We structured it*' (50:6): '*Have they not looked at the camel – how it was created?*' (88:17) and: '*and in yourselves as well. Do you not then see?*' (51:21) Those who say that it is mandatory to look into His Signs and reflect on His creation said that Allah censures the one who does not look and strips them of the benefit of their senses and says: '*They have hearts they do not understand with.*' (7:179)

Scholars disagree about which obligation is first, looking and seeking evidence or belief, which is affirmation in the heart for which recognition is not a precondition. The Qāḍī and others believed that the first of the obligations is to look and deduce because Allah Almighty is not known a priori. He is known by reflection and by deduction from evidence which He has set up in order for Him to be recognised. This is what al-Bukhārī believed when he made a chapter in his book entitled 'Chapter: Knowledge before speaking and acting by the words of the Almighty: "*Know that there is no god but Allah.*" (47:19)' The Qāḍī said, 'Whoever does not know Allah is ignorant, and whoever is ignorant of Him is an unbeliever.' Ibn Rushd said in the *Muqaddimāt*: 'This is not clear because belief is made sound by the certainty which is attained at a later date by someone whom Allah has first guided through *taqlīd* and then by his reflection on other signs which Allah has guided him to reflect on.'

He said, 'Al-Bājī used as this as evidence for the one who says that the consensus of the Muslims is that reflection and deduction is a primary obligation at all times, although the common people and those who imitate (*muqallidūn*) are still called believers.' He added, 'If they did not believe *taqlīd* was sound, it would only be sound to call a person who obtained knowledge by investigation and deduction a believer.' He further said, 'If faith were only valid after reflection and deduction, it would be permitted for the unbelievers, if the Muslims conquer them, to say, "You are not allowed to kill us because part of your *dīn* is that faith is only sound after reflection and deduction. Therefore you must give us more time to look and reflect."' He said, 'This would lead to leaving them with their unbelief. They could not be killed until they had looked and deduced.' This is sound. The Messenger of Allah ﷺ said, 'I was commanded to fight people until they say, "There is no god but Allah," and believe in me and what I have brought. When they do that, their blood and property are protected from me except for a right, and their reckoning is up to Allah.'

Ibn al-Mundhir said in the *Kitāb al-Ashrāf*, concerning the description of the perfection of faith: 'There is a consensus from the people of knowledge that when an unbeliever says, "I testify that there is no god but Allah and I testify that Muḥammad is His slave and Messenger, and that all that Muḥammad brought is true, and I am quit of every *dīn* different from the *dīn* of Islam," and he is adult and sane, then he is a Muslim. If he recants after that and displays unbelief, he is an apostate who must be judged as an apostate is judged.'

Abū Ḥafṣ az-Zanjānī said, 'Our shaykh, Qāḍī Abū Ja'far Aḥmad ibn Muḥammad as-Samnānī, said, "The first of the obligations is to believe in Allah and His Messenger and all that he brought. Then reflection and deduction which lead to true knowledge of Allah Almighty."' So he put belief in Allah Almighty first before knowledge of Allah. He said, 'This is closer to what is correct and kinder to people because most of them do not grasp the reality of recognition, investigation and deduction. If we were to say, "The first of the obligations is knowledge of Allah," that would lead to calling the majority and greatest number unbelievers. Only a few people would enter the Garden. That is unlikely because the Messenger stated that most of the people of the Garden would be from his community, and that all the other nations of the Prophets would form one row and his community eighty rows.' This is clear and unambiguous. Praise belongs to Allah.

Some of the later and former *mutakallimūn* believe that anyone who does not recognise Allah Almighty by the means which they have laid out and the investigations which they have followed, does not have sound belief and is an unbeliever. According to this, most Muslims are unbelievers and the first of those they call unbelievers are their fathers, forebears and neighbours. This is reported from some of them who said, 'Do not condemn me by the great number of the people of the Fire.' Such a statement could only issue from someone ignorant of the Book of Allah and the *Sunnah* of His Prophet ﷺ because it is restricting the vast mercy of Allah at the behest of a very small group of the *mutakallimūn*, who proceed to declare the bulk of the Muslims to be unbelievers.

This is seen in the words of the Bedouin who uncovered his genitals to urinate. The Companions of the Prophet ﷺ chided him. He said, 'O Allah, have mercy on me and Muḥammad and do not have mercy on anyone else with us!' The Prophet ﷺ said, 'You have limited what is limitless.' Al-Bukhārī, at-Tirmidhī and other Imams transmitted it. Do you think that this Bedouin knew Allah by means of proof, evidence, and clarification? His mercy encompasses all things. How many like him are rightly judged to be believers! The Prophet ﷺ was satisfied with many who professed their Islam by just articulating the two *shahādahs*, and he was content with that. Do you not see that he asked the black woman, 'Where is Allah?' She said, 'In the sky.' He asked, 'Who am I?' She answered, 'You are the Messenger of Allah.' He said, 'Free her. She is a believer.' There was no investigation or deduction. He judged that she was a believer immediately, even though she had no reflection or recognition. Allah knows best.

The beautiful faces of youths and women cannot be considered as valid subjects for this kind of reflection. Abū al-Faraj al-Jawzī said that aṭ-Ṭabarī said, 'It reached me that it was attributed to this group who listen to *samā'* that they would look at beardless youths, and would sometimes adorn them with jewellery and dyed garments and claim that their intention was to be increased in faith by looking, reflecting, and seeking evidence of the work of the Creator. This is the furthest limit of following lower desires, delusion of the intellect and opposition to true knowledge.'

Abū al-Faraj further said that Imām Abū al-Wafa' ibn 'Aqīl said that Allah only made it lawful to look at a form when the self did not incline to it and desire had no part of it. Rather it is a type of learning that is not mixed with desire nor accompanied by pleasure. That is why Allah did not send a woman with the Message and did not make women *qāḍīs*, *imāms* or *mu'adhdhins*. All of that is because she can be a focus of lust and temptation. If anyone says, 'I find lessons in beautiful forms,' we say he is lying. If anyone distinguishes himself with having a nature outside of our natures, we say he is lying. This is how *shayṭān* tricks those who make that claim. A wise man said, 'Everything in the macrocosm has a like in the microcosm. That is why the Almighty says: "*We created man in the finest mould*" (95:4) and: "*and in yourselves as well. Do you not then see?*" (51:21)' We explained the nature of this resemblance at the beginning of *al-An'ām* (6:2).

An intelligent person must look at himself and reflect on his creation: from being a spurting fluid to the point of becoming a fully formed creature, helped by foods, taught with kindness, and preserved with gentleness until he gained faculties and reached maturity. Then he says, 'Me! Me!' and forgets: '*a point of time when he was not something remembered*' (76:1) and that he will be buried in the ground. Woe to him if he is regretful! Allah Almighty says: '*We created man from the purest kind of clay, then made him a drop in a secure receptacle; then formed the drop into a clot and formed the clot into a lump and formed the lump into bones and clothed the bones in flesh; and then brought him into being as another creature. Blessed be Allah, the Best of Creators! Then subsequently you will certainly die. Then on the Day of Rising you will be raised again.*' (23:12-16) He sees that he is a slave with a Lord and is responsible and threatened with the punishment if he falls short, and hopes for the reward if he does as he is commanded. So he occupies himself with the worship of his Master – knowing that if he does not see Him, He sees him – and does not fear people. It is more fitting to fear Allah. He does not think that he is superior to any of the slaves of Allah. He is formed from impurity and filled with soil, going to the Garden if he obeys or otherwise to the Fire. Ibn al-'Arabī said, 'Our shaykhs recommend a person look at these wise verses which contain these aspects of knowledge:

How can someone be arrogant
when he will always return to his resting place [the earth]?
He comes from it and goes back to it,
and is its brother and suckling babe.
It calls on him to use it as a latrine
when he is a child and he obeys.

and what Allah has created

This is added to what was before it, meaning and in the other things which Allah has created: '*and seen that it may well be that their appointed time is near*?' that the end of their life may be near. It is in the position of the genitive added to what is before it. Ibn 'Abbās said, 'By the nearness of the time He means the Day of Badr and the Day of Uḥud.'

In what discourse after this will they believe?

What Revelation will they affirm other than the one Muḥammad ﷺ has brought? It is said that the *hā'* is for the fixed term according to the meaning of 'What words will they believe after their life ends when belief will not help because the Next World is not the Abode of responsibility?'

مَن يُضْلِلِ ٱللَّهُ فَلَا هَادِيَ لَهُۥ وَنَذَرُهُمْ فِي طُغْيَٰنِهِمْ يَعْمَهُونَ ١٨٦

186 If Allah misguides people, no one can guide them. We will abandon them to wander blindly in their excessive insolence.

It is clear that their turning away is because Allah misguided them. This refutes the Qadariyyah. '*We will abandon them to wander blindly*' is in the nominative for the inceptive. It is related in the appositive applied to the position of the *fā'* and what is after it. The verb '*wander*' means 'to be confused' and it is also said that it means to go back and forth. It was adequately discussed at the beginning of *al-Baqarah* (2:16).

يَسْـَٔلُونَكَ عَنِ ٱلسَّاعَةِ أَيَّانَ مُرْسَىٰهَا ۖ قُلْ إِنَّمَا عِلْمُهَا عِندَ رَبِّى ۖ لَا يُجَلِّيهَا
لِوَقْتِهَآ إِلَّا هُوَ ۚ ثَقُلَتْ فِى ٱلسَّمَٰوَٰتِ وَٱلْأَرْضِ ۚ لَا تَأْتِيكُمْ إِلَّا بَغْتَةً ۗ
يَسْـَٔلُونَكَ كَأَنَّكَ حَفِىٌّ عَنْهَا ۖ قُلْ إِنَّمَا عِلْمُهَا عِندَ ٱللَّهِ وَلَٰكِنَّ أَكْثَرَ
ٱلنَّاسِ لَا يَعْلَمُونَ ١٨٧

187 They will ask you about the Hour: when is it due? Say: 'Knowledge of it rests with my Lord alone. He alone will reveal it at its proper time. It hangs heavy in the heavens and the earth. It will not come upon you except suddenly.' They will ask you as if you had full knowledge of it. Say: 'Knowledge of it rests with Allah alone. But most people do not know that.'

They will ask you about the Hour: when is it due?

Ayyān is a question about time. A poet said:

When (*ayyān*) will you grant what I need?
Do you not see that there is time for its success?

The Jews used to say to the Prophet ﷺ, 'If you are a Prophet, then tell us when the Last Hour will occur.' It is related that the idolaters said that out of extreme denial. The phrase, '*When is it due?*' is in the nominative for the inceptive according to Sībawayh, and the predicate is *ayyān*. It is an adverb based on the *fatḥah* because it has the meaning of a question. When the verb *arsā* is used of Allah, it means that He made it firm, implying 'When will it be made firm?' meaning 'When will it occur?' *Rasā* means to make firm and stop. It can be seen in the words: '*built-in (rāsiyāt) cooking vats*' (34:13). Qatādah said that it means 'firm'.

Say: 'Knowledge of it rests with my Lord alone. He alone will reveal it at its proper time. It hangs heavy in the heavens and the earth. It will not come upon you except suddenly.'

It has not been made clear to anyone so that a person should always be cautious regarding it. '*Reveal*' means 'disclose'. '*Its proper time*' means at the time it is due.

Revealing (*tajliyah*) is to disclose something. The meaning of '*It hangs heavy in the heavens and the earth*' is that its knowledge is hidden from the people of the heavens and the earth. Everything whose knowledge is hidden is heavy on the heart. It is said that its coming is terrible for the people of the heavens and the earth, as al-Ḥasan and others said. Ibn Jurayj and as-Suddī said that its description is terrible for the people of the heavens and the earth. Qatādah and others said that the heaven and the earth cannot bear it because of its immensity because the heaven will split open, the stars scatter and the sea run dry. It is said that the meaning is that asking about it is heavy. '*It will not come upon you except suddenly*' without warning. *Baghtah* is a verbal noun used as a *ḥāl*.

They will ask you as if you had full knowledge of it

As if you knew it because of the frequency of their questions about it. Ibn Fāris said that *ḥafiyy* means someone who knows something. *Ḥafiyy* is someone who asks often. Al-A'shā said:

If you ask about me, how many an asker
has full knowledge (*ḥafiyy*) of al-A'shā wherever I ascend.

It is said that *aḥfā* is used in asking and in seeking, so it is *muḥfī* and *ḥafiyy* for doing it a lot. Muḥammad ibn Yazīd said, 'The meaning is: "they ask you as if you were someone often asked about it," in other words, persistently asked. He believed that there is no alternation in the normal order of the words. Ibn 'Abbās and others said that there is a reversal in the normal order. The meaning is that they will ask you about it as if you had full knowledge of it, i.e. full knowledge of their piety and delight in your answer. That is because they said, 'There is kinship between us and you, so confide to us the time of the Hour.'

Say: 'Knowledge of it rests with Allah alone. But most people do not know that.'

This is not repetition, but one of the two items of knowledge: one is its occurrence and the other is what it is.

قُل لَّآ أَمْلِكُ لِنَفْسِى نَفْعًا وَلَا ضَرًّا إِلَّا مَا شَآءَ ٱللَّهُ ۚ وَلَوْ كُنتُ أَعْلَمُ ٱلْغَيْبَ
لَٱسْتَكْثَرْتُ مِنَ ٱلْخَيْرِ وَمَا مَسَّنِىَ ٱلسُّوٓءُ ۚ إِنْ أَنَا۠ إِلَّا نَذِيرٌ وَبَشِيرٌ لِّقَوْمٍ
يُؤْمِنُونَ ١٨٨

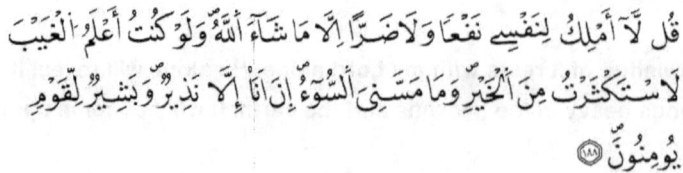

188 Say: 'I possess no power to help or harm myself, except as Allah wills. If I had had knowledge of the Unseen, I would have sought to gain much good and no evil would have touched me. I am only a warner and a bringer of good news to people who believe.'

Say: 'I possess no power to help or harm myself, except as Allah wills.

This means 'I have no power to bring myself good or to repel evil from myself, so how could I have knowledge of the Hour?' It is said that it means 'I do not possess guidance or misguidance for myself.' The phrase '*except as Allah wills*' is in the position of the accusative for the inceptive. The meaning is: 'Except what Allah wishes to give me power over.' Sībawayh recited:

He does whatever He wishes to people.

If I had had knowledge of the Unseen, I would have sought to gain much good

The meaning is: 'If I had known what Allah Almighty desired of me before He let me know it, I would have done it.' It is said, 'If I had known when I would be victorious in war, I would have fought and not been overcome.' Ibn 'Abbās said, 'If I had known the year of the drought, I would have prepared what would be enough for me for it in the time of fertility.' It is said that the meaning is, 'If I had known what goods would sell well, I would have bought them at the time when they were cheap.' It is said that the meaning is: 'If I had known when I would die, I would have done a lot of righteous actions,' as al-Ḥasan and Ibn Jurayj said. It is said that the meaning is 'If I had known the Unseen, I would answer all that I am asked about.' All of that is meant and Allah knows best.

and no evil would have touched me. I am only a warner and a bringer of good news to people who believe.'

These are new words, meaning 'I am not mad,' because they attributed madness to him. It is said that it is connected and the meaning is: 'If I had known the Unseen, evil would not have touched me, and I would have been cautious.' This indicates the words of Allah: '*I am only a clear warner.*' (26:115)

هُوَ ٱلَّذِى خَلَقَكُم مِّن نَّفْسٍ وَٰحِدَةٍ وَجَعَلَ مِنْهَا زَوْجَهَا لِيَسْكُنَ
إِلَيْهَا فَلَمَّا تَغَشَّىٰهَا حَمَلَتْ حَمْلًا خَفِيفًا فَمَرَّتْ بِهِۦ فَلَمَّآ أَثْقَلَت دَّعَوَا ٱللَّهَ
رَبَّهُمَا لَئِنْ ءَاتَيْتَنَا صَٰلِحًا لَّنَكُونَنَّ مِنَ ٱلشَّٰكِرِينَ ﴿١٨٩﴾ فَلَمَّآ ءَاتَىٰهُمَا صَٰلِحًا
جَعَلَا لَهُۥ شُرَكَآءَ فِيمَآ ءَاتَىٰهُمَا فَتَعَٰلَى ٱللَّهُ عَمَّا يُشْرِكُونَ ﴿١٩٠﴾

189-90 It is He Who created you from a single self and made from him his spouse so that he might find repose in her. Then when he covered her she bore a light load and carried it around. Then when it became heavy they called on Allah, their Lord, 'If You grant us a healthy child, we will be among the thankful!' Then when He granted them a healthy, upright child, they associated what He had given them with Him. But Allah is far above what they associate with Him!

It is He Who created you from a single self and made from him his spouse so that he might find repose in her.

The majority of commentators said that what is meant by '*a single self*' is Ādam. '*His spouse*' is Ḥawwā'. '*So that he might find repose in her*' means be familiar with her and at peace. All of this was in the Garden.

Then when he covered her she bore a light load and carried it around.

Then Allah introduces another state which is in this world after they descended. He says: '*Then when he covered her,*' which is an allusion to sexual intercourse, '*she bore a light load*'. Every load which is in the womb or on a tree is called *ḥaml*. When it is on the back or the head, it is called *ḥiml*. Ya'qūb related that *ḥiml* is used for dates. Abū Sa'īd as-Sayrāfī said, 'Both are used for pregnancy, sometimes alluding to the hiddenness of the burden of the women and sometimes by its similar appearance to the burden of the animal.' *Ḥaml* is also a verbal noun of *ḥamala, yaḥmilu.*

'*Carried it around*' refers to the sperm, meaning she continued with that light burden. Allah is saying, 'She stands, sits and moves about, and does not feel its burden greatly as being heavy,' as al-Ḥasan, Mujāhid and others said. It is said that the meaning is: 'She continues with the burden,' and so it is a reversal, as you might say, 'I put on my head the hat.' 'Abdullāh ibn 'Umar recited *mārat* with an *alif* and single *rā'*, from *māra, yamūru*, 'to come and go and move'. Ibn 'Abbās and Yaḥyā ibn Ya'mar recited *marat* from *miryah*, i.e. complained about what afflicted her, which is a burden or illness or the like.

Then when it became heavy they called on Allah, their Lord, 'If You grant us a healthy child, we will be among the thankful!'

'*When it became heavy*' means it became a burden, as used for the fruit of the date palms. It is said that it began to be heavy as the verbs *aṣbaḥa* and *amsā* are used. '*They called on Allah, their Lord*': the pronoun '*they*' refers to Ādam and Ḥawwā'. According to this view it is related in accounts of this *āyah* that when Ḥawwā' became pregnant the first time, she did not know what it was. This is strengthened by the reading of *marat*. She was alarmed by that and Iblīs found a way to her.

Al-Kalbī said, 'When she became heavy the first time, Iblīs came to Ḥawwā' in the form of a man. He asked, 'What is that in your belly?' She answered, 'I do not know!' He said, 'I fear it is an animal.' She told Ādam about that and they continued to worry about it. Then Iblīs returned to her and said that he had a position with Allah: 'If I pray to Allah and you bear a human will you name him after me?' 'Yes,' she replied. He said, 'I will pray to Allah.' He came to her when she had given birth and said, 'Give him my name.' She asked, 'What is your name?' 'Al-Ḥārith,' he answered. If he had named himself to her, she would have recognised him, and so she called him 'Abd al-Ḥārith.

Something similar to this is mentioned in a weak *ḥadīth* in at-Tirmidhī and elsewhere, and there is a great deal in the Israelite sources which are not firm and should not be relied on by someone who has a heart. Even though Ādam and Ḥawwā' had been deluded previously, a believer is not bitten from the same hole twice, although it is recorded and written. The Messenger of Allah ﷺ said, 'He deceived them twice: in the Garden and on the earth.'

when He granted them a healthy, upright child, they associated what He had given them with Him

The meaning of '*ṣāliḥ*' (*healthy*) is 'a balanced child'. Scholars disagree about the interpretation of the *shirk* here ascribed to Ādam and Ḥawwā'. Commentators said, 'The *shirk* was in the naming and attribute, not in worship and lordship.' The people of meanings said, 'They did not believe that al-Ḥārith was their Lord by their naming their son 'Abd al-Ḥārith, but they believed that al-Ḥārith was the reason for the deliverance of their child and so they named him after him, as a man names himself the slave of his guest by way of humility to him, not meaning that the guest is his actual lord. It is as Ḥātim said:

I am the slave of the guest as long as long he stays with me,
although my disposition contains none of the nature of a slave.'

Some people said that this refers to the Adamic genus and clarification of the state of the idolaters among the descendants of Ādam. It is that which is relied on. Allah's words, '*associated with Him*' [which is in the dual] refer to the male and female unbelievers, and means both sexes. This is indicated by the words: '*But Allah is far above what they associate with Him*!' and He uses the plural not the dual here. This is a good position.

It is said that the meaning of '*It is He Who created you from a single self*' is in one form and shape, and '*and made from him his spouse*' is from the same species. '*When he covered her*' means the two sexes. According this view, Ādam and Ḥawwā' are not mentioned in the *āyah*. When Allah gives them a child who is healthy, upright and balanced as they wanted, they turn that child from the natural form of the *fiṭrah* to *shirk*. This is what the idolaters do. The Prophet ﷺ said, 'There is no child but that he is born on the *fiṭrah* – (one transmission has 'on this religion') – and his parents make him a Jew or Christian or Magian.' 'Ikrimah said, 'Allah did not single out Ādam here, but made it general to the human race after Ādam.' Al-Ḥusayn ibn al-Faḍl said, 'This is considered more appropriate by the people who employ reason since the first words contain ascription of terrible things to the Prophet of Allah, Ādam.'

The people of Madīnah and 'Āṣim recite '*shirkan*' in the singular. Abū 'Amr and the rest of the people of Kufa recited in the plural *shurakā'*, the plural of *sharīk*. Sa'īd al-Akhfash do not recognise the first reading, but it is valid with the elision of the *muḍāf*, meaning 'they assigned Him the quality of having a partner'. The meaning means that they assigned Him partners.

The *āyah* indicates that pregnancy is an illness. Ibn al-Qāsim and Yaḥyā related that Mālik said, 'The beginning of pregnancy is ease and joy, and the end of it is an illness.' Mālik said that it is an illness as can be seen from the apparent implication of Allah's words: '*They called on their Lord*.' Pregnant women do this as well as other people in grave situations and severe danger. Furthermore death as a result of pregnancy is considered martyrdom, as is related in *ḥadīth*.

Since the fact of pregnancy being an illness is confirmed by the apparent implication of the *āyah*, the situation regarding the actions of a pregnant woman is the same as that of a sick person. No scholar from any region disagrees about the fact that a sick person may not gift away or otherwise dispose of more than a third of their property. Abū Hanīfah and ash-Shāfi'ī said that that only refers to a pregnant woman when she has been divorced. If she has not been divorced, that is not the case. Their argument for this is the fact that pregnancy is normal and one usually recovers from pregnancy. We say that that is the case with most illnesses. People usually recover from them. And people who are not ill may also die.

Mālik said, 'When a pregnant woman is more than six months pregnant, she is not permitted to dispose of more than a third of her property. If someone divorces his wife while she is pregnant and then, when she is six months pregnant, he wants to take her back, he cannot do that because she is considered to be ill, and the marriage of someone ill is not valid.'

Yaḥyā said, 'I heard Mālik say about a man who is present during fighting: "When he is pressed in the battle line, he is not permitted to decide anything about the disposal of his property except for a third. He is in the position of a pregnant woman, a sick person who it is feared may die, and anyone else in a similar situation."' This also applies to someone in prison who is to be killed in retaliation. Abū Ḥanīfah, ash-Shāfi'ī and others disagree about this. Ibn al-'Arabī said, 'After proper investigation, it is clear that someone imprisoned for killing is in a worse state than someone who is ill. To deny that is wrong thinking. The cause of death exists in both cases, as illness is also a cause of death. Allah Almighty says: "*You were longing for death before you met it. Now you have seen it with your own eyes.*" (33:143)' Ruwayshid aṭ-Ṭā'ī said:

O rider with a slow mount!
    Ask the Banū Asad what this sound is.
Tell them to make haste with excuses
    and seek words to prove your innocence. I am death.

This same state is also indicated by the words of the Almighty: '*When they came at you from above you and below you, when your eyes rolled and your hearts rose to your throats.*' (33:10)

How can ash-Shāfi'ī and Abū Ḥanīfah say that the critical situation is simply being in the battle line? Allah Almighty has reported that confronting the enemy when the two groups approach one another is the critical situation which results in this terrible state where the hearts rise to the throats, people have an evil opinion of Allah, and the hearts are shaken and bewildered. Is this state seen in a sick person or not? This is undoubtedly correct. This was the case with those who were firm in their faith, strove for Allah as one should strive, and witnessed the Messenger and His Signs. So how is it with us?

Our scholars disagree about someone who embarks on the sea at a time of great fear and whether his ruling is that of a healthy person or a pregnant woman. Ibn al-Qāsim said that the ruling of such a person is that of a healthy person. Ibn Wahb and Ashhab said that his ruling is that of a pregnant woman when her pregnancy reaches six months. Qāḍī Abū Muḥammad said, 'Their view is more analogous because that is a state in which one fears for one's life, as is also case with heavy pregnancy.' Ibn al-'Arabī said that Ibn al-Qāsim did not sail on the sea nor did he 'see worms in his staff'. Anyone who wants to be certain that Allah alone is the Doer and there is no other doer with Him, and that secondary causes are ineffectual and cannot be relied on, and to have true reliance on Allah and entrustment of his affairs to Him, should go on a sea journey.

أَيُشْرِكُونَ مَا لَا يَخْلُقُ شَيْـًٔا وَهُمْ يُخْلَقُونَ ﴿١٩١﴾ وَلَا يَسْتَطِيعُونَ لَهُمْ نَصْرًا وَلَآ
أَنفُسَهُمْ يَنصُرُونَ ﴿١٩٢﴾

191-2 Do they make things into partner-gods which cannot create anything and are themselves created; which are not capable of helping them and cannot even help themselves?

Do they worship something that does not have the power to create anything? The words '*and are themselves created*' refer to the idols which are created. He said *yukhlaqūna* because they believed that the idols can harm and help, so giving them the status of human beings as in His words: '*...swimming in a sphere*' (21:33) and: '*Ants! Enter your dwellings*' (27:19). Allah's words: '*...which are not capable of helping them and cannot even help themselves?*' mean that idols cannot help anyone nor do they respond to calls for help.

وَإِن تَدْعُوهُمْ إِلَى ٱلْهُدَىٰ لَا يَتَّبِعُوكُمْ سَوَآءٌ عَلَيْكُمْ أَدَعَوْتُمُوهُمْ أَمْ أَنتُمْ
صَٰمِتُونَ ﴿١٩٣﴾

193 If you call them to guidance they will not follow you. It makes no difference if you call them or stay silent.

Al-Akhfash said that the words: '*If you call them to guidance, they will not follow you*' mean: if you call the idols to guidance, they will not follow you. Aḥmad ibn Yaḥyā said that it is '*ṣāmitūn*' because it is the end of the *āyah* and so did not say '*ṣamattum*'. According to Sībawayh '*ṣāmitūn*' and '*ṣamattum*' are the same. It is said what is meant is that Allah already knew that they would not believe.

Both *yattabiʿūkum* and *yatbaʿūkum* are recited which are two dialectical forms with the same meaning. Some of the people of language say that *atbaʿa* is used when one follows someone and does not catch him up and *ittaba'a* is when he goes after him and catches him up.

إِنَّ ٱلَّذِينَ تَدْعُونَ مِن دُونِ ٱللَّهِ عِبَادٌ أَمْثَالُكُمْ فَٱدْعُوهُمْ فَلْيَسْتَجِيبُوا۟
لَكُمْ إِن كُنتُمْ صَٰدِقِينَ ﴿١٩٤﴾ أَلَهُمْ أَرْجُلٌ يَمْشُونَ بِهَآ أَمْ لَهُمْ أَيْدٍ
يَبْطِشُونَ بِهَآ أَمْ لَهُمْ أَعْيُنٌ يُبْصِرُونَ بِهَآ أَمْ لَهُمْ ءَاذَانٌ يَسْمَعُونَ
بِهَا قُلِ ٱدْعُوا۟ شُرَكَآءَكُمْ ثُمَّ كِيدُونِ فَلَا تُنظِرُونِ ﴿١٩٥﴾ إِنَّ وَلِـِّۧىَ ٱللَّهُ
ٱلَّذِى نَزَّلَ ٱلْكِتَٰبَ وَهُوَ يَتَوَلَّى ٱلصَّٰلِحِينَ ﴿١٩٦﴾

194-6 Those you call on besides Allah are slaves just like yourselves. Call on them and let them respond to you if you are telling the truth. Do they have legs they can walk with? Do they have hands they can grasp with? Do they have eyes they can see with? Do they have ears they can hear with? Say: 'Call on your partner-gods and try all your wiles against me and grant me no reprieve. My Protector is Allah Who sent down the Book. He takes care of the righteous.'

Those you call on besides Allah are slaves just like yourselves.

Allah is arguing with them about the worship of idols. To '*call on*' is to worship. It is said that it is 'you call them gods'. The expression '*besides Allah*' means those who are other than Allah. Idols are called slaves because they are owned and subject to Allah. Al-Ḥasan said that the meaning is that the idols are created like you. Since the idolaters believed that the idols harm and help like people, Allah uses the pronoun *hum* (the masculine plural) rather than *hunna* (feminine plural) [which would normally be the case]. He also said '*slaves*' ('*ibād*) and used *alladhīna* and not *allātī*. The meaning is: 'seek benefit and harm from them'.

let them respond to you if you are telling the truth.

If they are telling the truth in saying that the worship of idols gives benefit. Ibn 'Abbās said, 'The meaning of "call on them" is "worship them".'

Do they have legs they can walk with? Do they have hands they can grasp with? Do they have eyes they can see with? Do they have ears they can hear with?

Then Allah refutes them and says that they are foolish: '*Do they have legs they can walk with?...'* This means: 'you are better than them and so how can you worship them?' What is meant is to make their ignorance clear because that which is worshipped is described with limbs.

Sa'īd ibn Jubayr recited the *āyah* with '*in*' rather than '*inna*' because of the two silent letters and '*slaves*' in the accusative and '*like*' in the accusative. It means: 'Those on whom you call other than Allah are slaves like you,' meaning that they are stones and wood. So you are worshipping something when you are nobler than what you worship. An-Naḥḥās said, 'This reading should not be used for three reasons. One is that it is contrary to the vast majority. The second is that Sībawayh prefers the nominative as the predicate of "*in*" when it means "what" (*mā*). That is because the effect of "*mā*" is weak and that of "*in*" is weaker still. The third is that al-Kisā'ī claims that "*in*" hardly ever means "*mā*" in Arabic unless it is followed by an affirmation as in Allah's words: "*The* (*in*) *unbelievers are only living in delusion.*" (67:20)'

The basis of '*let them respond to you*' is *lām* with a *kasrah* (*fa-li*) and the *kasrah* is elided to make it light. Then it is said that there is something elided in the words, meaning 'Call on them to follow you so that they can respond to you if you are speaking the truth about them being gods.' Abū Ja'far and Shaybah recited '*yabṭushūna*' which is a dialectical form. '*Yad*' (hand), '*rijl*' (foot) and *udhun* (ear) are all feminine nouns which take a *hā'* in the diminutive.

Say: 'Call on your partner-gods and try all your wiles against me and grant me no reprieve.

The partner-gods are their idols. He says, 'You and they should try all your wiles against me and do not delay in doing so.' The root of '*try your wiles*' (*kīdūni*) has a *yā'* elided because the *kasrah* indicates it. The same is true in '*Grant me no reprieve*' (*tunẓirūni*). *Kayd* (*wiles*) means deceit and *kayd* also means war. It is said, 'He raided and did not encounter fighting (*kayd*).'

My Protector is Allah Who sent down the Book.

It means: 'the One who undertook to help me and preserve me is Allah.' The *walī* of something is the one who preserves it and prevents harm from reaching it. The Book is the Qur'an.

He takes care of the righteous.

'He preserves them.' In *Ṣaḥīḥ Muslim*, 'Amr ibn al-'Āṣ said, 'I heard the Messenger of Allah ﷺ say more than once, "The family of my father are not my protectors.

My protector is Allah and the righteous believers."' Al-Akhfash said that is recited as '*inna waliyya-llāhi*' (the friend of Allah) meaning Jibrīl. An-Naḥḥās said that that is the reading of 'Āṣim al-Jaḥdarī. The first recitation is clearer by His words, '*He takes care of the righteous.*'

وَالَّذِينَ تَدْعُونَ مِن دُونِهِۦ لَا يَسْتَطِيعُونَ نَصْرَكُمْ وَلَآ أَنفُسَهُمْ يَنصُرُونَ ﴿١٩٧﴾ وَإِن تَدْعُوهُمْ إِلَى الْهُدَىٰ لَا يَسْمَعُوا۟ وَتَرَىٰهُمْ يَنظُرُونَ إِلَيْكَ وَهُمْ لَا يُبْصِرُونَ ﴿١٩٨﴾

197-8 Those you call on besides Him are not capable of helping you. They cannot even help themselves. If you call them to guidance, they do not hear. You see them looking at you, yet they do not see.

The phrase '*Those you call on besides Him*' is repeated to make it clear that what they worship cannot help or harm anything. '*If you call them to guidance*' is a precondition whose apodosis is '*they do not hear.*' '*You see them*' is a new sentence. '*Looking at you*' is in the position of an adverbial *ḥāl*, and refers to the idols. The meaning of '*looking*' is to have eyes open as if looking at something and so it is as if they were looking at the person who is looking at them. It is said that they had eyes made from gems, which is why Allah says '*them*' (using the masculine plural). It is also said that the idolaters are meant by this. Allah says that they did not see since they did not benefit from their eyesight.

خُذِ الْعَفْوَ وَأْمُرْ بِالْعُرْفِ وَأَعْرِضْ عَنِ الْجَٰهِلِينَ ﴿١٩٩﴾

199 Make allowances for people, command what is right, and turn away from the ignorant.

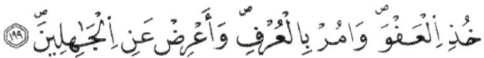

This *āyah* consists of three statements which encompass the rules of the *Sharī'ah* in respect of commands and prohibitions. The words '*make allowances for people*' include maintaining ties of kinship with relatives who cut one off, pardoning wrongdoers, being kind to the believers and other traits of the good character which are found in those who obey Allah. The words, '*command what is right*', include maintaining ties of kinship, fearing Allah regarding both what is lawful and what is unlawful, lowering the eyes, and preparing oneself for the Abode of Permanence. The words '*turn away from the ignorant*' encourage one to attach oneself to knowledge, turn from the people of wrongdoing, remain aloof from arguing with foolish people and colluding with the ignorant rich, and other praiseworthy traits of character and guided actions.

These qualities require further explanation, and the Messenger of Allah ﷺ put them all together in what he said to Jābir ibn Sulaym. Abū Jurayy Jābir ibn Sulaym said, 'I mounted my young camel and then went to Makkah and looked for the Messenger of Allah ﷺ. I made my camel kneel at the door of the mosque and they directed me to the Messenger of Allah ﷺ who was sitting down, wearing a woollen cloak which had red stripes on it. I said, "Peace be upon you, Messenger of Allah." "And upon you peace," he replied. I said, "We are a company of the people of the desert, an uncouth people, so teach me something by which Allah will help me." He said, "Come near," three times. I approached him and he said, "Say that again." I repeated it to him and he said, "Fear Allah and do not disdain anything known to be right. Meet your brother with a cheerful face. Pour your bucket into the vessel of someone who asks for water. If a man abuses you by saying something he does not know about you, do not abuse him by saying what you know of him. Allah will allot a wage for you and that person will bear a sin. Do not abuse anything which Allah Almighty gives you."' Abū Jurayy stated, 'By the One who has my soul in His hand, after that I did not abuse even a sheep or a goat.' Abū Bakr al-Bazzār transmitted something with the same meaning in his *Musnad*.

Abū Sa'īd al-Maqbūrī related from his father from Abū Hurayrah that the Prophet ﷺ said, 'You do not enrich people through your property, but your cheerful face and good character expands them.' Al-Bukhārī related from the *ḥadīth* of Hishām ibn 'Urwah from his father that 'Abdullah ibn az-Zubayr said about Allah's words: '*Make allowances for people and command what is correct*,' 'Allah only revealed this *āyah* about people's character.' Sufyān ibn 'Uyaynah related that ash-Sha'bī said, 'Jibril descended to the Prophet ﷺ and the Prophet ﷺ asked him, "What is this, Jibrīl?" He answered, "I will not know until I ask the All-Knowing." (One variant has, "I will not know until I ask my Lord.") So he went and remained away for a time and then returned and said, "Allah Almighty commands you to pardon those who wrong you, to give to those who deprive you and maintain times with those who cut you off."' One of the poets composed about this:

Noble character is found in three.
    If someone possesses all of them, that is the truly gallant youth.

Giving to the one who deprives you, maintaining ties with someone
who cuts you off, and pardoning the one who transgresses against you.

Ja'far aṣ-Ṣādiq said, 'In this *āyah*, Allah commanded his Prophet ﷺ to have good character, and the Qur'an does not contain anything more comprehensive about good character than this *āyah*. The Prophet ﷺ said, "I was sent to perfect good character."' A poet said:

All matters depart from you and come to an end
except for praise. It remains for you.
If I were to be given a choice between all virtues,
I would choose only good character.

Sahl ibn 'Abdullāh said, 'Allah spoke to Mūsā on Mount Sinai. He was later asked, "What did He command you?" "Nine things," he replied. "To fear Him both secretly and openly, to speak the truth in times of both pleasure and anger, moderation both when wealthy and when poor, and I was commanded to maintain ties with those who cut me off, to give to those who deprive me, to pardon those who wrong me, and that my speech should be remembrance, my silence reflection, and my glance a lesson."'

It is related that our Prophet Muḥammad ﷺ said, 'My Lord commanded me to have nine qualities: sincerity both in secret and in public, fairness both when pleased and when angry, moderation in both wealth and poverty, and that I pardon those who wrong me, maintain ties with those who break with me and give to those who deprive me, and that my speech be remembrance, my silence reflection and my glance a lesson.'

It is said that the verb '*Make allowances*' refers to *zakāt* because it is a little from a lot, but that is unlikely because someone wipes out (*'afā*) when he makes allowances (literally effaces). It is said that the phrase 'make allowances for him' means 'Do not speak ill of him, but make allowances for him.' The reason for its revelation rejects that, and Allah knows best. When Allah commanded the Prophet ﷺ to reason with the idolaters, He was directing him to have good character. That is a means of bringing the idolaters to faith, implying 'accept from people in spite of what you see of their character and be easy on them. Say, "I take my right with pardon and ease," i.e. easily.'

command what is right,

This means what is good and correct. 'Īsā ibn 'Umar recited '*al-'uruf*' with two *ḍammah*s, like *ḥukum*. They are two dialectical usages. *Ma'rūf* and *'ārifah* designate every good quality which is pleasing to minds and with which souls are at rest. A poet said:

If someone does good, his repayment will not go lacking.
The correct does not disappear before Allah and people.

'Aṭā' said, '"*Command what is correct*" means "There is no god but Allah."'

and turn away from the ignorant.

When you have presented the argument against them and commanded them to what is right and then they display rash ignorance towards you, simply turn away from them. This is modesty before them and being too noble to respond to them. Even though this is addressed to Allah's Prophet ﷺ, it teaches correct behaviour to all of His creation. Ibn Zayd and 'Aṭā' said, 'It was abrogated by the *Āyah* of the Sword.' Mujāhid and Qatādah said, 'It is an unabrogated *āyah*.' That is sound based on what al-Bukhārī related that 'Abdullāh ibn 'Abbās said, "Uyaynah ibn Ḥisn ibn Ḥudhayfah came and stayed with his nephew, al-Hurr ibn Qays, who was one of the group whom 'Umar brought near to him. The reciters were the people of the assembly and council of 'Umar no matter whether they were older men or younger men. 'Uyaynah said to his nephew, "Nephew, you have access to this ruler, so ask him for permission for me to see him." He said, "I will ask him for permission for you to see him." He asked permission for 'Uyaynah and 'Umar gave permission. When he entered where he was, he said, "O Ibn al-Khaṭṭāb! By Allah, you do not give enough to us and you do not judge justly between us." 'Umar was so angry that he wanted to punish him. Al-Ḥurr said to him, "Amīr al-Mu'minīn, Allah Almighty said to His Prophet ﷺ, '*Make allowances for people, command what is right and turn away from the ignorant.*' This is one of the ignorant." By Allah, 'Umar did not do more than that when he recited it to him. He acted in accordance with the Book of Allah.'

'Umar's application of this *āyah* and the suggestion of al-Ḥurr indicated that it is an unabrogated *āyah*, not an abrogated one. That is how al-Ḥasan ibn 'Alī ibn Abī Ṭalib applied it as will be explained. When someone is deliberately coarse towards a ruler and deliberately makes light of what is due to him, he can punish him (*ta'zīr*). If it is other than that, then there should be turning away, overlooking and pardon, as the just caliph did on that occasion.

وَإِمَّا يَنزَغَنَّكَ مِنَ ٱلشَّيۡطَٰنِ نَزۡغٞ فَٱسۡتَعِذۡ بِٱللَّهِۚ إِنَّهُۥ سَمِيعٌ عَلِيمٌ ٢٠٠

200 If an evil impulse from *Shayṭān* provokes you, seek refuge in Allah. He is All-Hearing, All-Knowing.

When Allah Almighty revealed, '*Make allowances*,' the Prophet ﷺ asked, 'How, O Lord, when there is anger?' So there was revealed, '*If an evil impulse from Shayṭān provokes you…*' *Shayṭān* provokes and whispers. There are two dialectical forms of '*provokes*': *nazagha* and *naghaza*. It is said, 'Beware of the malevolent slanderer (*nuzzāgh*) and backbiter. They provoke strife.' Az-Zajjāj said, 'The impulse (*nazgh*) is the closest movement there is, and in the case of *shayṭān* it is the closest whispering.' Sa'īd ibn al-Musayyab said, 'I was with 'Uthmān and 'Alī when there was a provocation between them caused by *Shayṭān*, and neither of them spared his companion anything. Then they did not leave until each of them had asked for his companion's forgiveness.'

The meaning of '*provokes you*' is to strike you and expose you to whisperings urging you to do what is not lawful when you are angry. To '*seek refuge in Allah*' is to seek deliverance from that by Allah. Allah tells us that whispering can be repelled by resorting to Him and seeking refuge in Him, and Allah's is the Highest Example. One only seeks refuge from dogs with the owner of the dogs. It is related that a man of the early generations asked one of his students, 'What do you do with *Shayṭān* when he makes mistakes seem attractive to you?' 'I strive (against him),' he answered. He said, 'And if it recurs?' 'I strive (against him),' he replied. He asked, 'And if it recurs?' 'I strive (against him),' he repeated. The teacher said, 'There is no end to this. What do you think you would do if you went by some sheep and their dog barked at you and kept you from passing?' He answered, 'I would strive to repel him by my effort.' He said, 'You would have to keep doing that endlessly. Rather seeking refuge in the owner of the sheep will spare you that.'

Naghz, nazgh, hamz and whispering are the same. Allah Almighty says: '*Say: "My Lord, I seek refuge with You from the goadings of the shayṭāns*"' (23:97) and He says: '… *from the evil of the slinking whisperer.*' (114:3) The root of *nazgh* is corruption. One uses the verb for causing dissension between people. Allah says: '*Shayṭān had caused dissent (nazagha) between me and my brothers*' (12:2) which means 'he corrupted things'. It is said that *nazgh* is causing to err and deluding, and the meanings are similar. Something similar to this *āyah* is found in *Ṣaḥīḥ Muslim* from Abū Hurayrah. He said that the Messenger of Allah ﷺ said, '*Shayṭān* comes to one of you and says,

"Who created such-and-such?" until he says to him, "Who created your Lord?" When it reaches that, he should seek refuge with Allah turn from it.'

In it, 'Abdullāh said, 'The Prophet ﷺ was asked about whispering and said, 'That is pure belief.' In the *ḥadīth* of Abū Hurayrah, 'That is explicit faith,' which means sincere faith. This does not accord with its literal meaning since it is not the case that whispering itself is part of faith because faith is certainty. It is indicating the fear of Allah they experienced, fear of the punishment they might receive for what occurred in themselves. It is as if he was saying that alarm at this is pure and sincere faith because the soundness of your faith and your knowledge has told you that it is wrong. So such whispering is called faith since faith repels it, turns from it, rejects it and does not accept it. The alarm felt because of it results from strength of faith.

As for the command to seek refuge, that is because those whisperings are the effects of *Shayṭān*. As for the command to stop, it means to not rely on whisperings and to not pay any attention to them. If someone has sound faith and uses what his Lord and Prophet have commanded him to use, that will help and benefit him. If his faith is mixed with doubt and the sensory dominates him and he is not able to get free of sensory preoccupations, then he must use logical proofs as the Prophet ﷺ did when he said to the one who mentioned to him the example of mangy camels, 'There is no contagion.' The Bedouin asked, 'What about the camels which are like gazelles in the sand and then a mangy camel comes and goes in among them and they get mange?' The Prophet ﷺ answered, 'Who infected the first one?' So he removed the doubt at its root.

When *Shayṭān* despaired of deluding and misguiding the Companions of Muḥammad ﷺ, he began to try to confuse them with these promptings. Whisperings are false sayings (calamities, clouds). Their hearts were averse to them and they found it terrible when they occurred to them, so they went, as it says in the *Ṣaḥīḥ*, and said, 'Messenger of Allah, we find in ourselves things which we think it too terrible to speak about.' He asked, 'Have you experienced that?' They answered, 'Yes.' He said, 'That is clear faith to spite *Shayṭān* as the Qur'an says: "*You have no authority over any of My slaves.*" (15:42).' So the thoughts which are not steady and which are not brought about by doubt are those which are repelled by turning away from them. Such thoughts are called whisperings. Allah knows best. This matter was mentioned at the end of *al-Baqarah* (2:285-86). Praise be to Allah.

إِنَّ ٱلَّذِينَ ٱتَّقَوْا۟ إِذَا مَسَّهُمْ طَٰٓئِفٌ مِّنَ ٱلشَّيْطَٰنِ تَذَكَّرُوا۟ فَإِذَا هُم مُّبْصِرُونَ ﴿٢٠١﴾ وَإِخْوَٰنُهُمْ يَمُدُّونَهُمْ فِى ٱلْغَىِّ ثُمَّ لَا يُقْصِرُونَ ﴿٢٠٢﴾

201-2 As for those who are godfearing, when they are bothered by visitors from *Shayṭān*, they remember and immediately see clearly. But as for their brothers, the visitors lead them further into error. And they do not stop at that!

As for those who are godfearing, when they are bothered by visitors from *Shayṭān*,

'*Those who are godfearing*' means those who are fearful of *shirk* and acts of disobedience. In the phrase '*when they are bothered by visitors (ṭayf) from Shayṭān*,' this *ṭayf* is the reading of the people of Basra and the people of Makkah. The reading of the people of Madīnah and the people of Kufa is *ṭā'if.* It is related as *ṭayyaf* from Sa'īd ibn Jubayr. An-Naḥḥās said, 'In instances such as this the Arabic language takes *ṭayf* as the verbal noun of the verb *ṭāfa, yaṭīfu.*' Al-Kisā'ī said that it is a lightening of *ṭayyif*, like *mayyit* and *mayt*. An-Naḥḥās said that the meaning of *ṭayf* linguistically refers to something that is imagined in the heart or is seen while one is sleep. That is also the meaning of *ṭā'if.* Abū Ḥātim said, 'I asked al-Aṣma'ī about *ṭayyif* and he said that the form *fay'il* is not one of the verbal nouns.' An-Naḥḥās said that it is not a verbal noun but has the meaning of the active particle. The meaning is: 'When something [from *Shayṭān*] attaches itself to those who fear disobedience, they reflect on the power of Allah and His blessings to them, and so they abandon disobedience.' It is also said that *ṭayf* and *ṭā'if* have two different meanings. *Ṭayf* is imagination and *ṭā'if* refers to *Shayṭān* himself. The first is a verbal noun for the wandering of the imagination from the verb *ṭāfa, yaṭīfu, ṭayf,* and they do not use this *ṭā'if* as an active participle. As-Suhaylī said that it is a fantasy without reality. As for His words: '*So a visitation (ṭā'if) from your Lord came upon it*' (68:19), *ṭayf* is not used for it because it is an actual active particle. It is also said that it refers to Jibrīl.

Az-Zajjāj said, 'One says "I came upon (*ṭuftu, aṭūfu*) them," and "a phantom came (*ṭāfa, yaṭīfu*)".' Ḥassān said:

> 'Leave this. But whoever has a phantom (*ṭayf*)
> which makes him sleepless when evening has gone.'

Mujāhid said that *ṭayf* is anger. It designates insanity, anger and whispering which visits someone, because it is a touch from *Shayṭān* which resembles the touch of imagination.

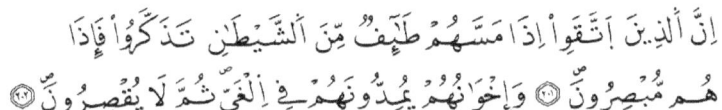

they remember and immediately see clearly.

'Immediately see clearly' means they stop. It is said that they have insight. Sa'īd ibn Jubayr recited *tadhdhakkarū*, but there is no sense to it in Arabic. An-Naḥḥās mentioned that. 'Iṣām ibn al-Muṣṭaliq said, 'I visited Madīnah and saw al-Ḥasan ibn 'Alī. I admired his bearing and good appearance and envy arose in me due to the hatred that my heart harboured towards his father. I said, "You are the son of Abū Ṭālib!" "Yes," he replied. I began to go to great lengths in insulting him and insulting his father. He looked at me with a kind and compassionate look and then recited, "I seek refuge with Allah from the accursed *Shayṭān. In the Name of Allah, the All-Merciful, Most Merciful. 'Make allowances for people, command what is right, and turn away from the ignorant'* as far as *'and immediately see clearly'*." Then he said to me, "Take it easy. I ask Allah's forgiveness for both me and you. If you ask us for help, we will help you. If you ask us for a gift, we will give you a gift. If you ask us for guidance, we will guide you." I began to repent of my excess and he quoted the words of Allah: "*'No blame at all will fall on you. Today you have forgiveness from Allah. He is the Most Merciful of the merciful.'* (12:92) Are you one of the people of Syria?" "Yes," I replied. He said, "An attribute I recognise as being from Akhzam (i.e. innate)."[1]

'And then he continued: "May Allah make you and your parents thrive and give you well-being and help you. Tell me your needs and anything else that you want. You will find us according to your best opinion, Allah willing."' 'Iṣām said, 'The earth seemed narrow to us after it had been wide and I wished it would swallow me up. I sought refuge and there was then no one on the surface of the earth I loved more than him and his father.'

But as for their brothers, the visitors lead them further into error.

It is said that it means their brothers among the *shayṭān*s, who are the deviants among the people of misguidance who are reinforced by *shayṭān*s in their error. It is said that it is the deviants who have brothers among the *shayṭān*s because they accept what comes from them. *Shayṭān* was mentioned before in this *āyah*. This is the best of what is said about it. This is the view of Qatādah, al-Ḥasan and aḍ-Ḍaḥḥāk.

1 This became an Arab proverb. The poem is by Abū Akhzam aṭ-Ṭā'ī, who was the grandfather or great-grandfather of Abū Ḥātim. He had a son called Akhzam who was very rebellious towards his father. When Akhzam died, leaving sons behind, they eventually attacked their grandfather and caused him to bleed and he said this.

And they do not stop at that!

This means that they do not repent nor return. Az-Zajjāj said that there is a change of order in the words, the meaning being: 'those you call on apart from Him cannot help you nor help themselves, while their brothers among the *shayṭān*s reinforce them in their error because the unbelievers are the brothers of the *shayṭān*s.' The meaning of the *āyah* is that when a visitation from *Shayṭān* touches a believer, they immediately take note. As for the idolaters, *Shayṭān* reinforces them. The words '*they do not stop at that*' are said to refer to the idolaters according to both views. It is also said that they refer to *Shayṭān*. Qatādah said that it means: 'Then they do not abstain from them nor show mercy to them.' 'Stopping short' is to cease doing something, i.e. the *shayṭān*s do not cease to help the unbelievers to err.

The words 'into error' can be added to Allah's words, '*lead them further*' and it can be connected to '*brothers*'. *Ghayy* is ignorance. Nāfi' recited *yumiddūnahum* while the rest recite it as *yamuddūnahum*, which are two dialectical usages from *madda* and *amadda*. *Madda* is the more frequently used. Makkī said that. An-Naḥḥās said, 'A group of scholars of Arabic, including Abū Ḥātim and Abū 'Ubayd, reject the reading of the people of Madīnah. Abū Ḥātim said, "I do not know of any reason for it but that the meaning is 'increase them in error'." A group of the people of language, including Abū 'Ubayd, related that it is said that when there is a lot of the thing itself, Form I is used and when there is a lot of something else, Form IV is used. It is related from Muḥammad ibn Yazīd that he used as evidence for the reading of the people of Madīnah the fact that one says, "I helped him (FORM I) in something," in other words made it seem attractive to him, and invited him to do it, and "I helped (Form IV) him in the like of that," i.e. helped him with an opinion or something else.'

Makkī said, 'The *fatḥah* of Form I is preferred because it is said that Form I is used for evil and form IV for good. Allah Almighty says: "*...and drawing them on* (Form IV) *as they wander blindly in their excessive insolence.*" (2:15 et al.) This indicates the strength of the *fatḥah* on this letter because it is about evil. Error (*ghayy*) is evil. It is also because that is the position of the community.' 'Āṣim al-Jaḥdarī recited, '*yumāddūnahum*'. 'Īsā ibn 'Umar recited '*yaqṣurūna*' while the rest have '*yuqṣirūna*'. They are two dialects. [POEM]

وَإِذَا لَمْ تَأْتِهِم بِـَٔايَةٍ قَالُوا۟ لَوْلَا ٱجْتَبَيْتَهَا ۚ قُلْ إِنَّمَآ أَتَّبِعُ مَا يُوحَىٰٓ إِلَىَّ مِن رَّبِّى ۚ
هَـٰذَا بَصَآئِرُ مِن رَّبِّكُمْ وَهُدًى وَرَحْمَةٌ لِّقَوْمٍ يُؤْمِنُونَ ﴿٢٠٣﴾

203 If you do not bring them a Sign, they say, 'Why have you not come up with one?' Say, 'I follow only what has been revealed to me from my Lord.' This is clear insight from your Lord, and guidance and mercy, for people who believe.

'*If you do not bring them a Sign*' means 'recite one to them'. *Lawlā* in '*Why have you not come up with one?*' means 'why not?' and when it has this meaning it is only followed by a verb, actual or implied, and this was already discussed at length in *al-Baqarah*. (2:118) The meaning of *ijtabā* is to create it by oneself. He informed them that the Signs are from Allah, and he ﷺ only recites to them what has been revealed to him. The meaning of *ijtabā* is to extemporise, devise and invent something from oneself.

Say, 'I follow only what has been revealed to me from my Lord.'

It is from Allah, not from myself.

This is clear insight from your Lord,

'*Clear insight from your Lord*' means the Qur'an. *Baṣā'ir* is the plural of *baṣīrah*, which is the proof and lesson, meaning 'that to which I have directed you is that Allah Almighty is One.' *Baṣā'ir* are that by which He is seen. Az-Zajjāj said that it means 'paths'. *Baṣā'ir* also means blood duties. Al-Ju'fī said:

They went with their blood duties (*baṣā'ir*) on their shoulders,
but my blood (*baṣīrah*) is a ready and swift steed that runs with it.

'*Guidance*' is right guidance and clarification, and '*mercy*' is blessing.

وَإِذَا قُرِئَ ٱلْقُرْءَانُ فَٱسْتَمِعُوا۟ لَهُۥ وَأَنصِتُوا۟ لَعَلَّكُمْ تُرْحَمُونَ ﴿٢٠٤﴾

204 When the Qur'an is recited listen to it and be quiet so that hopefully you will gain mercy.

It is said that this was revealed about the prayer. That is related from Ibn Mas'ūd, Abū Hurayrah, Jābir, az-Zuhrī, 'Ubaydullāh ibn 'Umayr, 'Aṭā' ibn Abī

Rabāḥ and Sa'īd ibn al-Musayyab. Sa'd said, 'The idolaters used to come to the Messenger of Allah ﷺ in Makkah when he was praying and say to one another, as Allah tells us: "*Do not listen to this Qur'an. Drown it out so that hopefully you will gain the upper hand,*" (41:26) and so Allah revealed in answer to them: "*When the Qur'an is recited listen to it and be quiet.*"'

It is said that it was revealed about the *khuṭbah.* Sa'īd ibn Jubayr, Mujāhid, 'Aṭā', 'Amr ibn Dīnār, Zayd ibn Aslam, al-Qāsim ibn Mukhaymarah, Muslim ibn Yasār, Shahr ibn Ḥawshab and 'Abdullāh ibn al-Mubārak all said that. This is because the Qur'an in it is little while silence is obliged in all of it. Ibn al-'Arabī said that. An-Naqqāsh said that the *āyah* is Makkan, and there was no *khuṭbah* or *Jumu'ah* in Makkah.

Aṭ-Ṭabarī mentioned from Sa'īd ibn Jubayr that this is about silence on the Day of Sacrifice, and the day of Fiṭr and *Jumu'ah*, and is general to whatever the *imām* says aloud. That is sound because it includes all of what this *āyah* and other things from the *Sunnah* say regarding remaining silent. An-Naqqāsh said, 'Commentators agree that this listening applies to the obligatory and non-obligatory prayers.' An-Naḥḥās said that linguistically it must apply to everything unless evidence indicates that something in particular is singled out.

Az-Zajjāj said, 'It may well mean: "Learn its import and do not exceed it."' *Inṣāt* is 'being silent in order to listen, hear and observe'. The verb is *anṣata* and *naṣata.* A poet said:

The *imām* said, 'You must follow the command of your master.'
We did not disagree. We listened in silence (*anṣatanā*) as he spoke.

It is said that *anṣata* can take a direct object or use the particle *li.* [POEM]

Some people have said that it means, 'Listen to the Messenger of Allah ﷺ in particular' so that his Companions will listen and understand him. This is unlikely. The sound view is that it is general and undefined since Allah continues: '*...so that hopefully you will gain mercy*' and specificity requires a proof.

'Abd al-Jabbār ibn Aḥmad said in *Fawā'id al-Qur'ān* that the idolaters used, in their recalcitrance, to make a great clamour and tumult and to cause annoyance, as shown by Allah's words about them: '*Those who disbelieve say, "Do not listen to this Qur'an. Drown it out so that hopefully you will gain the upper hand."*' (41:26) So Allah commanded the Muslims that, while the revelation was being delivered, they should be different to this state and should listen. He praised the jinn for doing that saying: '*And We diverted a group of jinn towards you to listen to the Qur'an.*' (46:29)

Muḥammad ibn Ka'b al-Quraẓī said, 'When the Messenger of Allah ﷺ recited in the prayer, those behind him responded to him when he said, "*In the Name of Allah, the All-Merciful, Most Merciful*" repeating what he said until he finished the *Fātiḥah* of the Book and the *sūrah*. That continued for as long as Allah wished it to continue and then the revelation came: "*When the Qur'an is recited listen to it and be quiet,*" and then they were silent.' This indicates that the meaning of being silent is to not speak aloud as they used to do when repeating the words of the Messenger of Allah ﷺ. Qatādah said about this *āyah*, 'A man would come and find them in the prayer and ask them how much they had prayed and how much remained, and so Allah revealed this.'

Mujāhid also said that they used to speak about their needs in the prayer and Allah revealed: '*…so that hopefully you will gain mercy.*' We already mentioned the disagreement about the follower reciting behind the imam in *al-Fātiḥah*. (1:9) The rulings regarding the *khuṭbah* will be dealt with in *al-Jumu'ah*, Allah willing.

وَاذْكُر رَّبَّكَ فِي نَفْسِكَ تَضَرُّعًا وَخِيفَةً وَدُونَ الْجَهْرِ مِنَ الْقَوْلِ بِالْغُدُوِّ وَالْآصَالِ وَلَا تَكُن مِّنَ الْغَافِلِينَ ﴿٢٠٥﴾

205 Remember your Lord in yourself humbly and fearfully, without loudness of voice, morning and evening. Do not be one of the unaware.

Remember your Lord in yourself humbly and fearfully,

This is similar to Allah's words: '*Call on your Lord humbly and secretly.*' (7:55). Abū Ja'far an-Naḥḥās said that there is no disagreement that it is about supplication. It is related from Ibn 'Abbās that *dhikr* here means recitation in the prayer. It is said that the meaning is: 'Recite the Qur'an while reflecting and considering.' '*Taḍarru'*' is a verbal noun, and it is in the position of the adverbial *ḥāl*. '*Khīfah*' is added to it. The plural of *khīfah* is *khiwaf* because it means 'fear'. An-Naḥḥās mentioned it. The root of *khīfah* is *khiwfah* and the *wāw* has been changed into the *yā'* because of the *kasrah* before it. The verb is *khāfa, yakhāfu*, and the nouns are *khawf, khīfah* and *makhāfah*. The active participle is is *khā'if* and the plural is *khuwwaf* following the root and *khuyyaf* in usage. Al-Farrā' also related that the plural of *khīfah* is *khīf*. Al-Jawharī said, '*Khīfah* is fear and the plural is *khīf*. It has a *wāw* in the root.

without loudness of voice, morning and evening.

'*Without loudness of voice*' is less than being actually out loud, implying 'hearing yourself,' as Allah says elsewhere: '*...try to find a way between the two*' (17:110), between being out loud and being silent. This indicates that raising the voice in *dhikr* is forbidden according to what was said elsewhere. Regarding '*morning and evening*', Qatādah and Ibn Zayd said that the word *āṣāl* refers to evenings and *ghuduw* is the plural of *ghudwah*. Abū Miljaz recited *īṣāl*, which is the verbal noun, implying entering into the evening.' *Āṣāl* is the plural of *uṣul*. It is a plural of plurals, that is *aṣīl*, which is the plural of *uṣul*, as az-Zajjāj says. Al-Akhfash said that *āṣāl* is the plural of *aṣīl*. Al-Farrā' said that *āṣāl* is the plural of *aṣīl*. *Uṣul* is the singular as is used by a poet:

There is none better than her when evening (*uṣul*) approaches.

Al-Jawharī said that *aṣīl* is the time after *'Aṣr* up until *Maghrib*. Its plurals are *uṣul*, *āṣāl* and *aṣā'il* like the plural of *aṣīlah*. A poet said:

By my life, you are a House with the noblest of people.
Sit in its courtyards in the afternoons (*aṣā'il*).

It is also the plural of *uṣlān*. The diminutive is *uṣaylān* and then change the *nūn* to a *lām* and say *uṣaylāl*. We see this is a verse of an-Nābighah. The verb 'Do not be unaware' means do not neglect *dhikr*.

إِنَّ ٱلَّذِينَ عِندَ رَبِّكَ لَا يَسْتَكْبِرُونَ عَنْ عِبَادَتِهِۦ وَيُسَبِّحُونَهُۥ وَلَهُۥ يَسْجُدُونَ ۩

206 Those who are in the presence of your Lord do not consider themselves too great to worship Him. They glorify His praise and they prostrate to Him.

Those who are in the presence of your Lord

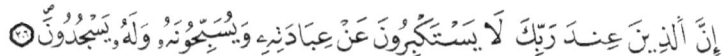

The consensus is that this refers to the angels. Allah says: '*...in the presence of your Lord*,' and Allah Almighty is at (*bi*) every place because they are near to His mercy, and everyone who is near to Allah is in His presence, as az-Zajjāj said. Another said that it is because they are in the position of only having the decision of Allah carried out on them. It is said that it is because they are the messengers of Allah, as one says, 'There is a large army with the caliph.' It is said that it is by way of honouring them and that they are in an honoured place, and so it designates their nearness in respect of nobility, not space. '*They glorify*' means they esteem Him and proclaim Him pure of any evil. '*They prostrate to Him*' is said to mean 'they pray,' or 'they are humble,' which makes them different from the people who commit acts by which they disobey Allah.

The majority of scholars say that this is a place of prostration for the reciter. They disagree about the numbers of the prostrations of the Qur'an. The largest number that is said is fifteen. The first is at the end of *al-A'rāf* and the last is at the end of *al-'Alaq*. That is the view of Ibn Ḥabīb and Ibn Wahb in one transmission, and Isḥāq. Some scholars add the prostration of al-Ḥijr in His words: '*Be among those who prostrate*' (15:97) as will be explained, Allah willing. According to this view, there are sixteen prostrations. It is also said that there are fourteen. Ibn Wahb said that in another transmission from him and he omits the second prostration of *al-Ḥajj*. That is the view of the People of Opinion. The sound position is that it is omitted because the *ḥadīth* which affirms it is not sound.

Ibn Mājah and Abū Dāwūd related in their *Sunan* from 'Abdullāh ibn Munayn of the Banū 'Abd Kulāl from 'Amr ibn al-'Āṣ that the Messenger of Allah ﷺ recited fifteen prostrations in the Qur'an, three of which were in the *Mufaṣṣal* and two in *al-Ḥajj*. 'Abdullāh ibn Munayn is not used as evidence. Abū Muḥammad 'Abd al-Haqq said that. Abū Dāwūd related that 'Uqbah ibn 'Āmir said, 'I asked, "Messenger of Allah, are there two prostrations in *Sūrat al-Ḥajj*?" He answered, "Yes, and whoever does not prostrate them has not recited them." 'Abdullāh ibn Lahī'ah is in the *isnād*, and he is very weak. Ash-Shāfi'ī affirmed it and dropped the prostration in *Ṣād*. It is also said that there are eleven prostrations, and this omits the last one of *al-Ḥajj* and three in the *Mufaṣṣal*. That is the well-known position of Mālik. It is related from Ibn 'Abbās, Ibn 'Umar and others.

In the *Sunan* of Ibn Mājah, Abū ad-Dardā' said, 'I prostrated eleven prostrations with the Prophet ﷺ: *Sajdah*, *al-Furqān*, *Sūrat an-Naḥl*, as-*Sajdah*, *Ṣād*, and the prostration of the *Ḥāmīms*.' It is said that it is ten, and the last one of *al-Ḥajj*, *Ṣād* and the three of the *Mufaṣṣal* are omitted. That is mentioned from Ibn 'Abbās. It is even said that there are only four: as-*Sajdah*, *Fuṣṣilat*, *an-Najm* and *al-'Alaq*.

The reason for this disagreement is the differing transmissions in *ḥadīths* and practice, and their disagreement about whether the simple command to prostate in the Qur'an refers to the prostration of recitation or to the obligatory prostration in the prayer. There is disagreement about the obligatory nature of the prostration of recitation. Mālik and ash-Shāfi'ī said that it is not mandatory. Abū Ḥanīfah said that it is obligatory. That is connected to the fact that the general command to prostrate is obligatory and to the words of the Prophet ﷺ, 'When the son of

Ādam recites a [verse of] prostration and prostrates, *Shayṭān* withdraws weeping, saying, "Woe is me!'" The variant of Abū Kurayb has 'O woe!' It is also because the Prophet ﷺ reported Iblīs, may Allah curse him, as saying: 'Allah commanded the son of Ādam to prostrate and he prostrated, so he has the Garden. I was commanded to prostrate and refused, so I have the Fire.' Muslim transmitted it. It was also because the Prophet ﷺ used to persist in doing it.

Our scholars rely on the confirmed *ḥadīth* of 'Umar which al-Bukhārī transmitted in which he recited an *āyah* of prostration on the *minbar* and then descended and prostrated and the people prostrated with him. Then he recited it in another *Jumuʿah* and the people were ready to prostrate but he said, 'People, take it easy! Allah has not written it for us unless we wish.' That was in the presence of the Companions, the Anṣār and Muhājirūn, may Allah be pleased with all of them. None of them objected to it, and so the consensus on it was established. As for the statement: 'The son of Ādam was commanded to prostrate,' that refers to the obligatory prostration, and the Prophet ﷺ continued to indicate that it was recommended. Allah knows best.

There is no disagreement that the conditions for the prostration of the Qur'an are the same as those required for the prayer: being pure of ritual impurity, intention, facing *qiblah* and the time, except for what al-Bukhārī mentioned about Ibn 'Umar who used to prostrate without being in a state of purity. Ibn al-Mundhir mentioned it from ash-Shaʿbī. Does it, in the view of the majority, require *taḥrīm*, raising the hands in it, the *takbīr* and *taslīm*? There is disagreement about that. Ash-Shāfiʿī, Aḥmad and Isḥāq believe that the person concerned should say the *takbīr* and raise their hands for the *takbīr*.

It is related in a report from Ibn 'Umar that the Prophet ﷺ said the *takbīr* when he prostrated and said the *takbīr* when he came up. The well-known position in the school of Mālik is that one says the *takbīr* for it in going down and coming up from it in the prayer. There is disagreement about the *takbīr* for it in other than the prayer. The majority scholars say that there is a *takbīr* but there is no *salām* for it. A group of the early generations and Isḥāq believed that the *salām* should be said for it. According to this view, it is certain that the *takbīr* at the beginning is for the *iḥrām*, and according to the view of the one who does not say the *salām*, it is for the prostration, and that is enough. The first is more likely by the words of the Prophet ﷺ, 'The key of the prayer is purity and its *taḥrīm* is the *takbīr* and its *taḥlīl* is the *salām*.' This act of worship has a *takbīr*, and it is more likely that it have *taḥlīl* like the *janāzah* prayer. Rather it is more proper because it is an action, and the *janāzah* prayer consists of words. This is what Ibn al-ʿArabī preferred.

As for its time, is said that one prostrates no matter what the time is because it is a prayer for a reason, and that is the view of ash-Shāfiʿī and a group. It is said that it should be done as long as the morning sky is not yet yellow nor the sun not yet yellow after *ʿAṣr*. It is said that there is no prostration after *Ṣubḥ* nor after *ʿAṣr*. It is said that one may prostrate after *Ṣubḥ* but not after *ʿAṣr*. These are the three views in our school. The reason for the disagreement is the conflict between what is demanded by the reason of recitation of a *sajdah āyah*, and the prostration incurred by it, and the general prohibition against praying after *ʿAṣr* and after *Ṣubḥ*. Their disagreement is about the reason why it is forbidden to pray at these two times. Allah knows best.

When someone prostrates, he should say in his prostration, 'O Allah, lower from me this burden, write for me a reward for it and make it stored up for me.' Ibn ʿAbbās related that from the Prophet ﷺ. Ibn Mājah mentioned it.

If someone recites a *sajdah āyah* in the prayer, and it is a *nāfilah* prayer, he prostrates if he is alone or in a group, provided he is safe from confusing people by doing so. If he is in a group in which one is not safe from that, then according to the text, it is permitted to prostrate. It is also said that he should not prostrate. As for in the obligatory prayer, the well-known position from Mālik is that it is forbidden in it, whether the prayer is silent or aloud, in a group or alone. The reason is that it entails increasing the number of prostrations of the obligatory prayer. It is said that the reason is out of fear of confusing the group. This is doubtful. According to this, it is not forbidden for someone alone or in a group that is safe from confusion.

Al-Bukhāri related that Abū Rāfiʿ said, 'I prayed *ʿIshā'* with Abū Hurayrah and he recited "*When the sky bursts open*" (84:1) and he prostrated. I asked, "What is this?" He answered, "I prostrated for it behind Abū al-Qāsim ﷺ and I will continue to do so until I meet him."' He alone transmitted it. We read in it, "Imrān ibn Ḥusayn was asked, "What if a man listens to a *sajdah* [verse] when he did not sit down in order to listen to it (the recitation)?" He answered, "What do you think if he did sit down in order to listen to it?" It was as if he did not oblige him to prostrate.' Salmān said [when he passed by some people who recited a verse of prostration], 'We did not come for this,' [and he did not prostrate.]

'Uthmān said, 'The prostration is for the one who hears it.' Az-Zuhrī said, 'You should only prostrate if you are in a state of purity. If you prostrate and while you are at home, face the *qiblah*. If you are riding, then you may perform it in whatever direction you face. Someone walking does not prostrate for the prostration of someone at a distance.' Allah knows best.

Table of Contents for Āyats

Sūrat al-An'ām – Cattle

1 Praise belongs to Allah Who created the heavens and the earth... 2
2 It is He Who created you from clay and then decreed a fixed term... 5
3-5 He is Allah in the heavens and on the earth. He knows... 8
6 Have they not seen how many generations We destroyed before them... 9
7 Even if We were to send down a book to you on parchment pages... 11
8-10 They say, 'Why has an angel not been sent down to him?'... 12
11-12 Say: 'Travel about the earth and see the final fate of the deniers.' ... 13
13-16 All that inhabits the night and the day belongs to Him.... 15
17 If Allah touches you with harm, none can remove it but Him.... 17
18-19 He is the Absolute Master over His slaves. He is the All-Wise... 18
20 Those We have given the Book recognise it as they recognise... 20
21-22 Who could do greater wrong than someone who invents lies... 20
23 Then they will have no recourse except to say, 'By Allah, our Lord... 21
24 See how they lie against themselves and how what they invented... 22
25 Some of them listen to you but We have placed covers on... 24
26 They keep others from it and avoid it themselves... 25
27 If only you could see when they are standing before the Fire and... 28
28 No, it is simply that what they were concealing before... 30
29 They say, 'There is nothing but this life and we will not be raised again.' 31
30 If only you could see when they are standing before their Lord.... 31
31 Those who deny the meeting with Allah have lost... 32
32 The life of this world is nothing but a game and a diversion.... 34
33-34 We know that what they say distresses you. It is not that they are... 36
35 If their turning away is hard on you, then go down a tunnel... 38
36-37 Only those who can hear respond. As for the dead, Allah will ... 39
38 There is no creature crawling on the earth or flying creature, flying... 40
39-41 Those who deny Our Signs are deaf and dumb in utter darkness.... 43
42 We sent Messengers to nations before you, and afflicted those nations... 45
43-45 If only they had humbled themselves when Our violent force came... 46
46-47 Say: 'What do you think? If Allah took away your hearing and ... 49
48 We do not send the Messengers except to bring good news and... 50
49 The punishment will fall on those who deny Our Signs because... 51

50 Say: 'I do not say to you that I possess the treasuries of Allah, nor do I...51
51 Warn by it those who fear they will be gathered to their Lord... 52
52 Do not chase away those who call on their Lord morning and evening...53
53 In this way We try some of them by means of others... 56
54 When those who believe in Our Signs come to you, say, 'Peace... 57
55 In that way We make the Signs plain so that you may clearly see... 59
56 Say: 'I am forbidden to worship those you call upon besides Allah.'... 60
57 Say: 'I stand on a Clear Sign from my Lord and yet you have denied.... 60
58 Say: 'If I did have in my possession what you are in such haste... 62
59 The keys of the Unseen are in His possession. No one knows them... 62
60 It is He Who takes you back to Himself at night, while knowing... 66
61-62 He is the Absolute Master over His slaves. He sends angels... 68
63-64 Say: 'Who rescues you from the darkness of the land and sea? ... 70
65 Say: 'He possesses the power to send you punishment from above... 71
66-67 Your people deny it and yet it is the Truth. Say: 'I am not here as... 74
68 When you see people engrossed in mockery of Our Signs... 74
69 Their reckoning is in no way the responsibility of those who are... 77
70 Abandon those who have turned their *dīn* into a game and... 78
71-73 Say: 'Are we to call on something besides Allah which can... 80
74 Remember when Ibrāhīm said to his father, Āzar, 'Do you take idols... 84
75 Because of that We showed Ibrāhīm the dominions of the heavens... 86
76 When night covered him he saw a star and said, 'This is my Lord!'... 87
77 Then when he saw the moon come up he said, 'This is my Lord!'... 89
78 Then when he saw the sun come up he said, 'This is my Lord! ... 90
79 I have turned my face to Him Who brought the heavens and earth... 90
80 His people argued with him. He said, 'Are you arguing with me... 91
81-82 Why should I fear what you have associated with Him... 92
83 This is the argument We gave to Ibrāhīm against his people.... 93
84-86 We gave him Isḥāq and Ya'qūb, each of whom We guided.... 94
87 And some of their forebears, descendants and brothers; We chose... 96
88 That is Allah's guidance. He guides by it those of His slaves He wills.... 97
89 They are the ones to whom We gave the Book, Judgment and... 97
90 They are the ones Allah has guided, so be guided by their guidance.... 98
91 They do not measure Allah with His true measure... 99
92 This is a Book We have sent down and blessed, confirming... 101
93 Who could do greater wrong than someone who invents lies... 102
94 'You have come to Us all alone just as We created you at first... 105
95 Allah is He Who splits the seed and kernel. He brings forth... 107
96 It is He Who splits the sky at dawn, and appoints the night as a time... 107

97 It is He Who has appointed the stars for you so you might be guided... 109
98 It is He Who first produced you from a single self... 109
99 It is He Who sends down water from the sky from which... 110
100 Yet they make the jinn co-partners with Allah when... 115
101 He is the Originator of the heavens and the earth.... 116
102-3 That is Allah, your Lord. There is no god but Him... 117
104 'Clear insights have come to you from your Lord. Whoever sees... 120
105 That is how We vary the Signs, so that they say, 'You have been... 120
106 Follow what has been revealed to you from your Lord – there is no... 122
107 If Allah had willed, they would not have associated anything with Him....122
108 Do not curse those they call upon besides Allah, in case... 123
109 They have sworn by Allah with their most earnest oaths that if a Sign...124
110 We will overturn their hearts and sight, just as when... 127
111 Even if We sent down angels to them, and the dead spoke to them... 128
112 In this way We have appointed as enemies to every Prophet... 129
113 so that the hearts of those who do not believe in the Next World... 131
114 'Am I to desire someone other than Allah as a judge when it is He... 132
115 The Words of your Lord are perfect in truthfulness and justice.... 133
116-7 If you obeyed most of those on earth, they would misguide you... 134
118 Eat that over which the name of Allah has been mentioned... 135
119 What is the matter with you that you do not eat that over which... 135
120 Abandon wrong action, outward and inward.... 136
121 Do not eat anything over which the name of Allah has not been... 137
122 Is someone who was dead and whom We brought to life... 141
123 And likewise in every city We set up its greatest wrongdoers... 142
124 When a Sign comes to them, they say, 'We will not believe until... 143
125 When Allah desires to guide someone, He expands his breast to Islam....144
126 This is the path of your Lord – straight. We have made the Signs... 146
128 On the Day He gathers them all together: 'Company of jinn... 147
129 In that way We make the wrongdoers friends of one another... 148
130 Company of jinn and men! did not Messengers come to you... 149
131 That was because their Lord would never have destroyed the cities... 151
132 All have ranks according to what they did. Your Lord is not unaware...151
133 Your Lord is the Rich Beyond Need, the Possessor of Mercy.... 152
134 What you are promised will come about and you can do nothing... 152
135 Say: 'My people, do as you are doing, just as I am doing.... 152
136 They assign to Allah a share of the crops and livestock... 153
137 In the same way their associates have made killing their children... 155
138 They say, 'These animals and crops are sacrosanct.... 157

139 They say, 'What is in the wombs of these animals is exclusively for... 158
140 Those who kill their children foolishly without any knowledge... 159
141 It is He Who produces gardens, both cultivated and wild... 161
142 And also animals for riding and for haulage and animals... 173
143-4 There are eight in pairs: a pair of sheep and a pair of goats... 175
145 Say: 'I do not find, in what has been revealed to me, any food... 178
146 We made unlawful for the Jews every animal with an undivided... 186
147 If they call you a liar, say: 'Your Lord possesses boundless mercy... 189
148 Those who associate others with Allah will say, 'If Allah had... 190
149 Say: 'Allah's is the conclusive argument. If He had willed... 191
150 Say: 'Produce your witnesses to testify that Allah made this... 191
151-3 Say: 'Come and I will recite to you what your Lord... 192
154-5 Then We gave Mūsā the Book, complete and perfect for him... 204
156-7 So you cannot say: 'The Book was only sent down to the two... 205
158 What are they waiting for but for the angels to come to them... 206
159 As for those who divide up their *dīn* and form into sects... 211
160 Those who produce a good action will receive ten like it.... 212
161-3 Say: 'My Lord has guided me to a straight path, a well-founded... 213
164 Say: 'Am I to desire other than Allah as Lord when He is the Lord... 217
165 It is He Who appointed you caliphs on the earth... 219

Sūrat al-A'rāf – The Ramparts

1-2 Alif Lām Mīm Ṣād. It is a Book sent down to you... 221
3 Follow what has been sent down to you from your Lord... 222
4-5 How many cities We have destroyed! Our violent force came... 223
6-7 We will question those to whom the Messengers were sent... 224
8-9 The weighing that Day will be the truth. As for those whose scales... 225
10 We have established you firmly on the earth and granted you... 228
11 We created you and then formed you and then We said to the angels... 229
12 He said, 'What prevented you from prostrating when I commanded... 230
13 He said, 'Descend from Heaven. It is not for you to be arrogant in it.... 233
14-15 He said, 'Grant me a reprieve until the day they are raised up.'... 233
16-17 He said, 'By Your misguidance of me, I will lie in ambush for them... 234
18 He said, 'Get out of it, reviled and driven out. As for those of them... 236
19 'Ādam, live in the Garden, you and your wife, and eat of it wherever... 237
20 Then *Shayṭān* whispered to them, disclosing to them their private... 237
21 He swore to them, 'I am one of those who give you good advice.' 239
22-24 So he enticed them to do it by means of trickery.... 239

25 He said, 'On it you will live and on it die and from it you will be... 241
26 Children of Ādam! We have sent down clothing to you... 241
27 Children of Ādam! do not let *Shayṭān* tempt you into trouble... 245
28 Whenever they commit an indecent act, they say, 'We found... 246
29-30 Say: 'My Lord has commanded justice. Stand and face Him... 247
31 Children of Ādam! wear fine clothing in every mosque and eat and... 248
32 Say: 'Who has forbidden the fine clothing Allah has produced... 254
33 Say: 'My Lord has forbidden indecency, both open and hidden... 259
34 Every nation has an appointed time. When their time comes... 260
35-36 Children of Ādam! if Messengers come to you... 261
37 Who could do greater wrong than someone who invents lies... 262
38-39 He will say, 'Enter the Fire together with the nations of jinn and... 263
40-41 As for those who deny Our Signs and are arrogant regarding... 265
42 As for those who believe and do right actions – We impose... 267
43 We will strip away any rancour in their hearts. Rivers will flow... 267
44 The Companions of the Garden will call out to the Companions... 269
46 There will be a dividing wall between them and on the ramparts... 270
48-49 The Companions of the Ramparts will call out to men... 274
50 The Companions of the Fire will call out to the Companions... 275
51 those who took their *dīn* as a diversion and a game, and were deluded... 276
52 We have brought them a Book elucidating everything... 277
53 What are they waiting for but its fulfilment? The Day its fulfilment... 277
54 Your Lord is Allah, Who created the heavens and the earth in six... 278
55 Call on your Lord humbly and secretly. He does not love those who... 283
56 Do not corrupt the earth after it has been put right. Call on Him... 286
57 It He is who sends out the winds, bringing advance news of His mercy... 288
58 Good land yields up its plants by its Lord's permission... 290
59 We sent Nūḥ to his people and he said, 'My people, worship Allah!... 291
60-62 The ruling circle of his people said, 'We see you in flagrant error.'... 293
63-64 Or are you astonished that a reminder should come to you... 294
70-72 They said, 'Have you come to us to make us worship Allah alone... 297
73 And to Thamūd We sent their brother Ṣāliḥ, who said, 'My people... 298
74 Remember when He appointed you successors to 'Ād and settled you... 299
75-76 The ruling circle of those of his people who were arrogant said... 300
77-79 And they hamstrung the She-Camel, spurning their Lord's... 300
80 And Lūṭ, when he said to his people, 'Do you commit an obscenity... 303
81 You come with lust to men instead of women.... 306
82-83 The only answer of his people was to say, 'Expel them ... 306
84 We rained down a rain upon them. See the final fate of the evildoers! 307

85-87 And to Madyan We sent their brother Shu'ayb who said... 308
88-89 The ruling circle of those of his people who were arrogant said... 311
90-93 The ruling circle of those of his people who disbelieved said... 312
The ruling circle of those of his people who disbelieved said... 313
94-95 We have never sent a Prophet to any city without seizing its people... 314
96 If only the people of the cities had believed and been godfearing... 314
97-98 Do the people of the cities feel secure against Our violent force... 315
99 Do they feel secure against Allah's devising? No one feels secure... 316
100 Is it not clear to those who have inherited the earth after... 316
101 These cities – We have given you news of them. Their Messengers... 316
102 We did not find many of them worthy of their contract. 317
103 And then, after them, We sent Mūsā with Our Signs... 317
104-12 Mūsā said, 'Pharaoh! I am truly a Messenger from the Lord... 318
113-4 The magicians came to Pharaoh and they said... 320
115-7 They said, 'Mūsā, will you throw first or shall we... 321
118-22 So the Truth took place and what they did was shown to be false.... 322
123-6 Pharaoh said, 'Have you believed in him before I authorised you... 322
127-8 The ruling circle of Pharaoh's people said, 'Are you going to... 324
129 They said, 'We suffered harm before you came to us and after... 326
130 We seized Pharaoh's people with years of drought and scarcity... 327
131 Whenever a good thing came to them, they said, 'This is our due.'... 327
132 They said, 'No matter what kind of Sign you bring us to bewitch us... 330
133 So We sent down on them floods, locusts, lice, frogs and blood... 330
134-6 Whenever the plague came down on them they said, 'Mūsā, pray... 334
137 And We bequeathed to the people who had been oppressed... 335
138 We conveyed the tribe of Israel across the sea and they came upon... 336
139-40 What these people are doing is destined for destruction.... 336
141 Remember when We rescued you from Pharaoh's people... 337
142 We set aside thirty nights for Mūsā and then completed them... 337
143 When Mūsā came to Our appointed time and his Lord spoke to him... 341
144 He said, 'Mūsā, I have chosen you over all mankind for My Message... 343
145 We wrote about everything for him on the Tablets... 344
146-7 I will divert from My Signs all those who are arrogant in the earth... 346
148 After he left, Mūsā's people adopted a calf... 347
149 When they took full stock of what they had done and saw... 349
150-1 When Mūsā returned to his people in anger and great sorrow... 350
152-3 As for those who adopted the Calf, anger from their Lord... 355
154 When Mūsā's anger abated he picked up the Tablets... 357
155 Mūsā chose seventy men from his people for Our appointed time ... 358

156 Prescribe good for us in this world and the Next World.... 360
157 those who follow the Messenger, the Unlettered Prophet... 361
158 Say: 'Mankind! I am the Messenger of Allah to you all... 365
159 Among the people of Mūsa there is a group who guide by the truth... 366
160-2 We divided them up into twelve tribes – communities.... 367
163-4 Ask them about the town which was by the sea when... 368
165 Then when they forgot what they had been reminded of... 372
166 When they were insolent about what they had been forbidden to do... 373
167 Then your Lord announced that He would send against them... 373
168 And We divided them into nations in the earth. Some of them are... 374
169 An evil generation has succeeded them, inheriting the Book... 375
170 As for those who hold fast to the Book and establish the prayer... 377
171 When We uprooted the mountain, lifting it above them like a canopy... 378
172-4 When your Lord took out all their descendants from the loins... 378
175 Recite to them the tale of him to whom We gave Our Signs... 383
176-7 If We had wanted to, We would have raised him up by them.... 386
178 Whoever Allah guides is truly guided; but those He misguides... 388
179 We created many of the jinn and mankind for Hell.... 389
180 To Allah belong the Most Beautiful Names, so call on Him by them... 389
181 Among those We have created there is a community who guide... 393
182 But as for those who deny Our Signs, We will lead them... 393
183 I will give them more time. My strategy is sure. 394
184 Have they not reflected? Their companion is not mad.... 394
185 Have they not looked into the dominions of the heavens... 394
186 If Allah misguides people, no one can guide them.... 398
187 They will ask you about the Hour: when is it due? Say: 'Knowledge... 399
188 Say: 'I possess no power to help or harm myself, except as Allah.... 401
189-90 It is He Who created you from a single self and made from him... 402
191-2 Do they make things into partner-gods which cannot create... 406
193 If you call them to guidance they will not follow you.... 406
194-6 Those you call on besides Allah are slaves just like yourselves.... 407
197-8 Those you call on besides Him are not capable of helping you.... 409
199 Make allowances for people, command what is right... 409
200 If an evil impulse from *Shayṭān* provokes you, seek refuge in Allah.... 413
201-2 As for those who are godfearing, when they are bothered by... 415
203 If you do not bring them a Sign, they say, 'Why have you not come... 418
204 When the Qur'an is recited listen to it and be quiet so that hopefully... 418
205 Remember your Lord in yourself humbly and fearfully... 420
206 Those who are in the presence of your Lord do not consider... 421

Glossary

Abū-l-'Abbās: Muḥammad ibn Yazīd al-Mubarrad, a leading philologist and grammarian of the school of Basra. He died in Baghdad in 285/898. He wrote many books, including *al-Kāmil* and *al-Kitāb.*
Al-Abwā': a place between Makkah and Madīnah.
Abū Ḥātim: Sahl ibn Muḥammad al-Jushanī as-Sijistānī, d. 255/869, a prominent Basran philologist.
Abū Ḥaywah: Shurayḥ ibn Yazīd al-Ḥaḍramī, the Qur'an reciter of Syria from Homs. He has a *shādhdh* reading, and died in 203/818.
Abū Isḥāq: Ibrāhīm ibn as-Sarī az-Zajjāj, author of *I'rab al-Qur'ān.*
Abū Ja'far: aṭ-Ṭabarī.
Abū Jahl: 'Amr ibn Hishām, one of the important men of Quraysh who was violently opposed to Islam.
Abū Lahab: One of the Prophet Muhammad's uncles, who was a great enemy of Islam.
Abū 'Ubayd: al-Qāsim ibn Sallām al-Harawī or al-Baghdādī, d. 224/838.
Abū 'Ubaydah: Ma'mar ibn al-Muthanna at-Taymī, d. 209/824, author of *Majāz al-Qur'ān*, the first book on the linguistic analysis of the Qur'an.
'Ād: an ancient people in southern Arabia to whom the Prophet Hūd was sent.
Aḍḥā: *see* **'Īd al-Aḍḥā**.
Al-Akhfash: Abū-l-Khaṭṭāb 'Abdu'l-Ḥamīd ibn 'Abdi'l-Majīd al-Akhfash al-Kabīr, a grammarian in Basra, one of the first to study Arabic poetry as well as contributing to philology and lexicography and recording Bedouin vocabulary. He revised *Kitāb*, the first book on Arabic grammar, written by his student Sībawayh. He was a client of the Qays tribe and died in 177/793.
Allāhu akbar: the Arabic expression 'God is greater.'
Āmīn: 'Ameen', a compound of verb and noun meaning 'Answer our prayer' or 'So be it'.
amīr: the one who commands; the source of authority in a situation; a military commander.
Amīr al-Mu'minīn: 'the Commander of the Believers', the caliph.
'āmm: generally applicable, used in reference to a Qur'anic ruling.
Anṣār: the "Helpers", the people of Madīnah who welcomed and aided the Prophet ﷺ.

'āqilah: the paternal kinsmen of an offender who are liable for the payment of blood money.
al-'Aqīq: a valley about four and a half miles west of Madīnah.
'araḍ: plural *a'rāḍ*, an accidental or non-essential, ontic quality. The opposite of *jawhar*.
'Arafah: a plain fifteen miles to the east of Makkah. One of the essential rites of the ḥajj is to stand on 'Arafah on the 9th of Dhū'l-Ḥijjah.
'arīyah: a kind of sale by which the owner of an *'arīyah* is allowed to sell fresh dates while they are still on the palms by means of estimation, in exchange for dried plucked dates.
'aṣabah: male relatives on the father's side.
Al-Aṣma'ī: Abū Sa'īd ibn 'Abdi'l-Malik ibn Qurayb, 122/740-213/820, an early philologist and Arabic grammarian of Basra. He also wrote on genealogy, natural science and zoology and was a scholar of Arabic poetry in the court of Hārūn ar-Rashīd. He spent a great deal of time recording the language of desert Bedouins.
'Aṣr: the mid-afternoon prayer.
athar (plural *āthār*) lit. impact, trace, vestige; synonym of *khabar*, but usually reserved for deeds and precedents of the Companions.
awliyā': the plural of *walī*.
āyah: a verse of the Qur'an.
'Ayr: the second largest mountain in Madīnah after Uḥud, located to the south of Madīnah.
Ayyūb: the Prophet Job.
Bāb al-Ḥalbah: one of the gates of Baghdad, also known as Bāb aṭ-Ṭalsim. It was destroyed by the Ottomans in 1917.
Badr: a place near the coast, about 95 miles to the south of Madīnah where in 2 AH, in the first battle fought by the newly established Muslim community, the 313 outnumbered Muslims led by the Messenger of Allah overwhelmingly defeated 1000 Makkan idolaters.
baḥīrah: in the Jāhiliyyah period, a female camel which had given birth five times, the last being a male. Its ears were slit and it was let free to graze.
Balqā': the area of the eastern plateau of the Jordan valley.
Banū: lit. sons, meaning a tribe or clan.
Bāṭiniyyah: those who engage in esoteric interpretation.
Dajjāl: the false Messiah whose appearance marks the imminent end of the world. The root in Arabic means 'to deceive, cheat, take in'.
ḍammah: the Arabic vowel 'u'.
Dāwud: the Prophet David.

dhikr: lit. remembrance, mention. Commonly used, it means invocation of Allah by repetition of His names or particular formulae.
dhimmah: obligation or contract, in particular a treaty of protection for non-Muslims living in Muslim territory.
dhimmī: a non-Muslim living under the protection of Muslim rule.
Dhū'l-Ḥijjah: the twelfth month of the Muslim calendar, the month of the hajj.
Dhū'l-Qa'dah: the eleventh month of the Muslim calendar.
dīn: the life-transaction, lit. the debt between two parties, in this usage between the Creator and created.
Ditch: the Battle of the Ditch (or Trench), which took place in 627 CE/5 AH in which the combined forces of Quraysh and their allies unsuccessfully laid siege to Madīnah for thirty days.
Dīwān: originally the register of soldiers and pensions under 'Umar. Subsequently it became a governmental department for the finance and records of the government.
Fadak: a small, rich oasis in the north of the Hijaz near Khaybar.
Fajr: the dawn prayer.
faqīh: pl. *fuqahā'*, a man learned in knowledge of *fiqh* who by virtue of his knowledge can give a legal judgment.
farḍ: an obligatory act of worship or practice of the *dīn* as defined by the *Sharī'ah.*
Al-Farrā': Abū Zakariyyā Yaḥyā ibn Ziyād, ca. 144/761- 207/882, a noted grammarian of Kufa. Al-Farrā' lit. means 'he who skins/scrutinises language'. He wrote *Majāz al-Qur'an*.
fāsiq: pl. *fussāq*, impious, someone not meeting the legal requirements of righteousness. The evidence of such a person is inadmissible in court.
fatḥah: the Arabic vowel 'a'.
Fātiḥah: "the Opener," the first *sūrah* of the Qur'an.
fatwa: an authoritative statement on a point of law.
fidyah: a ransom, compensation paid for rites or acts of worship missed or wrongly performed because of ignorance or ill health. Also the amount paid by a woman in the *khul'* divorce.
fiqh: the science of the application of the Sharī'ah. A practitioner or expert in *fiqh* is called a *faqīh.*
fisq: deviant behavior, leaving the correct way or abandoning the truth, disobeying Allah, immoral behavior.
fitnah: civil strife, sedition, schism, trial, temptation, also *shirk*.
Fiṭr: *see* **'Īd al-Fiṭr**.

fuqahā': plural of *faqīh.*
gharīb: a *ḥadīth* which has a single reporter at some stage of the *isnād.*
ḥabūs: see *waqf.*
ḥadd: Allah's boundary limits for the lawful and unlawful. The *ḥadd* punishments are specific fixed penalties laid down by Allah for specified crimes.
ḥadīth: reported speech of the Prophet ﷺ.
hady: sacrificial camel.
ḥāfiẓ: pl. *ḥuffāẓ*, someone who has memorised the Qur'an by heart.
hajj: the annual pilgrimage to Makka which is one of the five pillars of Islam.
ḥāl: In Arabic grammar, a circumstantial adverb in the accusative case which describes something happening at the same time as the action or event mentioned in the main clause.
ḥalāl: lawful in the *Sharī'ah.*
ḥām: a male camel which had fathered ten females in succession which was then in pre-Islamic times freed from work for the idols.
hamzah: the character in Arabic which designates a glottal stop.
ḥanīf: someone following the primordial religion of *tawḥīd* and sincerity to Allah.
Ḥanīfiyyah: the religion of the Prophet Ibrāhīm, the primordial religion of *tawḥīd* and sincerity to Allah.
ḥarbī: a belligerent.
harām: unlawful in the *Sharī'ah.*
Ḥaram: Sacred Precinct, a protected area in which certain behavior is forbidden and other behaviour necessary. The area around the Ka'bah in Makkah is a Haram, and the area around the Prophet's Mosque in Madīnah is a Ḥaram. They are referred to together as *al-Ḥaramayn*, 'the two Ḥarams'.
ḥarf: (plural *aḥruf*) one of the seven modes or manners of recitation in which the Qur'an was revealed.
Hārūn: the Prophet Aaron, the brother of Mūsā.
Hārūt and Mārūt: the two angels in Babel mentioned in the Qur'an (2:102), from whom people learned magic. Some commentators state that they are two kings rather than two angels (*malikayn* rather than *malakayn*).
ḥasan: good, excellent, often used to describe a *ḥadīth* which is reliable, but which is not as well authenticated as one which is *ṣaḥīḥ.*
Hāshim: the Banu Hāshim is a clan of the Quraysh tribe of which the Prophet ﷺ was a member, the name coming from his great-grandfather, Hāshim ibn 'Abd Manāf.

Ḥawwā': Eve, the first woman.
Hijaz: the region along the western seaboard of Arabia in which Makkah, Madīnah, Jidda and Ta'if are situated.
Hijrah: emigration in the way of Allah. Islamic dating begins with the Hijrah of the Prophet Muḥammad ﷺ from Makkah to Madīnah in 622 AD.
Hubal: a pre-Islamic idol worshipped by Quraysh at the Ka'bah.
Hūd: the Prophet sent to the people of 'Ād.
Ḥudaybīyah: a well-known place ten miles from Makkah on the way to Jiddah where the Homage of ar-Riḍwān took place.
Hudhayl: a tribe which lived in the hills between Makka and Ṭā'if and were linked genealogically with Quraysh.
ḥudūd: plural of *ḥadd.*
Ḥums: an alliance in the pre-Islamic period, centred on the Ka'bah in Makkah and based on the religion of the Prophet Ibrāhīm. It included the tribe of Quraysh as well as some other tribes. It was based on strictness in their religion. It came about around the year of the Elephant (522 CE).
Iblīs: the personal name of the Devil. He is also called *Shayṭān* or the 'enemy of Allah'.
Ibrāhīm: the Prophet Abraham.
'Īd: a festival, either the festival at the end of Ramadan or at the time of the Hajj.
'Īd al-Aḍḥā: a four day festival at the time of hajj. The *'Īd* of the Sacrifice, it starts on the 10th day of Dhū-l-Ḥijjah (the month of Hajj), the day that the pilgrims sacrifice their animals.
'Īd al-Fiṭr: the festival at the end of the month of fasting (Ramadan).
iḍāfah: a possessive construction in Arabic in which the first noun is indefinite and the second usually definite. It is used to indicate possession. The first word is called *'muḍāf'* and the second is *'muḍāf ilayhi'*.
'iddah: a period after divorce or the death of her husband for which a woman must wait before re-marrying.
idghām: in Qur'an recitation, to assimilate one letter into another. Thus *an-ya'bud* becomes *ay-ya'bud*, *qad rabayyan* becomes *qattabayyan*, etc.
Idrīs: a Prophet, possibly Enoch.
'ifrīt: a powerful sort of jinn.
iftitāḥ: the opening supplication of the prayer.
iḥrām: the conditions of clothing and behaviour adopted by someone on hajj or *'umrah.*
ijtihād: to exercise personal judgment in legal matters.

'illah: underlying reason, effective cause.
'Illiyūn: 'the High Places', a name for the upper realm of Paradise, where the register of people's good actions is kept, or the register itself.
Ilyās: also Ilyāsīn, the Prophet Elijah or Elias.
imālah: a vowel shift in Arabic where an open vowel rises, *ā* towards *ī*, and short *a* towards *i*.
imam: Muslim religious or political leader; leader of Muslim congregational worship.
īmān: belief, faith.
'Īsā: the Prophet Jesus.
Isfandyar: Persian Esfandiyār, a legendary Persian hero who is known for his battle with Rustam (Rostam) in Ferdowsi's *Shahnameh.*
'Ishā': the obligatory evening prayer.
Isḥāq: the Prophet Isaac.
Ismā'īl: the Prophet Ishmael.
isnād: a *ḥadīth*'s chain of transmission from individual to individual.
Isrāfīl: the archangel who will blow the Trumpet which announces the end of the world.
Jāhiliyyah: the Time of Ignorance before the coming of Islam.
jalālah: animals that have been eating filth and impurities.
jawhar: literally 'jewel', substance, specifically the essence or the intrinsic being of a thing.
Jibrīl: the angel Gabriel.
jihad: struggle, particularly fighting in the way of Allah to establish Islam.
jinn: inhabitants of the heavens and the earth made of smokeless fire who are usually invisible.
jism: physical body.
jizyah: a protection tax payable by non-Muslims living under Muslim rule as a tribute to the Muslim ruler.
Jumāda-l-Ākhir: the sixth month of the Muslim calendar.
Jumāda-l-Ūlā: the fifth month of the Muslim calendar.
Jumu'ah: the day of gathering, Friday, and particularly the Jumu'ah prayer which is performed instead of *Ẓuhr* by those who attend it.
juz': pl. *ajzā'*, a thirtieth part of the Qur'an.
Ka'bah: the cube-shaped building at the centre of the Ḥaram in Makkah, originally built by the Prophet Ibrāhīm. Also known as the House of Allah.
kaffārah: atonement, prescribed way of making amends for wrong actions, especially missed obligatory actions.

kāfir: (pl. *kāfirūn* or *kuffār*): an unbeliever, a person who rejects Allah and His Messenger. The opposite is believer or *mu'min.*

kasrah: the Arabic vowel *i.*

Kawthar: abundance, a river in the Garden.

Al-Khalīl: Abū 'Abdu'r-Raḥmān ibn 'Amr al-Farāhidī, 110/718-170/786, born in Oman, a leading grammarian, philologist and lexicographer of Basra. He compiled the first Arabic dictionary: *Kitāb al-'Ayn*, and the first to codify the metres of Arabic poetry. His students included Sībawayh and al-Aṣma'ī.

kharaj: tax imposed on agricultural land.

Khārijites: the earliest sect, who separated themselves from the body of the Muslims and declared war on all those who disagreed with them, stating that a wrong action turns a Muslim into an unbeliever.

Khaybar: Jewish colony to the north of Madina which was laid siege to and captured by the Muslims in the seventh year after the Hijra because of the Jews' continual treachery.

Khorasan: Persian province southeast of the Caspian Sea; a centre of many dissident movements in early Islamic history.

Khuzā'ah: an Azdī tribe who were concentrated around Makkah.

Kilāb: Banū Kilāb, a tribe that dominated central Arabia, originating from Najd.

kitābah: a contract for a slave to buy his freedom in instalments.

Kitābī: Someone who is one of the People of the Book, i.e. a Jew or Christian.

kufr: disbelief, to cover up the truth, to reject Allah and refuse to believe that Muhammad ﷺ is His Messenger.

kunyah: a respectful but intimate way of addressing people as "the father of so-and-so" or "the mother of so-and-so."

Kunāsah: a vast marketplace in Kufa, located outside the walls, which was a centre for caravans and a site for poetry recitation, storytelling, history and other activities.

Lā ilaha illā 'llāh: 'There is no god but Allah.'

Lakhm: a large tribe that originated in Yemen and in pre-Islamic times created the Lakhmid kingdom in al-Ḥīrah, near Kufa, which acted as a buffer between the Arab tribes and Persian empire.

al-Lāt: an idol worshipped by Thaqīf at Ṭā'if.

li'ān: mutual cursing, a form of divorce in which the husband and wife take oaths when he accuses her of adultery and she denies it.

Lūṭ: the Prophet Lot.

maddah: prolongation. There are three letters which are subject to prolongation in recitation of the Qur'an: *alif*, *wāw* and *yā'*.
Madīnat as-Salām: the round city of Baghdad which was the original core of the city, built by the Abbasid caliph al-Manṣūr in 145/762.
Madyan: Midian, the people to whom the Prophet Shu'ayb was sent.
Maghrib: the sunset prayer; also the western part of Muslim lands. Today it means Morocco.
mann: an Iraqi measure of weight, two *raṭl*s.
Maqām of Ibrāhịm: the place of the stone on which the Prophet Ibrāhīm stood while he and Ismā'īl were building the Ka'bah, which marks the place of the two *rak'ah* prayer following *ṭawāf* of the Ka'bah.
marfū': 'elevated', a narration from the Prophet ﷺ mentioned by a Companion, e.g. 'The Messenger of Allah ﷺ said...'
Marr az-Zahrān: site of one of the pre-Islamic marketplaces, located near a mountain, al-Aṣghar, about 24 Km from Makkah.
Maryam: Mary, the mother of 'Īsā.
Mash'ar al-Ḥarām: a venerated place in the valley of Muzdalifah where it is a sunnah to stop when performing *ḥajj*.
Masjid al-Ḥarām: the great mosque in Makkah.
mawqūf: 'stopped', a narration from a Companion without mentioning the Prophet ﷺ.
Mīkā'īl: the angel Michael.
mithqāl (plural *mathāqīl*): 'miskal', the weight of one dinar, the equivalent of 72 grains of barley (equals 4.4 grams).
mu'adhdhin: someone who calls the *adhan* or call to prayer.
muḍāf: in Arabic grammar in a possessive phrase, the *muḍāf* is the 'added' and *muḍāf ilayh* is what it is added to
Muḍar: the ancestor of the Arabs.
mudd: a measure of volume. approximately a double-handed scoop.
muftī: someone qualified to give a legal opinion or fatwa.
Muhājirūn: Companions of the Messenger of Allah ﷺ who accepted Islam in Makkah and made hijrah to Madīnah.
Muḥarram: the first month of the Muslim lunar year.
muḥkam: perspicuous, a word or text conveying a firm and unequivocal meaning.
muḥrim: a person in *iḥrām*.
muḥṣan (or *muḥṣin*): a person who has been previously legally married.
mujtahid: a scholar who is qualified to carry out *ijtihād*.

munkar: "denounced", a narration reported by a weak reporter which goes against another authentic *ḥadīth.*
Munkar and Nakīr: the two angels who come to question a person in their grave.
mursal: a *ḥadīth* where a man in the generation after the Companions quotes directly from the Prophet without mentioning the Companion from whom he got it.
Mūsā: the Prophet Moses.
Musaylimah: the false prophet of the Banū Ḥanīfah in Najd.
musnad: a collection of *ḥadīth*s arranged according to the first authority in its *isnād*; also a *ḥadīth* which can be traced back through an unbroken *isnād* to the Prophet.
mutakallimūn: those who study the science of *kalām*, the science of investigating theological doctrine.
Mu'tazilite: someone who adheres to the school of the Mu'tazilah which is rationalist in its approach to existence. Originally they held that anyone who commits a sin is neither a believer nor an unbeliever. They also held the Qur'an to be created.
Muzdalifah: a place between 'Arafah and Minā where the pilgrims returning from 'Arafah spend a night in the open between the ninth and tenth day of *Dhū-l-Ḥijjah* after performing *Maghrib* and *'Ishā'* there.
nabīdh: a drink made by soaking grapes, raisins, dates, etc. in water without allowing them to ferment to the point of becoming intoxicating. Once it is intoxicating, it is *nabīdh.*
nāfilah: (plural *nawāfil*): supererogatory act of worship.
An-Naḥḥās: Abū Ja'far Aḥmad ibn Muḥammad an-Naḥḥās, d. 338/949, an Egyptian scholar of grammar and *tafsīr* in the Abbasid period.
nafs: the lower self.
Najd: the region around Riyadh in Arabia.
Najrān: a region in the Arabian peninsula which borders Yemen.
Negus: a generic term for the ruler of Abyssinia.
niṣāb: the minimum amount of wealth of whatever kind that *zakāt* can be deducted from.
Nūḥ: the Prophet Noah.
People of the Book: principally the Jews and Christians whose religions are based on the Divine Books revealed to Mūsā and 'Īsā; a term also used to refer to any other group who claim to be following a Book revealed prior to the Qur'an.

People of Ḥadīth: 'the adherents of Ḥadīth', the movement who considered only the Qur'an and *ḥadīth* to be valid sources of *fiqh*.
People of Opinion (*ra'y*): a term used to describe those who use personal opinion to deduce judgment. It was a term used particularly to describe the early Ḥanafīs.
Preserved Tablet: *al-Lawḥ al-Mahfūẓ*, also referred to as the *Umm al-Kitāb*, the source of the Qur'an, and the place where decrees are recorded.
qabā': a calf-length over-garment with sleeves.
Qābīl: Cain.
Qadariyyah: sect who said that people have power (*qadar*) over their actions and hence free will.
qāḍī: a judge, qualified to judge all matters in accordance with the Sharī'ah and to dispense and enforce legal punishments.
Qārūn: the Biblical Korah who was famed for his incredible wealth and became arrogant on account of it. The earth swallowed him up.
qasāmah: an oath taken by fifty members of a tribe or locality to refute or establish accusations of complicity in unclear cases of homicide.
Qayrawān: a town in north-central Tunisia, founded in 50/670. It was chosen as the capital of the Maghrib by the Aghlabids in about 182/800. It was an important centre of learning.
Qays: a major tribal confederation.
qiblah: the direction faced in the prayer which is towards the Ka'bah in Makkah.
Qubā': a village on the outskirts of Madīnah (originally about 5 km/3 miles outside the city) where the first mosque in Islam was built, also known as the Masjid at-Taqwā (Mosque of Fear of God).
Quraysh: one of the great tribes of Arabia. The Prophet Muḥammad ﷺ belonged to this tribe, which had great powers spiritually and financially both before and after Islam came. Someone from this tribe is called a Qurayshī.
Qushayr: Banū Qushayr, an Arab tribe that was a branch of Ka'b, originating from the area of Yamāmah.
Rabī'al-Awwal: the third month of the Muslim calendar.
Rabī'al-Ākhir: the fourth month of the Muslim calendar.
Rabī'ah: one of the two main branches of North Arabian tribes, the other being Muḍar.
Rāfiḍites: the Rawāfiḍ, a group of the Shi'ah known for rejecting Abū Bakr and 'Umar as well as 'Uthmān. It is a nickname, meaning "deserters".
Rajab: the seventh month of the Muslim calendar.

rak'ah: a unit of the prayer consisting of a series of standings, bowing, prostrations and sittings.
Ramadan: the month of fasting, the ninth month in the Muslim lunar calendar.
Rāshidūn: 'Rightly Guided', the title given to the first four caliphs in Islam: Abū Bakr, 'Umar, 'Uthmān and 'Alī.
ra'y: opinion, personal discretion. (see also People of Opinion.)
ridā': an ample form of mantle.
riṭl: or *raṭl*, a measurement of weight, approximately one pound.
Riyāḥ: the Banū Riyāḥ, a branch of Tamīm.
rūḥ: (plural *arwāḥ*) the soul, vital spirit. 'The Purest Rūḥ' can also refer to 'Īsā or Jibrīl.
rukū': the bowing position in the prayer.
Rustam: Persian Rostam, the famous Persia hero of Ferdowsi's *Shahnameh*.
ṣā': a measure of volume equal to four *mudd*s.
Sabaeans: a group of believers. It is not entirely clear who they were. Possibly they were Gnostics or Mandaeans.
Sacred Months: the months of Rajab, Dhū'l-Qa'dah, Dhū'l-Ḥijjah and Muḥarram in which fighting was forbidden.
ṣadaqah: charitable giving in the Cause of Allah.
sadd adh-dharā'i': a legal term for the blocking of a means which might lead to undesired consequences.
Ṣafā and Marwah: two hills close to the Ka'bah.
Ṣafar: the second month of the Muslim lunar calendar.
ṣaḥīḥ: healthy and sound with no defects, used to describe an authentic *ḥadīth*.
Ṣaḥīḥ: "the Sound", the title of the *ḥadīth* collections of al-Bukhārī and Muslim.
Sahm: the Banū Sahm is a clan of Quraysh.
sā'ibah: in the Jāhiliyyah, a she-camel let loose to graze, usually as a result of a vow to idols.
sajdah: prostration, particularly in the prayer.
Salaf: the early generations of the Muslims.
salām: the expression, *'as-salāmu 'alaykum,'* or 'Peace be upon you,' used as a greeting and to end the prayer.
Ṣāliḥ: the Prophet sent to the people of Thamūd.
Salsabīl: the name of a spring in the Garden.
Sha'bān: the eighth month in the Muslim calendar.
shaddah: doubled letter.

shahādah: bearing witness, particularly bearing witness that there is no god but Allah and that Muhammad is the Messenger of Allah. It is one of the pillars of Islam. It is also used to describe legal testimony in a court of law.
Sham'ūn: Simon.
Sharī'ah: The legal modality of a people based on the revelation of their Prophet. The final *Sharī'ah* is that of Islam.
Shawwāl: the tenth month of the Muslim calendar.
Shayṭān: devil, particularly Iblīs, one of the jinn.
shirk: the unforgiveable wrong action of worshipping something or someone other than Allah or associating something or someone as a partner with Him.
Aṣ-Ṣiḥāḥ: the famous dictionary *Tāj al-'Arūs wa-ṣ-Ṣiḥāh al-'Arabīyah*, by Ismā'īl ibn Ḥammād al-Jawharī.
Shīth: Seth, Ādam's third son.
Shu'ayb: the Prophet Jethro.
ṣiddīq: a man of truth, the *ṣiddīq* is the one who believes in Allah and His Messenger by the statement of the one who reports it, not from any proof except the light of belief which he experiences in his heart and which prevents him from hesitating and prevents any doubt entering him about the word of the Messenger who reported.
Sijjīn: the register where the actions of the evil are recorded, or the place where it is kept.
Sīrah: biography, particularly biography of the Prophet ﷺ.
Ṣirāṭ: the narrow bridge which spans the Fire and must be crossed to enter the Garden. It is described as sharper than a sword and thinner than a hair. It will have hooks over it to catch people as they cross it.
siwāk: a small stick, usually from the arak tree, whose tip is softened and used for cleaning the teeth.
subḥāna'llāh: the Arabic expression, 'Glory be to Allah'.
Ṣubḥ: dawn prayer
sujūd: prostration.
sukūn: a diacritic mark that means that there is no vowel sound after a consonant.
Sulaymān: the Prophet Solomon.
sunan: plural of sunnah.
sunnah: the customary practice of a person or group of people. It has come to refer almost exclusively to the practice of the Messenger of Allah ﷺ.
sūrah: a chapter of the Qur'an.

tā' marbūtah: a letter at the end of words which is not pronounced except when annexed to another word. It is written as a *hā'* with two overdots.
Tābi'ūn: the second generation of the early Muslims who did not meet the Prophet Muhammad ﷺ but learned the *dīn* of Islam from his Companions.
tadbīr: a contract given by a master to a slave whereby the slave will be freed after the master dies.
tafsīr: commentary or explanation of the meanings of the Qur'an.
Ṭā'if: a walled town south of Makkah known for its fertility. It was the home of the tribe of Thaqīf.
takbīr: saying *'Allāhu Akbar,'* 'Allah is greater'.
talbīyah: saying *'Labbayk'* ('At Your service') during the hajj.
Tamīm: one of the largest of the Arab tribes, located in Najd.
tanwīn: nunnation.
taqiyyah: concealment of one's views to escape persecution.
taqdīs: proclaiming Allah's sanctity, often by certain formulae.
taqwā: awe or fear of Allah, which inspires a person to be on guard against wrong action and eager to do actions which please Him.
tasbīḥ: glorification of Allah by saying *'Subhāna'llāh'*.
tathwīb: a repetition, the expression 'Prayer is better than sleep' pronounce twice in the adhan for *Fajr*.
ṭawāf: circumambulation of the Ka'bah, done in sets of seven circuits.
tawḥīd: the doctrine of Divine Unity.
tawjīh: orientation, a supplication formula recited before starting the prayer.
Tayy': a large, ancient Arab tribe.
Thamūd: a people to whom the Prophet Ṣāliḥ was sent, possibly a group of Nabateans. Madā'in Ṣāliḥ is located at al-Ḥijr in Najd about 180 miles north of Madina. The inscriptions on the tombs there date from 3 BC to 79 CE which are probably after the culture which once flourished there was destroyed.
Uḥud: a mountain just outside of Madīnah where five years after the Hijrah, the Muslims lost a battle against the Makkan idolaters. Many great Companions, and in particular Ḥamzah, the uncle of the Prophet, were killed in this battle.
Umayyah: the Banū Umayyah, the Umayyads.
Umm al-Kitāb: literally 'Mother of the Book'. It has a number of meanings, one of which is the celestial prototype of the Qur'an. It is also used for the Fātiḥah.
Umm al-Mu'minīn: literally 'Mother of the Believers', an honorary title given to the wives of the Prophet.

Umm al-Qur'ān: literally 'the Mother of the Qur'an', the opening *sūrah* of the Qur'an, *al-Fātiḥah*.
umm walad: a slavegirl who has had a child by her master and is freed after his death.
Ummah: the body of Muslims as one distinct Community.
'umrah: the lesser pilgrimage to the Ka'bah in Makkah performed at any time of the year.
uqiyyah: unit of measurement equal to a 12th of a *raṭl*.
uṣūl: plural of *aṣl*, the basic principles of any source used in *fiqh*.
uṣūlī: someone well-versed in the study of the fundamental principles (*uṣūl*) of Islamic law.
'Uzayr: Ezra.
Al-'Uzzā': a female idol worshipped by the pagan Arabs in the Hijaz in the Jāhiliyyah.
Waddān: a settlement about eight miles from al-Abwā' where an expedition took place in 2/623.
Wādī-l-Qurā: located near the Gulf of 'Aqabah north of the Red Sea where a Jewish settlement was located in the time of the Prophet ﷺ.
wakālah: agency, delegated authority..
walā': the tie of clientage established between a freed slave and the person who frees him, whereby the freed slave becomes integrated into the family of that person as a client (*mawlā*).
walī: (plural *awliyā'*) someone who is a 'friend' of Allah, thus possessing the quality of *wilāyah*. Also a relative who acts as a guardian.
waṣīlah: in the Jāhiliyyah, a she-camel that has given birth to two females with no male in between them. It was set loose to graze.
wasq: a measure of volume equal to sixty *ṣā'*s.
witr: literally 'odd', a single *raka'h* prayed at night after the *shaf'* which makes the number of sunnah prayers uneven.
wuḍū': ritual washing to be pure for the prayer.
Yahūdha: Judah.
Yaḥyā: the Prophet John the Baptist, the son of Zakariyyā.
Yamāmah: a region to the east of the plateau of Najd.
Ya'qūb: the Prophet Jacob, also called Isrā'īl (Israel).
Yūnus: the Prophet Jonah.
Yūsuf: the Prophet Joseph.
Zabūr: the Psalms of Dāwud.
Zakariyyā: the Prophet Zachariah, the father of Yaḥyā, John the Baptist, and guardian of Maryam.

zakāt: a wealth tax, one of the five pillars of Islam.
zakāt **al-fiṭr:** a small obligatory head-tax imposed on every Muslim, who has the means, for himself and his dependents. It is paid at the end of Ramadan.
zandaqah: heresy. This is an Arabicised Persian word. The term had been used for heterodox groups, especially Manichaeans, in pre-Islamic Persia, and hence it was originally applied to Magians.
ẓihār: an oath by a husband that his wife is like his mother's back to him, meaning she is unlawful for him. It was a form of divorce in the Jāhiliyyah.
zindīq: a term used to describe a heretic whose teaching is a danger to the community or state.
Ẓuhr: the midday prayer.
Zuṭṭ: a nomadic people from northern India who were in Iraq possibly before the Arab conquest.